ENCYCLOPEDIA
OF THE
STATELESS NATIONS

ENCYCLOPEDIA OF THE STATELESS NATIONS

Ethnic and National Groups Around the World

VOLUME I
A–C

James Minahan

GREENWOOD PRESS
Westport, Connecticut • London

Library of Congress Cataloging-in-Publication Data

Minahan, James.
   Encyclopedia of the stateless nations : ethnic and national groups around the world /
James Minahan.
      p. cm.
   Includes index.
   ISBN 0–313–31617–1 (set : alk. paper)—ISBN 0–313–32109–4 (v. 1 :
alk. paper)—ISBN 0–313–32110–8 (v. 2 : alk. paper)—ISBN 0–313–32111–6 (v. 3 :
alk. paper)—ISBN 0–313–32384–4 (v. 4 : alk. paper)
   1. World politics—1989—Dictionaries. 2. Nationalism—History—20th century—
Dictionaries. 3. Ethnic conflict—History—20th century—Dictionaries. 4. Stateless-
ness—Dictionaries. I. Minahan, James. Nations without states. II. Title.
D860.M56   2002
909.82'9'03—dc21   2001033691

British Library Cataloguing in Publication Data is available.

Library of Congress Catalog Card Number: 2001033691
ISBN: 0–313–31617–1 (set)
          0–313–32109–4 (Vol. I)
          0–313–32110–8 (Vol. II)
          0–313–32111–6 (Vol. III)
          0–313–32384–4 (Vol. IV)

First published in 2002

Greenwood Press, 88 Post Road West, Westport, CT 06881
An imprint of Greenwood Publishing Group, Inc.
www.greenwood.com

Printed in the United States of America

The paper used in this book complies with the
Permanent Paper Standard issued by the National
Information Standards Organization (Z39.48–1984).

10 9 8 7 6 5 4 3 2 1

CONTENTS

Contents

Contents

PREFACE

This volume is an updated and greatly expanded sequel to the award-winning *Nations without States: A Historical Dictionary of Contemporary National Movements*, which was published in 1996 and contained information on over 200 national groups and their homelands. Since that time, many new national groups have emerged as part of the nationalist revival that began with the end of the Cold War a decade ago. The purpose of this encyclopedia is to provide readers with an easy-to-use, accurate, up-to-date guide to the many national groups in the contemporary world. It is being published at a time when national identity, ethnic relations, regional conflicts, and immigration are increasingly important factors in national, regional, and international affairs.

Encyclopedia of the Stateless Nations: Ethnic and National Groups Around the World follows the development of over 300 national groups from the earliest periods of their histories to the present. That collection of national surveys is an essential guide to the many emerging groups and the national groups that the world ignored or suppressed during the decades of the Cold War, the longest and most stable peace in the history of the modern world. The Cold War did give the world relative peace and stability, but it was a fragile peace and a stability imposed by force. When reading the descriptions of national groups and the analyses of their histories, it is important to keep in mind the broader context—the growing role of national identity worldwide. This encyclopedia, like its 1996 predecessor, addresses the post–Cold War nationalist resurgence, by focusing on the most basic element of any nationalism, the nation itself.

This encyclopedia contains 350 national surveys, short articles highlighting the historical, political, social, religious, and economic evolution of the many national groups that are now emerging to claim roles in the post–Cold War world order. The worth of this encyclopedia in part derives from its up-to-date information on the often virtually unknown national groups that are currently making news and on those that will produce future headlines, controversies, and conflicts.

In this book I have followed the same general approach taken in the previous book for choosing which national groups to cover. Selecting the national surveys to be included in the encyclopedia again presented numerous problems, not the least of which was the difficulty of applying a uniform criteria that could accommodate language, religion, common history, occupational specialization, regional localization, common culture, self-identification, and identification by others. In general, strict adherence to official government lists of ethnic groups has been avoided, as the compilation of such lists is often driven by political considerations. If government criteria were followed, national groups in such states as Turkey or Japan would not be included, because of government claims that there are no national minorities within their borders.

The national groups chosen for inclusion represent a perplexing diversity that share just one characteristic—they identify themselves as separate nations. The arduous task of researching this diversity has been made more complicated by the lack of a consensus on what constitutes a "nation" or "nation-state." There is no universally accepted definition of "nation," "country," or "state." The subject continues to generate endless debate and numerous conflicts.

An attempt to apply the criteria used to distinguish independent states foundered on the numerous anomalies encountered. Size is definitely not a criterion. Over 40 states recognize a building in Rome, covering just 108.7 acres, as an independent state. Nor is United Nations membership the measure of independence; Ukraine and Belarus (Byelorussia) were founding members of the United Nations in 1945 yet became independent only in 1991. Membership in such international organizations as the International Olympic Committee (IOC) or the Organization of African Unity (OAU) does not necessarily signify political independence. Antarctica issues postage stamps but has no citizens; Palestine has citizens and embassies in dozens of countries but is not in practice an independent state; and so on.

Webster's Unabridged Dictionary defines the word *nation* as "a body of people, associated with a particular territory, that is sufficiently conscious of its unity to seek or possess a government particularly its own." On the basis of this definition, the criteria for selecting nations for inclusion was narrowed to just three important factors, modified by the diversity of the nations themselves. The three factors are self-identity as a distinctive group, the display of the outward trappings of national consciousness (particularly the adoption of a flag, a very important and very emotional part of any nationalism), and the formation of a specifically nationalist organization or political grouping that reflects its claim to self-determination. Many stateless nations were eliminated from the encyclopedia when one of these three factors could not be found during the exhaustive research process. National identity is often difficult to define and is very tricky to measure. For that reason this definitive volume of twenty-first-century nationalism contains a number of national groups whose identity is disputed but that met the criteria.

In any compilation, the selection process for choosing which material to include is a complex evolution of subtractions and additions. Estimates of the number of national groups in the world run as high as 9,000, making the selection process truly a process of elimination. The nations included in these volumes therefore represent only a fraction of the world's stateless nations.

Each national survey is divided into several parts or headings: the name and alternative names of the group; population statistics, incorporating the total national population and its geographical distribution; the homeland, including location, size, population, capital cities, and major cultural centers; the people and culture; the language and religion; a brief sketch of the national group's history and present situation; the national flag or other pertinent flags; and a map that places the national homeland in a local geographic setting.

Most of the nations included in this encyclopedia played little or no role in international politics before the end of the Cold War. Some of the national groups will be familiar, historically or more recently as news items, but the majority are virtually unknown and do not have standardized names or spellings in English. Familiar names often were, or are, the colonial or imposed names that in themselves represented a particularly harsh form of cultural suppression. That situation is now being reversed, with scholars, cartographers, and geographers attempting to settle on the definitive forms of the names of national groups, territories, and languages. Until that process is completed, many of the names used in these volumes will not only be unfamiliar but will not appear in even the most comprehensive reference sources.

The population figures are the author's estimates for the year 2002. The figures are designated by the abbreviation "(2002e)" before the appropriate statistics. The figures were gleaned from a vast number of sources, both official and unofficial, representing the latest censuses, official estimates, and—where no other sources were available—nationalist claims. Where important disparities over group size exist, both the official and the claimed population figures are included. Official rates of population growth, urban expansion, and other variables were applied to the figures to arrive at the statistics included in the encyclopedia. Since very few of the world's national groups are confined to one territory, the population statistics also includes information on geographic distribution.

Information on the homeland of each national group includes the geographic location and general features of the territory. Most of the national groups are concentrated in defined national territories—a state, province, region or historical region, department, etc. The corresponding features are included in this section, even though most territorial claims are based on historical association, not modern ethnic demographic patterns, provincial boundaries, or international borders. The geographic information incorporates the size of the territory, in both square miles (sq. mi.) and square kilometers (sq. km). The population figures for the larger cities cover the populations within city limits, and where appropriate, populations of surrounding urban or metropolitan areas. The two figures are included in an effort to reconcile the vastly different methods of enumerating urban populations used by the various governments and international agencies. A list of the principal statistical sources is provided at the end of this section.

Current political events have graphically demonstrated that the overall numbers are much less important than the level of national sentiment and political mobilization. A brief sketch of the people and their culture accompanies each entry, highlighting the cultural and national influences that have shaped the primary national group. A related section covers the linguistic and religious affiliations of each national group.

Each of the stateless nations has its own particular history, the events and conflicts that have shaped its national characteristics and level of mobilization. The largest part of each national survey is therefore devoted to the national history, the historical development of the national group. The national history survey follows the evolution and consolidation of the nation from its earliest history to the present. Although meticulous attention has been paid to the content and objectivity of each national survey, the polemic nature of the subject and, in many cases, the lack of official information have made it impossible to eliminate all unsubstantiated material. The author apologizes for the unintentional inclusion of controversial, dubious, or distorted information gathered from myriad and often unsatisfactory sources.

The national flags and other flags intimately associated with national groups are images of the actual flags; however, due to the informal use of these flags and a lack of information on actual size, all are presented in the same format. In many cases more than one flag is presented, particularly when a national flag has not been adopted or when other flags are equally important. The maps are the author's own, provided to complement the text. They are simple line drawings provided to aid the reader and as supplements to a comprehensive atlas.

The two appendices will allow the reader to develop a better understanding of the historical evolution of national sentiment over the past century and of the rapid proliferation of national organizations that has attended the post–Cold War wave of nationalism. Appendix A sets the numerous declarations of independence in a historical and chronological context, explicitly illustrating the waves of nationalism that have paralleled or accompanied the momentous trends and events of contemporary history. Appendix B provides a geographic listing, by region and nation, of the ever-expanding number of national organizations that herald the mobilization of national sentiment. The number of groups that exist within each national movement graphically illustrates the range of nationalist opinion, although little is known or published about the ideologies, aims, or methods of the majority of these national organizations.

Very few of the stateless nations developed in isolation; they were shaped by their relations with various governments and neighboring peoples. Accordingly, nations mentioned in the various entries that are themselves the subjects of separate entries appear with an asterisk (*). An extensive subject index is provided at the end of the last volume. Each encyclopedia entry also includes a short bibliographic list of sources.

This historical encyclopedia was compiled to provide a guide to the nations in the forefront of the post–Cold War nationalist resurgence, a political process all too often considered synonymous with the more extreme and violent aspects of nationalism. This work is not presented as an assertion that a multitude of new states are about to appear, even though political self-rule is the ultimate goal of many the national groups included in the survey. This encyclopedia is presented as a unique reference source to the nonstate nations that are spearheading one of the most powerful and enduring political movements in modern history, the pursuit of democracy's basic tenet—self-determination.

PRINCIPAL STATISTICAL SOURCES

1. National Censuses 1998–2001
2. *World Population Chart*, 2000 (United Nations)
3. *Populations and Vital Statistics*, 2000 (United Nations)
4. *World Tables*, 2000 (World Bank)
5. *World Demographic Estimates and Projections*, 1950–2025, 1988 (United Nations)
6. *UNESCO Statistical Annual*, 2000
7. *World Bank Atlas*, 1998
8. The Economist Intelligence Unit (Country Report series 2000)
9. *World Population Prospects* (United Nations)
10. *Europa Yearbook*, 2000
11. U.S. Department of State publications
12. *CIA World Factbook*
13. *United Nations Statistical Yearbook*, 2000
14. *United Nations Demographic Yearbook*, 2000
15. *The Statesman's Yearbook*, 2000
16. *Encyclopedia Britannica*
17. *Encyclopedia Americana*
18. Bureau of the Census, U.S. Department of Commerce 2001
19. National Geographic Society

20. Royal Geographical Society
21. *Webster's New Geographical Dictionary*, 1988
22. *Political Handbook of the World*
23. The Urban Foundation
24. *The Blue Plan*
25. Eurostat, the European Union Statistical Office
26. Indigenous Minorities Research Council
27. The Minority Rights Group
28. Cultural Survival
29. World Council of Indigenous Peoples
30. Survival International
31. *China Statistical Yearbook* (State Statistical Bureau of the People's Republic of China)
32. Arab Information Center
33. CIEMEN, Escarré's International Centre for Ethnical Minorities and Nations, Barcelona
34. International Monetary Fund
35. American Geographic Society

INTRODUCTION

The human race has never been a uniform whole, composed of rigorously identical individuals. There are a certain number of characteristics common to all human beings, and other attributes belonging to each individual. Besides the division of the human race by sex, age groups, and class divisions of economic origin, there is another very important separation, which is of a linguistic, ethnic, religious, or territorial type: the division into discernible national groups. Just as social classes are defined by economic criteria, even though they include global human realities and not just economic parameters, national groups are characterized not simply by linguistic or ethnic realities but also by global human realities, such as oppression or other forces of history.

The emphasis on the rights of states rather than the rights of the individuals and nations within them has long dictated international attitudes toward nationalism, attitudes buttressed by ignorance and failure to understand the "nation" versus the "nation-state." The use of condemnatory labels—separatist, secessionist, rebel, splittist, etc.—has been a powerful state weapon against those who seek different state structures on behalf of their nations. The rapid spread of national sentiment, affecting even nations long considered assimilated or quiescent, is attracting considerable attention, but the focus of this attention is invariably on its impact on established governments and its effect on international relations. As the Cold War withered away, it was replaced by a bewildering number and variety of nationalisms that in turn spawned a global movement toward the breakdown of the existing system of nation-states.

Current trends toward decentralization of government and empowerment of local groups inadvertently fragment society into often contending and mutually unintelligible cultures and subcultures. Even within a single society, people are segmenting into many self-contained communities and contending interest groups, entities that often take on the tone and aims of national groups.

The human race was divided into national groups long before the division of labor and, consequently, well before the existence of a class system. A class is defined by its situation in relation to production or consumption, and it is a universal social category. Each individual belongs to a horizontally limited human group (the economic class) and to a vertically limited group (the nation or national group). People have had identities deriving from religion, birthplace, language, or local authority for as long as humans have had cultures. They began to see themselves as members of national groups, opposed to other such groups, however, only during the modern period of colonization and state building.

An offshoot of the eighteenth-century doctrine of popular sovereignty, nationalism became a driving force in the nineteenth century, shaped and invigorated by the principles of the American and French revolutions. It was the Europeans, with their vast colonial possessions, who first declared that each and every person has a national identity that determined his or her place within the state structure. Around the world colonial and postcolonial states created new social groups and identified them by ethnic, religious, economic, or regional categories. Far from reflecting ancient ethnic or tribal loyalties, national cohesion and action are products of the modern state's demand that people make themselves heard as groups or risk severe disadvantages. Around the world, various movements and insurgencies, each with its own history and motivations, have typically—and erroneously—been lumped together as examples of the evils of nationalism.

Over the last century, perhaps no other subject has inspired the passions that surround nationalism and national sentiment. We can distinguish two primary kinds of nationalism, often opposed: unifying or assimilative nationalism; and separatist nationalism, which seeks to separate to some degree from the nationalism of the nation-state. Unifying nationalism shades off gradually into assimilation and imperialism, which reached its apex in the nineteenth century and continues to the present. Nationalism, in its most virulent forms, has provoked wars, massacres, terrorism, and genocide, but the roots of nationalist violence lie not in primordial ethnic and religious differences but in modern attempts to rally populations around nationalist ideas. Nationalism is often a learned and frequently manipulated set of ideas rather than a primordial sentiment. Violent nationalism in political life is a product of modern conflicts over power and resources, not an ancient impediment to political modernity.

The question of what a nation is has gained new significance with the recent increase in the number of claims to self-determination. The legitimacy of these claims rests upon the acceptance of a group in question as a nation, something more than just a random collection of people. The international community primarily regards nations as territorially based, and the consolidation of nations within specific territories has lent legitimacy to self-determination struggles in many areas. Yet this limited definition can give both undue influence to territorially consolidated groups seeking full sovereignty and independence, as well as undermine equally legitimate claims for self-determination among nonterritorial groups that do not aim for statehood but aim, rather, at greater control over their own lives.

National identity becomes nationalism when it includes aspirations to some variety of self-government. The majority of the world's stateless nations have embraced nationalism, but even though nationalists often include militant factions seeking full independence, most nationalists would probably settle for the right to practice their own languages and religions and to control their own territories and resources. Although the nationalist resurgence has spawned numerous conflicts, nationalism is not automatically a divisive force; it provides citizens with an identity and a sense of responsibility and involvement.

The first wave of modern nationalism culminated in the disintegration of Europe's multinational empires after World War I. The second wave began during World War II and continued as the very politicized decolonization process that engulfed the remaining colonial empires, as a theater of the Cold War after 1945. The removal of Cold War factionalism has now released a third wave of nationalism, of a scale and diffusion unprecedented in modern history. In the decade since the end of the Cold War, regionalist movements across the globe have taken on the tone and ideology of nationalist movements. The new national awakening, at the beginning of the twenty-first century, in many respects resembles the phenomenon of the turn of the twentieth century. Ethnicity, language, culture, religion, geography, and even economic condition—but not nationality— are becoming the touchstones of national identity.

Nationalism is often associated with separatism, which can be an offshoot of nationalism, but the majority of the world's national movements normally mobilize in favor of greater autonomy; separatism and separatist factions usually evolve from a frustrated desire for the basic tenet of democracy, self-determination. The conflicts resulting from this latest nationalist upsurge have reinforced the erroneous beliefs that nationalism is synonymous with extremism and that separatism is confined to the historical "hot spots" in Europe and Asia. One of the basic premises of this encyclopedia is that the nationalist resurgence at the end of the twentieth century is spreading to all corners of the world and is likely to mold the world's political agenda for decades to come. Academics too often define nationalism in terms of its excesses, so that its very definition condemns it.

The post–Cold War revival of nationalism is not limited to any one continent, nor is it a product of any particular ideology, geographic area, religion, or combination of political or historical factors. The latest wave of nationalism affects rich and poor, large and small, developed and developing, indigenous and nonindigenous peoples. National diversity is often associated with political instability and the likelihood of violence, but some of the world's most diverse states, though not without internal nationalisms, have suffered relatively little violence between national groups, while countries with relatively little cultural or linguistic diversity, including Yugoslavia, Somalia, and Rwanda, have had the bloodiest of such conflicts.

Nationalism has become an ascendant ideology, one that is increasingly challenging the nineteenth-century definition of the unitary nation-state. The worldwide nationalist revival is an amplified global echo of the nationalism that swept Europe's stateless nations in the late nineteenth and early twentieth centuries, now including the indigenous-rights movements that are major moral, political, and legal issues in many states, and a growing number of groups based on religious distinction that have taken on the characteristics of national groups.

The United Nations estimates that only 3% of the world's 6,000 national groups have achieved statehood. Although the last decade has seen the emergence of an unprecedented number of new states, the existing world order remains conservative in the recognition of new states. There is no perfect justice in dealing with nationalist aspirations; each case should be viewed as separate and distinct. Joining the club of independent states remains a privilege of few of the world's national groups.

The failure to understand national identity and nationalism is often reinforced by the view that nationalism represents a tribal, waning stage of history. The world's insistence that national structures conform to existing international borders for the sake of world peace was one of the first casualties of the revolution brought on by the world's new enthusiasm for democracy and self-determination. Between the end of World War II and the end of the Cold War, nationalism spawned only three new states—Iceland, Singapore, and Bangladesh—while the decolonization process created many more. However, between 1991 and 2001 nationalism accounted for the splintering of the Soviet Union and Yugoslavia, and the partitions of Czechoslovakia and Ethiopia, leading to the emergence of twenty-two new states. The belief that political and economic security could be guaranteed only by the existing political order faded as quickly as the ideological and political divisions set in place after World War II.

The world is in the midst of an extended post–Cold War transition that will last well into the present century. The community of democratic states is expanding, but this era of transition remains complex and dangerous. In much of the world there remains a potentially explosive mix of social, demographic, economic, and political conditions that run counter to the global trends toward democracy and economic reforms. The transition has taken the lid off long-simmering ethnic, religious, territorial, and economic disputes and has stimulated the growth of national identities on a scale unimaginable just a decade ago.

The definition of a "nation" remains controversial and undecided. The nineteenth-century French scholar Ernest Renan stated that a nation is a community of people who have endured common suffering as a people. National identity and nationalism are highly complicated and variable phenomena that resist simple diagnoses of any kind. The most basic premise remains that nations are self-defining. In a broad sense, a nation may be defined as any group of people that perceives itself to be a nation.

The growth of national sentiment can be based on a common origin, language, history, culture, territorial claims, geographical location, religion, economics, ethnicity, racial background, opposition to another group, or opposition to bad or oppressive government. The mobilization of national sentiment is most often a complicated mixture of some or all of these components. No one of these factors is essential; however, some must be present if group cohesion is to be strong enough to evolve a self-identifying nationalism. None of the world's national groups is a hermetically sealed entity. All are influenced by, and in turn influence, other national groups. Nor is any national group changeless, invariant, or static. All national groups are in states of constant flux, driven by both internal and external forces. These forces may be accommodating, harmonious, benign, and based on voluntary actions, or they may be involuntary, resulting from violent conflict, force, or domination.

Democracy, although widely accepted as the only system that is able to provide the basis of humane political and economic activity, can be a subversive force. Multiparty democracy often generates chaos and instability as centrifugal forces, inherent parts of a free political system, are set loose. The post–Cold War restoration of political pluralism and democratic process has given rise to a rebirth of ethnicity and politicized national identity, while the collapse of communism in much of the world has shattered the political equilibrium that had prevailed for over four decades. The Cold War blocs had mostly succeeded in suppressing or controlling the regional nationalisms in their respective spheres, nationalisms that now have begun to reignite old national desires and ethnic rivalries. Around the globe, numerous national groups, their identities and aspirations long buried under decades of Cold War tensions, are emerging to claim for themselves the basic principle of democracy, self-determination. The centrifugal forces held in check by the Cold War have emerged to challenge accepted definitions of a nation and its rights. The doctrine of statism is slowly being superseded by a post–Cold War internationalism that is reshaping the world's view of the unitary nation-state and, what is more important, the world's view of who or what constitutes a nation.

Two main trends are vying to shape the post–Cold War world. One is the movement to form continental or regional economic-political groupings that would allow smaller political units as members. The other is the emergence of smaller and smaller national units as older states are broken up. The two trends are not mutually exclusive. The nation-state, with its absolute sovereignty, is fading and giving way to historical trends—the nation rather than the nation-state in one direction, and supranational bodies, such as the United Nations, the European Union, and even

NAFTA, in the other. The rapidly changing political and economic realities have swept aside the old arguments that population size, geographic location, and economic viability are deterrents to national self-determination. The revival of nationalism is converging with the emergence of continental political and economic units theoretically able to accommodate ever smaller national units within overarching political, economic, and security frameworks.

The third wave of modern nationalism, with its emphasis on human rights and democratic self-determination, is set to top the international agenda for decades to come. The nationalist revival, global in scope, has strengthened submerged national, ethnic, and regional identities and has shattered the conviction that assimilation would eventually homogenize the existing nation-states. The nationalist revival is now feeding on itself, as the freedom won by many historically stateless nations has emboldened other national groups to demand greater control of their own destinies.

A unique feature of this current wave of nationalism is the growing mutual cooperation and support among and between the stateless nations, both nationally and internationally. A number of national groups in countries such as Russia, China, and Myanmar have joined together to work for common goals. Many of the nations selected for inclusion in the encyclopedia are members, or aspiring members, of two organizations that for the first time provide legitimate forums in which to gain strength through numbers and to publicize causes without recourse to violence. The larger of the organizations, the Unrepresented Nations and Peoples Organization (UNPO), was formed in 1991 by six stateless nations, four of which have since been recognized as independent states. The organization, its membership now swollen by the representatives of dozens of stateless nations, is already referred to as an alternative United Nations, representing over 100 million people. The second group, the Free Europe Alliance, is less global in scale but, like the UNPO, is inundated by membership applications.

The political and cultural renaissance spreading through the world's national groups is inexorably moving global politics away from the present system of sovereign states, each jealously defending its authority, to a new world order more closely resembling the world's true national and historical geography. A world community dominated by democracy must inevitably recognize the rights of the world's stateless nations, including the right of each to choose its own future. The twin issues of national identity and self-determination will remain at the forefront of international relations. The diffusion and force of contemporary national movements make it imperative that the nationalist phenomenon be studied and understood. One of the most urgent concerns of our time is to fashion a principled and effective policy toward all national groups.

ENCYCLOPEDIA
OF THE
STATELESS NATIONS

Abaza

Abazian; Abazin; Abazinians; Apsua; Apswa; Ashuwa; Beskesek Abkhaz; Kuban Abkhaz; Ashvy

POPULATION: Approximately (2002e) 38,000 Abaza in Russia, concentrated in the Abazashta region of the Karachayevo-Cherkess Republic in southern Russia. There is an Abaza community of about 10,000 in Turkey and small communities in the Middle East, Germany, and the United States.

THE ABAZA HOMELAND: The Abaza homeland lies in the northwestern area of the North Caucasus region of southern European Russia. The homeland, called Abazashta, forms a district of the Karachayevo-Cherkess Republic of the Russian Federation lying in the foothills of the main range of the Great Caucasian Mountains on the upper reaches of the Big and Little Zelenchuk, Kuban, and Kuma Rivers. A majority of the Abaza live in 13 towns and villages in Abazashta, with small communities in neighboring Kuban and as far away as Kabarda, Adygea, and in two towns near Kislovodsk, farther north in Stavropol Krai. In recent years the Abaza have rallied to the call for a separate autonomous republic of Abazashta, or autonomy

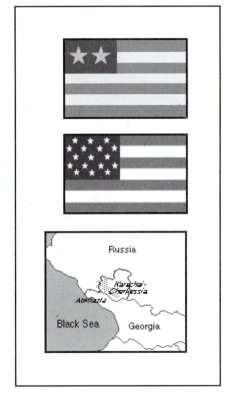

within a proposed Cherkessia-Abazashta state as an independent member state of the Russian Federation. The Abaza capital and major cultural center is Teberda, (2002e) 13,000.

FLAG: The Abaza national flag has seven green and white vertical stripes bearing a red canton charged with two gold five-pointed stars on the upper hoist. The flag of the Confederation of Caucasian Peoples, to which the Abaza belong, has seven green and white stripes bearing a blue canton charged with seventeen small white five-pointed stars.

PEOPLE AND CULTURE: The Abaza are a West Caucasian people closely related to the Abkhaz* of the Black Sea coast to the west. The Abaza call themselves Ashvy or Apsua, a name also used by the Abkhaz. Part of the Balkano-Caucasian race, the Abaza have the features of the

Pontic and Caucasian types—light skin, round heads, and medium stature. The small Abaza nation is traditionally divided into two distinct kinship groups, the Tapanta and the Ashkharaua. In the tradition of most European Muslims, the Abaza's lifestyle is basically European, and Abaza women are liberated and unveiled, even though the majority continue to live in isolated rural settlements and work as farmers or herders. An estimated 30% of the total now live in urban areas. The Abaza highly value hospitality, and the arrival of a guest is accompanied by a ritual feast. Providing hospitality is a source of family and community pride.

LANGUAGE AND RELIGION: The Abaza language, called Abazin, belongs to the Northwest Caucasian or Abkhazo-Adyghian language group of Caucasian languages. The language is close to Abkhaz but also shows elements characteristic of the Circassian language of the Kabards.* Phonetically and morphologically, the Abaza language is practically the same as neighboring Abkhaz and is noted for its great number of distinctive consonants and its limited number of distinctive vowels. The language is spoken in three major dialects and five subdialects, some of which are partially intelligible to Abkhaz speakers: Abazakt, Apsua, Kubin-Elburgan, Kuvin, and Psyzh-Krasnovostok. Tapanta is the main dialect and is the source of the Abaza literary language. The Ashkharaua speak two closely related dialects called the Ashkharawa dialects. The language is the mother tongue of about 95% of the Abaza, a very high percentage among Russian nationalities. Abazin has literary status in Russia and is written in a modified Cyrillic script; however, in Turkey the Abaza minority use Turkish as their literary language. Abaza phonetics are considered the most difficult of all the languages spoken in the Russian Federation.

The majority of the Abaza are Sunni Muslims of the Hanafite rite, with a small Christian minority making up about 3% of the population. The Muslim religion was embraced between the seventeenth and nineteenth centuries under Turkish influence; however, the Abaza's earlier Christian and pagan beliefs and customs can still be observed in their distinct Muslim traditions. A significant number of Abaza, particularly the Ashkaraua, remained nominally Christian until the mid-nineteenth century.

NATIONAL HISTORY: The Abaza nation is descended from the proto-Abkhazian tribes, a broad conglomerate of Caucasian tribes that populated the eastern shores of the Black Sea in ancient times. Archeological evidence of their presence goes back to between 4000 and 3000 B.C. Four of the tribes, the Apsil, Abazgi, Svanig, and Misimian, slowly merged to form the Abkhaz nation in the eighth century, and by the late eighth century or early ninth century, a distinct offshoot had formed, the Abaza nation. The center of the Abaza nation lay in the traditional territory of the Abazgi tribe in the northwestern part of Abkhazia, from the Bsybyu River to the present city of Tuapse.

Some individual clans had been moving into the Caucasian highlands since the eighth century, but the resettlement of the whole Tapanta tribe began in the thirteenth century, followed by that of the Ashkaraua tribe. In the fifteenth and sixteenth centuries, the Abaza were known as a strong and militant nation, their mountain strongholds nearly impossible to take by force, although intertribal quarrels and constant wars with neighboring peoples in the seventeenth century reduced the small nation to vassalage to Kabard princes. From the fourteenth to the seventeenth centuries, the Abaza migrated to the valleys of the Laba, the Urup, the Big and Little Zelenchuk, the Kuban, and the Teberda Rivers in present Karachai-Cherkessia. The Abaza who remained on the coast of the Black Sea were assimilated by the Abkhaz and Cherkess.*

Turkish expansion into the Caucasus brought a new religion to the region, Islam. Under Turkish influence the Abaza converted to Sunni Islam between the sixteenth and eighteenth centuries, although there were still Christian Abaza up to the nineteenth century. The Abaza nobility first embraced the Islamic religion, which was spreading to their homeland from Abkhazia. For about a century after the Abaza majority's conversion to Islam, the rural people retained their pagan and Christian traditions, only slightly changed to accommodate the prevailing religion.

Cossack, Ukrainian, and Russian settlements began to appear in the river valleys among the Abaza as early as the sixteenth century. The expanding borders of the Russian Empire reached the Abaza homeland in the late eighteenth century, making Abazashta of strategic concern to both the Russians and the Turks of the Ottoman Empire. To overcome Abaza resistance to outside authority, both powers used force of arms, but the most effective way became deportation. Whole villages were forcibly resettled in territory controlled by Russia or Ottoman Turkey.

Already outnumbered by immigrant communities in the eighteenth century, the Abaza were involved in frequent smaller conflicts over land rights and cultural differences. During the Russo-Turkish wars in 1828–29, the Abaza joined the other Circassian peoples to fight against the Russians. The Abaza living on the open steppes were especially vulnerable to exterminatory attacks by Russian forces. The Russian victory led to reprisals and further deportations.

During the widespread Shamil revolt against Russian rule from 1834 to 1858, the small nation was split, as the Tapanta sided with the Russians, while the Ashkharaua supported Shamil and the Muslim rebels. After the Caucasus wars of 1817–64, some 30–45,000 Abaza emigrated to Turkey. A government order of 1862 ordered all Abaza living in the area between the Laba and Belyi Rivers to resettle in the Kuban or leave the Russian Empire. Also in the 1860s, many Abaza were moved or deported from the mountains to the plains, where bigger villages were established artificially. By 1900, the Abaza had been drastically reduced in numbers, while emigration had destroyed their former tribal structure. The territories emptied by the emigrants were colonized by immigrants from other parts of Russian, mostly ethnic Slavs. An estimated two million acres of historically Abaza land were confiscated for Slav settlement.

The way of life of the Abaza was shaped by their environment. Before the 1860s, they lived in the mountains, with the emphasis on raising livestock in the rich upland pastures. They were famed for their flocks and herds, particularly their pedigree horses. The Tapanta, who lived in the flatter steppe, were more involved in field cultivation. Land reform in the late nineteenth century reduced their traditional lands, and herding was curtailed as pastures passed into private hands and rents became prohibitive. Most Abaza turned to farming to survive.

The Russian Empire was swept by revolution in February 1917, leaving Abazashta effectively independent as local government collapsed. A movement to unite with the separatist republic set up in neighboring Abhkazia, however, was put down by local Slav militias. Although there were Abaza soldiers fighting in both the Red and White Guard units, two White mounted regiments, Tapanta and Baskhyag, had achieved considerable fame as fierce fighters before the final White defeat in 1920.

The new Soviet authorities divided the Abaza homeland between the Karachai* and Cherkess national areas, while collectivization and the cultural revolution radically changed the Abaza way of life. The Soviet solution to Abaza opposition was found in the deportation and execution of the "class enemies" unacceptable to the new authorities. Russification of the Abaza culture was pressed by local Soviet officials. A rebellion in 1930 was brutally suppressed and its leaders liquidated.

In 1923 a Latin-alphabet Abaza script was created, and education in the Abaza language was made available for the first six years of schooling; thereafter, Russian was to be used. In 1938 the Soviet authorities ordered that the Abaza literary language adopt the Cyrillic alphabet and that Russian be made the official language of education. In spite of the Russification of education and administration, a notable literature developed; an Abaza theater was established, and a newspaper was published in the language.

Joseph Stalin, an ethnic Georgian and particularly suspicious of the small Muslim nations of the Caucasus, prepared in 1943 a plan to deport the Abkhaz and Abaza to Central Asia, but the plan was later postponed. In 1944 the Karachayevo-Cherkess Autonomous Oblast was abolished, following the deportation of the entire Karachai nation. Preparations for the mass deportation of the Abkhaz-Abaza began again in 1953, but due to Stalin's death in that year the two small nations were spared the horrors experienced by other Caucasian peoples deported from their homelands on his orders. Abazashta remained administratively divided between the Stavropol Krai of the Russian Federation and the Georgian Soviet Socialist Republic from 1944 until 1957, when the Karachai-Cherkess Autonomous Region was reconstituted and the Abaza were reunited in one political unit.

Communist policy and propaganda left a marked impact on both the daily lives and the mentality of the Abaza people. The way of life in Abazashta is now basically European, with the Abaza's clothing and household goods reflecting the advance of European culture. During the Soviet era, homes could be built only in one of three standardized designs approved by the state, and urban settlements were restructured from the traditional haphazard placement to the Russian-style grid pattern.

Two tendencies emerged in the 1960s that threatened the Abaza culture even more than decades of Russification and suppression—mixed marriages and urbanization. By 1979 an estimated 21% of the Abaza lived in urban areas, as against the near-zero figure of 1900. Surrounded by peoples of predominately Russian culture, the Abaza were rapidly assimilating.

In spite of increasing urbanization, liberalization of Soviet life in the late 1980s initiated a period of reculturation, and a religious revival began to slowly reverse the inroads made by the official atheism of the Soviet period. Many Abaza crossed the new international border to fight alongside their Abkhaz kin in neighboring Georgia in 1992. A militant nationalist organization, the Confederation of Caucasian Peoples, supported by most of the small nations of the North Caucasus, organized fighting units to support the Abkhaz bid for independence.

The defeat of the candidate supported by the Cherkess and Abaza in republican elections in September 1999 set off a round of violence and increased demands for the partition of the Karachai-Cherkess Republic into two. Stansilav Derev, the Cherkess-Abaza candidate, charged that the election had been unfair and vowed to separate the Cherkess-Abaza region from Karachai. The Abaza leaders supported the move but demanded their own national homeland within the proposed Cherkess autonomous *okrug*. Twenty-six people were injured when supporters of Derev and the Karachai candidate, Vladimir Semenov, clashed in Cherkess.

The Abaza have begun to take a greater interest in their own history and culture as the effects of decades of imposed Soviet culture fade. Following the contested election in the republic, representatives of the Abaza, at a meeting of the region's non-Karachai ethnic groups, voted for autonomy as part of a separate Cherkess-Abaza state. Abaza and Cherkess leaders in November 1999 drafted a legal document providing for a separate Abaza-Cherkess autonomous republic within Russia. The controversy increasingly pits the Abaza and Cherkess against the republic's Karachai and the large Russian population.

Abaza and Cherkess members of the republican legislature walked out in January 2000. They refused to return for budget and other debates in March-April, claiming that their participation would be invalid, as their regions would soon secede from the joint republic. Abaza autonomy within a new Cherkess-Abaza republic would give them greater say in local government and end the growing ethnic confrontations between the Circassian peoples, the Cherkess and the Abaza, and the Turkic Karachais in the Karachai-Cherkess Republic.

SELECTED BIBLIOGRAPHY:

Abtorkhanov, Abdurahman, and Marie Bennigsen Broxup. *The North Caucasus Barrier: The Russian Advance towards the Muslim World.* 1992.

Baddeley, John F. *Russian Conquest of the Caucasus.* 1997.

Coppieters, Bruno, ed. *Contested Borders in the Caucasus.* 1996.

Olson, James S. *An Ethnohistorical Dictionary of the Russian and Soviet Empires.* 1994.

Abkhaz

Abkhazi; Abkhazians; Abxazo; Apsua; Apswa; Ashuwa; Ashvy

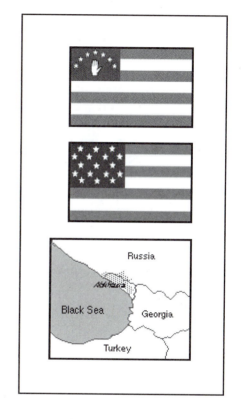

POPULATION: Approximately (2002e) 123,000 Abkhaz in the Caucasus, mostly in the breakaway Republic of Abkhazia and adjacent areas of Russia. There are an estimated 35,000 in Turkey. Other large populations live in Syria and Jordan. Smaller communities live in the United States, Israel, Yugoslavia, Canada, Egypt, the Netherlands, and Germany. The Abkhaz diaspora, called the Mokhajirs, is claimed by nationalists to number over 500,000.

THE ABKHAZ HOMELAND: The Abkhaz homeland occupies a narrow coastal lowland on the Black Sea, backed by a spur of the western Caucasus Mountains. The steep mountain slopes give way to a central area of foothills and river valleys that descend to a narrow coastal lowland along the shores of the eastern Black Sea. This narrow strip of land is characterized by an extreme variety of natural conditions, including subtropical lowlands, mountain lakes, mineral strings, and abundant forests. The Abkhaz republic, while virtually independent, legally remains an autonomous republic within the Republic of Georgia. *Republic of Abkhazia (Apsny Respublika)*: 3,320 sq. mi.—8,599 sq. km, (2002e) 270,000. The population breakdown is based on 1992 population estimates made prior to the outbreak of fighting in the region: (1992e) 537,000—Georgians 44%, Abkhaz 20%, Russians 16%, Armenians 6%, Ukrainians 2%, Pontian Greeks 2%. The Abkhaz capital and major cultural center is Sukhumi, called Aqua by the Abkhaz, (2002e) 65,000.

FLAG: The Abkhaz national flag, the official flag of the breakaway republic, has seven green and white stripes with a red canton on the upper hoist bearing a white hand below an arch of seven white five-pointed stripes. The flag of the Confederation of Caucasian Peoples, to which the

Abkhaz belong, has seven green and white stripes with a blue canton charged with seventeen small, white five-pointed stars on the upper hoist.

PEOPLE AND CULTURE: The Abkhaz are a Northern Caucasian nation encompassing four major geographical and cultural groups: the Muslim Gudauta, Abzhui, and Abaza,* and the Orthodox Samurzakan. The Abkhaz call themselves Apsua, and their ancient territory they call Ashvy or Apsny, the Land of the Abkhaz. Anthropologically the Abkhaz belong to the West Caucasian group of the Balkano-Caucasian race. They are characterized by above-average height, a lean build, relatively fair skin, sharp features, and dark eyes. The Abkhaz population grew very slowly until after World War II. From 1926 to 1939 the population grew by 2,000, which graphically reflects the impact of collectivization and the excesses of the Soviet repression. The Abkhaz culture is based on the ancient traditions of the Caucasus, a warrior ethos, and an emphasis on ritual hospitality. The skill of making eloquent speeches is highly prized and cultivated. It is the primary requirement of any village elder or community leader.

LANGUAGE AND RELIGION: The Abkhaz language belongs to the Northwest or Abkhazo-Adyghian group of Caucasian languages. Rich in consonants, at least 68, the Abkhaz language is considered the world's fastest phonetically, with complete information, such as word root and tense, often conveyed by a single consonant. There are few borrowed words from other languages. The language is considered one of the most difficult of the languages of the region to learn, which probably explains why the Abkhaz are extremely adept at learning foreign languages. The large variety of consonants and vowels enables the Abkhaz to pronounce foreign languages fairly precisely. The three major dialects of the language are Abzhui, Samurzakan, and Bzyb. The modified Russian Cyrillic alphabet currently in use does not fully represent the traditional sounds, which include a wavering trill, whistling noises, and a prolonged buzz. The Abkhaz language retains many proverbs that guide everyday behavior and values.

The majority of the Abkhaz are Sunni Muslims of the Hanafite school; however, the rites and rituals often mix ancient Christian and pagan traditions. Christianity was brought to the region by missionaries in the first century A.D., and the Abkhaz greatly helped the spread of the new region throughout the Caucasus region. In the sixteenth century the Turks introduced Islam, which rapidly supplanted the earlier Christianity among a majority of the population. Neither of these religions ever completely eroded pagan beliefs, which still remain strong in the region. Many Abkhaz mark both Islamic and Christian holidays and conduct pagan rituals, particularly those associated with the supreme god, Antzva, the plural form of the word for "mother." There are several sacred sites in Abkhazia where families and individuals go to pray to the traditional Abkhaz pantheon.

NATIONAL HISTORY: The early Abkhaz tribes, the Apsil, Misiman,

Abazg, and Svanig, were known to the ancient Greek and Roman historians. Greeks colonized the coastal regions as early as the sixth century B.C. Latinized following the Roman conquest of the Greek cities in 65 B.C., the tribes adopted much of Rome's Latin culture and language, and Christian missionaries later became active in the region.

In the first century A.D., the early Abkhaz tribes organized in petty states, which united in the Lazika principality in the fourth century. The tribes soon came under Byzantine cultural and political influence. During this period the first evidence of a local Christian congregation was recorded, when Stratophilus, the archbishop of Pitsunda, took part in the first Council of Nicaea, held in A.D. 325. Orthodox Christianity was brought to the region from Byzantium in the seventh century.

The consolidation of the Abkhaz nation in the seventh and eighth centuries began with the separation of Abkhazia from Lazika in 740. Prince Leon II united all of present western Georgia into a unitary state, with his capital at Kutaisi. Weakened by wars and internal strife, the state declined, and in 978 the Abkhaz throne passed to the dynasty that ruled Georgia, although the Abkhaz regained their independence in 1463.

During the rule of the Shervashidze dynasty, Turkish influence became paramount, and in 1578 Abkhazia became a protectorate of the Turkish sultanate. Over the next decades a majority of the Abkhaz abandoned Christianity for the Islamic religion of the Turks. In the eighteenth century the Turks attempted to annex Abkhazia. The Shervashidze rulers turned to Russia for help, and in 1810 Abkhazia became a Russian protectorate.

The Crimean and Caucasian wars, fought mostly in the Black Sea and Caucasus regions, allowed the Abkhaz to demand greater rights. However, following the final Russian victory over the Caucasian peoples to the east in 1864, Abkhaz autonomy became unnecessary to the Russian government. The last Prince Shervashidze was sent into exile, and Abkhazia was annexed to the Russian Empire.

Russian attempts to promote assimilation, particularly official efforts to convert the Muslim Abkhaz to Orthodox Christianity, incited a popular uprising in 1866. The Russian military quickly defeated the poorly armed Abkhaz army of 20,000 and subjected the majority of the defeated Abkhaz to virtual serfdom on Russian and Georgian estates established on confiscated Abkhaz lands. As a result of the brutal suppression following the Abkhaz uprising, many Abkhaz emigrated to Turkish territory, in the so-called Manadzhir Movement. Over 70,000 Abkhaz are believed to have left Abkhazia between 1866 and 1878. The government resettled the abandoned lands with ethnic Slavs.

Health resorts along the coast became fashionable among the tsarist nobility in the late nineteenth century. Overall economic prosperity spurred the growth of a local intelligentsia and eventually the rise of Abkhaz national consciousness. By the early 1900s a strong nationalist and separatist sentiment had developed among the educated Abkhaz. Following the February Revolution in 1917, Abkhazia became effectively independent as the tsarist bureaucracy collapsed. Abkhaz leaders formed the Abkhaz National Council and asserted their nation's right to autonomy.

Occupied by Georgian troops following the Bolshevik coup in October 1917, the Abkhaz mobilized and in February 1918 rose to expel the Georgian invaders. The rebels proclaimed Abkhazia independent on 8 March 1918. Their independent state lasted just 42 days before Bolshevik troops invaded from the north. In desperation, the Abkhaz leaders appealed to the neighboring Georgians for military aid. Having defeated the Bolsheviks, the Georgians stayed to incorporate the unwilling Abkhaz nation into their new republic. The Abkhaz revolted against Georgian rule in early 1921. The resulting chaos within Georgia provided a pretext for the Red Army's subsequent invasion and conquest of both Abkhazia and Georgia.

The Abkhaz language and most national institutions were suppressed in 1931 following the incorporation of Abkhazia into Soviet Georgia. The Soviet period saw the collectivization of the Abkhaz homeland and, from 1937 to 1953, an official policy of settling large numbers of ethnic Georgians in the region and of deporting many Abkhaz. In spite of the hardships and oppression, agricultural production in Abkhazia increased rapidly, which in turn spurred the growth of the cities and the urbanization of the Abkhaz nation. Only 5% of the Abkhaz lived in urban areas in 1926, but by 1939 over 15% were urban.

A Latin-based alphabet, devised in 1862, spurred the early growth of Abkhaz education. The first books were published in the Abkhaz alphabet in 1865, and by 1912 a vernacular prose had developed. Soviet policy decreed a change of alphabet to Roman letters in 1928, then to the Georgian alphabet in 1938, and the Cyrillic alphabet in 1954. Abkhaz periodicals, in Cyrillic script, started to appear only in the mid-1950s.

The Soviet leader Joseph Stalin, himself an ethnic Georgian and particularly suspicious of the small Muslim nations of the Caucasus, prepared in 1943 a plan to deport the Abkhaz to Central Asia, but the plan was later postponed. Preparations for the mass deportation of the Abkhaz began again in 1953, but due to Stalin's death in that year the Abkhaz were spared the horrors experienced by other Caucasian peoples deported from their homelands on his orders. However, massive Georgian immigration to Abkhazia, undertaken under Stalin's long dictatorial rule, reduced the Abkhaz to minority status in their homeland by the end of World War II. Resentment of their minority status provoked resentment of all Georgians, whom the Abkhaz associated with Stalin and suppression.

Resentment of the dominant status of the ethnic Georgians in Abkhazia led to serious rioting in 1957 and 1967, and it stimulated an Abkhaz national revival in the 1970s and 1980s. Led by the educated urban population, Abkhaz nationalist sentiment developed as a popular anti-Georgian movement. Beginning in 1978, the Soviet government, in an effort to head off growing Abkhaz demands for separation from Georgia, set aside as many as 67% of government and party positions in Abkhazia for the native Abkhaz minority.

In 1988, during the liberalization of Soviet life, a nationalist popular front organization known as Aiglara (Unity) formed, and for the first time since 1921 the Abkhaz National Council was convened. On 18 March 1989, the council called for Abkhaz secession from Georgia, which provoked a strong Georgian nationalist reaction.

The Republic of Georgia, which regained its independence at the disintegration of the Soviet Union in 1991, claimed Abkhazia as part of its national territory. An ethnocentric Georgian national government exacerbated tensions between Georgians and Abkhazians, whose sense of national identity is as strong as that of the Georgians. On 23 July 1992 the Abkhaz legislature, with widespread support, reinstated the republic's 1925 constitution, effectively declaring Abkhazia an independent republic. In response, the Georgian military occupied the region, setting off a bitter war of secession.

The Abkhaz forces slowly drove the Georgian military from the region and in September 1993 took control of the capital, Sukhumi. Some 200,000 Georgians fled or were driven from Abkhazia into western Georgia. In June 1994 the Georgian government reluctantly accepted 3,000 Russian troops on the Abkhaz border, effectively making Abkhazia independent under the de facto protection of Russia. On 26 November 1994, the Abkhaz parliament formally proclaimed the sovereign Republic of Abkhazia. The parliament then elected as the republic's first president the parliament chairman, Vladislav Ardzinba.

In May 1997, following several rounds of inconclusive talks under UN auspices, Georgian Eduard Shevardnadze offered increased autonomy but ruled out the Abkhaz demand for Georgian recognition of their independence. In July Shevardnadze called for a larger United Nations peacekeeping force during UN-sponsored talks that also included delegates of the Russian government.

The republic remains effectively independent, although its sovereignty has not been recognized by any world body or national government; the Abkhaz continue to exist in a diplomatic no-man's-land, their fragile independence guaranteed only by the presence of Russian peacekeeping troops. In spite of agreement on a UN-sponsored cease-fire in May 1998, in the summer of 1998 thousands of ethnic Georgians were expelled from the Gali region, near the Abkhaz-Georgian border, following renewed fighting between Abkhaz military forces and Georgian paramilitary groups.

The Georgian parliament in April 1998 rejected a new Abkhaz appeal for recognition of Abkhazian independence. In May there was a new outbreak of hostilities in the Gali region between the Abkhaz forces and Georgian groups known as the White Legion and the Forest Brothers, the worst fighting in over five years. The Georgian government denied any knowledge of the two unofficial paramilitary groups operating in the border region.

President Shevardnadze stated that he would be prepared to grant the region the highest status of political autonomy within an integral Georgian federation in September 1998. The Abkhaz leadership rejected the proposal and reiterated its demand for recognition of the region's independence as a precondition to further negotiations between the Abkhaz and Georgian governments.

The status of the Abkhaz homeland remains undecided, with both sides seemingly unwilling to compromise. One of the outstanding issues is that of the tens of thousands of Georgian refugees who wish to return to their homes in Abkhazia. In May 1999, President Shevardnadze appealed to the Abkhaz leadership to fulfill resolutions passed by the UN Security Council and other international organizations directed at returning the refugees to Abkhazia. Spokesmen for the Security Council demanded that both the Abkhaz and Georgians widen their commitments to the UN-led peace process by respecting the 1998 cease-fire agreement, adding that the UN expected a settlement on the political status of Abkhazia within the state of Georgia. Vladislav Ardzinba again rejected the idea that Abkhazia must remain part of Georgia, even with a large measure of autonomy.

Talks on the status of the Abkhaz homeland continued in 1999–2000, with little progress except for minor agreements on border controls, smuggling, and peacekeeping forces. The more difficult questions of the Georgian refugees, Abkhaz demands for recognition of their independence, and the ultimate status of the region remain as intractable as they were following the 1994 declaration of independence. In October 2001 fighting again broke out in the border region, threatening the fragile armed peace between the Azkhaz and the Georgians.

SELECTED BIBLIOGRAPHY:

Akaba, N. *Abkhazia and Georgia*. 1990.
Chervonnaeiia, Svetlana Aleksandrovna. *Conflict in the Caucasus: Georgia, Abkhazia, and the Russian Shadow*. 1994.
Coppieters, Bruno, ed. *Contested Borders in the Caucasus*. 1996.
Lordkipanidze, Mariam. *The Abkhazians and Abkhazia*. 1990.

Aborigines

Aborigines; Torres Straight Islanders

POPULATION: Approximately (2002e) 330,000 Aborigines in Australia, including the Torres Straits Islanders. Most Aborigines continue to live in rural areas, including the arid outback, but since the 1950s urbanization has accelerated, particularly to the large cities of the east coast.

THE ABORIGINAL HOMELAND: The Aboriginal homeland extends across the huge island continent of Australia, with concentrations of Aborigine population in the Northern Territory and Queensland. The continent on the whole is exceedingly flat and dry, particularly the traditional Aborigine lands in the vast Australian outback. Some of the Aborigine lands have local status as reserved lands, particularly in northern Queensland, but most traditional territory has been lost. About three-quarters of the Aborigines live in rural towns and in the reserved lands of the outback and the far north; the rest live in cities and urban slums. The Torres Strait Islands are located in the Torres Strait, which separates mainland Australia from

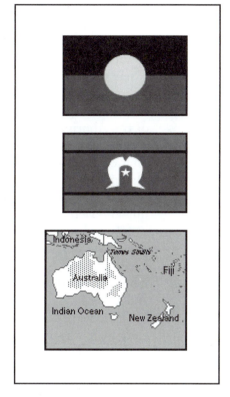

New Guinea. The islands have a distinct population of Melanesian descent, although they have established close relationships with the Aborigines of the mainland.

FLAG: The Aboriginal national flag, the flag of the national movement, is a horizontal bicolor of black over red bearing a centered yellow disk. The flag of the Torres Strait Islanders has horizontal stripes of green, blue, green, the blue broader than the green stripes and bearing a stylized white *dhari*, a dancer's headdress, and a white, five-pointed star centered.

PEOPLE AND CULTURE: Australia is the only continent where the entire indigenous population maintained a single kind of adaptation—hunting and gathering—into modern times. There are about 300 distinct communities. The two major indigenous groups are the Aborigines and the Torres Strait Islanders. Although they have many cultural traits in common with other hunter-gatherer peoples, the Aborigines are unique in the degree of contrast between the complexity of their social organization and the relative simplicity of their material culture. Myth and ritual are expressed in Aboriginal art, poetry, music, and dance. The Aborigines traditionally were divided into numerous tribes, subtribes, and clans, often regionally based. The tribal system remains intact in the rural areas, but in urban areas chiefly authority and clan ties have weakened considerably.

LANGUAGE AND RELIGION: The Aboriginal languages include dialects of 31 language groups, most of which are not mutually intelligible. Only about 10% of the 250 languages and 600 dialects estimated to have been in use prior to European settlement remain in use. When first encountered by Europeans, the Aborigines did not have a written language. Their songs, chants, and legends were passed on as a kind of oral literature of considerable subtlety and complexity. In the 1970s and 1980s a dialect called Aboriginal English arose, an English obedient to traditional forms of the Aboriginal dialects.

The majority of the Aborigines are nominally Christian, mostly Protestant, with many continuing to practice traditional beliefs known as Dreamtime. The myths and ritual constituting Dreaming, or Dreamtime, signify continuity of life unlimited by space and time. Only clan elders had full knowledge of the Dreaming and, therefore, authority in traditional rituals and social behaviors.

NATIONAL HISTORY: The ancestors of the Aborigines are thought to have migrated from Southeast Asia between 60,000 and 40,000 years ago. They spread throughout Australia and lived mostly in isolated small clan and tribal groups. It is not known whether there was a single wave or multiple waves of migration into Australia. Aboriginal hunter-gatherer society as it was at the time of European settlement emerged about 5,0000 years ago. Control of ritual lore and ecological knowledge, not ownership of possessions, was the basis of respect and status in Aboriginal societies. The Aborigines lived in about 650 distinct groups, each with its own dialect, political system, social system, laws, and territory. The land was essential to culture and religious life.

The Aboriginal population is estimated to have numbered between 300,000 and one million when the first shipload of Europeans disembarked at Sydney Harbor on 26 January 1788. Some groups claim an indigenous population of between 750,000 and 3 million in 1788. Over the next century the Aborigines were systematically decimated through violence, disease, and expulsion from their traditional homelands. The so-called pacification by force culminated in the 1880s, with massive depopulation and the extinction of some groups of Aborigines. Introduced diseases exacted a terrible toll and probably killed many more than did direct conflict. The best known of those who died were the Tasmanian Aborigines, who numbered about 4,000 when the European arrived. By the late nineteenth century, they had disappeared.

The estimated number of persons of predominantly Aboriginal descent declined from 180,000 in 1861 to less than 95,000 in 1901. The disappearance of the Aborigines in southeast Australia was so rapid that many white Australians believed that the Aborigines would die out, and they acted so as to ensure that outcome. After 1900 violence continued, and even intensified, particularly among the larger Aboriginal populations of northern Australia. By 1930, the aboriginal population had dwindled to some 30,000; the Aborigines were tagged a "dying race."

Since the 1930s, mostly due to their ability to survive in the Australian outback and with the support of a substantial urban population of mixed-race Aborigines, the Aboriginal nation has experienced a remarkable recovery and resurgence. In 1932, the formation of the Australian Aborigines League marked the beginning of Aborigine activism. It was not until the 1960s that the frontier period finally ended, with the move into permanent settlements of the last few nomadic groups.

Traditionally, primary responsibility for Aboriginal policy has rested with the individual states in the Australian federation, except in the federally administered Northern Territory. As a result, the status of the Aborigines has varied markedly from state to state. Policies of malignant or benign neglect were only slowly replaced by policies aimed at assimilation, particularly of the large "mixed blood" portion of the Aboriginal population. This policy, from the 1930s to the 1960s, involved the forcible removal of tens of thousands of Aboriginal children from their parents for placement in white-run schools and institutions. By the 1940s, most of the remainder had been sequestered as low-paid laborers with limited economic and legal rights in squalid settlements controlled by the state governments.

Until the mid-1960s, the Aborigines were not considered Australian citizens and were denied the vote, full social benefits, and inclusion in the census. The civil rights movement in the United States in the 1960s inspired a few urban Aborigines to organize and mobilize politically. Initially these "assimilated" Aborigines focused on status issues, beyond the narrow parochial issues that had characterized Aboriginal dissent previously. Popular pressure from white Australian groups, including churches and organized labor, brought the first moderating reforms in the legal status of the Aborigines, including in 1962 the right to vote in every Australian state.

The movement to upgrade the dismal status of the Aboriginal population culminated in the 1967 Constitutional Referendum, which mandated that the Australian government was to take the initiative in the definition of Aboriginal legal status. "Integration" was promoted by the federal government, while Aboriginal activists increasingly pressed for land and civil rights. The establishment of an Aborigine "embassy" in a tent on the parliament grounds in Canberra in 1972 began a spate of protests that mobilized popular support. Land issues continued to divide the movement, while in the Northern Territory well-funded land councils became effective instruments of local Aboriginal autonomy.

The electoral victory of a Liberal–National Country coalition in 1975 modified the Australian government's position on Aboriginal affairs in favor of "self-management." The Aboriginal Land Rights Act was passed in 1976, but the federal administration has consistently, if not actively, defended commercial and mining interests against the demands of the Aboriginal groups. During the 1980s the legal status of the Aboriginal deteriorated, and despite protests by about 15,000 Aborigines during the Australian Bicentennial (called "Invasion Day" by activists) in January 1988, the government has refused further concessions.

Aborigines are among the poorest people in Australia, inhabiting the least desirable areas and living in the worst housing. They have the highest infant mortality rate, the highest death rate, and the shortest life expectancy in the country. The Aboriginal population continues to suffer from discrimination, high unemployment, low levels of education, and involvement in violent crimes. Alcoholism is a major social problem among both urban and rural communities; Aborigines are twenty times more likely to be arrested than non-Aboriginals, mostly for drunken behavior.

In July 1990, Aboriginal leaders from all over Australia met in a remote bush camp in the Northern Territory to form a provisional independent Aborigine government. They claimed to have no choice but to form a separate national state, because the Australian government had failed to fulfill its promises to guarantee Aboriginal rights. However, many Aborigines in the Northern Territory, who already control about a third of the state's lands and earn millions from land-rights royalties, refused to join the new national government.

Increasingly asserting their national rights, in October 1991 a number of Aboriginal leaders traveled to London to press the United Kingdom government for millions of dollars in compensation for the contamination of traditional hunting grounds between 1953 and 1957 by British nuclear testing. In 1994, Aborigine groups affected by nuclear testing agreed to a multimillion-dollar settlement from the federal government.

The Australian federal government, in response to Aborigine activists, in 1992 announced sweeping plans for judicial, economic, and social reforms intended to improve the lives of Aborigines. These attempts to legislate reforms, while enacted in good faith and with considerable investment of resources, have been generally unsuccessful. In one important decision, what became known as the Mabo ruling of June 1992, the High Court found that Aboriginal traditional rights in the Murray Islands off Australia's northeast coast had not been extinguished by European settlement. This ruling negated the long-held legal concept of *terrus nullius*, which claimed that Australia had been uninhabited before European settlement, and it opened the way to major land claims by Aborigines across Australia.

In October 1993 the Australian government reached an agreement with the Aborigines over land rights, agreeing to protect native titles where the Aborigines could show a continuous link to traditional lands, but rejecting claims by to such territories as the national capital, Canberra, and heavily populated urban areas like the central district of Brisbane. The government in August 1994 gave back title to 8,800 sq. mi. (23,000 sq. km) of land in a remote part of central Australia; pastoral leases granted between 1975 and 1993 had automatically extinguished native land titles. The government created tribunals to adjudicate land claims, but the Australian states retained exclusive control over economic use of the land. Many Aborigines celebrated the agreement as historic, but some militants rejected the plan as failing to give them a veto over economic development of their land.

The public flogging of six Aborigines accused by their tribal elders of stealing cars opened a legal debate over whether Australia's judicial system could accommodate traditional Aboriginal justice. Many Aborigines feel that traditional punishment is part of Aboriginal self-determination.

Over 600 Aborigines who had been taken forcibly from their parents from the 1950s through the early 1970s launched a test case for compensation against the government in October 1994. Thousands of Aborigine children had been adopted by white Australian families as part of government assimilation policies. One in 10 Aborigines over the age of 30 had been separated from their mothers. Individuals removed from their families and cultures account for a disproportionate number of people arrested or imprisoned and of those who commit suicide. In June 1997, 1,500 Aborigines removed from their homes as children sued the government for reparations. Polls show that most white Australians do not believe that the federal government should apologize for the policy. Nonetheless, an official report issued in 1997 described the government's past policies of removing children from their families as genocide.

A 1995 national survey of Aborigines, the first of its kind, found that past government racial policies have left devastating social scars, including low levels of education, poor housing, poor health, higher risk of suicide, and a disproportionately great risk of arrest and imprisonment. Although the High Court's Mabo ruling has greatly facilitated land rights, the situation of the Aborigines has not much improved. Despite official efforts, including hundreds of millions of dollars in social programs, the situation for Aborigines remains more or less the same today as in 1950.

A court case brought by the Wik people of north Queensland in the early 1990s claimed title to lands leased to white farmers in 1915. The court decided by a narrow margin in favor of the Wik people, raising the possibility that almost 80% of Australia's land could be subject to

Aboriginal land claims. It applied to swathes of outback where colonial leases had allowed the farming of properties the size of small European countries. By 2000, about 40% of Australia's landmass had been subjected to Aborigine land claims.

Aboriginal leaders are divided over the issue of autonomy. While some press for a special status within Australia, others want to form an independent national state in northern Australia. At the turn of the twenty-first century, the Aborigines have no special status in Australia akin to that of the Native Americans in the United States and Canada, as no treaty has ever been signed giving them such a legal status. The idea of a treaty giving the Aborigines special rights has been branded as separatism by several Australian politicians. The Australian government refused to accept a finding by the UN that Australia's native title amendments are discriminatory and in conflict with the International Convention on Elimination of Racial Discrimination. In October 1999 Aboriginal leaders took their case to the United Nations Human Rights Commission.

Activists protested the establishment of the Ku Klux Klan in Australia in June 1999. Intimidation and attacks by Klan members increased in 1999–2000. Members of the Aborigine and Torres Straight Islander Commission called on the government to ban the Klan in Australia.

The Australian parliament expressed its regret for the policy of removing Aboriginal children from their homes as part of the policy of assimilation. The August 1999 statement, however, avoided the words "sorry" and "apology," and it did not offer compensation to the 100,000 victims of the "Stolen Generation."

SELECTED BIBLIOGRAPHY:

Bennett, Scott. *Aborigines and Political Power*. 1989.
Blainey, Geoffrey. *Triumph of the Nomads: A History of Aboriginal Australia*. 1982.
Coombs, H. C., ed. *Autonomy: Issues and Strategies*. 1998.
Povinelli, A. *Labor's Lot: The Power, History, and Culture of Aboriginal Action*. 1994.

Acadians

Acadiens; Maritime French; Fransaskois

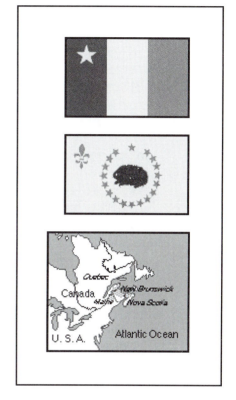

POPULATION: Approximately (2002e) 385,000 Acadians in Canada, primarily in the Maritime Provinces of New Brunswick, Nova Scotia, and Prince Edward Island, but with a large community in southeastern Gaspé region of Quebec and some 20,000 in the state of Maine in the United States.

THE ACADIAN HOMELAND: The Acadian homeland lies in eastern Canada and the northeastern United States. The region, lying on the Atlantic Ocean, includes the Canadian provinces of New Brunswick, Nova Scotia, Prince Edward Island, part of Quebec, and the northeastern corner of the American state of Maine in the basin of the Madawaska River. Most of Acadia borders the Gulf of St. Lawrence and the Bay of Fundy, with fishing as an important occupation. Much of the region is rolling countryside traversed by many rivers. Forests cover much of the territory, including about 90% of New Brunswick. The Acadian homeland has no official status in Canada or the United States. The Acadian capital and major cultural center is Moncton, New Brunswick, (2002e) 61,000. The other important cultural center is Edmundston, called Madawaska by the Acadians, (2002e) 13,000. The major cultural center in Maine is Madawaska, (2002e) 5,000, just across the St. John River from Edmundston.

FLAG: The Acadian national flag, adopted in 1884, is a horizontal tricolor of blue, white, and red, like the French flag, but with the addition of a single five-pointed gold star on the upper hoist. The flag of the Madawaska Acadians of northern Maine is a white field bearing a porcupine surrounded by eighteen small gold stars centered, and a gold fleur-de-lis on the hoist.

PEOPLE AND CULTURE: The Acadians, against all odds, have preserved their unique cultural inheritance, particularly in New Brunswick, where they account for about 250,000 of the total population of (2002e) 761,000. Their national identity is founded on their history, which includes their abandonment by the mother country and the horrors of the deportation and the return to their homeland. There is education in both standard French and the quite different Acadian dialect; however, the official language acts of 1969 and 1981 weakened the Acadian community by integrating it more fully into Canada's national culture. Some of the Acadians in western New Brunswick are assimilating into the Québecois culture, but most Acadians maintain their distinct Francophone culture and dialects.

LANGUAGE AND RELIGION: The Acadians' unique dialect, called Français Acadien, interchanges French and English words and forms but is still considered a French patois, separate from the Quebec dialect. The dialect also shows borrowings from the local Algonquian languages, particularly that of the Micmacs,* who aided the first French settlers, and from English. Only in 1968 were the Acadians allowed access to secondary education in French. Official language acts passed in 1969 and 1981 have given French and English equal status throughout Canada. New Brunswick was declared officially bilingual in 1981. The Acadian minority in Quebec has retained its separate dialect and has resisted assimilation into the larger Québécois French-speaking population.

The Acadians remain devoutly Roman Catholic, the religion that played such a large part in the formation of their national character. The yellow star on the Acadian flag is said to represent the papacy and its place in Acadian national history. In rural areas cultural life continues to revolve around the church, which is both the religious and secular center of village life. The Roman Catholic Church has served as a major force in preserving Acadian culture. The church often provided French-speaking schools when the government was unable or unwilling to provide them.

NATIONAL HISTORY: Acadia, Acadie in the French language, was colonized in the seventeenth and eighteenth centuries. Centered in what is now Nova Scotia, French colonization spread through the region around the Gulf of St. Lawrence and the Bay of Fundy. The first organized French settlement in Acadia was founded in 1604 on an island in Passamaquoddy Bay, on the present U.S.-Canadian border. Founded by Pierre de Monts and Samuel de Champlain, in 1605 the colony was moved to Port Royal and became the center of the colonization of Acadia. The majority of the settlers in New France were Bretons* and Normans,* from the poorer, neglected western provinces of France.

In 1613 Port Royal was destroyed, and its inhabitants were dispersed by an English military expedition from Virginia. In 1621, King James I of England awarded the Acadian lands taken from the French to Sir William Alexander for the purpose of founding the colony of Nova Scotia, but in

1632 James's son, Charles I, ceded Acadia back to France, and under the Company of New France a renewed period of French colonization began.

A bitter struggle for control of Acadia broke out between two of the leading French officials of the colony in 1636. The conflict, which eventually resulted in a local civil war, weakened the French defenses, and the region was again under English rule from 1654 to 1670, when Acadia again reverted to French rule and settlement from France accelerated.

On 16 October 1710, Port Royal was captured by British troops. By the terms of the Treaty of Utrecht in 1713, Nova Scotia was given to Great Britain, but Île-Royale, Cape Breton Island, and Île St. Jean, later called Prince Edward Island, were left to France. The Acadians under British authority were ordered to swear allegiance to the British crown or to withdraw to French territory. The Acadians did neither, although they carefully remained neutral in the ongoing British-French war, and continued to prosper in their small towns and rolling farmlands. Under growing pressure, many Acadians finally signed the oath in 1730, but they were exempted from bearing arms against the French forces. In spite of the war, the period from 1713 to 1748 is considered the golden age of the Acadian nation and culture.

The French crown granted the fief of Madawaska in 1683 to Sieur Charles-Aubert de la Chenaye. In 1763 the Madawaska region was sold to Gen. James Murray, the governor of Quebec. Madawaska was largely unsettled by Europeans prior to the mid-1700s. When the British deported the Acadians from the Atlantic region, some of the Acadians moved south and settled along the St. John River.

In 1755 the British capture of Fort Beauséjour began the expulsion of the Acadian population, an apparent attempt to reduce French influence in the area. For obscure reasons the British, at bayonet point, forced between 6,000 and 8,000 Acadians to abandon their homes between 1755 and 1762. The Acadians, often separated from their families, were stripped of all rights and forced on board overcrowded vessels bound for destinations unknown. The traumatic events of the deportation deeply scarred the Acadian national memory.

In 1763, at the conclusion of the Seven Years' War, the British authorities incorporated most of the former Acadia into Nova Scotia. With the end of hostilities, the British authorities, beginning in 1764, allowed exiled or imprisoned Acadians to return to the region. The British colonists, however, had taken the best of the region's farmlands so many Acadians settled in the coastal regions, a pattern that persists to the present. The largest concentration of French-speaking communities remaining in the area became part of New Brunswick when it was separated from Nova Scotia in 1784.

The Acadians, mostly rural and Catholic, remained apart from the English-speaking mainstream in the Maritimes but also refused to assimilate into the predominate Québécois culture to the west. Education became the primary national issue, particularly after 1864 when there was introduced an English-language curriculum that taught the glories of the British Empire but completely ignored the Acadians' history and culture.

In 1884 the Acadians, at their first national convention at Miscouche, Prince Edward Island, adopted national symbols, including their national flag. In the nineteenth century the Acadians put considerable effort into resisting assimilation into the dominant Anglophone culture as well as efforts by the Québécois to incorporate their small nation. The Catholic Church, with its focus on the parish, served as a major force in preserving the Acadian culture. Often the church provided French-speaking schools when local governments were unable or unwilling to provide them. In 1890 the first institute of higher education in the French language was opened in Nova Scotia.

In 1912 there was considerable resistance to the infamous Rule XVII, which abolished French as the medium of instruction and communication in schools outside Quebec. The rule was not reversed until 1968, when Acadians in some areas gained access to secondary education in French. In 1969 the Official Languages Act made English and French equal in throughout Canada.

During the Great Depression of the 1930s, assimilation began in earnest. Families having difficulty feeding themselves stopped supporting the Catholic institutions that had been the bedrock of French culture in the region. Education increasingly came under the control of the dominant Anglophones before and during World War II. Due to the mechanization of farming that began during the 1940s, many small farmers from Acadian parishes sold their farms and moved to the English-speaking cities.

By the 1950s, many Acadians had begun to assimilate into the dominant English-speaking culture of the Maritime Provinces. However, the activism of the 1960s began to reverse the trend. The term "French-Canadians" began to be replaced by new forms of identity, both in Quebec and among the Acadian communities of the Maritimes. In the 1970s many Acadians, who had been assimilating into the dominate English-speaking culture, acquired a new appreciation of their unique culture and dialect. Over the next decade a strong movement developed to preserve their culture. The movement focused on the provision of, and control over, French-language education. A limited form of bilingualism was incorporated into New Brunswick's constitution. In 1980 the Parti Québécois announced its support for a separate Acadian state for the French-speaking Acadians of Canada's Maritime Provinces.

The federal parliament introduced a resolution in 1989 to reconfirm its commitment to bilingualism in all of Canada. In March 1990 the Canadian Supreme Court ruled that Francophone minorities should have some control over their children's education, at least where population size warranted. On 21 January 1992, the first Francophone school and community center in Nova Scotia was opened.

In 1994, Quebec's nationalist leadership admitted that the rights of Acadians and other French minorities in Canada would probably suffer if Quebec separates from Canada, but it promised to honor historical obligations to the other Francophone communities whatever should happen. In spite of their fears for the future, in August 1994 about 70,000 Acadians from all over the Maritimes and from the United States met for the first time in New Brunswick in a celebration of their culture.

The language issue in Canada remains unresolved and highly politicized, especially in the area of French-language education. There are major national political parties on both sides of the issues, and it is likely that most contention over the issue will continue to be played out through these parties and the courts. In 1997 resistance broke out against the closure of Acadian schools in New Brunswick, which were met by violent attacks by the Royal Canadian Mounted Police riot squad. The conflict mobilized the Acadians of the province to demand greater cultural and educational rights.

The issue of Quebec separatism is strongly intertwined with the situation of the Francophone Acadians. Accordingly, any eventual solution (or lack thereof) of the Quebec issue will play a strong role in determining the status of the Acadian nation The Acadians, like the Québécois, increasingly see themselves as an oppressed nation. Unemployment in Canada is highest among the Acadians, up to 25% in some areas of northeastern New Brunswick

In March 1998, in an annual report to parliament, the commissioner of official languages, Victor Goldbloom, criticized the Canadian federal government for not enforcing the official-languages policy. He noted that there was no one in charge of enforcing the language program, particularly in the French-speaking areas of the Maritime Provinces.

The increasing mobilization of the Acadians has aided the revival of the Acadian national identity. Demands for equality with their English-speaking neighbors has led to a new militancy and renewed contacts with other French-descended groups around the world. In September 1999, the Acadians hosted the annual Francophone meeting of French-speaking states and communities in Moncton, New Brunswick. They are building toward the World Acadian Congress in 2004, the 400th anniversary of the arrival of Acadians in Canada.

Queen Elizabeth II is scheduled to visit New Brunswick in the fall of 2002, when the Acadians hope that she will bring an official apology for the expulsion of their ancestors from Nova Scotia. An Acadian activist, Warren Perrin, filed a lawsuit against the queen demanding an apology in 1990. The lawsuit he filed asked only for an apology and a cancellation of the expulsion order from 1755.

SELECTED BIBLIOGRAPHY:

Davidson, Donald. *Regionalism and Nationalism in the United States.* 1990.
Gallant, Melvin. *The Country of Acadia.* 1986.
Griffiths, Naomi E. S. *The Contexts of Acadian History, 1686–1784.* 1992.
Mahaffie, Charles D., Jr. *Land of Discord Always: Acadia from Its Beginnings to the Expulsion of Its People 1604–1755.* 1997.

Acehnese

Achinese; Atchinese; Atjehnese

POPULATION: Approximately (2002e) 3,970,000 Acehnese in Indonesia, mostly concentrated in the Aceh district in northern Sumatra. Small Acehnese communities live in other parts of Indonesia. Some nationalists claim a national population of up to 25 million in Indonesia.

THE ACEHNESE HOMELAND: The Acehnese homeland occupies a strategic position on the northwestern tip of the island of Sumatra, the farthest west of the islands of the Malay Archipelago. Lying in the Indian Ocean just southwest of the Malay Peninsula, the region is mountainous, with thick tropical forests, except for a wide coastal plain where the majority of the population is concentrated. The Acehnese homeland is subject to the *bohorok*, a hot, dry wind that blows during the monsoon season, a wind the Acehnese claim has shaped their national character. Aceh forms a special autonomous district of the Republic of Indonesia, the only one of its kind in the country. *Special Autonomous District of Aceh (Daerah Isti-*

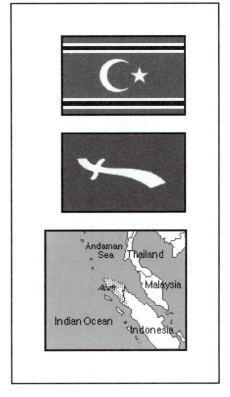

mewa Aceh*): 21,305 sq. mi.—55,180 sq. km, (2002e) 4,399,000—Acehnese 90%, Javanese 8%, Batak 1%. The Acehnese capital and major cultural center is Banda Aceh, often called Kuta Radja, (2002e) 262,000, commonly known as the "doorway to Mecca," because the city has been a stopping place for pilgrims journeying by ship to the Muslim holy sites in Saudi Arabia.

FLAG: The Acehnese national flag, the flag of the national movement, is a red field bearing a centered white crescent moon and five-pointed star and with black horizontal stripes, outlined in white, near the top and bottom. The flag of the major nationalist organization, the Free Aceh Movement, is a red field bearing a centered white sword.

PEOPLE AND CULTURE: The Acehnese are a nation of mixed Malay,

Arabic, and Indian ancestry, physically resembling the other Malay peoples but with pronounced Indian and Arabic features, almond-shaped eyes, and long, straight Semitic noses. They are a blend of many races and tend to be taller and fairer skinned than other Indonesians. They are famous throughout Indonesia for their devotion to Islam and their militant resistance to both Dutch and Indonesian rule. The majority of the Acehnese population are rice growers in the coastal regions. Descent is traced through both the maternal and the paternal lines, and the position of the unveiled women is extremely high for a Muslim society.

LANGUAGE AND RELIGION: The Acehnese speak a western Malayo-Polynesian language, with a marked Arabic admixture, written in its own alphabet, a modified Arabic script. The language is spoken in seven major dialects, not all of which are mutually intelligible. Most Acehnese speak the Banda Aceh dialect along with local variations, while only about half are able to speak Bahasa Indonesia, the national language of the Indonesian republic. Until the overthrow of the Suharto dictatorship in 1999, the Acehnese were forbidden to use their language in the written form.

The Islam practiced by the Acehnese is more orthodox than that of other parts of the Indonesian Archipelago, and the Acehnese have sought to protect their strong religious character. Undiluted by the Hindu and Buddhist influences farther east, the Acehnese practice a form of Islam more closely related to the practices of the Islamic peoples of the subcontinent and the Middle East. Aceh's staunchly Islamic character has long been a driving force within the campaign for an independent Acehnese state.

NATIONAL HISTORY: The first recorded history of the region concerns Pole, a Buddhist state that flourished about A.D. 500 in northern Sumatra. A powerful ancient Malay state, Aceh often controlled parts of the nearby Malay Peninsula. Aceh's power was eventually curbed by the Indianized states established on Java and Sumatra by Hindu immigrants in the seventh century A.D. Muslim Arabs settled the Acehnese coast in the twelfth century, soon converting the Acehnese to their Islamic religion. An independent Muslim sultanate, Aceh maintained strong ties to the west, ties strengthened by continued Arabic immigration and the arrival of Gujarati Muslims from northwestern India.

The sultanate's political and military power, gradually diminished by wars with neighboring states, recovered under the rule of Ali Mubhayat Syah in the early sixteenth century. During the reign of Iskander Shah in the later seventeenth century, Aceh experienced a great flowering of culture and political power, a golden age financed by a virtual monopoly on the lucrative Sumatra pepper trade.

Wealthy Aceh, visited by Portuguese fleets under De Cunha in 1506 and Sequeira in 1509, was the goal of the first Dutch expedition to the Indies in 1599, as well as of an English East India Company expedition in 1602. European encroachments and a devastating civil war began a long period of Acehnese decline in the seventeenth century. The state, in a situation unusual in the East, was ruled by a succession of four female monarchs between 1641 and 1699.

The Acehnese established formal treaty relations with Great Britain in 1819, and Aceh was recognized as a sovereign state by both Britain and the Netherlands in 1824. The two European powers, despite their formal recognition of the sultanate, continued to vie for influence and for control of the important spice trade. An Anglo-Dutch treaty of 1871 acknowledged Dutch supremacy in the Indies and effectively relegated Aceh to the Dutch sphere of influence.

Negotiations between the American consul in Singapore and Acehnese ministers in 1873 provided a pretext for Dutch aggression. Dutch gunboats shelled the Acehnese capital, while colonial troops landed on the coast, setting off the longest and bloodiest colonial war in Dutch history, a war that continued up to World War I. Sultan Tuanku Danel Syah finally surrendered to the Dutch in 1903 and was exiled in 1905.

Until the end of Dutch rule during World War II, however, the Acehnese were never fully pacified. Japanese military forces, advancing on the islands in 1942, inspired an Acehnese uprising; the Japanese drove the Dutch forces from the sultanate, but the conservative Acehnese rejected Japanese overtures. Following the Japanese surrender in 1945, many Acehnese joined the anticolonial forces fighting Dutch attempts to regain control of their colonial possessions in the East Indies.

Initially rejecting inclusion in a united Indonesia, the Acehnese were finally persuaded to accept the status of an autonomous state within a federal Indonesia in 1949. The United States of Indonesia, dominated by the numerically predominant Javanese of the central island of Java, soon began to disintegrate as opposition mounted to attempts to abolish the autonomy of the member states. After 1950 the Acehnese quickly became disillusioned with the Indonesian leadership, which was generally perceived as corrupt and un-Islamic. Resentment grew when Aceh's provincial status was removed. Rejecting direct rule from Java, the Acehnese rebelled in early 1950. The Acehnese rebel leaders declared Aceh independent of Indonesia on 11 February 1950, but in spite of fierce Acehnese resistance, Indonesian troops overwhelmed the poorly armed rebels and the secession collapsed.

The rebellion resumed in September 1953 under Daud Beureu'eh, a popular Muslim activist. In an effort to undermine the nationalist movement, the Indonesian government granted Aceh additional autonomy in 1956. Two years later, alarmed by the growing communist influence in Java, Acehnese leaders demanded full autonomy. Aceh was granted the status of a special territory, with considerable religious and educational autonomy, in 1959. Javanese economic and political domination of Indonesia continued, however, pushing militant nationalists to mobilize in the

1960s. The separatists gained majority support only following the imposition of a new transmigration policy, a government-sponsored resettlement of population from the seriously overcrowded Java to less-populated islands of the republic.

The Acehnese separatists, led by Tenku Tjhik di Tiro Muhammad Hassan, called Hassan di Tiro, the eighth head of the dynasty established in Aceh in 1874, fought bloody battles with government forces throughout the 1970s. Supported by a large portion of the population, di Tiro proclaimed the independence of Aceh on 4 January 1977. The government responded by killing several leaders of the Free Aceh Movement and driving others into exile in Europe. On 4 December 1976, nationalists raised the rebel flag and reiterated their loyalty to the exiled Acehnese government. Fighting erupted in several areas of Aceh, bringing violence to many noncombatant villages caught in the cross fire. The Indonesian government prematurely announced the end of the Acehnese separatist movement in 1986.

Fighting resumed in the province in 1989 between separatists and security forces. The Indonesian government sent special combat forces into the province to put down the small separatist movement. In the process, according to human rights organizations and most Acehnese, the soldiers killed, raped, and tortured thousands of people. Large-scale human-rights violations were committed by the military, including illegal executions, disappearances, and imprisonment of nonviolent activists and the families of separatists. Thousands were killed, and over 2,000 are still missing. Many activists or suspected sympathizers simply disappeared into mass graves.

Acehnese nationalists in 1991 asserted that the advantages of Indonesian citizenship were outweighed by mistrust and the indiscriminate violence of the government forces, and that independence was the only solution for Aceh. Some combat troops were withdrawn in August 1998, but violence returned in December, and security forces were returned to Aceh. Thousands of Acehnese fled their homes to the security of temporary displaced-persons camps.

To many Acehnese, the Indonesian army is the enemy. The army's role in the brutal suppression of the 1980s remains an open wound, even though the army has apologized for its past misdeeds. Its role in safeguarding the authority of the Indonesian government in the region remains unchanged, and the army still retains control of most Acehnese territory. In August 1998 Indonesian military leaders apologized for excesses and promised to withdraw all combat troops from the province.

The Acehnese point to their extensive natural gas reserves, vast forests, and mineral deposits as the foundations of an independent Aceh. The uncontrolled exploitation of these natural resources by the Indonesian government has become one of the main nationalist issues in the region.

Javanese migrants settled in Aceh through government transmigration policies are alleged to be the main beneficiaries of development schemes, while roads, schools, and hospitals are still rudimentary in rural areas where the majority of the Acehnese live.

The underdevelopment of their fertile and mineral-rich homeland is another source of deep antagonism toward the Indonesian government. The region is home to a natural gas plant that is one of Indonesia's biggest earners of foreign currency. It is an economic asset that the Indonesian government is very reluctant to lose.

The Acehnese majority support nationalist demands for a referendum on independence from Indonesia similar to that allowed the East Timorese* in mid-1999. In spite of military suppression, thousands participated in demonstrations demanding independence, or at least a referendum to allow the Acehnese to decide their own future. The word "referendum" has been painted in huge letters on buildings across the province. In November 1999 over 100,000 Acehnese gathered in Banda Aceh to listen to nationalist leaders openly demand a referendum on secession from Indonesia. The Indonesian military forces did not interfere, but the government is faced with a serious decision—to allow a referendum or take the chance that the Acehnese will unilaterally declare their independence. Should Aceh secede, Indonesia could well unravel.

In early 2000, rebels of the Free Aceh Movement launched attacks on the remaining troops in the province. When the special forces left the city of Lhokseumawe, an angry crowd rampaged through the city, smashing and burning shops and government buildings. Reinforcements were ordered back into Aceh. By late 2000 about 150,000 Acehnese had fled their homes, fearing violence by the Indonesian troops.

The plight of the devoutly Muslim Acehnese has long found sympathy among Indonesia's Muslim majority, unlike the mainly Christian East Timorese, Ambonese,* and West Papuans.* In response to increasing unrest in many parts of Indonesia, the government has promised to devolve greater powers to the provinces, but the Acehnese are not disposed to settle for autonomy. The Acehnese rejected a government autonomy plan in 1999 and have demanded a greater share in the revenues from their natural resources, particularly the natural gas deposits, as an interim measure until the province's future is decided.

In early 2000, random identity checks and detentions remained a daily hazard. Soldiers continued to attack villages, singling out individuals for arrest or killing. Although the Acehnese rebels are not blameless in the widespread violence, the police and army are responsible for most of the atrocities occurring in Aceh. The level of outrages, including rapes and abductions, has not been seen in the region before, not even during the nine-year operation against the rebels between 1989 and 1998. Since the operation ended, fighting has expanded as news of the horrors spreads across the region.

A cease-fire agreement was signed by representatives of the Indonesian government and the leaders of the Acehnese separatist movement in Geneva in May 2000. The agreement, called a "memorandum of understanding," is a humanitarian agreement, not a political agreement. The nationalists signed in the hopes that the human-rights abuses would be ended. In June, an exiled nationalist leader, Teuku Don Zulfahri, the secretary-general of the Free Aceh Movement, was assassinated in Kuala Lumpur just before the agreement took effect. In spite of the agreement, violence in the region continued.

Campaigners for a vote on self-determination in mid-2000 proposed to the Indonesian government that an agreement be negotiated that would lead to the withdrawal of all soldiers and national police from Aceh and the disarming of all rebel fighters as a prelude to a United Nations–supervised referendum on Aceh's future. In April 2001 the Indonesian president, Abdurrahman Wahid, authorized a military offensive in the province. The murder of Achenese activists during the offensive aroused a renewed nationalist fervor in the region.

The Acehnese nationalists and the Indonesian government have not yet found enough common ground to start useful talks. The Indonesian armed forces have threatened to fight to the last man to keep Aceh from seceding from Indonesia.

SELECTED BIBLIOGRAPHY:

Griffiths, Michael. *Indonesian Eden: Aceh's Rainforest.* 1990.
Kell, Tim. *The Roots of Acehnese Rebellion, 1989–1992.* 1995.
Sjamsuddin, Nazaruddin. *The Republican Revolt: A Study of the Acehnese Rebellion.* 1988.
Smith, Holly S. *Aceh: Art and Culture.* 1998.

Acreaños

Acreans

POPULATION: Approximately (2002e) 424,000 Acreaños in South America, mostly in the northwestern Brazilian state of Acre, but with smaller communities in northern Bolivia and eastern Peru.

THE ACREAÑO HOMELAND: The Acreaño homeland lies in north-central South America in the basin of the Acre River on the border between Brazil, Peru, and Bolivia. The territory takes its name from the Acre River, which rises near the Peruvian border. Most of the region is Amazonian lowlands; some of it has been cleared of the dense jungle that covers about 90% of the region. Acre produces the highest-quality rubber in Brazil. The largest portion of the original Acre territory forms a state, the most western of the Federal Republic of Brazil. *State of Acre (Estado do Acre)*: 59,343 sq. mi.—153,698 sq. km, (2002e) 578,000—Acreaños 68%, Bolivians 7%, Peruvians 2%, other Brazilians 23%. The Acreaño capital and major cultural city is Rio Branco, Rio Blanco in the Acreaño dialect, (2002e) 236,000.

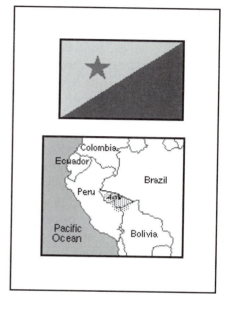

FLAG: The Acreaño national flag, the official flag of the state, is a diagonal bicolor yellow at the hoist and green on the fly bearing a single red five-pointed star on the upper hoist.

PEOPLE AND CULTURE: The Acreaños are a unique South American people of mixed background, incorporating influences from both the Spanish-culture Bolivians, the Portuguese-culture Brazilians, and the indigenous Amerindians. Their culture, which developed in the isolation of their Amazonian homeland, is a mixture of both Spanish and Portuguese elements, with borrowings from the local indigenous populations. The indigenous peoples are divided into six linguistic groups: Tupi, Karib, Tukano, Jê, Pano, and Aruaque. They belong mainly to the Pano and Arauque groups. The indigenous peoples, like other Acreaños, live by hunting, fishing, agriculture, and gathering.

LANGUAGE AND RELIGION: The language of the Acreaños is a local dialect of Brazilian Portuguese, with major borrowings from the Spanish spoken in neighboring Bolivia and Peru and also from the local indigenous languages. The dialect, quite different from the Portuguese spoken in the more populous coastal states, is intelligible to Portuguese speakers only with difficulty. Most Acreaños also speak Spanish, and many speak the standard Brazilian Portuguese.

The Acreaños, with the exception of the small indigenous portion of the population, are overwhelmingly Roman Catholic. In all communities there are native healers, called *paje*, who pass their spiritual and medicinal knowledge on to their successors. Some traditional rites that have become part of their Catholic beliefs involve hallucinogenic brews.

NATIONAL HISTORY: The region was sparsely inhabited by Amazonian tribes when the first Spanish colonists, pushing north from Bolivia, settled the area in the seventeenth century. Under Spanish rule Acre covered a larger area than the present state, forming parts of the Spanish *audencia* of Cuzco, in present-day Peru, and the *audencia* of Charcas, in modern Bolivia. Unimportant economically, the region grew slowly, with only scattered settlements during the Spanish colonial period. Portuguese settlers moving into the region from the east came to the Acre River basin in the late 1700s and early 1800s. By 1820 the region had a mixed population of indigenous peoples and Spanish and Portuguese settlers.

In 1825, during the South American rebellions against Spanish rule, the leaders of the *audencia* of Charcas declared the region independent of Spain, as the Republic of Bolivar. The new state claimed the vast Acre region. The territorial claims brought the new Bolivian republic into acrimonious border disputes with both Peru and Brazil.

In 1867, the larger northern territory of Acre was formally ceded to Brazil and was joined to the Amazonas area, in spite of the conflicting territorial claims. The arrival of Brazilian colonists in considerable numbers dates from the establishment of the first official colony on 3 April 1877. Throughout most of the nineteenth century, the ownership of the remaining Acre territory remained unsettled, but it was generally considered to form part of Bolivia. The territorial disputes sparked the first stirrings of communal feeling among the diverse population of the region.

The demand by North American and European industry for rubber sparked outside interest in the region. In the 1880s the rubber boom in Acre drew an influx of both Brazilians and Bolivians, leading to renewed violence and territorial claims by Brazil, Bolivia, and Peru. The owners of the new rubber companies, called the Seringalistas, appropriated huge areas of rain forest for extracting raw latex from the rubber trees. The indigenous peoples tried to resist, but their bows and arrows were no match for the armed gangs employed by the rubber barons. The new immigrants organized groups called *Correrias* of about 50 men each for assaulting indigenous villages. As the settlers were generally bachelors, they killed only the men, taking the captured women as wives. Most of the indigenous peoples were exterminated or perished from diseases brought to the region by the immigrants.

In 1898, the Bolivian government attempted to take control, provoking an armed revolt of the Brazilian inhabitants. Supported by the authorities in neighboring Amazonas, and in defiance of the governments involved, the revolutionaries extended their authority across the territory, and on 14 July 1899 they declared the region independent, as the Estado Independente do Acre—also called the Republic of Acre. The independence declaration, a political effort to protect the booming rubber trade developed by the Acreaños from both Brazilian, Peruvian, and Bolivian encroachment, angered all three governments. Violence soon broke out, aggravated by an agreement between the Bolivian government and an American syndicate for the exploitation of Acre's valuable wild-rubber reserves. The governments of Brazil and Bolivia laid formal claims to Acre, and in 1900 the two states came close to war over the issue of Acreaño independence.

Bolivian troops invaded Acre and quickly overthrew the republican government; however, in August 1900 the Acreaños revolted and drove the Bolivian troops from the region. On 7 August 1902, under a government dominated by President Luis Galvez Rodriguez de Arias, the Acreaños again declared the independence of their contested homeland. The independent republic embraced territory west to the Madeira River in present Brazil, into the northwestern corner of Pando Province of Bolivia, and a small territory in present-day eastern Peru. In 1903, over the protests of the Acreaños, the governments of Bolivia and Brazil signed the Treaty of Petropolis, which divided the territory, giving the Brazilians the larger portion and Bolivia a smaller territory and an indemnity of ten million dollars. Brazilian troops moved into the territory and quickly suppressed the Acreaño government. On 24 January 1903 Acre was formally annexed to Brazil. In 1909 the Peruvians formally renounced their claim to the region.

The rubber boom, which had sustained the Acreaño rebellion, proved to be short-lived, and by 1912 the region had lost its economic importance due to production of rubber in British Malaya. Many people who had hoped for quick riches left the region, leaving behind the small, mixed Acreaño population. After the end of the rubber boom the region was neglected and ignored by successive Brazilian governments; there was very slow economic growth and little in the way of development during the 1920s and 1930s. After the outbreak of the Second World War in 1939, there was renewed interest in the natural products of the region, especially when access to rubber in the Far East was cut off. At the end of the war the region began to attract Brazilians from the crowded east coast and, especially, from the drought-stricken and extremely poor northeastern states.

The government of Brazil ignored the Amazon regions until the 1960s, when a new capital, Brasilia, was constructed in the interior to spur development there. Acre remained a federal territory until 1963, when it was raised to the status of a full state in the Brazilian federation, partly in response to Acreaño regionalism and complaints of official neglect. A small nationalist movement charged the Brazilian government with treating the region as an internal colony to be exploited for its natural resources.

Arbitrary government practices that exploited the region's natural wealth but returned little to the Acreaños exacerbated the alienation of the Acreaños during the 1970s. Acre was virtually controlled by eight powerful families and misunderstood and neglected by the federal government; a movement for autonomy grew, making demands for local control of natural resources and for autonomy to deal with mounting problems. The autonomy movement gained support in response to more and more cattle ranches established by mostly absentee landlords with generous government subsidies.

In the early 1980s disputes intensified between large landowners, who had cleared vast tracts of Amazonian rain forest for grazing lands to raise beef for the fast-food market in the United States, and local rubber trappers, the descendants of the early Acreaños. The Acreaño rubber trappers charged the government with allowing the destruction of Acre's natural resources to satisfy short-term greed. An average of one murder a day marked the growing conflict. The dispute increasingly pitted the Acreaños, mostly small farmers and rubber trappers, supported by the local churches, against the large landowners, backed by the state and federal governments. In 1982 opposition candidates overwhelmingly won state elections in Acre, reflecting Acreaño dissatisfaction with government policies.

In late 1988 a leading Acreaño environmentalist, the leader of a union of 30,000 Acreaño rubber trappers, was murdered by assassins later tied to ranching interests. The murder of Francisco "Chico" Mendes Filho revived feeling and resentment mostly dormant since the turn of the twentieth century, when local rubber barons had financed a rebellion that took Acre from Bolivian control. The Acreaños, backed by human-rights organizations, charged that the local state police were unreliable, as they worked with or received payoffs from the wealthy landowners. The situation became so explosive that federal police stepped in to hunt for the killers.

Tensions eased somewhat in January 1990, when one of Mendes's dreams was signed into reality; a 2,000 sq. mi. (5,180 sq. km) tract designated as Brazil's first "extractive reserve" was set aside for the sustainable exploitation by the native Acreaños. Mendes saw such reserves as economically and socially viable means of preserving the rain forest and the traditional way of life of the Acreaños. A new federal government in March 1990 promised greater protection for Acre's remaining rain forests; however, uproar over Francisco Mendes's murder forced the government to order investigations into other unsolved murders of Acreaño activists in the region. Acknowledgment of some of its grievances somewhat dampened the region's antigovernment sentiment, but in the decade since his murder Chico Mendes has become a martyr to the Acreaño regionalist movement.

In late 1991 the murderers of Chico Mendes, a wealthy rancher and his son, were sentenced to 19 years in prison. The trial, the first ever in Acre for the murder of an environmentalist, rubber worker, small farmer, or Amerindian, was closely watched by the Acreaño activists, human-rights organizations, and foreign governments.

A growing autonomy movement, led by the Forest Alliance, demands Acreaño control of the region's fragile environment, mineral wealth, and local economy. Autonomist and environmental groups support the creation of a reserve, including parts of historical Acre in other states, which would include Amerindian areas and government-protected national parks. In response to pressure from the Acreaño activists, the Brazilian government has eliminated federal subsidies for ranchers that made it profitable to cut down virgin forests for farming and ranching, and it has begun to tax agricultural income. The Acreaños have begun to use their organization for political means, and having ousted the former state government, they have consistently voted for pro-Acreaño and environmentalist candidates.

In spite of good intentions, however, the Brazilian rain forest continues to disappear at an alarming rate, threatening both the Acreaño way and the fragile ecology of the entire Amazon River basin. The Acreaño demand for local control has gained widespread support both within Brazil and internationally since the early 1990s; however, the Acreaños' regionalist government has often been at odds with the neighboring states, where forest clearance and control by wealthy oligarchies continue.

SELECTED BIBLIOGRAPHY:

Barbosa, Luiz C. *The Brazilian Amazon Rainforest: Global Ecopolitics, Development, and Democracy*. 1999.
Burch, Joann J. *Chico Mendes: Defender of the Rain Forest*. 1994.
Kelly, Robert C., ed. *Brazil Country Review 1999/2000*. 1999.
Viveiros de Castro, Eduardo, ed. *From the Enemy's Point of View: Humanity and Divinity in an Amazonian Society*. 1992.

Adyge

Adygeny; Adyghe; Adyghei; Adygei; Adijei; West Circassians

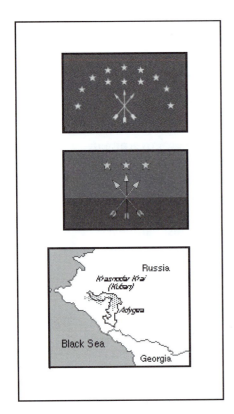

POPULATION: Approximately (2002e) 131,000 Adyge in Russia, mainly in the Adyge Republic of the Russian Federation and the adjoining Krasnodar Territory. A large Adyge population, estimated to number over 130,000, live in Turkey, with smaller numbers in Syria, Jordan, Iraq, Israel, the United States, and Germany. Adyge nationalists estimate the total number of Adyge in the world at between 275,000 and 300,000.

THE ADYGE HOMELAND: The Adyge homeland lies in the North Caucasus region of southern European Russia, surrounded by territory belonging to Krasnodar Krai (Kuban), and separated from the territories of the other Circassian peoples, the Cherkess* and Kabards,* by the Slav-populated Laba region just east of Adygea. Its terrain consists of rolling plains in the Kuban River valley and mountains and foothills in the south. The region, rich in agricultural output, also produces oil and natural gas. Adygea, formerly the Adygei Autonomous Oblast, became a member state of the Russian Federation in 1991. *Republic of Adygea (Respublika Adygea/Adyge Respublik)*: 2,934 sq. mi.—7,599 sq. km, (2002e) 445,000—Russians and Kuban Cossacks* 68%, Adyge 24%, Cherkess and Kabards 6%, Nogais* 2%. The Adyge capital and major cultural center, Maykop (Maikop), called Myjeqwape in the Adyge language, has a population of (2002e) 169,000.

FLAG: The Adyge national flag, the official flag of the autonomous republic, is a green field bearing three crossed yellow arrows surmounted by three yellow stars under an arc of nine yellow stars. The flag of the pan-Circassian nationalists of the Adyge Khase organization is a horizontal bicolor of red over green bearing three crossed gold arrows surmounted by three gold stars.

PEOPLE AND CULTURE: The Adyge, also known as the Lower or

Western Circassians or Kiakhs, are the most westerly of the three main divisions of the Circassian peoples. The small Adyge nation, which first emerged as a distinctive group in the thirteenth century, is divided into ten cultural and geographical subgroups. The *tlapq*, or clan, descended from the same male ancestors and, sharing a common name, remains the basis of the extended family outside the urban areas. Traditionally an Adyge man is never without his dagger, and few things are more important to him than his weapons. This is reflected in the past prevalence of blood feuds. Adyge folklore is rich and varied, and it has served as the basis of the modern Adyge literature and poetry. The Adyge are known throughout the region for their skills in breeding horses, cattle, and sheep, and they are renowned horsemen noted for their marksmanship. Their sheepskins and leathers are prized far beyond their homeland.

LANGUAGE AND RELIGION: Their language, Adyge or Adygebze, also called West Circassian or Kiakh, belongs to the Northwestern Caucasian languages and is a Lower Circassian language of the Abkhazo-Adyghian group of Caucasian languages. The language, although dialectical differences remain, can be understood by the other Circassian peoples, but the written form of the language employs a different Cyrillic alphabet. An alphabet based on the Arabic script was created in 1918, but it was replaced by Latin script in 1927, and Cyrillic was imposed in 1938. The language is the mother tongue of an estimated 96% of the Adyge population and is spoken in four major, mutually intelligible dialects and several subdialects. Adyge, which became a literary language only after the 1917 revolution, was made an official language, along with Russian, in Adygea in 1994 and is now taught in the republic's schools. The literary language is based on the Temirgoyev dialect.

Overwhelmingly and fervently Sunni Muslim, the Adyge adhere to the Hanafi rite, a moderate form of Islam that eschews fundamentalist extremes. The Islamic religion, with strong pagan and Christian influences, remains an important part of the Adyge's everyday life. Ancient cults associated with thunder, fertility rites, and sacred groves remain to the present. The Adyge tend to be nonfanatical and to maintain a strong attachment to the Adat, or Adyge-Habze, customary law.

NATIONAL HISTORY: The Circassian peoples probably settled the region of the north Caucasus before the sixth century B.C. Possibly the earliest representative of the Caucasian peoples, the Circassian peoples populated a wide area north of the Caucasus Mountains, an area that figured prominently in the legends of ancient Greece. The handsome Circassians, valued in harems and as slaves, developed a warrior society as protection against the region's frequent invaders and against raids by slavers.

The fierce Circassian tribes, often warring among themselves, were feared by neighboring peoples. The intertribal wars eventually scattered the tribes across a wide area, from the Black Sea to the Kuban River and the Greater Caucasus Mountains. The Adyge homeland, whose rivers drain into the Black Sea, not the Caspian, has a long history of contact with the Mediterranean world. Greek and Roman writers described them as fine horsemen. The Adyge tribes traded with Byzantium in horses, honey, agricultural products, and fine jewelry. Christianity, introduced to the Adyge tribes by Greek monks, began to take hold in the sixth century A.D. A common religion facilitated the tribes' trade and diplomatic ties to the Byzantines and the early Slav state of Kievan Rus, to the north.

Contact with Byzantium ended with the thirteenth-century Mongol invasion. Weakened by the Mongol conquest of 1241–42, the tribes came under the rule of Christian Georgia, although inaccessible mountain strongholds frustrated Georgian efforts to subdue the Adyge completely. The tribes, seeking allies, sought aid from the expanding Ottoman Empire of the Turks, and Turkish influence soon became predominant in much of the region.

Russian expansion into the North Caucasus in the sixteenth century was fiercely contested by the Ottoman Turks. The Adyge, along with the other Circassian tribes, generally sided with the Turks in the series of wars with Russia. By the seventeenth century, the majority of the tribes had adopted the Turks' Islamic religion. In 1774 the Russians finally established their authority in the region, which prompted fierce Adyge resistance over the next decades. Zaporozhye Cossacks from the Ukraine were settled in the newly conquered lands in 1792. These Cossacks, the ancestors of the Kuban Cossacks, adopted many fighting techniques and cultural traditions from the native Adyge tribes. Relations between the two peoples, often united against the hated tsarist administration, were generally good.

The Russian government, in the Treaty of Adrianople in 1829, forced the weakened Turks to give up all claims to the region. The treaty was only a formality, as rebellions, skirmishing, and reprisals continued for several more decades. In 1857 the Russian military established a fort at Maykop, in Adyge territory. The Muslims of the eastern Caucasus region rebelled in 1859, and although the Adyge were not directly involved in the war, they did take advantage of the Russians weakness to raid and harass the forts in their homeland. An influx of freed serfs seeking lands following the abolition of serfdom in Russia in 1861 led to violent confrontations between the Adyge and the new arrivals. In 1864 the Russians, after years of sporadic fighting, finally conquered the Circassian peoples and took direct control of Adygea.

The defeated Circassians, including the Adyge, were given a choice between settling on the plains among the growing Russian population, under Russian military control, or emigrating to Turkish territory. An estimated 400,000 Circassians, rejecting Christian domination, fled or were expelled to Ottoman territory. Relegated to a marginal existence in the rural areas, the remaining Adyge proved an enduring problem for the Russian military and civil authorities.

Openly sympathetic to the Muslim Turks when war began in 1914, the Adyge enthusiastically welcomed the news that revolution had overthrown the hated tsar in February 1917. Vehemently opposed to the antireligious stance of the new Bolshevik government installed after a coup in October 1917, the Muslim leaders of the Caucasus region organized an autonomous state called North Caucasia. In January 1918 Soviet rule was established at Maykop, but the region remained chaotic. Threatened by both sides in the Russian Civil War, the Muslim leaders declared North Caucasia independent of Russia on 11 May 1918. A rival government, set up by the Kuban Cossacks, also laid claim to Adygea.

The breakaway Republic of North Caucasia was overrun by the White forces of Gen. Anton I. Deniken in January 1919. The Whites' vehement opposition to the secession of the region from Russia and their poor treatment of the non-Slav population pushed the Adyge and other Muslim tribes into an alliance with the opposing Reds. Promised independence in a Soviet federation of states, most of the Adyge went over to the Bolshevik forces. In January 1920, the Red Army defeated the last White units.

In 1922, a part of the traditional Adyge homeland was established as an autonomous district under the Soviet nationalities policy. Most mosques and all religious schools were closed by the government. Before the revolution the Circassians had been a single mostly undifferentiated nation, with only a vague sense of national identity. Following the revolution, they were divided into separate autonomous units under regional or tribal names. The Soviet authorities, following the populist approach to language planning, created two different alphabets for the Circassian peoples, one for the Adyge and one for the central and eastern Circassians. Geographically, the Adyge were separated from the other Circassian peoples.

Soviet repression, particularly of religion, provoked sporadic rebellions, with two serious rebellions in 1929 and 1937. In 1936, in an effort to diffuse Adyge nationalism, the Soviet government upgraded Adygea's status to that of an autonomous region, with redrawn borders and a new capital at Maykop. However, Russian was made the only official language of the region in 1938, as part of the promotion of a new community, the "Soviet people."

Thinking to capitalize on the Circassians' grievances, the Nazi Germans, after taking the Kuban region during the Caucasus campaign of 1942, offered the Adyge an alliance and promoted anticommunist solidarity. The Germans held Adygea from August 1942 to January 1943, but the Adyge view that the Germans represented just another in a long series of invaders spared them the brutal deportations suffered by neighboring Muslim peoples when the Red Army retook the Caucasus region.

The reform of Soviet society under Mikhail Gorbachev in the late 1980s allowed the Adyge to voice decades of frustrations and grievances. The three Circassian peoples—the Adyge, the Cherkess or Circassians, and the Kabards—separated under tsarist and Soviet rule, demanded unification and the dissolution of the hybrid territories that the Cherkess and Kabardin had been forced to share with the Turkic Karachai and Balkar peoples for most of the twentieth century. In the Circassian homelands, finally under their own flags, an effort is now being made, through land grants and other incentives, to persuade the scattered Circassian diaspora to return to their ancient homelands.

SELECTED BIBLIOGRAPHY:

Bennigsen, Alexandre, and S. Enders Wimbush. *Muslims of the Soviet Empire: A Guide.* 1986.

Goldenberg, Suzanne. *Pride of Small Nations: The Caucasus and Post-Soviet Disorder.* 1994.

Lapidus, Gail W., ed. *The New Russia: Troubled Transformation.* 1995.

Olson, James S. *An Ethnohistorical Dictionary of the Russian and Soviet Empires.* 1994.

Afars

Afarafs; Afar Af; Denakils; Dankalians; Denkels; Adals; Afar-Sahos

POPULATION: Approximately (2002e) 1,660,000 Afars in northeastern Africa, divided among the states of Ethiopia (with 1,075,000), Eritrea (with 445,000, including 140,000 Sahos), and Djibouti (with 310,000). Afar nationalists claim a regional population of 3.2 million.

THE AFAR HOMELAND: The Afar homeland lies in the Danakil Basin of East Africa's Great Rift Valley in eastern Ethiopia, northern Djibouti, and southern Eritrea. The so-called Afar Triangle is one of the world's hottest regions, at its lowest point 383 feet below sea level, and is mostly desert east of the coastal mountains that front the Red Sea. The Afar homeland has no official status in Eritrea or Djibouti. In Ethiopia the region forms a state of the Federal Democratic Republic of Ethiopia. *Afar National Regional State*: 105,019 sq. mi.—272,000 sq. km, (2002e) 1,374,000—Afars 92%, Amharas 4%, Argoda 1%, as well as Tigreans,* Oromos,* other Ethiopians. The Afar capital and major cultural center is Asayita in Ethiopia, (2002e) 20,000. The most important center of the Eritrean Afars is Assab (Aseb), (2002e) 56,000, and the major Afar center in Djibouti is Tadjoura, (2002e) 12,000. The traditional Afar capital is Aussa, in Ethiopia, (2002e) 10,000.

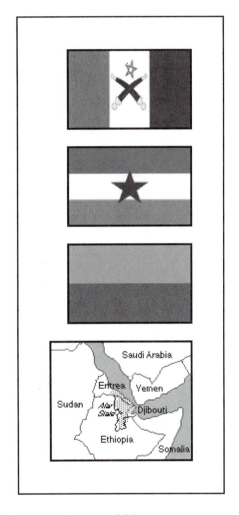

FLAG: The Afar national flag, the official flag of Afar state in Ethiopia, is a vertical tricolor of green, white, and blue, bearing crossed swords centered under a five-pointed star. The flag of the Afar national movement, and the official flag of the Afar Liberation Front, is a horizontal tricolor of blue, white, and green, charged with a centered red star. The traditional Afar flag, which is used in many areas, is a pale blue over green bicolor.

PEOPLE AND CULTURE: The Afar, including the closely related Saho, are a nation of mixed ancestry, the descendants of ancient Semitic and Hamitic peoples with a later Arabic admixture. Divided into tribes, sub-tribes, and clans, the Afar are also identified by a class system that segregates the population into two distinct divisions, the *Asimara* (Red) nobles and the *Adoimara* (White) commoners. The Saho, although often considered a separate people, form ten small tribal groups and account for some 10% of the national population. Most Afars live as herders, although there are some fishermen in coastal areas, salt miners, and farmers in the Aussa Oasis. The proud, highly individualistic Afar-Saho tribes are much feared by outsiders; cooperation in larger units is usually induced only by warfare against a common enemy. Afar culture emphasizes a man's strength and bravery, and prestige comes traditionally from killing one's enemy. The strikingly beautiful Afar women will usually not consider courtship with a man who has never killed another man. They hope for a husband who wears the iron bracelet indicating that he has killed ten men. Marriage to outsiders is very rare.

LANGUAGE AND RELIGION: The Afar language is a language of Afar-Saho group of the Eastern Cushitic branch of the Afro-Asiatic languages. The Afar language forms a dialect continuum with Saho and shows little dialectical difference. The major dialects are Central Afar, Northern Afar, Aussa, and Baadu. The language, particularly in the coastal regions, has been influenced by Arabic, Somali, and other languages used in the region. Saho, often called Sah or Sao, although closely related, is considered a distinct language and is mostly spoken in Eritrea. Literacy is very low, averaging about 8% in all areas. The major Saho dialect is Irob.

The Afars are nominally Muslim, but particularly in the interior regions practice is very relaxed, although Islam is held in great esteem. Religious practices are imbued with earlier pre-Islamic traditions, such as reverence for sacred trees and groves. Although Muslims are permitted to have four wives, Afar marriages are usually monogamous, and traditionally a man was not allowed to marry until he had killed another man. There is a small Christian minority, mostly in Ethiopia.

NATIONAL HISTORY: The Afar homeland is thought to be the site of the origin of the human species; a 4.4 million-year-old humanoid was found there in the 1990s. The Afars claim to be descendants of Ham, the son of Noah as recorded in the Bible. An ancient Semitic people, migrants from southern Arabia, Afars settled the Danakil Basin thousands of years ago. Mixing with the indigenous Hamitic peoples, the migrants developed a nomadic, tribal culture in the hot, dry desert. The forbidding landscape of their homeland discouraged most invaders, although at times the tribes came under the nominal rule of the ancient Ethiopian Empire, and coastal tribes had early contact with other peoples.

Seafaring Arabs, spurred by missionary zeal to spread their new Islamic religion, converted the coastal tribes to Islam in the seventh century. Carried by caravans and raiders, the new religion spread to the isolated interior tribes between the tenth and twelfth centuries. Modeled on the Muslim tradition, small Afar sultanates flourished, eventually forming a powerful confederation, called Adal by the Ethiopians, in the twelfth century.

An Afar military leader, Ahmad ibn Ghazi, in the sixteenth century organized a *jihad* (holy war) against the Christian Ethiopians. Leading a combined army of Afars, Sahos, Somalis, and other Muslim peoples, Ghazi scored a decisive victory in 1529, utterly destroying the Ethiopian states except for a few mountain strongholds. However, with the assistance of Portuguese soldiers, a resurgent Ethiopia defeated the Muslims in 1541, causing the Afar-Saho to withdraw to their desert homeland and to avoid contacts with outsiders over the next century.

Italian colonial forces established a base on the coast at Assab in 1869 and slowly expanded their conquests at the expense of the Egyptians and Turks. In 1882 the Italians created a colonial administration for the region, although the forbidding interior desert mostly confined their authority to the Red Sea coast. The Ethiopians, fearing further European expansion in the region, conquered the Muslim stronghold of Harar and sent an army against the Afar Sultanate of Aussa, thus adding the first Afar territory in the eastern lowlands to their expanding empire. The Afar-Saho homeland was eventually divided by three colonial powers: the Italians took the northern Coastal area, Ethiopia the lowlands, and the French gained control of the Afar Sultanate of Tadjoura. The three powers agreed to new boundaries in 1896 that effectively divided Adal into three parts, the partition reflected by a new name, the Afar Triangle.

The scattered Afar tribes, nominally ruled by three sultanates—one of which, Tadjoura, lay wholly within French territory—refused to recognize the imposed international borders and continued to move their herds across the colonial frontiers; except for those living near the larger towns, they were little affected by the colonial administrations. Not until 1928 did the first European cross the huge Danakil Basin, while most of the enormous natural depression remained outside government controls until after World War II.

The French administration of the Territory of the Afars and Issas openly favored the less difficult Afars against the Issas, who openly favored the unification of all Somali lands in a single state. In 1967 the then-dominant Afars voted in a referendum to retain the region's ties to France, rejecting independence for the territory.

The Afars of Italian Eritrea, under British administration after World War II, were the first of their nation to encounter modern education and ideas, and they later provided the leadership of the Afar national movement that formed after Eritrea was federated with feudal, Christian Ethiopia in 1952. Afar nationalism gained some support over the next two decades but became a popular movement only after the 1974 Ethiopian revolution, which ended the feudal monarchy.

By the 1970s the sultans' roles had become largely ceremonial, and the social divisions within the traditonal Afar heirarchy were of diminished importance. The Afars, having initially backed the overthrow of Ethiopia's monarchy in 1974, were outraged by the new Marxist government's response to an Afar petition for famine aid and protection of their traditional grazing lands—that is, to order Marxist land reform, parceling out the best of the Afar grazing lands to farmers, many from outside the region. The violent suppression of Afar protests provoked a mass exodus. Led by Sultan Ali Mirah Anfere, thousands of Afars fled to French territory, where they formed the first openly separatist national organization, the Afar Liberation Front (ALF).

The overthrow of Ethiopia's Marxist government in 1991 was followed by the creation of an autonomous Afar state within newly democratic Ethiopia, but limited autonomy has failed to satisfy the growing Afar demands for unification and independence.

A serious Afar revolt in northern Djibouti, launched in November 1991, has mobilized Afar nationalists in all areas of the divided nation, particularly following the massacre of up to 40 civilians in a crowded Afar quarter of Djibouti City in December 1991. The Front for the Restoration of Unity and Democracy (FRUD) led a widespread Afar rebellion in northern Djibouti. Ties with Afar groups active in Ethiopia and Eritrea increased with military aid and political support from Afars outside Djibouti.

The independence from Ethiopia of Eritrea in May 1993 and a major offensive against the Afars in Djibouti in July 1993 strengthened demands for a united, independent Afar state. The Afars rejected Eritrean independence as a further partition of their national territory.

In 1994 the Afars of Djibouti split, with one faction joining the Djibouti government, another continuing to fight. In September 1997, rebels of the FRUD movement resumed military activities against the Djibouti government. Previously FRUD fighters had engaged the military only when attacked by government forces. Several FRUD leaders were arrested in Ethiopia and deported to Djibouti, where they were charged with inciting violence.

A border dispute between Ethiopia and Eritrea led to war in the region in May 1998. Much of the fighting over the next two years took place in Afar territory, displacing thousands of Afar civilians. The Afar groups, careful not to be drawn into the fighting, declared a cease-fire and demanded that both governments end the fighting and withdraw their troops from the region. The war was brought to an end in mid-2000, but thousands of troops remain in the border region, severely curtailing Afar nationalist activities in the region.

At the turn of the twenty-first century the Afars remain split—physically, between three different governments; and ideologically, between groups seeking peace and showing willingness to work with regional governments and others seeking reunification and an independent Afar state in the Horn of Africa. The rebels of the FRUD group in Djibouti, led by Ahmed Dini, demanded negotiations with the newly elected Djibouti government in April 1999, but their demands were rejected. The Afar community in Djibouti, weary of years of fighting, has not overwhelmingly supported the renewed militancy of FRUD and other groups since 1997.

The Afars and the closely related Sahos, although a traditionally nomadic people, are a highly cohesive group and reject the partition of their traditional territory among three states. Guerrilla activity in all three countries continues, with the stated aim of the reunification and independence of the Afar homeland. One of the major problems faced by the national movement is the factionalism and division caused by the partition of the Afar lands between Ethiopia, Eritrea, and Djibouti. Unemployment, illiteracy, and violence are widespread in all three regions.

SELECTED BIBLIOGRAPHY:

Harbeson, John W. *Post–Cold War Politics in the Horn of Africa: The Quest for Political Identity.* 1995.
Haskins, Jim, ed. *From Afar to Zulu: A Dictionary of African Cultures.* 1998.
Lewis, I. M. *Nationalism and Self-Determination in the Horn of Africa.* 1984.
Lewis, Ioan M. *Peoples of the Horn of Africa: Somali, Afar and Saho.* 1998.

Afrikaners

Boers; Boerevolk

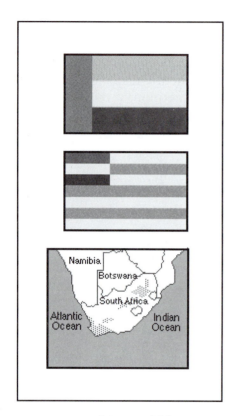

POPULATION: Approximately (2002e) 3,180,000 Afrikaners in southern Africa, 2,185,000 in South Africa, 150,000 in Namibia, and smaller numbers in Zimbabwe, Zambia, and other neighboring African states.

THE AFRIKANER HOMELAND: The Afrikaner homeland covers nearly the whole of modern South Africa; however, the historic Afrikaner districts lie in the southwestern Cape of Good Hope and the central and northern areas that formed the historic Afrikaner republics of Transvaal and Orange Free State. The Cape has a Mediterranean climate and is famed for its produce, particularly wines, but most of the Afrikaner homeland is flat or rolling savanna land called veld or velt, rising to mountains that separate the Afrikaner homeland from the English-dominated territory on the Indian Ocean. The major Afrikaner cultural centers are South Africa's major cities of Johannesburg, Pretoria, and Cape Town.

FLAG: The Afrikaner national flag, the former flag of the Transvaal, is a tricolor of red, white, and blue stripes and a broad vertical green stripe at the hoist. The flag of the former Orange Free State is also used by some groups—seven horizontal stripes of white and orange, bearing a canton of the Dutch flag, horizontal red, white, and blue, on the upper hoist. Other nationalist groups and political organizations use a variety of flags.

PEOPLE AND CULTURE: Afrikaners are the descendants of Dutch, Germans, and French Huguenots who settled in southern Africa between the seventeenth and nineteenth centuries. Afrikaner scholars categorize Afrikaner ancestry as 50% Dutch, 27% German, 18% French, and 5% other, mostly Flemish.* They are commonly known as Boers, meaning "farmers" in the Afrikaner language, although this term is sometimes used derogatorily by others. Isolated from later European influences, they Africanized, developing a distinct culture and language and gradually fusing as the so-called white tribe of Africa. A very strong sense of identity and destiny has inspired both noble accomplishments and tragic mistakes. The Afrikaner contributions to the development of southern Africa are undeniable, although these have been overshadowed by their association with the policy of apartheid.

LANGUAGE AND RELIGION: The Afrikaner language, Afrikaans, is principally derived from the South Holland dialect of the mid-seventeenth-century Dutch settlers in south Africa. Borrowings from Malay, English, French, German, and indigenous African languages, as well as the grammatical simplification that occurred over several centuries, greatly changed the language. Until the mid-nineteenth century Afrikaans was a spoken language only, with standard Dutch used as the Afrikaners' literary language. A movement to make Afrikaans the literary language gradually gained support, with increased use in newspapers, schools, and churches in the late nineteenth and early twentieth centuries, and in 1925 Afrikaans officially replaced standard Dutch as the Afrikaner literary language. It is now one of eleven official languages in South Africa.

The majority of the Afrikaners belong to various Protestant sects, primarily the Dutch Reformed Church, which has become an integral part of the Afrikaner culture. The traditionally rural Afrikaner culture revolved around the village or regional churches, which became the center of both the religious and secular life of the communities. Churches still retain considerable influence on the Afrikaner culture.

NATIONAL HISTORY: In 1652, the Dutch East India Company sent out a party of soldiers and officials under Jan van Riebeeck to establish a support station on the Cape of Good Hope for shipping between the Netherlands and the Far East. In the first years the company encouraged immigration, but after the first decade of the eighteenth century Cape Colony grew largely by natural increase, as large families were the norm.

The colonists gradually expanded into the lush farmlands of the Cape, but with the Cape Town market for agricultural produce glutted and slaves doing most of the work of the colony, there was growing pressure to disperse and to become self-sufficient pastoral farmers. In the early 1700s, Dutch explorers from the Cape visited the area north of the Orange River and returned with tales of a nearly uninhabited but very rich land beyond the frontiers of the colony. Small groups of farmers began moving out of the colony to settle the vast lands of the interior.

In 1707 the European population of Cape Colony, including the dispersed farmers, stood at 1,779, largely Dutch, Germans, Flemish, and French Huguenots. The three immigrant groups, sharing the same Protestant roots, gradually merged into a new nation, which by the late eighteenth century spoke its own language, Afrikaans.

The Cape Colony became the center of a constant struggle between an expanding European population and the various indigenous peoples. Classified by the Europeans as non-Europeans, these groups included the African ethnic groups, but eventually the category was extended to include peoples of mixed background and laborers imported from the Dutch East India colonies. The Boers were hostile toward both the indigenous Africans, with whom they fought frequent wars, and the government of the Cape, which attempted to restrain their movement and commerce.

Although the colony prospered, over half the immigrant European population eventually turned to the life of the *trekboeren*, or wandering farmers. They developed their own subculture, based on self-sufficient patriarchal communities. Wandering across the highlands east of the Cape, the Afrikaner farmers began to compare their way of life to that of the Hebrew patriarchs of the Old Testament. Staunch Calvinists, the Afrikaners saw themselves as the children of God in the wilderness, a Christian elect divinely ordained to rule the land and its backward indigenous tribes.

The British occupied the Cape to prevent its capture by the French in 1795. Dutch rule was restored in 1803, but as a result of the Napoleonic Wars in Europe, Cape Colony became a permanent British possession in 1806. Although at first the Afrikaners accepted British administration, resentment quickly surfaced over British liberal policies, specifically in regard to the frontier and the freeing of slaves. Tensions between the Afrikaners and the authorities greatly increased after the British landed 5,000 British settlers in 1820. In 1833 slavery was prohibited in the British Empire, an action that directly threatened the Afrikaner's way of life.

Small groups began to "trek" north out of British jurisdiction in 1831, and between 1835 and 1843 over 12,000 Afrikaners left the colony in the Great Trek, heading for the relatively empty spaces of the high velt and southern Natal. In the frontier districts the Afrikaners established a number of autonomous states, the most important being those of the Transvaal, the Orange Free State, and Natalia (Natal). The settlers from the Cape were called "Voortrekkers," and their numbers grew following the defeat of all indigenous groups standing in the way of the trekkers. The legends and lore of the Great Trek became important parts of Afrikaner culture and heritage, much like the expansion of America into the lands to the west.

In 1848, the British authorities laid claim to the regions colonized by the Boers, and British troops defeated Afrikaner efforts to deny the British access to the veld. Unable to maintain effective administrations in the face of stiff Afrikaner resistance, however, in 1852 the British government agreed to recognize the independence of the settlers in the Transvaal, later the South African Republic, and in 1854 it recognized the independence of the Orange Free State. Both Afrikaner republics committed their domestic policies to "apartheid," a policy of strict inequality in church and state between the white immigrant populations and the indigenous black tribes. Between 1862 and 1864 civil war erupted between rival Afrikaner groups in the Transvaal, seriously weakening resistance to British expansion.

The discovery of diamonds and gold between 1867 and the end of the nineteenth century set the stage for confrontation between the Afrikaners and the British of the Cape. The discovery drew in thousands of foreigners, *uitlanders* in the Afrikaner language, with growing demands for the same rights as the Afrikaner population. The refusal of the Afrikaner republican governments to grant civil rights to the largely British foreign population of the gold and diamond fields raised tensions in the 1870s.

In 1877 the British took direct control of the South African Republic and the Orange Free State. The Boers rebelled in December 1880, setting off the First Anglo-Boer War, which ended with British defeat and renewed independence for the Boer republics in August 1881. New gold strikes in 1886 brought a new influx of foreigners to the states, setting off a new crisis with the British authorities of the Cape. The British financed foreign agitation against the Boer governments, and in December 1895 a British force of 660 raided into the Transvaal, bringing the region close to war. In October 1899 the Second Anglo-Boer War broke out, pitting the British against the two Boer republics, which had the support of a large part of the Afrikaner population of the British Cape Colony. The Boers, initially successful, were armed and supported by Germany, but thousands of troops sent from Britain forced the Boers to give up direct confrontations and to move out onto the veld to fight a guerrilla war.

The British defeated the last Boer army in mid-1900 but were unable to end the effective guerrilla tactics of the Boer fighters. A new policy was initiated that involved burning thousands of Afrikaner farms and herding 120,000 civilians into the first concentration camps of the twentieth century. Inefficient administration and poor sanitation made the camps notorious; and an estimated 27,000 Boers, mostly women and children, died of hunger and disease. The camps caused tremendous bitterness among the Afrikaners, feelings that persist to the present. In 1902 the last Boer fighters were forced to surrender.

The Afrikaners, led by the first nationalist organization, Het Volk, agitated against British rule and demanded responsible government and autonomy. In 1906 the Transvaal was granted an autonomous government, followed by the Orange Free State in 1907. In local elections the Het Volk won majorities. In 1910 the states were merged with the British South African territories into the new Union of South Africa. After the bitterness of defeat, the Afrikaners experienced a surge of nationalism in the early twentieth century and mostly supported the new Nationalist Party.

Part of the Afrikaner population supported Germany during World War I, but a secessionist rebellion in October 1914 was defeated by moderate Boers and British troops. In the postwar years the Afrikaners gradually gained control of the South African government and in 1948, after World War II, gained complete control of the government. Throughout the 1950s the Afrikaners became increasingly urbanized, and by 1960 an estimated 84% lived in urban areas, even as the old Boer farm culture hardened into the restrictive and repressive policy of apartheid. The 1960s saw a massive increase in Afrikaner nationalism as the world increasingly opposed the government's racial policies. The increasing isolation of South Africa in the 1970s forced the Afrikaners into a "laager" mentality, emulating the old circled wagons of the pioneer era to show solidarity against world opinion.

Several extremist organizations grew out of the first tentative government moves to ease the more odious apartheid laws in the late 1970s and early 1980s. In 1988, when the Afrikaners marked the 150th anniversary of the Great Trek, they were already divided into opposing camps, with some favoring a gradual relaxation of the policy, others wanting to return to rigid segregation. The split led to a revolt in the Afrikaner press, which largely favored change, and to turmoil in other institutions, including the churches. Amid growing violence in 1985 the government announced an indefinite state of emergency, but by 1989 it had begun to dismantle the apartheid policy and to free political prisoners. South African whites, including a majority of the Afrikaners, approved constitutional racial equality, setting the stage for the end of Afrikaner domination and the hated apartheid. In 1994, free and democratic elections brought a longtime political prisoner, Nelson Mandela, to the presidency of the country.

The end of apartheid, although opposed by a minority of the Afrikaners, allowed the Afrikaner nation to renew ties to Europe and opened new opportunities for Afrikaners in neighboring parts of Africa.

For the most part, the Afrikaner nation is descended from those enumerated as such by the colonial authorities in 1707. The Afrikaners constitute roughly 8% of the South African population and roughly half the white population of the country, which means that they are unable to influence national policy seriously. To survive as a "volk," the Afrikaners are seeking ways to protect their culture and language, including demanding autonomy to protect their unique heritage and identity. The majority want some form of cultural autonomy, but small groups have established small territories that they claim will grow into independent Afrikaner homelands in South Africa. Shorn of their former privilege and power, the Afrikaners have begun a new era. Possessing a language and culture unique to southern Africa, the white tribe has no other home, and its future is inextricably linked to the fortunes of South Africa.

The consequences of having lost political power began to catch up with the Afrikaners in the late 1990s. Once pampered by the apartheid state, the Afrikaners have seen their privileges curtailed, particularly preferential access to employment and superior public services. Their language no longer has the significance it once did. In public employment and state-run enterprises, such as television, Afrikaners have been relegated to a subordinate role. Their new circumstances, among them widespread crime, have led many to consider emigration. Many Afrikaners have the feeling of having become strangers in their own homeland.

Many Afrikaners cling to a belief in territorial self-determination in a federal South Africa as the only way to safeguard their language and culture. Only an extremely small number have actually set out for the sparsely populated expanse of the Northern Cape Province, where militants have begun laying the foundations of a future Afrikaner state of "Orania." Orania is seen as the first growth-point in an area between the west coast and the Oranje River that will eventually become the volkstaat, the homeland of the Afrikaner nation.

SELECTED BIBLIOGRAPHY:

Davis, R. Hunt, ed. *Apartheid Unravels*. 1991.
de Klerk, W. A. *The Puritans in Africa: A Story of Afrikanerdom*. 1975.
Degenaar, J. J. *Afrikaner Nationalism*. 1994.
Suzman, Mark. *Ethnic Nationalism and State Power: The Rise of Irish Nationalism, Afrikaner Nationalism and Zionism*. 1999.

Ahmadis

Ahmedis; Qadianis; Qadyanies

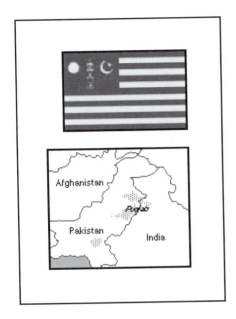

POPULATION: Approximately (2002e) 8,202,000 Ahmadis in southern Asia, with 4,910,000 in Pakistan, and smaller communities in northern India, Bangladesh, Afghanistan, and Iran. Other Ahmadi communities live in Europe, the United States, Canada, Indonesia, and Africa. The total population of Ahmadis in the world is estimated at over 10,000,000.

THE AHMADI HOMELAND: The Ahmadi homeland lies in northern Pakistan, mostly in the Punjab, the vast plain that stretches westward into India. Before the partition of 1947, the Ahmadis also inhabited areas that now form part of present India, including the birthplace of the founder of Ahmadiyya, at Qadian, in Indian Punjab. In 1947 they officially relocated from Qadian to Rabwah, in Pakistan. The Ahmadi capital and major cultural center is the city of Rabwah, (2002e) 48,000, in the Punjab province of Pakistan.

FLAG: The Ahmadi national flag, the flag of the Ahmadiyya movement in Pakistan, has thirteen green and white stripes with a green canton on the upper hoist bearing a yellow sun, a white tower, and a white crescent moon and five-pointed star.

PEOPLE AND CULTURE: The Ahmadis are an ethnoreligious national group, having developed from what is considered by most Muslims to be a heretical sect. The highly organized national community, which has a considerable financial base, consolidated only in the twentieth century. Having suffered persecution since the founding of Pakistan in 1947, the Ahmadis have coalesced into a national group, one of many in Pakistan. Culturally the Ahmadis share the general culture of the Indian subculture but have also incorporated cultural traits borrowed from the Christian minority. An estimated 99.9% of the Ahmadis are converts or descendants of converts from Islam. Discrimination and segregation have isolated most Ahmadis in separate villages or neighborhoods.

LANGUAGE AND RELIGION: The Ahmadis, many being refugees or the descendants of refugees from northern India, mostly speak Urdu, while the majority of the Punjabi population around them speak Punjabi. The Urdu language is the language of their religious beliefs and has become something of a national language since persecution increased in the 1970s. The Ahmadis speak several dialects, often using borrowed words from Punjabi and other regional languages. Many Ahmadis speak English, reflecting the location of the Ahmadi diaspora.

The Ahmadiyya religion, which is claimed by its adherents to be a sect of Islam, incorporates beliefs and traditions from earlier Muslim, Christian, and Hindu forms. Branded unbelievers by the civil and religious authorities of Pakistan, the Ahmadis have come under increasing persecution since the 1970s. They are zealous missionaries, preaching Ahmadi beliefs as the one true Islam, with Mohammed and Mirza Ghulam Ahmad, the founder of the sect, as its true prophets. Ahmadis in Pakistan have been prevented from performing the religious pilgrimage to Saudi Arabia, because the government classifies them as non-Muslims on their passports. Unlike other religious communities in Pakistan, the Ahmadis are totally denied freedom of religion.

NATIONAL HISTORY: The Ahmadiyya movement within Islam, called by other Muslims Qadianism, was founded in the Muslim village of Qadian in the Punjab in 1889 by Mirza Ghulam Ahmad. He claimed to be the *mahdi*, a figure expected by some Muslims at the end of the world, as well as the Christian messiah, an incarnation of the Hindu god Krishna, and a reappearance of Mohammed. Ahmad was the son of a prosperous Urdu-speaking family but refused to go into the British civil service as urged by his father. He lived a life of study and contemplation and claimed to hear voices. He spoke of a revelation and soon gathered a small group of devoted followers. From then on his influence and following steadily increased, as did opposition from the Muslim community in the Punjab.

The Ahmadi doctrine, in some aspects, is quite unorthodox. For example, it holds that Jesus feigned death and resurrection and later escaped to India, where he died at the age of 120 and was buried in Kashmir. One of Ahmad's major differences with orthodox Islam was his belief that *jihad*, or holy war, had become un-Islamic, that the struggle against unbelievers must be waged by peaceful methods.

Ahmad died in 1908, and in 1914 a schism over succession occurred among the Ahmadiyya followers. One group seceded, headed by the son of the founder, Ahmad; it disowned the prophetic claims of Ghulam Ahmad and established its center in Lahore. The main group, called the Qadiani, after the village of Qadian, moved its headquarters to Rabwah, in what was then West Pakistan, in 1947. Both groups are noted for their missionary work.

Mohammed Ali Jinnah, the founder of Pakistan, accepted the Ahmadis as a Muslim sect, but many of the new country's leaders and clerics rejected his approval. Since the creation of Pakistan in 1947 and Jinnah's death in 1948, more fundamentalist Islamic groups have agitated against accepting the Ahmadis within the pale of Pakistani Islam. In spite of fundamentalist opposition, the Ahmadis, who are relatively well educated as a group, have been well represented in both the pre- and postindependence administrations in Pakistan and have held many high government offices. Yet despite their success in many fields, their status has remained uncertain at best. More than any other national group in Pakistan, they have been the victims of the lack of ethnic unity in modern Pakistan, which gave rise to the perceived need for the "unity of Islam" as a tenet of Pakistani nationalism.

Anti-Ahmadi agitation first exploded in the spring of 1953 in several urban centers in the Punjab, with destruction of Ahmadi property and mosques. Government action to restrain the fundamentalist Muslim clergy resulted in a period of relative calm that lasted until 1970. In that year, in national elections, the Ahmadis mostly allied themselves with the Zulfika Ali Bhutto regime and entered the Punjabi legislature in significant numbers. As Pakistan came under intense secessionist pressure, first from the Bengalis in East Pakistan, then from the Baluchis* and Pushtuns,* the demands for Islamic unity in West Pakistan resulted in increased violence against "non-Muslim" groups. Following severe rioting in April and May 1974 in Punjab, a constitutional amendment officially declared the Ahmadis to be unbelievers.

Late in 1974, after an exhaustive examination of all evidence for and against the Ahmadis, the Muslim World League (Rabita Alame Islami), which represents religious scholars from most Muslim countries, passed an unanimous resolution declaring the Ahmadiyya movement as apostate, outside the family of Islam. It further declared that the Ahmadiyya movement was a man-made organization, with no divine authority or guidance.

A martial-law decree issued on 26 April 1984 declared the Ahmadis *kafirs*, or infidels, and mandated the active persecution of the Ahmadi minority. All manifestations of Ahmadi religious and traditional practices were declared punishable by law, and the Ahmadis were singled out for discriminatory treatment within the corrupt and ineffective government bureaucracy. The return of a civilian government in the late 1980s, under the leadership of Benazir Bhutto, the daughter of the country's former political leader, did not result in any major changes in the status or condition of the Ahmadi minority in Pakistan. In early 1990 the Pakistani government rejected charges by human rights organizations that persistent religious and job discrimination against the Ahmadi community continued unabated.

Many of the more affluent Ahmadis have left Pakistan since the 1984 decree, including Hazrat Mirza T. Ahmad, who was elected caliph of the Ahmadiyya movement in 1982. He left Pakistan for the United Kingdom in 1984 and has blamed orthodox Muslim clerics for stirring up anti-Ahmadi sentiment in Pakistan.

The Pakistani government in 1992 announced that a column that indicates religion would be added to each Pakistani citizen's identity card. The government had reportedly succumbed to pressure from Islamic fundamentalists of the majority Sunni population that the Ahmadis should not be identified as Muslims and that all Ahmadis should be removed from important government jobs. Pakistan's small Christian minority vehemently opposed the new law; the government officials stated that the law was not aimed at Christians but at the Ahmadis, as they can hide behind Muslim names.

An important court judgment in 1994 guaranteed the Ahmadis freedom of expression, but in practice persecution continued unabated. One consequence of the continued suppression of the Ahmadi community in Pakistan has been the growth of a particular Ahmadi national consciousness, when before the Ahmadis had considered themselves part of the vast Muslim majority of the country.

The Islamization of Pakistan's laws, begun by the military dictator Gen. Zia ul Haq in 1978, continues to undermine freedom of religion in the country and has led to massive abuses against the Ahmadis and other religious and ethnic minorities. Islamization has been extended to all areas of political and social life. The country's blasphemy laws have been used to bring politically motivated charges of blasphemy and other offenses against the Ahmadis. In many cases local officials and police have encouraged acts of violence against the Ahmadis. Changes to the Pakistan penal code introduced in the 1990s make it a criminal offense for Ahmadis to profess, practice, or propagate their faith or to call themselves Muslim. In one amendment to the code, the death penalty became the mandatory punishment for defiling the name of the Prophet Mohammed. Any reference to the Prophet by an Ahmadi is considered by orthodox Muslims as a defilement of his name and is punishable by death.

The Ahmadis, by accepting Mirza Ghulam Ahmad as a prophet, reject the finality of the prophecy of Mohammed, a view that infuriates more orthodox sects. Ahmadis also resist the politicization of Islam and therefore the concept of the Islamic state, which has been the symbol of national unity in Pakistan.

Virtually all Muslim denominations, organizations, scholars, and nations have declared the Ahmadis *kafirs*. Particularly in Pakistan, where the majority of the Ahmadis live, Qadianism, Ahmadiyyat, is considered a form of unbelief. The Ahmadis have even been accused of acting as agents of Israel, though the Ahmadi leadership opposed the creation of the Israeli state in 1947–48.

Disenfranchised as Muslims, the Ahmadis can vote only for their single representative allowed in the Pakistani parliament. Since 1985, elections in Pakistan have been held under an electoral system that compartmentalizes the different religious groups. The majority of seats in the legislature are reserved for Muslims, while the Christians have four, the Hindus four, and the Ahmadis one.

The Lahore High Court in April 1994 extended the blasphemy law to include defilement of the names of "all the true prophets of Allah mentioned in the Koran," including Abraham and Jesus. The ordinance made the Ahmadis liable to a penalty of up to three years' imprisonment for a range of activities that identified their faith with the orthodox Islamic faith or involved its propagation. According to a 1997 U.S. State Department report, the Ahmadis suffer from the violation of their places of worship; denial of freedom of faith, speech, and assembly; restrictions on their press; social boycott; and alleged officially sanctioned extremist acts against their community. Further, they are barred from burying their dead in Muslim graveyards. According to a press report of 1998, there were 658 prosecutions in 1997, involving 2,467 individuals, under the blasphemy and anti-Ahmadi laws. The systematic discrimination suffered by the Ahmadi people has been compared to apartheid in South Africa.

The number of prominent Ahmadis murdered by unknown assailants since 1974, when the Ahmadis were declared non-Muslim, reached 68 in 1999, with little done to investigate or bring the assailants to justice. The continuing persecution of the Ahmadis has pushed them to form a separate national group, with dire consequences for the already fragile social fabric of Pakistan, while many leading Ahmadis continue to emigrate to escape the hate stirred up by Islamic fanatics.

The Pakistani army staged a bloodless coup in October 1999, removing Prime Minister Nawaz Sharif and replacing him with Gen. Pervez Musharraf. Although the new government promised to review the blasphemy laws and to end the persecution of Ahmadis, discrimination and violence against them continue.

In 1999, Ahmadi leaders called on the Pakistani government to release immediately and unconditionally any Ahmadis currently imprisoned solely for practicing their religion, and to abolish all laws that make it a criminal offense for Ahmadis to profess, practice, or propagate their faith. Since the promulgation of an ordinance in 1984, it has been a criminal offense in Pakistan for Ahmadis to call themselves Muslim, to use Muslim practices of worship or Muslim phrases of greeting, or to propagate their faith. In practice Ahmadis can be imprisoned for calling their places of worship "mosques." In 2000, more than 2,000 Ahmadis faced various charges relating to their religious and cultural activities. New laws, adopted in 2000, made legalized persecution even more severe, including murder with impunity by ultra-faithful Muslims.

The Ahmadis, like other Pakistani groups, suffer from one of the highest illiteracy rates in the developing world. The masses are controlled by feudal politicians through religious-based politics. The dismal condition of the Ahmadis and the continuing discrimination against them has reinforced a cultural distinctiveness that began in the 1970s. Denied their places in the national fabric of Pakistan, the Ahmadis have become increasingly separate from the Sunni Muslim majority of the Pakistani nation.

SELECTED BIBLIOGRAPHY:

Copley, Antony. *Gurus and Their Followers: New Religious Reform Movements in Colonial India*. 2000.

Gualtieri, Antonio R. *Conscience and Coercion: Ahmadi Muslims and Orthodoxy in Pakistan*. 1989.

Lavan, S. *The Ahmadiyyah Movement*. 1974.

Malik, Iftikhar H. *State and Civil Society in Pakistan: Politics of Authority, Ideology, and Ethnicity*. 1997.

Ainu

Ainu Minzoku (Ainu Nation); Emishi; Yezo; Kurils; Kurilians

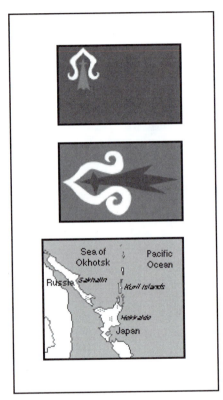

POPULATION: Approximately (2002e) 37,000 Ainu in eastern Asia, 27,000 in Japan, and around 10,000 in Russia. Since some Ainu do not identify themselves as ethnic Ainu for fear of the disadvantages of minority status, particularly in Japan, the exact Ainu population is a matter of conjecture, with estimates running as high as 300,000, including several thousand living in the Tokyo metropolitan area.

THE AINU HOMELAND: The Ainu homeland, called Ainu-Moshiri, which means "tranquil land of human beings," or "the earth where the Ainu live," includes parts of southern Sakhalin and the Kuril Islands in Russia and traditional lands on the northern Japanese island of Hokkaido, called Mosir by the Ainu. The islands are of volcanic origin and retain numerous active volcanoes and hot springs, considered sacred by the original Ainu inhabitants. The major cultural center of the Russian Ainu is Kurilsk, called Shana by the Ainu, in the Kuril Islands. The major cultural center on Hokkaido is Ashikawa, which once had an Ainu reservation in what are now the suburbs of the city.

FLAG: The Ainu national flag is a dark cerulean-blue field with the white and red Ainu national symbol on the upper hoist. The flag of the national movement is a lighter blue, bearing the same national symbol but much larger and shown horizontally.

PEOPLE AND CULTURE: The Ainu, which means "people" in the Ainu language, are the descendants of the original inhabitants of the region. The Ainu are traditionally round-eyed, short-statured, and brunette, with abundant body and facial hair compared to their Mongoloid neighbors. They are thought to be more closely related to the Caucasians or the Tungustic, Altaic, and Uralic peoples of eastern Siberia than to the Japanese or other Oriental peoples. Disease and a low birth rate have severely diminished their numbers over the past two centuries, and inter-marriage has brought about an almost completely mixed population. The men formerly wore heavy beards, and the women had mustache-like tattooing around the mouth. Of those still considered ethnic Ainu, most now closely resemble the Japanese in physical appearance. They are often referred to by the Japanese as *dojin*, a term for "indigenous" that connotes vulgarity and uncleanliness. Since the 1980s the Ainu have experienced a revival of their culture and language and have renewed demands for recognition of their unique heritage. Ainu culture is inseparably connected to their natural and spiritual environment. As noted, the number of Ainu in Japan may be much higher than official estimates; due to societal and economic discrimination, they tend to hesitate to express or define themselves as Ainu. In 1994, the first Ainu was elected to the Japanese Diet.

LANGUAGE AND RELIGION: The original Ainu language has been largely supplanted by Japanese or Russian in daily life. Their language is an isolated language group possibly related to the language of the Okinawans,* south of the Japanese main islands. Formerly spoken in up to 19 dialects, all but four are now extinct. The remaining dialects are Sakhalin (Saghilin), Taraika, Hokkaido (Ezo, Yezo), and Kuril (Shikotan). The language, however, is preserved in epics, songs, and stories transmitted orally to succeeding generations. Since the 1980s a concerted effort has been made to preserve the language as the Ainu national language, and since 1997 the language has been taught in Hokkaido schools.

The traditional religion of the Ainu centered on local forces of nature, which were thought to have souls or spirits. The most important ritual in the Ainu religion, the "Iyomante" or "Kuma Matsuri," involved the annual sacrifice of a sacred bear. Distinctive rhythmic music and dances characterize Ainu religious ceremonies, some of which have been preserved partly to attract the growing number of tourists visiting the region.

NATIONAL HISTORY: The Ainu, of unknown origin, inhabited the four major Japanese home islands, the Kuril Islands, and the southern part of Sakhalin for millennia. According to Ainu tradition, their ancestors populated the islands some three to four thousand years ago. Although known as a warrior people, the Ainu developed their culture and religion in harmony with nature. Holding their lands in common, various nomadic bands lived by hunting, fishing, gathering, and trading.

The Japanese began to colonize the Ainu lands in northern Honshu in the late Kamakura era, in the thirteenth and fourteenth centuries. The Ainu retreated northward before the expansion of the more advanced Japanese. In 1456, the first serious Ainu rebellion occurred, led by Koshamine; sporadic warfare with the Japanese decimated the Ainu population of Honshu. The Japanese moved across the Tsugaru Strait and began in the sixteenth century to colonize the southwest of the island they called Hokkaido. Commercial development of the newly conquered lands during the

Edo Era, from 1603, brought the total suppression of the Ainu population of the southern Japanese islands.

The Dutch navigator Martin de Fries was the first European to reach the region, in 1643. For about a hundred years the Kuril Islands were marked on the map as Dutch territory. The Russians, seeking furs, discovered Sakhalin Island in 1645 and the northern Kuril Islands in 1697. The Russians immediately levied a fur tribute on the Ainu population. "Slow-witted" Ainu were brought under control through violence, taken hostage, crippled, and massacred. Those who yielded were declared, as their reward, subjects of the Russian Empire. By the mid-eighteenth century the huge fur-bearing seal herds had been totally exterminated.

In 1669 the Ainu national hero, Shakushian, led the Ainu against the Japanese invaders of Hokkaido, only to suffer defeat once again. A century later, in 1789, another national hero, Kunashiri Menashi, led the Ainu in a final battle against harsh Japanese domination. Although their resistance ended in failure, the Ainu established their ethnic identity and thereafter were determined to maintain their heritage. The main cause of the Ainu collapse was their complete lack of any unifying social or political structure above the village level.

Until about 1800, the Ainu outnumbered the Japanese inhabitants of Hokkaido. Without any formal treaties or arrangements, the Japanese government incorporated the Ainu homeland and extended its authority over the Ainu people. Up to the 1868 Meiji Restoration, the government officially classed the Ainu as "foreign" and treated them as illegal foreigners living in the empire. After the restoration, a plan for government-sponsored Japanese emigration formed an integral part of the strategy for exploiting Hokkaido's rich natural resources. The surviving Ainu were confined to a small areas of the island similar to the reservations of the North American indigenous peoples.

The Japanese government adopted both a colonial and assimilationist policy in relation to the Ainu nation. Colonial authorities banned the traditional Ainu lifestyle and forced the Ainu to use the Japanese language and to adopt Japanese culture. The colonizers sought to obliterate the Ainu language and customs, but an English missionary, Dr. John Batchelor, gave the Ainu a written language and compiled their first dictionary.

In 1870, the government recognized the Ainu as Japanese but forced them to take up settled agriculture on communal lands, an activity totally alien to the Ainu tradition. An American, Horace Capron, inadvertently contributed to the decline of the Ainu by introducing scientific farming methods that greatly accelerated Japanese colonization of Ainu territory. The Meiji government in 1873 listed all of Hokkaido as "ownerless lands." The Hokkaido Colonization Commission nationalized Ainu communal lands, including lands on which Ainu houses sat, in 1877. The government ordered that all Ainu names be changed to recognizably Japanese names.

In 1885, when the Japanese population of Hokkaido had reached nearly 300,000, the Japanese government granted the island a separate provincial administration, which completely ignored the welfare and rights of the Ainu minority. The Law for the Protection of the Primitive Peoples of Hokkaido in 1899 described the Ainu as an inferior race and forced the remaining Ainu into the mountains and less productive lands. Thousands died from illness and starvation.

The Ainu began to assimilate as the only way to survive, and since the turn of the century they have increasingly adopted the Japanese language and culture and have attempted to hide their origins. The homogenous Japanese, extremely intolerant of minorities, have subjected the surviving Ainu to many forms of discrimination.

The Kuril Islands have been disputed by Japan and Russia since 1875, when the Russians gave the islands to Japan in exchange for northern Sakhalin. Just after the end of World War II, in September 1945, the Soviet Union violated its armed neutrality with Japan and occupied the Japanese territories in Sakhalin and the Kuril Islands. Two years later the Soviet government annexed the islands outright. The Japanese and some of the Ainu inhabitants of the islands left for nearby Hokkaido.

In the 1960s the Japanese government began construction of an industrial development area near the remaining Ainu lands in Hokkaido. The construction of a dam in the Nibutani region to supply water to the new development at first brought much-needed work and monetary compensation to the Ainu of the region, but later several Ainu leaders opposed the dam as destructive to the remaining Ainu culture in Hokkaido. The court case had still not been settled at the turn of the new century.

The position of the Japanese government is illustrated by its 1980 assertion to the United Nations regarding minorities and their freedom to practice their own religions and speak their own languages: "There are no minorities in Japan to which Article 27 of Section III of the International Covenant on Human Rights refers." Most Japanese officials continue to deny the existence of minorities in Japan.

In the late 1980s, a new nationalism took hold in the remaining Ainu population, spurred by renewed contacts between the Ainu of Japan and their remaining kin in the collapsing Soviet Union. The Ainu demanded cultural and economic autonomy. In 1984 the Ainu proposed scrapping the hated 1899 Ainu convention, to be replaced by recognition of Ainu political and cultural rights. Ainu delegates to a special meeting in Geneva of the United Nations in 1986 presented their case for indigenous status. In 1986 the total number of people in Hokkaido identifying themselves as Ainu was 24,381, although the number of part-Ainu in Japan may be in the hundreds of thousands.

The Japanese government, in the wake of the disintegration of the Soviet Union in 1991, began to press its claim to the Kuril Islands. The controversy over the disposition of the islands, part of the original Ainu patrimony, stimulated the growth of Ainu nationalism. Activists mobilized the Ainu population in one of the most remarkable revivals since the end of the Cold War. In 1991 the Ainu nationalist organization, Untari, formally laid claim to the Kuril Islands, on the grounds that both Russian and Japanese claims to the islands are predated by the Ainu by several millennia. The Japanese claim to have controlled the Kurils since the seventeenth century. The Russians claim that the Ainu of the Kurils paid taxes to the Russian Empire in the form of furs in the same century. The nationalists demanded "exclusive possession" of two or three of the smaller islands as a first step toward establishing a sovereign Ainu state.

The Ainu of Hokkaido mostly work as low-paid laborers, as their traditional pursuits, hunting and fishing, are prohibited. Of the millions of salmon caught in Hokkaido waters each year, the Ainu are allowed to take only 400 for ceremonial purposes, but not one for sustenance.

The Japanese government, after 1400 years of domination, continued to decline to recognize the existence of the Ainu until the late 1990s. The United Nations officially recognized the Ainu's indigenous status in December 1992. On 8 May 1997, the Lower House of the Japanese parliament recognized the Ainu people as an indigenous people of Japan, entitled to the protection of their distinct culture. The Ainu had been seeking this for many years from the Japanese government as redress for historical injustices and to replace the discriminatory 1899 Hokkaido Former Aborigine Protection Law. The new law is the first Japanese legislation acknowledging the existence of an ethnic minority in Japan, but it stopped short of actually acknowledging the Ainu's indigenous status, an omission that could raise questions about aboriginal rights, including those related to land and natural resources.

In 1998 Ainu nationalists again put forward a territorial claim to the disputed Kuril Islands. The Japanese government refuses to recognize the Ainu claim and pushes for the return of the Kuril Islands to Japanese sovereignty, even though polls show that the Japanese people do not care about the islands and do not see them as an important issue. For the Ainu, however, the claim to the islands is very important; a sovereign state in the islands would assure their survival as a separate nation.

SELECTED BIBLIOGRAPHY:

Partal, Vicent. *The Ainu Law of 1899*. 1992.
Peng, Fred C. C., and Peter Grier. *The Ainu: The Past and the Present*. 1977.
Sanders, Douglas. *Ainu as an Indigenous People*. 1986.
Shigeru, Kayano. *Our Land Was a Forest: An Ainu Memoir*. 1994.

Ajars

Ajarians; Adjars; Adzhars; Adzars; Achars; Ajhareli; Ach'areli; Laz; Zan

POPULATION: Approximately (2002e) 375,000 Ajars live in the southwestern Caucasus, mostly in Georgia, with 260,000, and another 105,000, called Laz, in adjacent areas of Turkey. Estimates of the Laz population range from 50,000 to 1.5 million.

THE AJAR HOMELAND: The Ajar homeland lies in southwestern Georgia, just north of the international border with Turkey. Two east-west ranges, the Ajar-Imeretinsky in the north and the Shavshetsky in the south, rise from the Black Sea coastal lowlands. Between the ranges lies the Ajaristskali River valley, which is closed at the eastern end by a third range, the Arsiyan Mountains. The coastal lowland area, which widens somewhat between Batumi and Rize and again in the north around Kobuleti, has a humid subtropical climate. In Turkey, the Ajar name for the region, Lazistan, is forbidden. The Ajar homeland in Georgia forms an autonomous republic within the Georgian republic. *Ajar Republic (Ajaria/Ajaristan)*: 1,160 sq. mi.—3,005 sq. km, (2002e) 386,000—Ajars 65%, Georgians 14%, Russians 6%, Armenians 6%, Greeks 2%. The Ajar capital and major cultural center, Batumi, (2002e) 144,000, lies on the Black Sea near the Turkish border. The center of the Laz Ajars in adjacent parts of Turkey is Rize, called Rizini by the Ajars, (2002e) 82,000.

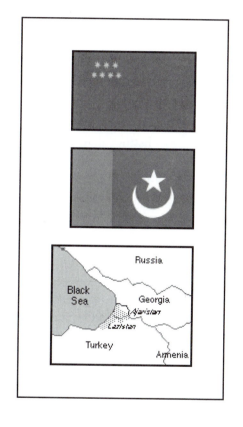

FLAG: The Ajar national flag, the flag of the autonomous republic, is a blue field bearing seven small seven-pointed gold stars on the upper hoist. The Ajar nationalist flag is a horizontal bicolor of green and red, the red twice the width of the green and bearing a centered white five-pointed star over a white crescent moon, pointing up.

PEOPLE AND CULTURE: The Ajars are a South Caucasian people who call themselves Ach'areli, or Ajareli. The majority of the Ajars are fishermen or farmers, and most live in rural areas. The Ajar nation is traditionally divided into the Ajars in the south and east, the Kabuletians in the north and west, and the Laz along the Black Sea coast in Turkey. The Ajars, not counted in Soviet or Georgian censuses since 1926, are not considered a separate ethnic group by the Georgian government, although they do have distinct religious and cultural traditions. Historically and religiously oriented toward Turkey, they have attempted to win greater autonomy within Georgia by peaceful means, while maintaining close family and cultural ties between the Ajar populations in both Georgia and Turkey. They consider themselves a separate nation, defined by their religion more than by ethnic origin.

LANGUAGE AND RELIGION: The Ajar language is a Gurian dialect laced with Turkish borrowings; it is called Guruli in Georgia and Lazuri in Turkey. The literary language of the Ajars in both Georgia and Turkey is standard Georgian, with 95% of the Turkish Laz being bilingual. The language, which is considered a subdialect of Georgian, is spoken in two distinct dialects, often referred to as Zan in Georgia and Laz in Turkey.

Religion has historically and emotionally divided the Ajar nation from the Georgians. The majority adhere to the Hanafite rite of Sunni Islam and remain devoted to their Muslim faith. The Ajar homeland formed part of the Turkish Ottoman Empire until the Russo-Turkish War of 1877–78 divided the region, bringing the majority under Russian rule but leaving a sizable minority in Turkey. Although their religion was suppressed under Russian and Soviet governments, their distinct Islamic traditions and their religious ties to Turkey remained. Since Georgian independence in 1991, the strong emphasis on Georgian Christianity and nationalism has frightened and alienated many of the Muslim Ajars, who have only recently regained their religious freedom.

NATIONAL HISTORY: The Ajar homeland, known to the ancient world as Colchis, flourished with the Greek colonization of the coastal region between the sixth and fourth centuries B.C. Celebrated in the Greek legends of Jason and the Argonauts and Medaea, Colchis remained part of the Greek world for centuries. In the first century B.C. Colchis formed an important part of the Greek kingdom of Pontus.

The region, conquered by the Romans in 62 B.C. and known by them as Iberia, became a prosperous, Latinized province that eventually adopted the new Christian religion in the fourth century A.D. The Christian Ajars formed part of the Roman kingdom of Lazica in the fourth century. Following the decline of Roman power, the region was contested by the Byzantine and Persian empires until the seventh century, when the Arab conquest of the Persian Empire brought a new power and a new religion to the region. Ajaria later became part of the Christian Armenian kingdom, and in the ninth century it nominally formed part of the expanding Georgian kingdom.

The Seljuks overran the region in the eleventh century, the Mongols followed in the thirteenth century, the forces of Timur (Tamerlane) invaded in the fourteenth century, and in the fifteenth century the Ottoman Turks conquered the area. The Ajars' ancestors, concentrated in the coastal plain and somewhat protected by high mountains, remained semi-independent until the Turkish conquest in the seventeenth century. Called Laz by the Turks, the Ajars prospered under Turkish rule. Over the next two centuries a majority adopted the Turks' Islamic culture and religion, their homeland forming an important part of the administrative district called Lazistan.

The northern part of Lazistan, called Ajaria or Ajaristan, with the important port of Batumi, was one of the prizes awarded to Russia by the Congress of Berlin at the end of the Russo-Turkish War of 1877–78. The region remained a frontier district between the Russian and Ottoman empires. Undeterred by the frequent Ajar uprisings and disturbances in the region, the Russians developed Batumi as a major Black Sea port and fostered the growth of subtropical agriculture in the region. In the late nineteenth and early twentieth centuries the port of Batumi grew rapidly, with an influx of Slavs and Georgians; it was linked by railways and pipelines to the important centers of Caucasian industrial centers.

The devoutly Muslim Ajars, restive under Christian Russian rule, rose during the 1905 Russian revolution and attacked the estates of the Georgian and Russian landlords who dominated their homeland. Subdued by imperial troops, the Ajars increasingly resented the privileges enjoyed by their Christian overlords, their resentment reinforced by their pro-Turkish sentiment as tensions mounted prior to World War I. Their homeland formed part of the frontline when war began in August 1914. Ajar nationalists in December 1914 rebelled in support of a Turkish invasion of the region. The entire Ajar nation suffered repression and restrictions when the Russian military defeated the invading Turks.

The revolution in Russia in February 1917 threw the region into chaos, as the local civil government collapsed. Armed bands of Russian soldiers and Ajar, Georgian, and Armenian nationalists roamed the area at will until Turkish troops took control in April 1918, with the active assistance of the Ajar nationalists. Encouraged by the Turks, the nationalists declared "Ajaristan" independent of Russia on 18 April 1918, calling their new state the Southwestern Caucasian Republic. An Ajar national council, the Showra, formally claimed the Muslim-majority districts of Batumi, Kars, Akhaltsikh, Skhalkalaki, Sharur, and Nakichevan, areas also claimed by the newly independent republics of Georgia and Armenia.

British troops occupied Batumi in December 1918. The British authorities promised to protect the new republic until its fate could be decided by the Paris Peace Conference. However, in April 1919, pressured by the governments of Georgia and Armenia, the British forcibly disbanded the

Showra and in June 1920 evacuated all British troops from the area. Quickly overcoming armed Ajar resistance, Georgian forces took Batumi and the north, while the Armenians incorporated Kars and the south into the new Armenian state.

The Red Army, victorious in the civil war, turned on independent Georgia in early 1921. Amid the ensuing disorder the Ajars declared their homeland independent of Georgia and requested Turkish military aid. In March, Turkish troops occupied the region and over vehement Ajar protests attempted to annex the region to Turkey. Pressed by the Soviet government, the Turks finally withdrew in May but retained control of Kars and the southern districts. Soviet Ajaristan, given the status of an autonomous republic in 1922, was incorporated into Soviet Georgia, although the Georgians disputed Ajar autonomy, claiming the Ajars as ethnic Georgians. The relatively tolerant early economic and cultural policies of the Soviet Georgian government ended with an attempted insurrection by the Ajar Underground Independence Committee. Cultural and religious organizations were suppressed as part of a campaign to element the Ajars' distinct cultural and religious traditions.

In 1926 the Ajars rose in rebellion against the Soviet anti-Muslim religious campaign and the forced collectivization of Ajar agriculture. In the late 1920s the suppression of Islam and compulsory collectivization led to new rebellions against the communist authorities. After crushing the Ajar rebellion, Joseph Stalin ordered large numbers of Ajars to be deported to Central Asia. In 1930, in a further punitive measure, Soviet ethnologists officially reclassified the Ajars as ethnic Georgians, a practice that continued throughout the Soviet era.

Counted as ethnic Georgians in Soviet censuses since 1926, the Muslim Ajars remained suspect as to their loyalty. Stalin drew up a plan for their deportation during World War II, but the plan was postponed and finally abandoned at Stalin's death in 1953. The Ajars then experienced a modest national revival that strengthened their resistance to attempts by Soviet Georgia during the 1960s and 1970s to eliminate their autonomy and to promote assimilation. Evidence collected following the Soviet collapse indicates that elements of the Georgian communist leadership pursued a long-term strategy of completely assimilating the Ajars within Georgian culture in the 1970s.

The relaxation of stern Soviet rule under Mikhail Gorbachev in the late 1980s encourage the Ajars to lobby for removal from Georgian authority in 1988–89. In 1989 the first openly nationalist organization formed in Batumi. In August 1989, the Soviet Georgian government published measures designed to increase the use of the Georgian language in all spheres of the republic's life. The Ajar nationalists considered this an act of repression.

In Turkey, in a sudden reversal of the government assimilation policy, the law banning the use of other languages was repealed in 1991. This relaxation allowed the Laz in region bordering Ajaristan to organize and begin publishing material in the Ajar language. Closer ties between the two parts of the Ajar-Laz nation progressed, with cultural exchanges, radio broadcasts, and demands for open borders.

In the wake of the failed Soviet coup in August 1991, the Georgians regained their independence under a nationalist, ethnocentric government that fanned ethnic and religious tensions in the new Georgian state established in January 1992. In spite of the overtures of the new Georgian government, the attitude of the radical Georgian nationalists—that the Ajars represent a threat to the Christian Georgian state—has come to dominate the Ajars' relations with the Georgians.

Officially designated an autonomous republic within Georgia in 1992, the region remains effectively independent in all but foreign and monetary policy. The only area of Georgia not to have experienced violent confrontations since Georgia regained its independence, the Ajar homeland—Ajaria, or Ajaristan—is increasingly going its own way. The Georgian government, already at odds with the Abkhaz* and Ossetians,* has been careful not to inflame Ajar nationalism.

Russia maintains a naval base near Batumi, and Russian soldiers patrol Ajaristan's border with Turkey. Russia's interest in the port of Batumi has not lessened since the collapse of the Soviet Union; accordingly, Russian support for Ajar separatism remains a threat to Georgia's hold on the area. In 1993 the Ajar leader, Aslan Abashidze, declared Russia the protector of the Ajars' national interests, but in September 1994 he denied allegations that he favored independence from Georgia.

The Georgian president, Eduard Shevardnadze, endorsed in November 1994 a statute establishing a free economic zone in Ajaristan. The zone, centered on Batumi, would give the Ajars greater access to foreign investment and would set up a rival to the Trabzon free economic zone, just across the frontier in Turkey. The region, quiet and calm by Caucasus standards, has become one of the most prosperous on the eastern shore of the Black Sea—but at a price. In November 1995, independent election monitors charged Abashidze's forces with gross voting violations; they accused Abashidze, who officially backed Shevardnadze, with using violence and other forms to intimidate and harass opposition Ajar groups.

In September 1996, the Ajar nationalist political party, Revival Union, in partnership with the Citizen's Union of Georgia, the ruling party in the national parliament, easily won the regional elections. The party, led by Aslan Abashidze, took 81.9% of the vote in the region. The Ajars, political analysts claim, are more interested in economic and political stability than are the other national minorities in Georgia, which is why Abashidze has increasingly separated the small region from the rest of Georgia.

President Shevardnadze of Georgia in June 1998 pledged to grant the ethnic regions of Abkhazia, Ajaria, and South Ossetia special status within a proposed Georgian federation. In September 1998, Aslan Abashidze warned that he would not allow Georgian troops to enter Ajaria. He announced that if Russian border troops leave, he would recall from civilian life the 5,000 Ajars who formerly served in the Soviet border troops to protect Ajaria's Black Sea coast and the land sector of Georgia's international border.

The Ajars of Georgia enjoy de facto independence under the protection of Russia's 90th Regiment, and under the region's post-Soviet political system. The Ajars have achieved this by political strategy, not military force, and the regional leaders continue to take care not to challenge the territorial integrity of the Georgian state, although small pro-independence organizations have proliferated as underground groups opposed to the authoritarian local government and Georgia's pro-Christian nationalism. Most Ajars support demands for greater political and cultural ties between the Georgian and Turkish portions of the small Black Sea nation.

The Ajars are grateful to Aslan Abashidze for keeping their homeland out of the Caucasian wars of the 1990s, and they tend to be indulgent of the excesses of the Abashidze family. The region is financially better off than neighboring parts of Georgia, although the Georgian government, in order to collect fees, is encouraging international trade in ports in central Georgia farther to the north. Too much pressure, financial or political, could stimulate demands for even more autonomy and perhaps a complete break with Georgia.

SELECTED BIBLIOGRAPHY:

Allen, W. E. *A History of the Georgian People*. 1978.
Ascherson, Neal. *Black Sea*. 1995.
Derluguian, Georgi M. *A Tale of Two Resorts: Abkhazia and Ajaria before and since the Soviet Collapse*. 1995.
Olson, James S. *An Ethnohistorical Dictionary of the Russian and Soviet Empires*. 1994.

Alanders

Ålanders; Aland Islanders

POPULATION: Approximately (2002e) 65,000 Alanders in Scandinavia, mostly in the Aland Islands and mainland Finland, with 25,000 in Sweden. Aland nationalists claim an Alander population of over 75,000 in the region.

THE ALANDER HOMELAND: The Alander homeland is an archipelago lying at the mouth of the Gulf of Bothnia between Sweden and Finland. Known as Åland or Ålandsöerna in Swedish, the islands are called Ahvenanmaa, the Land of Streams, in Finnish. The archipelago comprises 6,544 islands and islets in the Baltic Sea 15 miles west of the Finnish mainland and 15 miles east of Sweden. The islands, only some 700 of which are inhabited, take their name from the largest and most important island of the group, Åland, or Ahvenanmaa. The Alanders accepted in 1951 a statute of autonomy that has been widened in new legislation several times since. *Autonomous Province of Aland Islands (Åland Skärgärd)*: 581 sq. mi.—1,505 sq. km, (2002e) 26,000—Alanders 96%, Finns 3%. The Aland capital and major cultural center is Mariehamm, called Maarianhamina in Finnish, (2002e) 11,000.

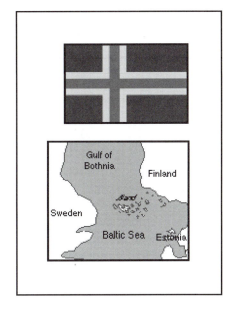

FLAG: The Aland national flag, the official flag of the autonomous state, is a blue field bearing a red Scandinavian cross outlined in yellow.

PEOPLE AND CULTURE: The Alanders, overwhelmingly of Swedish descent, now form a separate Scandinavian nation whose unique culture incorporates both Swedish and Finnish influences. The majority of the Alanders are of Swedish descent, but a minority are by tradition of Finnish ancestry. The population of the islands, following a sharp decline from nearly 30,000 in the 1950s, mostly due to immigration to Sweden, has stabilized over the last decade. The Alanders, following a long dispute between Sweden and Finland, have been recognized as a separate Scandinavian nation by the Nordic Council, a regional grouping of the Scandinavian states. They participate in several international organizations as a distinct nation. As a result of the official demilitarization and neutrality of the islands, military service is not obligatory for Alanders. Instead of military conscription, they may serve in the civil administration of the autonomous government.

LANGUAGE AND RELIGION: The Alanders speak a Swedish dialect that has a distinct pronunciation compared to the spoken language in Sweden, but there is no apparent difficulty in mutual intelligibility. Most Alanders are bilingual in Finnish. The Alander's Swedish language is the sole official language of the autonomous region and is the language of instruction in the Alander schools. The majority of the islanders are Protestants, mostly Lutheran, as are the majority in the other Scandinavian nations.

NATIONAL HISTORY: The Swedish kingdom began to expand in the twelfth century, first to the nearby territories of Finland and the Åland Islands. The Christian Swedes launched a military and religious crusade to conquer and Christianize the pagan Finns in 1154. The Aland Islands, colonized by the victorious Swedes, became thoroughly Swedish in culture and language, and they remained an integral part of the Swedish kingdom for over 600 years. In the sixteenth century the Alanders, along with the rest of Scandinavia, joined the Protestant Reformation.

The strategically important islands were contested by Sweden and Russia during the eighteenth-century wars for supremacy in northern Europe. The Russians, under Peter the Great, seized the archipelago in 1714 but returned the islands to Swedish rule in 1721. During the Napoleonic Wars the archipelago was finally ceded, along with Swedish Finland, to the Russian Empire in 1809.

The Swedish-speaking Alanders resisted Russian rule, and the islands were subject to international disputes and treaties. The Russian government militarized and fortified the islands, which remained the center of international disputes and treaties through much of the next century. Shelled by an Anglo-French fleet in 1854, during the Crimean War, the island's fortifications were later destroyed, and remilitarization was forbidden under the terms of the 1856 Treaty of Paris.

The energetic Alanders, stifled by the unpopular and repressive Russian bureaucracy, looked beyond their islands to sustain themselves. A large Alander merchant fleet of 30 fleet vessels dominated the nineteenth-century European-Australian grain trade and engendered a tradition of independence and self-reliance that has become an important part of the Alander national character.

Opposition to increasingly oppressive Russian rule fanned the growth of nationalism in the islands in the late nineteenth century. Affected by the wave of nationalist sentiment that swept Europe, the islanders developed a particularist Alander self-awareness. Alander resentment erupted in open conflict during the 1905 Russian revolution, but the rebellion was quickly crushed by troops hastily dispatched from the Finnish mainland.

With the outbreak of war in 1914, Aland's strategic military importance again became the subject of debate. With British and French consent, the Russians refortified the islands in 1915. The remilitarization of their islands and revolutionary sentiment spurred the growth of nationalism and pro-Swedish sentiment during the war. Agitation for autonomy grew as the war dragged on and the near-feudal Russian Empire began to collapse.

The Finns of the mainland, who became independent of Russian in 1917, claimed the islands as part of their national territory. Asserting their right to self-determination, the Alanders declared their autonomy and voted to secede from Finland and to unite with Sweden. In January 1918 the Swedish government recognized Finnish independence without reservation about the islands. The Swedish government gave no open support to the Aland separatists, but the Swedish public displayed considerable interest, especially when open revolt seemed inevitable.

Finnish democrats, involved in a bloody civil war with Red factions within the new country, were forced to ignore the islanders' demands. As the civil war dragged on, the Swedish military occupied the islands but were quickly withdrawn by the Swedish government. German troops, part of a multinational force sent to intervene in the Russian and Finnish civil wars, next occupied the islands. The Swedish people demanded that their government take action, and for a time in early 1920 it seemed that war would break out between Sweden and Finland. The Finnish government, victorious in the civil war, finally sent troops to occupy the islands. The leaders of the Aland secessionist movement were arrested. The Soviet Union, on historical grounds, also laid claim to the archipelago.

In July 1920, the League of Nations looked into the dispute, which Finland claimed was a domestic affair. In September of that year the dispute was referred to the new League of Nations, and a committee was dispatched to visit Sweden, Finland, and the archipelago. In June 1921, a League of Nations decision on the claims of Sweden, Finland, and the new Soviet Union favored Finland, which received sovereignty. The agreement provided for an autonomous Aland state in union with the Finnish Republic. The autonomy statute provided for full protection of the Alander's political, linguistic, and cultural rights, the right to private property, and the right to fly the distinctive national flag raised by the Aland nationalists in 1920. The islands were to remain neutral and unfortified, with their autonomy guaranteed by the League of Nations.

After World War I, the last of the great Aland sailing ships were laid up, and the era of Aland dominance of the Australian grain trade ended. The islanders turned to sheep herding, farming, and the growing trade between Finland and Sweden. The Finnish government, respecting the island's autonomy, generally left the Alanders to look after their own affairs.

In the late 1930s, as relations between Finland and the Soviet Union deteriorated, the Finnish government sought to remilitarize Aland, but in

May 1939 the Soviet Union blocked the League of Nations' approval of refortification. Finland and the Soviet Union fought a bitter war in 1939–40, following which they signed a new demilitarization agreement on the Aland Islands. The agreement was renewed following the end of World War II.

In the late 1940s, the Alanders again began a movement for separation from Finland, but as Finland established a democratic system the movement lost momentum. In 1951, under Soviet pressure, the Finnish parliament renounced the 1921 League of Nations guarantee of autonomy, but at the same time the Finnish government accorded the Alanders added rights of self-government. A new autonomy statute was approved and went into effect on 1 January 1952.

In the 1960s and 1970s traditional pro-Swedish sentiment persisted in the islands, and immigration to Sweden caused a population decline. The Aland economy, based on tourism, was buoyed by the duty-free goods sold on ships sailing between Aland and mainland ports in Finland and Sweden. Tourism gave the Alanders one of the highest average incomes in the region by the 1980s. Increased prosperity and closer ties among the Scandinavian nations stabilized the island's economy and population. Since 1970 the Alanders have had separate representation in the Nordic Council.

Aland nationalism, dormant for decades under liberal Finnish authority, again became an issue in the late 1980s, stimulated by the disintegration of the Soviet Union and Finland's application to join the European Union. The Alanders, already enjoying most of the trappings of independence, took a step closer in March 1991 with the endorsement of a proposal to introduce their own currency, the Aland daler. A revised autonomy statute that became effective on 1 January 1993 provides for greater economic and legislative freedom. The Finnish government retains responsibility over foreign affairs, the judicial system, customs, and monetary services.

Finland's entry in the European Union raised fears that membership will affect the island's demilitarized status and interfere with the duty-free tourism that contributes 70% of the Alanders' national income. The Alanders negotiated and won special concessions from the European Union. For tax purposes Aland counts as a country outside the Union, allowing the Alanders to go on selling duty-free goods after 1999, when duty-free sales became illegal in the rest of the Union. The deal also allows the Alanders to block other Europeans from buying properties or setting up industries in the islands. The negotiated concessions, finalized in November 1994, brought the Alanders a step closer to full independence within the European Union.

The majority of the Alanders are content with autonomy within democratic and prosperous Finland. The only proposed change to the small state's status that wins support is the idea of allowing Europe's small states to participate as full partners in integrated Europe.

SELECTED BIBLIOGRAPHY:

Hamalainen, P. K. *In Time of Storm: Revolution, Civil War and the Ethnolinguistic Issue in Finland.* 1979.

Hannikainen, Lauri, and Frank Horn, eds. *Autonomy and Demilitarisation in International Law: The Aland Islands in a Changing Europe.* 1996.

Matts, Dreijer. *History of the Aland People: From the Stone Age to Gustavus Wasa.* 1986.

Mead, W. R. *A Historic Geography of Scandinavia.* 1981.

Alaskans

POPULATION: Approximately (2002e) 482,000 Alaskans in North America, concentrated in the state of Alaska in the far northwest of the continent. There are Alaskans living in many other parts of the United States and in Canada.

THE ALASKAN HOMELAND: The Alaskan homeland forms the largest of the American states and covers an area about three times the size of France. Alaska is separated from the continental United States, locally called the "Lower 48," by over 600 miles of Canadian territory. The immense area of Alaska displays a great variety of physical characteristics, with nearly a third of the region lying within the Arctic Circle, an area of perennially frozen ground, called permafrost, and treeless tundra. The southern coast, the interior valleys, and the panhandle are areas of temperate climate and contain the majority of the population. Alaska is one of the United States of America. *State of Alaska*: 656,424 sq. mi.—1,700,135 sq. km, (2002e) 639,000—Alaskans 81%, other Americans 16%, Canadians, 3%. The major cultural center is the state's largest city, Anchorage, (2002e, city and metropolitan area) 265,000. The capital is at Juneau, in the panhandle; it is the largest city in area in the United States, (2002e) 31,000, lying 573 miles (922 km) to the southeast of Anchorage in the panhandle region.

FLAG: The official flag of the state is a dark blue field bearing seven small five-pointed gold stars in the form of the constellation known as the "Big Dipper" and a single larger five-pointed gold star on the upper fly. The flag of the Alaskan national movement is the same flag with the stars enlarged and with the blue field outlined on the upper, fly, and lower edges by a narrow white stripe. The flag of the Alaskan Independence Party (AIP) is a gray field bearing a centered circle with a black bear, eight yellow stars, and the name of the organization above the disk.

PEOPLE AND CULTURE: The Alaskans, the majority descendants of migrants from the other American states, claim that the "Alaskan experience" quickly turns people into Alaskans, with their traditional reverence for Alaska's traditions and culture—much of which comes from the state's indigenous population, which makes up about 16% of the total population. The Alaskan's heritage is culturally removed from the American mainstream, centering on the arts and crafts of the native Alaskans and on the remnants of Russian settlement. Alaskans, even first-generation descendants of migrants, often refer to new arrivals as "Cheeckakos," a name implying greedy, ignorant, and "just off the boat" people. New arrivals soon become the most fiercely Alaskan. By 1980 only about 20% of the nonindigenous population had been born in Alaska. A male-to-female ratio of five to one in 1910 has been reduced to near equality in 2000. In origin the Alaskans are about 75% white, 16% native Alaskan, 3.5% Asian or Pacific Islander, and 3% Hispanic.

LANGUAGE AND RELIGION: The official language of the state is English, although a number of native-Alaskan languages are used and are taught in area schools. The Alaskans speak a western dialect of American English, which includes many borrowings from indigenous languages and also reflects the dialects of adjacent Canada.

The majority of the Alaskans see themselves as religious, with all the major religions represented in the state. Native-Alaskan religions have become a source of spiritual learning in recent years. Historically, churches have formed the core of remote villages and towns, and they remain important to the smaller, less accessible villages, particularly as the centers of social and religious life during the long, hard winters.

NATIONAL HISTORY: The huge region is thought to have been inhabited by nomadic peoples from northern Asia who crossed the land bridge that once connected the continents some 30,000 years ago. The migrants adapted to the physical landscape and developed unique cultures based on the nature of the land. The name Alaska is derived from the Aleut name Alaxsxa, meaning "mainland."

The southern coast of Alaska was first explored by Europeans in the eighteenth century. Vitus Bering, a Dane in the employ of the Russian Empire, is credited with discovering Alaska in 1741. His explorations established Russia's claim to the vast region. The first European settlement was established in 1784 by Russian fur traders at Three Saints Bay on Kodiak Island. The Russian-American Company was created to administer the region as a trading monopoly in 1799. The Russian demand for the region's abundant supply of furs became the paramount reason for Russian administration. The native Alaskans suffered near genocide under harsh

Russian rule, with only 3,000 of the estimated 30,000 surviving Russian rule.

Russian administration ended on 30 March 1866, when the U.S. government purchased the huge region for a cash payment of $7,200,000. The American purchase was accomplished solely through the determined efforts of Secretary of State William H. Seward; for years afterward Alaska was called "Seward's Folly" or "Seward's Icebox," because of its perceived uselessness.

The treaty between the United States and Russia, ratified in 1867, was scoffed at by a majority of Americans, who viewed the new land as a wasteland of ice and snow until gold was discovered in 1898, setting off the legendary Klondike gold rush and a sudden increase in population. By 1900, Alaska boasted a population of 63,592, evenly divided between whites and native Alaskans, with smaller numbers of Japanese and blacks. The population declined with the end of the gold rush but began to grow again during the 1920s, reaching a total of 59,278 in 1930.

The fertile Matantuska Valley, near Anchorage, and other districts near Fairbanks in the interior were settled by farmers from the drought-stricken Midwest from 1935. The arrival of a settled farming population brought stability and permanence to Alaska's slowly growing population. The vast region became known as the "last frontier," a haven for misfits and adventurers from the continental United States.

Alaska's strategic importance was not appreciated until World War II and the Japanese occupation of the Aleutian Islands, the only American territory occupied by enemy troops. In 1942 the Alaska Highway, linking Alaska to the continental United States, was begun for military reasons, but it later became a major route for new immigrants. Between the end of World War II and 1960 the territory's population doubled, with many of the new migrants being military personnel unable to readapt to life in the "lower 48." In early 1958 Alaskans voted five to one for statehood, and on 7 July 1958 Alaska became the forty-ninth state of the Union, the first new state admitted since Arizona in 1912.

Enormous oil reserves, discovered in 1965, began to be developed during the 1970s with the construction of the 800-mile Alaska Pipeline from Prudhoe Bay, north of the Arctic Circle, to the southern port of Valdez. The rapid exploration of the state's oil wealth was increasingly opposed by many Alaskans who felt the pipeline spelled the end of their unique way of life.

The Alaskans, with a tradition of enjoying their wide-open spaces, resented interference with their freewheeling lifestyle by federal bureaucrats or anyone from the "lower 48." Alaskans generally feel that other Americans know more about the moon than about Alaska. In 1974, some of the more dissatisfied Alaskans formed a group called Alaskans for Independence, which polled over 5,000 votes in local elections.

Angered by the federal government's practices regarding their oil, minerals, land, and internal affairs, the Alaskans voted in 1980 to set up a commission to study the relationship between their state and the federal government, the first time since the Civil War in the 1860s that a state had questioned its ties to Washington. The two-year study, published in 1983, considered the benefits and liabilities of commonwealth, free association, or territorial status, and of partition or full independence by legal means. None of the options were found to be preferable to statehood at the time. Alaskans themselves remain divided over the issue, with a small but vocal independence movement gaining converts.

Land disputes, conflicts over fishing grounds, and the export of oil became major issues for the Alaskans in the 1980s. They want to export their oil to energy-hungry Japan but are prohibited by federal legislation, the Export Act of 1965, which was renewed in 1983. The act gives control of all oil to the U.S. government. The Alaskans' indignation over control of their natural resources increased following the poor federal response to a massive oil spill that polluted part of their pristine homeland in March 1989.

More than half of Alaska's inhabitants live in the Anchorage metropolitan area, about 15% in the Fairbanks area, and another 13% live scattered in the towns of the southeastern panhandle; nonetheless, in spite of increasing urbanization, Alaskans continue to see themselves as living on a frontier. The traditional Alaskan culture, incorporating both American and native-Alaskan customs and values, remains vital to the growing national consciousness of the state's population. Many frontier conditions persist in Alaska, and in many areas bars are as numerous as churches.

Historical ties to Siberia and the Russian Far East have been revived since the collapse of the Soviet Union in 1991. The Alaskans sent a gift of millions of pounds of excess salmon to their close neighbors in Russia to celebrate the triumph of democracy. In June 1991 the first scheduled air service was begun between Alaska and Siberia. The Alaskan authorities have signed a trade agreement with Russian authorities, and feasibility studies have been undertaken for a 56-mile rail tunnel under the Bering Straits to connect the Eastern and Western Hemispheres.

Alaskans, claiming that the United States is 49 states and a country, pay virtually no state taxes and receive dividends from their oil wealth but are increasingly dissatisfied with federal control of much of the state's land and wealth. Retention of vast tracts by the federal government and the awarding of other vast areas to fulfill the claims of the native peoples has further complicated the Alaskan's relations with Washington. The ongoing conflict over the Trans-Alaska Pipeline is a continuation of the century-long effort to find a balance between the conservation and development of the enormous Alaskan homeland. The nascent Alaskan independence movement is closely tied to environmental issues in the state. According to nationalist and environmental groups, Alaska's vast forests are being decimated even faster than Brazil's Amazon forests.

The terrorist attacks on New York and Washington, D.C., in September 2001 renewed demands for opening protected lands to oil drilling to reduce U.S. dependence on the Middle East. The demands gave new impetus to the long debate on control of Alaska's natural resources.

SELECTED BIBLIOGRAPHY:

Davidson, Donald. *Regionalism and Nationalism in the United States.* 1990.
Haycox, Stephen W., and Childers Mangusso, eds. *An Alaska Anthology: Interpreting the Past.* 1996.
Naylor, Thomas H., and William H. Williamson. *Downsizing the U.S.A.* 1997.
Wolfe, Art, and Nick Jans. *Alaska.* 2000.

Alawites

Alawis; Nusayriyah; Namiriyah; Ansariyah; Nusayris; Nusseiris

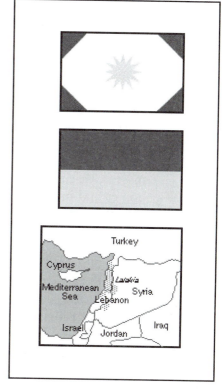

POPULATION: Approximately (2002e) 2,630,000 Alawites in the Middle East, with the largest concentration in Syria, 1,945,000, mainly in the Latakia region on the Mediterranean Sea and with smaller communities in Lebanon and Turkey. Outside the coastal Alawite homeland there are sizable communities in Damascus, other interior cities in Syria, and several areas of Turkey. Alawites often claim a national population representing 30% of Syria's total population, or about 3.5 million.

THE ALAWITE HOMELAND: The Alawite homeland occupies a wide coastal plain on the Mediterranean Sea backed by the Jebel an Nusayriyah Mountain in western Syria, between Turkey on the north and Lebanon on the south. Much of the mountainous region is covered in pine forests. The Alawites live chiefly along the Mediterranean coast and make up over 60% of the rural population of the province, while the city of Latakia has a Sunni majority. The Alawite homeland forms the provinces of Latakia and Tartus of the Syrian Arab Republic. *Al-Ladhiqiyah (Latakia)*: 1,617 sq. mi.—4,189 sq. km, (2002e) 2,004,000—Alawite 70%, Christian 14%, Sunni Muslim 12%, Ismaili Muslim 2%. The Alawite capital and major cultural center is the city of Latakia (Al-Ladhiqiyah), (2002e) 402,000.

FLAG: The Alawite national flag, the flag of the former republic, is a white field bearing a centered yellow sun with twelve rays and small red triangles at each corner. The flag used by Alawite nationalists is a vertical bicolor of red over yellow.

PEOPLE AND CULTURE: The Alawites trace their ancestry to the ancient Canaanites, who lived in the region before the time of Alexander the Great. The high incidence of fair hair and light eyes among the Alawite population is attributed to the conquest of the Phoenician city-states by the Greeks in the third century B.C. Alawite is a recent name that they have given themselves; it means "those who adhere to the teachings of Ali," the son-in-law of the Prophet Mohammed. They were formerly called Nusayris, after their mountains, which is now a derogatory name used by many of Syria's Sunni majority. Isolated by high mountains and avoiding intermarriage, the Alawites have survived for millennia and have retained distinct physical features. The Alawite nation comprises four ancient tribal confederations—Kalbiyah, Khaiyatin, Haddadin, and Matawirah—and retains a clan-based system similar to that of many nomadic peoples. Nearly half of the Alawites now live outside the coastal Alawite provinces, mostly in Damascus and other large Syrian cities in the interior. The Alawites are regarded by the majority Sunnis as more heretical than Jews.* Before they infiltrated the military and the government, they were victims of economic, social, and political discrimination.

LANGUAGE AND RELIGION: The Alawites speak a dialect of Levantine Arabic that uses many borrowings from other languages, particularly Turkish. The dialect, known as North Levantine Arabic or Lebanese-Syrian Arabic, belongs to the South Arabic group of dialects of the Arabic language. There is an urban standard dialect, based on the dialect of Damascus, that is used by many Alawites, but the language the group uses in homes and in the Latakia region is the Latakia dialect, which differs considerably from the standard dialect.

The Alawite religion, claimed by the Alawites to be a sect of Shi'a Islam, is considered by most Muslims as a non-Muslim or heretical sect. The Alawite liturgy is believed to have been derived from early Christianity; it observes Christmas, Easter, and Epiphany, and it uses ceremonial wine. The Alawites also observe certain Iranian traditions, such as Persian New Year. The roots of the Alawite religion lie in the teaching of Mohammed ibn Nusayr an-Namiri, a contemporary of the 10th Shi'ite imam in Basra in the ninth century. The Alawites are second in numbers in Syria to the dominant Sunni sect. The Alawites reject many of the dietary and social restrictions of traditional Muslim belief, and, unlike the Muslim majority, they are mostly secular and believe in the separation of religion and politics. Alawites do not set aside particular buildings for worship. In the past Sunni government officials forced them to build mosques, but these were invariably abandoned. Only Alawite men take part in active worship. They believe women, like objects and animals, lack souls, and that the soul of a sinful man may reincarnate into a woman after his death, so that he may spend one life span in the purgatory of a woman's soulless body. President Hafiz al-Assad persuaded a leading Lebanese cleric in 1975 to issue a declaration stating that the Alawites were Shi'a Muslims and therefore not heretics.

NATIONAL HISTORY: Included in the Roman province of Syria in 64 B.C., the rural coastal tribes retained much of their original culture, even after officially adopting Christianity. When Christianity flourished in the region, the people of the Nusariyah Mountains, isolated in their small communities, clung to their many pre-Christian religious traditions. Muslim Arab invaders conquered the region in A.D. 635, forcibly converting the population to Islam. The Nusayri tribes of the Syrian coast publicly practiced the Islamic religion of the Muslim empire while continuing to observe their pre-Islamic pagan and Christian practices in secret.

The conflict over the succession to the caliphate, which began at Mohammed's death in 632, eventually split the Muslim world. The Nusayri tribes, like the Shi'ites, favored Ali, Mohammed's nephew and son-in-law. The Alawites, unlike the Shi'ites, however, deified Ali and incorporated his worship into their Muslim and pre-Muslim religious practices. Originally they fled to the mountainous region of Latakia to escape repression by the Sunni Muslim majority. After hundreds of years of contact with the dissident Ismaili sect, the Alawites moved closer to traditional Islam.

Severely persecuted for their beliefs, the Alawites welcomed the conquest of Latakia by the Christian crusaders in the eleventh century and prospered under Christian protection. Reconquered by Saladin in 1188, the region declined, and the Alawites again suffered persecution. Devastated by the Mongol invasion of 1260, the Alawites had only begun to recover when the Ottoman Turks took the Latakia region in 1516.

Considered by the Turks as non-Muslim infidels and therefore not part of the general Muslim population, the Alawites were allowed to retain some autonomy under their own rulers, although subject to special taxes and restrictions and to the continued persecution of the Sunni Muslim majority in the region. In the mid-eighteenth century, the Turkish authorities abolished the Alawites' autonomy and imposed harsher restrictions under the direct rule of Turkish governors. For centuries, the Alawites constituted Syria's most repressed and exploited minority. By the nineteenth century, most were indentured servants or tenant farmers working for Sunni landowners. The Alawite national movement of the 1880s began as an anti-Turkish movement but gathered support as a movement for liberation from Sunni persecution.

Allied agents secretly entered Latakia after World War I began in 1914. Promising an end to centuries of virtual slavery, the agents encouraged Alawite nationalism as a way to disrupt the Turkish administration of the region. When French troops occupied Latakia in 1917, the Alawite leadership demanded the promised self-government. Disappointed by the French response, the Alawites rebelled in 1919 and launched attacks on French outposts and columns. The rebellion continued until reinforcements arrived from France in 1921 and the Alawite irregulars were routed.

Granted a League of Nations mandate in 1921, the French authorities divided Syria into several autonomous states, ostensibly to protect the minorities against the persecution of the Sunni Muslim majority, but also to gain minority support. The Republic of the Alaouites, declared an autonomous state under French protection on 1 July 1922, formed a member state of the French-sponsored Syrian Federation.

In 1924 the Alawite legislature voted for complete separation from Syria. Pressed by the non-Sunni minorities, the French dissolved the federation and created a unitary Syrian republic, but without the minority-dominated states of Latakia, Lebanon, and Jebel ed Druz. The Alawites, fearing and hating the Sunni majority, became fervently pro-French and provided willing recruits to the French colonial army. After centuries of discrimination and persecution, the Alawites greatly benefited from French rule. The French authorities raised Alawite education, health care, and social services to the level enjoyed by Syria's Sunni majority.

A Franco-Syrian treaty in 1936 that provided for a reunited Syrian state ended Alawite autonomy. Their homeland was soon dominated by Syria's majority Sunnis. The Alawites rebelled against Sunni domination in 1939, quickly driving all Syrian officials from the province. On 28 June 1939 the rebels declared Latakia independent of Syria. The rebellion gave the French a pretext to intervene without violating the 1936 treaty. French troops landed, and the French resurrected the autonomous Alawite Republic of Latakia. In 1942, during World War II, the French authorities, ignoring Alawite opposition, again ceded Latakia to Syria, and in 1944 the last French troops withdrew. The Alawites again rebelled in 1946 and unsuccessfully attempted to gain French support for an independent Alawite state.

Since most professions were closed to Alawites, thousands joined the Syrian military in the 1950s, as the only escape from grinding poverty and severe persecution. In 1954 the government of Syria was overthrown, and in the aftermath the Arab Socialist Resurrection Party (Ba'ath), consisting of an uneasy alliance of socialist and Arab unity groups, began to take form. Because of its secular ideology the Ba'ath gained many supporters among the Alawites, particularly those in the military.

A despised minority, the Alawites sought acceptance by embracing militant pan-Arab nationalism. The Ba'ath party, in power following a 1963 coup, offered equality in exchange for loyalty. The Alawites, dominant in the military officer corps and backed by the Ba'ath party, purged most non-Alawite officers between 1963 and 1969, and in 1970 they led a coup that installed Alawite strongman Hafiz al-Assad. The well-being of the Alawite minority in Syria improved considerably in the 1970s and 1980s, although an unusually large part of government spending since the 1970s has been allocated to military expenses.

Alawite military officers in the Ba'ath Party crushed domestic opposition by setting up a police state and appealing to the rural Syrian population, which had long resented the power of the politicians and large absentee landowners in Damascus and Aleppo. Ba'ath authoritarian rule enjoyed some popularity due to its policies of economic development, land reform, and the promotion of education. The Alawites, still seeking acceptance by the Sunni majority, strengthened the military while espousing radical pan-Arab nationalism and vehement opposition to the neighboring Israeli state. As these policies took effect, Syrian nationalists, peasants, and workers came to support the Assad regime. In contrast to the chaos of Syrian politics from 1945 to 1963, a remarkable continuity in government and society now rests upon the alliance of the Alawite-dominated Ba'ath Party, military, and bureaucracy.

The main opposition to Assad's Alawite-dominated regime came from the Muslim Brotherhood, based in the Sunni majority. The brotherhood mounted a serious challenge to the "heretical" Alawite regime in the 1970s. Sunni resistance to minority Alawite domination finally broke into open rebellion in the Sunni bastions of Hama and Aleppo in 1982. The Alawite-dominated military forces responded with large-scale violence to crush the rebellion. Over 20,000 Sunnis died, thousands were arrested, and all Sunni opposition was forced underground.

A revived Muslim Brotherhood launched a campaign of terrorism in 1986 to end Alawite rule in Syria, and Sunni resistance solidified following Syria's loss of Soviet support in 1989. The government responded by arresting large portions of the brotherhood, holding thousands without trial. In 1991 Assad won his fourth term as president. The only candidate in the rigged election, he received 99.98% of the vote.

The heavy concentration of power in Assad's hands combined with his poor health and chronic ambivalence concerning his successor placed the Alawite faction of the Ba'ath Party in extreme jeopardy in the 1990s. In January 1994, the president's eldest son, Basil al-Assad, was killed, eliminating the heir apparent. His death led to renewed fears among the Alawites about the future stability of the Alawite-dominated Syrian state. Assad's second son, Bashar, was trained as an eye doctor and seemingly had little interest in politics or power.

Syrian peace with Israel, part of the peace process that began in 1995, was blocked by President Assad over the issue of Israeli withdrawal from the entire Golan Heights, which had been captured by Israeli troops in 1967. The issue, which united Syrians behind the Assad regime, became a danger for the Alawite-dominated Syrian government, eliminating the possibility of compromise without provoking the Sunni majority.

Militant Alawites in adjacent areas of Turkey provoked violent confrontations between security forces and activists in March 1995. The violence left 28 dead and over 100 injured. Although the Alawites of Syria support their kin in Turkey, contact between the two groups has been limited by both the Turkish and Syrian governments. During the same period President Assad was the intended target of a bomb that exploded in Damascus. The suspected bombers were Turks living in Syria.

Assad replaced several high government officials with Alawites in 1997, reportedly anticipating the succession of his son Bashar. In February 1999, Assad was once more reelected as Syria's president in a referendum for a new constitutional term, with over 99% of the vote, again as the sole candidate. Moves to ensure that the close advisors were all Alawites continued until the death of Hafiz al-Assad in June 2000.

Bashar al-Assad, the heir to Hafiz al-Assad, was installed as interim president of Syria following his father's death. Many Alawites worry that Bashar will not be strong enough to safeguard their interests and position in Syria. The potentially explosive dimensions of Syrian politics reflect the country's recent history, in which Hafiz al-Assad built up a powerful security machine for the country, including its control of neighboring Lebanon, by relying on his own tightly knit Alawite group. If the Alawite clique fails, Syria has only shallow political, religious, or dynastic institutions to preserve the country's unity.

In November 2000, the new president ordered the release of over 600 political prisoners belonging to various banned groups. A draft law offered a wide amnesty, but opposition continues to grow in many areas, even among Bashar al-Assad's own clan, which has much to fear from reform. Evolution could easily become revolution, with the ruling Alawites as the chief targets.

The short-lived relaxation following the assent of Bashar al-Assad seemed to have ended in September 2001 with the arrests of leading Sunni dissidents. After nearly three decades of repressive Alawite rule, the majority Sunni hatred has been severely compounded. The minority Alawites remain in a precarious position as the hated ruling class in fragmented, coup-prone Syria.

SELECTED BIBLIOGRAPHY:

Heydemann, Steven. *Authoritarianism in Syria: Institutions and Social Conflict, 1946–1970*. 1999.

Mufti, Malik. *Sovereign Creations: Pan-Arabism and Political Order in Syria and Iraq*. 1996.

Rathmell, Andrew. *Secret War in the Middle East: The Covert Struggle for Syria, 1949–1961*. 1995.

Wedeen, Lisa. *Ambiguities of Domination: Politics, Rhetoric, and Symbols in Contemporary Syria*. 1999.

Alsatians

Elsassers; Alsatians and Lorrainers; Elsassers und Lotharingens

POPULATION: Approximately (2002e) 2,2237,000 Alsatians in France, concentrated in the Alsace and Lorraine regions of northeastern France. The Alsatians of Lorraine are traditionally considered part of the larger Alsatian national group. There are Alsatian communities in other parts of France, in adjacent areas of Germany, and in Luxembourg.

THE ALSATIAN HOMELAND: The Alsatian homeland lies in northeastern France, east of the Vosges Mountains. Most of Alsace-Lorraine lies in the valley of the Rhine River, which forms the frontier between France and Germany. The economy of the region depends as much on neighboring Germany, where many people who work in Alsace live, as it does on France. The region, forming the Bas-Rhin, Haut-Rhin, and Moselle Departments and the Territory of Belfort, is now divided among the planning regions of Alsace, Lorraine, and Franche-Comté, but there is little real autonomy. *Historical Region of Alsace-Lorraine (Elsass-Lotharingen)*: 5,842 sq. mi.—15,134 sq. km, (2002e) 2,955,000—Alsatians and Lorrainers 75%, other French 20%, Germans 4%. The Alsatian capital and major cultural center is Strasbourg, called Strassburg in the Alsatian dialects, (2002e) 269,000. The Lorrainers' most important cultural center is the capital of the French region of Lorraine, Metz, (2002e) 124,000.

FLAG: The Alsatian national flag, the flag of the Alsatian autonomy movement, is a vertical bicolor of red over white. The flag of the nationalist movement is the red over white bicolor bearing a gold Cross of Lorraine on the upper hoist. The official flag of the Alsatian region is a red field with a white and red stripe on the hoist and a gold stripe and six crowns on the fly. The official flag of Lorraine is a gold field bearing a red diagonal stripe charged with three alerions, heraldic eagles without beaks or claws. The official flag of the Territory of Belfort is a blue field with a gold fortress and six gold stripes.

PEOPLE AND CULTURE: The Alsatians, descendants of early Germanic peoples, are historically closely related to the inhabitants of Luxembourg and neighboring parts of Germany. The small nation is made up of a number distinct cultural and linguistic groups broadly grouped into two major divisions, the Alsatians and the Lorrainers. The region is densely populated, resulting in small and fragmented farms and landholdings, although it has a well-developed agricultural and light-industrial economy. Approximately a third of the Alsatians live in urban areas, particularly around the departmental capitals. A movement to revive the Alsatian culture, begun in the 1970s, has succeeded in saving many customs and traditions that were declining, particularly among the urban Alsatians. The culture and dialects remain strong, and younger Alsatians take pride in speaking their dialects and participating in cultural events and traditional celebrations.

LANGUAGE AND RELIGION: Historically the Alsatians are 90% German-speaking, with a small traditionally French-speaking minority. Most Alsatians are now effectively bilingual, speaking both French and one of the German vernaculars collectively called Alsatian (Elsaessisch) or Elsasserdeutch. About a million Alsatians continue to use their traditional dialects as the language of daily life. Alsatian includes a Franconian dialect spoken in northern Alsace and Lorraine and an Alemannic dialect in the southern districts of Alsace. The Alsatian dialects are akin to the Rhenish and Alemannic dialects spoken in the adjoining German states and in Switzerland, but they differ considerably from standard spoken German. The Alsatian dialects are approximately 40% intelligible to speakers of standard German, and they differ from most German dialects in not having undergone the second *lautverschiebung*, or vowel shift.

The linguistic division of Alsace approximates the region's religious division, with a large Roman Catholic Franconian majority in the north and the large Protestant Alemannic minority concentrated in the south. Protestantism made gains in the region during the Reformation, but the region's Protestant influence was countered by the resolute Roman Catholicism of the Habsburgs, who tried to eradicate the Protestant heresy in their holdings in Alsace and Lorraine. Church and state are not separated in Alsace as in the rest of France, and an hour of religious instruction weekly is required in regional schools.

NATIONAL HISTORY: Various Germanic tribes occupied the Roman frontier district west of the Rhine River as Roman power declined in the fourth and fifth centuries A.D. An early Frankish duchy, Alsace was eventually absorbed by Charlemagne's Frankish empire. Following Charlemagne's death in 814, control of the empire fell to squabbling heirs. The division of the empire among Charlemagne's three grandsons, formalized by the Treaty of Verdun in 843, was written in the earliest surviving examples of the French and German languages. By the terms of the treaty Alsace formed part of the middle kingdom of Lotharingia, named for Charlemagne's eldest son, Lothair, who inherited a long strip of territory extending from the Low Countries to Rome. Further division among Lothair's sons eventually divided the region into several distinct territories, including the separate duchy called Lotharingia, or Lorraine.

The Alsatian lands, incorporated by the Holy Roman Empire in 870, were gradually partitioned and by the fourteenth century had become a number of tiny feudal holdings, bishoprics, and independent municipalities, with some southern districts coming under Habsburg rule. Many of the free cities and small states formed military alliances with the Swiss Confederation. In the later Middle Ages the duchy of Lorraine came under strong French cultural and political influence. Noted for secular and ecclesiastical learning, the Alsatians produced many noted medieval scholars, including Martin Waldseemuller, who proposed naming the New World after Amerigo Vespucci in 1507.

The French kingdom began to subjugate the numerous small states on its borders at the end of the Thirty Years' War. By the terms of the 1648 Treaty of Westphalia, all the Habsburg lands in Alsace were annexed to France. Mulhouse and a few small holdings allied to the Swiss were not annexed until the French Revolution. Under French rule, Alsace retained considerable autonomy, with its own legislature or *parlement*, at Colmar. Lorraine remained a separate duchy until 1734. Religious freedom prevailed until the French Revolution, as the Edict of Nantes, which had been revoked in France in 1685, remained in effect in Alsace. Under Napoleon's highly centralized government Alsace lost its former autonomy, and the historical provinces disappeared into small administrative departments in 1789. The region's German-speaking inhabitants were subjected to intense assimilation pressures but clung tenaciously to their distinct dialects and culture.

The unification of Germany in the late nineteenth century—the goal of the most powerful of the numerous German states, Prussia—threatened France's hegemony in Europe and escalated the cultural and linguistic tensions in Alsace. German nationalists laid claim to Alsace and part of Lorraine as historically German-speaking lands.

Alsace and Lorraine were overrun by German troops in the war between Prussia and France that broke out in July 1870 and ended in a German victory in May 1871. Newly united Germany annexed Alsace and the German-speaking parts of Lorraine. A small part of Alsace, Belfort and its surrounding area, was left to France, partly as a gesture of respect to the Belfort garrison, which had fought bravely during a siege lasting 108 days. The annexation of Alsace-Lorraine at the end of the Franco-Prussian War was carried out on questionable historical and ethnic grounds and was opposed by many Alsatians.

The imperial German government instituted a program of severe Germanization. The Alsatians resisted official German efforts to eradicate their unique culture and dialects and developed a strong anti-German sentiment. Resistance to the Germanization of the region fostered a growing sense of the separateness of Alsatian culture and spurred the growth of Alsatian nationalism around the turn of the twentieth century.

In 1911 the German government granted limited autonomy to the region to counter rising nationalist sentiment. Anti-German rioting broke out at Zabern (Saverne) in November 1913, after Alsatian conscripts for the German military were repeatedly insulted by German officers. The rioting spread to the cities, where Alsatian leaders demanded political and cultural autonomy. New restrictions were imposed on the region to restore order. The cultural and linguistic restrictions heightened Alsatian resentment of German rule and exacerbated tensions between France and Germany.

Alsatian discontent with German rule and France's refusal to accept the loss of Alsace-Lorraine or to refrain from meddling in the region fueled a crisis between France and Germany. Both France and Germany, with rapidly growing arms industries, coveted the rich iron mines of Lorraine. The Alsatian Question added to the distrust and tension that eventually led to the outbreak of World War I in 1914.

During World War I, thousands of Alsatian conscripts were sent to the eastern front. Thousands more assisted the Allies against their German masters. By the Treaty of Versailles, signed on 28 June 1919, Alsace-Lorraine was ceded to France. By 1918, however, only a quarter of the region's inhabitants were able to speak French. A nationalist minority, hoping for independence from both Germany and France, began a campaign of agitation against the returning French administration. Nationalists pointed out that the French annexation of Alsace-Lorraine violated the principle of self-determination of European minorities contained in U.S. president Woodrow Wilson's Fourteen Points, the conditions he believed were necessary to ensure continued peace in Europe.

French authority, although initially welcomed by the majority of the Alsatians, proved as harsh and restrictive as that of the Germans. The French government in 1919 promised not to interfere with traditions, customs, language, or local rights but soon began a program of Gallicization of the region. Many supporters of French rule joined the nationalists in demanding self-determination. A minority supported complete independence. Separatist sentiment, fanned by the suppression of Alsatian newspapers, cultural institutions, schools, and local government, provoked massive demonstrations led by the growing nationalist movement. In May 1926 the various nationalist organizations united in the Heimatbund, the Home League, which pressed for cultural and political autonomy, and for the supremacy of the Alsatian dialect in schools and local government. The government's response to increased nationalist activities culminated in the trial of 22 nationalists at Colmar in 1928.

In spite of the French government's attempts to crush the movement, Alsatian nationalism retained widespread support up to World War II. However, with the fall of France in 1940, the majority of the Alsatians opposed annexation to the Third Reich. The stubborn resistance and growing discontent in Alsace-Lorraine soon led to harsh measures by the Nazi administration. Thousands of reluctant Alsatians conscripts were drafted into the German military. There were very few volunteers among the more than 100,000 Alsatians sent to fight on the Russian front. Many Alsatian nationalists were arrested and sent to concentration camps.

German restrictions on the French language and Alsatian culture were so harsh that the former assimilation efforts of the French government were mostly forgotten. Generally hailed as liberators, French and American troops occupied Alsace in 1944, and the region officially reverted to French rule when the war in Europe ended. As in 1919–20, the French government stressed assimilation in an effort to eliminate the Alsatian Question that had plagued Franco-German relations since 1870. In 1945 the French government banned the use of the Alsatian dialects in the area's schools.

Alsatian nationalist sentiment declined with rising prosperity and the beginning of European integration and Franco-German cooperation. In 1949 President Charles de Gaulle and Chancellor Konrad Adenauer chose Strasbourg as the symbol of Franco-German reconciliation. The city, with its bilingual population and distinct Franco-German Alsatian culture, became the home of the 23-nation Council of Europe. In 1958 Strasbourg was chosen as the site of the future parliament of a united, federal Europe.

The decline of the iron and steel industries led to agitation, mass demonstrations, and violent confrontations in the region in 1978–79 and 1984–85. The agitation took on a definite nationalist sentiment as Alsatians and Lorrainers accused the French government of neglecting the region while lavishly financing the regeneration of aging industries in the French heartland.

In 1980, under socialist rule, the highly centralized French government began to devolve some autonomous powers to 22 newly created planning regions that loosely mirrored France's historical regions. In spite of Alsatian demands for unification, the new regions included historical Alsace, but Alsatian Lorraine remained part of the larger Lorraine region, and the Territory of Belfort was included in the region of Franche-Comté.

In 1990 only about half the Alsatians and Lorrainers spoke their Alsatian dialects as their first languages, a drop from about 90% in 1922. In February 1991, the municipal authorities of Strasbourg decreed that the Alsatian dialect should be revived on all street signs. The move was widely denounced in the rest of France as a "Teutonic takeover," reviving memories of the Nazi occupation of World War II.

A number of nationalist organizations emerged between the 1970s and the 1990s, but there has been little of the violence characteristic of other ethnic conflicts in Europe. Small militant groups have used sabotage or demonstrations to press for greater self-government, but violence has been rejected by all but very tiny fringe movements.

The continuing process of European unification has given the Alsatians a new focus, an Europeanized Alsace, a bilingual and bicultural federal state at the heart of united Europe. Large German investment in the region has spurred the renewal of German-language education. The assimilation of the Alsatians into French culture has begun to reverse, with new emphasis on their distinct dialects and culture. Opinion polls in 1998 found that the Alsatians expressed loyalty to their commune, Alsace or Lorraine, Europe, and then France, in that order.

Talk of moving the European parliament to Brussels or Luxembourg is enough to arouse Alsatian nationalism and it has renewed demands for an autonomous, neutral Alsatian enclave between France and Germany. Alsatian national pride has become closely tied to Strasbourg's status as a European capital, and the attachment of Alsatians to their homeland is demonstrated by the practice of speaking of France as a neighboring state. When Alsatians leave their region they speak of going to France.

Considered too French by the Germans and too German by the French and having been forced to change nationality four times in the twentieth century, the fervently pro-European Alsatians look to a continental federation that will allow them finally to be themselves, a distinct European nation. A growing pro-European nationalist movement, supported by cultural associations and municipalities, has sought greater autonomy, the unification of the Alsatian lands, and protection and recognition of the unique Alsatian dialects and culture.

SELECTED BIBLIOGRAPHY:

Duijker, Hubrecht. *Alsace*. 1995.
Kahn, Bonnie M. *My Father Spoke French: Nationalism and Legitimacy in Alsace, 1871–1914*. 1990.
Northcutt, Wayne. *The Regions of France*. 1996.
Vassberg, Liliane M. *Alsatian Acts of Identity*. 1993.

Altai

Altai-kizhi; Altay; Oirots; Oyrots; Sayan Turks

POPULATION: Approximately (2002e) 77,000 Altai in Russia, mainly in the Altai Republic in western Siberia. Smaller communities live in the former Soviet republics of Kazakhstan and Uzbekistan.

THE ALTAI HOMELAND: The Altai homeland lies in Central Asia on the Russian Federation's southern borders with Kazakhstan, China, and Mongolia. A mountainous region, Altai embraces a complex series of ranges and high plateaus, divided by deep valleys and broad basins. Most of the Altai population live in the Sayan uplands. The Altai Mountains, sloping down to the Abakan Steppe in the north, include Russia's highest mountain, Mount Belukha, so sacred to the Altai that no one would dare to climb it. Formerly known as Gorno-Altay or Mountain Altai, the region became a member state of the Russian Federation in 1992. *Republic of Altay (Respublika Altai)*: 35,753 sq. mi.—92,600 sq. km, (2002e) 204,000—Russians 54%, Altai 31%, Ukrainians 11%, Tuvans* 4%. The capital and major cultural center of the Altai is the capital of the republic, Gorno-Altaysk, called Ulala by the Altai, (2002e) 54,000.

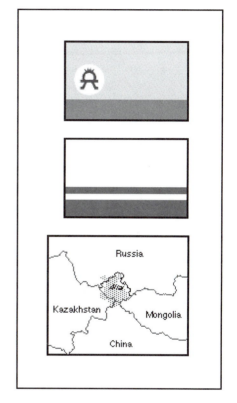

FLAG: The Altai national flag, the flag of the national movement, is a yellow field with a narrow pale green stripe across the bottom and charged with a white circle bearing a traditional symbol in red. The official flag of the Altai Republic has a white field with narrow blue and white stripes over a wider blue stripe at the bottom.

PEOPLE AND CULTURE: The Altai nation, of mixed Turkic and Mongol background, is made up of two cultural and linguistic groups comprising several tribal and clan organizations, the most important being the Tabulars, Chelkans, and Kumandas of the northern Altai, and the Telengits, Teles, Taleuts, and Altai of the southern Altai group. The two groups also show physical differences, with the southern tribes resembling the Mongols, while the northern tribes more closely resemble the Uralic nations. The Altai consolidated as a nation not until the Soviet era. Prior to the 1920s, they were not a homogeneous ethnic group and did not have a common name for themselves. Over the centuries the Altai have tenaciously clung to their Old Turkic culture and their traditional way of life. They have urbanized since the 1930s, but this has not diminished the importance of their clan and tribal ties. The tribes have remarkable skill in mining and smelting iron and have traditionally fashioned high-quality harnesses, helmets, spears, hunting gear, sabers, and implements for daily use.

LANGUAGE AND RELIGION: The Altai speak two dialects of the Sayan Turkic groups; the dialects are not mutually intelligible, and the Altai peoples consider them two distinct languages. Northern Altai, also called Telut or Telengut, and Southern Altai, called Oirot or Oyrot, belong to the northern group of Turkic languages of the Uralic-Altaic linguistic family. Both Altai languages are spoken in several dialects, with the northern dialects closer to the language of the Uighurs,* and the southern belonging to the Kipchak language group. The southern dialect is the literary language of the small nation. The vocabulary of the written language has been influenced by Mongolian and to a lesser extent by Arabian and Iranian.

The Altai peoples are mostly Orthodox Christian or adhere to an indigenous religion, Burkhanism, which combines aspects of early shamanist beliefs with later Christian and Buddhist influences. Burkhanism, prohibited during the Soviet era, has been revived since the collapse of the Soviet government in 1991. In rural areas many Altai, mostly sheepherders, still worship fire and milk and continue to respect the wisdom of the traditional shamans. Evangelical groups, particularly Baptists, have been gaining converts in the region since the early 1990s.

NATIONAL HISTORY: Remains have been found of a primitive communal society that existed in the Altai Mountains as early as the third millennium B.C.; however, little is known of the region until the arrival of the Pazyryks, the near-mythical ancestors of the Altai. The Pazyryks were of mixed Europoid and Mongoloid descent and are known to have created an advanced civilization in the highlands of the Altai Mountains between 600 and 300 B.C.

The Altai were first mentioned in fifth-century A.D. records as nomadic Mongol tribes, although the southern Altai tribes first emerged between the sixth and eighth centuries, the descendants of the ancient Turkic tribes of the Saiano-Altais. The Altai tribes formed from the gradual mixture of ancient Turkic tribes of Uighurs, Oguz, Kimak-Kipchaks, Yenisey-Kyrgyz, and others.

The expanding Mongol empire absorbed the Altai lands in the thirteenth century, and the Altai tribes remained under nominal Mongol rule for over two centuries. In the fourteenth century the Altai region was overrun by the forces of Tamerlane. Some Altai tribes moved west and invaded Kazakh territory, reaching almost to the Ural Mountains.

A powerful tribal confederation, dominated by the Oirot tribe, formed in the sixteenth century and eventually extended its sway far into Central Asia. The Oirot/Altai confederation controlled Dzungaria until the arrival of Chinese forces in the region. When the Chinese incorporated Dzungaria into Sinkiang in 1758, they launched a war of extermination against the ferocious Altai tribes, reducing their numbers to only a few thousands, most in isolated strongholds in the Altai Mountains, which came under Russian control.

Slavic Cossacks, the vanguard of Russian expansion, began to penetrate the region, and by the late sixteenth century they regularly collected a fur tax from the northern tribes. Control of the growing trade in furs allowed the Russians to slowly extend their influence among the southern mountain tribes over the next century. In 1756 the southern Altai tribes accepted Russian protection. The Russians established a civil government in the region, collected taxes in the form of furs, and occasionally put down uprisings but generally left the nomadic tribes to govern themselves under their traditional rulers. Russian sovereignty was finalized with the formal annexation of the region in 1866.

Traditionally the Altai tribes were nomads, but under Russian influence many settled. A Russian Orthodox mission was established, and a majority of the Altai were converted to Christianity, often forcibly. In the 1840s a written language, based on the southern Teleut dialect and using the Cyrillic alphabet, was created by Russian missionaries. The Bible and other works were produced. The Altai literary language existed until 1922.

Burkhanism, a distinctly anti-Russian messianic faith, spread through the tribes in 1904. At its center was the mythical Oyrot Khan, who promised to liberate the Altai from Russian domination and to restore them to their pre-Russian and pre-Chinese greatness. The creed served as a foundation for a new nationalist liberation movement. Russian colonization, facilitated by the completion of the Trans-Siberian Railroad, further aggravated ethnic tensions in the region. In 1905 the Japanese defeated the Russian Empire in the Russo-Japanese War, and Burkhanism acquired a decidedly pro-Japanese orientation.

In 1911 a related people, the Tuvans, declared their independence as revolution swept the Manchus from power in China. Tuvan independence greatly affecting the growth of Altai nationalism, leading to the first attempts to unite the related tribes of the Altai Mountains in the years leading up to World War I.

The Altai tribes were left effectively independent when Russian civil government collapsed in the wake of the Russian Revolution in February

1917. A more secular nationalism emerged, with demands for the creation of an independent republic to include the neighboring Khakass* and Tuvans. United for the first time, the tribes organized to resist attempts by local Bolsheviks to take power as chaos and civil war spread throughout the disintegrating Russian Empire. On 26 January 1918 the victorious Altai declared their homeland independent of Russia and laid claim to the lower Yenisei River valley, the Abakan Steppe, the Altai Mountains, and the huge Altai Steppe to the west.

Allied to the anti-Bolshevik White forces of Adm. Alexander V. Kolchak, the Altai participated in some of the fiercest battles of the Russian Civil War. In 1920 the Red Army finally defeated the Whites, leaving the Altai to fight on alone. The Altai tribes held out against overwhelming odds until 1922.

Partly as punishment for their support of the Whites, the new Soviet government designated the Altai Steppe a Russian settlement area. The move restricted the tribes to a newly created autonomous province, called Oirot after the largest of the tribes, in the southern Altai Mountains. Soviet industrialization brought a large influx of ethnic Slavs to the region, reducing the Altai to nearly 50% of the population of the autonomous province by 1930. Burkhanism and talk of Altai nationalism were tolerated until 1933, when the Altai nationalist movement was denounced as an anti-Soviet conspiracy.

The Soviet authorities supplemented the Altai alphabet with several Russian characters in 1922, in order to convey accurately the growing number of words borrowed directly from Russian. In 1931 a Latin alphabet was adopted, but in 1938 the Russian Cyrillic script was officially adopted as the official alphabet of the Altai dialects.

The small nomadic nation, devastated by war and forced to settle and collectivize in the 1930s, began to decline and rapidly lose population. Alcohol abuse became a major social problem as pressure increased to embrace a universal Soviet culture. During World War II, the Soviet government accused the Altai leadership of being pro-Japanese. As a result, many of the top Communist Party leaders in the region were eliminated or sent to forced-labor camps. In 1948, the Soviet government banned the use of the word "Oirot" as counterrevolutionary. The Oirot Autonomous Oblast was renamed the Mountain Altai Autonomous Oblast, and the name of the capital was changed from Oirot-Tura to Gorno-Altaisk.

In spite of the problems created by Soviet rule, the Altai made great gains in education and gradually produced a new generation of leaders well aware of past glories and injustices. A modest national revival took hold in the more relaxed atmosphere following Stalin's death in 1953, a revival that began to reverse the long Altai decline. In the 1960s the Altai nation again began to increase in numbers.

The liberalization of Soviet life under Mikhail Gorbachev in the late

1980s prompted Altai demands for greater autonomy and redress of the Stalinist injustices. The proposed construction of a hydroelectric dam became a nationalist rallying point. The dam was intended to flood the Katun Valley, destroying the last bastion of the traditional Altai way of life. Altai protests eventually persuaded Gorbachev to terminate the project.

Following the disintegration of the Soviet Union in 1991, Altai demanded full republic status within the newly democratic Russian Federation. Under the terms of Russia's new constitution, Altai gained republic status in March 1992, but nationalist demands for greater autonomy continue to be ignored. A free-trade zone was set up in the republic in 1995, but the Altai have received little economic benefit.

In 1993 Russian archeologists discovered the mummified remains of a high-born, tattooed woman in the region where the Russian, Chinese, Kazakh, and Mongol borders meet on the Ukok Plateau of the Altai Mountains. The discovery, which confirms long-held Altai beliefs of an advanced civilization, the Pazyryks, in the region at the time of Alexander the Great, led to a controversy between functionaries of the Russian government, who wished to continue the work, and Altai officials, who accused the archeologists of plunder and disrespect for their ancestors. Republic officials, with the support of nationalist groups in the region, banned further excavations, claiming that the Russians, who ultimately took the mummy, along with others to Moscow, did so without permission and cared little for the cultural value of the find to the indigenous Altai. Altai leaders have demanded that the mummified princess and other mummies found in the region be returned.

The burial mounds of the vanished Pazyryk people had acted like freezers, preventing decay for over 2,500 years. Water had dripped through the wooden burial chambers through gaps between the small stones making up the mound, freezing the sarcophagi. The Ukok Plateau lies 8,000 feet (2,438 m.) above sea level and is only accessible by helicopter. The region had been the site of the "southern steppe road," which carried great migrations of peoples in the pre-Christian era. A recent survey has revealed thousands of burial mounds, hundreds of them from the Pazyryk period, from 600 to 300 B.C.

The mummies were taken by the Russians on tours in South Korea and Japan, where they were met by admiring crowds, as both the Koreans and Japanese believe that their roots lie in the Altai region. The Altai complain that they received nothing from the archeological tour. Many of the objects found with the mummies are on display at the archeological institute at Novosibirsk. The issue became so sensitive that a Belgian team, with official permission to work in the region, was prevented from doing so by local nationalist groups.

The Altaic intelligentsia has constantly been accused of nationalism and anti-Russian sentiment. In 1997, official sources in the Russian government reported that corruption in the Altai Republic, which is entirely dependent on federal subsidies, has reached astronomically high levels even by the dismal Russian standards. The officials also warned of secessionist tendencies among the Altai population. The combination of separatism and corruption, they warned, could lead to a "second Chechnya."

SELECTED BIBLIOGRAPHY:

Bainbridge, Margaret. *The Turkic Peoples of the World.* 1993.
Forsyth, James. *A History of the Peoples of Siberia: Russia's North Asian Colony, 1581–1990.* 1992.
McCagg, William O., and Brian D. Silver, eds. *Soviet Asian Ethnic Frontiers.* 1979.
Thomas, Nicholas, and Caroline Humphrey, eds. *Shamanism, History, and the State.* 1994.

Ambonese

Melayu Ambon; South Moluccans; Siwa-Rima

POPULATION: Approximately (2002e) 1,340,000 Ambonese in Indonesia, mostly in the Molucca Islands (Maluku) in eastern Indonesia. The only important community outside Indonesia is an exile population dating from the early 1950s, now numbering over 50,000 in the Netherlands.

THE AMBONESE HOMELAND: The Ambonese homeland, the Molucca Islands, known as the Spice Islands during the Dutch colonial era, form an island group of some 1,000 islands spread across the Banda and Ceram Seas in eastern Indonesia. The islands are mostly of volcanic origin and are covered in dense forests with luxuriant vegetation. The homeland in the Maluku islands, popularly called the Moluccas, forms Maluku province of Indonesia. *Maluku (Moluccas)* (2002e) 2,385,000—Ambonese 44%,

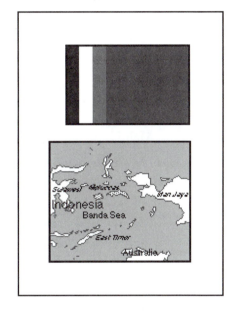

Muslim Moluccan 36%, South Sulawesis* 5%, Javanese 4%, other Indonesian 11%. The Ambonese capital and major cultural center, the city of Ambon, had a population of (1998e) 350,000, prior to the outbreak of religious and ethnic violence in January 1999, but by 2002 the population is estimated to have fallen to about 260,000.

FLAG: The Ambonese national flag, the flag of the national movement and the flag of the former republic, is a red field with three vertical stripes of black, white, and green at the hoist.

PEOPLE AND CULTURE: The Ambonese, known as South Moluccans in the Netherlands, are a people of mixed Malay, Melanesian, Dutch, and African background. They show the ethnic and racial transition between the Malays to the west and the Papuans to the east. Due to intermarriage with the Dutch, Portuguese, and Javanese, there is great diversity of racial types. The Ambonese culture, through close contact during the colonial period, has incorporated more European influences than it has the cultures of neighboring peoples. The Ambonese nation includes the Christian coastal peoples living around the Banda Sea and a number of distinct subgroups, particularly in the islands around the southern edge of the Banda Sea. Ambonese culture acquired traditions and customs from neighboring peoples, but basically the culture is Melanesian. The Ambonese see the destruction of the sacred area of Manusela in the middle of Seram, the mythical origins of the nation, as the most serious modern threat to their culture. Designated a nature park, Manusela was under the auspices of the World Wildlife Fund and a tourist attraction until the outbreak of serious fighting in January 1999.

LANGUAGE AND RELIGION: The Ambonese language, called Ambonese Malay, is the first or second language of well over a million people living around the Banda Sea in eastern Indonesia. The language, a Malayan language of the Malayo-Polynesian language group, is only marginally intelligible to speakers of standard Indonesian, which is also spoken by most Ambonese. The language developed from Bazaar Malay, with many Dutch, Portuguese, and African words and archaic Malay forms. The language further diverged by adopting elements from the various vernaculars of the Maluku peoples. The language, considered by the Ambonese as a national language, is often considered a Malay-based creole by language experts.

The majority of the Ambonese belong to Protestant sects brought to the islands by the Dutch. Although the Ambonese national group is closely associated with Protestant Christianity, smaller Roman Catholic, Sunni Muslim, and animist minorities in the more remote islands have historically and culturally formed parts of the Ambonese people. Religion is closely related to the culture and the nationalist movement. The churches, called *baileos*, formed the center of Ambonese life until most were destroyed by the Indonesian military, which forbade the people to rebuild them.

NATIONAL HISTORY: The original inhabitants of the islands, a Papuan people called Afuros, were absorbed or pushed into the island interiors by ancient Malay settlers. They were often ruled by the powerful Hindu empires that dominated the islands to the west, but their earlier religions had mostly given way to Islam by the fifteenth century. Valued for their produce, mainly exotic spices, the islands came under the rule of the Muslim sultanate of Ternate in the northern Moluccas soon after Islam spread through the region.

A Spanish expedition led by Ferdinand Magellan explored the islands in 1511–12. Sailors returning to Europe told stories of the abundant spices then prized for preserving food. The Portuguese established trading posts in 1521 and won a virtual monopoly on the spice trade after defeating Ternate in a long war, 1550–87. Portuguese missionaries, expelled from the northern islands in 1574, began the Christian conversion of the southern islands. The Dutch expelled the Portuguese in 1605 and annexed the southern Moluccas in 1660. A separate residency of the Dutch East Indies, the islands became a center of clove production. Dissatisfied with the Ambonese as plantation workers, the Dutch authorities imported African slaves to work the clove plantations.

Mostly converted to Protestant sects, the Ambonese became a favored people of the Dutch colonial authorities. Ambonese moved easily into the colonial administration and the colonial army, the Koninklijk Nederlands Indisch Leger (KNIL), was founded in 1830. The KNIL consisted almost entirely of Ambonese and other Moluccans.

Better educated and more prosperous than the other East Indians, the Ambonese readily adopted much of the Dutch European culture, further widening the rift with the neighboring Muslim peoples. In 1860 slavery was abolished, and the freed slaves of the area were gradually absorbed into the Christian Ambonese community.

Fervently pro-Dutch, Ambonese nationalists in the early twentieth century focused on the creation of a separate Christian state in union with the Netherlands. In 1920 students formed the first nationalist organization, called the Ambonese Union. After unification with the northern residency, Ternate, to form a separate government of the Moluccas in 1927, serious religious conflicts developed in the region. The conflicts were aggravated by the growth of Muslim Indonesian nationalism in the northern Ternate region.

An important naval base, the port of Ambon was overrun by the Japanese in 1942. The islands became the scene of an Ambonese guerrilla war against the invaders until the Japanese surrender in 1945. At the end of the war, Indonesian nationalists laid claim to all the islands of the Dutch East Indies. Vehemently opposed to Muslim rule, the Christian Ambonese joined the returning Dutch forces to fight the Indonesian nationalists from 1945 to 1949. The Ambonese, many educated in Christian schools and with experience in the Dutch colonial administration, rejected the economic and social projects of the proposed state of Indonesia. A negotiated settlement finally allowed Indonesian independence as a federation of autonomous states in 1949.

The Ambonese, persuaded to join the federation, won a provision allowing peaceful secession if they felt their interests were jeopardized. The Indonesian government, soon after independence, began to centralize the government over the objections of the peoples of the islands other than the central island of Java. In 1950 the Ambonese announced their intention to secede from Indonesia. The Indonesian government retaliated by dissolving the local administration and imposing direct rule from Djakarta.

The Dutch-trained Ambonese army rebelled and drove the Indonesians from the southern islands. On 25 April 1950 the Ambonese leaders declared the independence of the South Moluccas and appealed to the United Nations and the Dutch government. The Muslim states blocked United Nations intervention, and the Dutch refused to be drawn into yet another Indonesian war. Abandoned by the Dutch, the Ambonese were left to face the threat of the millions of Muslims in the islands around their isolated homeland.

In November 1950, Indonesian troops invaded the breakaway state, setting off heavy fighting. The republic collapsed after nine months of independence. The Ambonese leaders, faced with imminent defeat, accepted a Dutch offer of humanitarian aid. The Dutch evacuated 12,000 South Moluccans threatened by Indonesian reprisals. Another 23,000 fled to neighboring Dutch New Guinea and Portuguese Timor. The Dutch government housed the refugees in former Nazi concentration camps in the Netherlands. The Ambonese revolt resumed in 1956, but with most military leaders in exile in the Netherlands the rebellion collapsed in 1958. In 1966 the Indonesians executed the captured former president of South Moluccas as a warning to the South Moluccan nationalists, who set up a government in exile the same year.

A policy of "transmigration," immigration from the more heavily populated islands to the west, funded by the government, was instituted in the Moluccas in 1954. Between 1954 and 1988 over 60,000 were moved to the islands, mostly from the Muslim regions of Sulawesi or from Java and Bali.

The refugees in the Netherlands resisted assimilation and continued to work for the restoration of their republic. Young Ambonese born in Europe formed the South Moluccan Liberation Front (SMLF) in 1973. In December 1975 radical militants attacked the Indonesian embassy in Holland and hijacked a Dutch train, holding scores of hostages to force Dutch support for a resurrected South Moluccan republic. In 1977 the group struck again, taking over a hundred children hostage at a Dutch elementary school. The Dutch parliament voted in 1978 to regard the case of the South Moluccas as a closed issue. In April 1990, on the 40th anniversary of South Moluccan independence, thousands of Ambonese demonstrated in the Netherlands. Several hundred Ambonese, still living in a Nazi-era concentration camp, have refused to leave for state housing, as they feel it would lessen their commitment to an independent Moluccan state.

The Indonesian government ignored minor incidents in the region until a group of nationalists raised the forbidden flag of the Republic of the South Moluccas in April 1988. The nationalists, on the island of Saparua, were arrested by security forces and were imprisoned and tortured. In 1990 a number of local leaders were arrested to prevent incidents on the 40th anniversary of the declaration of independence.

The Indonesian government's controversial transmigration policy brought an influx of Muslims to the Ambonese homeland, particularly from the nearby island of Sulawesi. The immigrants not only changed the demographic balance from a Christian-majority Maluku province to a Muslim majority but began to dominate commerce. After the appointment of a Muslim governor for the province in 1992, the Muslims from Java and Sulawesi began to dominate local government and the civil service as well.

Ambonese nationalism in the islands, dormant for decades, resurfaced in the late 1980s as Muslim militancy threatened their Christian heritage. On 25 April 1992, the "Government of the Republic of the Moluccas in Exile" was formed, with J. Sounauwe as president. The new Ambonese government was formed on the initiative of the political organization Homeland Mission 1950. In late 1994 Ambonese nationalists formed a working group with the nationalist forces of the neighboring regions of East Timor and West Papua to coordinate their responses to the increasing violence against ethnic and religious minorities in Indonesia.

General Suharto's brutal and despotic rule crumbled in May 1998, releasing separatist and nationalist tensions across the Indonesian archipelago. The growing political and ethnic tensions in Indonesia reached the Moluccas in November 1998. As Christmas and Ramadan approached, both Christian and Muslim groups prepared for trouble. When a minor conflict broke out in mid-January 1999 between a Christian bus driver and two Muslim youths, the tension burst into violence.

In January 2000, Muslim activists in Jakarta demonstrated in favor of *jihad*, or holy war, against the Ambonese Christians. Some Muslim leaders, supported by Islamic activists, claim an Ambonese Christian plot to drive out the Muslim transmigrants. They even suggest that Christian militants are reviving the campaign for an independent South Moluccan state, just as the East Timorese* have done to the south.

An estimated 5,000 people have died in the ethnic and religious violence that erupted in January 1999, and over 100,000 have become refugees. Community leaders are at a loss to explain the sudden collapse of peace in the region. Some talk of foreign or government agents stirring up trouble; others point to increased tension between the Ambonese and the ever-growing population of Muslims settled in their homeland as part of the transmigration program. The Ambonese fear not just the pogroms but the great influx of Muslim migrants, which will eventually leave them a powerless minority in their homeland. Whenever the violence dies down, there seems to be a new incident, a new provocation; more churches, mosques, and villages are burned, and more people are killed, leading many to suspect deliberate provocation.

The Moluccan Islands have been torn apart by the repeated bouts of violence. Christians and Muslims have retreated into enclaves guarded by informal militias and served by separate hospitals, schools, banks, markets, harbors, and government services. Some soldiers appear to have taken sides, further alienating the Ambonese. Firefights have been reported between soldiers and elements of the local police who support the Ambonese Christians.

The actions of the Indonesian government are not encouraging, according to Ambonese leaders. Both the president and vice president of Indonesia visited the region in early 2000, but to little effect. The problems in the area are too complex and deeply rooted to be addressed in the short term in any effective way, leaving the Ambonese to look after themselves. The Maluku province has a population of over two million, about 54% Muslim and 44% Christian. Many seek separation from the Muslim-dominated province and the creation of a separate South Maluku province, but many are increasingly retreating into nationalism, seeing secession, on the model of East Timor, as the only way to save their small nation from annihilation.

In early April 2000, over 5,000 armed Muslims, many from Java and central Indonesia, most belonging to the Komondo Jihad group, marched through the region calling for holy war against the Ambonese Christians. The Indonesian government established a naval blockade to intercept Muslims trying to reach the islands, but many were already preparing for violence in the northern islands. In June 2000 the Indonesian government declared emergency rule in the islands and stepped up security following a new round of violence. The arrival of the Muslim commandos raised fears among the Ambonese that they would become the victims of an effort to cleanse the Moluccas of all Christians.

The Ambonese received renewed interest and support following the September 2001 terrorist attacks on the United States. Financial and military ties between the Islamic radicals fighting for Muslim domination in the Maluku region was reported by Western diplomats in Indonesia to lead to Osama bin Laden. Sympathy as fellow victims of Islamic terrorism gave the Ambonese hope that their cause would not again be forgotten by the outside world.

SELECTED BIBLIOGRAPHY:

Chauvel, Richard. *Nationalists, Soldiers, and Separatists: The Ambonese Islands from Colonialism to Revolt, 1880–1950*. 1994.

Palmer, L. H. *Indonesia and the Dutch*. 1962.

Van Kaam, Ben. *The South Moluccans: Background to the Train Hijackings*. 1981.

Wittermans, Tamme. *Social Organization among Ambonese Refugees in Holland*. 1991.

Amhara

Abyssinians

POPULATION: Approximately (2002e) 19,400,000 Amhara in Ethiopia, mostly concentrated in the Ethiopian Highlands in the central and northeastern parts of the country. There are Amhara communities in other parts of Ethiopia, legacies of the former Amhara domination of the empire and later socialist republic.

THE AMHARA HOMELAND: The Amhara homeland lies in the highlands in northeastern Ethiopia along the border with Sudan. The region is topographically divided into highlands and lowlands. The highlands are characterized by chains of mountains and plateaus. The original home of the Amhara is in the lowlands east of the Ethiopian Highlands, but the Amhara consider the highland regions of Gojjam and Begemdir as the heartland of the Amhara nation. The region is organized as a state of the

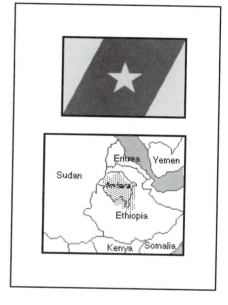

Federal Democratic Republic of Ethiopia. *State of Amhara*: 65,928 sq. mi.—170,752 sq. km, (2002e) 17,105,000—Amhara 91%, Oromos* 3%, Agew/Awi 3%, Kimant 1.5%, Agew/Kamyr 1%, other Ethiopians 0.5%. The Amhara capital and major cultural center is Bahir-Dir, (2002e) 123,000. Other important cultural centers are Gondar, (2002e) 142,000, and Addis Ababa, (2002e) 2,643,000, the federal capital of Ethiopia, which forms a separate administrative region.

FLAG: The Amhara national flag, the flag of the Amhara region in Ethiopia, is a yellow field bearing a broad red diagonal stripe from the upper fly to the lower hoist charged with a single five-pointed yellow star.

PEOPLE AND CULTURE: The Amhara are a Semitic people of mixed Arabian, Hamitic, and black African ancestry. Amhara means "mountain people" in the Amharic language. They are not a cohesive group, politically or culturally, but comprise a number of distinct groups united by culture and language. The Amhara claim to be the descendants of ancient Jews,* and, like the Jews, the Amhara consider themselves to be a "chosen people." Over the centuries the Amhara have absorbed conquered peoples, which has given them a broad range of physical types, but culturally the Amhara of the core areas of Gondar and Gojjam in the Ethiopian Highlands are considered the true Amhara. They enjoyed a privileged status under numerous emperors from the Amhara group, but gradually they divided between the pure Amhara and the Shoa Amhara, the more mixed population in the lowlands around Addis Ababa. The Amhara had served the emperors and, more importantly, increased their group's power but viewed the Shoans as not being true descendants of the ancient Amhara. The Amharic language and culture formed the "official" Ethiopian language and culture, though they did not constitute a majority of the population.

LANGUAGE AND RELIGION: The Amhara language, Amharic or Amharanya, is a Semitic language written in its own script. The language is very complex; estimates of the number of letters in the Amharic alphabet vary between 247 and 259. Amharic belongs to the South Ethiopic group of Ethiopian Semitic languages, a branch of the Southeast Semitic division of the Semitic family of languages. Amharic is widely spoken outside the Amhara homeland and is the official language of the Ethiopian state. It was formerly the language of primary-school instruction in all of Ethiopia but has been replaced in many areas by local languages since 1995. The total number of Amharic speakers, including those using Amharic as a second language, may still constitute as much as 50% of the total Ethiopian population.

The majority of the Amhara belong to the Ethiopian Coptic Church, the ancient Christian religion of the Ethiopian Highlands. The religion, retaining many traditions and rites that have disappeared from other Eastern Christian religions, is a vital part of the Amhara culture. Orthodox Ethiopian Christianity was formerly the state religion, imposed throughout the country.

NATIONAL HISTORY: In the first millennium B.C., the Sabeans of southern Arabia developed a flourishing agricultural civilization. The queen of the Sabeans, while on a visit to Jerusalem, was quite taken with Solomon, the king of Israel. The fruit of their union, Menelik, according to Amhara tradition, became the first leader of Semitic migrants from southern Arabia who around 700 B.C. crossed the Red Sea to settle in the region of present Ethiopia and Eritrea. The migrants conquered the indigenous peoples and erected a strong empire based in Aksum. The Semitic Aksumites eventually split into two related but distinct nations, the Amhara and the Tigreans.* The Amhara spread from their traditional lands to conquer much of the highlands.

Missionaries from Egypt and Syria introduced Christianity in the fourth century A.D. The Amhara accepted Christianity at a time when the Christian religion was increasingly split along ideological lines. In 475, the Amhara, along with the Egyptian Copts,* broke with the authorities in Rome.

The Amhara clung to their religion, a core institution of their unique culture, which in turn formed the center of the early Ethiopian state. The Amhara resisted the spread of Islam in the seventh century and remained a great power until their defeat by invading Muslims in 675. Their highland homeland was cut off from the Christian world by the Muslim conquest of the surrounding regions, but the Amhara preserved their culture and religion in their mountain strongholds.

Gondar became the capital of the Abyssinian Empire, a loose confederation of mostly Christian states in the Ethiopian Highlands. Some Amhara moved south into the Shoa region, where they mixed with the Hamitic Oromos and other peoples. Conflict over power in the state began a long enmity between the "pure" Amhara of the highlands and the more mixed Shoa Amhara of central Ethiopia.

The prominence of the Amhara developed from their great expansion in the thirteenth century. The Amhara language spread and became the mother tongue of much of north and central Ethiopia. Amhara monks spread Christianity among the peoples incorporated into the empire through marriage and assimilation. After contact with Christian Europe was resumed by Portuguese explorers in 1493, the Amhara empire was believed to be the site of the Christian kingdom of Prester John.

Long wars between the Amhara and the Muslims of Harar and Somalia, who were supported by their fellow Muslims the Turks, continued incessantly from about 1520. Nearly conquered in 1541–43, the Amhara were saved by the intervention of the Portuguese, who came as rescuers of the Christian kingdom. The Amhara recovered and reconquered much of their former empire, keeping the Muslims at bay. The region was a center of European missionary activity until the missionaries were expelled from the empire in 1633, after a century of conflict between pro- and anti-Roman Catholic factions. The Amhara heartland in the highlands formed a principality within the empire ruled by a *ras*, or prince, who claimed direct descent from Menelik. The Amhara gradually lost contact with Europe and became a subject of conjecture and legend. James Bruce, an eighteenth-century European explorer, reported a decayed empire in the region north of the Blue Nile.

Hostility against foreign Christians and Europeans, which persisted after the religious conflict of the seventeenth century, was a factor in Amhara-dominated Ethiopia's isolation until the mid-nineteenth century. In the 1850s the Amhara became the preeminent nation in the multinational Abyssinian Empire, as the kingdom began to emerge from its medieval isolation. The imperial government of Emperor Haile Selassie I focused on the Amharization of the entire Ethiopian population. He consolidated the feudal-bureaucratic hierarchy but failed to establish political unity in the entire country. Many remote regions, with various ethnic groups, had little connection with the Amhara-dominated central government.

The Amhara emperor Menelik II led the forces of the empire in defeat of the invading Italians at Adwa in 1896, the first defeat of an European colonial army in northern Africa. The territorial integrity of the Amhara-dominated empire was recognized by the European powers in 1906.

The Italians again invaded from their colony of Eritrea in 1935 and quickly overran Ethiopia. The Amhara heartland was set up as the state of Italian East Africa. During the Italian occupation, Ras Hailu of Gojjam collaborated and was branded a traitor, but his motivation, based on Amhara nationalism, was to oppose the domination of the Ethiopian emperor and the Shoa Amhara of the lowlands. In 1941 Allied troops drove the Italians from Ethiopia, and the empire was restored under traditional Shoa Amhara domination.

The Amhara, in spite of their dominant position in Ethiopia, were mostly farmers with a small educated and privileged minority. Anti-Shoan sentiment and dissatisfaction over high taxes fueled a regionalist movement in Gojjam in the 1940s, until 3,000 troops were sent to the region to arrest the Amhara leadership. Antigovernment feeling related to taxes and the domination of the Shoans again led to serious disturbances in the region in 1967.

After a period of civil unrest that began in February 1974, the aging Emperor Haile Selassie I was deposed. A provisional council of soldiers, known as the Dergue or Derg, meaning "committee," seized power and installed a socialist government. The Dergue summarily executed members of the royal family, former government ministers, and generals of the royal army and their families. Emperor Haile Selassie was strangled in the basement of his palace on 22 August 1975. Marxism was officially adopted as the state ideology in the late 1970s and early 1980s, under the rule of Mengistu Haile Miriam.

The culture of the Amhara remained static and semifeudal up to the 1974 revolution and the overthrow of the imperial government, which ended the domination of the provincial Amhara nobility. Most Amhara supported the end of the feudal, corrupt imperial government, but the traditional enmity between the "pure" Amhara and the Shoans escalated after the revolution as the Shoans continued to dominate the new communist government of Ethiopia. The militarization of the country and communist reforms alienated a large portion of the traditionally conservative Amhara. Many Amhara, however, supported the Marxist-Leninist regime due to sensitivity about Eritrean nationalist movements and the possibility of further disintegration of their ancient empire.

The Mengistu government quickly moved to disestablish the church, the nobility, and large landholdings. The alienated Amhara found themselves discriminated against by the ruling clique. In 1975, armed units of the Ethiopian Democratic Union (EDU) became active in the Amhara heartland provinces of Gojjam, Begendir, and western Tigray. The EDU reflected traditional Amhara opposition to land reform and to the excesses of the Mengistu regime. In May 1976 roughly 40,000 peasants from the Amhara regions, poorly armed and trained, were dispatched to fight Eritrean separatists. Thousands died; the Ethiopian forces were decimated. Many Amhara soldiers made their way home harboring hatred for the ruling Dergue. The EDU, however, was defeated by the Soviet-armed Ethiopian army in 1978; many Amhara leaders were executed, while others fled into exile.

In December 1977, the Dergue launched a "Red Terror" against monarchists, republicans, the church, and Amhara nationalist organizations. Over 10,000 people, mostly ethnic Amhara, were killed. Relatives of those executed were forced to pay the cost of the bullets before claiming the bodies. The Amhara-led Ethiopian People's Party began a war of words against the Dergue and in 1979 made a complete break with the communist government. In March 1979 the government began a new drive against the church, forcing many Christians to register with the government and others to renounce their faith. Executions of Christian Amhara leaders were reported. The ethnic vendetta against the Amhara in 1978–80 alienated a great part of the Amhara population of Ethiopia. A major effect of the government's land reform was to take lands away from ethnic Amhara for distribution to the more loyal Oromos, and for a time the revolution was suspected of being an Oromo plot. Violence escalated as famine struck the region in the early 1980s.

Local loyalty to the Amhara nation has always taken precedence over loyalty to the Ethiopian state. The regionalism of the Amhara grew with the persecutions of the Amhara Christian population by the Dergue. The revolution galvanized Amhara nationalism as the Amhara nation fell from a position of dominance to that of a persecuted minority. In the early 1980s the national movement split between those seeking cultural and economic autonomy and others advocating the secession of the Amhara homeland from the increasingly oppressive communist Ethiopian state. In December 1983, hundreds of Amhara leaders were rounded up in Addis Ababa on charges of alleged ties to rebel groups.

In 1985 the Amhara rebels, after gains in the core Amhara provinces, consolidated their gains and established ties to other rebel ethnic and dissident groups fighting the Dergue. In 1989 the Tigreans, having taken control of much of northern Ethiopia, organized the Amhara forces as the Ethiopian People's Democratic Movement (EPDM). Together the two groups formed the Ethiopian People's Revolutionary Democratic Front (EPRDF), which eventually became an alliance of six ethnically based opposition groups. The EPRDF finally defeated the communist forces and overthrew the Dergue in 1991. Mengistu fled to exile in Zimbabwe. A transitional government, dominated by minority Tigreans, was formed, leaving many Amhara in opposition to the new government.

The new government's recognition of the independence of Eritrea in 1993 sparked a new nationalism among the Amhara. The All-Amhara People's Organization (AAPO) led a drive for autonomy. In 1995 the Amhara heartland in the northwest of Ethiopia was set up as an autonomous region with a regional assembly. Violent confrontations between Amhara and other ethnic groups have increased since the division of Ethiopia into nine states in 1995, particularly over control of Addis Ababa. Amhara leaders charge that their people have been stigmatized as *neftegna*, settlers, in areas where they have lived for centuries. The Amhara, once the rulers of a vast empire, are now a national minority in a federation of many ethnic groups. Frustration and discontent are fueling nationalism and ethnic sentiment for self-rule.

SELECTED BIBLIOGRAPHY:

Donham, Donald L. *Marxist Modern: An Ethnographic History of the Ethiopian Revolution.* 1999.

Gish, Steven. *Ethiopia.* 1996.

Pankhurst, Richard, and Barbara Pankhurst. *The Ethiopians.* 1998.

Shack, William A. *The Central Ethiopians: Amhara, Tigrina, and Related Peoples.* 1995.

Andalusians

Andalucians; Andaluz

POPULATION: Approximately (2002e) 9,447,000 Andalusians in southwestern Europe, concentrated in the Andalusia region of Spain but with sizable communities in other parts of Spain and smaller communities in France, Switzerland, Luxembourg, Germany, and Latin America.

THE ANDALUSIAN HOMELAND: The Andalusian homeland lies in the southern Iberian Peninsula in southwestern Europe at the mouth of the Mediterranean Sea opposite North Africa. The region is traversed by mountain ranges, including the Sierra Morena and the Sierra Nevada. Geographically, Andalusia is divided into two zones, Upper Andalusia (the valley of the upper Guadalquivir River) and Lower Andalusia (the valley of the lower Guadalquivir). The region is celebrated for its fertility and is often called the "granary of Spain," although agriculture remains backward and underdeveloped. Andalusia forms an autonomous region of the Spanish kingdom, comprising eight provinces—Almeria, Cadiz, Cordoba, Granada, Huelva, Jaen, Malaga, and Seville. *Autonomous Region of Andalusia (Comunidad Autónoma de Andalucía):* 33,694 sq. mi.—87,267 sq. km, (2002e) 6,795,000—Andalusians 86%, Roms* (Gypsies) 10%, other Spaniards 4%. The Andalusian capital and major cultural center is Seville, called Sevilla in Spanish, (2002e) 703,000 (metropolitan area 1,115,000).

FLAG: The Andalusian national flag has three horizontal stripes of green, white, and green. The same flag, with a centered red star, is the flag of the nationalist movement. The official flag of the autonomous region is the same, with the addition of the state seal, centered.

PEOPLE AND CULTURE: The Andalusians are a distinct Iberian cultural group, the descendants of the Iberian peninsula's many conquerors and immigrants. Moorish and Castilian strains predominate, while the large Roman population, called Gitanos, has had great influence on the Andalusian character, language, music, and culture. Theirs is the poorest of the nations of Spain, and emigration has long been the solution to the region's high unemployment and lack of opportunities. Centuries of emigration have established a numerous Andalusian diaspora across other regions of Spain and in other parts of Europe and the Americas. The Andalusian culture, characterized by Flamenco music and dance, bullfights, and survivals of their Moorish heritage, reflects crosscurrents from Europe, Africa, the Atlantic, and the Mediterranean. Andalusian culture is often seen by non-Spaniards as the typical culture of multicultural Spain. Moorish influence, so strong in the character, language, and customs of the Andalusians, may partly account for the hostility other segments of the Spanish population feel toward them, although the Andalusians tend to overlook the eight centuries of Moorish rule that shaped their homeland and people.

LANGUAGE AND RELIGION: The language of the Andalusians, popularly called Andaluz, is a dialect of Castilian Spanish spoken in number of subdialects that correspond to the region's historical provinces. Andalusian nationalists claim that the dialect is a distinct Romance language. Castilian speakers counter that the dialect, rather than a separate language, is simply carelessly articulated Castilian.

The majority of the Andalusians are Roman Catholics. Their observance is heavily ceremonial; many towns host elaborate processions during Holy Week, and guilds stage ostentatious *romerías*, pilgrimages, throughout the year. Pre-Christian superstitions and traditions have long formed part of Andalusian Christianity and since the colonial era have spread throughout Latin America.

NATIONAL HISTORY: The southern Iberian Peninsula is thought to have been first settled fifteen hundred years before the time of Christ, by the early Iberians. In the latter half of the second millennium B.C., the region formed the kingdom of Taressus, the biblical Tarshish. Phoenicians founded colonies along the coast, including Gadir, later called Cadiz, around 1100 B.C. The Phoenician's descendants, the Carthaginians of North Africa, destroyed Taressus and established themselves as the dominant power in the region in 480 B.C.

The Romans, victorious over the Carthaginians in the Punic Wars, took control of the region in 209–206 B.C. Called Baetica by the Romans, the land was parceled out in large agricultural estates, a legacy that persists to the present. The decline of Roman power in the fifth century A.D. was followed by invasions of Germanic Goths and Vandals. The English word "vandal," meaning a person inflicting senseless and wanton destruction, originated with the Vandal conquest of the Roman province. The Vandals crossed the narrow strait into North Africa, but left their name, Vandalusia.

Muslim Berbers, popularly called Moors, defeated the Goths and settled Vandalusia from North Africa in 711. The region, now called Al-Andalus, flourished under the Muslim Ommiad dynasty, which ruled from 756 to 1031. The Moors created a brilliant civilization in which religious tolerance, cultural autonomy, science, and literature flourished. Large Christian, Jewish, and Muslim communities existed side by side. Many non-Muslims attained wealth and power under the enlightened rule of the Moors. Cordoba, the Moorish capital, was one of the largest and most advanced cities of the known world. While other European capitals remained backward and filthy, Cordoba was known for its beauty and architecture; it boasted over two miles of street lamps. Agriculture, trade, and universities sustained Europe's most advanced culture.

Internal conflicts weakened the Moorish hold on the region, however, and by the thirteenth century Andalusia had been divided into a number of separate kingdoms based respectively on Seville, Cordoba, Jaen, and Granada. In 1212, Castilian Christians from the north conquered Lower Andalusia and gradually extended their authority over several of the small kingdoms. The infamous Inquisition, introduced in the region in 1478, ruthlessly persecuted the more sophisticated non-Christian populations of Al-Andalus. The Jews, a respected segment of the population under Moorish rule, were the first targets of Spanish Christian intolerance. Their extensive properties were confiscated, and they were finally forcibly driven from Spanish territory in 1492, many taking refuge in the more tolerant Ottoman Empire.

The last of the Moorish kingdoms, Granada, fell to the victorious Christians in 1492, bringing an end to the brilliant civilization of Moorish Spain. It was at a camp outside the walls of Granada that the monarchs of Catholic Spain agreed to sponsor Christopher Columbus's expedition in search of the Indies. Jewels and gold from the looted Moorish towns helped to finance the expedition.

The Christian conquest of Moorish Andalusia brought about an immediate decline in the standard of living in the region. Magnificent monuments and religious structures were destroyed or converted to Christian churches, and libraries were destroyed.

The Moors, called Moriscos by the Spaniards, rebelled in 1568 and appealed to the Turks for aid. The Spanish solution to the problem of large Moorish populations in Andalusia was the same as with the Jews—expulsion. The Moors' properties, including vast rice and cereal plantations, were confiscated, and in 1609 the Moors were expelled from Spain. The expulsion of the Jews and the Moors led to a sharp decline in trade and agriculture. The extensive irrigation system that had sustained Andalusia's golden age was destroyed or neglected. Once-flourishing agricultural regions were used for sheep herding or were abandoned.

The area partially recovered with the exploration of the New World and the subsequent rise of the commercial centers of Seville and Cadiz. The Andalusian monopoly on trade with the Americas made the area wealthy and a meeting place between cultures. Due to Andalusia's position as the gateway to the New World, the Andalusian dialect, rather than the Castilian spoken in Madrid, spread to much of Latin America and became the basis for the dialects spoken throughout much of present Latin America.

The region, still split into numerous large estates, became progressively less productive and fostered a pattern of rural poverty and illiteracy. In 1833 the province of Andalusia was divided into provinces, in order to dilute the traditional Andalusian regionalism and to centralize all power in the Spanish capital, Madrid. Although the land was celebrated for its fertility, the control wielded by the large landowners, and backward farming methods, made Andalusia one of the poorest regions of Spain. In the largely rural region, the lack of education in Castilian and the retention of folk traditions perpetuated a separate Andalusian dialect and culture that remains to the present.

Flourishing vineyards, agriculture, and mines spurred the growth of the local economy during a period of relative prosperity in the latter half of the nineteenth century. The period of prosperity ended about 1900, when vine diseases and a drop in mining output again left Andalusia a poor, backward, and underdeveloped region, in which large estates, many owned by absentee landlords, continue to dominate. This economic and cultural system produced a distinctive outlook that involved suspicion of outsiders, class consciousness and conflict, and significant emigration. Early in the twentieth century, the region became a center of an anarchist movement, fueled by the region's backward economy.

In August 1932, led by reactionary elements, the Andalusians rebelled against the central government, but they were quickly crushed by government troops. The rebellion, the harbinger of the Spanish Civil War, left much devastation, as well as resentment that continues to the present.

In 1936, when the civil war broke out, much of Andalusia was held by the pro-Fascist Nationalist rebels, although eastern Andalusia was held by the Loyalists until March 1939. The civil war left behind prejudices and hatreds that persist in the region to the present. The victory of Francisco Franco's Nationalists in 1939 was followed by the imposition of a strict dictatorial regime; Andalusia was the scene of several serious anti-Franco demonstrations between 1939 and the outbreak of World War II. Under Franco's fascist rule, which stressed the lessening of regional differences, the Andalusians were subjected to intense pressure to accept Castilian speech and culture.

Andalusia remained neglected, underdeveloped, and backward after

World War II, while the Spanish government developed the richer northern regions into the state's industrial heartland. Emigration, long an outlet for poor Andalusians, accelerated in the 1950s and 1960s. Many emigrated to Latin America or settled as low-paid laborers in wealthier parts of northern Europe. Hundreds of thousands, in government-sponsored migrations, settled in the industrialized northern regions of Spain, where they were dubbed "Franco's Legions." During the 1960s, Andalusia lost around 14% of its population, in what has been described as the greatest European exodus in peacetime in the twentieth century.

Andalusia began the 1970s as Spain's poorest region, pitiably poor and underdeveloped. Sorry transport links, antiquated farming, and almost nonexistent industry were exacerbated by a lack of skilled workers. Even in the mid-1980s, only a third of all Andalusians had finished secondary schools. Emigration, mostly to the richer regions of northern Spain, remained the traditional outlet for excess, unskilled workers until the late 1980s.

A growing antifascist movement in the late 1960s triggered a new awareness of the Andalusians' distinct dialect and culture. Activities and events in the region reflected the emergence of a national awareness in Andalusia, a totally new political and cultural phenomenon in the region. With the return of democracy in 1975, at Franco's death, an active autonomy movement emerged. The low level of economic development in the region was a major contributing factor in the rising nationalist demands.

The Andalusians looked back on periods of greatness, which were the basis of the subcultural nationalist movement of the 1970s and 1980s. In 1979–80, strikes and demonstrations in support of regional autonomy swept the region. In October 1980 a referendum was organized in Andalusia; 89% of the voters favored home rule. In 1981 the region was granted autonomy. Self-government for the Andalusians put an end to over three centuries of centralized rule from Madrid.

Andalusia was particularly hard hit, however, during the worldwide recession of the 1980s, which was made more difficult by the worst drought of the century, although the growth of tourism somewhat offset agricultural losses. In spite of the great natural wealth of the region and the phenomenal growth of tourism, the Andalusians remain among the poorest people of Europe. Further, many Andalusians have begun to question the booming tourist industry, which has brought unbridled construction to the southern coast. The tourist industry has grown faster than any other part of the local economy.

In the late 1980s, several regionalist political parties emerged, including the Partido Andalucista (PA), the Andalusian Party, and an openly separatist organization, Liberación Andaluza. In early 1989 the PA demanded the recognition of Andaluz as a separate language, insisting that the language has become distinct enough from spoken Castilian to be a separate language. Nationalists also insisted that the dialects spoken throughout Latin America are in fact dialects of the Andaluz language, not of Castilian Spanish.

In the 1990s, Andalusians living outside their homeland, particularly in other parts of Spain, maintained their culture through strong cultural associations. The antipathy they felt from other peoples helped them to maintain their separate identity. In 1992 the first encyclopedia of Andalusian culture was presented at the World Exposition in Seville. The region continues to suffer from backward and inefficient farming methods.

A new militancy and closer ties to the central government won financial aid from Madrid in 1999–2002, but the Andalusians increasingly look to Brussels, not Madrid, as the center of power and regional finance. Although European Union subsidies support antiquated and backward agriculture, many areas have prospered to the point that foreign workers have had to be imported. Many of the emigrants of the mid-twentieth century are returning to the area from Catalonia and the Basque country, no longer needing to live outside their homeland in order to work and prosper.

SELECTED BIBLIOGRAPHY:

Douglass, Carrie B. *Bulls, Bullfighting, and Spanish Identities.* 1997.
Kean, George. *Andalucia.* 1993.
Kern, Robert W. *The Regions of Spain: A Reference Guide to History and Culture.* 1995.
Mead, Rowland. *Andalucia Handbook.* 1997.

Andhrans
Andhras; Andhra Telugu

POPULATION: Approximately (2002e) 38,500,000 Andhrans in India, concentrated in the 12 coastal and southern districts of the Indian state of Andhra Pradesh. Outside the region there are sizable Andhran communities in the state capital, Hyderabad; in the Telengana region; and in other parts of India. There are Andhran populations in other parts of Asia and in Europe, the United States, and Canada.

THE ANDHRAN HOMELAND: The Andhran homeland lies in east-central India, in the Coastal and Ralalseema regions of the state of Andhra Pradesh. The region, lying partly in the Deccan Plateau and partly in the lowlands along the Bay of Bengal, is mostly fertile and flat, except for the highlands in the southeast. Andhra comprises the 12 southern and eastern districts that were amalgamated with the Telengana region to form the state of Andhra Pradesh in 1956. *Region of Andhra*: 61,273 sq. mi.—158,696 sq. km, (2002e) 39,150,000—Andhrans 84%, Tamils* 10%, Kanarese 3%, Gonds 1%, other Indians 2%. The Andhran capital and major cultural center is Kurnool, called Karnul in Telugu, (2002e) 323,000, in the interior Rayalseema region. The other important Andhran cultural center is the port city of Vishakhuaptnam, in the Northern Circars region of northern Andhra, (2002e) 1,081,000, metropolitan area 1,692,000.

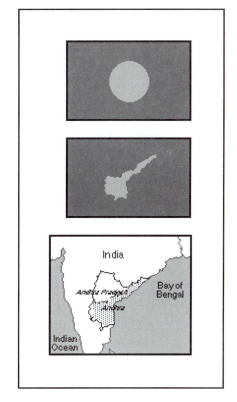

FLAG: The unofficial Andhran national flag is a green field bearing a centered yellow disk. The flag of the Jai Andhra movement is a green field charged with an outline map of the 12 Andhran districts in yellow.

PEOPLE AND CULTURE: The Andhrans are a Dravidian people, the descendants of India's pre-Aryan inhabitants pushed south by the Aryan conquest of northern India. The Andhrans, generally smaller and darker than the Aryan peoples to the north, form part of the larger Telugu nation, which is divided into two historically and culturally groups, the Andhra

Telugu in the east and south of Andhra Pradesh state, and the Telengana Telugu in the northwestern region of Telengana. The first references to the Andhrans as a distinct nation are found in writings from around 1000 B.C. They are mentioned as a southern people inhabiting the region south of the Vindhyas.

LANGUAGE AND RELIGION: The Andhrans speak a Dravidian language, Telugu, part of the great language family spoken across southern India. The language, which is the official language of Andhra Pradesh state, is spoken in three distinct dialects, Rayalseema, Coastal, and Telengana, and a number of subdialects. Rayalseema and Coastal are spoken by the Andhrans. The language is described as the "Italian of the East." Next to Hindi, Telugu is the most widely spoken language in India. The earliest recorded version of the language appeared in the seventh century A.D., but it did not become a literary language until in the eleventh century. It exhibits a dichotomy between the written and spoken styles, and it has sharply distinct dialectical differences. Telugu is written in its own script, which forms the basis of the important Andhran literary tradition.

The Andhrans are overwhelmingly Hindu, although many ancient traditions and customs remain important in local ceremonies and rites. The Brahminism of northern India is opposed by the less rigid Dravidian Hinduism of the region, and the Andhra region lies on the fault line between the Aryan north and the Dravidian south.

NATIONAL HISTORY: The Dravidian peoples, originally inhabiting most of ancient India, were pushed south by the Aryan invasions of northern India between 1700 and 1200 B.C. The Dravidians erected numerous small states, including a Telugu Dravidian state of Andhra, which flourished from about 250 B.C. to 250 A.D. The Andhra homeland, overrun by several invading armies, remained under Telugu control until the Muslims conquered much of the region in the thirteenth and fourteenth centuries.

The political history of the Andhrans began with the sprawling Mauryan empire in the third century B.C. The Greek ambassador in the court of Chandra Gupta Maurya made a number of references to the Andhrans in his book *Indica*. According to his account, the Andhrans were an independent and militarily very strong nation. The Roman Pliny, in the first century A.D., wrote of a powerful king of Andhra who had trading and political relations with Rome.

Around 300 A.D., the Ikshvakus extended the Andhra kingdom to the Krishna and Godavari deltas, with their capital at Vijayapuri. This kingdom was eventually absorbed into the Pallava kingdom, which ruled Andhra from Vengipura, near present Eluru. The Andhran kingdom split into a number of small, warring states in the sixth century.

The Kakatiya dynasty of Warangal rose to power in the region about 1000 A.D. on the ruins of the earlier Andhran kingdoms. The Kakatiya rulers were great patrons of learning and builders of temples. The thousand-pillared temple at Warangal is a testimony to the architectural skills that the Andhrans patronized. The Kakatiyas were also known for the construction of an extensive irrigation system.

A powerful Telugu Hindu state established at Vijayanagar in 1336 protected the Hindu south against Muslim incursions for over two centuries. An important center of Brahmanist Hindu culture and Dravidian art, the city of Vijayanagar was reputed in the fourteenth century to have a population of over half a million, rivaling Renaissance Rome. The Vijayanagar state finally fell to the Muslims in 1565.

The British established their first settlement on the Telugu coast at Machilipatnam in 1611, and, following the founding of Madras to the south in 1640, they gradually took control of the southern Telugu regions south of the Krishna River. The region became part of the Madras Presidency in 1653. British influence led to the rapid modernization of the Andhrans, the southern and eastern branches of the Telugu nation.

The northern part of the Telugu homeland was joined to the powerful Delhi sultanate of the Muslim Moguls in 1687–88. In 1713 a Mogul general had himself named viceroy, or governor, of the Mogul domains in the Deccan. Following the collapse of the Mogul state in 1722, he declared the region the independent state of Hyderabad, giving himself the title Nizam ul-Mulk. The state, a center of Muslim culture in central India, became a British ally during the intense British-French rivalry in India. The coastal region, the Northern Circars, was ceded to direct British rule in 1766. In 1800 Hyderabad became a British-protected feudal state.

Andhran nationalism developed in the early twentieth century, particularly after the establishment of the first Andhran political-cultural organization, the Andhra Jana Sangh (AJS), in 1921. Eminent Andhran leaders associated with the AJS established Telugu-language libraries, opened language schools, published books, and promoted research into the language and history of the Andhran nation. In 1931 the AJS formed part of the new, more militant political grouping, the Andhra Mahasabha, with Suravaram Prathapa Reddy as its first president.

The Andhra Telugu, under a British-educated elite, developed as a relatively modern, educated population, while the Telengana Telugu of Hyderabad, dominated by the Muslim minority, remained backward and uneducated. The coastal Andhrans played an active part in the Indian national movement, which, however, never extended to the feudal Hyderabad state. The disparity between the two halves of the Telugu nation widened up to World War II.

In the postwar era, the disposition of the British-protected states became a controversial issue. When India achieved independence in 1947, the Andhra Telugu region formed part of the newly created Madras state, but in Hyderabad the Nizam refused to accede to India's sovereignty despite the state's large Hindu majority. On 17 February 1947 the Nizam proclaimed

Hyderabad an independent state, setting off rioting in both Hyderabad and in the Andhra region of Madras. Fighting between Telugu irregulars and Muslim insurgents in Hyderabad galvanized the entire Telugu nation. Indian troops invaded the breakaway state, which was joined to newly independent India in September 1947. The backward Telengana region of Hyderabad, with a Telugu-speaking population, was the scene of a communist-backed insurgency from 1946 to 1951. Telugu rebels, using communist Chinese rebel tactics, set up a Soviet underground in the Telengana.

The rise of Telugu nationalism, mostly in the Andhran districts, led to demands for a separate Telugu-language state within India in 1950. A leader of the Andhra Telugu, Patti Sreeramulu, an ascetic believer in linguistic autonomy, fasted in an attempt to dramatize the demand for a separate Telugu state. He died in December 1952, and his death set off severe communal violence. In 1953 the Indian government separated the Telugu-speaking region of northern Madras to create the state of Andhra, the first linguistic state formed in India. In 1956 the state of Hyderabad was divided along linguistic lines; the Telengana Telugu region was added to Andhra to form Visalandhra, or Greater Andhra. On 1 November 1956 the state of Andhra Pradesh was formed, with its capital at the city of Hyderabad, where 40% of the population spoke Urdu. The more sophisticated coastal Andhrans took over most civil service positions and bought property in the Telengana, where land was still inexpensive.

The Andhrans at first welcomed the formation of a state embracing the entire Telugu-speaking population of India, but friction soon erupted between the more advanced Andhrans and the Telenganas, who had lived under feudal conditions in Hyderabad. Rioting and fighting between the Andhrans and Telenganas periodically swept the state in the 1960s and 1970s, leading to the suspension of the state government and the imposition of direct rule from New Delhi in 1973. A nationalist minority in the Telugu Desam (Telugu Nation) Party proposed greater autonomy or even independence as the only way to reconcile the two halves of the Telugu nation.

Small cultural differences between the Andhrans and Telenganas—such as the many Urdu words in the Telengana dialect, the Andhran preference for coffee (the Telenganas drink tea), and the differences between the traditional Telugu cuisine in Andhra and Muslim-influenced Telengana cooking—became issues that could spark bloody riots. The Telenganas in 1969 proposed the separation of their region, the former heartland of Hyderabad, from Andhra Pradesh state, but by 1971 their opposition to the union had waned, following concessions in education, employment, and other aid to their underdeveloped region. The concessions brought a nationalist backlash among the Andhrans, who resented the massive transfer of state funds to the Telengana. By the late 1970s the coastal Andhrans were agitating for a separate Andhra state.

New violence broke out in 1982–83, both between the Andhrans and Telenganas and between supporters of the nationalists and pro-Indian groups. In 1983 the Telugu Desam Party won state elections under the leadership of Nadamuri Taraka Rama Rao, whose first priority was to calm the tension between the two Telugu peoples. In 1988 N. T. Rama Rao was convicted of abusing his official position to enrich himself and his family members. The conviction, seen in the state as an Aryan plot, briefly united the two Telugu peoples, but tension resurfaced in the early 1990s. Telugu Desam was defeated in 1991 and became an opposition party in the state.

An upsurge of violence in 1990–92, based in the Telengana, was led by leftist groups seeking land reform and social justice in the still-backward region. The violence, which quickly spilled over into the Andhran regions, added to Andhran demands, led by the Jai Andhra movement, for separation of prosperous, sophisticated Andhra from the backward, poverty-stricken Telengana. At the turn of the twenty-first century, the vast differences between the Andhrans and the Telenganas remain, and, although communal violence has lessened, renewed violence and demands for the separation of the two peoples remain just below the surface.

SELECTED BIBLIOGRAPHY:

Chadda, Maya. *Ethnicity, Security and Separatism in India*. 1997.
Devi, Yashoda. *History and Culture of the Andhras*. 1994.
Rao, Narayana. *Emergence of Andhra Pradesh*. 1974.
Rao, Raghunadha. *History of Modern Andhra Pradesh*. 1988.

Anguillans

POPULATION: Approximately (2002e) 15,000 Anguillans in the Caribbean area, concentrated on the island of Anguilla. Other Anguillan communities live on St. Kitts, Jamaica, the United Kingdom, and in the southern United States.

THE ANGUILLAN HOMELAND: The Anguillan homeland lies in the eastern Caribbean Sea. The most northerly group of the Leeward Islands in the Lesser Antilles, the territory of the Anguillan state includes Scrub, Seal, Dog, and Sombrero Islands, the Prickly Pear Cays. The island is relatively flat and is covered with sparse, dry woodlands fringed with white-sand beaches. Numerous bays and inlets indent the shoreline of the long and narrow island. The nearest island neighbors are Saint Martin, which lies five miles (eight kilometers) to the south, and St. Kitts, about 60 miles (100 kilometers) to the southeast. *Territory of Anguilla*: 35 sq. mi.—91 sq. km, (2002e) 13,200—Anguillans 94%. The Anguillan capital and major cultural center is The Valley, a port town of about 1,000 inhabitants.

FLAG: The Anguillan national flag, the flag of the independent republic of 1969, is a white field with a broad pale-blue stripe across the bottom and three orange dolphins in a circle centered on the white.

PEOPLE AND CULTURE: Most of the Anguillans are blacks or mulattos, the descendants of African slaves. The few white inhabitants are mostly Europeans drawn to the island's tranquility and year-round fine weather. The Anguillan population is young, with more than a third of the population being younger than 15 in 2000. The birth and death rates are moderate, so population growth is relatively stable. Emigration to other Caribbean islands, the United States, or the United Kingdom is the traditional escape from unemployment and a lack of opportunity. The Anguillans live under somewhat poor conditions, and employment is seasonal or unsteady; however, housing conditions are generally better than average for the Caribbean. The island's dry climate and its unsuitable soil limit the importance of agriculture, although crops are grown for domestic consumption. Livestock and fishing have traditionally been the basis of the local economy, but tourism has become the dominant economic factor in recent years.

LANGUAGE AND RELIGION: The official language of the Anguillan state is English, which is widely used; however, a patois of mixed English, African, and French is the language of daily life. Education in English is compulsory between the ages of five and 14, and it is provided free by the Anguillan government. Advanced education is available elsewhere in the Caribbean region or in the United Kingdom.

The Anguillans are mostly Christian. The largest religious groups are the Protestant denominations, particularly the Anglicans and Methodists. Officially the breakdown is Anglican 40%, Methodist 33%, Seventh-Day Adventist 7%, Baptist 5%, Roman Catholic 3%, other 12%. Many pre-Christian traditions and customs have been retained, however, by the islanders.

NATIONAL HISTORY: Historians believe that Anguilla was not populated by the Carib Indians for any length of time, and it is uncertain whether or not the island was visited by Columbus in 1493. Several European explorers visited the island; the French named the long and narrow island *anguille*, or eel.

Anguilla was first colonized between 1632 and 1650 by settlers from the island of St. Kitts. The island was placed under the political control of St. Kitts and has remained British almost continuously since 1650. The population increased very slowly; most islanders engaged in fishing or salt gathering. The island was attacked in 1699 by a party of Irish, who eventually settled and whose surnames are still evident on the island.

The island changed hands several times before becoming permanently British by the terms of the Treaty of Utrecht in 1713. The French attempted to conquer the island twice in the eighteenth century, in 1745 and 1796, but were repelled. The Treaty of Paris in 1783 definitively awarded Anguilla to the British.

Of little economic importance, Anguilla remained sparsely populated throughout the nineteenth century. Black slaves, imported from nearby islands in the eighteenth and nineteenth centuries, formed the majority of the population, most working on plantations owned by the small number of white residents.

The territory had been administered by the British authorities as part of the Leeward Islands since its colonization, and from 1825 it was closely associated with St. Kitts, a situation the Anguillans have long resented. In 1875 the Anguillans petitioned for separate status but were turned down. St. Kitts, Nevis, and Anguilla were united as a single colony in 1882.

Anguilla remained a very minor outpost of the British Empire well into the twentieth century, neither politically nor economically important. The island became part of the Leeward Islands Colony in 1956, and in 1958 the island, in association with St. Kitts and Nevis, joined the British-sponsored Federation of the West Indies. The federation was dissolved in 1962, when the major islands opted for separate independence. In 1967 St. Kitts-Nevis-Anguilla became a British-associated state, independent except for defense, foreign affairs, communications, and currency.

The Anguillans, still unhappy with rule from St. Kitts, repudiated their ties to the associated state on 39 May 1967, demanding self-government. Negotiations with both the British and St. Kitts governments failed to find an acceptable compromise. On 10 February 1969 the Anguillans announced the severance of all ties to the United Kingdom and declared themselves the independent Republic of Anguilla.

The British government refused to accept the secession or Anguilla's independence, and on 19 March 1969 troops and London "bobbies" (police) landed. On 30 March, the islanders were forced to sign a truce and again to accept British rule. The Anguilla invasion was dubbed the "Bay of Piglets" by local residents. In August 1969 the British authorities granted a new constitution as a separate, self-governing British dependency. Although Anguilla technically still remained a part of the Federation of St. Kitts-Nevis-Anguilla, the seat of the representative from Anguilla remained empty.

The new Anguillan government provided for a seven-member House of Assembly and a chief minister, but the British government retained authority over defense, police, civil service, and foreign affairs. In 1971, two months after the new self-government agreement, all British troops were withdrawn. The ruling political party, the Anguilla United Party, sought to sever all ties to the government of St. Kitts–Nevis and demanded a separate government for the island. In the 1980s and 1990s, the movement for separation from St. Kitts–Nevis animated local politics. On 19 December 1980, Anguilla was finally separated from St. Kitts–Nevis, which achieved separate independence in 1983.

The island, with some of the Caribbean's finest beaches, was slow to attract tourism, due to its lack of development, but by the late 1980s new hotels and facilities were bringing increasing numbers of European and North American visitors and providing employment for much of the local population. However, one of the island's leading sources of income is cash sent by the several thousand Anguillans living overseas.

In 1989 the Anguillans voted to retain their ties to the British government, which provides economic aid and stability. The vote reflected a new British policy of allowing the inhabitants of the dependencies access to the National Health Service, including treatment in the United Kingdom for serious illnesses.

A severe hurricane in September 1996 devastated the island and destroyed about half the houses on the island, in the worst Atlantic hurricane season in decades. British aid in rebuilding the ravished island reinforced the Anguillan desire to retain their ties to the British government. In 1997 plans for a new airport, with almost double the present runway length, were announced, to be financed by private investors.

Hubert Hughes, the chief minister of the islands, during a serious political crisis verbally attacked the London-appointed governor, who called a general election in March 2000, four years early, in an effort to break a constitutional deadlock over Anguillan self-government. In early 1999, Hubert Hughes won reelection, with four of the seven seats in the House of Assembly. That dropped to three in June, when a coalition partner switched allegiances. The opposition then boycotted the House of Assembly, leaving it one short of a quorum. Without an assembly there was no legislation and no budget; Hughes tried and failed to get the island's court to order the speaker to convene the assembly.

The Anguillans have not expressed a desire for full independence but have asked the British government for wider self-government. Some Anguillans have expressed interest in joining a proposed political and economic community made up of the English-speaking Caribbean states.

SELECTED BIBLIOGRAPHY:

Hammett, C. J. *Anguilla: Consolidated Index of Statutes and Subsidiary*. 1986.
Jones, S. B. *Annals of Anguilla 1650–1923*. 1979.
Morten, Neil. *Theirs Not to Reason Why: A Study of the Anguillan Operation as Presented to Parliament*. 1969.
Webster, Ronald. *Scrap Book of Anguilla's Revolution*. 1973.

Anjouanis

Nzwanis; Nzwani Comorians; Mohelis; Mwali Comorians; Anjouanais

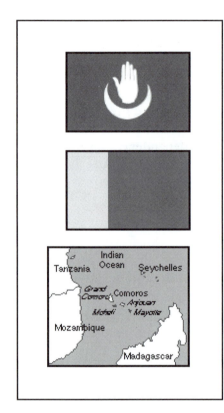

POPULATION: Approximately (2002e) 270,000 Anjouanis, including the Mohelis, in the Comoro Islands. Outside the region there are Anjouani communities in Madagascar, Kenya, and Mauritius in the Indian Ocean area and in France.

THE ANJOUANI HOMELAND: The Anjouani homeland is a collection of islands lying in the Mozambique Channel of the Indian Ocean about 310 miles (500 kilometers) west of the northern tip of Madagascar, and 185 miles (300 kilometers) east of Mozambique. Though the islands are of volcanic origin and are mountainous, the island of Anjouan has one of the highest population densities in the world. Anjouan is roughly triangular, rising to a central volcanic massif at Mtingui. Although the soil is good, much erosion has occurred, and many areas are no longer arable. Mohéli is the smallest of the Comoro Islands, mostly a plateau with fertile valleys and hillsides are covered with thick forests; it has a population of only 25,000. Officially the islands form part of the Islamic Republic of the Comoro Islands, but since declaring independence in 1997 their status has remained undecided. *State of Anjouan/L'État d'Anjouan (Anjouan-Mohéli/Mwawana)*: 201 sq. mi.—521 sq. km, (2002e) 268,000—Anjouanis 84%, Mohelis 11%, other Comorians 5%. The Anjouani capital and major cultural center is the city of Mutsamudu, (2002e) 28,000. The major cultural center on Mohéli is the capital, Fomboni, (2002e) 13,000.

FLAG: The Anjouani national flag, the flag of the separatist state, is a red field bearing an open white right hand in red above a white crescent moon, pointing up. The flag of the Mohelis is a red field with a broad yellow stripe at the hoist.

PEOPLE AND CULTURE: The Anjouanis and Mohelis are a blend of the different peoples who settled the islands—Iranian traders, mainland black Africans, Arabs, and Malay Malagasy from nearby Madagascar. Arab Muslim culture is well established, and polygamy is an accepted practice among the islanders, although the practice is declining due to the expense of maintaining a large household. Most of the islanders work as farmers or fishermen, with some engaged in herding cattle, sheep, goats, or donkeys. A small number work in industry or in jobs related to tourism. Housing, both in rural and urban areas, is usually shared by several generations. Educational levels are low, and over half the population is estimated to be illiterate. The birth and death rates are both high in the islands, and, although infant mortality is a major problem, the growth of population is about twice the world average. Almost half the population is less than 15 years of age.

LANGUAGE AND RELIGION: Arabic and French are the official languages of the Comoros, but the language of daily life is a group of island dialects called Shikomoro or Comorian, a variety of Swahili. Each of the islands has a distinct dialect, named for its respective island—Shindzwani or Anjouani and Shimwali or Moheli. Malagasy is also widely spoken as a trade language.

The islanders are overwhelmingly Muslim, belonging to the Shafiite rite of Sunni Islam. A small number of Roman Catholics recall the former French presence in the islands. Although an estimated 99.9% of the Muslim islanders adhere to Shafiite ritual, attendance at local mosques is very low. Strong pre-Islamic traditions, involving occultism and spirit possession, remain important parts of the religious beliefs. Koranic schools for children reinforce Islam's influence.

NATIONAL HISTORY: The population of the islands was formed by successive waves of settlement over at least 1,000 years. Early immigrants from Madagascar were followed by Arabs in the eighth century and in the ninth century by Omani Arab settlers, whose ruling elites were related to the rulers of Kilwa and Zanzibar, islands farther to the south, and to the Arabs of the Arabian Peninsula. The islands remained under Omani Arab rule until the sixteenth century.

The islands became trade centers for dhows that traded throughout the Indian Ocean. Trading towns were built, and black African slaves, brought from the mainland, were employed as plantation workers on the more fertile southern islands of the group.

Portuguese explorers reported sighting the islands in 1505, at about the time that Shirazi Muslim migrants from Persia established separate dynasties and introduced Islam there. The Comoro Islands were shown on the world map of Portuguese cartographer Diego Ribero of 1527, but the first European known to visit them was the English explorer James Lancaster, about 1591. Each of the islands was ruled by a local family, supported by small oligarchies of Arab landowners.

The Comoro Islands, long a bastion of Arab culture off the east African coast, were an early base for Arab exploration and for the extension of the Islamic culture and religion in east Africa. Early in the nineteenth century, there were fresh incursions from Madagascar, and Mohéli was ruled by a Malagasy dynasty. Slaves were regularly imported from Mozambique, and at the end of the nineteenth century their descendants probably constituted the majority of the population of the islands.

Slave raids by Malagasy pirates led in the nineteenth century to fortification of the towns and to appeals for French aid in combating the slavers. The sultan of Anjouan approached the French authorities and offered to sell them his island in exchange for protection from pirates, an annual rent, and free education for his many children.

Between 1866 and 1902 the French established colonial rule over the islands of Anjouan and Mohéli. The three islands of Grand Comoro, Anjouan, and Mohéli were proclaimed a French protectorate in 1886. All of the Comoro Islands—Grand Comoro, Anjouan, Mohéli, and Mayotte—were organized as a colony attached to Madagascar in 1914. French settlers, French-owned companies, and wealthy Arab merchants established a plantation-based economy that utilized about a third of the land area for export crops. French plantation companies obtained forced labor from the islands' peasants, who had to lease land from the companies.

In 1947, the islands became a French overseas territory and were represented in France's National Assembly. Internal political autonomy was granted in 1961. An agreement was reached in 1973 by which the Comoros would become independent in 1978. In 1974 the National Assembly, following demands for individual-island autonomy, decided to allow each of the four islands to determine its own fate. On 4 February 1974, the islands, except for Mayotte (called Mahore by its inhabitants), voted 95% in favor of independence from France. The three islands, dominated by Grand Comoro, unilaterally declared a sovereign republic on 6 July 1975. Efforts to incorporate Mahore into the new republic dominated local politics and led to instability and inter-island feuding in the republic.

The Comoro Islands, after 15 years of economic decline, political conflict, and finally French military intervention, held their first democratic elections, but the chronic instability continued. Each of the three islands elected its own governor and governing council, but their authority was limited, and in reality the republic was controlled by a political elite on Grand Comoro.

After independence the Comoros suffered a brutal reign of terror, which French-protected Mahore escaped. Coups and countercoups established several unstable governments that agreed on only one issue, that France should surrender prosperous Mahore to Comorian rule. Increasing dissatisfaction with the plundering of natural resources by a small oligarchy led to separatist, pro-French sentiment, particularly on Anjouan. Rivalries between the islands became more important than ethnic differences or the

Mahore issue, with accusations of unfair distribution of power and development among the islands.

Yet another coup, in September 1995, led by French mercenary Bob Denard, overthrew the Comorian government. France again intervened in the islands and arrested Denard; new elections were held. The new Comorian government drafted a constitution that extended the authority of the president and established Islam as the basis of all legislation. Resistance by the impoverished Anjouanis to rule from Grand Comoro became more pronounced. An openly nationalist organization, the Anjouan Liberation Movement (MLA), was formed in 1996.

To escape grinding poverty, over 20,000 Anjouanis immigrated to more prosperous Mahore between 1975 and 1995. Unemployment on the two Anjouani islands remained around 90%, while nearby French Mahore (former Mayotte) enjoyed a guaranteed wage, free education, and modern health care. The islanders became envious of the better conditions on Mahore; thousands of migrants crossing the shark-infested waters were turned away from Mahore by the French authorities each year.

Civil unrest broke out across the islands in early 1997 as civil servants demanded payment of salary arrears. The financial and political crisis fueled secessionist movements on both Anjouan and Mohéli. Large antigovernment demonstrations shook the islands. A Koranic scholar, Abdallah Ibrahim, the leader of the Anjouani separatists, accused the Comorian government of abandoning Anjouan and of leaving the Anjouanis impoverished and underdeveloped. On 5 August 1997, Ibrahim, with the support of the majority of the Anjouanis, declared Anjouan independent of the Comoros. On 11 August the leaders of the Moheli people announced that their island would join the new state.

The separatist leaders declared that they would prefer independence or a return to French control; they refused to consider rejoining the coup-prone, impoverished Comoros. The French government refused to talk to the separatists and reiterated its support of the integrity of the Comoro Islands. A factional split among the separatists divided the movement into two groups, those favoring independence and the pro-French minority favoring a return to French rule.

The government on Grand Comoro dispatched troops to subdue the separatists on Anjouan, but the islanders repulsed the soldiers, killing many and taking 80 prisoners. The crisis led to yet another coup on Grand Comoro and the installation of a new military government. The Organization of African Unity (OAU) tried to mediate the conflict but made little progress. The OAU and the United Nations officially recognize Mahore as part of the Comoros federation, which the separatists point out is no more realistic than the Comoro government's claims upon Anjouan and Mohéli.

The new head of the Comoro state, Col. Azali Ansumani, in January

2000 ruled out elections in the country until a solution is found to the separatist crisis in the southern islands. Little information of the ongoing is available, as the government has cut telephone lines as part of its embargo of the secessionist islands. Separatist leaders have accused the Grand Comoro government of trying to starve the islands into submission and of having offered them little more than decades of poverty and coups. A new proposal for a loose federation of the islands of the Comoros was rejected by the Anjouanis in mid-2000 as not going far enough to address the separatists' demands.

A coup by pro-Comorian soldiers briefly overthrew the Anjouani separatist government in August 2001, but a counter-coup six weeks later reinstated the military group that had ruled Anjouan and Mohéli since 1997. The Anjouanis have refused mediation by the Organization of African States (OAS) on rejoining the Comoros, but their unsettled political status has added to the already serious economic and social problems in the islands.

SELECTED BIBLIOGRAPHY:

Djabir, Abdou. *The Comoros: A State in Construction*. 1997.
Kelly, Robert, ed. *Comoros Country Review 1999/2000*. 1999.
Newitt, Malyn. *The Comoro Islands: Struggle against Dependency in the Indian Ocean*. 1980.
Ottenheimer, Martin, and Harriet Ottenheimer. *Historical Dictionary of the Comoro Islands*. 1994.

Ankole

Banyankole; Banyankore; Nkole; Nkore; Ankore; Nyankole; Ulunyankole; Ulunyankore

POPULATION: Approximately (2002e) 3,608,000 Ankole in Uganda, divided into two cultural groups, the 2,084,000 Ankole and the 1,524,000 Kiga. Outside the homeland the only large community is in the Ugandan capital, Kampala.

THE ANKOLE HOMELAND: The Ankole homeland lies in southwestern Uganda, flat savanna west of Lake Edward and south of Lake George in the highland lakes district of East Africa. The fertile plains slope down to the wet lowlands toward Lake Victoria in the east. The only mountainous area is in the southwestern Kigezi region on the Rwanda border, the homeland of the Kigas. In 1993 nationalists unilaterally proclaimed the restoration of their former kingdom, but the government has yet to authorize the political changes necessary. The

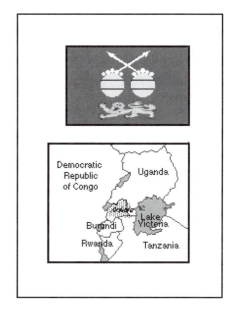

region, formerly the Southern Province, now forms the districts of Bushenyi, Mbarara, Kabale, Rakai, Ntungamo, and Rukungiri. *Kingdom of Ankole*: 8,062 sq. mi.—20,886 sq. km, (2002e) 3,437,000—Ankole 58%, Kiga 39%, other Ugandans 2%, Rwandans 1%. The Ankole capital and major cultural center is Mbarara, (2002e) 54,000, the historical capital of the kingdom. The other important cultural center is Kabale, (2002e) 38,000, the center of the Kiga.

FLAG: The Banyankole national flag, the flag of the former kingdom, is a green field bearing a crouching white lion surmounted by two white drumheads crossed by horizontal black stripes and backed by crossed white spears.

PEOPLE AND CULTURE: The Banyankole, called Ankole or Nkole, are an amalgamation of distinct peoples—the Iru, a Bantu agricultural people; the Hima, Nilotic pastoralists who account for some 5% of the population; and the Kiga, concentrated in the southwest region of Kigezi, a Bantu people closely related to the Bairu. The three peoples of the region mixed very little, and intermarriage was forbidden between the Nilotic Hima and the Bantu Iru and Kigauntil after Ugandan independence in 1962. The Hima are generally tall and have lighter skin and more aquiline features than the Bantu Iru and Kiga. They are generally believed to be the descendants of pastoralists who migrated to the region from the northeast. The Iru and Kiga are the descendants of agricultural populations that preceded the Hima in the region. Like the other Bantu peoples of southern Uganda, their origins can be traced to the Congo region. The three Ankole peoples are found in mixed populations throughout the southwest, and clan ties cut across historical differences, helping to unite the three people of the kingdom.

LANGUAGE AND RELIGION: The Ankole language is a Bantu language of the Southern Nyoro-Ganda group of Benue-Niger languages. The language, classified as a Western Lacustrine Bantu language, is spoken in four major dialects—Hororo, Orutagwenda, Hima, and Chiga. Chiga and Ankole are basically the same language, but, in Bantu fashion, each group calls it after its own name. Spoken in the southwestern districts, Kiga is 85–94% intelligible to speakers of central Ankole dialects. The Ankole language, although of clear Bantu origin, shares a Nilotic influence in vocabulary, particularly relating to animal husbandry. The language is used in primary schools and for local radio and newspapers. Education of children over 10 years old is in English. The standardized dialect of Nyankore-Chiga, the literary language of the Ankole-Chiga people, is called RuNyakitara and is taught at the regional university.

The majority of the Ankole profess Christianity and observe its rituals but continue to adhere to earlier spiritual beliefs. They consider the rituals of the different Christian sects, Islam, and their traditional religions all valuable sources of power. Many purchase and use charms to protect their homes, children, and gardens from curses. The spirits of ancestors or former kings are often called upon in times of trouble. The Catholic Church claims 38% of the population and the Anglican Church 55%, but in the 1990s evangelical Protestant sects began winning converts. About 5% of the population has a cultural commitment to Islam.

NATIONAL HISTORY: Bantu migrations from the northeast populated the region between 1000 and 1200 A.D. The Bantu farmers and fishermen, originally organized in village and clan groups, formed a unified state in the region in the fourteenth century, part of the semilegendary Bacwezi kingdom thought to have incorporated lands now in Uganda and northwestern Tanzania. The region grew rich on agriculture and trade. Around 1500, tall Nilotic herdsmen, the Hima, conquered the kingdom from the north and relegated the more advanced Bantu peoples to a serflike condition, forbidden to own cattle, which was the measure of wealth, or to intermarry with the Hima aristocracy.

Ankole legend tells of the first occupant of Ankole, Ruhanga the Creator, who is said to have come from heaven with three sons, Kairu, Kakama, and Kahima, to rule the earth. There is a story of how Ruhanga gave a test to determine which of his three sons would become the heir. The test consisted of keeping milk-filled pots on their laps throughout the night. At dawn, the youngest son, Kahima, had passed the test. Ruhanga ordered Kairu to serve his brother, leaving Kakama, or Rugaba as he was called, to rule in Ankole with the advice of Kahima. The legend portrayed the social stratification of Ankole society and gave the stratification divine sanction.

The Hima Abahinda dynasty based their wealth on herds of long-horned Ankole cattle tended by Iru herdsmen. The Hima aristocracy, headed by a king, the *omugabe*, formed a relationship with the Iru similar to that between the Tutsi and Hutu peoples of neighboring Rwanda. Later, the Kiga were incorporated into the kingdom under a system of provincial chiefs known as *abakuru d'ebyanga*. The Hima vested power in a royal drum, called the *Bahyendanwa*, revered as the symbol of Ankole nationhood; the belief was that as long as the drum remained in the kingdom, Ankole would prosper. Ankole society evolved with two separate but closely intertwined supports, the agricultural and the pastoral.

The Hima provided cattle products that would otherwise not have been available to farmers. Because the Hima population was much smaller than the Bantu population, the gifts and tribute demanded by the Nilotic aristocracy could be supplied fairly easily. These factors probably made Hima-Bantu relations tolerable, but they were reinforced by the superior military organization and training of the taller Hima warriors. By the end of the nineteenth century, particularly in outlying areas of the kingdom, the distinctions between the Hima and the Bantu agriculturists had lost their importance.

Originally Ankole was known as Kaaro-Karungi; the name "Ankole" was adopted during the seventeenth century during a devastating invasion by the Nyoros.* The kingdom recovered and expanded, incorporating the formerly independent kingdoms of Igara, Sheema, Buhweju, and parts of Mpororo.

European explorers visited the kingdom in the 1860s, amazed at the sophisticated and cultured societies they encountered in Ankole and the neighboring kingdoms. European missionaries followed the explorers and converted a majority of the population to Christianity, the Hima generally adopting Protestant beliefs and the Iru and Kiga mostly Roman Catholic.

British officials, in an attempt to cut off the arms trade with German East Africa, signed a treaty with Ankole in 1894 and then proceeded to proclaim the kingdom a British protectorate. The Ankole bitterly opposed British attempts to extend their authority to the kingdom; sporadic skirmishes culminated in a general uprising in 1897. Crushed by British troops sent from nearby colonies, Ankole's leaders signed a formal protectorate agreement that left most government functions to the *omugabe* and a partially elected assembly, the Eishengyero.

British colonial policy in the 1920s and 1930s greatly reduced the power of the king and the political independence of the Ankole kingdom. Unpopular British rule, more concerned with the economy than with the cherished trappings of monarchy, reduced Ankole to a vast labor pool. Ankole was less developed than other parts of British Uganda, and resentment fostered the rise of nationalism during World War II. Iru activists, seeking to exploit British rule, formed the Kumayana Movement in the early 1950s and demanded that the British authorities end Hima domination and disparities in the allocation of local government jobs and in education. The Iru rights movement later merged with the growing Ankole national movement.

The kingdoms of southern Uganda increasingly opposed inclusion in Uganda as the British territory moved toward independence in the decade after World War II. The growing opposition to domination by Uganda's non-Bantu northern tribes pushed the Hima, Iru, and Chiga to bury old differences and begin to identify with Ankole nationalism. In the late 1950s, agitation for autonomy or separate independence swept the kingdom, but after extensive negotiations the Ankole finally accepted semifederal status within independent Uganda.

The independence government of Milton Obote, a non-Bantu northerner installed as Uganda's first president in 1962, quickly moved to curtail the powers of the southern kingdoms, over vehement Bantu opposition. In 1966, amid growing tension and moves toward secession, the Obote government ended all Ankole autonomy and in 1967 abolished the four southern Bantu kingdoms.

Firmly opposed to the Obote government, most Ankole supported the revolt, led by Idi Amin Dada, that overthrew Obote in 1971. Quickly disillusioned with the mercurial Dada, whose administration became even more repressive than Obote's, the Ankole withdrew their support. Following an abortive secessionist revolt in 1972, Dada loosed his mainly Muslim army on Ankole. Thousands died in brutal massacres, and refugees streamed across the borders into Zaire and Rwanda. Its leadership decimated, murdered, or disappeared, the Ankole national movement collapsed.

Idi Amin Dada, one of Africa's most brutal dictators, was finally overthrown in April 1979 and fled the country, but several successor governments lasted only short periods until Milton Obote again became president of Uganda in 1980. The Ankole, with vivid memories of Obote's earlier rule, gave their support to a southern Bantu rebel movement led by an ethnic Ankole Hima, Yoweri Musaveni. The rebels drove Obote from office in 1986 and installed Musaveni as the head of Uganda's first Bantu-dominated government.

Relative peace since 1986 has, paradoxically, allowed Ankole nationalism to resurface even though firmly opposed by President Musaveni. Led by the more militant Protestant minority, the nationalist movement is buoyed by nostalgia for the former monarchy and the memories of the peace and prosperity the kingdom enjoyed until 1967. Ankole nationalism is sustained by the belief that an independent Ankole would have been spared the horrors and desolation of the years since 1962.

In 1992 the Ugandan government announced a radical decentralization of government, transferring power to councils in local areas, prompting calls for the restoration of the Ankole kingdom. In July 1993 a new law restored all the former Bantu kingdoms except for Ankole. Firmly opposed to the restoration of the Ankole kingdom, President Musaveni refused to listen to Ankole arguments. In November 1993, in defiance of the president, John Barigye was crowned king, and the restoration of the kingdom declared. The proclamation, declared illegal by the Musaveni government, set off a serious crisis between the Ankole government, backed by the nationalists, and Uganda's central government.

The Bantu majority of Ankole support the restoration of the monarchy as a means of safeguarding their unique culture but have refused to consider the restoration of the Hima institutions of domination that formerly were an integral part of the monarchy. In February 2000, President Museveni stated that he would consider the restoration of the monarchy if the majority of the people in the concerned districts demanded it. The Nkore Cultural Trust (NCT), a pro-monarchy organization, began consulting leading members of the Ankole community about the delayed process of restoring the Ankole monarchy. Nationalists want the restoration of the monarchy partly for tradition but also to unite the Ankole people, as politics and religion have failed to do.

The Ankole remain bitterly divided over the future of their homeland. Some want a restoration of the kingdom and autonomy or independence, others, mostly non-Ankole, but also many Ankole, in the outer areas of the old kingdom, reject the monarchy but support greater autonomy. In 2001 nationalists proposed the creation of a new Ankole to include the Ankole-populated districts of Mbarara, Bushenyi, and Ntungamo. Nationalists also claim the Rujumbura and Rubado counties of Rukungiri District, which is inhabited by ethnic Ankole.

Economic and political instability in the Great Lakes region of Africa has fueled the growth of Ankole nationalism. The prohibition on political organizations in Uganda and a lack of even the traditional democratic traditions of the Ankole kingdom makes nationalism an attractive alternative to many young Ankole. The largest nationalist organization, the Banyankore Cultural Foundation (BCF), although openly nationalist, rejects the monarchy as an antiquated caste system that divided Ankole into classes or castes. Reviving the monarchy, according to the group, means reviving social injustice and endangering the unity that has been growing in Ankole.

SELECTED BIBLIOGRAPHY:

Bwengye, Francis. *The Agony of Uganda: From Idi Amin to Obote.* 1986.

Doornbos, Martin R. *Not All the King's Men: Inequality as a Political Instrument in Ankole, Uganda.* 1979.

Karugire, Samwiri Rubaraza. *A History of the Kingdom of Nkore in Western Uganda to 1896.* 1988.

Mukherjee, Ramkrishna. *Uganda: A Historical Accident? Class, Nation, State Formation.* 1985.

Antilleans

Netherlands Antilleans

POPULATION: Approximately (2002e) 276,000 Antilleans, mostly concentrated in the five Caribbean islands of the Netherlands Antilles but with a sizable community of over 60,000 living in the Netherlands.

THE ANTILLEAN HOMELAND: The Antillean homeland is made up of five islands divided into two widely separated groups of islands in the Caribbean. The northern group lies at the northern end of the Lesser Antilles chain and consists of Sint Eustatius, the southern part of Saint Martin, called Sint Maarten, and Saba. The southern islands lie about 500 miles (800 kilometers) to the southwest, off the coast of Venezuela, and consist of Bonaire and Curaçao. *Federation of the Netherlands Antilles (Nederlandse Antillen/Antianan Ulandes)*: 371 sq. mi.—961 sq. km, (2002e) 248,000—Antillean 84%, white 6%, other West Indians 5%, Surinamese 3%. The Antillean capital and major cultural center is Willemstad, on Curaçao, (2002e) 58,000, urban area 143,000, the capital of the federation. Other important cultural centers are Kralendijk, (2002e) 9,000, on Bonaire, and Philipsburg (2002e) 7,000, on Saint Martin.

FLAG: The Antillean is a white field with a blue horizontal stripe over a red vertical stripe charged with five small white stars. The flag of Curaçao is a blue field with a horizontal yellow stripe and two white stars on the hoist. The flag of Bonaire has orange, white, and blue diagonal stripes.

PEOPLE AND CULTURE: The racially mixed population includes strains of European, African, East Asian, and Native American stock. The predominantly black population of the northern group more closely resembles the population and culture of its English-speaking neighbors,

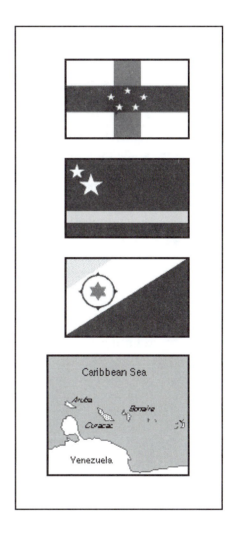

while the population of Curaçao and Bonaire, with stronger ties to Venezuela, show a marked Latin influence. Whites form small minorities on all the islands except Saba, where the population is about half white and half black. The Antilleans have a relatively high standard of living by comparison with other Caribbean peoples. Birth and death rates are low compared to other developing nations, and school attendance and literacy are high. More than 90% of the population is urban, and about three-quarters of the population lives on Curaçao, the most populous of the islands, (2002e) 181,000. Sint Maarten and Bonaire have populations of about 46,000 and 17,000 respectively, and the smaller islands have populations of less than 2,000 each.

LANGUAGE AND RELIGION: Dutch is the official language but is not widely spoken. The language of the southern islands, Papiamento or Papiamentu, also called Curaçoleño or Curassese, is commonly used, as is Spanish. Papiamento is a creole language, a mixture of Spanish, Portuguese, and Dutch, with about 25% of its vocabulary of Dutch origin. The language is spoken in three main dialects, which correspond to the three southern islands—Curaçao, Bonaire, and Aruba. Papiamento is taught during the first two years of primary school, although the language has no official status. English is also spoken, especially in the northern group, but throughout the federation the inability to speak Dutch hinders social and political mobility.

About three-fourths of the Antillean population is Roman Catholic, and a tenth belong to various Protestant denominations, mostly Lutheran, Dutch Reformed, and Methodist. There is a small Jewish community, said to be the oldest continuous Jewish community in the Americas. Many traditions brought to the islands by black slaves remain as religious or folk traditions, often mixed with Christian customs.

NATIONAL HISTORY: Peaceful Arawaks inhabited the southern islands prior to the European colonization of the Caribbean, while warlike Caribs populated Sint Maarten and the northern islands. Christopher Columbus reportedly sighted the northern islands in 1493. In 1499, Alonzo de Ojeda, a Spanish explorer, landed on Curaçao, and in 1527 the Spanish authorities took possession of Curaçao and Bonaire. Spanish rule did little to develop the islands but decimated the native peoples, who survived only in small, isolated pockets.

Soldiers in the employ of the Dutch East India Company captured Curaçao in 1634, and the first Dutch settlers arrived to colonize Curaçao and Bonaire in the next year. Curaçao was established as an entrepôt for the flourishing trade of the region, and Bonaire became the center of the growing trade in slaves, imported to work the European farms and plantations. On Sint Maarten, in 1648, Dutch and French prisoners of war, released by the departing Spanish administration, amicably divided the island, which was later recognized by a treaty between the Dutch and French governments.

The small island of Sint Eustatius, first colonized by the French and English in 1625, was taken by the Dutch in 1632. It became the center of the slave trade in the eastern Caribbean and by 1780 had a prosperous capital at Oranjestad. In 1781, the British sacked and burned the town after it gave the new United States flag its first salute by a foreign power. Nearby Saba, settled in 1632, never achieved any economic importance because of its inaccessibility and rugged landscape.

Except for brief periods of British rule during the Napoleonic Wars, the southern islands have remained Dutch since the seventeenth century. The northern islands, called the Windward Islands, changed owners numerous times but remained under Dutch control after the beginning of the nineteenth century. From 1828 to 1845 the islands were governed from Dutch Suriname, on the South American mainland. In 1845, the five islands and Aruba were formed into the separate colony of the Netherlands Antilles.

The emancipation of slaves in the Dutch islands in 1863 was a blow to the economy, particularly the lucrative slave trade. The island economies did not recover until the early twentieth century, with the discovery of the Venezuelan oil fields. In 1915 Shell Oil Company opened the first installation to refine Venezuelan oil. Others followed, and oil became the leading industry.

Venezuelan rebels in 1929 occupied Willemstad and claimed the southern islands as part of Venezuela's national territory before being driven out by Dutch police. The northern islands, with less population and industry, lived mostly on subsistence farming. The Dutch government in the 1930s began to develop all the islands to forestall radical political movements or claims by other governments.

The Nazi conquest of the Netherlands during World War II left the islands virtually independent. A competent government in Willemstad took control and extended its authority to the other islands. German submarines shelled the oil refineries in 1942, but generally the islands prospered with the increased demand for oil.

After World War II, negotiations began with the aim of conferring greater autonomy upon the island populations. The Netherlands Antilles Regulation, passed in 1951, provided for internal autonomy for the islands. On 15 December 1954, a charter was signed making the Dutch Caribbean islands an autonomous part of the Kingdom of the Netherlands.

The tourism boom of the 1960s provided needed income for each of the islands. The northern island territory of Sint Maarten, along with Curaçao, became an important stop for Caribbean cruise ships, but increased prosperity led to serious labor agitation. In 1969 labor conflicts on Curaçao resulted in rioting and arson, aggravated by separatist and racial tension. The rioting damaged the important tourist industry, and the islands recovered only in the mid-1970s. Curaçao developed into a major trade and financial business center in the Caribbean.

The decolonization of the Caribbean fueled the growth of nationalism in the 1970s, as neighboring islands gained independence. Discussions on complete independence were held intermittently. The Netherlands government began severing links to the islands, but the Antilleans, among the most prosperous in the Caribbean region, feared the economic consequences of independence. The Dutch authorities pressed for independence but insisted on preserving a federated structure embracing all the islands. In an unofficial referendum in 1977, the Arubans* voted to secede from the Antilles federation. In 1986 Aruba seceded but remained within the Netherlands.

By 1978 all the islands had accepted the concept of self-determination. Saba and Sint Eustatius, during the 1979 elections, refused to nominate candidates, in protest against the domination of the federation by Curaçao. In 1980, preparatory talks were held on independence referenda, which were to be held on each of the islands in 1988. Economic problems and the separation of Aruba led to delays, and the referenda were later postponed. The inhabitants of the smaller islands indicated that they preferred continued Dutch rule to independence in a federation dominated by Curaçao.

In 1989 the political leaders of Sint Maarten announced the island's desire to achieve full independence in the shortest possible time. Secessionist feelings on the islands were mostly fueled by animosity toward the central administration in Curaçao. Public protests erupted on Sint Maarten in 1993 because of dissatisfaction with how the local council was running the island's affairs, particularly their utilities. Efforts to placate secessionist sentiment in the islands by increasing insular autonomy have kept the federation together.

The Antilleans are largely self-governing, in the sense that only a limited number of responsibilities, such as foreign affairs and defense, remain the prerogative of the Dutch government—and the federation participates in them as well. During the mid-1990s, Antillean voters on all five islands approved measures to keep their islands within the Antilles federation. In November 1993 the people of Curaçao voted overwhelmingly not to follow the Arubans in separating from the federation but to remain a part of the Antilles federation. The governments of Curaçao and Sint Maarten collapsed in June 1994, pointing up continuing instability in the local island governments. In October 1994, the Antilleans of Bonaire, Saba, Sint Eustatius, and Sint Maarten followed the example of the inhabitants of Curaçao and voted to remain within the federation.

The federation government continues to fight for the cohesion of the islands and opposes separatist tendencies in the far-flung members. Each of the islands is largely autonomous, particularly in cultural matters, allowing the Antilleans of each island to develop as they wish. In spite of reassurances and offers of increased autonomy within the federation, the inhabitants of Sint Maarten, in June 2000, voted to separate from the Netherlands Antilles, which could lead to the breakup of the Caribbean federation into five separate states.

SELECTED BIBLIOGRAPHY:

Kruijt, Dirk. *Development and Poverty in the Netherlands Antilles: A Policy Evaluation of Sede Antia.* 1998.

Marshall, Nelson. *Understanding the Eastern Caribbean and the Antilles.* 1992.

Schoenhals, Kai, ed. *Netherlands Antilles and Aruba.* 1993.

Sedoc-Dahlberg, Betty, ed. *The Dutch Caribbean: Prospects for Democracy.* 1990.

Antioquians

Paisas; Antioqueños

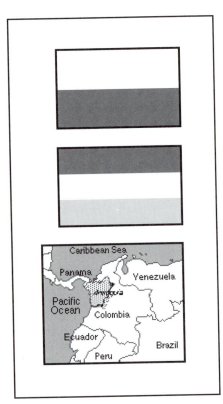

POPULATION: Approximately (2002e) 8,480,000 Antioquians in the Americas, concentrated in the Antioquian provinces of Colombia. Smaller communities live in other regions of Colombia, in other Central and South American states, and in the United States.

THE ANTIOQUIAN HOMELAND: The Antioquian homeland lies in northwestern Colombia, a mountainous region of high valleys in the Andes Mountains, extending west and north into the coastal lowlands on the Atlantic Ocean and the Caribbean Sea. Antioquia, as defined by nationalists, forms the Colombian departments of Antioquia, Caldas, Chocó, Quindío, Risaralda, and the northeastern districts of Valle Department. *Region of Antioquia (Region Antioquiana)*: 45,516 sq. mi.—123,098 sq. km, (2002e) 9,215,000—Antioquian 89%, other Colombian 11%. The Antioquian capital and major cultural center is Medellín, the capital of the department of Antioquia, (2002e) 2,201,000, metropolitan area 2,821,000.

FLAG: The Antioquian national flag, the official flag of Antioquia Department, is a vertical bicolor of white over green. The flag of the national movement is a vertical tricolor of green, white, and yellow.

PEOPLE AND CULTURE: The Antioquians, popularly called Paisas, are mostly descended from sixteenth-century Basque and Jewish refugees from Spain. Rejecting Indian and Negro slavery from the start, the Antioquians have remained a basically European culture, with little mixing with neighboring groups. They are readily recognizable in Colombia by their dress, diet, and speech. The Antioquians form the most important social group outside the Colombian capital, Bogotá; they include the Andean population who migrated from Antioquia south along the Cordilleras during the nineteenth century. The Antioquian birthrate, possibly the world's highest, with families of up to sixteen children, has rapidly increased the population and led to the expansion of the Antioquians from their core area, but without intermarriage with other Colombians or the loss of population at the center, a highly unusual phenomenon in Latin America. The Antioquians tend to feel superior to the other inhabitants of Colombia, seeing themselves as a first-world nation in a third-world country.

LANGUAGE AND RELIGION: Isolated in the valleys of the high Andes, the Antioquians developed a unique culture and preserved the purest Spanish spoken in the Americas. The Antioquian dialect, which preserves many words and forms that have disappeared from most other Spanish dialects, is closer to the Spanish spoken in southern Spain up to the middle of the nineteenth century.

The Antioquians are devoutly Roman Catholic, their religion forming an important part of their culture. Religious traditions and customs brought by the early settlers from Europe have been retained, including festivals and observances that have disappeared in Spain. In recent years Protestant sects have made inroads in the region.

NATIONAL HISTORY: The region was inhabited by various tribal groups when the first Spanish conquistadors, Rodrigo de Bastidas and Juan de la Cosa, explored the area from the Gulf of Urabá in 1500 and 1501. Refugee Basques and Jews, forced to convert to Catholicism and fleeing persecution in Spain, arrived in the New World in the 1530s. Deliberately choosing isolation in the Andean highlands, the refugees settled in newly discovered high valleys accessible only by mule trails through difficult mountain passes.

The immigrants founded the town of Antioquia in 1541 and took the name of the town as that of their new homeland. The isolated Antioquians were unusual in several ways—a very high birthrate, a refusal to intermarry with other Spanish groups during the colonial period, and their rejection of slavery. Dividing the land in the European manner, the Antioquians settled on small family farms that they worked themselves.

The Antioquians lived in isolation for over three centuries, a prosperous farming and mining community. The Antioquian heartland received no new immigrants after the first wave of arrivals, but unusually large families increased the population rapidly. In their first century they increased from less than 100,000 to over two million. The prolific Antioquians soon expanded in all directions from the original settlements, taking with them their unique culture and their strong ties to the Antioquian nation.

The region, rich in minerals, particularly gold, became an important mining center in the seventeenth century. Smuggling developed as a means to avoid paying the Spanish king his fifth of the value of gold exports, and it remains a tradition in the area to the present. Political instability in the

Spanish possessions reinforced the Antioquian desire for isolation and fostered a culture of independence.

Antioquia was included in the Federation of New Granada when Spanish rule ended in 1819. The Antioquians at first moved to separate themselves from the new state, but their leaders were persuaded to accept substantial autonomy rather than to follow Ecuador and Venezuela in seceding from the federation. The Colombian constitution of 1855 created a loose confederation of autonomous states, satisfying Antioquian demands for extensive self-government. A bloody civil war between 1860 and 1862 was fought between the procentralists and the federalists, who sought a loose federation of independent states. Another rebellion broke out in Antioquia in 1876, led by conservative forces.

The Antioquian population expansion continued to spread along the fertile mountain valleys. Manizales was founded in 1848, Pereira in 1863, and Armenia as late as 1889. To dilute the power of the expanding Antioquian homeland and to undermine national sentiment in the region, the Colombian government instituted a policy of separation. The regions of Caldas, Risaralda, and Quindío were hived off from Antioquia as they became settled; however, the inhabitants of these new departments retained their Antioquian identities.

The abolition of state sovereignty in 1886 led to a sharp deterioration in the relations between the Antioquian provinces and the central government in Bogota. In 1899, civil war erupted between advocates of a loose confederation and supporters of a strong central government. Antioquian rebels, many demanding secession, continued to fight government troops until they were finally subdued in 1902. Government suppression of nationalist and regionalist tendencies escalated following civil war and the secession of neighboring Panama in 1903.

After 1914, the completion of the Panama Canal and the arrival of the railroad led to rapid economic growth and the industrialization of the Antioquian provinces. Coffee, introduced around the turn of the century, brought stability to the Antioquian expansion; twenty years later the Antioquian provinces were producing the majority of Colombia's exported coffee. Textiles, produced in Antioquia's growing industrial cities, followed coffee as the region's major product.

Devoutly Roman Catholic, prosperous, and middle-class, the Antioquian provinces were profoundly shaken by *La Violencia*, the civil war that engulfed Colombia from 1946 to 1958. The conflict marked the beginning of modern Antioquian nationalism and raised demands for autonomy, even independence, in order to escape Colombia's chronic instability. Although many of Colombia's politicians and leaders came from the Antioquian provinces, the population of the Andean homeland remained a nation within a nation.

In the 1960s, the Antioquians spread into the highlands above Cali in the Cauca Valley, and in 1966 yet another region was split off, to form the Department of Risaralda. The growing industrialization of the Antioquian provinces produced some highly progressive social schemes, including model housing estates for industrial workers. The Antioquian economy began to falter in the late 1970s, damaged by industrial recession and the end of the coffee boom. A new boom crop, drawing on the Antioquian tradition of smuggling contraband, appeared—drugs.

This new growth industry, taken up by the lowest rungs of Antioquian society in the 1960s, spread through the Antioquian provinces during the economic recession of the late 1970s, and by the late 1980s it involved all social classes. The developed, prosperous Antioquian provinces rapidly degenerated into a killing ground for various armed groups—the military, leftist guerrillas, and gangs in the pay of local drug barons. The drug producers in the 1960s backed fanatical anticommunist death squads in a spiraling local "dirty war" with Marxist guerrillas operating in the mountainous regions in the south.

Since the early 1980s, the Antioquian provinces have experienced a "positive revolution" due to the drug money pumped into the regional economy, affecting, directly or indirectly, over 15% of the economically active population of Colombia. Illegal drugs have created wealth and jobs, and they have allowed hundreds of thousands of Antioquians to escape poverty. The region has a dynamic, drug-fueled economy, in a continent with chronic financial problems, but at a very high price in destroyed lives and property.

The Antioquian heartland, near the Panamanian border, is the hub of the Colombian drug trade. The drug-related groups have ensured that few guerrilla organizations operate in the area, an achievement that has won them some popular support among the Antioquians, who are weary after decades of civil war. Even the United States, which presses the Colombian government on drug eradication in the southern regions, has mostly ignored the Antioquian drug lords since the mid-1990s.

The Colombian government has pursued an unannounced coexistence with the drug barons of the Antioquian region. The drug producers control television and radio stations, car dealerships, supermarkets, office buildings, discount drug stores, and at least six professional soccer teams. The government in Bogota has refrained from confronting the powerful drug barons, fearing that if pressed they might support Antioquian separatism.

In the 1990s, small nongovernmental groups began to organize against the ills they saw as results of the breakdown in Colombian security, but the groups themselves were seen by the Colombian government as subversive. Historically isolated, the Antioquians feel that the problems of modern Colombia have been magnified in their homeland, the most prosperous and efficient in the country. The powerful drug lords have much support among the urban poor and the corrupt political class but little among the predominantly middle-class and clannish Antioquians.

The region remains mostly agricultural, and European pattern of farming family properties persist. The small-to-medium-sized farms are a notable exception to the inequality conspicuous in Colombia outside the Antioquian region, where the top 10% of society holds 80% of the land. Besides their industries, the Antioquians produce an agricultural surplus in a country where other areas of which are unable to feed themselves. Many complain that they feed the country, receiving little but violence and instability in return.

Antioquian nationalists view the drug barons as foreigners in their homeland and point to the fact that even in Medellin, with its rows of luxury apartment blocks, the standard of living has fallen. The region's famed textile mills are working well below capacity, and the factories face declining prospects. Skilled workers are unemployed or work as waiters or domestics. Emigration, particularly to the United States, has increased dramatically. Critics claim that beneath the superficial prosperity most of the drug profits have been invested outside Antioquia, primarily in more developed countries.

The region's geographical isolation and distinctive historical experiences have fostered a strong regional loyalty. Narco-terrorism is destroying the democratic tradition of Colombia that allowed an outlet for Antioquian regionalism. Antioquian nationalists, who claim that their homeland is paying for past government mistakes, admit that independence and the elimination of the drug trade would bring a massive economic depression but are adamant that with international assistance Antioquia, which resembles Europe to a remarkable degree, would rank among the hemisphere's richest states within three to five years.

The Colombian government's policy of ceding autonomy to leftist guerrilla groups in the south of the country increased demands for autonomy for the traditional Antioquian provinces in northern Colombia. In early 2000 there were demonstrations across the region demanding the same treatment as the enjoyed by the murderous, drug-trafficking guerrilla groups.

The sense of Antioquian isolation continues, with roads to the coast and other parts of Colombia often blocked by guerrilla groups or government paramilitaries. The traditional of federalist, anti-clerical liberalism remains a strong strain in the region. Although the Antioquian provinces are not coca producers, the drug industry, rebel guerrilas, and equally violent paramilitaries have disrupted national life across the region. The violence has mostly been confined to the rural areas, but in early 2001 a series of bomb blasts in Medellin and other cities alarmed the complacent urban majority. Unstable Colombia gains momentum each time violence erupts support for separation from violent, unstable Colombia gains momentum.

SELECTED BIBLIOGRAPHY:

Brew, R. J. *Aspects of Politics in Antioquia, 1850–1865.* 1977.
Kline, Harvey F. *Colombia: Portrait of Unity and Diversity.* 1983.
Oquist, Paul. *Violence, Conflict and Politics in Colombia.* 1980.
Vellinga, Menno. *Industrialization and Regional Development in Colombia.* 1988.

Anyi
Agni; Anyin; Sefwi; Sehwi

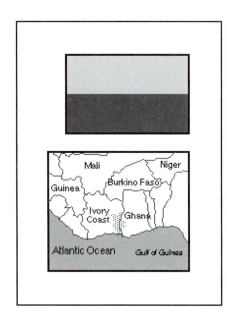

POPULATION: Approximately (2002e) 1,720,000 Anyi in West Africa, about 1,375,000 in the Côte d'Ivoire (the Ivory Coast), and 240,000 in Ghana. Outside the homeland, the largest Anyi population lives in and around the Ivorian capital, Abidjan.

THE ANYI HOMELAND: The Anyi homeland lies in coastal West Africa on the border between the Côte d'Ivoire and Ghana. The region is mostly tropical forest, the remnants of the once-vast rain forests, with wetlands along the coast. Due to the arbitrary division of colonial territories, the Anyi homeland is divided between the Côte d'Ivoire and Ghana, with about 80% in the Côte d'Ivoire and 20% in Ghana. The Anyi region of Ghana lies between the international border west of the Tano River. The majority of the Anyi population remains rural, while the region's cities have mixed populations, including large Baule elements. The homeland includes territory in the Aboisso, Abengourou, Agnibilekrou, Tanda, M'bahiakro, and Daoukro Departments of the Côte d'Ivoire and the Anyi-Nzima region of the Western Province of Ghana. The homeland has a population of about 1,800,000. The Anyi capital and major cultural center is the city of Abengourou, (2002e) 96,000, the capital of the kingdom of Indenié and residence of the Anyi paramount chief. The other major cultural center is Abiosso, the capital of the kingdom of Sanwi, (2002e) 41,000. The major cultural center of the Anyi in Ghana is the town of Enyi, (2002e) 21,000.

FLAG: The Anyi national flag, the flag of the national movement, is a vertical bicolor of gold over red.

PEOPLE AND CULTURE: The Anyi are a Bantu people of the Akan subgroup, closely related to the Ashanti* of central Ghana. Its six major ethnic divisions—Sanwi, Betie, Indenié, Aboure, and Abron in Ivory Coast, and Nzima in Ghana—and a number of subclans inhabit both sides of the international border. The Anyi are a matriarchal people, an Anyi man inherits his status and property from his mother's brother; women have a relatively high social status in both the political and economic lives of the nation. In recent years the Ivorian government has tried to change Anyi inheritance traditions, but with only limited success. Most Anyi live in neighborhoods of family housing complexes or in dispersed homesteads of nomadic cultivators producing cocoa and coffee. Although they have accepted many aspects of European material culture, the traditional elements of their social structure remain the basis of Anyi political organization. The Anyi have a highly stratified society that includes a hierarchical political administration; also, as in other Akan nations, the ownership of a symbolic chair or stool remains central to Anyi political life. The ritual stools are seen as vital to the existence of the Anyi nation.

LANGUAGE AND RELIGION: The Anyi speak dialects of Anyi-Ashanti, a Kwa language of the Tano group of the Niger-Congo language family. The language, like Chinese, is a tonal language and is spoken in thirteen dialects, three of which—Aowin (also called Brissa or Brosa), Sehwi, and Nzima or Nzema—are mostly spoken in Ghana. The most important dialects are Sanvi, Indenyé, and Moronou. The Anyi are mostly bilingual, speaking their own language along with the official national languages, French in the Côte d'Ivoire and English in Ghana. Historically, the Anyi language existed only in oral form. Various people, mainly trying to make Bible portions available, have tried to introduce written forms of the language, but none have taken root and been widely accepted. The New Testament, published in the Anyi Sanvi dialect, which was dedicated in April 1998, was the first major document published in any of the Anyi dialects.

The majority of the Anyi respect and practice elements of their traditional religious beliefs, although officially they are divided—about 50% Roman Catholic, 15% Muslim, and 5% Protestant, particularly in Ghana, the remainder adhering to traditional beliefs. Organized religions, particularly Catholicism, which maintains a bishopric in Abengourou, have greatly influenced the Anyi, who accept Christianity or Islam; most, however, still venerate ancestors and spirits that live in rocks, trees, and rivers. Islam has made inroads in the cities and towns but has only marginally infiltrated the villages. Traditionally, the Anyi have shown indifference toward Islam. An estimated 75% of the Anyi, whatever their professed religion, participate in traditional religious ceremonies and rituals.

NATIONAL HISTORY: The forefathers of the Anyi people presumably bore the name Nta and came from the Black Volta region. Various Akan peoples, moving from the east between the eleventh and thirteenth centuries, settled in the forest zone along the coast and mostly absorbed the small tribes already living there. The rise of the early Akan states began in the thirteenth century, probably related to the opening of trade routes established to move gold throughout the region. Gradually brought under the rule of the expanding Ashanti, the tribes became part of the powerful Ashanti confederation in the late seventeenth and eighteenth centuries.

Small clan and tribal groups began moving west in the sixteenth century, but the great Anyi migration came in the mid-eighteenth century. The wars associated with the rise of the Ashanti in the late seventeenth century led to the migration of numerous Akan groups into the forest country of the southeast, where they created a number of small city-states. To increase the size and power of their states, refugees and immigrants were welcomed. Exogamy, the practice of marrying outside one's clan, was encouraged or required. The practice also served to absorb surrounding peoples.

Around 1740, following a dispute with the dominant Ashanti, the Anyi moved westward out of the confederation and in their new homeland established four distinct kingdoms—Sanwi, Moronou, and Indenié in present Côte d'Ivoire, and Comoenou in Ghana. The kingdoms, never as powerful as the neighboring peoples, were often under the indirect rule of the Ashanti and Baule peoples. The Anyi installed themselves mostly between the Tano and the Comoé Rivers. As they prospered and successive waves arrived in the region, the Anyi principally filled the area between the Tano and Comoé Rivers from Aboisso in the south, then along the eastern side of the Comoé from the Abengourou area into the northern plains.

The Anyi kings, called *ohenes*, each possessed a royal stool, the incarnation of the sovereignty and dignity of their respective kingdoms. The kingships were closely tied to the Anyi culture and religion; the Anyi states were administered by an aristocratic bureaucracy that governed subordinate tribes and regulated the labor of the slaves captured from less advanced peoples to the north. The kingdoms established trade and cultural ties as far away as present Nigeria, while carrying on a long series of wars with the rival Baule tribe to the west.

The Anyi were particularly successful at assimilating other groups into their political organization, with the result that many present Anyi trace their ancestry both to Anyi chiefdoms and to smaller, distinct societies that fell under Anyi control. One mechanism of Anyi assimilation was by grouping semiautonomous chiefdoms under an Anyi paramount chief.

Europeans visited the coastal regions as early as the sixteenth century, but the Anyi kingdoms, established in the eighteenth century, had little contact with colonial powers until the early nineteenth century. In 1842 the French established a fort at Assini and signed with the Sanwi kingdom a treaty providing for the cession of the land around the fort in exchange for tribute. A year later, threatened by the resurgent Ashanti, the Sanwi king, Amon Ndoffou, placed his kingdom under French military protection. The advancing Ashanti conquered the Nzima kingdom, Comoenou, but the French halted further Ashanti incursions. French explorers, missionaries, trading companies, and soldiers extended French control to the interior regions, extending protectorate status to the inland Anyi kingdoms in 1887.

During European colonization, land occupied by the Anyi along the Comoé River was territory claimed by the French and later became the Republic of Côte d'Ivoire. However, Anyi land adjacent to the Tano River was in territory controlled by the British and later became Ghana.

The final British conquest of Ashantiland in 1900 ended the Ashanti threat to the Anyi kingdoms. No longer in need of French protection, the Anyi tried to reassert their independence but failed to dislodge the French military. The Anyi peoples, traditionally holding their lands in common, fiercely resisted French efforts to acquire land for export crops. French land taxes and demands for forced labor pushed the Anyi to rebel during World War I. Anyi resistance collapsed as the French artillery reduced village after village; the rebels finally surrendered in 1916.

The Anyi kingdoms were administered as part of the French Ivory Coast after World War I. Under French influence the Anyi became the most advanced of the tribes in the colony, and eventually the most pro-French. Under Vichy rule following the fall of France in 1940, many Anyi crossed into the British Gold Coast to join the Free French, and they helped the Free French forces to liberate their homeland from the Vichy French in 1943. Although the Anyi welcomed the returning Free French authorities, the kingdoms remained the focus of Anyi loyalty.

In 1948 severe rioting erupted over French attempts to interfere in the succession to the throne of Indenié. The Anyi claimed that their treaties with France covered only military matters and demanded the separation of the Anyi homeland from the Ivory Coast as a separate Anyi state in French West Africa.

Anyi nationalism grew rapidly in the 1950s, fanned by conflicts with the colony's predominant Baule tribe. Early in 1959, as it became clear that the Ivory Coast colony would become an autonomous state, King Amon Ndoffou II of Sanwi asserted the Anyi right to separate independence based on the 1843 and 1887 treaties. The king established a provisional government and sent emissaries to Paris to argue the Anyi case for separation.

The French government rebuffed the Anyi delegation, and the Anyi kingdoms moved toward secession. In early 1960, as the Ivory Coast prepared for the independence scheduled for August, the Anyi nationalists mobilized. On 5 February 1960, the king of Sanwi declared his kingdom independent of France and the Ivory Coast. The other Anyi kingdoms voted to join Sanwi in an independent Anyi state, provoking an armed response from the new Ivorian government. Unable to halt Ivorian soldiers moving into the region, many Anyi fled to Ghana, but the Sanwi king and over 400 supporters were arrested. King Amon Ndoffou II and his head of government, Ehoumou Bile, received prison sentences of 10 years followed by 20 years of banishment. In 1962 the Ivorian government, to quell separatist disturbances, released the king and the other Anyi political prisoners, but it banned all Anyi tribal rituals.

Ivorian recognition of the secessionist republic of Biafra of the Ibos* in 1969 provoked a new crisis in Anyiland. Nationalists claimed the same right the Ivorian government had acknowledged in Biafra and prepared to declare independence in December 1969. The secessionists hoped to demonstrate Anyi autonomy from the powerful Baule tribe. Ivorian soldiers moved in quickly to crush the movement, carrying out a secret war denied by the Ivorian government. It is still not known how long the operation lasted or how many Anyi died in the conflict and the repression that followed.

The one-party Ivorian state allowed little dissent or opposition until faced with a severe economic and political crisis in 1989–90. Anyi nationalists, suppressed for nearly two decades, organized amid the growing tumult. In 1991 nationalist leaders asserted that the Anyi kingdoms, separate French protectorates until forcibly incorporated into the Ivorian state in 1960, had a legal right to decide democratically whether to continue their ties to the Côte d'Ivoire or to separate under the terms of the protectorate agreements of the nineteenth centuries. The death on 7 December 1993 of Félix Houphouet-Boigny, the president of the Côte d'Ivoire since independence, released long-suppressed regional and tribal rivalries in the country.

Traditionally the Anyi have not been highly mobile, but a trend began in the late 1990s for the youth and those without land to leave the homeland for education or work. New influences and global nationalist resurgence since the end of the Cold War have fueled the growth of regional and national sentiment in the region. Ethnic violence has become more common, particularly against non-Anyi who settled in the region since the 1960s, many from outside the Côte d'Ivoire.

Government efforts to stifle dissidence and opposition to the continuing Baule domination of the country led to a severe political crisis and serious riots in late 1999. The Côte d'Ivoire, once one of Africa's economic success stories, slowly collapsed in a severe economic and political crisis. The military coup that deposed the civilian government in late December 1999, for the first time in the country's history, was sparked by a dispute over military pay but also reflected the rising regional and tribal tension. The United States, Canada, and other Western nations suspended bilateral assistance and all arms transfers to the Ivorian government.

The instability spreading across the country provoked increasingly violent ethnic and regional confrontations in 2000. The major divide, roughly between the Muslim north and the Christian south, was made more serious by the dramatic growth of tribal and regional identities that had been submerged for decades.

Political instability, coupled with a sharp decline in prosperity since 1985, have fueled a resurgence of Anyi nationalism and calls for the recognition of the Anyi kingdoms as the representatives of the Anyi nation in both West African countries. The kingdoms still evoke strong loyalties and ethnic pride. National boundaries in the region reflect the impact of colonial rule as much as present political realities, bringing modern nationalism into conflict with centuries of evolving ethnic identification that for the Anyi supersedes their inclusion in modern Côte d'Ivoire and Ghana. Nationalism, particularly in the Côte d'Ivoire, where a corrupt government spent its way into bankruptcy, has become a major issue in the Anyi homeland.

The specter of tribalism and ethnic divisions, long absent from Ivorian politics and life, returned during the presidential elections in late 1998. A military coup led to increasing violence between tribal and religious groups in 1999–2000. In November 2001, a leading member of the Anyi exile community in Ghana called for the establishment of an autonomous Anyi state as a prelude to a future referendum on reunification and sovereignty.

SELECTED BIBLIOGRAPHY:

Lewis, Barbara. *The Ivory Coast*. 1990.
Mundt, R. J. *Historical Dictionary of the Ivory Coast*. 1987.
Parin, Paul. *Fear Thy Neighbor as Thyself: Psychoanalysis and Society among the Anyi of West Africa*. 1970.
Riboud, Michelle. *Ivory Coast: 1960–1986*. 1987.

Apache
N'de; Inde; Tinde

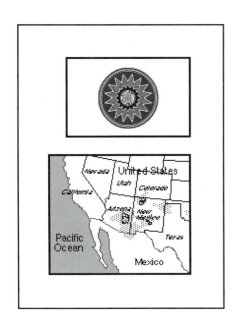

POPULATION: Approximately (2002e) 74,000 Apache in the southwestern United States, concentrated in the states of Arizona and New Mexico, the site of the largest Apache reservations—San Carlos and White Mountain in Arizona and Jicarilla and Mescalero in New Mexico. Other small communities live in Oklahoma, California, and Florida. Only about 12,000 Apache are on the tribal lists, but in the 1990 census over 50,000 responded as Apache. Some Apache activists claim a national population of up to 100,000.

THE APACHE HOMELAND: The traditional Apache homeland embraces large parts of the states of Arizona and New Mexico and small parts of the neighboring states of Colorado and Texas, but the Apache now control only small reservations in Arizona and New Mexico. The Western Apache live on the Fort Apache and San Carlos reservations in east-central Arizona. The Chiricahua (except a small band living in Oklahoma), the Mescalero, and the Lipan live on the Mescalero and Jicarilla reservations, in New Mexico. Most Apache now live in mixed communities and engage in farming or have assimilated into the large urban populations of the southwestern states. The major Apache cultural centers are Whitewater and San Carlos, Arizona, and Dulce, Mescalero, and Ruidoso, New Mexico.

FLAG: The flag of the Apache Survival Coalition (ASC), the largest of the pan-Apache organizations, is a white field bearing a central circular traditional design of blue, white, and red.

PEOPLE AND CULTURE: The Apache are a Native American nation of the southwestern United States and northwestern Mexico. The name is thought to come from the Yuma word for "fighting men," or from the Zuni word meaning "enemy." Their name for themselves, Inde or Tinde, means "the people." The nation is composed of six regional groups—the Western Apache, Chiricahua, Mescalero, Jicarilla, Lipan, and Kiowa

Apache or Gataka. The Western Apache traditionally live in eastern Arizona, and the Chiricahua in southwestern New Mexico, southeastern Arizona, and adjacent areas of the Mexican states of Chihuahua and Sonora. The Mescalero, also known as Faraon, live east of the Rio Grande in southern New Mexico, while the Jicarilla live in northern New Mexico and parts of Colorado and Texas, with the Lipan occupying territory east of the Jicarilla in New Mexico and Texas. The Kiowa Apache, long associated with the Kiowa, a people of the Great Plains, live in Colorado, Oklahoma, and Texas. Of the estimated population of 55,000, only about 12,000 are on the tribal registries. The once-nomadic people now occupy permanent dwellings, often outside reservation boundaries, and depend on livestock, agriculture, tourism, and various tribal enterprises for their livelihood. The Apache minority on reservations have become the heart of tribal life, keeping traditional social and ritual activities alive for the entire nation. Present Apache culture is a mixture of traditional beliefs, such as witchcraft, and contemporary American culture.

LANGUAGE AND RELIGION: The Apache belong to the Southern Athapaskan linguistic family, which also includes the neighboring Dine or Navajo.* The language belongs to the Navajo-Apache branch of the Athapaskan languages, which are also spoken in Alaska and western Canada. Most adults speak the language and many can understand it, but education in the language is a recent accomplishment; younger Apache, who often speak English as their first language, are now learning the language as a matter of pride. Spoken in several dialects, including the Eastern Apache dialects of Jicarilla, Lipan, Kiowa Apache, and Mescalero-Chiricahua and Western Apache or Coyotero, the language is reviving, except for the Kiowa Apache and Lipan dialects, which are almost extinct.

The Apache religion, centered on sacred geographical monuments and traditional rituals, retains its appeal and is often combined with modern Christian sects, primarily Protestant. The controversy over Mount Graham has revived the traditional beliefs as a form of protest in the late 1990s. Religion remains a fundamental part of Apache culture. Among the best known of the traditional spirits are the *ga'ans*, the protective mountain spirits represented in religious rites.

NATIONAL HISTORY: The Apache are thought to have originated in western Canada, although many claim they have always lived in their southwestern homeland. The migration of the Athapaskan bands from Canada, in the fourteenth and fifteenth centuries, brought the migrants down along the eastern flanks of the Rocky Mountains. The bands then scattered throughout present New Mexico, Arizona, and northern Mexico.

The immigrants lacked any centralized tribal organization. The primary organization was the band, which in turn was divided into smaller local groups. The bands were small enough to allow every individual to be aware of kinship ties to all other members. The bands remained nomadic or seminomadic and lived as farmer-raiders, primarily hunters of buffalo, but also practiced limited farming. Continuous wars with other tribes and with invaders from Mexico created a warlike Apache reputation.

When the Apache bands confronted the Spanish explorer Francisco Coronado in 1540, they mostly lived in present eastern New Mexico. The Spanish called the Apache tribes *Vaqueros*. The Spanish established a mission near modern Taos, New Mexico, but it did not succeed. In the 1600s, several bands moved west into Arizona. The Apache, in spite of their warlike reputation and refusal to accept outside authority, were described by early Spanish explorers as a gentle people, faithful in friendship.

When New Mexico became a Spanish colony in 1598, hostility increased between the Apache and the Spaniards. As early as the seventeenth century, the Apache were raiding Spanish missions and ranches. An influx of Comanche into traditional Apache territory in the early 1700s forced the Lipan and other groups to move south of their main food source, the buffalo herds. As late as 1700, Plains Apache farmers were still living along the Dismal River in Kansas. With the introduction of the horse by the Spanish, these and other Plains Apache were pressed south and west by the Comanche and Ute. By the mid-eighteenth century the majority of the Apache were concentrated in the dry, mountainous southwest. In 1821 their homeland was claimed by the new Mexican government, as the successor to the Spanish territorial government of the region

Culturally, the Apache bands divided into eastern and western groups, which were often influenced by neighboring peoples. Characteristic of both groups, with the exception of the Kiowa Apache, was the lack of a centralized tribal organization. The band, an autonomous collection of small local groups within a given geographic area, was the primary political unit as well as the primary war and raiding unit. The strongest headman of the local group was recognized as an informal chief, and several bands might unite under one leader, particularly when faced with a powerful enemy.

The Apache attained their greatest fame as guerrilla fighters, defending their mountain homelands under a string of famous leaders in the nineteenth century. Although the Apache wars with the expanding United States were among the fiercest fought on the frontier, the Apache attempted, as they had with the earlier Spanish and Mexicans, to remain friendly with the Americans. The territory of the Apache was acquired, without their consent, by the Americans through agreements with Mexico—the Treaty of Guadalupe Hidalgo in 1848 and the subsequent Gadsden Purchase in 1853.

In 1848, when gold was discovered in California, the Apache were threatened by incursions of American fortune seekers on their way to the gold fields. In an incident at a mining camp, Mangas Colorado, a chief of the Chiricahua, was whipped, an act that increased enmity against the invaders. In 1858 a meeting between Americans and Apache took place at Apache Pass in the Dragoon Mountains, resulting in a peace that lasted until 1861—when Mangas Colorado's nephew, Cochise, who had long resisted fighting the Americans, was unjustly accused of crimes.

Cochise had worked as a woodcutter at the Apache Pass stagecoach station until 1861. A raiding party from another Apache band drove off cattle belonging to an American rancher and abducted the child of a ranch hand. A prejudiced and inexperienced military officer, Lt. George Bascom, sent to investigate the incident, ordered Cochise and five other Apache to surrender for questioning. When they denied guilt, Bascom ordered his men to arrest them. In the ensuing struggle, the soldiers killed one of the men and captured four others, but Cochise, suffering from three bullet wounds, escaped. He captured a number of whites to exchange for his friends, but Bascom retaliated by hanging six Apache, including several of Cochise's relatives. The "Bascom Affair" marked the beginning of the Apache wars, which lasted nearly a quarter of a century.

Avenging the deaths of their kinsmen, Cochise and his uncle ravaged the Southwest. The Apache fighters were so fierce that troops, settlers, and traders all withdrew from the region. The recall of regular troops to fight in the American Civil War practically abandoned the territory to the Apache, but Mangas was captured and killed in 1863, leaving Cochise as the principal chief of the Apache. The wars divided the bands, with some, particularly in the east, remaining at peace and even working as scouts for the American military.

Despite their adept use of swift horses and their knowledge of the terrain, the superior arms of the federal troops outmatched the Apache. Most Apache surrendered in 1871–73 and agreed to settle on reservations, but large numbers of warriors refused to yield their nomadic ways or to accept what they saw as permanent confinement. Intermittent raids continued, led by Geronimo and Victorio, provoking renewed military campaigns against the Apache. The last of the Apache wars ended in 1886, with the surrender of Geronimo and his few remaining warriors.

Reservations were established for the Jicarilla and Mescalero Apache in New Mexico, and in 1891 Fort Apache Indian Reservation was established in Arizona. By an act of Congress in 1897, the reservation was divided into the White Mountain and San Carlos reservations. The Chiricahua, including Geronimo, were evacuated from the Southwest and were held as prisoners of war—successively in Florida, Alabama, and finally at Fort Sill in Oklahoma—for a total of 27 years. Geronimo died in 1909, and in 1913 the tribe members were allowed either to accept land allotments in Oklahoma or to move to the Mescalero Reservation in New Mexico.

The Apache, like the other Native peoples of North America, have been since World War II more likely than members of any other American racial or ethnic group to be victims of violent crime—at twice the rate for blacks and two and a half times the national average. They are also more likely to be victims of interracial crime. Some 70% of violent crimes against the Apache are committed by offenders of different races, usually white Americans. Only 19% of crimes against blacks and 31% of crimes against whites are interracial. The Apache Americans are not only victims of crimes; on average, roughly one in 25 is in jail, on parole, or on probation, twice the rate for white Americans. Alcohol abuse is a prominent factor in these figures, with arrests related to alcohol being double the national average.

In 1996 the Apache bands united and organized to face a new threat to their culture and sovereignty. Mount Graham, the most sacred mountain of the San Carlos Apache—called Dzil Nchaa Si An in the Apache language, meaning "Big Seated Mountain"—is being desecrated by an astronomical telescope project sponsored jointly by the University of Arizona, the Vatican State, Germany's Max Planck Institute, and Italy's Arcetri Observatory. The telescope, which could not be built in Italy because of air pollution, is based on a "Star Wars" prototype developed for the U.S. Army by the University of Arizona. The university gave it to the Vatican observatory in exchange for 25% gratis viewing time by university personnel.

The mountain is considered a living focus of spiritual energy, not just a geographical location or geological formation. The controversy opened many long-standing wounds between the Apache, the U.S. Forest Service, and the University of Arizona, with the complication of the involvement of foreign governments and institutions. The differences in cultures and attitudes are very real. In the desert, the Apache pray for rain and praise their sacred mountains when they are covered with clouds. The astronomers, who need clear viewing, hope there will be no rain and no clouds but dry desert skies.

The Apache, outraged at the desecration, formed their first national organization, the Apache Survival Coalition (ASC), in 1989. The ASC is the first organization since the end of the Apache wars in which some Apache feel able to confront the world around them without fear of repercussion; it represents a rare display of solidarity between secular and traditional Apache leaders. The Forest Service has chosen to ignore the Apache claims to the sanctity of the mountain.

In 2000, in a surprising move that aroused widespread opposition, the leaders of the Mescalero Apache signed an agreement that was the "first step" toward building a private waste storage site on their reservation in south-central New Mexico. The agreement, with the Northern States Power of Minnesota, would provide for the storage of high-level nuclear waste. The Mescalero president, Wendell Chino, stated that the agreement would provide for the long-term economic self-sufficiency for his people. Estimates of revenues from the venture go up to $50 million a year. Although the state government of New Mexico is opposed to the deal, the

Mescaleros are a sovereign entity and do not need state approval to enter into agreements. The most intense opposition came from indigenous environmental groups, including Mescaleros, who traveled to Minnesota to protest the transfer of nuclear waste to the Southwest.

The nuclear-waste deal was not put to a tribal vote, which excluded opposing opinions among the Apache. Indigenous environmental groups claim that the history of the nuclear industry and of nuclear waste storage within indigenous territories is a devastating account of deception, danger, and short-term gain. The controversy opened a heated debate on how the Apache are governed, including calls for a united Apache political entity.

SELECTED BIBLIOGRAPHY:

Haley, James L. *Apaches: A History and Culture Portrait.* 1997.
Laurie, Ben, ed. *Apache: The Definitive Guide.* 1999.
Lund, Bill. *The Apache Indians.* 1997.
Perry, Richard J. *Apache Reservation: Indigenous Peoples and the American State.* 1993.

Arabistanis

Arabestanis; Ahvazis; Ahwazis; Iranian Arabs; Khuzestan Arabs

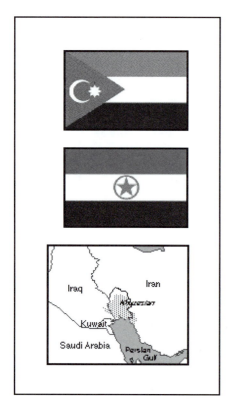

POPULATION: Approximately (2002e) 3,460,000 Arabistanis in Iran, concentrated in the southeastern province of Khuzestan. Outside the region there are Arabistani communities along the coast of the Persian Gulf, in Baghdad, and in southern Iraq.

THE ARABISTANI HOMELAND: The Arabistani homeland lies at the eastern end of the Fertile Crescent, the valley of the Tigris and Euphrates Rivers. The region, at the western end of the Persian Gulf, is mostly fertile lowland west of the Zagros Mountains, which divide the region from the rest of Iran. Arabistan is rich in natural resources and is the center of the Iranian petroleum industry. The region, called Arabistan or "Land of the Arabs" or Ahwaz by nationalists, forms the province of Khuzestan in the Islamic Republic of Iran. Some Arabistani nationalists claim a larger area, including a wide strip of territory extending from Khuzestan along the Persian Gulf (Arab Gulf) east to the Strait of Hormuz. *Province of Khuzestan (Arabistan/Ahvaz)*: 25,688 sq. mi.—66,532 sq. km, (2002e) 4,526,000—Arabistani 74%, Iranian 20%, Lur 3%, Turk 1%. The major Arabistani capital and major cultural center is the city of Ahvaz, also called Ahwaz, (2002e) 970,000, the center of Arab culture in the region.

FLAG: The Arabistani flag, the flag of the national movement, is a vertical tricolor of green, white, and black bearing a red triangle at the hoist charged with a white crescent moon and an eight-pointed white star. The flag of the largest national organization, the Ahwaz Liberation Organization (ALO), is a vertical tricolor of red, white, and black bearing a centered green five-pointed star surrounded by a green circle.

PEOPLE AND CULTURE: The Arabistanis are a Semitic Arab people made up of thirty tribal groups that are ethnically and culturally related to the Arab peoples to the west, but they are not closely related to Iran's majority Aryan population. About 40% of the Arabistanis are urban, concentrated in the large cities of Abadan, Ahvaz, and Khorramshahr. The majority of urban Arabistani males work as unskilled laborers in the region's important petroleum industry. Some urban Arabistanis and the rural population are still tribally organized. The rural Arabs of Khuzestan are mainly farmers and fishermen or herdsmen in the coastal plains along the Persian Gulf. Both urban and rural Arabistanis have intermingled with the Iranians, Lurs, and Turks and often intermarry; however, the Arabistanis see themselves as separate and distinct. Outside Khuzestan there is little ethnic solidarity among the Arabistani groups of Iran.

LANGUAGE AND RELIGION: The Arabistanis speak a Semitic language, an Arabic dialect with a marked Farsi (Iranian) admixture called Mesopotamian Gelet Arabic. The dialect is the language of daily life of the Arabistani population but has no official status in the region, where the Iranian language, Farsi, is the only official language and is widely spoken as a second language. The Arabistani dialect is related to the dialects spoken by the mainly Shi'a population of southern Iraq, but with its pronounced Farsi admixture it is considered a separate regional dialect.

The Arabistanis are mostly Shi'a Muslims, adhering to the branch of Islam predominant in Iran; a Sunni Muslim minority is concentrated in the coastal areas. They are closely related religiously and culturally to the large Shi'a population west of the Shatt-al-Arab in neighboring Iraq. The division between the Shi'a and Sunni communities has hampered ethnic solidarity in the Arabistan region.

NATIONAL HISTORY: The region is thought to have been inhabited by ancient civilizations as far back as 8000 B.C. The land known to the ancients as Elam was conquered many times and by many nations, including the Macedonians of Alexander the Great, who called the area Susiana after its ancient capital at Susa. Under the rule of the ancient Persians, the region's name was changed to Khuzestan, the Land of the Khuz, the name of the descendants of the ancient Elamites of the Old Testament era.

Arabs, invading from the southwest, added Khuzestan to the Muslim caliphate in the seventh century A.D. To ensure the loyalty of the frontier district, the Arab authorities settled Arab colonists among the native Khuz, and the name of the region was changed from Khuzestan to Arabistan, the Land of the Arabs. Forming the eastern extension of Arab culture, the region became one of the wealthiest districts of the Arabs' extensive empire. The region boasted a vast irrigation system that sustained a large settled population and also wealthy, sophisticated cities, renowned seats of Muslim learning. By the eleventh century the native Khuz had disappeared, having either died out or been absorbed by the Arab majority.

The region's prosperity ended with the thirteenth-century Mongol invasion. The marauding Mongols slaughtered much of the population, laid waste vast stretches of fertile farmland, and destroyed the region's renowned irrigation network. The territory eventually recovered, but it never regained its former glory. Without irrigation most of the area reverted to barren desert, with agriculture restricted to the wetlands along the rivers and the coast.

Weakened by conflicts with the growing Ottoman Empire, the Arab empire lost Arabistan to the Persians in the sixteenth century. The region eventually formed a frontier district between the Persians and the Turkish-ruled Arab lands. Backward and neglected, Arabistan continued a long decline, and by the nineteenth century it was one of the poorest and least-developed areas of the Middle East.

In 1821 the Arabs of the region established an emirate under traditional rulers, who enjoyed considerable political autonomy under the Persian government. An imperial decree, signed by Shah Nasr al-din Qadjar in 1857, recognized the internal autonomy of the region, under the rule of the emir of Mohammerah (Khorramshahr), and the right of the Arabistanis to establish diplomatic relations with other states.

The Arabistan region, disputed between the Iranians and Arabs for nearly four centuries, has been the subject of numerous treaties since 1639, but they have proved to be little more than momentary truces. The Treaty of Erzerum in 1847 and the Constantinople Protocol of 1913 finally defined the border between Turkish and Persian territory on the eve of the First World War. The treaties, protested by the Arabs, left a large Arabic population under Persian rule.

Persian settlers, favored by the government, enjoyed the benefits of Persia's late-nineteenth-century modernization, leaving the Arabistanis economically deprived and thus exacerbating the traditional hostility between the two peoples. Oil, discovered in 1908, radically changed the province's historical population pattern, as the mainly rural Arabistanis migrated to the rapidly growing cities near jobs in the oil fields.

Arab liberation, supported by the Allies as a way to undermine the Ottoman Empire when war began in 1914, reverberated in Arabistan, one of the few Arab populated territories not under Turkish rule. After centuries of harsh Persian domination, the Arabistanis enthusiastically embraced the call for Arab emancipation. After the war the Arabistanis received aid and support from the Arab countries that emerged from the collapse of the Ottoman Empire in 1918.

Arabistani leaders, with the help of the British, revolted against Persian rule and took control of the major towns in the region. On 18 August 1923, the Arabistani *shaik* declared the independence of Arabistan. Persian troops intervened in 1924, driving the rebel government into British territory in Iraq.

Reza Shah Pahlevi, a military officer, overthrew the old Persian dynasty in 1925 and proclaimed himself the new ruler of the country, which he renamed Iran. The centralization of government under the Pahlevi dynasty involved the official elimination of the privileges of the Iranian state's numerous ethnic and religious minorities. Arabistan's traditional autonomy under its own emir was rescinded, and the region was brought under the direct rule of the new Iranian government. In 1928 the inhabitants of Arabistan, again rechristened Khuzestan, came under intense pressure to assimilate. Ethnic clothing was outlawed, Arabic-language publications were banned, and all schools were ordered to teach only in Farsi, Iran's official language. The last Arabistani emir, Sheikh Khazaal, the emir of al-Mohammarah, was imprisoned in Tehran and strangled in his prison cell in 1936. The Iranian government systematically encouraged Iranian emigration to the region in an effort to dilute the Arab majority of Khuzestan.

The chiefs of the tribes of Arabistan appealed to the new Arab League in 1946, pleading for aid and support against the Iranians. The El Saadeh Party was established as a first attempt to win independence for the region. The chiefs complained of neglect and the lack of rights afforded the Iranian majority. The profits of the burgeoning oil industry, centered in the region, were used for development projects elsewhere, while the Arabistanis lived in poverty. The province, called Arabistan by the nationalists and most Arab countries, remained one of the focal points of Arab nationalism throughout the 1950s.

In 1958 a radical, Arab nationalist government took power in neighboring Iraq and drastically increased outside support for the nascent Arabistani nationalist movement. Exile nationalist organizations, based in the Iraqi capital, Baghdad, directed operations in the province; strikes, demonstrations, and the sabotage of pipelines and oil refineries becoming common. The Iraqi government, however, temporarily suspended overt aid to the national movement following the resolution of a long-standing border dispute in in the Shatt-al-Arab region in 1975.

The revolution that overthrew the hated Iranian monarchy in 1979 at first allowed the Arabistanis to form a provincial council; the new regime prepared to grant limited autonomy, but leading Islamic clerics in the new government, viewing the Arabistanis as potential agents for rival Iraq, refused to make concessions. Renewed suppression of the Arab population was initiated. The Islamic Revolution proved a disappointment to even its most ardent Arabistani supporters, and the presence of brutal Revolutionary Guards in the region caused growing unrest. Betrayed by the revolutionary government, the Arabistanis launched a renewed campaign of sabotage in the oil fields. On 30 April 1980, militants seized the Iranian embassy in London in order to free 91 Arabistanis imprisoned in Iran.

The Iraqi dictator, Saddam Hussein, citing the harsh treatment of the Arabistanis, declared the 1975 border agreement void. On the same day, 22 September 1980, he launched a military invasion of Iranian Khuzestan. The conflict soon bogged down; it became an eight-year war of attrition. Many of the Arabistanis, fearing the radicalism of the Iraqi regime, refused to support the Iraqis, which split the Arabistani national movement. By 1988 Arabistan's cities, ports, and oil fields lay in ruins, still under Iranian control.

The end of the Iran-Iraq War in 1989 also ended most outside support for the Arabistanis. Abandoned by Saddam Hussein's Iraq, which turned its attention to nearby Kuwait in 1990, the Arabistanis have looked to the other Arab states for support. Drawing on Arab sympathy and monetary aid, the Arabistani nationalists compare their situation to that of the people of Palestine, another Arab nation under foreign military rule. An Iranian military crackdown forced several Arabistani leaders, including Faleh Abdullah al-Mansouri, the chairman of the Ahwaz Liberation Organization (ALO), to flee to Europe.

The Arabs suffer from political, cultural, and economic discrimination, particularly the Sunni Muslim minority. The highly centralized Iranian government, in spite of signs of liberalization in the late 1990s and the early part of the new century, has refused to consider even limited autonomy for the country's many ethnic or religious minorities.

Renewed tension between Iraq and Iran over the disposition of the region has resulted in a series of border incidents and skirmishes. In February 2000, the Iranian government complained to the United Nations about Iraqi border incursions and Iraqi support of antigovernment Iranian groups raiding the region.

Conservative Shi'a Iranian parliamentarians lost seats for the first time in April 1996, marking the beginning of the gradual relaxation of the strict rule of the Islamic government. In 1997 a more moderate leader became president of Iran, beginning a period of hesitant reform, with reduced censorship and support of a diversity of attitudes. Reformers, promising a further relaxation of the harsh Islamic rule of the past twenty years, but holding out little hope for greater self-government for the Arabistanis, won elections in February 2000.

The Arabistanis continue to suffer cultural, economic, political, and—where Sunnis are in the majority—religious discrimination. The highly centralized Iranian Islamic state allows little freedom of choice, and resistance to Arabistani demands for cultural and political autonomy remains firm. Although most Arabistanis in exile reject armed insurrection due to the overwhelming firepower of the Iranian army, low-level sabotage and resistance continues to disrupt the region.

SELECTED BIBLIOGRAPHY:

Haseeb, Khair El-Din, ed. *Arab-Iranian Relations*. 1998.
McLachlan, K. S. *The Boundaries of Modern Iran*. 1994.
Rajaee, Farhang. *The Iran-Iraq War: The Politics of Aggression*. 1993.
Tapper, Richard, ed. *The Conflict of Tribe and State in Iran and Afghanistan*. 1983.

Aragonese

Aragonés; Patués; Manyas

POPULATION: Approximately (2002e) 2,045,000 Aragonese in Europe, mostly concentrated in northeastern Spain. Large Aragonese populations live outside the autonomous region, particularly in neighboring Catalonia, Navarra, and in Madrid.

THE ARAGONESE HOMELAND: The Aragonese homeland is roughly coextensive with the historical kingdom of Aragon. Lying just south of the Pyrenees, which form the border with France, the Pyrenean foothills, or the pre-Pyrenees, slope southward to the Ebro River. Most of Aragon lies around the Ebro River basin, a semi-arid plain that bisects Aragon into northern and southern portions. The Iberian Cordillera, or the Sierra de Goedar, covers most of the southern and southwestern districts of the region. Much of the region is sparsely

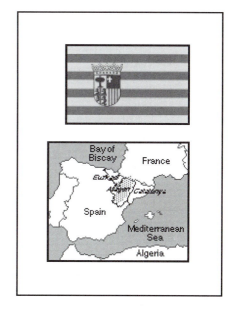

populated and desertlike. Aragon forms an autonomous region of the Spanish kingdom, comprising the three provinces of Huesca, Zaragoza, and Teruel. *Autonomous Region of Aragon (Comunidad Autonoma de Aragón/ Aragoi)*: 18,382 sq. mi.—47,609 sq. km, (2002e) 1,194,000—Aragonese 93%, Catalans* 5%, other Spanish 2%. The Aragonese capital and major cultural center is Zaragoza, called Saragossa in the Aragonese language, (2002e) 605,000, metropolitan area 841,000. The other important cultural center is Huesca, called Uesca in Aragonese, (2002e) 45,000, the center of the Aragonese-speaking region.

FLAG: The Aragonese national flag, the official flag of the region, has nine yellow and red horizontal stripes charged with the quartered Aragonese shield surmounted by a golden crown.

PEOPLE AND CULTURE: The Aragonese are an Iberian people historically and culturally related to the neighboring Catalans. The Aragonese tend to be concentrated in the irrigated zones of the Ebro River basin and are much sparser in the adjoining mountains. The population of the mountainous areas of Huesca and Teruel Provinces has declined steadily since the early twentieth century, while the city of Zaragoza has grown at the expense of the rural areas. The population of the region continues to decline, due to a lack of arable land and opportunities.

LANGUAGE AND RELIGION: The Aragonese language, the original language of the region, has been superseded by the Aragonese dialect of Castilian Spanish since about 1800. The language is a Navarro-Aragonese dialect of the Ibero-Romance language family, spoken in four major dialects—Western, Central, Eastern, and Southern. Most modern speakers use the Eastern dialect, but the literary language is based on Central and Eastern. In 2000 only about 15,000 used the Aragonese language as their first language, although between 50,000 and 100,000 have some knowledge of it or use it as a second language. The active speakers live mostly in the high Pyrenean valleys of northern Aragon. The oldest texts written in any of the Iberian Romance languages are in Aragonese. The *Glosas Emilianenses* and *Silenses*, dating from the tenth century, are explanations, in Aragonese, of words written in Latin. *Glosas* from the ninth century have recently been discovered but have yet to be published. There are similarities in the language to Catalan and Occitan. Since the mid-1980s there has been a campaign to revitalize the language and extend its use as the national language of Aragon.

The Aragonese are officially mostly Roman Catholic, and the elaborate medieval cathedral of the Pilar in Zaragoza is the center of Aragonese Catholicism. However, since the late 1970s the Aragonese have become increasingly secular, while others have abandoned Catholicism for the evangelical Protestant sects that offer a more intimate religious experience than the stately Spanish Catholicism.

NATIONAL HISTORY: The first mention of the region comes from Carthaginian records of Carthage's possessions in Spain, including the Celtiberian town of Salduba, the predecessor of Zaragoza. After the overthrow of Carthaginian power in Spain by the Romans, Aragon formed part of the Roman province of Hispania Tarraconensis, although Roman power was never very strong in the region, particularly in the highlands in the north. In the third century A.D., Salduba, called Caesaraugusta by the Romans, was made an episcopal see of the new Christian church.

The decline of Roman power was followed by invasions of Germanic peoples, particularly the Visigoths, who settled the region in the fifth century. In 714, Muslim Moors overran the Visigoth holdings in Aragon and established their rule at Zaragoza. In the early eighth century the Carolingian Franks pushed the Muslims from the region, which was incorporated into the kingdom of Navarre.

Classical Latin, the language of Rome, continued to be used as the literary language of the region, although several distinct dialects emerged that were loosely based on the vulgar Latin of the colonists and soldiers that inhabited the region. The Hispanic Romance dialects spoken in the region gradually extended themselves southward, along with the occupation by the Christian kingdoms of lands formerly held by the Muslims. Castilian Spanish, originally spoken in the region of Cantabria, began to absorb the other regional languages—Aragonese, Leonese,* and Mozarabic—in the early Middle Ages. Castilian was considered less elegant than Aragonese, and many literary works continued to be written in the language of Aragon.

The principality of Aragon had its origins in 1035, when Sancho III of Navarre left part of the region to his illegitimate son, Ramiro I. Ramiro and his successors, as kings of Aragon, extended the Aragonese territory southward at the expense of the Moorish emirate of Zaragoza, and in 1118 Zaragoza replaced Huesca as the kingdom's capital. In 1137 the ruler of Catalonia married the heiress of the kingdom. The union of Aragon and Catalonia principally benefited the Catalans, who dominated the state until 1412.

The reconquest of present-day Aragon from the Moors was completed by the late twelfth century. In 1179 the Aragonese reached an agreement with the neighboring Castilians under which the parts of Spain remaining in Muslim hands were to be divided into two zones, one for each kingdom to reconquer. While the Aragonese kings took an active role in the reconquest, as counts of Barcelona they also had important relationships in southern France, where several lordships were vassal states. The French conquered the vassal states north of the Pyrenees in 1196.

Having completed the conquest of the territories allocated to them by the treaty of 1179, the Aragonese began expanding into the Mediterranean area, a move made possible by the considerable sea power of their partners in the kingdom, the Catalans. In 1229, Catalan naval power was utilized to conquer the Muslim kingdom of Mayurqah, later called Majorca, the first significant step in the Catalan expansion in the Mediterranean. The Aragonese kings in 1238 conquered the rich kingdom of Valencia from the Muslims. By the early fifteenth century, the Aragonese kingdom ruled Navarre, Sicily, Sardinia, and part of mainland Italy.

The increasing power of the Catalans within the state weakened the Aragonese kingdom in the fifteenth century. Many Aragonese nobles came to favor union with Castile, in order to counterbalance the power of the mercantile Catalans. Their chance came in 1412 with the extinction of the house of Barcelona. They procured the election of a Castilian prince, Ferdinand, to the vacant Aragonese throne over strong Catalan opposition. One of Ferdinand's successors, John II, countered renewed Catalan resistance by arranging for his heir, Ferdinand, to marry Isabella, the heiress of Castile. In 1479 the kingdoms of Aragon and Castile were united to form the nucleus of modern Spain. It was Isabella and Ferdinand who, outside the walls of the newly conquered Granada, received Christopher

Columbus. Treasure from the looted Moorish city helped to pay for his expedition to the New World.

Construction of an irrigation system, begun by the Moors, was resumed in the sixteenth century. Two lateral canals of the Ebro River became most important in reviving agriculture in the semi-arid region. In the oases and the irrigated districts the Aragonese culture revived, including the standardizing of the language in the sixteenth and seventeenth centuries, in spite of the inroads made by Castilian Spanish.

The Aragonese lands retained considerable parliamentary and administrative autonomy until the early eighteenth century, when their constitutional privileges were abrogated. The old kingdom of Aragon survived as an administrative unit until 1833, when it was divided into the three provinces of Huesca, Zaragoza, and Teruel.

The region remained relatively isolated until the arrival of the railroad in 1864, which opened the way to Mediterranean ports and to trade with other parts of Spain. The population began to decline when grape phylloxera destroyed the numerous foothill vineyards in the early twentieth century. The migration of the population, particularly from the rural areas in the Pyrenees and the Aragon highlands, left many areas virtually depopulated. Only the city of Zaragoza continued to grow in population.

Increased prosperity around Zaragoza, based on irrigated agriculture in the Ebro River valley, ended during the Spanish Civil War of the 1930s; many of its fiercest battles were fought in Aragon. The Aragon front, which extended across the region into the mountains, remained a battleground for most of the civil war, driving thousands of Aragonese from the region. Many settled in Catalunya or other neighboring regions. By 1939 much of the region was in ruins, and the important irrigation system was inoperative.

The Aragonese were mostly ignored during the long fascist dictatorship of Francisco Franco. The region lost population due to underdevelopment and poor transport and communications links. The more rural provinces of Huesca and Teruel saw particularly sharp declines in population as young Aragonese, with few prospects locally, left for Madrid, Barcelona, or northern Europe in search of work.

Franco's death in 1975 finally allowed the Aragonese to voice their many grievances. A particularly Aragonese political party, the Aragonese Regionalist Party (PAR), founded in 1978, formed part of a popular coalition in the provincial governments; it channeled Aragonese complaints to the lower levels of government and championed Aragonese demands for autonomy. The Spanish government granted a statute of autonomy on 10 August 1982.

In 1986 the PAR stood alone and in regional elections won 19 parliamentary seats. In 1990 the party changed its name to Aragonese Party, in order to show its nationalist character. In the late 1990s the Aragonese campaigned for greater autonomy, similar to that granted to more nationalistic nations—the Catalans, Basques,* Galicians,* and Andalusians.*

In September 1999, a national water plan was unveiled, a huge scheme to transfer a cubic kilometer of water a year from the Ebro River in Aragon to the dry regions in southeastern Spain. The Aragonese were outraged by the plan. Mobilization of the population led to massive demonstrations. Activists claimed that Aragon has a desert of its own and many depopulated villages, some without piped water. A huge protest march in the Aragonese capital was led by nationalists, along with the city's conservative mayor, in defiance of his party, and the region's socialist premier. The conflict over Aragon's water is likely to sour relations between the region and the center for years to come. Militants vow that none of the annual cubic kilometers of water will ever leave Aragon.

Mass demonstrations in Zaragoza in early 2000 drew tens of thousands of Aragonese demanding political and cultural equality with the more advanced autonomous areas of the Spanish state. Regional disputes over water and other resources stimulated the growth of particular Aragonese nationalism. A parallel movement aims to revive Aragonese culture and language as part of the new national identity emerging in the region. The Aragonese, although a historical nation, are among the newest to create a national identity in southwestern Europe.

SELECTED BIBLIOGRAPHY:

Bisson, Thomas A. *The Medieval Crown of Aragon: A Short History.* 1991.

Chaytor, Henry J. *History of Aragon and Catalonia.* 1979.

Kelsey, Graham. *Anarchosyndicalism, Libertarian Communism and the State: The CNT in Zaragoza and Aragon, 1930–1937.* 1991.

Lourie, Elena. *Crusade and Colonization: Muslims, Christians, and Jews in Medieval Aragon.* 1990.

Arakanese

Maghi; Mogh; Mormas; Marmas; Mash; Rakhain; Yakhaing; Yakan

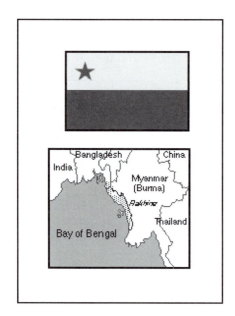

POPULATION: Approximately (2002e) 5,110,000 Arakanese in Myanmar, concentrated in the southwestern state of Arakan. Other sizable Arakanese communities live in adjacent areas of Bangladesh, in India, and in other parts of Myanmar.

THE ARAKANESE HOMELAND: The Arakanese homeland occupies a long, narrow plain on the Bay of Bengal in northwest Myanmar stretching from the Naf estuary on the Bangladesh border in the north to the Gwa River in the south. Arakan is separated from the rest of the Myanmar by the mountain range called the Arakan Yoma. The coast has several sizable offshore islands, including Cheduba and Ramree. Only a tenth of the region is cultivated, mostly in the delta areas, where most of the population is concentrated. Long accessible only by sea due to the impenetrable range of mountain jungles, the Arakan region is now linked by air and road with the rest of Myanmar. Nationalists claim a territory of over 20,000 square miles in western Myanmar. Arakan, officially called Rakhine, forms a state of the Socialist Republic of the Union of Myanmar, formerly known as Burma. It is the only state of Myanmar with a Muslim majority. *State of Rakhine (Arakan)*: 14,194 sq. mi.—36,772 sq. km, (2002e) 2,943,000—Arakanese 77%, Bengali 6%, Zomis* 5%, other Burmese 12%. The Arakanese capital and major cultural center is Akyab, called Sittwe by the Burmese, (2002e) 165,000.

FLAG: The Arakanese national flag, the flag of the national movement, is a vertical bicolor of white over red charged with a five-pointed red star on the upper hoist.

PEOPLE AND CULTURE: The Arakanese are a people of Bengali, Arab, and Burman ancestry. The Arakanese are generally darker than Myanmar's dominant Burmans, and racial animosity against them is exacerbated by the fact of their Muslim majority. The Arakanese Muslims, called Rohingya—from Mrohang, or Rohang, the ancient name of

Arakan—make up about 70% of the Arakanese population, while Arakanese Buddhists constitute over 20%, although both groups wear Burmese dress and share the distinct regional culture. The Rohingyas are claimed by the Myanmar military government to be descendants of Bengalis who settled the region under British rule. In spite of their religious differences, the Arakanese, who share a long history and culture, have united against the hated military government. The traditional animosity between the Arakanese and the Burmans is illustrated by a popular Burman proverb, "If you meet an Arakanese and a poisonous snake, first kill the Arakanese."

LANGUAGE AND RELIGION: The dialect spoken by the Arakanese is a dialect of Burman (Myanmarese) that incorporates borrowings from Bengali and other languages. The long maritime tradition of the Arakanese and their historical isolation led to the differentiation of their dialect from standard Burmese. Considered a southern dialect of Burman, Arakanese, also called Rakhain or Rakhine, is a nonstandard dialect with profound pronunciation and vocabulary differences from standard Burman. Many Arakanese speak and read Burman, and a minority also speak Bengali.

The conflict between the Burmans and the Arakanese is aggravated by religious conflict, as the Arakanese are predominantly Muslim, where Myanmar's majority is Buddhist. The Arakanese Muslims are mostly in the north and west, while the Arakanese in the southern and eastern districts are mostly Buddhist. There is a small Hindu minority concentrated in the port cities. In 1982 a law declared that only Buddhists could be citizens of Myanmar, disenfranchising the majority of the Arakanese population. No new mosques have been allowed in the region, the most recent having been constructed in 1975. Since 1995, the military junta has imposed various restrictions against the Muslims, including regulating the size of gatherings for religious purposes, levying special taxes on the slaughter of animals for traditional festivals, and new limitations on the maintenance or building of mosques. Many mosques and cemeteries have been demolished in order to build roads, army bases, and other projects.

NATIONAL HISTORY: The Arakanese trace their history to the establishment of an independent state in the region in 2666 B.C. They count a lineal succession of as many as 227 Arakanese princes and claim that their empire once extended across Myanmar into China and Bengal. Although most historians do not corroborate these claims, the most sacred Arakanese image of the Buddha, the huge Mahamuni statue, now in Mandalay, is alleged to predate the earliest Burman kingdom by a millennium.

Settlers from India's Coromandel Coast probably established an independent Arakanese kingdom as early as the fourth century A.D. The ancient maritime state had strong ethnic, economic, and religious ties to India. Islam, introduced by Arab invaders in the late seventh century, soon became the religion of the majority, further separating Arakan from the Buddhist nations on the eastern side of the Arakan Yoma.

The Burmans, a warrior people related to the Tibetans, conquered the Arakanese state in the eleventh century. After several unsuccessful rebellions, the Arakanese finally drove the Burmans from their homeland in 1238. In 1433 King Narameikhla established a new capital at Mrohaung. The city, which remained the Arakanese capital until the eighteenth century, gave its name to the kingdom and later to the Muslim majority.

The resurgent Arakanese quickly expanded and by the fifteenth century controlled an extensive empire on the northern shore of the Bay of Bengal. In 1495 the Arakanese kingdom extended its borders westward and took control of the important port city of Chittagong, in present Bangladesh, but Arakan's expansion was then checked by the rise of the powerful Mogul Empire on the kingdom's western border. In 1531 the first European ships appeared in the region, and Portuguese freebooters settled in the coastal towns. With Portuguese assistance, the Arakanese navy became the terror of the Ganges River delta, where so many slaves were taken that depopulation became a serious problem.

The Arakanese were defeated by the Mogul rulers of India in 1666, and the coastal areas were annexed, leaving a truncated kingdom under King Sandathudamma. When he died in 1684, the Bengalis increased their influence, but the Arakanese kingdom retained considerable autonomy, again becoming virtually independent as Mogul power declined in the late eighteenth century. The Burmans invaded again in 1785, deposed the last king, Thamada, and carried off the huge Mahamuni Buddha to Mandalay. In 1793 the Burmans returned to conquer the kingdom, but after only two years of harsh Burman rule the Arakanese rebelled. Brutally crushing the rebellion, the Burmans deported over 20,000 Arakanese to slavery in Upper Burma. Thousands fled Burman reprisals by crossing the Naf River to seek protection in British Bengal.

A second Arakanese rebellion, 1811–15, greatly increased tension on the frontier between British territory and the Burmese kingdom. Repeated border clashes culminated in the first Anglo-Burmese War in 1824. The terms of the 1826 Treaty of Yanbu forced the defeated Burmans to cede Arakan and other districts to the British Empire. The territories of the former Burmese kingdom, reunited under British rule in 1886, formed part of British India for decades. In 1937, however, under pressure from the majority Burmans, the British authorities separated the historical region of Burma, including Arakan, from India.

The outbreak of World War II pitted the British, aided by the Arakanese and other minority peoples, against the invading Japanese and the initially pro-Japanese Burmans. Arakanese nationalists, promised separate administration at war's end, felt betrayed when the British ignored the promise following the Burmans' defection to the Allied cause in 1943. Postwar preparations for the independence of Burma motivated Arakanese demands for separate independence. In 1947 the Mujahid Rebellion broke out in northern Arakan. The rebellion, led by the North Arakan Muslim League, failed in its bid to join Muslim northern Arakan to newly independent Muslim Pakistan. A negotiated compromise, autonomy for all the Arakanese within a Burmese federation, was abrogated soon after Burmese independence in 1948.

Ethnic and religious polarization intensified social cleavages between the Arakanese and the dominant Burmans. Poor treatment of minorities by the Burmese Buddhists solidified the region's perceptions of social separateness. Arakanese nationalism, particularly after the military takeover of Burma in 1962, became a potent force in the region. The formation of the Arakan Liberation Front (ALF) in 1974 marked a major escalation of the sporadic Arakanese rebellion against Burman domination. Led by Khaing Mo Lin, the ALF launched a coordinated military campaign against the powerful and ruthless Burmese army. Thousands fled into Bangladesh to escape Burmese military reprisals. The death in battle of Khaing Mo Lin in 1977 provoked a massive exodus of 200,000 rebels and their supporters to sanctuary in neighboring Bangladesh. In 1979 the majority returned to their homes, but the Burmese military government refused to accept some 50,000 known Arakanese separatists.

Severe economic problems, the result of decades of inept military rule, have impoverished potentially rich Arakan. Over half the Arakanese population lead miserable existences as sharecroppers on estates mostly owned by ethnic Burman absentee landlords. In 1982 Burma's ethnocentric military rulers, following the announcement of the law that only Buddhists were eligible for citizenship, declared Arakan's Muslim majority a stateless people, classifying them illegal immigrants from Bengal, now independent Bangladesh. Theoretically unprotected by state institutions, the Rohingyas suffered confiscation of property, forced labor, and religious persecution. The 1982 citizenship law is still used to deny Rohingyas and members of other ethnic minorities basic rights in Myanmar. In 1987 Burma, once the richest state in southeastern Asia, was assigned least-developed-country status by the United Nations.

The military government, claiming that Arakanese nationalists were preparing to declare independence in 1991, launched a massive military offensive in the region. Unable to locate the elusive Arakanese nationalists, the military turned on the most visible target, the unarmed Muslim Rohingyas in northern Arakan. Rohingya refugees, numbering over 200,000 by the end of 1992, streamed across the Bangladesh border, taking with them tales of persecutions and horrors, including extrajudicial executions, torture, and forced service as porters and other labor. Hundreds of mosques were closed, demolished, or put to other uses, such as military barracks or warehouses. The treatment of the Muslim Arakanese increased solidarity among the Arakanese nation in the face of government repression.

In the early 1990s the government of Myanmar, seeking to change its international image as one of the world's most brutal regimes, made concessions to the sensibilities of Arakan's population. In spite of its new attitude to Arakanese nationalism, the Myanmar government failed to persuade the growing number of armed national organizations to begin negotiations. Arakanese leaders accuse the Burmans of massacring over 200,000 Arakanese, mostly Muslims, in the last 50 years, but the current military regime is guilty of more death and destruction than any of its predecessors.

In February 1994 the United Nations began the repatriation of some of the Rohingyas in the dismal refugee camps on the Bangladeshi border. The government of Myanmar agreed to accept some 130,000 of the over 200,000 refugees but continues to insist that the remainder are illegal immigrants and must stay in Bangladesh where they originated.

Torture was reportedly customary for prisoners of the military in the region, including civilians accused of supporting the Arakanese separatists. Prisoners held in Maungdaw Prison, near the Bangladeshi border, which held many separatists and suspected separatists, were later sent to hard labor camps, where the death rate topped 60% during the early 1990s.

Two Arakanese Muslim groups, the All Burma Muslim Union and the Arakan Liberation Party, were expelled in 1995 from the Democratic Alliance of Burma (DAB), the umbrella group opposing the military government. The two groups were among five expelled for reportedly signing cease-fire agreements with the military authorities. The cease-fires, which never took effect, were later repudiated.

The Arakanese joined 17 ethnic groups at a meeting hosted by the Karens* in January 1997. The groups signed the Mae Tha Raw Hta Agreement, which calls for the establishment of a democratic, federal union in Burma. The various nationalist organizations formed an alliance known as the National Democratic Front (NDF), a revival of a group that fought the Burmese military in the 1970s and 1980s. Several of the groups had signed cease-fire agreements with the Burmese government, but with conditions deteriorating across Myanmar they joined the other national groups when fighting resumed in 1997–98. In December 1998, another meeting of antigovernment ethnic groups was attended by 23 delegations representing most of the non-Burman peoples of Myanmar.

Thousands of Rohingyas fled into southeastern Bangladesh in the first months of 1997. Unlike the refugees who came to Bangladesh in 1991–92, the new arrivals largely spread out across the border region, living in local Rohingya villages rather than in designated refugee camps. Sending them back to Myanmar is a problem the Bangladeshi government, which asserts that they are economic migrants, has so far not tackled. Rohingyas who returned to Myanmar have been subjected to forced labor and other hardships. The situation for the Muslim Arakanese has not changed in Myanmar: they are still discriminated against, they are not entitled to Burmese citizenship, and their freedom of movement is severely restricted. Since 1992, some 197,000 refugees have been returned to Arakan from Bangladeshi territory, but many attempt to go back to Bangladesh to escape the excesses of the Burmese military government. The Burmese military reportedly mined the border region to check cross-border violations.

In the late 1990s, thousands of Arakanese were forced to work as slave laborers on roads and other development projects and on military installations. The laborers, rounded up at random, include both peasants and professionals. The Muslims are particularly targeted for forced labor, portering for the military, and for forcible population reallocations. Anti-Muslim riots in mid-1997, reportedly instigated by the government, left many mosques and other properties destroyed.

Arakanese rebel groups acquired arms from Khmer Rouge members who fled to Thailand in 1999. The arms, although much needed, did little to redress the 10-to-1 ratio of government soldiers to ethnic rebels. Some of the arms later appeared in Bangladesh during a renewed influx of refugees fleeing repression and economic hardship in Arakan.

In February 2001, in a police action called Operation Leech, a number of Arakanese nationalist leaders were captured on Indian territory, and at least 6 were summarily executed according to Arakanese reports. The Indian government promised to investigate the incident.

SELECTED BIBLIOGRAPHY:

Fisher, Frederick, and Pauline Khng. *Myanmar*. 2000.
Phayre, Arthur. *History of Burma, Including Burma Proper, Pegu, Taungu, Tennasserim, and Arakan: From the Earliest Time to the End of the First War*. 1998.
Silverstein, J. *Burmese Politics: The Dilemma of National Unity*. 1980.
Smith, Martin. *Burma: Insurgency and the Politics of Insurgency*. 1991.

Aromanians

Vlachs; Vlasi; Volokhs; Arumun; Aromunians; Koutsovlachs; Koutzo-Vlachs; Torvlaks; Mavro-Vlachs; Tsintsars

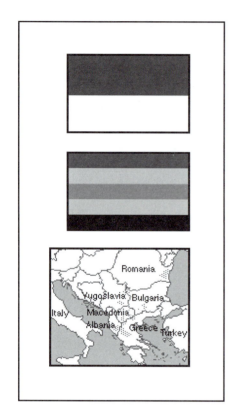

POPULATION: Approximately (2002e) 500,000 Aromanians in the southern Balkan states of Albania, Greece, Macedonia, Bulgaria, Romania, and Yugoslavia. Other estimates put the total Aromanian population between 150,000 and 1.5 million. The vast discrepancies between official numbers and estimates and the population figures put forward by nationalists and linguists are partly due to the respective methods of enumeration and partly a result of the fact that the Aromanians have traditionally assimilated in order to survive. Besides those in the Balkans, there are sizable Aromanian populations in western Europe, Canada, and the United States. The Aromanians include two smaller related populations—the Meglens in northern Greece, about 20,000, and the Istro-Romanians in Croatia, some 2,000.

THE AROMANIAN HOMELAND: The Aromanian homeland lies in the southern Balkan Peninsula, south and west of the Danube River, with pockets of Aromanians located in Greece, Albania, Macedonia, Yugoslavia, Bulgaria, and Romania. Greece has the largest Aromanian community and is the only country where Aromanians have a compact geographic distribution—in the Pindus Mountains in northwestern Greece, which is considered the core area of the Balkan Aromanians. The capital and major cultural center of the Aromanians in Greece is the town of Metzovo, called Aminciu by the Aromanians, (2002e) 5,000, the self-proclaimed "capital of the Aromanians." The other important cultural center in Greece is Tríkala, called Tricala by the Aromanians, (2002e) 48,000, whose population is swollen in winter by the annual migration of Aromanian herdsmen from the mountains. The cultural center of the Aromanians in Romania is Constanta, called Custanta in Aromanian. The center of the Macedonian Aromanians is the town of Krushevo, Crushova to the Aromanians. The cultural center of the Bulgarian Aromanians is the city of Sliven, where an annual Aromanian summer fair is held.

FLAG: The Aromanian national flag, used by most communities, is a vertical bicolor of navy blue over white. The nationalist flag of the nineteenth century, which was carried at the Paris Peace Conference in 1919, has five horizontal stripes of red, yellow, pale blue, yellow, and black.

PEOPLE AND CULTURE: Their Slav neighbors call them Vlach or Vlassi, but they call themselves Aromani or Aromuni, meaning Roman. Vlach or Vlah is now often used as a pejorative or generalized term, although the Meglens continue to call themselves Vlach. Traditionally the Aromanians were herdsmen, horse breeders, and shepherds, following their herds from pasture to pasture. Only about 20% continue to live the traditional seminomadic life, but only the Meglens adopted farming. The Aromanians are now mainly merchants, traders, and artisans. Like other national groups, the Aromanians have long linked their consciousness and primary loyalty to their villages, clans, valleys, or regions. The Aromanians, even in urban areas, tend to live apart, rarely intermarrying with Slavs, upholding an ancient tradition of superiority to the newer nationalities in the Balkans. They consider the Romanians as a separate but closely related nation. Until the beginning of the twentieth century, the Aromanians spent the period between Gherghiovden (St. George's Day, 23 April), and Krastovden (Day of the Cross, 14 September) in the Balkan, Rila, Pirin, Pindus, and Rhodope Mountains, before setting off with the vast migrations of the herds to the lowlands. The small nation has close ties to the Meglens, the Megleno-Romanians of Greece and Macedonia, and the Istro-Romanians, also called Morlakhs, in Croatia.

LANGUAGE AND RELIGION: The Aromanian language, called Arminesti or Aromaneashti, is a distinct Romance language, belonging to the southern or Balkan Romance group of the eastern Romance language family. It is structurally distinct from Romanian, and mutual intelligibility with standard Romanian is very low. The language is derived from late provincial Latin; it split from Romanian between A.D. 500 and 1000. Some linguists consider Aromanian, Megleno-Romanian, and Istro-Romanian as dialects of Romanian, but the majority consider them separate languages. Aromanian shares many common features with Bulgarian, Greek, and Albanian, but the lexical composition, though rich in Greek, Slavic, and Turkish borrowings, remains basically of the Romance type. The other important dialect, Meglen or Megleno-Romanian, spoken in Greece and Macedonia, is considered an intermediate dialect, between Aromanian and Romanian. There are numerous dialectical differences among the widely scattered populations. In the 1980s a separate alphabet, based on the Latin alphabet, was devised for the language. The number of Aromanians in the Balkans is estimated to number up to 1.5 million, but speakers of the

Aromanian language are estimated to have dropped from 500,000 in 1900 to around 250,000 in 2000.

The Aromanians are overwhelmingly Orthodox Christian, most belonging to the Greek Orthodox Church. Some Aromanians, particularly outside Greece, have suggested the creation of an autonomous Aromanian Orthodox Church to serve the needs of the widely scattered Aromanian diaspora.

NATIONAL HISTORY: The Aromanians claim descent from the ancient Romans who conquered Macedonia in the second century B.C. Some scholars believe they are descended from the aboriginal Thracians, Greeks, Illyrians, and others who amalgamated with the Latin colonists. Following the Roman evacuation of the region in A.D. 271, the area was subject to a series of barbarian invasions. The Romanized population survived, probably by taking refuge in the mountains, where they remained as shepherds and primitive farmers. They are thought to have returned to the plains when conditions improved in the sixth century, when the first mention of their distinct language was recorded. Another theory claims that they are descendants of Romanized Dacians who moved south of the Danube after the Roman evacuation.

The Slavs colonized the Balkans between the fourth and seventh centuries. They found two large and related tribal groups already established in the region—the Dacians north of the Danube River, and the Thracians south of the river. Both groups had adopted the Latin culture and spoke a Latin patois. North of the river, the Dacians absorbed the invading Slavs, but in the south the Thracians were either absorbed or pushed into the less accessible mountains. The Aromanian mountaineers were well known to the Byzantine military, who regarded the independent people as an unmitigated nuisance.

The Aromanians were instrumental in the formation of the Second Bulgarian Empire, also known as the Empire of the Vlachs and Bulgars, in 1184. In 1186 they rebelled against a tax increase imposed by the Byzantine emperor. In 1204, after the temporary collapse of Byzantine power, the Aromanians created their own kingdom, called Great Wallachia, in Thessaly and parts of Macedonia. They later established another state, Little Wallachia, in present northwestern Greece.

The Aromanian heartland in Thessaly was later absorbed by the Greek Despotate of Epirus, overrun by Serbs, and, with the coming of the Turks in 1393, incorporated into the Turkish Ottoman Empire. Aromanian caravans, made up of hundreds of packhorses, traveled freely across the Ottoman-ruled peninsula, and Aromanian traders established prosperous mercantile houses in the larger towns and as far away as Budapest and Vienna. By the end of the eighteenth century, the Aromanians all but controlled trade in the Ottomans' European territories.

Around 1700 an urban Aromanian culture formed in the Pindus Mountains, centered on the city of Gramostea, which boasted an Aromanian population of some 40,000. In the middle of the eighteenth century the Aromanians of Turkish Epirus, in present Albania, established a large urban population at Moscopole (Voskopoje) south of Lake Ohrid. At its height the walled city had up to 60,000 inhabitants, its own printing house, and a famous academy of learning. The city became the center of the Aromanian national and cultural revival and didactic literature. The first known inscription in Aromanian is dated 1731; it was found in the region in 1952. The destruction of the city by Albanian mercenaries in the pay of feuding beys in 1769 and again in 1788 dispersed its inhabitants as refugees and emigrants across the Balkans.

In the early nineteenth century, as nationalist ideas began to form in Europe, a small, educated minority began to see the Aromanians as a separate nation—not Greek, Romanian, Slav, or Albanian. A national movement began among wealthy Aromanian merchants in Vienna and Budapest, but the new Romanian state soon co-opted Aromanian nationalism, claiming the small south Balkan nation as long-lost kin and investing large sums in schools and churches that perpetuated Romanian but not Aromanian culture.

The Greek state, which became independent from the Ottoman Turks in 1821, opposed the Romanian movement, and the Aromanians were soon divided into pro-Greek and pro-Romanian factions. The development of a purely Aromanian national consciousness was hindered by the fact that Aromanians lacked a written language and had been taught to use the alphabets—Greek, Roman, or Cyrillic—of the countries in which they lived.

In the mid-nineteenth century, with the support of the Romanian government, the Aromanians of the Balkans began to define their national identity. The first cultural organization, the Macedo-Romanian Committee, based in the Romanian capital, Bucharest, from 1860, was able to open the first Aromanian school in Greece in 1867, with almost 100 schools operating in Greece, Macedonia, and Albania by the turn of the century. The Aromanians, with no written language and no national myth, were slow to develop a national consciousness in the late nineteenth century.

The cession of Thessaly by the Ottoman Turks to Greece in 1881, however, fueled Aromanian sentiment. A large number joined to petition the Ottoman sultan in protest, citing their fears of Greek assimilationist policy and the fact that the new border would cut across the traditional migration routes of the Aromanian herds. In 1905 the Ottoman Turkish government finally recognized the Aromanians as a separate community and allowed them to establish their own Orthodox church, but the church established by the nationalist Apostol Margarit was not successful, as most Aromanians had already adopted Greek identity.

The scattered Aromanians suffered dreadfully during the Balkan Wars from 1911 to 1913, when they and their herds were massacred by armed bands of Bulgarians, Greeks, and Serbs. Following the wars, in which the last Ottoman territories in Europe were lost, the Aromanians found themselves living in four different states—Albania, Serbia, Greece, and Bulgaria. Their centuries-old migration and trade routes were severed by the borders and customhouses of the new Balkan countries.

The increasingly hostile policies of the Greek state, which had to accommodate millions of displaced Greeks from Asia Minor, led to the dislocation of many Aromanian communities. Thousands of Greek Aromanians emigrated to Romania or abroad between 1923 and 1926. In 1925, not long after the Dobrudja was incorporated into Romania, the government gave land to immigrant Aromanians in which to settle. They have survived as a distinct community there despite their close cultural and linguistic ties to the neighboring Romanians.

In Greece, during the Ioannis Metaxas dictatorship of 1936–41, the Aromanians were forced to attend Greek-language night schools, and the Aromanian language was banned from public use. During World War II and the civil war that followed in Greece, Aromanian territory was fought over by several armies and guerrilla groups. During the war, Italian forces in Thessaly formed pro-fascist Aromanians into a "Roman Legion" and supported the creation of a separate Aromanian state. The autonomous "Principality of the Pindus," led by an extremist, Alcibiades Diamandi, faded with the withdrawal of the Italian fascists.

The Romanian communist government after the war had less interest in the Aromanians and ended its support. In 1951 the Greek census counted only 39,855 Aromanians; later they were left out of official statistics entirely. In 1952 the Greek government closed the last Aromanian churches and schools, centers of community life and culture. Aromanian assimilation was extensive and usually "voluntary," and it seemed that the Aromanians' disappearance as a distinct national group was imminent. The new communist governments of Bulgaria and Yugoslavia often branded the Aromanians "vagrants" and forced them to settle in towns and villages.

Under the rule of the Greek "colonels" in the 1960s and 1970s, Aromanians risked imprisonment for speaking their language even casually. The overthrow of the military regime in 1974 somewhat eased conditions, although they are today still not recognized as a national minority. The Greek government does not acknowledge the existence of national minorities within its borders, only religious minorities. The simple mention of Aromanian nationality is forbidden in a country that promotes a self-image as an ethnically pure and unique "Hellenic" state. As recently as August 1998, the speaker of the Greek parliament openly urged the homogenization of Greece's ethnic minorities.

The Romanian government's new interest in the Aromanians and Meglens in Greece recalls the controversy of the end of the nineteenth century.

Any intervention by outsiders in favor of the preservation of the Aromanian cultural and linguistic identity is viewed with great suspicion in Greece.

The situation of the Aromanian population in the other Balkan countries is also serious. In Albania the Aromanians are not counted as a separate ethnic group but are included in the Greek Orthodox minority. The Aromanians of the Timok Valley in Serbia are not recognized as an ethnic community but are regarded as Romanized Slavs. The 1991 Macedonian constitution officially recognized the Vlachs as a national minority, but the Macedonian language must be used in contacts with the government. Further, the government has refused to register the Aromanian Orthodox Church, on the grounds that there is already one Orthodox Church in the country. In 1995 the Aromanians were granted permission to teach optional courses in their language in Aromanian areas of Macedonia. In Bulgaria they enjoy few political or cultural rights, the legacy of the former communist government, which actively promoted the assimilation of national minorities. Although Romania is not one of the original areas inhabited by Aromanians, it now has an important community. The Aromanians in Romania are mostly descendants from émigrés of the first half of the twentieth century. They are considered by the Romanian state as constituting a linguistic and cultural community rather than an official minority. Romania, since the fall of communist governments in the Balkans, has reassumed to some extent the role of protector of the Aromanians.

In the early 1980s the Aromanians were thought to be on the verge of extinction, but during the international ethnic revival of the late 1980s their situation began to change. Émigré communities in Western Europe and North America took a new interest in their culture and language and encouraged their compatriots in the Balkans to do the same. Communities in the Balkans, along with groups in France, Germany, North America, and Greece, for the first time began to claim Aromanian identity. As renewed interest grew, the Iron Curtain collapsed, and many forgotten ethnic groups resurfaced. The Greek claim that all Aromanians in the Balkans are ethnic Greeks was set back by the emergence of large Aromanian populations in Albania and Macedonia speaking little or no Greek. Many Aromanians learned of their heritage only after the collapse of communism in the region.

The ethnic pride of the 1980s, however, gave way to ethnic cleansing in the Balkans in the early 1990s. The crisis between Greece and the former Yugoslav Republic of Macedonia fueled nationalist sentiment on both sides. In Greece the Macedonian problem made the assertion of a non-Greek identity almost impossible. Both the Greeks and the Macedonians made claims to the Aromanians' loyalty. A second blow to the new Aromanian identity came when relations between Greece and Albania deteriorated sharply in 1994 over the state of the Greek Epirotes* in southern

Albania. The Greeks set themselves up as protectors of the entire Orthodox population of the region, pitting the Christian population, Greek or not, against the Muslim Albanian majority.

However, throughout history the Aromanians, like chameleons, have disappeared only to reappear later with their language, culture, and traditions intact. A key element in their survival has been their ability to adopt social and cultural patterns of other national groups when their own survival has been threatened. The strategy of revealing Aromanian identity only when verifiably safe to do so ensured the Aromanians' remarkable survival of the turbulent twentieth century in the Balkans, but it makes it extremely difficult to estimate the population of the Aromanian nation in the region. Traditionally, by melting into their host nations, the Aromanians became the "best Greeks," the "best Macedonians," and the "best Albanians." Until the 1980s, even many Aromanian leaders were doing their best to convince the members of the small nation that they were either Greek or Romanian, but now most acknowledge that they are a unique nation of their own.

Since the collapse of totalitarian regimes in the Balkans in the early 1990s, and the establishment of more democratic regimes across the region, the situation of the Aromanians has improved considerably, except in Greece. Renewed ties to the diaspora has helped fuel a cultural and linguistic revival, especially among younger Aromanians. The Macedonian government has gone the farthest in supporting the preservation of the language and culture, but other regional governments have also begun to accede to Aromanian demands for protection of their unique culture and history. The national movement remains divided into rival groups, pro-Greek and pro-Romanian, while a growing number wish only to be Aromanian and to be recognized as a separate Balkan national group.

In 1991 the Albanian government recognized the Aromanians as a "cultural group," the second largest in the country after the Albanians, but refused them national-minority status. The first congress of the Aromanian nation was held soon after in Albania, with participants from the Balkan countries and the Aromanian diaspora. The congress is seen as marking the rebirth of the Aromanian national movement. The figure of 200,000 Aromanians in Albania seems to fill the huge gap between the figures concerning the Greek minority in Albania, given by the Albanian government as about 60,000, and Greek official statistics of "Greeks" in Albania at 300,000–400,000.

In the Balkans, to claim to be Aromanian and nothing else—neither Greek, Romanian, Bulgarian, Albanian, or Yugoslav—is tantamount to bomb throwing. But for many younger Aromanians, bomb throwing is a step up from the indifference of their parents, who were considered safely assimilated. In Macedonia there was pressure even in the 1995 census to declare oneself as Macedonian for reasons of political correctness. However, Aromanian activists in 1997 succeeded in convincing the parliamentary Assembly of the Council of Europe, without Greek participation, to recommend protection of the Aromanian culture and language in all their host countries.

SELECTED BIBLIOGRAPHY:

Murvar, Vatro. *The Balkan Vlachs: A Typological Study*. 1978.
Poulton, H. *The Balkans: Slavs and Minorities in Conflict*. 1994.
Winnifrith, Tom. *The Vlachs: The History of a Balkan People*. 1987.
———. *Shattered Eagles/Balkan Fragments*. 1995.

Arubans

Orubans

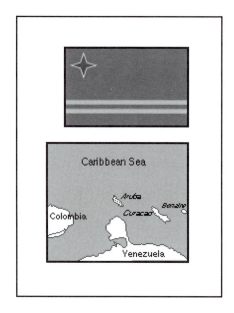

POPULATION: Approximately (2002e) 75,000 Arubans in the Dutch Caribbean, concentrated in the island state of Aruba. Another 14,000 live in the Netherlands, in the United States, and on other Caribbean islands.

THE ARUBAN HOMELAND: The Aruban homeland is a small island lying in the southwestern extreme of the Lesser Antilles in the Caribbean Sea. The island, lying 18 miles (29 kilometers) off the northern coast of Venezuela, is 19 miles long by 4 miles wide; it is mostly semidesert, surrounded by some of the Caribbean's finest beaches. The island lies outside the usual path of hurricanes. The natural vegetation consists of a variety of drought-resistant cacti, shrubs, and trees. Aruba forms an autonomous state in free association with the Kingdom of the Netherlands. *State of Aruba*: 69 sq. mi.—179 sq. km, (2002e) 71.000—Arubans 91%, Antilleans* 6%, other Caribbean islanders 3%. The Aruban capital and major cultural center is Oranjestad, (2002e) 21,000, the official capital of the state.

FLAG: The Aruban national flag, the official flag of the autonomous state, is a blue field with two narrow yellow stripes across the lower half charged with a red four-pointed star, outline in white, on the upper hoist.

PEOPLE AND CULTURE: The Arubans are a distinct Caribbean people, a mixture of Dutch, Arawak, and Spanish. Although they represent strains from many different people, including black African slaves, the physical appearance of the Arawak Indians continues to predominate. The mixture of the original Arawaks with the later Europeans developed the unique Aruban culture. Although tourism surpassed the oil industry as the mainstay of the Aruban economy in 1985, about 30% of the workforce continues to be employed at the huge oil refineries. The birth and death rates are both low, and the rate of natural increase is less than the average for the West Indies.

LANGUAGE AND RELIGION: The Arubans speak Papiamento, also spelled Papiamentu, the language of the southern Dutch islands in the

Caribbean, a patois based on a Spanish creole language but with strong Portuguese and Arawak elements, and more recently increased Dutch borrowings. An estimated 25% of the vocabulary is of Dutch origin. The official language of the island is Dutch, but the language of daily affairs remains Papiamento, which is also spoken in the Netherlands Antilles islands of Curaçao and Bonaire. Papiamento has no official status but is now recognized as a separate language, where formerly it was dismissed as a pidgin Spanish. The grammar and syntax have changed and become simplified from Spanish, the parent language. Papiamento is not intelligible to speakers of Spanish.

The major religion of the Arubans is Roman Catholicism. A minority adhere to various Protestant sects. The Church had great influence from early island history, but the advent of tourism and the secularization of Dutch society decreased its influence in the latter half of the twentieth century.

NATIONAL HISTORY: The island was inhabited by Arawaks when it was first discovered by Spanish explorer Alonso de Ojeda in 1499. It soon became a center of piracy and smuggling, but the Indians were not exterminated, as happened elsewhere in the Caribbean. Colonized in the early sixteenth century by Spanish settlers, Aruba remained a point of conflict among several of the European colonial powers. In 1634 the island was conquered by the Dutch, whose authority was confirmed by the other European powers two years later as compensation for the cession of New Amsterdam (New York) to the English. Aruba and five other islands in the Caribbean were united as the colony of Curaçao.

First the Spanish, then the Dutch, used the island as a huge cattle ranch, staffed by the native Arawaks. The Dutch later imported black slaves from Africa when the Arawaks proved a difficult workforce, but as no plantation economy ever developed on the island, the number of slaves was never large. The population grew slowly during the eighteenth century, with a few Europeans dominating the majority Arawaks and the black slaves.

Aruba was occupied by French forces during the Napoleonic Wars in the early nineteenth century. British forces, to protect the Caribbean from French domination, occupied the island in 1805–1806. Following the final French defeat and the liberation of the Netherlands, the island was returned to Dutch rule. Development of Aruba began only after its return to Dutch authority in 1816.

Gold was discovered in 1824 and remained the mainstay of the island's economy until after the turn of the twentieth century. In 1863 slavery was abolished in the Dutch possessions, and the island economy rapidly declined. Gold production ended in 1913, deepening the economic depression. Many Europeans left Aruba to return to Europe.

The economic turnabout came with the advent of oil production in nearby Venezuela. In 1924 the Lagos Oil and Transport Company, looking for a stable site for its business, established the first oil refinery on Aruba. Standard Oil built a second refinery in 1929. In 1930 Lagos became a subsidiary of Exxon, the giant American company. The huge oil refineries revived the economy of the island but also brought an influx of foreigners to work the refineries.

During World War II the Netherlands were overrun by the Germans, leaving the Caribbean Dutch islands self-governing under a local government based in Willemstad, the capital of Curaçao, 45 miles to the east. In 1942 German submarines shelled the refineries, causing some damage to the facilities, but the energy needs of the Allies brought tremendous prosperity to the Arubans.

At the end of the war a sense of separate Aruban nationality began to emerge, with increasing demands for cultural and political autonomy. In 1951, the Netherlands Antilles Regulation Act provided for self-government for the Dutch Antilles islands, and in 1954 the islands were granted autonomy as a federation under the Dutch government. From the beginning the Arubans resented rule from their rivals on Curaçao, which was the center of the autonomous government.

Tourism, beginning in the 1960s, became a new source of income, bringing renewed prosperity to the Arubans. Seeing themselves as a separate national group, the assertive Arubans, supported by a growing tourist income, demanded greater autonomy. Noted for its miles of white-sand beaches, duty-free shopping, friendly people, and casino gambling, the island became a center of Caribbean tourism, which replaced the oil industry as the Arubans' most important economic resource by 1985.

In the late 1960s the pro-independence People's Electoral Movement (Movimento Electoral di Pueblo, or MEP), was formed to promote separation from the Netherlands Antilles and independence for the Arubans. Initially the popular movement aimed merely at an end to Curaçaoan domination, but activists were soon promoting full independence from the Netherlands. Other political parties and organizations quickly formed, but the pro-independence groups won the widest support. Pro-independence sentiment in the 1970s led to a referendum organized by separatists in March 1977. Although only 57% of the electorate participated, 82% voted for immediate independence for Aruba. The Antilles government in Curaçao retaliated by removing the Aruban government. In August 1977 the separatist leader, Betico Croes, led a campaign of civil disobedience and a general strike. The strike closed the large tourist hotels, forcing over 1,500 tourists to leave the island.

Discussions between the Caribbean island dependencies and the Dutch government began in 1979. The Arubans pressed for and received local autonomy but continued to send delegates to the government on Curaçao. In 1981 they agreed to postpone a referendum on independence until

1988, following a Dutch agreement on separate independence for Aruba.

The islanders took on the trappings of independence while maintaining their economic and political ties to the Netherlands. A national flag was adopted, an anthem written, and official recognition of their Papiamento language was enacted. Anti-Curaçao feelings fueled a heated rivalry for tourist and oil income and intensified the Aruban national movement. On 1 November 1985 the Arubans elected their first parliament, in Oranjestad.

A 10-year agreement on autonomy, leading to complete independence in 1996, was negotiated with the Dutch government in the mid-1980s. On 1 January 1986 the Arubans officially seceded from the federation of Netherlands Antilles and assumed a new legal status as an autonomous state within the Kingdom of the Netherlands. Many nationalists pushed for a referendum on immediate independence and severance of all ties to the Dutch kingdom, but the major political parties preferred to wait, because the separation from the Netherlands Antilles caused an economic downturn, which cooled demands for complete independence. In fact, the prosperity of the island, underlined by Dutch control of only defense and foreign affairs, led many Arubans to question the need for full independence. In 1994 the Aruban government, in conjunction with the governments of the Netherlands and the Netherlands Antilles, decided to postpone indefinitely the transition to full independence.

In the 1990s offshore banking became the new growth industry, with Aruban banks competing with other Caribbean financial centers. The unregulated financial industry, although profitable for the Arubans, came under international scrutiny following several scandals and questionable financial dealings. Aruba was named the number one state for illegal money laundering in 1997

The Arubans handle their own internal affairs, directing their own civil service, judiciary, revenue, and currency. A governor appointed by the Dutch crown is the formal chief of state, but political power is in the hands of the Arubans themselves. The prosperous islanders celebrated the 500th anniversary of the first encounter between Europeans and Arawaks on Aruba in 1999.

The Aruban economy, based on tourism and banking, began to falter in mid-2000, partly due to the slowdown of the American economy. The Aruban government began to tighten banking regulations under pressure from the Dutch government and international agencies, but the new banking rules drove many investors to other Caribbean destinations, further slowing the economy. The economic situation, although not as serious as those facing other Caribbean nations, today underscores the Arubans determination to maintain their autonomy but also the important financial and military ties to the Netherlands.

The government of the United States, following the terrorist attacks in

New York and Washington D.C., in September 2001, pressured the Aruban government to tighten up lax banking laws when ties to Islamic radical groups were reported.

SELECTED BIBLIOGRAPHY:

Gastmann, Albert L. *Historical Dictionary of the French and Netherlands Antilles.* 1978.
Koulen, Ingrid. *Netherlands Antilles and Aruba: A Research Guide.* 1987.
Schoenhals, Kai, ed. *Netherlands Antilles and Aruba.* 1993.
Sedoc-Dahlberg, Betty, ed. *The Dutch Caribbean: Prospects for Democracy.* 1990.

Ashanti

Asante; Asanti; Achanti

POPULATION: Approximately (2002e) 2,812,000 Ashanti in West Africa, concentrated in the west-central part of Ghana and the eastern districts of the Côte d'Ivoire. Nationalists claim a population of over five million, accounting for about 28% of Ghana's total population and including such large related groups as the one million Brong (Abron) and the smaller Ahafo and Aowin groups.

THE ASHANTI HOMELAND: The Ashanti homeland lies in West Africa, called Asanteman in the Ashanti language, occupying the Kwahu Plateau west of Lake Volta in the west-central Ghana. The Ashanti Uplands stretch from the Côte d'Ivoire border in the west to the elevated ridge of the Volga Basin in the east. The region is the prime cocoa and gold producing region of Ghana. Ashantiland, the area claimed by nationalists, forms the Ghanaian regions of Ashanti, Brong-Ahafo, and a small part of Northern Region. Ashantiland is traditionally divided into 16 Ashanti states and 10 Brong states. *Ashantiland (Asanteman)*: 24,696 sq. mi.—

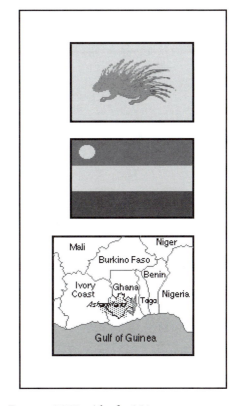

63,963 sq. km, (2002e) 5,247,000—Ashanti 61%, Brong 23%, Ahafo 3%, other Ghanaians 17%. The Ashanti capital and major cultural center is Kumasi, (2002e) 623,000, metropolitan area 1,100,000.

FLAG: The Ashanti flag, the traditional flag of the kingdom, is a gold field bearing a centered drawing of a red porcupine with gold quills. The flag of the national movement, is a vertical tricolor of red, yellow, and green bearing a gold geometric design representing a *mrammue*, a traditional gold weight, on the upper hoist.

PEOPLE AND CULTURE: Ashanti social organization is based on a matrilineal system, with localized clans claiming descent from a common ancestress. Members of the lineage traditionally assist their clans in such activities as building houses, farming, and funeral rites. The Ashantis believe that every individual is made of two elements, blood from the mother and spirit from the father. Every important lineage head—always males, due to menstrual taboos forbidding contact with sacred objects—has a sacred stool as a symbol of office. The Ashanti have urbanized since the 1950s, but a majority remain rural or village farmers. Much of the present knowledge about the history of the Ashanti comes in the form of oral histories that have survived for hundreds of years. The Ashanti, including the related Brong and Ahafo, represent numerous matriarchal clans that cut across tribal lines and are a closely related subgroup of the Akan peoples of West Africa.

LANGUAGE AND RELIGION: The Ashanti speak a Twi, or Agni-Ashanti, language of the Kwa branch of the Niger-Congo family of languages. The Twi languages, like the Chinese dialects, are tonal. All the Akan peoples of the region speak the common Twi language, but each ethnic and national group has its own dialect. The Ashanti language, called Ashante Twi, is spoken in the Ashanti heartland and is spoken as the unifying language across a large part of central and southern Ghana.

Traditionally the Ashanti have a complex religious system involving elaborate ceremonies, ancestor worship, witchcraft, and sorcery. Beliefs in many kinds of spirits form part of the concept and ritual. The most important and most frequent religious ceremonies recall the spirits of the departed rulers. These ceremonies, called *adae*, occur every twenty-one days. Funeral and mourning rites are also very important. The traditional ceremonies place great emphasis on ritual drumming; religious dance is a vital part of worship. The majority of the Ashanti now adhere to various Christian sects, but most continue to practice traditional religious rites. Islam has made little headway among the Ashanti proper, but associated subgroups, particularly the Brong, have a large Muslim minority.

NATIONAL HISTORY: The ancestors of the Akan peoples, thought to have migrated to the region from the east before the thirteenth century, established a number of small states or chiefdoms in the region. The foundation of the Ashanti nation is attributed to Osei Tutu, of the Oyoko clan, who established his capital at Kumasi in 1695. According to Ashanti legend, Osei Tutu plucked a golden stool from the sky; another legend has the stool rising from a lake near Kumasi. The Golden Stool, the *sika 'gua*, has became a politico-ritual symbol of Ashanti unity, embodying the spirit or soul of the Ashanti national group.

Two years after Osei Tutu established himself at Kumasi, he formed several of the small neighboring states into a loose confederation under his leadership as the Ashantene, the paramount chief of the Ashanti. After the death of Osei Tutu, in either 1712 or 1717, a period of internal chaos and factional strife ensued, ended by the accession of Opoku Ware. Under his rule the Ashanti confederation reached the apex of its power. The

Ashanti rulers established a strong state, with an efficient bureaucracy recruited by merit and a fine system of communications.

The success of the Ashanti empire depended on the trade in gold, not only with the coastal Europeans but with the Muslim states to the north. Gold dust was used as currency, measured against small weights. From the beginning of the eighteenth century, the Ashanti supplied slaves to British and Dutch traders on the coast. In return they received firearms, which they used to carry out further territorial expansion. The confederation, with its members and tributary states ruled by subkings, *omahenes*, steadily expanded over the next century to become one of West Africa's most powerful empires. The development of the empire was largely at the expense of the independence of the surrounding, related Akan peoples.

In the late eighteenth century the confederation ruled an area of over 100,000 square miles and boasted a population of between three and five million inhabitants. The Ashanti state was created and maintained by war, and a military ideology remained a central feature of its cultural orientation until its annexation of the confederacy to the British Empire in the early twentieth century.

A highly sophisticated Ashanti administration, rich on gold and slaves, collected taxes, took censuses, ordered commercial life, conscripted armies, and supported a constitution and courts of law. Led by Osei Bonsu, the Ashanti expanded southward in 1806–1807, finally conquering the coastal Fanti states. The expansion to the coast brought the Ashanti into conflict with the British, who had already established a foothold on the coast and now outlawed the slave trade. Declining trade relations and disputes over the Fanti states caused friction over the following decade that finally led to war.

Coveting the Ashanti's legendary mountains of gold and seeing the powerful Ashanti as a major threat to their domination of the Gold Coast, the British authorities prodded the Ashanti into open conflict. The British had miscalculated; they were defeated, though not decisively, in the first Anglo-Ashanti War of 1824–31. For over thirty years a tense peace prevailed, but in 1863, under Kwaku Dua, the Ashanti again challenged the British, sending forces to occupy the coastal provinces. In 1869 the British took possession of Elmina, also claimed by the Ashanti, and by 1873 the Ashanti were again at war with the British forces. An expeditionary force marched on Kumasi in 1874. Although the British managed to occupy the Ashanti capital only for one day, during which they burned and looted the city, the Ashanti were shocked to realize the inferiority of their own military and communications systems.

The British invasion of the confederation sparked numerous secessionist revolts in the northern provinces. Weakened by a devastating civil war from 1883 to 1888, the Ashanti were decisively beaten in the third Anglo-Ashanti War in 1893–94. Outraged by a British proclamation claiming the confederation as a protectorate, the Ashanti refused to surrender to the British authorities, thus provoking a fourth war in 1895–96. The defeated Ashantene, Prempeh I, his family, and many senior officials were exiled to the Seychelles, and the fabulous royal treasury was shipped to London. The only treasure missing from the looted goods, the Ashantene's sacred stool, remained hidden from the invaders. The subject peoples of the confederacy were quick to reassert their autonomy following the Ashanti defeat.

In 1899, Sir Frederick Hodgson, the governor of the Gold Coast, on a tour of the defeated confederation, demanded to use the Golden Stool for his seat. The outraged Ashanti rose in revolt rather than comply, and until 1901 they held off a superior British force. The war, the so-called War of the Golden Stool, resulted in the ultimate defeat of the Ashanti and their final incorporation into the British colonial system. On 1 January 1902, the Ashanti homeland was formally declared a British crown colony.

The Ashanti, politically mobilized after World War I, began to demand separation from the Fanti-dominated Gold Coast and establishment of a separate administration for Ashantiland. In 1935, responding to continued agitation and threats of violence, the British authorities resurrected the Ashanti confederation and installed a nephew of Prempeh I as the new figurehead Ashantene. The restored confederacy was made up of 21 constituent chiefdoms, designated as divisions of Ashantiland. Over Ashanti protests, the confederation was formally joined to the British Gold Coast colony in 1946.

By 1950 there had been no large-scale development of export crops, and subsistence farming remained the occupation of the majority of the Ashanti people. The growth of major commercial crops, such as kola nut and cocoa, transformed the economy of the region, making Ashantiland one of the most prosperous in West Africa.

After World War II, the Ashanti resisted the political advancement of the coastal peoples. Fearing domination by the former subject peoples, Ashanti nationalists mobilized in 1954 as the British began to move the colony toward self-government. Rejecting the unitary state dominated by their ancient Fanti enemies, the nationalists demanded separation from the Gold Coast. Kwame Nkrumah, advocating a centralized state, won the 1956 elections and demanded immediate independence for the entire Gold Coast colony.

Ashanti leaders pressed the British for separation, and the Ashanti secessionist crisis of 1956–57 forced the postponement of the scheduled grant of independence to the Gold Coast. After long negotiations, the Ashantis finally accepted a compromise, settling for autonomy and a separate regional assembly within a federal Ghana. The first African colony to win independence, Ghana was granted independence on 6 March 1957. Violent demonstrations broke in Kumasi and other Ashanti cities later in the year, following the arrest of the Ashanti political leaders, the closure of the Ashanti assembly, and the banning of regional political parties. A wave of antigovernment terrorist attacks shook the new Ghanian state as the Ashanti pressed for secession.

The Nkrumah government firmly crushed the Ashanti rebellion and in 1964 established a one-party dictatorship, notable only for squandering Ashantiland's enormous wealth and ultimately bankrupting Ghana. The overthrow of Nkrumah in 1966 inspired an Ashanti national revival. Fueled by growing disputes over the Brong states and the disposition of revenues from Ashantiland's important cocoa crop, Ashanti nationalism gained widespread support.

In the postcolonial coups in Ghana, the Ashantis and the Ewes* were the two major contenders seeking to expand their political influence. An attempted coup in 1967 is widely believed to have been supported by Ashantis and Fantis trying to reverse the growing domination of the Ghanaian state by the Ewes of the southeastern region. In 1972 Ignatius Acheampong, an Ashanti leader, seized power. During Acheampong's rule, from 1972 to 1978, the Ashanti played a key role in Ghanaian politics.

Flight Lt. Jerry Rawlings, associated with the Ewes, seized power in 1979, and the Ashantis were again largely excluded from the central government. Rawlings allowed presidential elections in late 1979 but again took power and banned all political parties. Although Rawlings attempted to balance ethnic rivalries, Ashanti demands for economic and cultural autonomy increased as the Ewes consolidated their power at a national level. By 1982 contention among the largest ethnic groups had intensified, and the armed forces were increasingly divided along ethnic lines, leading to yet more coup attempts.

In 1990 the Rawlings government, under pressure from Western nations and opposition groups, promised to restore multiparty civilian government. Ashanti leaders organized the Movement for Freedom and Justice (MFJ), which was denied permission to hold its inaugural rally in Kumasi due to growing antigovernment sentiment among Ashanti activists. Elections in 1992 led to rioting in Ashantiland over the results of the vote, which was won by the military ruler, Rawlings, with the support of the rival Ewes in the Volta region. In 1995, a mostly Ashanti organization known as the Alliance for Change was accused of leading anti-Rawlings demonstrations. Rawlings was again elected president in elections in 1996.

On 14 August 1995, the Ashanti king, Otumfuo Nana Opuko Ware II, celebrated his silver jubilee and the 300th anniversary of the Ashanti kingdom in Kumasi. President Rawlings, who is married to a member of the Ashanti royal family, attended the celebrations. The Ashantahene still plays an important role in Ghana today, symbolically linking the past with current Ghanaian political life. The Ashantahene's primary duties were traditionally religious and military, but since the 1930s the position has become increasingly secular.

An attempt to reassert Ashanti authority in the region of Techiman, which had once been part of the Ashanti empire but later became autonomous, led to rioting and the death of six people. The issue of tribute collections, which had been dormant, resurfaced in 1996 when the Ashanthene raised 17 subchiefs to the rank of paramount chiefs in regions outside the reduced Ashanti region. The king's move was seen as a ploy to reassert Ashanti authority in areas that had formerly been part of the Ashanti empire.

The Regional Security Council following violence between pro-government groups and Ashanti nationalists in December 1996 banned political activity in the run-up to elections. The ban included rallies, blockades of roads and streets, and songs or other acts that were likely to lead to violence.

Ashanti nationalism, suppressed under successive military governments, is again a potent force in the region as Ghana slowly moves toward real multiparty democracy. The heirs of one of Africa's most advanced political systems, the Ashanti claim that their historical right to separate nationhood is as strong as any in Africa.

Otumfuo Opuko Ware II, after ruling the Ashanti for 29 years, died on 19 March 1999. The succession, important to the stability and traditions of the Ashanti, was carried out with great ceremony. On 1 April 1999, amid great splendor, a new king of the Ashanti, Otumfuo Osei Tutu II, was inaugurated in Kumasi. Ghanian government attempts to influence the process of choosing the new Ashanti king outraged many Ashantis and prompted antigovernment demonstrations in Kumasi. The continuance into the new century of the monarchy, seen as one of the pillars of the distinctive Ashanti culture, was thus ensured. In late November 2000, Jerry Rawlings stepped down and allowed new presidential elections under a democratic system after 20 years in power. The Ashantis, who support a democratic system and a federal state in Ghana even though the Ghanaian government has never been popular in Ashantiland, welcomed the peaceful change of government, which is rare in Africa. The peace and relative prosperity of the 1990s lessened support by militants calling for complete separation from Ghana, although the end of the Rawlings era may give the nationalists new support among the masses, still suffering from economic excesses and government corruption.

SELECTED BIBLIOGRAPHY:

Allman, Jean Marie. *The Quills of the Porcupine: Asante Nationalism in an Emergent Ghana*. 1993.
Boateng, Faustine Ama. *Asante*. 1996.
Hetfield, Jamie. *The Asante of West Africa*. 1997.
Morrison, Minion K. *Ethnicity and Political Integration: The Case of Ashanti, Ghana*. 1982.

Asiris
Idrissis; Idrisis; Himyaris

POPULATION: Approximately (2002e) 2,590,000 Asiris in Saudi Arabia, mostly concentrated in the southwestern region of Asir. Outside the region there are Asiri communities in Riyadh and other areas of Nejd and along the coast in Hejaz.

THE ASIRI HOMELAND: The Asiri homeland lies in southwestern Saudi Arabia, lying on the Red Sea just north of Yemen. The most fertile region of Saudi Arabia, Asir is mostly a maritime plain backed by a highland plateau and high mountains that have isolated the region for centuries. The most mountainous region of the Arabian Peninsula, the region receives adequate rainfall for extensive cultivation, which is unusual in Arabia. It is a popular vacation area for Saudis from the deserts, because of its mountains, rainy weather, green

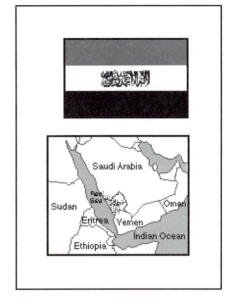

landscape, and life without air conditioning. The Emirate of Asir forms the provinces of Asir, Najran, and Jizan of the Kingdom of Saudi Arabia. *Emirate of Asir*: 40,130 sq. mi.—103,937 sq. km, (2002e) 3,258,000—Asiris 79%, Hejazis* 10%, Nejdis 8%, Yemenis 2%. The Asiri capital and major cultural center is the city of Abha, (2002e) 147,000, the official capital and the center of the most densely populated part of Asir, the highlands. The other important cultural center is Najran, (2002e) 118,000, the ancient capital of the Asiris.

FLAG: The Asiri national flag, the flag of the regional movement, is a vertical tricolor of green, white, and black, charged with the *Shahada*, the inscription in Arabic that reads "There is no God but God, Mohammed is the Prophet of God" and is written in black on the center stripe.

PEOPLE AND CULTURE: The Asiris are the descendants of the ancient Sabeans, the people of Biblical Sheba. They are often called Idrissi, after their former ruling dynasty. Although a large urban population has developed, the Asiris remain mostly tribal in nature and maintain their traditional tribal identity. The Asiris are geographically and culturally closer to the Yemenis than to the Saudis of the Nejd Desert, and their customs, culture, and architecture form part of their unique heritage. The most distinctive feature of Asiri architecture are shingles protruding from the sides of houses to deflect the frequent rains from the mud walls.

LANGUAGE AND RELIGION: The language of the Asiris is Himyaritic or Southern Arabian, an Arabic dialect with much pre-Arabic admixture. The language, not mutually intelligible with Nejdi Arabic, has become a rallying point for the anti-Saudi activists in the region in the 1990s. Himyaritic is spoken in three distinct dialects—Biishah, Najraan, and Coastal— reflecting the historical distribution of the Asiri population. The name "Himyaritic" comes from the ancient kingdom of Himyar that flourished in the region. The Asiris speak the standard Arabic based on the Riyadh dialect but retain their regional language as the language of daily life and of the family and home.

The majority of the Asiris follow the Shafai sect of Sunni Islam, a sect that is much less puritanical than the ruling Wahabi sect of Saudi Arabia. Wahabis, adherents of the puritanical sect that predominates in most of Saudi Arabia, form only a small minority in the northeast. The Wahabi interpretation of Islam is rooted in the Nejd Desert. To the majority of the Asiris it is a harsh and alien creed. Asiri beliefs retain many pre-Islamic traditions, including the belief in spirits and veneration of sacred wells, mountains, and oases.

NATIONAL HISTORY: Asir means "difficult to reach" or "inaccessible" in the Himyaritic dialect, a name given to the region due to its long isolation behind its high mountains. As the most fertile region of the Arabian Peninsula, Asir has been inhabited since earliest times. The Himyarites are thought to have settled the region about 250 B.C. A settled agricultural society developed a highly cultured civilization known as Sheba in the second century B.C. Legend tells of the journey of the queen of Sheba to ancient Israel to negotiate with King Solomon.

One of the earliest mentions of the area is that of a Roman, General Aelius Gallus, who was sent in 25 B.C. to conquer the incense-producing regions in present Yemen and Oman. His troops moved along the main caravan route east of the Asir Mountains and conquered Najran but failed to reach the incense areas because a lack of water forced them back. Under Roman rule, Asir formed part of Arabia Felix. The Romans were impressed with this green and fertile region on the Red Sea coast. After the departure of the Romans the Asiris established an independent state. In the sixth century the Asiris were Christianized, with an important bishopric at Najran, the capital of the kingdom of Himyar. In A.D. 523, the Christian establishment was destroyed by the Judaized King Yusuf.

Islam originated among the neighboring Hejazis, and with the explosive Muslim expansion of the seventh century the Asiris were converted to the new religion. With the removal of the Muslim center from Hejaz to Syria in the eighth century, the Arabian Peninsula again split into smaller sovereign tribal states. Protected by their high mountains, the Asiris developed as a prosperous agricultural and herding nation.

The puritanical Wahabis from the Nejd Desert overran Asir in the early nineteenth century. Egyptian troops, acting for the Ottoman sultan, drove the Wahabis from the region in 1818–19 and occupied the area until 1840, when they were replaced by Ottoman Turkish troops. Although under nominal Turkish rule, the Asiris continued under the direct rule of their own emirs and religious imams. The Turks divided Asir into two provinces, Highland Asir, with its capital at Abha, and Asir Tihama, in the maritime plain with its capital at Sabya. Coffee was introduced early, and the Asiris were among the major producers of coffee in the Ottoman Empire. In 1872 the Turks took direct control of the region, making Asir a *sanjak* of Turkish Yemen. In the 1880s, the Idrissi dynasty of Sabya became the predominant political force, ruling the region under the supervision of Turkish advisors.

In the early twentieth century, in 1906, the Idrisi leaders of Asir led a rebellion against Turkish rule. By 1910 the rebels controlled most of Asir, but the Turks, aided by the Hejazis, defeated the Asiris. The region, again under Turkish control, remained a Turkish province up to World War I, although Turkish control was limited to the lowlands. The Asiris, having withdrawn to the mountains, continued to control the Asiri highlands.

Turkish troops were withdrawn following the outbreak of war in 1914, and Turkish rule in Asir became even more tenuous. In April 1915, British agents, hoping to garner Asiri support for the Allies, signed a treaty with the Idrisi emir guaranteeing the independence and security of Asir upon the defeat of the Turks. Asiri troops fought the Turks as allies of the British forces. In January 1917, in a subsequent agreement the British government of India promised independence at the end of the war.

The Idrisi emir, Mohammed Ibn Ali Al-Idrissi, took refuge with King Abdul Aziz of Nejd following threats to Asir from Yemen and Hejaz. Hassan Al-Idrissi, the emir's uncle, with the defeat of the Turks, declared Asir independent on 3 August 1917. From 1917 to 1920 the Asiris fought off threats by the neighboring Yemenis and from the Wahabis of Nejd, but by late 1920 the Wahabis held highland Asir, while the forces of the Idrisi leaders held only the coastal region, the Tihama. The Asiris appealed to their former allies, the British, but the British refused to intervene between their former allies in Asir and Nejd. Asir, like neighboring Yemen, sought to maintain its separate independence against the forces of Ibn Saud of Nejd, who had conquered much of the Arabian Peninsula. The British military evacuated Asir in 1921, leaving the Asiris to fend for themselves.

Emir Mohammed died in 1923, setting off a succession crisis and civil war among factions backing rival candidates. His son, Ali bin Mohammed, succeeded but was quickly overthrown by Hassan al-Idrissi. Civil war lasted until 1926, when Hassan requested Saudi protection against the encroaching Yemenis, who claimed Asir on the grounds that it formed a *sanjak* of Yemen under Turkish rule. The Saudi king took control of Asiri foreign affairs, leaving the administration of the emirate to Hassan. Saudi forces ended the factional fighting and the immediate Yemeni threat, but many Asiris rejected the Wahabi Saudis and continued to fight a guerrilla war from the mountains.

Asiri discontent erupted into a full rebellion in 1933 under Hassan al-Idrissi. Asiri fighters, encouraged by the Yemenis, fought the Saudi forces across the region, particularly after the Saudi government announced the incorporation of Asir, to be known as Idrisi Province, into the Saudi Arabian kingdom. The Idrisi emir asked for help from Imam Yahya of Yemen, who sent troops into Asir. Ibn Saud, the leader of the Saudis, aided by American oil companies, invaded with a newly mechanized army of 45,000, quickly defeating the Asiris and their Yemeni allies. Imam Yahya was forced to withdraw and was only barely able to retain Yemeni independence. On 13 May 1934, Imam Yahya signed a treaty with the Saudis accepting peace conditions and recognizing Saudi authority in Asir. The Saudi authorities deposed the Idrisi emir Hassan and replaced him with a Saudi governor, effectively ending Asiri resistance.

From the late 1930s, the region remained an isolated agricultural province, appreciated by Saudi princes and government officials for its mild, cool climate and mountain scenery. Development of the province accelerated in the 1950s, although Asir was not recognized as an integral part of Saudi Arabia until the 1960s. The Yemeni civil war in the 1960s led to violence as troops violated the border regions, but the Asiris remained strictly neutral and refused to be drawn into the conflict.

The oil boom in Saudi Arabia in the 1970s brought material gain, but the Asiris refused to be assimilated into the Saudi culture. They retained their language and their Shafai religious beliefs in the face of Saudi efforts to extend their Wahabi creed to all parts of the kingdom. In the Saudi tradition, handouts and development projects were used to placate the inhabitants. The Asiris have their own Himyaritic-language television system, jobs, schools, and hospitals.

The coastal region, known for its scenery and beaches, began to be developed as a tourist resort in the 1980s, but Wahabi prohibitions on mixed bathing, drinking, or other vacation pursuits made the success of international tourism doubtful. In 1982 the Asir Kingdom Park, Saudi Arabia's first national park, opened in Asir.

Mineral finds in the mostly agricultural area held out the promise of even greater prosperity, but the Saudi economy began to falter in the mid-1980s, leading to a renewal of discontent and anti-Saudi feeling. In the 1990s, as the world economy became even more volatile, Asiri activists claimed that the ruling Saudis were paying more attention to their investments in London and Texas than to the welfare of the Asiris.

The Asiris continue to feel that they are a separate Arabian people, with their own language, religion, and history. Should Saudi Arabia disintegrate, it would most certainly do so along tribal lines. The Asiris mostly remain loyal to political units both bigger and smaller than the Saudi kingdom. Devout Muslims feel that they belong to the *umma*, the worldwide community of the faithful. But the Asiris also regard their tribal and regional ties as the vital badges of their identity.

In July 1998, Saudi warships fired on a Yemeni island in the Red Sea, killing three Yemenis and wounding nine. Though the island is insignificant, the incident was a reminder that the borders between the two states are not settled. The border, not delimited, wriggles through the Asir tribal highlands into the oil-rich desert beyond. Since the border was set by the Treaty of Taif in 1934, the Yemenis have mourned the loss of the three border provinces of Asir, Jizan, and Najran. An "understanding" reached in 1995 supposedly settled the border dispute, but skirmishes continue, keeping the question open.

The Saudi government set up a new company to promote tourism to the juniper-clad hills of Asir in 1998, but the prospect of no liquor, segregated sexes, and no nightlife whatsoever continued to make Asir a hard sell to Western tourists. The Asiris, less puritanical than the Wahabis of Nejd, proposed loosening the stringent rules, at least in areas of interest to tourists, but were overruled by the Saudi government.

Nobody understood the fragility of the new Saudi state better than Ibn Saud, who unified the peninsula tribes by conquest and intermarriage—or, as the Arabs put it, with a sword of steel and a sword of flesh. Ibn Saud was also aided by his alliance with the British. The tribal confederation was held together by regular handouts and the force of his determination. When he died in 1953, Ibn Saud left more than 40 sons. They lacked his personality but have continued the handouts. It was assumed that over time, and with its tremendous oil wealth, Saudi Arabia would gradually knit itself into a homogeneous Arabian nation. The Saudi ruling family has created the trappings of modern statehood, but the political reality remains a loose confederation of distinct tribal groups. In the past, oil wealth served to reduce regional discontent, but as the Saudi government curtails its role as the main provider, Asiri regionalism is again becoming a potent force.

Wahabi puritanical doctrines, spread from desert Nejd, with denunciations of royal corruption, indebtedness to the West, and American hold on the Saudi oil fields, have won wide support among the still anti-Saudi Asiris. Four of the hijackers implicated in the September 2001 terrorist attacks on the United States were Asiris. Sensitive to their nation's role in the attacks, Asiri officials have refused entry to journalists. Asiris were also implicated in the attack on the USS *Cole* in Aden harbor in 1999.

SELECTED BIBLIOGRAPHY:

Bang, Anne K. *The Idrisi State in Asir, 1906–1934: Politics, Religion and Person Prestige as Statebuilding Factors in Early Twentieth-Century Arabia*. 1996.

Cornwallis, Kinahan. *Asir before World War I: A Handbook*. 1975.

O'Fahey, R. S. *Enigmatic Saint: Ahmad Ibn Idris and the Idrisi Tradition*. 1990.

Saud, Noura bint Muhammad. *Asir: South-Western Region of the Kingdom of Saudi Arabia*. 1978.

Assamese

Asambes; Asamis

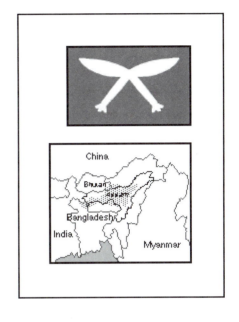

POPULATION: Approximately (2002e) 19,245,000 Assamese in south Asia, mainly in the Indian state of Assam. Sizable Assamese communities also live in neighboring Indian states and the adjacent areas of Bhutan and Bangladesh.

THE ASSAMESE HOMELAND: The Assamese homeland lies in northeastern India, a fairly isolated region separated from central India and linked by a land corridor between Bhutan, Bangladesh, and Nepal. The Brahmaputra River basin, mostly hilly plains, forms the major part of the state and is surrounded by upland tribal areas. The river valleys, with the richest soil, support the majority of the population. Assam forms a state of the Republic of India. *State of Assam (Swadin Asom)*: 30,285 sq. mi.—78,438 sq. km, (2002e) 27,060,000—Assamese 61%, Bengali 26%, tribal peoples 12%. The state capital is at Dispur, (2002e) 7,000, a suburb of the largest city and the center of Assamese culture, Gawahati, (2002e) 981,000 (metropolitan area 1,230,000).

FLAG: The Assamese national flag, the flag of the national movement, is a red field with two Assamese knives, in white, crossed in the center.

PEOPLE AND CULTURE: The Assamese are a people of mixed origins, descendants of early immigrants to the region, including the Austric Karbis, the Mongoloid Kirats, the Caucasian Aryans, and Drabir peoples, the Kaibartas and Banias. The physical diversity of the Assamese nation has resulted from a long history of invasion and conquest; the present Assamese nation is made up of several distinct ethnic groups. An estimated 10 million Assamese claim to be of Ahom descent. Being generally smaller and darker than the Indo-Aryan peoples of north India, they have often suffered discrimination. The culture of the Assamese has been greatly affected by the centuries of close contact with the neighboring Tibeto-Burman tribal peoples of the hills surrounding their great central valley.

They remain primarily rural, living in villages as rice farmers. Only a small fraction live in towns and cities.

LANGUAGE AND RELIGION: The Assamese language, the official language of the state, is the only Indo-Aryan language of the Assam valley. Called Asami, the language has been influenced by the vocabulary, phonetics, and structure of neighboring Tibeto-Burman languages and the now-extinct language of the early Ahoms. Several distinct ethnic groups collectively known as Assamese speak the language, which is divided into four major dialects and several subdialects. The language is written in the Bengali script. A strong literary tradition dates from the thirteenth century.

The majority of the Assamese, about 80%, are Hindu, with a substantial Muslim minority in the south, where converts from the Hindu lower castes have been influenced by the neighboring Bengalis. A majority of the Assamese Hindus accept Vaisnaivism, which is based on the deity Vishnu. Because of the various belief systems that have been integrated into their culture, the religious practices of the Assamese are often unorthodox, often combining animist traditions and customs. Other Assamese eat meat, which is strictly forbidden in Hinduism, while others refuse to worship elephants, as is customary among India's Hindu majority. Only about 1% are Christian, mostly belonging to evangelical Protestant sects.

NATIONAL HISTORY: Aryan invaders, originally from the Iranian Plateau far to the west, occupied the valley of the Brahmaputra River about 1200 B.C., pushing the earlier inhabitants into the less accessible mountain areas. Known as Kamarupa, the region was isolated from the mainstream of Indian civilization until the first century A.D. Ancient Assam's culture developed independently and incorporated influences from neighboring peoples, particularly the Tibetans to the north.

The Ahom, from neighboring Burma, conquered the Brahmaputra Valley in 1229 as part of the great expansion of the Tai peoples in southeastern Asia. The Ahom leader, Lung Sukapha, united the seven independent states in the region into one powerful kingdom under a Tai-speaking Ahom nobility. The power and prosperity of the Ahom kingdom reached its height under Rudra Singh, who ruled from 1696 and 1714. Gradually absorbed by the Aryan Assamese of the river valleys, the Ahom formed an aristocratic nobility, but they had disappeared as a separate people by the seventeenth century. The Ahom influence on the language and culture of the region remains strong to the present.

The Assamese kingdom, often at war with the neighboring Muslim Bengalis to the south, finally turned to the new power in the region, the British, for protection from their many enemies. Instability brought an invasion from present Myanmar in 1817. The Burman invaders, repulsed in 1822 with British military aid, returned later to conquer the kingdom, a major cause of the first Anglo-Burmese War of 1824–26. Taken from the defeated Burmans, Assam was added to the British province of Bengal.

By 1842 the remaining Assamese territories had come under British rule. Resistance to British rule continued in many areas, particularly in the less accessible hill regions.

The British authorities, to overcome a labor shortage in the underpopulated region, encouraged migration from Bengal. The inflow of migrants to northeastern India continued unabated, raising ethnic tension and demands for protection of the majority Assamese culture and language and for a separate Assamese province in British India. Assam remained part of British Bengal until the authorities created a separate autonomous province in 1937. The growth of nationalism in Assam became part of the Indian national movement against continued British colonial rule in the 1930s. Small groups advocated a return to Assam's precolonial independence, but the majority joined the Indian nationalist movement. Opposition to the Muslims of neighboring Bengal was the focus of local Assamese interest.

Assam's oil fields became important resources in British India and were the objects of an unsuccessful Japanese offensive during World War II. Japanese promises and inducements failed to attract many Assamese to their cause but did open the discussion of autonomy and spurred the growth of postwar Assamese nationalism.

The postwar partition of British India into predominantly Hindu India and Muslim Pakistan in 1947 created a chaotic situation in Assam, as refugees streamed across the newly established international borders, which divided the region. Assam's Muslim-majority region of Sylet went to the new Pakistani state, forming part of the eastern half of the Muslim republic, East Pakistan, which later seceded from Pakistan as the Republic of Bangladesh in 1971.

The population of Assam increased from about 3.5 million at partition in 1947 to nearly 20 million in 1980. The increase, mostly through immigration, started with the arrival of several hundred thousand Hindus fleeing East Pakistan between 1947 and 1950. Since then the population of the state has grown with continuing immigration from Nepal, Bangladesh, and Indian states. The Indian government has often encouraged migration to the region.

Assam's numerous minorities, dissatisfied with Assamese domination of the state government following Indian independence in 1947, demanded separation, greatly reducing Assamese territory, as Nagaland, Mizoram, Meghalaya, and Arunchal Pradesh were hived off under separate administrations during the 1960s and 1970s. The Assamese majority in the truncated state, affected by the loss of what they considered traditional Assamese territory, demanded greater political autonomy and control of their national wealth, which includes India's only important source of petroleum. The capital of Assam was shifted from Shillong, now the capital of Meghalaya, to Dispur, a suburb of Guwahati, in 1972, when Meghalaya separated from Assam.

Muslim immigrants, fleeing poverty in Bangladesh, poured into the state in the 1970s, aggravating ethnic and religious tension. The illegals, perceived as a threat to Assamese culture and ethnic identity, provoked a strong Assamese nationalist backlash and raised demands for the expulsion of all illegal immigrants from the state. The United Liberation Front of Assam (ULFA) was formed in 1978 to liberate resource-rich Assam from Indian control and Bengali immigration. ULFA began its operations with grassroots developmental projects, winning widespread support. The group's fund-raising tactics, including extortion, kidnapping, and murder, brought an Indian military response and increased violence in the state. Many rebel commanders moved their operations to Assamese-populated regions of Bhutan or Bangladesh.

Turmoil in Assam in the 1980s was largely a result of Assamese charges of central government neglect and of the influx of illegal migrants. Resentment caused by chronic underdevelopment resulted in the targeting of the non-Assamese blamed for the region's economic situation. The lack of local control of the state's important petroleum reserves became a nationalist issue in the 1980s.

Amid growing violence, in 1981 the state government was dissolved, and direct rule from New Delhi was imposed. Many Assamese political leaders were imprisoned. New state elections were called, but the Indian government, fearing a nationalist victory, allowed the millions of illegal immigrants to vote in the election in February 1983. The vote, boycotted by the Assamese, established a pro-Indian state government. Violent clashes between Assamese nationalists and the Bengali migrants escalated in the 1980s into the most severe ethnic and religious confrontation since the partition of the subcontinent in 1947.

An Assamese nationalist party, supported by anti-immigrant and militant student groups, won a new state election in early 1985. Under an August 1985 accord, all those who came into India after 25 March 1971 would be treated as foreigners and all migrants who entered India before that date would qualify as Indian citizens, allowing the growing Bengali Muslim population to vote in subsequent elections.

The demands for separation from Assam by the Bodo* tribal minority in the 1980s strengthened the Assamese nationalists' determination not to surrender any more Assamese territory to newly formed ethnic states. Clashes between Assamese and Bodos in the late 1980s and the 1990s quickly reached the levels of violence of the continuing Assamese-Bengali confrontations.

In November 1990, the Indian federal government again dissolved the state government as separatist sentiment took hold in areas and among classes previously little affected. The Indian military made widespread use of the sweeping powers given it by the government to combat the separatists. The whole state was declared a "disturbed area." The deteriorating state of law and order, blamed on militant separatists, led to a crackdown on dissident activities. The major nationalist organization, ULFA, was outlawed, and many Assamese separatist leaders fled to Myanmar. In 1992 the Indian government suspended its military operation, and ULFA agreed to end its four-year campaign of violence; however, fighting resumed within months.

In the late 1990s, the Assamese rebels targeted government officials, both Assamese and those from minority groups or from outside the region. Attacks on police stations in several districts in 1996–97 led to government reprisals. The presence of several organized non-Assamese tribal groups in the region added to the general lawlessness and violence in Assam. A general strike called by the All Assam Students Union (AASU) paralyzed the state in September 1996. The AASU alleged that the state's voter lists were full of illegal Bangladeshi immigrants and wanted the list revised. In November 1996, the ULFA called a 24-hour strike that again crippled the state. The second strike was called to protest army atrocities and abuse of the civilian population. Strikes continued to disrupt the state in 1997–98.

Violence between Assamese nationalists and militant Bodos seeking to carve out a separate Bodo homeland from Assam increased in 1997–99. Conflicts between nationalists from the two groups left many dead and wounded. Attacks on trains, unarmed villages, and isolated homesteads continued in spite of military intervention. In February 1997, the ULFA rejected peace talks with the government in response to the army's crackdown in the state. Nearly 5,000 additional troops were deployed in Assam to combat the increasing violence.

On 15 August 1997, India celebrated 50 years of independence, but in Assam the celebrations were marred by strikes and attacks by Assamese dissident groups across the state. Although the ULFA had lost support due to the violence that surrounded it, the Indian forces in the region, acting with impunity, were accused of massive abuses, including the rapes of thousands of women and children. In 1998 human rights organizations began a campaign to expose the abuses and support demands that both the Indian government and the Assamese insurgents regain control of their respective military forces in the region. The Indian government asked the government of Bhutan for permission to attack ULFA bases in the tiny Himalayan state.

Militancy among the Bangladeshi Muslim immigrant population grew from 1998, reportedly aided by the government of Bangladesh. Demands for a Muslim state in the Muslim-dominated districts of southern Assam added to the violence in the state. The Indian government also accused Pakistan of supporting the growing Muslim insurgency and of aiding ULFA rebels in the region.

A government offer of amnesty led to the surrender of several hundred Assamese insurgents in 1998–99. To prevent the former militants from returning to violence, the Indian government established a new battalion in Assam, composed of ex-ULFA fighters. In October 1998, Paresh Barua, the military leader of ULFA, rejected a cease-fire with the government. He stated that the Assamese rebels would consider holding talks if they were held outside of the country and sovereignty were included on the agenda. In December the ULFA accused the federal government of attempting to trigger civil war by killing over 30 relatives of its top activists. In March 1999, six more relatives of ULFA leaders were killed, probably by former ULFA members. The death toll in the Assamese violence reached over 20,000 at the turn of the new year in 2000, following 21 years of fighting in the region.

Anti-insurgency operations in the state intensified in 1999–2000, even as the federal government made efforts to initiate a dialogue with the major militant groups, including the ULFA. Several groups reached agreements with the government, but the ULFA has steadfastly insisted on preconditions that are considered unacceptable, particularly demands for talks on the secession of Assam from the Indian union.

The continuing growth of the immigrant Muslim population gave five districts Muslim majorities by 1998, with several others having large numbers of Muslim inhabitants. The Assamese nationalists fear that they will soon be a minority in their homeland, outnumbered by the Muslim Bangladeshis and the mostly Christian tribal groups.

On 7 August 2001, the State Government initiated a week-long campaign aimed at mobilizing public opinion against all forms of insurgent violence and to create a congenial situation to enable the separatists to give up insurgency and return to the mainstream. The ULFA responded that it would hold peace talks with the Indian government only if they accept three conditions: talks should be held outside India, the dialogue should be held under UN supervision, and the core issue should be Assamese sovereignty.

SELECTED BIBLIOGRAPHY:

Baruah, Sanjib. *India Against Itself: Assam and the Politics of Nationality*. 1999.
Chattopadhyay, Dilip Kumar. *History of the Assamese Movement since 1947*. 1990.
Deaner, Janice. *Assam*. 2000.
Hussain, Monirul. *The Assam Movement: Class, Ideology and Movement*. 1993.

Assyrians

**Assurayee; Aturaya; Syriacs; Assyrian-Chaldeans;
Siro-Khaldei; Siriiytsy**

POPULATION: Approximately (2002e)
2,200,000 Assyrians in the Middle East, concentrated in Iraq and Syria but with sizable populations in other Middle Eastern states and Turkey. The Assyrian diaspora, with communities in Europe, North America, Australia and New Zealand, South Africa, and South America, numbers between 3 and 5 million.

THE ASSYRIAN HOMELAND: The Assyrian homeland, called Bet–Nahrain, lies in the Middle East, forming the so-called Assyrian Triangle between the Lower Zab and Tigris Rivers in northern Iraq, northern Iran, southeastern Turkey, and eastern Syria. The region claimed by the Assyrians as their traditional homeland includes territory west to the Euphrates River in Syria, north to the Hakkari Mountains in Turkey, east to Lake Urmia, and south to central Iraq. The Assyrian homeland has no official status in the countries that control the region. Major Assyrian cultural centers include Mosul, Irbil, and Kirkuk in Iraq, Qamishliye and Haseke in Syria, Urfa and Hakkiri in Turkey, and Orumiyeh in Iran.

FLAG: The Assyrian flag, the flag of the national movement, is a white field bearing wavy blue, white, and red stripes from the corners to the center and is charged with a centered blue four-pointed star around a yellow disc, outlined in white and surmounted by the red national seal. The flag of the Chaldeans is a very pale blue field bearing crossed pale blue stripes surmounted by a four-pointed orange star with a yellow center within a orange circle centered and two vertical blue stripes on the hoist and fly. The flag of the Syriacs in Syria and Jordan is a red field bearing a stylized golden bird with outstretched wings.

PEOPLE AND CULTURE: The Assyrians claim descent from the ancient Assyrians of the Middle East. They are not Arabs but a Semitic people indigenous to Mesopotamia and have maintained a continuous and separate identity that predates the Arabization of the Middle East. A Christian people, the Assyrians are the adherents of a bewildering variety of Christian sects, united by their minority status and their alienation from Muslim domination. Their national identity entails an inextricably intertwined combination of language, culture, history, religion, and ethnic heritage. The Syrian Orthodox or Jacobite community, numbering over 50,000, ranks as the largest Christian denomination in Turkey. There are social differences between the Assyrians and their Muslim neighbors, as most Assyrians are urbanized and more prosperous, with relatively more of them in the professions.

LANGUAGE AND RELIGION: The Assyrian language, also called Neo-Syriac, Chaldean, or Syriac, is Semitic in origin, having evolved from ancient Aramaic, the language of Christ. The language is spoken in two major dialects, Western and Eastern, with numerous subdialects. A related language, Turoyo, spoken in Turkey, is often called a Northern dialect, but it is distinct. An Assyrian literary language developed in the 1840s on the basis of the Urmiye alphabet, using the same 22 letters as Hebrew. In the early centuries of the Christian era, Aramaic divided into eastern and western varieties. West Aramaic is still spoken in a few villages in Lebanon; the largest number of Assyrians speak the Syriac language, the only surviving dialect of the East Aramaic languages. The language is related to Hebrew and Arabic but is claimed to predate both. The earliest Syriac inscriptions date from the first half of the first century A.D., and the earliest documents not inscribed on stone date from the year 243.

The Assyrians, although closely associated with their Christian religion, are divided among a number of Christian sects. The largest denominations are the Chaldean Catholic Church with about 45% of the Assyrian population, the Syriac Orthodox with 26%, the Assyrian Church of the East with 19%, the Free Assyrian Orthodox Church of Antioch or Syrian Catholics with 4%, and various Protestant sects with a combined 6%. A small minority, around 1%, has converted to Islam but remain Assyrian in culture and language.

NATIONAL HISTORY: The Assyrians claim direct descent from the ancient inhabitants of the Assyrian empire that flourished in Mesopotamia from about 2500 to 612 B.C. Some historians claim that genocide explains the disappearance of the ancient Assyrians, but others maintain that they remained in their homeland after the fall of Nineveh, the Assyrian capital, in 612 B.C. Subject to new rulers, the Assyrians again emerged during the first years of the Christian era. Christianity spread from its roots in Palestine and Syria throughout the Roman Empire, with the Assyrians among the first converts. The Assyrian Church of the East, established in the

Assyrian city of Edessa, present Urfa in Turkey, claims to be the first and oldest church in the world. Christianity became a leading factor in strengthening the ethnicity of the early Assyrians.

The young religion, rent by controversies and schisms, began to divide into opposing sects in the first centuries of its rapid expansion. Nestorius, the patriarch of Constantinople, in A.D. 428 objected to the term "Mother of God," thus opening a 200-year controversy within the church. The followers of Nestorius organized themselves as a separate sect in Syria in 435, but to escape persecution by Byzantine church authorities dispersed to Mesopotamia, Persia, and Asia. Nestorian refugees spread their doctrine as far east as India and China.

The Church of Antioch, popularly called the Jacobites, established by Jacob Baradeaus in the sixth century, grew under the patronage of the Byzantine empress Theodora. The opposition of the other Syriac Christian sects to rule by the Orthodox Christian Byzantines weakened the empire's response to the sudden threat from the Arabian lands to the south. Arab Muslims, fired by missionary zeal, defeated the Byzantines in 634–36. Forced conversion to Islam, accompanied by massacres, decimated the Christian population. The survivors lived as despised minorities among the Muslim majority, subject to special restrictions and taxes. The Assyrian language, the lingua franca of the Middle East until about 900, was completely supplanted by the Arabic language adopted by the Muslim majority.

Invading Mongols overran the Middle East in 1258, and once again the Christians suffered massacres and dispersal. The devastated Christian population, just beginning to recover from the Mongol massacres, again faced eradication from Tamerlane's marauders in the fourteenth century. Nearly eliminated for their refusal to accept Islam, the survivors fled into the mountains of Kurdistan. The remnant of the Nestorian Christians, sheltering in the mountains, were the first to be called Assyrians.

Jesuit missionaries, followed by Orthodox and eventually Protestant denominations, made converts in the region but only among the already Christian populations, leading to a proliferation of sects and rites. The Assyrian Church of the East divided in 1550, creating the Chaldean Church of Babylon. The Chaldeans, while retaining most of the Nestorian rites and practices, accepted the authority of Rome in 1551. The Jacobites that formed a union with Rome are the Syrian Catholics; the Arabic-speaking Orthodox reunited with Rome are the Melchites.

The various Christian sects began to unite after the Turkish conquest of the Middle East in 1638. Denied the benefits of citizenship and excluded from many aspects of public life in the Ottoman Empire, the Christians also suffered periodic persecutions. The mutually antagonistic sects began to unite and to put aside old grievances in order to reaffirm their common heritage as Christians, aliens, and infidels in the Muslim world.

The Assyrian Christians became the center of the international conflicts and power struggles in the nineteenth-century Middle East. The European powers tried to exploit the fact that they shared the Christian religion with the Assyrians and other Christian minorities, which raised the suspicion and enmity of the Ottoman authorities. The corrupt and feudal Ottoman Empire increased persecution of its large Christian population in response to European overtures. The number of Assyrians killed in the 1895 massacres in the Ottoman Empire is estimated as up to 100,000.

The Christian populations at the turn of the twentieth century lived primarily in the rural areas of the Ottoman Empire, the only large urban populations being at Mosul in Mesopotamia and Antioch in Syria, the ecclesiastical seats of several of the sects. In the early twentieth century, a cultural and national revival that had begun a half-century before rapidly spread through the Christian communities. The Assyrian revival finally united the disparate peoples and sects as a nation. The ancient dialects gave way to a modern literary language with the appearance of an Assyrian dictionary that updated its usage and syntax.

An Assyrian national movement, growing out of the cultural revival, led to a widespread revolt against Turkish rule in 1908. Thousands of Assyrians died in savage reprisals and massacres of noncombatants. When world war began six years later the Assyrians again rebelled, assured by the British, French, and Russians that their support of the "Christian" powers would bring them an independent homeland in the Assyrian Triangle at war's end. For their support of Turkey's enemies, the Assyrians, like their fellow Christian Armenians, suffered massacres, persecution, and expulsions.

By the time the war ended in 1918 over half the prewar Assyrian population had perished, some 750,000 people. The surviving Assyrians, following revolutionary Russia's withdrawal from the war, isolated and without ammunition, again came under attack. The large population around Urmia, in Turkey, fled attacks by the Turkish military. Thousands perished during the panicked evacuation through the Zargos Mountains to the protection of British forces in Iraq. Over a third of the population that joined the exodus was lost to attacks by hostile Muslims, severe weather, epidemics, and hunger. Other Turkish Assyrians were forced from their homeland into French-controlled Syria.

The Assyrian leaders, expecting the allies to keep their promises, sent a delegation to the 1919 Paris Peace Conference. The representatives of the Assyrian-Chaldean nation put forward a claim to an independent state in their ancient homeland. Ignored by their former allies, the 250,000 surviving Assyrians in the Middle East came under renewed attack from Turks, Kurds, and Arabs, all claiming the same territories for their new states. Thousands of Assyrian refugees fled abroad; only those in the Jhezeira District of Syria, controlled by France, were given a measure of autonomy.

The Mosul Commission, appointed by the League of Nations to investigate the plight of the Assyrian refugees in 1924, recommended that they be settled in the Mosul District with a large measure of autonomy. Both Turkey and Iraq, with rival claims to Mosul, rejected the commission's recommendations. Although the claim to a homeland had failed, the Assyrian claim to Mosul delayed the settlement of the territorial dispute until 1925, when the commission awarded the district to Iraq, with Great Britain responsible for minority rights for 25 years.

Years of dreadful repression followed the Allied betrayal. Destitute and dependent on hostile Muslim governments, the Assyrians survived only through the support of the far-flung diaspora. Tension between the Assyrian population in Iraq and the new Iraqi government, in which the British refused to intervene, culminated in a massacre of unarmed Assyrians at Simeil in 1933. In all, some 3,000 Assyrians were massacred during August 1933. The massacres sparked a massive emigration, mostly to North America but also to countries throughout the world.

In 1968 nationalists formed the Assyrian Universal Alliance (AUA) as a global organization to work for a semi-autonomous state in the Assyrian ancestral homeland. Nationalists in the United States, insisting that only an independent Assyria will assure the ultimate survival of their beleaguered nation, formed the Bet–Nahrain Democratic Party (BNDP) in 1976, with the creation of a separate Assyrian state in their ancient homeland as its stated aim. The International Confederation of the Assyrian Nation, founded in 1977, organized a provisional Assyrian government.

The Assyrian population continues to be drawn into the continuing conflicts in the Middle East. During the Lebanese civil war from 1975 to 1991, many Lebanese Assyrians fought side by side with the Maronites* against the Muslim forces. The third-largest ethnoreligious group in Iraq, the Assyrians formed an alliance with an old enemy, the Kurds, during the uprisings in northern Iraq in the 1960s and 1970s. In 1988 over 2,000 Assyrians died when the Iraqi military, which was also shelling Kurdish villages, bombarded five Assyrian villages with chemical weapons.

The Assyrians in Iraq suffered renewed persecutions during and after the 1991 Gulf War. Many Assyrians joined the Kurdish uprising that followed Iraq's defeat, and over 250,000 fled into the mountains with the Kurds when the rebellion collapsed. After the Gulf War their situation in Iraq worsened. In spite of discrimination, however, the Assyrians often amass wealth and even obtain high government positions.

In January 1999, the Assyrian Patriotic Party (APP) documented an increasing spiral of violence directed at the Assyrian community in northern Iraq. The violence included bomb attacks on convents, churches, and clergy. The violence exemplified the precarious position of the Assyrians in the Middle East.

The oppressive regimes in Iraq and Syria deny the existence of the Assyrians as a distinct ethnic group, while in Turkey the remnant of a once-sizable population continues to emigrate to escape discrimination and the violence of the separatist war being fought by the Kurds. The existence of the Assyrians continues to be precarious in several Middle Eastern countries, where they remain suspect. The Assyrians, like their Kurdish allies, fear that without their own state they will eventually disappear in the very lands that were Christianity's cradle.

Fears that they are suspect as a Christian minority has grown in the wake of the September 2001 terrorist attacks on the United States. Like Muslims living in the West, they are often seen as an alien group in their ancient homeland. Two decades of growing influence by Islamist movements has threatened the fragile security the Assyrians enjoyed under secular governments in Iraq and Syria, where they were prominent in the anti-colonial struggles, as well as founders of the Baath Party that rules in both countries.

Islamic religious sentiment that is replacing national identities has increased persecution, including growing violence against Assyrians. Ties to the Assyrian diaspora has prompted greater numbers to emigrate, a trend that accelerated in late 2001. Although once more pro-Western than their Muslim neighbors, the Assyrians, particularly in Iraq, now see themselves as much the victims of American policy as the Muslims.

SELECTED BIBLIOGRAPHY:

Booko, John. *Assyria: The Forgotten Nation in Prophecy*. 1998.
Dadesho, Sargon. *The Assyrian National Question*. 1987.
Dalrymple, William. *From the Holy Mountain: A Journey among the Christians of the Middle East*. 1998.
White, Craig. *Assyrians in the Modern World*. 1995.

Asturians

Astur; Asturianos

POPULATION: Approximately (2002e) 925,000 Asturians in Spain, concentrated in the northwestern province of Asturias, with smaller communities in neighboring regions and the industrial cities of Castile, Madrid, and Catalunya.

THE ASTURIAN HOMELAND: The Asturian homeland lies in northwestern Spain, with about 90% of the territory included in the autonomous Principality of Asturias and smaller territories included in the neighboring autonomous regions of Castile-Leon and Cantabria. Mountains cover about four-fifths of the land, effectively isolating Asturias from the neighboring provinces. Hills surround the central region, the valley of the Nalón River, where the majority of the Asturians are concentrated. Precipitation is high, and many in the mountainous area are snowbound during the winter. Asturias forms an autonomous community, coextensive with the province and the principality, within the Kingdom of Spain. *Principality of Asturias (Principato de Asturias/Asturies)*: 4,079 sq. mi.—10,565 sq. km, (2002e) 1,073,000—Asturians 68%, Galicians* 14%, Cantabrians* 3%, other Spanish 15%. The Asturian capital and major cultural center is Oviedo, called Uviéu in the Asturian language, (2002e) 200,000. The other important Asturian cultural center is Gijón, called Xixón in Asturian, (2002e) 268,000, the region's largest city.

FLAG: The Asturian national flag is a blue field bearing the Asturian Cross in yellow. The flag of the nationalists is a pale blue field with the Asturian Cross, moved to the left, and charged with a single red five-pointed star on the upper hoist. The flag of the Conseyu Nacional Asturies

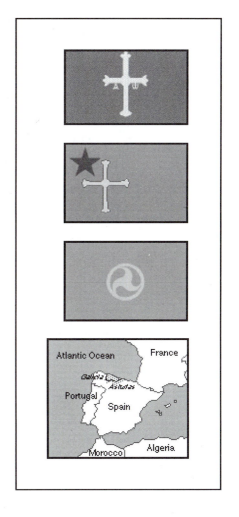

(CNA), the largest of the nationalist organizations, is a pale blue field bearing a centered "flower of Asturies" in yellow.

PEOPLE AND CULTURE: The Asturians are a Spanish nation, the descendants of Iberian and Celtic peoples who inhabited the region prior to the Roman conquest. The Asturian population has doubled since 1900, but its percentage of the Spanish total has steadily declined, and emigration has left behind an aging population. Emigration to the industrialized areas of Spain and other European Union states has also kept the Asturian population growth below the national average, except in the industrial triangle of Oviedo, Avilés, and Gijón. The population of the region continues to decline, making rural depopulation a serious problem. The regional culture, quite distinct from that of the Castilian plains, is basically an alpine culture, with traditions and customs that have been handed down since Celts controlled the mountains, including dress, bagpipes, and traditional dances. The Asturians are known for their stubborn courage and independence.

LANGUAGE AND RELIGION: The Asturian language, Asturianu, often called Bable in Spain, is made up of several closely related dialects spoken throughout the province. The language, which combines features of both Galician and Castilian, retains many forms and words that disappeared in the related Romance languages. In the mid-1990s there were an estimated 100,000 first-language speakers of Asturian, plus at least half a million others able to speak or understand it. However, since the language was not taught for decades, only 57% of speakers can read it, and only 38% can write it. The language is spoken in three major dialects—Central Asturian or Bable, Western Asturian, and Eastern Asturian. The language is as different from standard Spanish as is Galician or Catalan, with only about 80% mutual intelligibility with Spanish. Children aged six to 16 are obliged to study Asturian in regional schools, but it is voluntary from ages 16 to 19. The Academy of the Asturian Language was formed in 1981 to revive a famed academy of the eighteenth century. The language has had official status since 1998, with teaching in the language and some use of it in local administration.

The observance of the Roman Catholic religion tends to be less intense among Asturians than in Castile and central Spain. Local folklore preserves many pre-Christian superstitions and customs. As the Catholic Church had become identified with the mine and land owners in the nineteenth century, anticlerical sentiment became part of the culture of the region. Since the late 1970s evangelical Protestant sects have gathered a substantial number of converts in the region.

NATIONAL HISTORY: The region, populated by Celtic tribes, was conquered by Roman troops under Emperor Augustus in 25 B.C. The name "Asturias" derives from the major tribe that inhabited the region at the time of the Roman conquest. As always, when faced with a superior military force, many of the region's inhabitants withdrew to mountain strongholds, where Roman rule remained only nominal.

The Muslim conquest of Spain, beginning in A.D. 711, quickly overran the southern and central parts of the Iberian Peninsula. Thousands of Visigoths, mostly Christian nobles, fled north to the sanctuary of the Asturian mountains. They established a small kingdom in 718 under the successor to the Visigothic ruler of Spain, Pelayo, and established a capital at the town of Cangas de Onís, called Cangues d'Onís locally.

The kingdom expanded to include Galicia to the west and Cantabria to the east before the end of the eighth century. The capital was transferred to Pravia in 780 and finally to Oviedo, a strategically sited new city. During the reign of Alfonso III, from 866 to 910, the frontiers of the kingdom were pushed south to Duero River, from the Atlantic Ocean to Osma. By the tenth century, the kingdom had become too large to be controlled effectively from the northern mountain capital at Oviedo, and in 910 García I made Léon, to the south, his new capital. García's successors styled themselves kings of Leon and Asturias, and the center of the kingdom shifted south they dropped the Asturian title and called themselves kings of Leon.

John I of Castile, which had united with Leon in 1230, created a principality of Asturias for his eldest son, Prince Henry, later King Henry III, in 1388. The crown princes throughout the Spanish monarchy have held the title "prince of Asturias," much as the title "prince of Wales" remains in the British royal family.

During the French invasion of Spain during the Napoleonic Wars in the early nineteenth century, the Asturians gained widespread fame for their stubborn defiance of the French conquerors. In 1838 Asturias was created as a province of the Spanish kingdom. In the late nineteenth century, Anarcho-Syndicalist political parties and organizations gained a wide following among the poor working classes. Serious strikes and uprisings, usually put down with severe force, kept the region in turmoil.

In 1931 the Spanish monarchy was overthrown, and a republic was declared in Madrid. The title "prince of Asturias" lapsed when revolution swept Spain. New elections held in 1933 showed a definite shift to the right across most of Spain, which outraged the mostly leftist population of Asturias.

A miners' uprising in the region in October 1934 was met with overwhelming force. Government troops fought pitched battles with the miners, and the uprising quickly became a revolution, with growing support for independence from the corrupt and backward Spanish republic. On 18 October 1934, Asturian leaders, with the support of the majority of the population, declared Asturias independent of Spain. The separatists were quickly and bloodily suppressed. The repression of the revolt devastated the region and left much destruction and poverty.

In the years before the outbreak of civil war in 1936, Asturias was one of Republican Spain's most politically radical provinces. Unions and other working-class organizations kept firm control over Asturian policy. This problem was exacerbated by the independent attitude of provincial government. In the midst of a fresh Nationalist offensive in the summer of 1936, Madrid declared that the central government would assume control over provincial military and production decisions. The Asturians, calling themselves the Asturias Commune, by this time completely cut off by Franco's forces, repudiated Madrid and declared themselves independent in August of that year. The young republic succumbed to a Nationalist siege during the winter. In the wake of the Asturian Commune's destruction, the province remained wary of central administration.

After the Spanish Civil War the Asturians have tenaciously fought to retain their autonomy against the centralizing Franco government. Labor unions, persecuted by the Franco regime, gained widespread support among the mine workers in the region. In 1962 a series of strikes, beginning in the Asturian coal fields, gave indication of widespread discontent in the region. Student demonstrations took to the streets in support of the strikers. The confrontation quickly turned violent, with many killed and injured in running battles in the region's industrial cities. The conflict is considered by Nationalists to be the inception of the modern Asturian National movement.

Franco's death in 1975 ushered in an era of rapid democratization in Spain. The sudden liberalization of political life allowed the voicing of decades of grievances and raised demands for regional self-government across the country. The Asturians, after years of pressing the Spanish government, were granted a statute of autonomy in 1981, but with fewer powers than some other Spanish regions.

Nationalists claim that the government of the autonomous region continues to reject greater autonomy for the region. They also blame the Spanish and Asturian governments for the region's massive industrial pollution and increases in tourism, both of which they claim are destroying their national heritage. Their culture is being marginalized in favor of the dominant Castilian culture of Spain, and young Asturian youths continue to be jailed for refusing to serve in the Spanish army. Strikes and continuing emigration are often the Asturian responses to government inaction and neglect.

Asturian agriculture and industry have traditionally had a collective orientation; the extensive pastures in the mountains were mostly held collectively until the early twentieth century. The wealth of the region, although agriculture remains important, is in its extensive coal fields, which extend throughout the Nalón River basin. Asturias is the most important mining and metallurgical region of Spain, although the undeveloped infrastructure has hindered industrial expansion.

In 1998 the Asturian language was given official status but was not raised to the status of an official language as demanded by Nationalists. Teaching of the language, though not in the language, is guaranteed, and administrative uses are mandated. The Asturian language, long considered a dying rural dialect, has become one of the major issues of the growing Nationalist movement in the region.

The Asturian Party (PAS), the largest of the regional political organizations, has gained widespread support for its campaign to win greater self-government for Asturias. The party has elected members to the national legislature, local mayors in Asturian municipalities, and many members of regional and local councils. The Asturians seek the same rights as the neighboring region of Galicia, which has been granted greater autonomy within Spain, along with the regions of Catalonia, the Basque Country, and Andalusia. The Asturians see themselves as a national group with a distinctive identity as strong as those of other regions having large measures of autonomy.

SELECTED BIBLIOGRAPHY:

Kern, Robert W. *The Regions of Spain: A Reference Guide to History and Culture.* 1995.
Rose, David. *Beneath the Mountain.* 1988.
Ruiz, David. *Contemporary Asturias 1808–1936.* 1982.
Schubert, Adrian. *The Road to Revolution in Spain: The Coal Miners of Asturias 1860–1934.* 1987.

Avars

Maarlulal; Magarulal; Avarskiy; Avaros; Dagestanis

POPULATION: Approximately (2002e) 744,000 Avars in the Caucasus region of southeastern Europe, 584,000 in the Dagestan Republic of the Russian Federation, over 50,000 in neighboring Azerbaijan, and smaller communities in neighboring Russian provinces and republics. An estimated 45,000 ethnic Avars live in Turkey and the Middle East.

THE AVAR HOMELAND: The Avar homeland is in the mountainous highlands of southeastern European Russia. They are concentrated in west-central Dagestan and extend across the international border into northern Azerbaijan and southeastern Chechnya. The Avars inhabit the valleys of the Avar-Koisu and Andi-Koisu Rivers and their tributaries. The region, which includes the high peaks of the eastern Caucasus Mountains, was nearly inaccessible until the early twentieth century. The 50,000 Avars in the Belakan region of northern Azerbaijan have been working for the unification of Belakan with Avaristan. Avaristan, the Avar homeland, has no official status. Avar nationalists claim that the traditional Avar capital and major cultural center is the town of Khunsakh, (2002e) 15,000, in southwestern Dagestan. The other major cultural center is Makhachkala, the capital of Dagestan, (2002e) 336,000, where Avars now make up about 20% of the population.

FLAG: The Avar national flag, the flag of the national movement, is a green field bearing a white crescent moon and three four-pointed white stars.

PEOPLE AND CULTURE: The Avars are the largest of the Dagestani peoples of the Dagestan Republic of southern European Russia. The Avars, historically and linguistically united, actually encompass a complex mix of related, though quite distinct, ethnic communities. The Avars are further divided into tribes, clans, subclans, and village communities. The majority of the Avars live in the river valleys, where they have traditionally dominated commerce and trade. The basic unit of their society is the village community, which is administered by an assembly and a council of elders. Some scholars doubt the modern Avars' connection to the historical Avars, who dominated much of Russia and Eastern Europe until defeated by Charlemagne, though Avar nationalists claim direct descent. They are among the most fiercely loyal to their ethnic identities in the Caucasus. Historically, the Avars have dominated commercial relations in the region, especially in Dagestan. Since the mid-nineteenth century, the Avars have prided themselves on their heritage of resistance to Russian rule, much like their ethnic kin, the Chechens.*

LANGUAGE AND RELIGION: The Avaro-Andi-Dido Peoples is a generic reference to the 17 ethnic groups who are considered part of the Avar nation, each speaking its own dialect. The Avar language is a Caucasian language that forms part of the northeast branch of the Caucasian languages, and it has considerable borrowings from Turkic languages, Arabic, and Persian. Over 99% consider one of the four Avar dialects as their first language. Only about 60% speak Russian as a first or second language. The Avar literary language, based on the Khunzakh dialect, is called Bolmat's or Bolmata. The other peoples of the Avar, Dido, and Archi groups speak related languages but use Bolmat's as their literary language. Because the town of Khunzakh has historically been the political and cultural center of the Avars as well as of the entire region, the Khunsakh dialect is the dominant spoken dialect. Russian and Bolmat's Avar serve as lingua francas between the different national groups in Dagestan. In order to avoid conflict, the Dagestani government has refused to make a decision on an official state language.

The Avars are fervently Sunni Muslim, the majority adhering to the Shafi rite, or school. Despite Soviet pressure of 70 years to renounce their religion, since 1991 the Avars have experienced a marked religious revival. The Avar peoples, particularly those in the more isolated mountains, have nurtured many pagan beliefs that have been adapted to their Islamic faith. Classical Arabic and Koranic teaching has been available in area schools since 1992.

NATIONAL HISTORY: The first historical mention of the Avars was by Pliny the Elder in the first century A.D., when Avaristan was known as Serir. The Avars were recorded in the fourth and fifth centuries as a mounted, nomadic Turkic people who dominated the steppes of Central Asia. Displaced by more powerful tribes, the Avars in the sixth century were pushed west, their formidable army increasing rapidly by incorporating conquered peoples. Reaching their greatest power in the late sixth century, they plundered all of present southern Russia and the Balkans; their empire stretched between the Adriatic and Baltic Seas and the Elbe and Dnieper Rivers.

In 626 the Avars invaded Byzantine territory and laid siege to the Byzantine capital, Constantinople. Although unsuccessful, in the process they extended their dominion over lands formerly subject to Byzantium. Internal discord in the second half of the seventh century resulted in the expulsion of about 9,000 opponents of the Avar leadership from the Avar empire. The empire was further weakened by a revolt precipitated by the creation of the Bulgarian state in the Balkans in 680.

To the west the Avars controlled the Hungarian Plain and moved into territory that formed part of Charlemagne's Frankish empire. In 796 Charlemagne's forces defeated the Avars, who in 805 formally submitted to Charlemagne's authority. By the ninth century they had virtually disappeared from history. According to Avar tradition, remnants of the defeated nomads moved south to refuges in the Caucasus Mountains. Since the seventh century Avaristan has suffered foreign invasions. In their isolated valleys and mountain strongholds, the Avars resisted all invaders of their homeland.

Between the fifth and twelfth centuries, Georgian Orthodox Christianity was introduced to the Avar valleys, but the religion remained mixed with earlier pre-Christian beliefs. In the first half of the eighth century Arabs invaded the region, bringing the Islamic religion with them. The consolidation of Islam was inhibited by the simultaneous advance of Christianity from the west, but the weakening of the Christian Georgians, following the invasion of the region by the Turkic forces of Tamerlane, allowed Islam to prevail.

The Mongol Golden Horde overran the region in 1241, but by the fourteenth century independent states, particularly the Avar Khanate, began to break the hold of the Horde. In the fifteenth century the region was the center of a fierce struggle for control by the Ottoman Turks and the Persians. Under Turkish influence, in the seventeenth century the majority of the Avar tribes adopted the Islamic religion. The consolidation of Islam in Avaristan in the eighteenth century resulted in a series of religious wars with the Christians of Georgia.

The Avar Khanate, a tributary state of the Ottoman Empire, extended its power by incorporating neighboring peoples and territories in the fifteenth and sixteenth centuries. The ruler of the consolidated Avar state took the title of "khan." The khanate rose to the height of its power in the seventeenth and eighteenth centuries. The peoples of the high mountains were mostly left to their own devices during the period of Avar domination. The Avar khans wielded their powers in the name of the Ottoman sultans.

The Russians, moving south into the Caucasus, established a protectorate over the Avar Khanate in 1803. The remaining Avar territories and those of the subgroups came under Russian rule in 1806. After the Napoleonic Wars, the Russian government tried to extend its authority to the Caucasus. Growing Russian influence in their homeland pushed the

Avars to rebel in 1821. In response, the Russian authorities abolished the protectorate and imposed direct control. The Caucasian War, from 1816 to 1856, is the most celebrated period in the history of the Avars. Large numbers of ethnic Slav settlers poured into the rich valleys of Avaristan. The Avars' religious leader, Imam Shamil, led a holy war against the Christian invaders, gaining widespread support among the other Caucasian Muslims. In 1834 he declared the Muslim North Caucaus independent of the Russian Empire, beginning a quarter-century of war.

After 1856, at the end of the Crimean War, the Russian government was able to concentrate troops against the Muslims. The Shamil Revolt finally collapsed in 1858–59, but Avar hatred continued to color relations with the Russian authorities. In 1864, the Russians changed the Avar Khanate into the Avar District, but effective Russian rule was not imposed until the 1870s.

Government pressure to Russianize followed the imposition of strict Russian rule, which intensified the anti-Russian sentiments of the Avar. The Avars lost much of their most productive land to Slavic settlers; the majority lived in abject poverty in the isolated mountains. Resistance to Russian rule continued, mostly by Avars who moved from their valleys to the high mountains, beyond the reach of the Russian administration.

The Avars were mostly untouched by World War I, although pro-Turkish sentiment was widespread. The Russian Revolution, which overthrew the monarchy in February 1917, was slow to be felt in the region. When news of the event arrived, the majority of the Avars thought their nation would finally be free of hated Russian rule and that old wrongs would be righted, including the return of their confiscated lands.

Regional leaders of the northern Caucasus convened a congress at Vedens, Shamil's old capital, on 27 October 1917. They elected a national committee of sheiks, officers, and merchants to govern as the Russian civil government collapsed. In December the new Muslim army captured several important Russian cities, which were looted. Pressed by Cossack troops, the Muslim leaders declared the independence of the Republic of North Caucasia on 11 May 1918. The following month, the new republic signed a treaty with Turkey and was recognized by the Central Powers, Germany and Austria-Hungary.

During the Russian Revolution, the Avars, promised autonomy by the Bolsheviks, often actively supported them. The promises of autonomy made by Lenin were more attractive to the Avars than the Christian and Russian nationalism of the anti-Bolshevik White forces. The defeat of the Whites in 1919–20 brought a bloody suppression of the Cossack settlements in the region. Avar and other Caucasian volunteers often assisted the Red Army commissars assigned to the suppression of the Cossacks.

The North Caucasian republic collapsed with the final Red victory. Soviet power was officially established in Dagestan on 20 January 1920 but was immediately faced with severe problems. An autonomous Mountain Republic was erected to replace the independent North Caucasia. In August and September 1920, the Avars, not having received the promised autonomy, rebelled against their new Soviet masters, but they were defeated and brutally punished in 1921. The Mountain Republic lasted only 20 months, due to ethnic tensions that eventually forced the Soviets to partition the region along ethnic grounds. The Dagestan Autonomous Soviet Socialist Republic was established on 20 January 1921, under tight Soviet control.

Soviet policy, particularly collectivization, provoked a renewed rebellion in Avaristan in 1930. The rebellion, centered in the highland Ando-Dido villages, was crushed with widespread destruction. Imposed collectivization enabled the Soviet authorities to eradicate their last opponents in the Avar communities.

From the early 1960s until the mid-1970s, government policy in the region pressed for resettlement of mountain peoples to the lowland plains. The resettlements involved all Caucasian ethnic groups, but the Avars in particular. The forced migration to the plains led to the domination of both urban society and the rural lowlands by the Avar nation, bringing them into conflict with the indigenous populations, particularly the former nomadic Turkic tribes of the plains.

In the 1980s, an Avar held the post of secretary-general of the Dagestan Communist Party and rewarded Avars with most positions of power in the autonomous republic. They had played a very important role in the North Caucasus for centuries and had historically dominated commercial relations in the region. Resentment of the Avars' position spread among the other Dagestani peoples following the relaxation of Soviet rule in the late 1980s.

The loss of isolation, the growth of industrialization and urbanization, and the rise in educational standards resulted in marked changes in Avar culture. Elements of European urban culture, particularly the material culture, penetrated even the most remote corners of the Avar homeland. The Sovietization of Avar society led to severe social problems, particularly alcoholism and divisions between the older and younger generations.

Following the collapse of the Soviet Union, Dagestan was declared a member of the new Russian Federation, but ethnic tension has been increasing since 1991. Avar political power, tied to Soviet domination, has been declining during the 1990s. Their loss of status and the many administrative positions formerly held by Avars has led to ethnic clashes and a new political mobilization of the Avar nation. The revival of the story of Shamil in the mid-1980s provided the Avar national movement with a cultural icon.

In 1995 a potential conflict with the Kumyks* over a land dispute led to the mobilization of 30,000 Avars. The dispute, caused by the forced

Soviet migration of the Avars from their mountain homeland to the traditional steppe lands of the Turkic Kumyks, continues to sour relations between the two peoples and to fuel the growth of Avar separatism. Calls for Muslim unity have been disregarded, as ethnic allegiances are stronger than the idea of Islamic brotherhood.

The loss of traditional Avar dominance in Dagestan has raised ethnic tension among the Dagestani peoples and continues to fuel the growth of national movements in the region. Increased inter-ethnic violence in Dagestan in the 1990s increased support for the idea of a separate federation republic, to be called Avaristan. The Avars have been pushing for greater sovereignty for Avaristan within Dagestan or for recognition as a separate republic within the Russian Federation. An Avar nationalist organization, the People's Front Iman Shamil, was formed to lead the fight for greater Avar independence and the unification of the Avar nation.

On 11 July 1994, troops of Azerbaijan clashed with armed Avars in northwest Azerbaijan after the seizure of arms reportedly smuggled into the region from Dagestan. The armed Avars were reportedly linked with separatist Avars active on both sides of the Russian-Azeri border. In 1995 Azeri press reports accused the Russians of supporting separatism among the Avar population of northern Azerbaijan. At the turn of the twenty-first century they remain vigilant, but should Dagestan descend into violence—as has the homeland of the related, neighboring Chechens—separatism could become a central issue of the growing Avar national movement.

The leader of the Avar People's Movement announced in August 1999 that his organization had put 1,500 fighters under arms. The volunteers were deployed along the Chechen border, where the war between the Chechens and Russians continued to destabilize the region. In spite of sympathy with the Chechens, the Avars opposed participation in the war, which destroyed much of the neighboring republic.

The position of the Avars is one of precarious advantage. Although they no longer dominate the Dagestani political system, they remain the most powerful national group politically. They retain some advantages based on their traditional positions in the hierarchy of the region, even though these advantages are now shared with other national groups. The Avars have not pressed their historical position and have yielded considerably to other groups, seeing their interests served best by a stable and peaceful Dagestan. The other national groups in Dagestan, at least for now, have neither the power nor the will to challenge seriously the Avar position in the republic. The gravest issue is the growing Avar separatism in the northern Belakan and Zaqatala districts of Azerbaijan.

SELECTED BIBLIOGRAPHY:

Abtorkhanov, Abdurahman, and Marie Bennigsen Broxup. *The North Caucasus Barrier: The Russian Advance towards the Muslim World.* 1992.

Bremmer, Ian, and Ray Taras, eds. *Nations and Politics in the Soviet Successor States.* 1993.

Chenciner, Robert. *Dagestan: Tradition and Survival.* 1997.

Matveeva, Anna. *The North Caucasus: Russia's Fragile Borderland.* 2000.

Azoreans

Açoreanos

POPULATION: Approximately (2002e) 320,000 Azoreans in Europe, the majority in the Azores, but with a substantial numbers living in mainland Portugal. Large Azorean immigrant populations live in the United States, Canada, and Brazil, and emigration to mainland Europe continues as the poor economy offers few opportunities to young Azoreans. The immigrant populations have maintained their ties to the islands and are often more nationalistic than the islanders themselves.

THE AZOREAN HOMELAND: The Azorean homeland lies in the eastern Atlantic Ocean 745 miles (1,200 kilometers) west of the Portuguese mainland. The nine volcanic islands and several islets, rising from the Mid-Atlantic Ridge in the North Atlantic Ocean, are mostly mountainous, being of fairly recent origin geologically. The islands are still thought by many to be the remnants of ancient Atlantis. The islands were granted autonomy as a special region within the Portuguese state in 1976. The three groups of islands correspond to the three administrative districts of Ponta Delgada, Angra do Heroísmo, and Horta. *Autonomous Region of the Azores (Açores)*: 905 sq. mi.—2,344 sq. km, (2002e) 243,000—Azoreans 96%, other Portuguese 4%. The Azorean capital and cultural center, the capital of the autonomous region, is Ponta Delgada, (2002e) 21,000, on São Miguel.

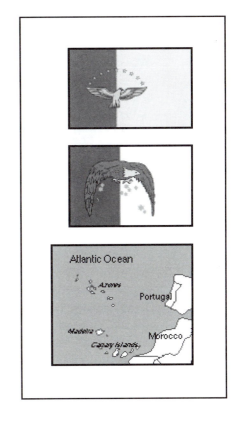

FLAG: The Azorean national flag, the official flag of the islands, is a horizontal bicolor, the third nearest the hoist dark blue, the remainder white. Overlaying the color division is a golden hawk, *açor* in Portuguese, its spread wings surmounted by nine gold stars arranged in an arc, wing to wing. The same blue and white flag but with the *açor*'s wings spread downward around nine stars as a map of the islands is the flag of the largest nationalist organization, the Front for the Liberation of the Azores (FLA).

PEOPLE AND CULTURE: The Azoreans are an Atlantic island people descended from fifteenth-century colonists from Europe, mostly Portuguese and Flemish.* The combination of the fair Flemish and the Iberian Portuguese was the foundation of the Azorean nation. Flemish physical traits, light hair and blue eyes, can still be seen in the features of many Azoreans. Each island has a certain uniqueness, due to the different nationalities that originally settled the archipelago. The Azoreans claim that hardship built their national character. They have had to survive earthquakes, volcanic eruptions, fierce storms, crop failure and crop disease, European wars, and pirate raids. Due to their isolation in the mid-Atlantic, they have had to become self-reliant and independent in order to survive. Azorean loyalties have always been to the family, the village, the island, and only indirectly to Portugal, the distant authority on the European mainland. In a 2000 poll, the majority stated that they viewed themselves as Europeans, but not necessarily as Portuguese.

LANGUAGE AND RELIGION: The Azorean language, the language of daily life, is a dialect of Portuguese that forms part of the Madeira-Azores subgroup. The dialect incorporates borrowings from Flemish, English, and African languages. Nationalists claim that the Azorean dialect is so different from mainland Portuguese that it constitutes a separate Romance language. The people of São Miguel have a harsher accent because of their Iberian heritage, while among the inhabitants of the Flemish-settled islands the spoken language is softer and more sophisticated. The Azorean language is different from mainland Portuguese in tone, vocabulary, and style; it represents a Portuguese dialect that is older and more conservative than standard Portuguese, due to the isolation of the archipelago.

The Azoreans are devoutly Roman Catholic. Historically, to be Azorean was to be Roman Catholic, but in recent decades small Jewish and Protestant minorities have been established. Although the Portuguese Jews are accepted, the Protestants are merely tolerated and at times are viewed with suspicion. The Catholic Church gives the Azoreans a sense of security because of its conservatism. To the Azoreans a static society and a steady income mean survival. The Church remains the center of traditional Azorean society, providing not only spiritual but also social and cultural support. Most public festivals are related to their religion, and church gatherings are often the only social contact for rural villages.

NATIONAL HISTORY: Ancient writings suggested that mythical lands existed beyond the narrow seas known to the Europeans. These myths drew adventurers and explorers to venture farther and farther from mainland Europe. The actual date of the discovery of the Azores is lost in history, but their existence was known in Europe as early as the fourteenth century; the islands appear on a map drawn in 1351. The uninhabited islands, rediscovered by Diego de Sevilla in 1427, were explored by Gonzalo Velho Cabral, sailing under the orders of King Henry, known as Henry the Navigator, between 1432 and 1444.

At some point following the discovery of the largest island, sheep were let loose to provide for future settlers, as there were no native animals. The islands received colonists from Portugal beginning in 1445. The first settlers were a mixed group of Portuguese from Algarve and Minho, Madeirans,* Moorish prisoners, black slaves, French, Italians, Scots,* English, and Flemish. For centuries the archipelago was called the Flemish Islands, stemming from the gift of the island of Faial to Isabela of Burgundy in 1466. Her Flemish subjects, dispatched to establish farming communities on Faial, later spread to all of the islands, and by 1490 over 2,000 Flemings were living in the Azores. The capital of Faial, Horta, was named for a Flemish leader called Horter. The Flemish language disappeared, and the settlers gradually adopted Portuguese names.

The remote islands, used as a place of exile by the Portuguese government, later developed as important stops on the sea routes between Europe and the New World. The first Azoreans emigrated westward during the colonial period, the forerunners of an exodus to the Americas that continued for centuries. The large immigrant Azorean populations fostered ties to the United States and other American republics, ties that were often stronger than the island's connections to metropolitan Portugal.

The islanders often played a considerable part in Portuguese history. They fiercely resisted the accession of the Spanish heir, Philip II, to the Portuguese throne in 1580–83, and they suffered under the so-called Spanish captivity from 1580 to 1642. By 1640 the population of the islands had risen to over 100,000, making them a valued prize on the trade routes between Europe and the American colonies.

Around 1800 the Portuguese government introduced mandatory military conscription for 14-year-olds, and later for 16-year-olds, which convinced thousands of young Azoreans to emigrate legally or illegally. The discovery of gold in California fueled the outflow in the mid-nineteenth century. American whaling ships, which often stopped at the islands to take on supplies and hire sailors, provided a means for young Azoreans to leave the islands.

In 1877, the Hawaiian* government needed cane workers and offered to pay transportation for emigrants from the Azores. From 1879 to 1899 nearly 13,000 islanders sailed for Hawaii. The immigrants eventually spread through the Hawaiian Islands, where they bought land, raised cattle, and generally prospered. In 1920 there were over 20,000 Azoreans living in Hawaii, but ties to the home islands in the Atlantic remained strong.

Administered as colonial possessions until the 1930s, the islands remained neglected, overcrowded, and underdeveloped. High unemployment and the pressure of a rapidly growing population escalated the importance of the Azoreans' traditional escape, emigration. Families of 10 to 15 children were typical, making overpopulation a chronic problem. In 1940 the islands had a population of 484,278, according to official census figures, far too large to be supported by the agricultural output of the region. Few Azorean families have not felt the effect of emigration.

Azorean immigrant communities, retaining strong emotional ties to their island homeland, were the first to develop a sense of Azorean national awareness. Although they often lived alongside immigrant Portuguese communities in the Americas, they retained their dialect and customs, their distinct group consciousness reinforced by continuing emigration from the home islands.

During World War II the neutral Portuguese government granted the Allies access to bases in the islands in 1943. A military and economic agreement, signed in 1951, established joint American and Portuguese military facilities in the islands, particularly Lajes Air Base on Terceira, a North Atlantic Treaty Organization (NATO) base. The agreement, renewed many times since, financially benefits the Portuguese government but conveyed few advantages to the Azoreans. Resentment of the continued colonialism kindled the first stirrings of national sentiment within the islands.

Political instability in mainland Portugal continued to hamper modernization of the islands in the early twentieth century. Although the islands had been known as the breadbasket of Portugal, farming methods remained rooted in the nineteenth century. Modern conveniences and technology were slow to reach the remote islands. Only in the 1970s was electricity and tap water made available on the more remote islands.

The devoutly Catholic and conservative Azoreans, alarmed by the popular revolution that installed a leftist government in Lisbon in 1974, quickly organized to resist the new government's nationalization of banks, industries, farms, and fisheries. Nationalists mobilized the population against the revolutionary excesses of the new government in Lisbon.

The Portuguese government's announced intention to free the last of Portugal's colonial empire incited a rapid growth of support for the nationalists. Several nationalist organizations formed as separatist demonstrations rocked the islands. By the summer of 1975 the Azoreans had driven every leftist official from the islands and had burned the headquarters of the Communist Party in Ponta Delgada. Considering their islands a colony, although officially they formed an integral part of the Portuguese republic, Azorean nationalists prepared for the independence granted the other overseas Portuguese provinces.

Disappointed at the Portuguese government's refusal to grant the Azores the same right to self-determination as the African colonies, nationalists gained widespread popular support. In January 1976 a poll of islanders indicated that 45% favored immediate independence while 55% favored varying degrees of autonomy, fearing that premature independence would aggravate the island's chronic economic problems and its lack of trained technicians and administrators.

Popular support for independence declined following a grant of autonomy by a newly installed democratic Portuguese government in 1976. Rejecting independence for the time being, the regional government negotiated new agreements bringing major development funds and a larger share of the money earned from the island's American military bases. Although autonomy satisfied the majority of the Azoreans, separatist demonstrations continued sporadically until 1980.

The island's leaders, including the nationalist leader João Mota Amaral, although putting aside the issue of independence until the islands were prepared economically and politically, set about winning more autonomy from Lisbon. The aims of the Azores regional government were to slow emigration and promote local development not dependent on funds sent from Azorean communities in the United States. (An estimated 1.5 million Azoreans and their descendants live in the United States and Canada.)

In the early 1980s the regional government had brought local unemployment down to less than 2%, compared with mainland Portugal's 12%, and prices of commodities, such as gasoline, were held at about half the price on the mainland. With relative economic prosperity, the population stabilized in the early 1980s for the first time since the 1950s. Azoreans returning to the islands from the Americas offset emigration.

Portugal's entry into the European Economic Community in 1986 and rising prosperity in the islands—although incomes are still only a third of Economic Community levels—animated a resurgent nationalist movement in the late 1980s. Disputes over the use of the Azorean flag and anthem, and over the disposition of Azorean properties confiscated in 1975, have become major nationalist issues. The Lisbon government views the Azorean's preference for their own flag and anthem as evidence of continuing separatist sentiment in the islands.

In 1991 Azorean nationalist leaders claimed that 74% of the Azoreans favored independence within the context of a united, federal Europe. The nationalists often receive the backing of local government officials, as support for secession is a useful tool when the Azorean government wishes to pressure Lisbon, though advocating secession is a grave offense in Portugal. The majority of the Azorean nationalists have participated in demonstrations, strikes, and boycotts, but few have been associated with clandestine activities or violence. The 1976 autonomy statute and subsequent legislation have given the Azoreans wide powers of self-government and have reduced the appeal of separate independence, although groups advocating independence within what is now the European Union (EU) receive considerable support.

The economic situation of the Azoreans, although improved since Portugal joined united Europe in 1986, remains precarious. The average income in the islands in 2001 is still just 50% of the European average, leading to continuing high unemployment and sporadic unrest. Economic grievances have replaced political grievances, but to the Azoreans the two are closely intertwined.

SELECTED BIBLIOGRAPHY:

Guill, James H. *A History of the Azores Islands: Handbook*. 1993.
Ludtke, Jen. *Atlantic Peaks: An Ethnographic Guide to the Portuguese-Speaking Islands*. 1989.
Rogers, Francis M. *Atlantic Islanders of the Azores and Madeira*. 1979.
Smith, Karine R. *Until Tomorrow: Azores and Portugal*. 1978.

Bahais

Bahai; Baha'i; Bahá'í; Babis

POPULATION: Approximately (2002e) 425,000 Bahais in Iran, concentrated in the northern provinces of the country. Outside Iran there are large Bahai communities in India, North America, and Europe. The number of Bahais in Iran, never counted separately in official censuses, is an open question, with estimates ranging from 95,000 up to 1.5 million. The Bahai diaspora numbers over 6.5 million. There are an estimated 140,000 Bahais in the United States and Canada, including many refugees from Iran.

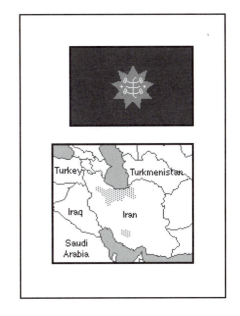

THE BAHAI HOMELAND: The traditional Bahai homeland lies in northern Iran, south of the Elburz Mountains in Zanjan, Mazandaran, and Tehran provinces. Other Bahai communities are located in southern Iran around the city of Neyriz, in the province of Fars. The majority of the Bahais are urbanized, living in the larger towns and cities, particularly Tehran and Zanjan.

FLAG: The Bahai flag, the flag of the Iranian Bahai, is a blue field bearing a nine-pointed red star centered.

PEOPLE AND CULTURE: The Bahais of Iran are the people of the heartland of the Bahai faith. A century and a half of hostility and persecution has formed the national identity of the Bahais. Forced into isolation, they retained many customs and traditions that were considered alien and anti-Muslim by the clerics and faithful of Iran. The development of a distinct Bahai culture, including a separate nineteen-month calendar, began in the 1850s and continues to the present. The spread of the religion to India and other parts of the world has brought many influences to the Bahais in Iran, which have become part of their developing culture. The Bahai religion remains the core of the culture, much as Islam is an integral part of Muslim cultures.

LANGUAGE AND RELIGION: The language of the Bahais is a dialect of Farsi, or Iranian, that developed after the founding of the Bahai religion in the mid-nineteenth century. Influences from the many languages spoken by Bahai converts around the world have influenced the speech of the Bahais in the heartland in Iran.

The Bahai faith began as a reformist movement within Shi'a Islam, but the Bahai were soon considered apostates because of their claim to a valid religious revelation subsequent to that of Mohammed. The Bahais have no organized clergy, sacraments, or rituals. Group meetings and religious education, which often take place in private homes and offices, are severely curtailed. Bahais believe in world peace, universal education, and sexual equality. There are significant restrictions on freedoms of individual members. These are enforced through shunning or expelling nonconforming adherents. Membership in the faith is not automatic at birth but must be assumed consciously once a child reaches maturity. The largest of Iran's non-Muslim religious minorities, the Bahais are not mentioned in the Iranian constitution and suffer the status of unprotected infidels. Since the beginning of the Islamic Revolution in 1978, more than 200 Bahais, mostly community leaders, have been executed. Bahai institutions remain disbanded, community properties confiscated, holy places destroyed, and cemeteries desecrated.

NATIONAL HISTORY: The Bahai faith originated in Iran during the 1840s as a reformist movement within Shi'a Islam. Initially it attracted a wide following among the Shi'a clergy. The Bahai faith emerged from Islam in a way similar to that in which Christianity arose from Judaism. Siyyid 'Ali-Muhammad assumed the title of Bab (Gate) on 23 May 1844, claiming to be not only the return of the twelfth imam expected by the Shi'ites but also a prophet, the herald of God, a messenger, the bearer of a new revelation that would fulfill the prophetic expectations of all the great religions. He claimed to be the forerunner of the Promised One. The Bab's claim to prophethood could not be reconciled with the traditional interpretation of the Islamic belief that Mohammed was "the seal of the prophets" and that Islam was the ultimate religion. In 1848 the Bab announced the sect's complete secession from Islam and all its rites; his adherents were known as Babis.

The Bab was imprisoned for several years but refused to recant. In June 1850 he was publicly executed in Tabriz. The political and religious authorities, feeling threatened by the ethnoreligious nature of the new beliefs, joined to suppress the movement. Since then the hostility of the Shi'a hierarchy to the Bahai has remained intense.

Historically reviled as heretics, the Bahais often have suffered increased levels of persecution during times of political ferment. In the latter half of the nineteenth century the Shi'a clerical class saw its spiritual monopoly threatened by the spread of the new Babi religion. Attacks on Babis spread across northern Iran in the early 1850s. The Babis resisted, and fighting ensued; thousands perished in the unequal conflicts in Zanjan, Neyriz, and Mazandaran, the centers of the Bahai community. An estimated 20,000 were killed in the massacres.

In 1852 an unsuccessful attempt on the life of Naser ed-Din Shah by three Babis as revenge for the execution of the Bab precipitated a massacre of scores of innocent men, women, and children. Most of the community leaders were murdered, leaving the surviving adherents dispirited and disorganized. The Shi'a clergy smugly announced the destruction of the upstart Babi community.

One of the Babis arrested in connection with the attempted assassination of the shah, Mirza Hoseyn Ali Nouri, later known as Baha'u'llah, was found not guilty of participation after four months in a subterranean dungeon, but he was nevertheless exiled to Baghdad, in the Ottoman Empire, in 1863. There he proclaimed himself to be the Promised One whose advent had been prophesied by the Bab. He was accepted by most Babis. Although he was removed by the Ottoman government from Baghdad to Constantinople at the urging of the Iranian ambassador, he continued to preach. He was later moved to Adrianople, and finally in 1868 to the prison-city of Acre (Akko), in Palestine. There he gathered the Babi remnant and founded what became known as the Bahai faith. His emissaries traveled through Iran, rallying the surviving Babis and spreading the new doctrine. Because of his exile to the Holy Land, the world headquarters, or Universal House, is located in Haifa, Israel.

The revitalized community of Babis-Bahais in Iran once again began to attract the attention of the clergy and the government. Baha'u'llah commanded his followers to spread his teachings only through peaceful means, to be loyal to the government, and to obey the Iranian authorities. Although he was forbidden to return to Iran, he taught that the purpose of his religion was the promotion of amity and concord among all peoples, races, and religions; that, however, did not lessen the fear and hatred of the more conservative elements dominant within the conservative Shi'a clerical establishment.

The first half of the twentieth century was relatively peaceful for the Bahais, but they were always treated as second-class citizens. They gradually united as a cultural and later as an ethnoreligious group, maintaining their separate traditions and culture. Threatened by prejudice and discrimination, they turned inward, refusing to marry outside the group. They slowly developed a distinct national identity, based on their religion but reinforced by their isolation and the hostility of the majority of the Iranian population.

Attacks on the Bahais increased after the coup of 1955. Although they benefited from the shah's program of secularization, the Bahais were summarily denied many civil rights under the Pahlavi monarchy. Bahai groups have alleged that prior to the 1979 Islamic Revolution, the shah's government used the Bahais as scapegoats for various difficulties, allowing elements within the Shi'a clerical establishment to repress Bahai activities and cultural events.

The Islamic Revolution that swept Iran in 1979 began a period of severe persecution of the estimated one million Bahais. The new Islamic government restricted freedom of religion and culture. The new constitution declared that the "official religion of Iran is Islam and the doctrine followed is that of Ja'fari (Twelver) Shi'ism." It also stated that other Islamic denominations were to be accorded full respect, but it designated Zoroastrians, Jews, and Christians as the only "recognized religious minorities." The rights of non-Shi'a Muslims and other religious minorities were curtailed, although they were officially permitted to perform their religious rites and ceremonies and to have a limited degree of control over personal affairs and religious education.

The Iranian Islamic constitution stated that the "investigation of individuals' beliefs is forbidden" and that no one could be molested simply for holding a certain belief, but that the adherents of religions not specifically protected under the constitution do not enjoy freedom of activity. This situation most directly affected the Bahais, as the largest non-Muslim minority. The Bahais were defined by the Islamic government as a political sect historically linked to the former monarchy and therefore counterrevolutionary. The government accused the Bahais of espionage activities for the benefit of foreign entities, particularly Israel.

Thousands of Bahais were dismissed from government positions in the early 1980s but were denied unemployment benefits and were required to repay the government for salaries or pensions received since the first day of employment. Those unable to pay were often imprisoned. All Bahai property, including places of worship, schools, and hospitals, as well as many of their privately owned businesses, were confiscated. The professions were closed to Bahais, including law, medicine, nursing, and teaching, and discrimination made employment in other fields very difficult.

Bahais were subject to arbitrary arrest and detention by Iranian authorities throughout the 1980s. Many of those detained were tortured and executed. Over 200 Bahais were executed during the 1980s, and thousands were arrested. The government claimed that these arrests and executions were for "criminal offenses," but the majority of the offenses were fabricated or the detainees were never charged with crimes. The level of persecution dropped after the widespread violence of the mid-1980s. The number of arrests and detainees as well as the amount of mob violence declined, but economic, cultural, and religious persecution continued unabated.

In August 1983 the Iranian government officially declared membership in a Bahai institution to be a criminal offense. Bahais are now forbidden to teach or practice their faith or to maintain links with coreligionists abroad. The fact that the world headquarters is situated in the state of

Israel exposes the Bahais to government charges of espionage on behalf of Zionism. Those caught communicating with or addressing monetary contributions to the Bahai faith headquarters in Haifa are subject to arrest and are often imprisoned.

The broad restrictions on Bahais in Iran appear to be geared to destroy them as a distinct cultural community. They repeatedly have been offered relief from persecution in return for recanting their faith and assimilating into the Iranian Shi'a culture. The government, leaving Bahai women open to charges of prostitution, does not recognize Bahai marriages. Children of Bahai marriages are not recognized as legitimate and are denied inheritance rights. Bahai sacred and historical properties have been confiscated systematically.

A Bahai community leader, Bahman Samandari, was executed on 18 March 1992. He had been arrested and held without charge. Iranian officials later claim he was a Zionist spy. Following international protests against the execution, Iranian Bahais were not allowed to attend a congregation of the Bahai religion in New York.

A 1993 law prohibits government workers from membership in groups that are viewed as counterrevolutionary or that deny the "divine religions," terminology used to label Bahais. The law also stipulates penalties for government workers who do not observe "Islamic principles and rules." A UN special representative reported the existence of an official directive on the Bahais ordering government agencies to block the progress and development of the Bahai community, expel Bahais from universities, cut the Bahai links to the diaspora, restrict employment opportunities, and deny Bahais positions of influence in education or government. The government denied the existence of the directive, but it appears to reflect current Islamic government practices.

A more moderate government was elected in Iran in 1997, but little changed for the persecuted Bahais. They are not allowed to bury or honor their dead in keeping with their traditions. Historical Bahai cemeteries have been confiscated and in many cases desecrated or destroyed. In October 1998, three Bahais were arrested in Damavand, a city north of Tehran, on the grounds that they had buried their dead without government authorization.

Public and private universities continue to deny admittance to Bahai students, a particularly demoralizing situation for the Bahai community, which traditionally has placed a high value on education. Official denial of access to higher education appears aimed at the eventual impoverishment of the Bahai national group.

A Bahai man, Ruhollah Rowhani, was executed in July 1998 after serving nine months in solitary confinement on a charge of apostasy, stemming from allegedly having converted a Shi'a Muslim woman to the Bahai faith. The woman concerned asserted that her mother was a Bahai and that she herself had been raised a Bahai. Rowhani was not accorded a public trial or sentencing for his allegedly crime, and no sentence was announced prior to his execution. Two other Bahais were tried alongside Rowhani and were later sentenced to death by a revolutionary court for the exercise of their Bahai faith. In March 1999 reports received by Bahais outside Iran indicated that the death sentences of other two had been lifted.

In September 1998, the Islamic authorities launched a widespread operation to disrupt the activities of the Bahai Institute of Higher Learning, also known as the "Open University." The institute had been established as a cultural organization shortly after the 1979 revolution to offer higher educational opportunities to Bahai students denied access to the country's high schools and universities. The organization employed Bahai faculty and professors, many of whom had been dismissed from teaching positions by the government. Classes were conducted in homes or offices owned or rented by Bahais. In the assault, which took place in at least 14 different cities, many teachers were arrested, and Bahai property, including books, papers, and furniture, was destroyed or confiscated. In March 1999, four of the detainees, accused of having established a secret organization and teaching against Islam and the government, were sentenced to prison terms ranging from three to 10 years.

In 1999 some of the most severe restrictions were lifted, allowing some Bahais access to food-ration booklets and primary schooling. The Iranian government, in 1999–2000, appeared to adhere to a policy of keeping a small number of Bahais in arbitrary detention, some at risk of immediate execution, at any given time. This manner of attempting to control and suppress the Bahais is accompanied by widespread persecution and the denial of access to justice. Bahais regularly are denied compensation for injury or criminal victimization. Government ministries declare that only Muslim plaintiffs are eligible for compensation in these circumstances.

The Iranian government, in response to UN and human rights demands, continues to classify the Bahais as a political group, not as a religious minority. They are still associated with the shah's pre-1979 regime and are believed to be against the Islamic Revolution and to be engaged in espionage activities against the Iranian state. The Bahais have no civil rights, and they may not hold government jobs, enforce legal contracts, practice law, collect pensions, attend institutions of higher learning, belong to political parties, or practice their faith.

Bahais continue to be the victims of attacks, looting, and arson by the Iranian populace, incited by Shi'a clerics. They are generally denied identity cards and passports. They are also subject to vilification by the state-controlled media. In the years since the Islamic Revolution in 1979, the Iranian Bahais, rejected, persecuted, and forced into isolation, have taken on the characteristics of a distinct national group, including the longing for a safe place to live, a homeland.

SELECTED BIBLIOGRAPHY:

Afnan, Abul-Qasim. *Black Pearls: Servants in the Household of the Bab and Bahaullah*. 1999.
Cooper, Roger. *The Baha'is of Iran*. 1985.
Hatcher, W. S., and G. D. Martin. *The Baha'i Faith: The Emerging Global Religion*. 1986.
Kazemzadeh, Firuz. *The Baha'is in Iran: Twenty Years of Repression*. 2000.

Bahians

Bahianos

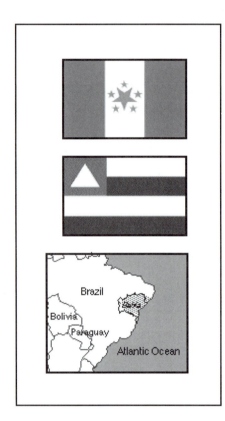

POPULATION: Approximately (2002e) 11,590,000 Bahians in Brazil, concentrated in the northeastern state of Bahia. Outside the region there are Bahian communities in Rio de Janiero and the industrial cities of the southern Brazilian states.

THE BAHIAN HOMELAND: The Bahian homeland lies in northeastern Brazil, encompassing a fertile coastal plain (the Reconcavo), a semicircle of land bordering Baía de Todos os Santos (Bay of All Saints). Inland the land rises abruptly to the Bahian Plateau, a flat, fertile agricultural region with forests in the west. Bahia forms a state of the United States of Brazil. *State of Bahia (Stado do Bahia)*: 216,613 sq. mi.—561,026 sq. km, (2002e) 13,206,000—Bahians 82%, other Brazilians 17%. The Bahian capital and major cultural center is Salvador, also called São Salvador or Bahia, (2002e) 2,493,000 (3,121,000).

FLAG: The Bahian national flag, the historical flag of the Bahian national movement, has three vertical stripes of blue, white, blue bearing a centered five-pointed red star, pointing down, surrounded by five smaller red stars. The official flag of the state of Bahia has four horizontal stripes of red and white charged with a blue canton bearing a white triangle on the upper hoist.

PEOPLE AND CULTURE: The Bahians are the descendants of the mixed population of colonial Bahia; Amerindians, mostly Portuguese Europeans, and black slaves from Africa. Less prejudiced than other Europeans, the Portuguese freely mixed with the other groups, with the present Bahian national group an intricate mixture of the three groups. Bahian society is characterized by a strongly developed class structure, with little vertical mobility. The influence of the class system permeates all aspects of the culture, including marriage, labor, and housing. The four distinct classes are the upper class, the descendants of the former plantation aristocracy, mostly of pure European heritage; the local upper class, comprising the educated government bureaucrats, technicians, merchants, and professionals—mostly Caucasians or *brancos da terra*, whites with known or suspected black ancestry; the working classes, generally blacks, mulattos, and dark-skinned *mesticos*; and urban workers, domestics, and day laborers—mostly blacks, mulattos, and some *brancos da terra*. Bahia was a major center of the African slave trade in the colonial period, and the state still has one of the largest black and mulatto concentrations in Brazil. These groups have contributed many of the traditions and distinctive foods that form part of the Bahian culture.

LANGUAGE AND RELIGION: The Bahians speak a dialect of Brazilian Portuguese that utilizes many borrowings from Tupi, the dominant Indian language in the early colonial period, and the lingua franca of the colony until the eighteenth century. Other borrowings come from Nago, a composite African language that emerged from the interaction of various groups of black African slaves. Nago was spoken in the region until the early twentieth century. Educated Bahians speak standard Brazilian Portuguese, but the language of the streets, the home, and the family is still the Bahian dialect, which is understood only with difficulty by outsiders.

During the nineteenth century, various African cults came together as Candomble (Candomblé), representing a particular Bahian fusion of Catholic beliefs and rituals associated with African mythology and religious traditions. Although the vast majority of the Bahians see themselves as Roman Catholics, most also participate in Candomble ceremonies, which continue to grow in popularity among the middle class, partly because of the reputed healing powers of the Candomble mediums. Protestantism has made little headway in the region, although in the 1990s evangelical sects have gained some converts. In Salvador, with its 365 Catholic churches, there were an estimated four times as many Candomble temples.

NATIONAL HISTORY: Bahia, along with the rest of western South America, was theoretically allotted to Portugal by the Treaty of Tordesillas in 1494, although the territory was virtually unknown to the Europeans and was not formally claimed until Portuguese navigator Pedro Alvars Cabral accidentally touched there in 1500. Portuguese explorers entered the large bay on All Saints Day, 1 November 1501, naming it Baía de Todos os Santos, All Saints' Bay. In 1503 Amerigo Vespucci encountered the Bahia coast, the first territory in Brazil to be explored. Ignored until 1521, the region was colonized in the 1530s to forestall other European claims, particularly by the French, whose activities in the region menaced Portuguese control.

Between 1532 and 1536 Bahia was created as a feudal hereditary captaincy under a *donatario*, with virtual sovereign authority. A more centralized Brazilian administration under a governor-general was set up in 1536.

The colony of São Salvador was founded in 1549 as a center of European colonization. European cattle, grains, and fruits were introduced, and the foundations of the sugar industry were laid. The town of Salvador became the seat of the Portuguese government in Brazil.

An important early development in the colony of Bahia was the work of the Jesuits. Missionaries sent by the Jesuits devoted their lives to the protection and conversion of the Amerindian population of the region. The converted Indians were settled in villages similar to the missions of Spanish America. Jesuit control over the valuable labor supply aroused the ire of the colonists, who wished to enslave the indigenous population. The conflict was finally taken to Lisbon, where the Jesuits, in a royal decree of 1574, were granted control of the village Indians while permitting the colonists to enslave Indians captured in legitimate warfare. Restrictions on indigenous labor stimulated the importation of black African slaves.

By 1600 Bahia had a population of 2,000 Europeans, with more than twice as many black African slaves and converted Indians. The ethnic groups, crops, animals, and agricultural institutions that were to become characteristic of Bahia were already evident. By the middle of the seventeenth century, these institutions had been greatly expanded, and Bahia became the leading province in Brazil for both sugar and tobacco.

European rivalries often threatened the existence of the Bahia colony. English privateers attacked in the late 1500s, and in 1624 troops of the Dutch West India Company captured Bahia (but were driven out by a Spanish fleet). By 1645 the Dutch threat to the region had ended, but the threat from pirates and privateers of many nationalities remained. The Portuguese, as allies of the British during the War of the Spanish Succession, were attacked by French forces between 1701 and 1713.

Black slaves, mostly from the Guinea coast and Angola, were imported to work the sugar plantations. The Portuguese settlers, less race conscious than other Europeans, mixed freely with the indigenous peoples and the African slaves, forming the basis of the later Bahian national group.

Poor administration, heavy taxes, and reactionary government fueled unrest among the powerful Portuguese planters of Bahia. The removal of the Brazilian capital from Bahia to Rio de Janiero, farther south, was a blow to the local colonists, although as a sop to local patriotism some national courts were established in Salvador. The transfer of the seat of the colonial government began a period of decline from which Bahia would not really emerge until after 1900. The ideals of the French Revolution in 1789 further strained relations between the Bahians and the Portuguese government.

Brazil became independent of Portugal on 7 September 1822. In 1823 Bahia was created as a province of the newly created Empire of Brazil. Bahian discontent grew quickly over economic and political differences with the government in Rio. A group of Bahian leaders in 1824 attempted the secession of Bahia from Brazil and the creation of a new independent state, to be called the Confederation of the Equator. The secession was stopped, but revolt among the Bahians again flared in 1831–40.

In November of 1837 a group of discontented military officers and civilians, under the leadership of Francisco Sabino, took control of Salvador and declared the independence of the Republic of Bahia. The revolutionary forces, known as the Sabinada, were soon joined by thousands of black and mulatto volunteers. The new recruits began agitating for the adoption of an antislavery posture. A fleet of Brazilian warships blockaded Salvador's harbor, and in March 1838 soldiers besieged the city, which finally surrendered. Several hundred Sabinada members, including Sabino, were executed for treason.

In the 1820s, the British government began to press the Brazilians to end the slave trade, and a treaty was finally consummated in 1826. It was another quarter-century, however, before the Brazilians began to honor their treaty obligations. After 1852 almost no slaves were landed in the Bahian ports, making slave breeding an important economic activity.

The sugar-based slave economy prospered after 1840, although a movement for the abolition of slavery in Bahia began in the 1850s. Finally, in 1888, the Brazilian government passed a law giving complete and immediate freedom to slaves, without compensation to the slave owners. The abolition of slavery brought an immediate economic decline to Bahia, fueling renewed antigovernment sentiment. In 1889 the Brazilian monarchy was overthrown, and the Republic of Brazil was proclaimed. Bahia joined the new republic under a local government with wide powers of autonomy. In 1891 Brazil was changed to a federation called the United States of Brazil.

Immigration from Europe, heavy in southern Brazil, had little impact in Bahia. Very few new immigrants settled in Bahia, sustaining the development of the distinct Bahian national heritage of Amerindian, black African, and Portuguese strains. The unique culture of the region developed in relative isolation, with its own dialect, cuisine, and traditions. The area, still not recovered from the abolition of slavery, was a poor peasant area of mostly subsistence farmers. The Bahians, in the first decades of the twentieth century, with their traditional sugar economy still dominant, were reluctant to accept technological innovations in agriculture or industry.

Antonio Conselheiro, a wandering preacher and mystic, settled in the Bahian town of Canudos in 1893. He began preaching that a holy land would rise up in the Bahian wilderness. Thousands of Bahians, with nothing left to lose, migrated to Canudos. The surrounding towns and communities called Conselheiro's followers *fanaticos* and feared the growing unrest among the poorest segment of the population. The politically powerful landowners resented Conselheiro's depletion of their supply of cheap labor. The Bahian government denounced Conselheiro for several years, but political infighting prevented any action. In 1896, after confrontations in the region, military expeditions were rapidly deployed against Conselheiro and his followers. Canudos finally fell to the military forces on 5 October 1897. Over 15,000 people were killed on both sides, and 150 women and children were taken prisoner. The soldiers cut the throats of male prisoners, and the prettiest of the female prisoners were picked over by the soldiers. The Canudos rebellion is considered the beginning of radical political and religious movements in the region.

In the 1930s, communist agitation won support among the poverty-stricken Bahian population. In 1935 martial law was declared to forestall a communist coup in the region. Bahian regionalism began to be an issue, with calls for recognition of their distinct religious, cultural, and racial mixture.

After World War II, communist sympathies and a strong autonomy movement led to violence in the region. In the 1950s, as education became more widespread and communications improved, the Bahians were influenced by anticolonial nationalism. The nascent national movement, comparing Bahia to a classical exploited colony, won support among the urban poor. The imposition of military rule in Brazil added to the grievances of the Bahians.

Regionalist loyalty in the 1970s and 1980s was reinforced by the growing sense of being a unique national group, with a history, a culture, and traditions quite different from those of the rest of Brazil. The Bahian cuisine, the second most complicated in the world, was recognized as an integral part of the distinct Bahian culture. In 1982 state elections were held, the first since 1965. The return of legal politic organizations, outlawed under the previous successive military governments, allowed some voicing of grievances. In the agricultural areas of the state rural unions sprang up, often heavily politicized.

The Bahians claim that their homeland is economically viable, but it continues to suffer from the overall Brazilian economic disaster. In spite of much natural wealth, Bahia remains among the poorest areas of Brazil. Bahia yields the majority of Brazil's industrial diamonds, as well as gold and other valuable minerals. The state is the leading producer of cattle, hogs, sheep, and agricultural products, particularly cocoa, tobacco, and coffee. Droughts in the 1990s added to the growing poverty, and poor government response increased local tension. Radical landless movements became part of a larger antigovernment movement in Bahia. The rural population is mostly made up of subsistence farmers.

In the 1970s modern industry was established, particularly in the larger urban areas, including an important petroleum complex near Salvador. Bahia's industrial output, which grew 64% between 1980 and 2000, was better than the Brazilian average of just 18%, but the long-awaited prosperity continues to elude the Bahians. The first planned resort, at Sauipe, on the coast 75 miles (120 km) from Salvador, is under construction in an effort to boost earnings from tourism.

The faltering Brazilian economy and the abject poverty of much of the Bahian population in the 1990s fueled renewed discontent. In February 1990, amid growing unrest, rioting and looting broke out in the region, particularly in Salvador and other coastal cities. In 1997, a small nationalist organization issued a call for the complete separation of Bahia from Brazil, asking how Bahia would be worse off by going it alone. They pointed out that Bahia would be neither the smallest, poorest, nor least developed state in South America and that, free of Brazil's economic policies, the Bahian homeland could take its place among the more developed countries of the continent.

SELECTED BIBLIOGRAPHY:

Harding, Rachel E. *A Refuge in Thunder: Candomble and the Creation of Black Identity in Nineteenth Century Bahia.* 2000.

Kraay, Hendrik, ed. *Afro-Brazilian Culture and Politics: Bahia, 1780s to 1990s.* 1998.

Megenney, William W. *A Bahian Heritage: An Ethnolinguistic Study of African Influences on Bahian Portuguese.* 1974.

Pierson, Donald. *Negroes in Brazil: A Study of Race Contact at Bahia.* 1967.

Balawaris

Balawaristanis; Baltistanis; Balts and Gilgitis; Sbaltis

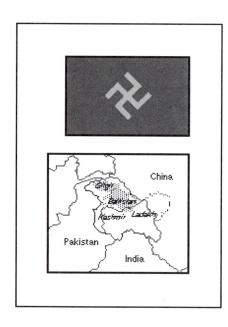

POPULATION: Approximately (2002e) 785,000 Balawaris in the Pakistani zone of Kashmir concentrated in the Northern Areas, which include the former Gilgit Agency and Baltistan. There are sizable Balawari communities in central and southern Pakistan, particularly in the cities of Rawalpindi and Karachi, and some 70,000 in Indian-controlled Ladakh. Nationalists claim a Balawari population of 2 million in the region.

THE BALAWARI HOMELAND: The Balawari homeland lies at the historical junction of the Buddhist and Islamic worlds. It occupies an extremely mountainous region in the Karakoram Range of the Himalayas in the disputed region of Kashmir in northern Pakistan. The area includes the former Gilgit Agency, with the old principalities of Hunza an Nagir; the governmental districts of Punial, Yasin, Kuh, Ghizer, and Ishkoman; and the administrative districts of Chilas and Baltistan. Legally Balawaristan is neither a constitutional part of Pakistan nor a part of Pakistani-controlled Azad Kashmir. There is no local government administration, and the region remains officially a disputed area under tight military control. *Northern Areas/ Gilgit-Baltistan (Balawaristan)*: 27,990 sq. mi.—72,495 sq. km, (2002e) 1,007,000—Balawaris (Balts, Shins, Hunzakuts, Vashkuns) 67%, Punjabis 14%, Pushtuns* 8%, Khowaris and Kashmiris* 11%. The Balawari capital and major cultural center is Skardu, called Skardo locally, (2002e) 35,000. The other important cultural center is Gilgit, (2002e) 17,000.

FLAG: The Balawari national flag, the flag of the national movement, is green field with a centered yellow swastika, the *yung drung*, the ancient Bon symbol of prosperity.

PEOPLE AND CULTURE: The Balawaris represent a variety of cultural and ethnic groups that are culturally, politically, and socially closely related. The Balts, who call themselves and their language Balti in both Indian and Pakistani zones, are the largest of the Balawari ethnic groups.

The Shins (Shina), or Gilgitis, are the largest of several distinct ethnic groups in Gilgit. The Iranian Revolution and opposition to Pakistan's Punjabi-dominated culture have shaped Balawari identity since the early 1970s. The agrarian communities that inhabit the high valleys have cultural affinities that stretch from Tibet to Iran. Although the Muslim culture that dominates the region has greatly influenced the culture, there is another aspect of Balawari identity that locals cling to—pre-Islamic linguistic and cultural ties to Tibet and Ladakh. Cultural links to the Kashmiris or the Pakistanis are few.

LANGUAGE AND RELIGION: The Balti language is considered by many scholars to be an archaic form of spoken Tibetan, written in a Perso-Arabic script. Balti is one of the most archaic forms of spoken Tibetan; its closest relatives are Purig, spoken in Kargil region in Indian-held territory, Ladakhi, and the Amdo dialect of eastern Tibet. Over the centuries, the language became a mixture of Tibetan, Persian, Urdu, and Arabic, being at the juncture of the Buddhist and Islamic worlds. Each valley in the high mountains developed its own dialect as part of its local culture. English-medium schools are further confusing the language issue. The Shina language is the most widespread in Gilgit, with five major dialects and numerous subdialects. Gilgit or Gilgiti is the standard dialect. The inhabitants of the Yasin and Ishkhoman Valleys speak Khowari, another Dardic language of the Indo-Aryan language group that is related to the language spoken by the Kashmiris. The Hunzakuts (Burusho) of Hunza and Nagar speak Burushaski, an isolated language not known to be related to any other. Most Balawaris speak at least one other language along with Urdu, the official language of Pakistan. Government schools in the region use Urdu as the medium of instruction, so most children learn their mother language at home.

The Balawaris are about 60% Shi'a Muslims of the Ismaili (Sevener) or Ithna 'Ashariyah (Twelver) sects. There is a large Sunni Muslim population, mostly in the eastern districts, and a small Buddhist minority. The Shi'as look mainly to Iran for education and guidance. Shi'a imams also offer formidable resistance to the cultural changes sweeping South Asia. The process of Islamicization was gradual. Buddhism and Bon shamanism were replaced over the course of several centuries, but absorption into Pakistan and improved communications have quickened the pace of change. The Shi'as of the region often face discrimination by Pakistan's majority Sunni Muslim population, as Pakistan's political and religious line is anti-Iranian and anti-Shi'a. The small Balawari population in the Suru Valley of Indian-controlled Ladakh faces considerably less discrimination and has more access to religious facilities.

NATIONAL HISTORY: The inhabitants of the Karakoram Range were first mentioned in Chinese chronicles of the eighth century. The indigenous population is thought to have been the Aryan Dards. The region, called Bolor, was once a center of Bon shamanism, the indigenous religion of the high Himalayas. The region served as the conduit for the diffusion of Mahayana Buddhism from India into China and Mongolia. Buddhism was introduced with the arrival of the Mons, an Indo-Aryan tribe led by Buddhist missionaries in the second century A.D. The peoples of the region, living in high, isolated mountain valleys, remained predominantly Buddhist until the fifteenth century, when most were converted to Islam by Kashmiri invaders.

The inhabitants of the high valleys were most often governed as distinct principalities under the rule of *maqpons*, or princes. Ali She Khan Anchan, who ruled from 1590 to 1625, unified Baltistan and briefly extended its frontiers to Ladakh and western Tibet in the east and Chitral in the west. The Muslim Balts destroyed the lamaseries and shrines in the Buddhist regions. A generation later, the Balts were conquered by the Ladakhis,* but the Ladakh kingdom was divided among heirs and soon lost power. An invasion of Tibetans* in the seventeenth century forced the Ladakhi kings to ask for aid from the Mogul emperor in 1650. Called Tibet-i-Khurd, or Little Tibet, the remote region sent annual tribute in exchange for a military alliance.

In 1840, Baltistan was annexed by the Dogra rulers of Jammu as part of their conquest of Kashmir. Their rule is chiefly remembered for its exploitation, with tribute to the Dogras paid in forced labor and heavy taxes. After the British conquered the neighboring Punjab, they allowed the Dogra rajas to keep nominal control over Baltistan under the 1846 Treaty of Amritsar. Russia was then extending its influence into Central Asia, making Gilgit and Skardu key listening posts in the "Great Game." Gilgit was established as a special agency under a British agent in 1889 and was officially leased to the British in 1901 by the Dogra raja.

In 1947, as the British left the subcontinent and partition created the two new states of India and Pakistan, the Pakistanis claimed religious affiliation with the Muslim Balawaris, while the Indian government laid claim to the region based on tribute sent to the Mogul emperors in the seventeenth century. The British authorities handed control of Gilgit to the Hindu maharaja Hari Singh of Kashmir two weeks before the partition. The Muslim majority of Gilgit and Baltistan favored joining Pakistan; when they heard that the maharaja had acceded to Hindu India, they were outraged. Local leaders appealed for assistance from Pakistan's ailing founder, Mohammed Ali Jinnah, who regretted his inability to send military help due to the pressing problems faced by his new government.

On 1 November 1947 the Balawaris rebelled against the Dogra rulers of Jammu and Kashmir. They imprisoned the Dogra governor and the Gilgit Scouts; along with a Muslim company of Kashmir State troops, they took control of the local garrison. A provisional government was established at Gilgit under the presidency of Raja Shah Rais Khan, a member of the former ruling dynasty of the region. The Gilgiti troops soon reached Skardu, where the Balts joined the uprising.

Negotiations between the new Indian and Pakistani governments dragged on. During this diplomacy, the leaders of the Gilgit region threw off the Kashmiri raja's rule and declared the region part of Pakistan. The Balawaris fought through the winter of 1948, pushing far into Ladakh before being driven back by Indian troops. In 1949 a cease-fire was signed between Pakistan and India, and the region was divided, with Gilgit, most of Baltistan, and a small part of Ladakh remaining under Pakistani control.

The Pakistani government issued a decree on 28 April 1949 officially separating the what became known as the Northern Areas from Jammu and Kashmir and placed the districts under the administration of the central government. Until 1972 the Pakistani government ruled the region under the Frontier Crimes Regulation (FCR). The arrangement was remarkably similar to the one that had existed under British administration, with local rajas and mirs allowed to maintain their power. For the Balawaris, little had changed.

In the 1970s, Zulifikar Ali Bhutto, the Pakistani prime minister, abolished the FCR and ended the oppressive system of land revenue. By then, the political entity of the Northern Areas had been formed, comprising the Skardu and Ganche districts of Baltistan and Gilgit, Ghizar, and Diamar districts of the former Gilgit Agency. In spite of Bhutto's reforms, little was done to alleviate the political bonds that held the Balawaris.

The completion of the Karakoram Highway in 1978 brought rapid change to the once-isolated region, including government-sponsored settlement of Sunni Muslim Punjabis and Pushtuns. The region emerged as Pakistan's chief destination for tourists and trekkers. Bolstered by the success of the Iranian Revolution in 1979, the Shi'a imams became politically active. They formed the Tehrik-i-Jaffaria Pakistan (TJP), a party that promotes Shi'a political interests. The religious issue fueled Balawari nationalism as tension increased between the mostly Sunni Muslims in Pakistan and Kashmir and the Shi'a Muslim Balawaris.

The Shi'a and Sunni communities in Gilgit and Baltistan had lived harmoniously for centuries. In the 1970s, reportedly activated by government agents, the two groups met in increasingly violent confrontations that culminated in a bloody conflict in 1988. In May 1988, Shi'a Muslims in the Gilgit region rebelled. The military brought in Pushtun soldiers from the North-West Frontier Province. These tribesmen invaded Gilgit and went on an unchecked rampage of lynching, looting, and raping that remains unpunished to the present. Activists in the region charged that the Pakistani government covertly sponsored the violence beginning in 1970–71, during the civil war that led to the secession of Bangladesh, in an effort to take the people's minds off political issues. Another violent clash in 1992 left several dead, but no judicial inquiry has ever been held.

In 1994 Sunni Muslim groups in the eastern districts of the Northern Areas began a campaign to legally join Pakistan, while the mainly Shi'a Muslim Balawaris demanded a separate Karakoram province with real executive and legislative powers. The region has no constitutional rights, democratic representation, or separation of powers. The Balawaris have long protested the withholding of their civil and political rights, especially the right to democratic representation. Pakistani nationals hold all top positions in the area.

A number of Balawari leaders were arrested in June 1996 after demanding that the people of Gilgit-Baltistan be given the same right to vote as the Kashmiris. Peaceful demonstrations in Gilgit and Skardu protested against Pakistani domination and the discriminatory recruitment practices that disadvantaged the Balawaris. Pakistani police opened fire, and over a dozen people were injured or killed. More than 800 were arrested, and the region was placed under a continuous curfew.

Moderate Balawari leaders demanded that the Pakistani government grant the self-rule provided for under a United Nations resolution passed on 13 August 1948. The demand marked the launching of the Balawari nationalist movement, which aimed to focus international attention on the Balawaris' plight. The Balawaris stated that their demands had nothing to do with the Indian-Pakistani conflict over Kashmir. The demands included a political status similar to that of Azad Kashmir, which is self-governing, and a separate legislative assembly that would serve the region pending the settlement of the Kashmir issue.

The Balawaris, after over 50 years of Pakistani rule, still have fewer rights than they had under the rule of the Dogra maharajas of Kashmir and Jammu prior to 1947. They also have less political freedom than the peoples of Indian Kashmir or Pakistani-controlled Azad Kashmir. Still ruled as a disputed territory, the Northern Areas have no official status. The Pakistani government, following the 1999 fighting along the dividing line in Kashmir, promised that it would soon come out with a package of reforms to give the Balawaris basic rights. A decision by the Pakistani Supreme Court in March 1999 directing that legislative and administrative powers be granted the Northern Areas Council remains unimplemented.

In mid-1999 Pakistani irregulars crossed the demarcation line into Indian-held territory around the town of Kargil in the Ladakh District of Kashmir. The majority of the fighters sent to the region by the Pakistani government were Balawaris of the Northern Light Infantry, the successor to the British-raised Gilgit Scouts. Nationalist leaders continue to denounce the government use of the local troops as cannon fodder. The growing resentment in the region came into focus following the Kargil conflict. The Pakistani government refused to accept back the bodies of over 250 soldiers of the Northern Light Infantry. Another 500 Balawaris are believed to have been killed in the conflict. The ill-conceived adventure in Kargil resulted in more Balawari casualties than any conflict since the war between Pakistan and India in 1965.

One of the long-term consequences of the Pakistan's Kargil debacle is the rapid rise of Balawari nationalist sentiment. In early 2000 nationalists in the region raised a demand for the creation of an independent state, to be called Balawaristan. Activists presented their case at a human rights conference in Geneva, distributing material outlining alleged massive human rights abuses of the Balawari people of Pakistan.

The Gilgit-Baltistan region is stunningly beautiful, and the people are friendly and hospitable, but tourism, the hope for the poverty-stricken population, has proved impossible without the necessary infrastructure. Except for the Gilgit-Skardu road, which is in poor repair, there are only dirt tracks connecting the valleys and villages of the region. Most of the region remains under the strict control of the Pakistani army. In response to the growing discontent, the Pakistani government in March 2000 added extra funds to the development budget for the Northern Areas, a move derided by the nationalists. The region's high birth rate and small land holdings force many Balawari men to migrate south in search of work. Most return on a seasonal basis, but resentment of the need to leave their home regions to find work in the culturally and ethnically different south, where they face religious discrimination as Shi'ites and ethnic prejudice as non-Aryans, has added to the growing list of grievances since the 1970s.

Shi'a imams offer formidable resistance to the cultural changes sweeping South Asia. There are no movie theaters, satellite dishes are frowned upon, and even video shops are scarce. There are numerous reminders to visitors to keep their bodies covered. As in other parts of Pakistan, however, the growing number of educated but unemployed youths is fueling the transformation of local culture via religious politics.

Younger Balawari nationalists who lament the loss of pre-Islamic cultural practices, which have disappeared under the religious pressure of the imams, have focused on the renaissance of the Balawari culture. Nationalists want to reestablish ties to the Ladakhis and Tibetans that were severed by the Pakistani takeover in the late 1940s in an effort to save their culture from total Iranian-style Islamicization. To the growing Balawari national movement their culture is more than Islamic or non-Islamic. Wearing the traditional woolen cloths or even speaking local languages are considered signs of backwardness by the Pakistanis.

Over a half-century of oppressive Pakistani rule has left a legacy of hatred and suspicion among the Balawaris. An indifferent government bureaucracy, oppressive military occupation, and a lack of recourse to the administration or the courts have brought the continuing Pakistani control of the region into question as the unhappy Balawaris increasingly embrace separatism as the only means of survival.

In November 2000 nationalist leaders charged the Pakistan government with financing the settlement of terrorists, drug and arms smugglers, and Taliban activists in the region in an effort to convert the Balawaris into a minority in their own homeland. In early August 2001 nationalists appealed to the United Nations to charge Pakistani President Pervez Musharraf as a war criminal for his part in the genocide campaign against the people of Balawaristan.

During the pro-Taliban disturbances that swept Pakistan following the terrorist attacks on New York and Washington on 11 September 2001 there were reports of widespread attacks on Balawaris, including assaults, rapes, forced conversions to Sunni Islam, and murders of religious leaders. In many cases the police failed to take necessary precautions, investigate, or prosecute those responsible.

SELECTED BIBLIOGRAPHY:

Ali, Shaheen Sardar, and Javaid Rehman. *Indigenous Peoples and Ethnic Minorities in Pakistan: Constitutional and Legal Perspectives.* 2000.

Dani, Ahmad Hasan. *History of Northern Areas of Pakistan.* 1989.

Malik, Iftikhar H. *State and Civil Society in Pakistan: Politics of Authority, Ideology, and Ethnicity.* 1997.

Rizvi, B. R. *The Balti: A Scheduled Tribe of Jammu and Kashmir.* 1993.

Balkars

Bolkars; Taulu; Malkars; Malkaris; Mallqarlis; Balkalar; Balkary; Five Mountain Tatars

POPULATION: Approximately (2002e) 95,000 Balkars in Russia, the majority in the Kabardino-Balkaria Republic in the North Caucasus. Outside Europe there are small Balkar populations in the Central Asian republics of Kazakhstan and Kyrgyzstan, where they were exiled during the Stalin era.

THE BALKAR HOMELAND: The Balkar homeland lies in southern European Russia, a rugged area in northern foothills of the western Caucasus Mountains. Balkaria, known as the Five Mountains, is an alpine region of high river valleys and towering peaks, some of the highest in the Caucasus. The Balkars are concentrated in the high valleys of the Baksan and Malka Rivers. The region contains many of the "five thousanders," the highest peaks of the Caucasus, many over 5,000 feet with glaciers on their crests. Officially, Balkaria forms part of the Republic of Kabardino-Balkaria, a state of the Russian Federation. In 1992 the Balkars proclaimed the autonomous Republic of Balkaria as a separate member state of the Russian Federation, but the Russian government has not recognized the state. *Republic of Balkaria (Malqar Respublika/Bolkaria)*: 950 sq. mi.— 2,461 sq. km, (2002e) 160,000—Balkars 57%, Karachais* 16%, Russians 14%, Kabards* 10%. The Balkar capital and major cultural center, Tyrny-Auz, called Tirni-Auds in the Balkar language, (2002e) 28,000, is in the valley of the Baksan (Bashan in the Balkar language) River.

FLAG: The Balkan national flag, the flag of the national movement, is a pale aquamarine-blue field charged with two narrow white stripes top and bottom, and bearing centered white mountain peaks. The traditional Balkar flag has three horizontal stripes of pale blue, white and pale blue

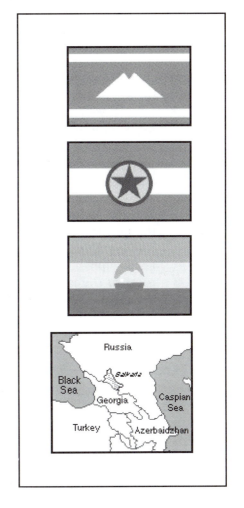

charged with a centered yellow disc, outlined in red, bearing a red five-pointed star. The official flag of the Kabardino-Balkar Republic is a vertical tricolor of pale blue, white, and green bearing a centered disc picturing a blue sky, white mountains, and green earth.

PEOPLE AND CULTURE: The Balkars are a small Turkic nation, ethnically, culturally, and linguistically related to the Karachais. Historical ethnologists believe that the Balkars are descendants of a complex fusion of Huns, Karachais, Kypchak, Khazar, Bulgarian, Alan, and Caucasian peoples and that they are among the most ancient nationalities of the Caucasus region. The Balkar nation comprises five major divisions, based on geographical location—Balkars, Bizingiyevs, Kholams, Ghegems, and Urusbiyevs. Among the Turkic peoples the Balkars are thought to be the group living highest in a mountain region. The Karachais and Balkars historically constitute two parts of a single nation, but since the fourteenth and fifteenth centuries they have become territorially isolated. Both national groups refer to themselves as Taulu. Most Balkar villages and towns are located on mountain slopes, lands not suitable for farming.

LANGUAGE AND RELIGION: The Balkars are a people of mixed Turkic and Caucasian background speaking dialects of the Karachai-Balkar language of the Kypchak group of the Uralo-Altaic language family. Balkar and Karachai are the two dialects of the Karachai-Balkar languages of the Ponto-Caspian language group. The two dialects are almost identical, although pronunciation is often different. The language is written in the Russian Cyrillic alphabet, although steps have been taken to adopt the Latin alphabet. Although classified as a Turkic language, the linguistic roots of the language are both Persian and Turkic. An estimated 97% of the Balkars use their language as the language of daily life, a high percentage in Russia.

The Balkars are overwhelmingly Sunni Muslim but retain strong elements of their indigenous animist traditions and are only sporadically devout. Their conversion to Islam in the nineteenth century is considered superficial, and the religion has been adapted to their earlier beliefs and traditions. Many still revere the spirits thought to inhabit trees, mountains, and other natural formations; festivals and ceremonies incorporate both Islamic and many pre-Islamic traditions.

NATIONAL HISTORY: Early Turkic tribes, possibly part of the Iranian-speaking Alan tribe, are thought to have migrated to the North Caucasus region by the end of the fourth century B.C. The Turkic tribes mixed with the indigenous Caucasian peoples and absorbed other migrating tribes in the region. In the third century B.C., the Turkic tribes began to penetrate the South Caucasus through the Derbent passage in Dagestan, and through the passes in the Kuban region. The gradual fusion of the Turkic and Caucasian tribes resulted in a settled agricultural and cattle-breeding community with an advanced culture.

The Balkars were first mentioned by Arabian sources of the tenth century A.D. as the Taulu-as, the Mountain-as, a tribe living in the far regions of Georgia. Many ethnographers and scientists believe the Balkars were already settled in their present homeland by the tenth century and were pushed into the high valleys of the Caucasus Mountains by the Mongol invasion of the thirteenth century. The conqueror Timur, or Tamerlane, who invaded the region in 1395–96, called the inhabitants "As," the same name presently used for the Balkars and Karachais by their immediate neighbors, the Ossetians.* Other scientists believe the Balkars and Karachai originated in the Crimea and migrated to their present homeland in the fifteenth century.

The Balkars lived as pastoral nomads dependent on sheep breeding, along with herds of cattle and horses. The products of their herds dressed, fed, and housed the people, while extra goods were traded to neighboring peoples for fabrics, crockery, salt, and other necessities. A highly developed mining industry provided metals, coal, and other raw materials. Since arable lands were scarce, terraces were used for agriculture on the mountain slopes, watered by ingeniously designed irrigation systems.

The Balkars maintained friendly cultural and economic relations with all the neighboring peoples. These contacts frequently resulted in numerous mixed marriages and interethnic kinship ties. The Balkar homeland, often overrun by migrating tribes, was the scene of much ethnic conflict. To escape marauding tribes, the Balkars gradually migrated to higher altitudes in the mountains, where they adopted less nomadic forms of farming and herding. Invasions and migrations, particularly in the fourteenth and fifteenth centuries, forced the Balkars and Karachais gradually to become territorially isolated.

In the sixteenth century, the Balkars became vassals of the Kabard princes. Over the next century Turkish influence in the region grew, and the nomadic Balkar tribes were brought under direct Ottoman Turkish rule in 1733. Until the mid-eighteenth century the Balkars were pastoral nomads, following an animist religion.

Islam was first introduced to the Balkars by the Crimean Tatars* and then by Nogai* nomads from the Kuban basin in the eighteenth century. By the beginning of the eighteenth century, the Balkars had already adopted Arabic as their literary language. The Balkar conversion to Islam accelerated during the Shamil rebellion against Russian rule between 1834 and 1858.

The first contact between the Balkars and the Russians is detailed in letters written by visitors to the region in 1629. Ten years later a Russian expedition explored the region, and in 1643 it passed through Balkaria. Russians moved into the territory of the declining Ottoman Empire in the eighteenth century and reached Balkaria in 1774. By 1827 Balkaria was under firm Russian control, and two years later the Russians forced the Turks to cede the Caucasian territories to the Russian Empire. Thousands of Balkars moved south to Turkish territory. Those that remained under

Russian rule took up arms against the tsarist authorities at every opportunity. Large-scale immigration of ethnic Russians took more and more of the Balkars' pastoral lands for farming, and the their former nomadic lifestyle changed more and more to farming and settled stock raising.

The Muslim peoples of the Russian Empire, their loyalty suspect, were exempted from military duty when war began in 1914. Even though a majority of the Muslim peoples openly favored Muslim Turkey, the Russian government, desperate for manpower, began conscripting young Muslims in 1916. The Muslim work units, sent to the front, came into contact with new revolutionary and nationalist ideas that took hold as Russia slipped into chaos. Balkar conscripts deserted the front to return home after the revolution of February 1917. As civil government collapsed, a Karachai-Balkar national committee took control of the region. The national committee gave its support to Russia's new Provisional Government, which vaguely promised autonomy for Russia's minority peoples.

The Muslim peoples of the North Caucasus attempted to unite in a cooperative independence following the Bolshevik coup in October 1917, but they faced tremendous problems with increasing disorder and pressure from rival political groups, including local Bolsheviks. The collapse of White resistance opened the way for the Red Army in August 1920. A detachment of the Ninth Soviet Army invaded Karachai-Balkaria in support of an uprising of local communists. The victorious Soviets overthrew the national committee government of "bourgeois nationalist exploiters" and divided the territory. In 1921 the Balkar District was established under Soviet power. In the next year, it was combined with Kabarda to form the new Kabardino-Balkar Autonomous Province. In 1936, Kabardino-Balkaria was made an autonomous republic of the Russian Federation, one of the union republics of the USSR.

During World War II, Nazi Germany turned on its Soviet ally in June 1941, and a German offensive drove into the Caucasus in mid-1942. Welcomed by many Balkars as liberators from hated Soviet rule, the Germans won thousands of recruits to their Turkish League, an anticommunist military unit under Nazi command. Nationalists convened a Karachai-Balkar national committee and formed a national government under Kadi Kairamukov. The new government moved to restore the region's traditional social and religious structure, opening closed mosques and decollectivizing rural life. However, horrified by German brutality, the Karachai-Balkar government increasingly distanced itself from German sponsorship and attempted to create a neutral state allied to Turkey. By early 1943 over a dozen Balkar guerrilla bands had taken up arms against the German occupation forces.

The Karachai-Balkar state collapsed with the Soviet reconquest of the Caucasus in October 1943. Stalin accused the two nations of treason and participation in Nazi atrocities. In November 1943, the 75,000 Karachai were shipped east in closed cattle cars. In March 1944, the 46,000 Balkars followed. Among the crimes allegedly committed by the Balkar nation was having sent a white stallion to Hitler. The Soviet guards dumped the deportees in the Central Asian wastes without provisions or shelter. Thousands died of exposure, hunger, and disease. The Balkars virtually disappeared as a distinct Soviet ethnic group. Their homeland in the upper Baksan River valley was ceded to Soviet Georgia.

The survivors, officially rehabilitated in 1956, returned to their Caucasian homes, where they lived under close surveillance by the security organs until the Soviet liberalization in the late 1980s. The Balkars turned to education and by the 1970s had one of the highest ratios of higher education in the Soviet Union. Renewed contact between the two peoples of the small nation, forbidden for over three decades, spurred a dramatic resurgence of Karachai-Balkar culture and a renewed nationalism in the late 1980s.

The Soviet collapse in August 1991 stimulated demands for separation from the hybrid regions they had been forced into under communist rule. The republican leaders unilaterally raised the status of Kabardino-Balkaria to that of a member state of the new Russian Federation. The Balkars have long felt disadvantaged in the joint republic and object to Kabard plans to rename the republic Kabarda. In a referendum in December 1991, they voted to create a separate Balkar republic within the Russian Federation.

During the 1990s, as the Balkars' ethnic identity grew stronger, and demands for recognition of their separation from the joint Kabard-Balkar republic grew, but with only 9.4% of the republic's population, their political power is limited. Pan-Turkic nationalism, with stronger ties to other Turkic peoples, has become a growing factor in the region as the Balkars seek allies among the Turkic nations of the region.

A conference of Balkar leaders in 1994 called on the Russian government to allow the Balkars to sign the federal treaty as a separate republic of the Russian Federation. The request was rejected, but the Balkars continued to demand separation and the creation of a Balkar state. On 17 November 1996 the National Council of the Balkar People declared the secession of Balkaria from the joint Kabardino-Balkaria Republic and the establishment of a sovereign republic within the Russian Federation. The council elected a retired military officer, Lt. Gen. Sufeyan Beppaev, to chair the new Balkarian State Council. The president of Kabardino-Balkaria, an ethnic Kabard, accused the Balkars of nationalist extremism. In Moscow the move was denounced as a menace to stability in the region, and a criminal case was filed against the council.

Revelations from the newly opened files of the KGB, found by researchers in the early 1990s, became a focus of Balkar anger. The story of the Cherekskaya massacre of 1942 finally became known. Following the German advance on Rostov-on-Don, the Red Army fell back. Among the retreating troops were around 700 survivors of the shattered 115th Kabardino-Balkarian Cavalry Division, which had been engaged in running battles with German tanks and motor rifle units. When the retreating troops reached their homeland, many Balkars left to find their families. According to reports sent by the NKVD (the forerunners of the KGB) to police chief Lavrenty Beria in Moscow, the so-called deserters were largely ethnic Balkars who took refuge in settlements across the Caucasian foothills. Beria promptly dispatched "execution squads" to three Balkar villages—Sautu, Kyunyum, and Cheget-El—where they shot more than 1,500 men, women and children in the space of three days.

The upcoming anniversary of the NKVD massacre has given the new torch-bearers of the Balkar independence movement a golden opportunity to "honor the martyrs." In a bid to rally their ethnic kin in Kabardino-Balkaria, the Balkar nationalists have found that tales of past injustices are often more persuasive than promises of a better future. Over the past few years, Balkar leaders have been calling for Moscow to recognize the Cherekskaya massacre and admit that the commanders of the NKVD units were guilty of war crimes.

The Russian government, alarmed by separatism in Balkaria, has granted more state aid and development funds for the region. The funds, part of a bill passed in 1994 to complete the rehabilitation of the Balkars, have mostly been used to build roads and improve communications in the formerly isolated region. Funds have also been allocated to repatriate the Balkars remaining in Central Asia to their homeland.

SELECTED BIBLIOGRAPHY:

Ahmed, S. Z. *Twilight on the Caucasus*. 1997.
Nekrich, Alexander M. *The Punished Peoples*. 1978.
Ro'I, Yaacov, ed. *Muslim Eurasia: Conflicting Legacies*. 1995.
Tutuncu, Mehmet, ed. *The Turkic Peoples of the Caucasus*. 2001.

Baluch

Balooch; Baloch; Baluchis; Brahuis; Kur Galli

POPULATION: Approximately (2002e) 11,540,000 Baluch in southern Asia, with 6,460,000 Baluch and 2,310,000 Brahuis in Pakistan, 1,360,000 in Iran, and 375,000 in Afghanistan. Large populations live outside the homeland, particularly in the Pakistani port city of Karachi, where they make up the largest sector of the population of the district of Lyari, and minorities in Kerman and Khorastan Provinces. Other communities live in the Gulf States, Saudi Arabia, Turkmenistan, India, and the East African coast.

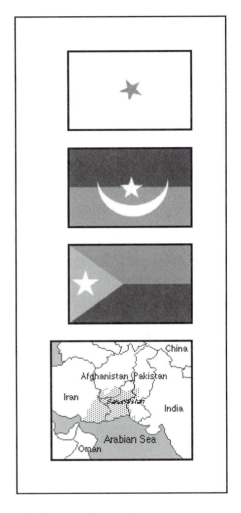

THE BALUCH HOMELAND: The Baluch homeland lies in southern Asia, straddling the borders of Pakistan, Afghanistan, and Iran. The region, often compared to a lunar landscape, is generally arid and lies outside the monsoon zone. Subsistence is difficult, and most Baluch are nomadic herders or engage in dry-land or irrigated farming and fishing. Politically, the Baluch of Pakistan have a degree of autonomy in Baluchistan, but in Iran, where they form the majority of the province of Seistan and Baluchistan, they have few group rights; in Afghanistan, they are spread across the southern provinces of Nimruz, Helmand, and Kandahar. "Greater Baluchistan," as defined by many nationalist groups, includes Pakistani Baluchistan, Iranian Baluchistan (the province of Baluchistan and Seistan), and Afghan Baluchistan (the regions of Seistan and Registan in the southern districts of the provinces of Nimruz, Helmand, and Kandahar). Pakistani Baluchistan forms a province of the Republic of Pakistan. *Province of Baluchistan*: 133,107 sq. mi.—344,863 sq. km, (2002e) 7,207,000—Baluch (including Brahuis) 71%, Pushtuns* 19%, Sindhis* 8%, other Pakistanis and Afghan refugees 2%. The capital of Pakistani Baluchistan and a major cultural center is Quetta, called Kwatah in the Baluch language, (2002e) 23,000. The major cultural center of Iranian Baluchistan is Zahedan, called Duzdab, (2002e) 507,000. The major center of the Baluch in Afghanistan is Zaranj, (2002e) 25,000.

FLAG: The Baluch national flag, the flag of the national movement, is a white field with a centered five-pointed red star. The flag of the Brahuis of Kalat is the red over green bicolor with a white five-pointed star above a large white crescent moon with its points extending into the red. The flag of the Baluch nationalists in Iran is a red over green bicolor bearing a pale blue triangle at the hoist charged with a single white five-pointed star.

PEOPLE AND CULTURE: The Baluch nation is made up of two distinct but culturally and historically related peoples, the Baluch (Nharhui Baluch, the formerly nomadic descendants of Iranian tribes), and the Brahui (Brahui Baluch, the traditionally settled population descended from the region's pre-Aryan Dravidian inhabitants). Kinship and social relations reflect the harsh physical environment and the division into numerous, often antagonistic, tribal groups broadly grouped into Western, Eastern, and Southern Baluch. The coastal Baluch tribes are in greater contact than those in the interior with the non-Baluch peoples of the Indian Ocean area and manifest a concomitantly greater sense of national solidarity. Baluch society is stratified and has been characterized as feudal militarism, an elaborate system of family, clan, and tribal ties. The Baluch are deeply committed to their personal honor and live by a code, the *baluchmyar*. The origins of the Baluch are subject to debate, although the most accepted myth among the Baluch is that they originated from Aleppo, in present Syria, shortly before the time of Christ. Some Baluch trace their origins to Nimrod, the son of Cush, Noah's grandson. The largest urban Baluch populations are in Iran and in Quetta and Karachi in Pakistan.

LANGUAGE AND RELIGION: The Baluch language, Balochi, is an Indo-Iranian language related to Farsi (Iranian) and Kurdish. The various dialects of Baluch, each with distinguishing characteristics, are divided into three broad groups—Eastern, Western, and Southern. The Brahui Baluch speak a Dravidian language related to the languages spoken in southern India, but with a heavy Baluch admixture. Linguistic evidence indicates the origin of Balochi to be in the ancient Median or Parthian empires of Persia, while the modern language incorporates elements and forms of Farsi (Iranian), Sindhi, Arabic, and a number of other languages. Under British colonial rule, Baluch intellectuals used Persian and Urdu scripts to transcribe Balochi into literary form, but since Pakistani independence and the rise of Baluch nationalism they have favored the Nastaliq script, an adaptation of the Arabic script.

The majority of the Baluch adhere to the Hanafi rite of the Sunni branch of Islam. Smaller Muslim minorities include Shi'a Muslims, mostly in Iran and Afghanistan, and a Zikri Muslim community, numbering over 800,000, in Pakistan. The Zikri are followers of a sect founded fifteenth century. The Zikri live in the coastal region of Makran and in Karachi. They believe in a messiah, Nur Pak, whose teaching they claim superseded those of the Prophet Mohammed. Their beliefs, often considered heretical, have led to intermittent Sunni repression of the Zikri minority. The Zikris do not generally marry outside their group. The Baluch believe that they were probably followers of Zoroaster prior to the introduction of Islam in the seventh century.

NATIONAL HISTORY: Dravidian peoples, once dominant across the subcontinent, were mostly driven into southern India by the Aryan invasions that swept across the north between 1700 and 1200 B.C. The Dravidian population of the upland valleys in the arid northwest escaped the onslaught as the Aryans bypassed their homeland to move farther east, leaving only a few small, nomadic Aryan tribes in the region. Various tribal groups, broadly known as Baluch, have inhabited the remote mountains and deserts of the region for over a thousand years.

Muslim Arabs occupied the land in the seventh century, bringing the Islamic religion to the Brahui population. Baluch nomads, driven from their homeland on the Iranian Plateau by the invading Seljuk Turks, migrated to the region in the eleventh and twelfth centuries. The Brahui, with a long history of settled government, remained the dominant people; the powerful Brahui khans of Kalat from the seventeenth century ruled the region.

Baluchistan was first explored by Europeans in 1810; the British occupied most of it during the first Anglo-Afghan War in 1839, justifying the occupation as a means of preventing the Russians from gaining access to the Indian Ocean through the region. In 1846 the British authorities divided British Baluchistan into three distinct areas: the settled areas under direct British administration, the Khanate of Kalat, and the tribal zones governed through various Baluch chiefs. In 1877 the British established the northern area as the Protectorate of British Baluchistan. The southern districts, Kalat and the tribal states, remained semi-independent, tied to British India by treaties and resident British advisers. The frontiers between British and Persian territory, settled by agreements in 1895–96, left a substantial Baluch population under Persian rule.

Periodic uprisings continued into the twentieth century, most seriously in the British zone during World War I. In the 1930s nationalist groups in both British and Iranian Baluchistan put forward demands for autonomy and the unification of all Baluch-populated territories. Reza Shah, in Iran, launched a series of pacification campaigns against the Baluch tribes, and by 1935 they had been subdued. During the 1940s rapid population growth extended the Baluch ethnic frontiers into southwestern Afghanistan.

The British authorities, preparing the subcontinent for independence in

1947, partitioned British India into predominantly Hindu India and Muslim Pakistan. Numerous states and territories had to choose which state they preferred to join. British Baluchistan attached itself to Muslim Pakistan, but the Baluchistan States, led by the Khanate of Kalat, refused to join either country. The khan, on 15 August 1947, one day after India and Pakistan became independent, proclaimed Baluchistan an independent state. In 1948, under intense pressure from the governments of Great Britain, Pakistan, Iran, and Afghanistan, the khan nullified the proclamation and chose Pakistan.

The Baluch leaders, accustomed to indirect rule and a substantial measure of autonomy under British rule, demanded the same under Pakistani rule, raising tension between the Baluch and the Pakistani government. The province of Baluchistan, Pakistan's largest in area, was abolished along with the other provinces in 1958 and became part of a unitary Pakistani state. Rejecting Punjabi domination of the new state system, the Khanate of Kalat again declared Baluchistan independent of Pakistan on 20 June 1958, with the support of most of the tribal leaders. Pakistani troops soon overran the rebel state and deported the khan, but he was allowed to return as the spiritual leader of the Baluch nation following a resumption of the Baluch uprising in 1962.

In 1970 Baluchistan's provincial status was restored, and the Pakistani government agreed to negotiations on Baluch autonomy in 1971. The government, shaken by the secession of East Pakistan, now Bangladesh, ordered the arrest of the Baluch leaders when they arrived for the scheduled meeting. Suspecting Baluch intentions to follow Bangladesh into secession, the Pakistani authorities clamped down on the Baluch autonomist and nationalist organizations, leading to a precipitous deterioration in relations between the Baluch and the central government.

In 1973, rebellion broke out in the province and soon spread to Iranian Baluchistan. The various tribes were able to put aside their differences to pursue a collective goal of an independent Baluchistan. At the movement's height in 1974, around 55,000 Baluch were engaged in battle with between 80,000 and 100,000 Pakistani and Iranian troops. Pakistani and Iranian military cooperation finally crushed the rebellion in 1977, razing whole villages and leaving over 10,000 Baluch dead. The revolt, pitting the Sunni Baluch against the new Shi'a Islamic government in Iran, resumed following the 1979 revolution, but once again it was brutally crushed. The revolt in Iran has continued sporadically to the present.

The overthrow of the Pakistani government in 1977 and the Soviet invasion of Afghanistan in 1979 greatly affected the entire Baluch nation. Refugees from Afghanistan established camps throughout the northern parts of Pakistani Baluchistan; the majority of the refugees were ethnic Pushtuns, a fact that raised tension in the region.

The Baluch revolt touched the lives of most Baluch in all three countries and politicized Baluch tribes long accustomed to the status quo. Original Baluch demands for greater regional autonomy escalated into a movement aimed at restructuring relations with state governments along confederal lines. By the mid-1980s, traditional cleavages among tribes and clans had declined in importance, as the Baluch increasingly saw themselves as a unified national group. Ethnic conflicts, mostly over land and water, became more frequent as non-Baluch peoples moved into the traditional homeland. In 1991 an indefinite curfew was imposed on Quetta, the capital of Pakistani Baluchistan, following three days of violent clashes between Baluch and Pushtuns that erupted following Baluch demands for the repatriation of up to a million mostly Pushtun refugees to Afghanistan.

The Baluch tribal leaders, the *sadars*, are slowly losing influence to younger, educated leaders who are determined to end the tribal system, which they blame for past Baluch defeats. A strong sense of Baluch identity and a desire to unite in a greater Baluchistan state reemerged with the end of the Cold War, in keeping with the new global emphasis on nationalism and self-determination.

In the early 1990s, local tribal leaders maintained a policy of local autonomy and of receiving government subsidies in exchange for keeping the peace. Political leaders of all ideologies continue to exploit the endemic anarchy of the Baluch areas of all three countries. Local practices of indenturing, virtual slavery, and the recruiting of young children for work in cottage industries remained severe problems in the 1990s. Due to the remoteness of the Baluch homeland, the smuggling of opium became a major cross-border industry in the region.

Serious clashes in Iran in the 1990s were blamed on drug traffickers or bandits, but Baluch nationalists continue to fight for self-rule. In October 1994, the Baluch National Council called for a special status for the Sunni-majority Sistan-Baluchistan region. In June 1995 a group of 97 Baluch "bandits," including many nationalists, surrendered to Iranian troops.

The divided Baluchistan remains among the poorest regions in all three countries. In Pakistan, the Baluch are underrepresented in the government, armed forces, and bureaucracy at both provincial and national levels. Pakistani Baluchistan contains large reserves of natural gas and coal, but the exploitation of these resources has not benefited the Baluch. Another nationalist issue is the large influx of non-Baluch to the province. The newcomers often take the best jobs in both the public and private sector, and their presence has heightened fears that the Baluch will become a minority in their homeland.

In October 1999, the Pakistani military overthrew the corrupt civilian government and declared a state of emergency. The military, traditionally centralist, ended the small amount of regional autonomy that the Baluchis had enjoyed during the 1990s. Unrest, always near the surface in the region, became a serious concern in 1999–2000.

Unrest in Pakistan following the Pakistani government's decision to support the attack on Afghanistan's Taliban following the terrorist attacks on the United States in September 2001 led to renewed tensions between the Baluch and the large Pushtun population, of both Afghan and Pakistani origin, that has colonized northern Baluchistan province. Violence in the region, particularly in Quetta, left many injured.

Recent cross-border contacts and a renewed sense of identity have added to the list of grievances that the Baluch harbor against all three governments. The dream of a "Greater Baluchistan" stretching from Iran into Pakistan is still very much alive. Maps published by various nationalist organizations show a projected Baluch state stretching from the Arabian Sea north to the border of Turkestan and west to include about a third of Iranian territory. The often-conflicting claims of the Baluch nationalist organizations in the three countries constitute one of the reasons that unification of the movement has so far eluded the Baluchi nationalists.

SELECTED BIBLIOGRAPHY:

Baloch, I. *The Problem of "Greater Baluchistan": A Study of Baluch Nationalism.* 1987.
Harrison, Selig S. *In Afghanistan's Shadow: Baluch Nationalism and Soviet Temptations.* 1988.
Matheson, Sylvia A. *The Tigers of Baluchistan.* 1987.
Titus, Paul Brian, ed. *Marginality and Modernity: Ethnicity and Change in Post-Colonial Balochistan.* 1997.

Bamilekes

Grasslanders; Bamileke Highlanders

POPULATION: Approximately (2002e) 4,250,000 in Cameroon, concentrated in the west-central provinces of Ouest (Western, the Bamileke heartland) and Littoral. There are important Bamileke communities in other parts of Cameroon, particularly around the capital, Yaoundé, and in the neighboring provinces of English-speaking Cameroon. Nationalists claim a Bamileke population of 8 million, which probably includes the many related ethnic groups in the French side of western Cameroon.

THE BAMILEKE HOMELAND: The Bamileke homeland, popularly called Bamilekeland, occupies a highland region in northwestern Cameroon, from the lower slopes of the Adamawa Plateau to the coastal lowlands and Mount Cameroon. During the twentieth century, the Bamileke expanded into areas surrounding their traditional homeland, including the large city of Douala on the coast, where the Bamilekes now make up about 70% of the population. The homeland, the region claimed by nationalists, has no official status in Cameroon; it forms the Cameroonian provinces of Ouest and Littoral. *Bamilekeland*: 13,170 sq. mi.—34,111 sq. km, (2002e) 4,165,000—Bamilekes 86%, Southern Cameroonians* and other Cameroonians 14%. The Bamileke capital and major cultural center is Bafoussam, (2002e) 151,000. The other important cultural center is Cameroon's largest city, Douala, (2002e) 1,239,000, urban area 1,520,000.

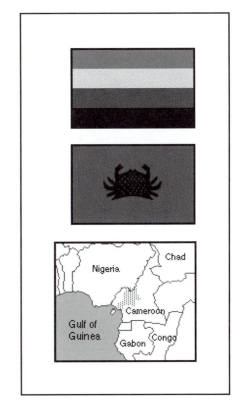

FLAG: The Bamileke national flag, the flag of the national movement, has four horizontal stripes of green, yellow, red, and black. The flag of the major Bamileke political party, Union of Cameroonian Peoples (UPC), is a red field bearing a centered black camaron, a local crab.

PEOPLE AND CULTURE: The Bamilekes, the most numerous of Cameroon's many ethnic groups, represent a loose agglomeration of Bantu-speaking peoples, some 90 related tribal groups. The Bamilekes usually do not refer to themselves as Bamileke but use the names of the individual kingdoms to which they belong, or refer to themselves as "grasslanders." They are considered the most energetic and enterprising of the Cameroonian peoples and dominate the cultural and economic life of much of western Cameroon. Descent, succession, and inheritance are patrilineal. Polygyny is practiced, and marriage often involves a substantial bride-price. The Bamileke population has expanded rapidly during the twentieth century, with excess population moving into nontraditional areas, including the large cities of Douala and Yaoundé, where they form much of the business community. In the savanna are many related peoples, divided into small kingdoms.

LANGUAGE AND RELIGION: The Bamilekes speak 17 related Bantu languages and dialects of the Bamileke division of the Mbam-Nkam group of Southern Bantu branch of the Benue-Congo languages. The most important of the languages are Fe'fe', Bandjoun, Medumba, Mengaka, Nda'nda, Ngiemboon, Ngomba, Ngombale, Ngwe, and Yemba. Each of the languages is further divided into numerous subdialects, but all are mutually intelligible with difficulty. The majority of the Bamilekes speak French, the country's official language, as a second language, and a minority, in the northwest, speak English, the former colonial language of the neighboring region in western Cameroon.

The Bamileke recognize a supreme god, Si, but ancestor worship remains the dominant form of belief. The head of the extended family preserves ancestral skulls and offers sacrifices to them. Indigenous practitioners prepare charms and medicines, also practicing divination, by interpreting an earth spider's manipulation of marked blades of grass. Some Bamileke, particularly in the northern districts and in Nigeria, have adopted Islam. Mostly French Roman Catholic missionaries have converted many of the Bamilekes in the southern districts to Christianity.

NATIONAL HISTORY: The Bantu peoples, thought to have originated farther to the north, began to migrate southward over 2,000 years ago. They settled the lowlands of Cameroon, displacing the earlier pygmy peoples. In the eleventh century A.D., they moved into the less accessible highlands to escape Muslim invaders.

Over several centuries numerous small chiefdoms emerged, often warring among themselves. Some 90 of the small tribal states united in the fifteenth and sixteenth centuries to form a powerful confederation in the southern highlands. The confederation took the name Bamileke, the name of the largest member state. A hereditary king, the *fon*, ruled each of the Bamileke kingdoms of localized patrilineal lineage, often assisted by a powerful queen mother, the *mafo*.

The confederation began to decline in the eighteenth century, its disintegration hastened by the secession of the Bamoun states in the west. The Muslim Fulanis during the late 1700s and early 1800s conquered most of northern Cameroon, subjugating or displacing the earlier Bantu peoples. The disruption of the Fulani invasion and ongoing slave raids further weakened the Bantu federation in the highlands.

Portuguese navigators explored the coast in the sixteenth century, opening the way for European colonization. British explorers, pushing inland from the slave ports, made contact with the Bamileke confederation in the early nineteenth century. Christian missionaries and merchant adventurers followed the European explorers between the 1840s and 1870s. The missionaries gained many converts but also, more importantly, brought Western education to the region. The Bamilekes embraced education enthusiastically, beginning a cultural evolution that continues to the present.

In 1884 several chiefs signed a protectorate agreement with German explorer Gustav Nachtigal, laying the foundation for Germany's annexation of the confederation to its Kamerun colony. The Germans built a capital at Buea but later moved the colonial government to Yaoundé. German rule, specifically its forced labor and curtailment of the powers of the traditional chiefs, proved harsh and unpopular. Bamileke rebellions were a near constant in the region from 1885 until World War I.

German Kamerun was taken by British and French troops in 1916, during World War I. After the end of the war, Germany was stripped of all its colonies. Kamerun was divided into two occupation areas, British in the west and French in the east, under an agreement signed on 22 June 1919. In 1922 the allied powers established mandate governments under the auspices of the new League of Nations. The boundary between the two mandates, drawn without consideration of the region's traditional frontiers, partitioned the traditional Bamileke lands.

The expansion of the Bamileke into the lowlands, beginning in the 1920s, presented the colonial authorities with a major challenge, as the dynamic Bamileke soon controlled regional commerce on both sides of the international border and increasingly demanded the reunification of the lands populated by the Bamileke and related tribes. The two Cameroon mandates, under different administrative systems and using different languages, had little in common except the Bamileke-Tikar-Bamenda ethnic community and a shared past as a German colony.

Bamileke nationalism grew rapidly after World War II; the first openly nationalistic organization, the Union Bamileke, was formed in 1948. The continuing partition of Bamilekeland, reinforced by a UN decision to establish trust territories within the old mandate borders in 1946, spurred the rapid spread of nationalist sentiment. Strikes and demonstrations demanding a separate administration for a united Bamilekeland brought commercial life in the region to a halt in the late 1940s. Bamileke demands included the reunification of East and West Cameroon, which would reunite the Bamileke nation.

The British and French authorities met in Kumba in May 1949 and again in December 1951 to try to work out a program that would satisfy Bamileke demands, but the sides failed to reach an agreement. In 1954 the British added their Cameroon trust territory to Nigeria as a quasi-federal state with its own administration. In 1955, the outlawed Union of Cameroonian Peoples (UPC), based largely among the Bamilekes, began an armed struggle for independence in French Cameroon.

Planned independence for the French Cameroon, announced in 1958, provoked savage rioting and demands for immediate Bamileke independence. A Bamileke rebellion, joined by several smaller tribal groups, paralyzed western Cameroon. The separatists formed a government-in-exile in Guinea in 1960, led by the outlawed UPC, which vehemently opposed domination by the northern Muslim tribes favored by the French administration. Undeterred by the continuing Bamileke rebellion, the French administration granted Cameroon independence in 1960. A northern Fulani, Ahmadou Ahidjo, was chosen as the president of the independent state. He favored the northern minority, recruiting them for the security forces and the civil service, although the Bamilekes retained their dominance in the commercial sector.

A February 1961 plebiscite gave the inhabitants of the British Cameroon a choice of joining independent Cameroon or neighboring Nigeria. In the largely Muslim northern Cameroons the vote favored Nigeria, but in the south the mostly Christian inhabitants voted for reunification with Cameroon—particularly the Bamilekes, who had been divided by the mandate boundaries. In 1962 the southern Cameroons of the British trust territory joined Cameroon as one of two states within a federal republic, a move that failed to address Bamileke demands for a separate autonomous state. A Bamileke insurgency paralyzed much of southwestern Cameroon.

Bamileke nationalists contended that Cameroon independence was a hidden form of continued French control through their Muslim allies from northern Cameroon. The Bamilekes were supported by many communist states and newly independent Ghana and Guinea. The rebels increasingly rejected the authority of their traditional rulers, creating a rift within the Bamileke rebels and supporters of the kingdoms. A civil war between the two factions further devastated the region and forced many to seek the relative security of large cities.

The Cameroonian government, with French military assistance, defeated the continuing Bamileke revolt in 1963. The five-year rebellion cost over 70,000 lives. The Bamileke homeland, formerly rich in coffee and cocoa, was in ruins. All political organizations except the ruling political party were outlawed in 1966. Ahidjo relied on a pervasive internal security apparatus to suppress political and ethnic dissent. Ethnic and religious tension leading to the slaughter of 235 Bamilekes by a rival ethnic group sparked a renewed Bamileke rebellion in 1967. Bamileke rebels, called Maquisards, continued to fight government troops until they were finally eradicated in 1971. After 1971 the Bamileke rebellion became a liberation movement, supported by many Marxist and socialist states.

In 1972 a new constitution abolished the federal system and established a unitary one-party state. Ahidjo was reelected in 1975 with 99% of the votes cast in an election widely denounced as unfair. Continuing Bamileke unrest led to the arrest of many leaders in 1979; they were accused of attempting to stir up revolution. In February 1980, President Ahidjo chose Bafoussam, the Bamileke capital, as the site of the third meeting of the ruling political party, the Cameroon National Union, a move viewed by the Bamilekes as a show of government strength.

In 1982, Paul Biya, a southern Christian, came to power in Cameroon, promising more freedom, an end to northern domination, and competent government. He gained much support among the Bamilekes with his promises to reduce ethnic outbreaks and tension. Biya soon proved as autocratic as his predecessor and lost support among the Bamilekes. An attempted coup by mainly northern elements began a period of political repression.

Africa's turn toward democracy following the end of the Cold War rekindled old tribal and regional tension. Public disorder spread, with demands for political reform and the end of one-party rule. Rioting swept the major cities, particularly in Douala and Yaoundé, where pro-government groups attacked Bamileke students. Violence between the Bamilekes and the Betis in Yaoundé left over 500 Bamileke businesses destroyed. Many Bamileke left the Cameroon capital to return to their homeland in Oueste and Littoral provinces.

The UPC, outlawed for 30 years, was legalized as part of democratization of Cameroon demanded by the international community. Supposedly free elections, boycotted by opposition parties in October 1992, polarized Cameroon and fueled a resurgent Bamileke national movement. The government responded by placing the Bamileke provinces under emergency military rule, but it failed to stem the resurgence of Bamileke national sentiment.

In the early 1990s, the Bamilekes joined the English-speaking Anglophones of the two western provinces in calling for greater political and social autonomy. The Bamilekes, with an English-speaking minority, cooperated with the Anglophone southern Cameroonians' demands for the return of a federal system and for guarantees of language and minority rights. A campaign of violence and harassment against the Bamilekes, mostly by the pro-government Betis, left many dead and injured. Bamileke leaders accused the government of selective repression, including newspaper censorship, arson attacks, and harassment and abuse of Bamileke students. Pro-government gangs continued to harass Bamilekes, based solely on their ethnic origin and alleged support of opposition political parties. Bamileke nationalists warned that if the repression continued, the Bamilekes would defend themselves forcibly.

General elections were held in Cameroon in May 1997, with opposition groups claiming massive vote rigging. Paul Biya's political party claimed to have won an absolute majority in the parliament. The fraudulent election increased tension in the country, particularly in Bamilekeland, where antigovernment demonstrations and nationalist activity increased.

The condition of the Bamilekes continued to deteriorate under Biya's rule in the 1990s, despite their initial support of Biya against Ahidjo in the early 1980s. They face discrimination and harassment due to their growing nationalist sentiment and to commercial competition with pro-government groups. Once again the Cameroon government is faced with the old "Problème Bamileke."

SELECTED BIBLIOGRAPHY:

Asiwaju, A. I. *Partitioned Africans: Ethnic Relations across Africa's International Borders, 1884–1984*. 1985.
Dongmo, J. L. *Bamileke Dynamism*. 1981.
Kago Lele, J. *Tribalism and Exclusion in Cameroon: The Case of the Bamilekes*. 1995.
Krieger, Milton H. *African State and Society in the 1990s: Cameroon's Political Crossroads*. 1998.

Barbudans

Barbuda Islanders

POPULATION: Approximately (2002e) 5,000 Barbudans in the island state of Antigua and Barbuda in the Caribbean. The majority of the Barbudans live on Antigua, where there is more opportunity, with about 1,800 living on Barbuda.

THE BARBUDAN HOMELAND: The Barbudan homeland is an island lying in the northern Caribbean, 25 miles north of Antigua. The Barbudan homeland is a flat, well-wooded coral island dominated by a large lagoon, called Codrington Lagoon, on its western side. Formerly called Dulcina, the island rises to Lindsay Hill in the northeast. The island has no streams or lakes and receives less rainfall than nearby Antigua. Much of the island is a game reserve, inhabited by a variety of wildlife. Nationalists also claim Redonda, the uninhabited third island of

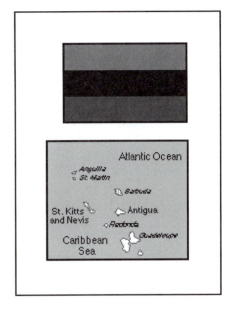

the group. Barbuda forms a special autonomous department of the Republic of Antigua and Barbuda. *Department of Barbuda*: 62 sq. mi.—160 sq. km, (2002e) 1,800—Barbudan 92%. The Barbudan capital and major cultural center is Codrington, (2002e) 1,000, the only settlement on Barbuda, which is situated on Codrington Lagoon.

FLAG: The Barbudan flag, the flag of the national movement, is a vertical tricolor of red, black, and blue.

PEOPLE AND CULTURE: The Barbudans are mostly the descendants of a nineteenth-century slave-breeding experiment on the island. The Barbudans, long isolated, are clannish, even when living on nearby Antigua, where many go for greater educational or work opportunities. They fear the expansion of private ownership, so different from their tradition of holding all land in common. Most Barbudans are farmers, raising sea-island cotton, although others sell sand to Martinique for the manufacture of cement.

LANGUAGE AND RELIGION: The daily language of the island is a West Indian creole dialect. English, taught in island schools, is spoken as a second language. The Barbudan dialect retains many African words brought to the island by slaves in the nineteenth century.

The majority of the Barbudans are Protestants, mostly belonging to the Anglican Church. There are minorities belonging to other Protestant sects and the Roman Catholic Church. The Barbudans are known for their simple faith and for choral singing, a legacy of nineteenth-century British clergy.

NATIONAL HISTORY: The island was uninhabited when it was first colonized from nearby Antigua in 1661. In 1678 European planters divided the island into several large plantations and imported black African slaves as labor. In 1691 the island was purchased by the English Codrington family. The island, flat and sandy, proved to be less productive than some neighboring islands, and, because of its exposed position, the island was the scene of many shipwrecks.

In the early 1800s, slaves were brought to the island for a slave-breeding experiment. With the increasing cost and availability of slaves, it was thought less expensive to breed slaves rather than depend on slaves brought from Africa. When slavery was abolished in the British Empire in 1834, the experiment was terminated, and the slave population on the island was freed. The freed slaves became self-reliant sailors, hunters, fishermen, and farmers who owned the land on Barbuda communally.

In 1860 Barbuda was officially annexed to Antigua. In 1872 it became a direct British territory and a dependency of the island of Antigua, ending the feudal control of the Codrington family. The island, with little economic promise, remained sparsely populated and neglected. The islanders, mostly self-sufficient, grew sea-island cotton and food crops, but in the mid-twentieth century they began to concentrate on livestock on land held in common by all Barbudans.

Antigua, with Barbuda as a dependency, joined the West Indies Federation in 1958; after the federation was dissolved in 1962, it sought to retain its ties to Britain. In 1967 the British colonial territories changed their status to that of associated states. Barbuda, as a dependency of Antigua, was included in the newly formed Associated State of Antigua. The Barbudans, opposed to their status as a dependency, formed the Barbuda Council, which worked for the exclusion of Barbuda from the new state.

Vehemently opposed to the private ownership, the casino gambling, and the high crime rate of tourist-oriented Antigua, the Barbudans in the late 1960s and the 1970s repeatedly petitioned the British government to grant them a separate, special administration to protect their unique culture and lifestyle. In 1976 Barbuda was made a semi-autonomous department of Antigua, with its own elected Council of Barbuda and a separate representative in the Antigua parliament.

The Barbudans continued to claim that they were treated as third-class citizens by the Antiguans. Barbudan objections and obstinacy delayed Antiguan independence for several years, as the two island peoples tried to work out an independence plan acceptable to both groups. Barbudan leaders tried to persuade the British to sever Barbuda from Antigua and to keep Barbuda as a British territory; when this failed, a delegation went to New York to try to block acceptance of the two-island nation to the United Nations. The Barbudans managed to delay independence until 1 November 1981, when the two-island state became independent as the Republic of Antigua and Barbuda. Some Barbudans appealed to the United States and Canada to accept them under a special territorial relationship.

The Barbudan delegation refused to sign the final independence agreement, its members insisting that they wished to secede and to establish Barbuda's own sovereignty. After the 400 eligible voters cast their vote in late 1981, the Barbuda Council announced the secession of their island from the new state. After long and often acrimonious negotiations, the Barbudans accepted a compromise, and the Barbuda Council took responsibility for certain island functions. Although the Barbudans won substantial autonomy, a sizable portion of the population continues to work for complete independence and to resist Antiguan efforts to develop the island. The islanders feel that adopting Antigua's tourist-happy attitude and unlimited growth would ruin their island. They have allowed a small airstrip, but only one small hotel.

In 1982 a resurrected medieval knightly order, the Sovereign Order of New Aragon, proposed setting up a sovereign state on half the island and selling land there to 400 knights of the order. One of the promoters of this scheme was the Italian actor Rosano Brazzi. Although some Barbudans would have welcomed the economic upsurge the New Aragon scheme would have brought the island, the Barbuda Council rejected the proposal as unsuitable for their small island.

The Barbuda People's Movement (BPM) formed as the most militant political organization on the island. The BPM is dedicated to the secession of Barbuda from the joint republic. Opposing the BPM is the Committee Working along with Antigua (CWAWA). The government of the republic has worked for closer cooperation between the two islands, but secessionist sentiment remains strong. Economic development, supported by the government, included installation of the first telephone service on Barbuda in 1986. In elections in 1985, the secessionist BPM lost support, and the Organization for National Reconciliation (ONR) gained a majority in the Barbuda Council, indicating less sentiment for separation.

In the 1990s Barbudan separatism again became a serious issue, mostly over the state of affairs on Antigua, which has become a center of money laundering in the Caribbean and a watering hole for Russian mobsters and Colombian drug barons. Some government officials, particularly from the Bird family and their Antigua Labour Party (ALP), which has ruled Antigua, with one brief break, since the 1940s, have been implicated in money laundering and vice scandals. Four Russian banks and a Ukrainian one operate in Antigua. In 1999 the United States warned the Antiguan government to reform its lax banking system and to crack down on drug trafficking.

In March 1999, control of the local government on Barbuda passed to the BPM when the party captured all five seats up for election. The party already controlled the other four seats on the Barbuda Council. At the turn of the twenty-first century, the Barbudans are again contemplating complete sovereignty for their small island. In July 1999, Vere Bird, the leader of the Antigua and Barbuda state for most of its post-independence period, died, severing one of the ties that bound the small islands together.

SELECTED BIBLIOGRAPHY:

Hall, Douglas. *Five of the Leewards, 1834–1870: The Major Problems of the Post-Emancipation Period in Antigua, Barbuda, Montserrat, Nevis, and St. Kitts.* 1978.
Kelly, Robert C. *Antigua and Barbuda Country Review 1999/2000.* 1999.
Lazarus-Black, Mindie. *Legitimate Acts and Illegal Encounters: Law and Society in Antigua and Barbuda.* 1994.
Lowes, Susan, ed. *Antigua and Barbuda.* 1995.

Bari

Beri; Bai; Mondaris; Mandaris; Kukus; Kakwas

POPULATION: Approximately (2002e) 610,000 Bari in the Lado area of west-central Africa, concentrated in the southern Equatoria region of Sudan, with about 80,000 in the West Nile District of Uganda and 40,000 in Haut-Congo region north and north west of Watsa in the Democratic Republic of the Congo.

THE BARI HOMELAND: The Bari homeland occupies a region in central Africa north of Lake Albert and on the west bank of the upper Nile River in southern Sudan. The region lies in the heart of Africa and controls the headwaters of the important Nile River. Most of the homeland is bushy savanna, with forests in the highlands and swamps along the Nile. The Lado region, the former Lado Enclave, claimed as a sovereign homeland by the Bari, has about 15,000 sq. mi.—38,850 sq. km, and a population of about a million. The Bari capital and major cultural center is Juba, in Sudan, (2002e) 147,000. The cultural center of the Ugandan Bari is Arua, the capital of the province of West Nile, (2002e) 31,000.

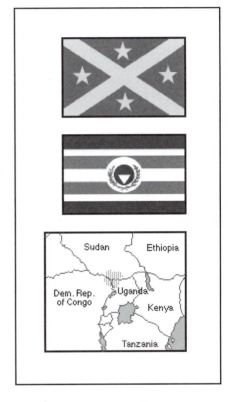

FLAG: The Bari national flag, the flag of the nationalist movement, is a blue field bearing a yellow St. Andrew's cross and charged with four yellow five-pointed stars. The flag of the Lado Defense Forces has seven stripes of blue, yellow, green, yellow, green, yellow, and blue, charged with the badge of the group centered.

PEOPLE AND CULTURE: The Bari comprise several closely related tribal groups living south and east of the Nilotic peoples of northeastern Africa. Most Bari live in the so-called Bari Triangle, called Lado by the Bari nationalists, on the borders of Sudan, Uganda, and Congo. Most live in small villages scattered across the hot, dry, flat plains of the Nile River valley. The Bari nation is divided into two major divisions the Bari and the Mandari, who number about 80,000 and live in the Sudanese portion of Lado. Many other small tribes in the region, including the Kakwa, Kuku, Fujulu, Nyangbara, and Nyepu, share the Bari culture and language. The Bari and Bari-related people in the region are estimated to number over a million. Traditionally Bari society has been divided into freemen and serfs, with blacksmiths, professional hunters, and similar groups forming castes. The Dupi (serfs), Kulu'ba, Liggi, Lui (freemen), and Tomonok (fishing, smithing) are the most important of the castes. The Marshia (Marsanit) are professional smiths who live in and around Rimo, mostly keeping to themselves. The majority of the 150 patrilineal Bari clans are composed of freemen. Both men and women undergo initiation by the extraction of the lower incisors and by scarring. The Bari villages are ruled by "big men" rather than chiefs. These include ritual functionaries, rainmakers, who are few in number but extremely powerful, and the "fathers of the earth," who are responsible for the magic that ensures successful crops, hunting, and warfare. Cultural and linguistic affinities point to a distant relationship between the Bari and the Maasai* of east Africa. The Bari belong to the group of east equatorial African nations that cannot be called either Bantu or Hamitic and have received no satisfactory collective designation.

LANGUAGE AND RELIGION: The Bari language is an Eastern Sudanic language, also called East Nilotic, of the Char-Nile branch of Nilo-Saharan language family. The Bari dialects of southern Sudan and northern Uganda form one of two linguistic branches that constitute the so-called Plain Nilotic branch of the Nilotic languages. Only distantly related to neighboring languages, the Bari language is more closely related to that of the Maasai, who inhabit the highlands far to the east. The ethnic Bari in northeastern Congo now speak a dialect of the Logo language. The Bari language is spoken in five dialects that correspond to the geographic areas of the Bari homeland, the Bari Triangle.

The Bari mostly adhere to traditional religious beliefs, which include magic, spells, and spirits that inhabit the physical features of the Bari homeland. A minority are Roman Catholic, although their religious practices incorporate both Catholic and pre-Christian beliefs. Recently evangelical Protestant sects have begun to win converts among urbanized Bari in Sudan and Uganda.

NATIONAL HISTORY: Europeans first visited the northern part of the region in 1841–42, when an expedition was dispatched by Mohammed 'Ali Pasha, the Ottoman sultan of Egypt. The neighboring settlements of Gondokoro, on the east bank of the Nile, and Lado soon became important stations for ivory and slave traders from Khartoum. After the discovery of Lake Albert in 1864, slave traders of diverse nationalities overran the whole region, and the Bari tribes were decimated.

Although Lado was claimed as part of Egyptian Sudan, nominally part of the Ottoman Empire, it was mostly ignored. The Ottoman Turks and their Egyptian vassals preferred to install foreigners in the African provinces, and it not until Sir Samuel Baker arrived at Gondokoro in 1870 as governor of the equatorial provinces that any attempt was made to control the slave traders. Under Egyptian administration the region was divided into provinces, with the Bari homeland mostly included in Equatoria, created in 1871. Only three years later, another British governor, Col. Charles Gordon, was dispatched to the troubled region. He established a separate administration for the province of Bahr al-Ghazal, further dividing the Bari homeland. Next an American, Col. Henry Prout, was placed in Lado as the governor, from 1876 to 1878.

Mehmed Emin Pasha, whose original name was Eduard Schnitzer, was born in Silesia, in central Europe, but later adopted a Turkish name and served in the Turkish army. In 1878 he was appointed governor of Equatoria Province, with the title of bey. Conducting an excellent and enlightened administration from the town of Lado, Emin made extensive and valuable surveys and brought slavery to an end in the province.

In the course of the Mahdist uprising in Sudan, the Egyptian government abandoned the region in 1884. Emin, though isolated in southern Equatoria, remained secure and was initially reluctant to be rescued by the famed explorer Henry Morton Stanley in 1888. Possibly owing to the arrival of Stanley and his forces, Emin was faced with discontent among his own troops. On 10 April 1889 he and Stanley, with over 1,500 others, left the region and crossed over to the eastern African coast. He later worked for the German authorities in East Africa and was ultimately murdered by slave traders.

The British and Belgians later occupied the territory, which they divided between themselves. The Belgians took the western Ituri-Uele region, which was added to the Congo colony. The British sector, called Nile-Equatoria, was later divided between Sudan and Uganda. The colonial authorities were followed by missionaries, mostly Roman Catholics. Jesuit priests, then Franciscan fathers, and even later Verona fathers set up mission stations and schools.

The British claimed the upper Nile region in February 1894, and in May of that year they leased to Leopold II of Belgium, as sovereign of the Congo Free State, a large area west of the upper Nile, which included the Bahr al-Ghazal and Fashoda. Pressed by the French government, Leopold agreed to occupy only that part of the area later known as the Lado Enclave. The British and French fought over the region between 1896 and 1899, but when the French withdrew from Fashoda in 1898, Leopold revived his claim to the whole area leased to him by the British government. Although he was unsuccessful, the lease was annulled as a result of a new agreement with Great Britain. In 1907 an Anglo-Belgian treaty determined the status of the Lado Enclave and established the border between British Sudan and the Belgian Congo. Leopold retained the enclave, with the stipulation that it should revert to the Anglo-Egyptian Sudan six months after the end of his reign. Leopold died in 1909, and the Lado Enclave was duly incorporated into the Anglo-Egyptian Sudan in 1910.

Since 1947 the strategic area called Lado has been eliminated from world maps, particularly by the UN recognition of the division of the Bari homeland. In 1962 the Bari leaders refused to sign a document attaching them to Uganda but they were ignored, and Uganda became an independent African state.

In the 1970s a nationalist group, the Lado Defense Forces, was formed by the Bari inhabitants of the region. Since then the Bari peoples of Lado have fought against Ugandan troops, the Sudan People's Liberation Movement (SPLM), and other rebel organizations operating in the Bari Triangle. The Bari peoples of Lado point to the fact that they never signed an agreement with any of the colonial powers, later African states, or any other power that would validate the division of their homeland.

In the 1990s, rebels from Sudan, Uganda, and Congo built bases in the region, where fighting has devastated the Bari villages. Thousands have been displaced or have died from hunger, shelling, or in battles. Ugandan troops occupied the region of Lado included in Congo in 1998, in their fight with the Congolese leader Laurent Kabila.

King John Bart Agami, the *agofe* of Lado, claims that Lado is the size of Sweden, with a population of some seven million, plus three million refugees who have fled the violence in the region. The Lado nationalists claim to have the support of Belgium in their quest for a separate state in the Congo-Sudan-Uganda border region. Nationalists claim that the region, rich in diamonds, copper, and gold, has been contested for over 300 years, first by tribal leaders, then slave traders, colonial powers, postcolonial African states, and now various rebel groups. King Agami sent three petitions to President Bill Clinton of the United States in an effort to win support for an independent Lado nation. He has also attempted to convince world leaders to convene a conference on Central Africa, where the warring parties of the region would sit around a negotiation table in an effort to end the devastation that has overwhelmed the region since the 1950s.

The Bari, divided by colonial borders, have retained a shared sense of identity that has sustained the small nation through the catastrophic events of the post-colonial period. Their experiences as part of Sudan, Congo-Zaire, and Uganda are comparable with those of the Caucasians in Russia or the Tibetans* in China. Bari nationalists argue that an independent Lado could at least provide the sense of security the Bari have lacked in the unstable Central African states.

SELECTED BIBLIOGRAPHY:

Casati, Gaetano. *Ten Years in Equatoria and the Return with Emin Pasha.* 1989.
Deng, Francis Mading. *War of Visions: Conflicts of Identities in Sudan.* 1995.
Price, Richard. *Equatoria.* 1994.
Rahim, Muddathir Abdel. *Imperialism and Nationalism in the Sudan: A Study in Constitutional and Political Development, 1899–1956.* 1987.

Bashkorts

Bashkurts; Bashkurds; Bashkyrs; Basqorts; Bashkirs

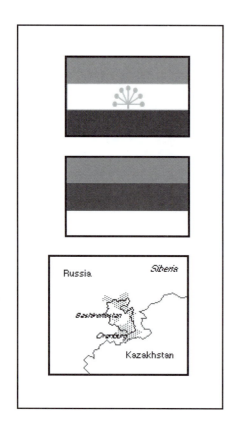

POPULATION: Approximately (2002e) 2,332,000 Bashkorts in Europe, concentrated in the southern Ural region of eastern European Russia, in the Bashkortostan and Tatarstan republics and Orenburg, Perm, Yekaterinburg, and Chelyabinsk regions. There are also sizable Bashkort populations in Central Asia, Ukraine, western Russia, and eastern Siberia.

THE BASHKORT HOMELAND: The Bashkort homeland lies in eastern European Russia between the Volga River and the Ural Mountains. Forming part of the divide between Europe and Asia, the republic extends from the western slopes of the Ural Mountains in the east to the Bugulma-Belebay Upland in the west. The republic, formerly called Bashkiria, formed an autonomous republic within Russia until the disintegration of the Soviet Union in 1991, when it became a member state of the newly independent Russian Federation. *Republic of Bashkortostan (Basqortostan Respublikahy)*: 55,443 sq. mi.—143,635 sq. km, (2002e) 4,095,000—Russians 36%, Bashkorts 28%, Tatars* 26%, Chavash* 4%, Maris* 3%. The population of the Bashkortostan Republic includes representatives of 106 distinct national groups. The Bashkort capital and major cultural center is Ufa, called Öfö in the Bashkort language, (2002e) 1,094,000.

FLAG: The Bashkort national flag, the official flag of the republic, is a vertical tricolor of pale blue, white, and green bearing a seven-petaled kurai, a reed that grows only in the Bashkort homeland. The seven petals stand for the seven tribes or clans of the Bashkort nation. The flag of the Bashkort Popular Party, the largest nationalist organization, is a vertical tricolor of pale blue, green, and white.

PEOPLE AND CULTURE: The Bashkorts, called Bashkirs by the Russians, are a Turkic people of mixed Finno-Ugric, Turkic, and Mongol background. Although the European strain is dominant, their background remains largely unclear. Traditionally the Bashkort nation comprises seven clans, further divided into numerous subclans and extended family groups. Assimilation of the Bashkorts living outside the republic is partly due to education, as the only Bashkort-language schools available to the Bashkort children are within the boundaries of the Bashkortostan Republic. The large number of Bashkorts living outside the republic are immersed in Tatar or Russian schools, media, and culture. Similarly, the rural dwellers have preserved their national identity almost intact, while the growing urban population has adopted to a considerable degree the culture and way of life of European Russia. Since the collapse of the Soviet Union, cultural clubs promoting the Bashkort language and culture have sprung up both in Bashkortostan and in the territories of the Bashkort diaspora. Even though many Bashkort have lost all contact with tribal structures, the sense of kinship and loyalty to kinsmen is still an important part of Bashkort culture. Two other smaller ethnic groups have recently been classified as Bashkorts—the Christian Bashkorts (called Nogaybak, or Nagaibak) and the Teptyar. Since 1991 many Bashkorts who had been assimilating into Tatar or Russian culture have registered as ethnic Bashkorts.

LANGUAGE AND RELIGION: The Bashkort language, called Basqort tele, is a Turko-Tatar language closely related to the language of the neighboring Tatars. The language, a Uralian language of the West Turkic language group, is spoken in three major dialects—Kuvakan (Mountain Bashkort), Yurmaty (Steppe Bashkort), and Burzhan (Western Bashkort). The literary language is based on the Kuvakan dialect and is written in the Cyrillic script. Bashkort did not become a separate literary language until 1919. The language is close to spoken Tatar and is considered by some as a dialect of Tatar, although this is denied by Bashkort nationalists. Until the reculturation that began to take hold in the late 1980s, many Bashkorts were assimilating into Tatar culture, and a minority still consider Tatar their first language. In 1959 only 62% of ethnic Bashkorts considered Bashkort their first language, with about 35% speaking Tatar as their mother tongue and the remainder using Russian. The decline of the language has slowly reversed since the national and cultural revival that has taken hold since the collapse of the Soviet Union. The forced introduction of the Bashkort language into state and public affairs led to protests by Russians and Tatars in the republic in the late 1990s.

The vast majority of the Bashkort are Sunni Muslims. They had originally adopted Islam in the tenth century, but many were forced by the Russians to convert to Orthodox Christianity between the sixteenth and eighteenth centuries. By the nineteenth century the majority of the converts had reconverted to Islam; however, at present about 3% of the Bashkort population are Christians. Polygamy, allowed by the Muslim religion, was outlawed during the Soviet era; however, some Bashkort men, particularly men of high social status, still have more than one wife. Foreign Christian sects have been active in the region since 1991, some claiming that the number of Christian Bashkorts has risen to around 7% of the total population.

NATIONAL HISTORY: The first records that mention the Bashkort, as nomadic herders in the southern Ural Mountains in the ninth and tenth centuries, list them as under the nominal rule of the Volga Bulgar state of the Chavash. Slavic monks, venturing into the pagan lands to the east, converted the Bashkorts to Christianity, traditionally in the year A.D. 922, but by the eleventh century most of the Bashkorts had abandoned Christianity for the Islamic religion brought north by traders from Central Asia.

The Golden Horde, Mongol and Turkic warriors of the Mongol's vast empire, overran the region in the thirteenth century. The Bashkort lands later came under the rule of the Tatar Khanate of Kazan, established as Mongol power declined in the fourteenth century. The period of Tatar rule drew the two Turkic peoples closer both linguistically and culturally. Some historians believe the Bashkorts moved into their present homeland between the thirteenth and fifteenth centuries.

A long series of wars with the growing Russian state ended with the khanate's conquest by Ivan the Terrible in 1552. Four years later the tsarist authorities took control of Bashkortostan and began actively to colonize the region, displacing many Bashkorts from their traditional lands. In 1574 Ufa was founded as a center of Slavic colonization of the region. The conquered Bashkort lands, settled by Slavic colonists and controlled by a string of Russian forts, formed the new frontier districts of the expanding Russian Empire.

The exploitation of the Bashkorts by tsarist authorities led to frequent disturbances and rebellions. In 1708 the Bashkorts rebelled and attacked the 3,000 Cossack and Russian settlements on their traditional lands, killing or capturing over 13,000 colonists. The revolt quickly spread from the Urals to the subject peoples of the Volga River basin, thus threatening Russian rule in the east until enough troops arrived to defeat the rebels in 1711. The most serious revolt occurred in 1773, led by the Bashkort national hero Salavat Yulay. Bashkort rebellions became so frequent that in the late eighteenth century smiths were forbidden to practice their trade, in order to prevent the fabrication of weapons. To counter the endemic Bashkort revolts the government established Cossack military colonies in the southern Bashkort lands. The Cossack colonists took the name of an important fort, calling themselves the Orenburg Cossacks.

In the late eighteenth and early nineteenth centuries, there was a great influx of Tatars, Russians, and other national groups into the Bashkort's traditional territory. The newcomers began buying or seizing the remaining pastoral land, severely damaging the Bashkort economy. The Bashkorts, impoverished and dispossessed of their lands, were forced to give up their formerly nomadic lives as herders and to settle in agricultural villages. The majority turned to agriculture to survive, some even moving into the growing Russian towns to find work.

The abolition of serfdom in Russia in 1861 brought a massive influx of freed serfs seeking land. The migration, seen as a threat to the Bashkorts' survival, fanned the growth of Bashkort nationalism in the late nineteenth century. Until then, they had lived in clans and identified with local tribal groups. Most considered themselves as ethnic Tatars, but that view gradually changed.

The Bashkorts again rebelled when news of the 1905 Russian revolution reached the area. Nationalists demanded the return of 5.4 million acres of stolen land, while more radical groups attacked Russian settlements and estates and assassinated tsarist officials, including the governor-general of Ufa. Loyal Orenburg Cossacks soon put down the revolt with great brutality.

The Bashkorts were largely untouched by World War I, and nationalists rapidly organized as revolution swept the empire in February 1917. Bashkort leaders formed the Bashkir National Movement, which called a national congress at Orenburg on 19 July 1917. The congress adopted an interim program favoring autonomy within a democratic Russian state and the expulsion of Slav colonists from the traditional Bashkort lands. Bashkort army units at the front deserted en masse and made their way home, where they formed the nucleus of the Bashkir National Army.

The Bolshevik coup in October 1917 forced Bashkorts into a reluctant alliance with their old enemies, the Orenburg Cossacks, who represented the anti-Bolshevik White forces in the region. The Bashkort Revolutionary Committee (Bashrevkom), in spite of White opposition to the secession of any part of "Holy Russia," declared the Bashkort homeland, called the Republic of Bashkiria, independent of the collapsing empire on 29 November 1917, claiming as national territory the provinces of Ufa and Orenburg. The claim to Orenburg ended the uneasy alliance with the Orenburg Cossacks, who fought and defeated the Bashkorts for control of the southern province. On 4 February 1918, Bolshevik forces moved into the region.

In the summer of 1918, Czech and Slovak prisoners of war held in Russia formed the Czech Legion, one of the strongest fighting forces in the region. The soldiers of the Legion, intent on getting back to their homeland via Siberia, swept the Bolshevik forces from the region in their march to the east. The Whites' insistence that Russia remain intact and their poor treatment of minority groups soon led to splits within the ranks of the anti-Bolsheviks. Despite White objections, the Bashrevkom drew up a series of plans for the expulsion of the Slav colonists and for the formation of Western-style state institutions in Bashkiria. Exposed to the persecutions of both the Whites under Adm. Alexander V. Kolchak and the Orenburg Cossacks under Hetman Dutov, the Bashkorts were often at odds with their allies, particularly over the Bashkorts' demands for self-government. Thousands of Bashkorts fled north from the Cossack-controlled lands in Orenburg province as violence again flared between the two groups.

The Bashkort leadership, believing a Bolshevik promise of independence within a Soviet federation of sovereign states, switched sides and went over to the Reds in March 1919. The Bashkorts prepared to send ambassadors to Moscow to represent the new Bashkurd Republic but were dismayed to find themselves treated as a conquered people rather than as allies. Betrayed by the Bolsheviks, the Bashkort turned on their new allies. At first the angry Bashkort troops were victorious, but the Red Army, following its victory over the Whites, was able to concentrate large numbers of troops in the region. The starving rebels finally surrendered in early 1922. The northern part of their traditional lands, the province of Ufa, called Little Bashkiria, became on 23 March 1922 the first autonomous republic erected for a national group within the Soviet Russian Federation. The Soviet government set up in the region in 1922 lacked even one ethnic Bashkort. The Bashkorts, under Soviet rule, enjoyed even less freedom than under the tsars.

The Bashkort nation lost about a third of its pre–World War I population in the suppression of their republic, the civil war, and the imposition of Soviet rule. Crop failure and famine in 1920–21 added to the massive death toll. However, Soviet rule, while oppressive, did bring some cultural and educational benefits, most immediately improved health care and the spread of literacy. The Bashkort language was widely used in education and the lower rungs of the local administration.

Many Bashkorts remained nomadic until forced collectivization in the early 1930s. Many died resisting the end of their traditional way of life. The Bashkorts were forced to settle in permanent villages or were moved to towns to which new industries and large Slavic populations were also being resettled. Oil was discovered in 1932, and the Bashkort homeland became the leading petroleum producer in the USSR.

During World War II, the *mufti* of Ufa and other Bashkort religious and political leaders were accused of spying for Germany and Japan and the Muslim Directorate was closed. They were deported to slave-labor camps in Siberia, but in 1941, in an effort to regain Muslim support, the Muslim Directorate of Ufa was revived.

Suppressed for over fifty years, Bashkort culture began to revive in the late 1970s, spurred by a renewal of interest in the Islamic religion. Led by Soviet intellectuals of Bashkort origin, the Bashkorts experienced a revival that glorified their past, emphasized their language, use of which had been declining since the 1920s, and revived their rich folk traditions. In 1980 a movement for the improvement of the political and legal status of the autonomous republic was formed. The growing Bashkort cultural and political movement coincided with the liberalization of Soviet society in the late 1980s, stimulating a resurgence of dormant Bashkort nationalism.

In the wake of the disintegration of the Soviet Union, demands for independence gained public support in the republic. In November 1991 the republican government reversed previous policy and announced an aim of eventual independence. In early 1993 Bashkort nationalists renewed their old claims to "Greater Bashkortostan," including Orenburg Oblast—which would give Bashkortostan, and the other republics in the Volga River basin a land border with the independent Republic of Kazakhstan on the south.

The Bashkortostan leadership in August 1994 negotiated extensive political and economic autonomy in a power-sharing agreement with the government of the Russian Federation. The agreements, which allow the republican government to retain a larger share of the oil revenue from the Bashkort fields, have given the Bashkorts within the republic greater financial security, but those outside its borders will not benefit. The republic has also asserted its right to enter into agreements with foreign governments; it signed an economic and political agreement with Iraq in March 1995.

The first serious clash between the Bashkort leadership and the federal authorities since the power-sharing agreement erupted in October 1997. The conflict grew out of the Bashkort assertion that presidential candidates in the Bashkortostan Republic must speak Bashkort, which many Russians claimed violated the Russian constitution. The language question in the republic remained one of the most contentious issues in the republic. Although the Bashkort population formed less than a third of the population of Bashkortostan, as the indigenous ethnic group the Bashkorts claimed the right to name their language, as well as Russian, as official. The large Tatar population objected, claiming that they outnumbered the Bashkorts in the republic and that Bashkort was merely a dialect of the Tatar language. The 1993 constitution was eventually adopted without reference to official languages. In early 1999 the lower house of the Bashkort legislature passed a bill, over the objections of the Tatar population of the republic and the government of neighboring Tatarstan, adopting Bashkort and Russian as official languages.

The president of the republic, Murtaza Rakhimov, rules with an iron fist, supported by the federation government in Moscow, which allows considerable autonomy in exchange for absolute political loyalty. Portraits of President Rakhimov adorn offices, hotels, and public buildings throughout the republic. His son, Ural Rakhimov, controls the important oil industry, making Bashkortostan virtually a personal fiefdom.

Population measurement has become a serious national issue in the region. According to official census figures the Bashkort nation, which had numbered some 1,500,000 in 1897, only returned to its pre-revolutionary size in 1989. The figure for 1926 had placed the Bashkort total at just one million; by 1959 it had dropped to 955,000. During the 1960s and 1970s, in spite of increasing assimilation, the overall numbers increased, and in 1970 there were an estimated 1,240,000 Bashkorts in the Soviet Union. By 1980 the number had increased to 1,380,000 in official estimates, and in 1989 the official census counted 1,345,000 Bashkorts. Unofficially, however, their numbers were considered to have passed the 1897 figure. Bashkort nationalists claim an ethnic population of some 2.5 million in the Russian Federation and the other states of the former Soviet Union.

Politicized ethnicity among the Bashkorts is not as strong or popular as among the neighboring Tatars, but, with closer ties between the scattered Bashkort communities and the migration of many Bashkorts to the republic in the 1990s, this is rapidly changing. Economic sovereignty has raised demands for greater cultural and political autonomy and for the redrawing of the Soviet-era borders, which artificially divided the Bashkort nation. The uneasy ethnic balance in the Bashkort homeland is an important issue for the regional Bashkort government.

Attempts by the Russian government to curtail the powers of the member states of the federation led to a nationalist backlash in Bashkortostan in 2000–2002. On the seventh anniversary of the signing of Bashkortostan's power-sharing agreement with Moscow on 3 August 2001, President Rakhimov announced that any attempt to annul the agreement would be a grave political error, perhaps even an irreparable one.

SELECTED BIBLIOGRAPHY:

Frank, Allen J. *Islamic Historiography and "Bulghar" Identity among the Tatars and Bashkirs of Russia*. 1998.
Kirkow, Peter. *Russia's Provinces: Authoritarian Transformation versus Local Autonomy*. 1997.
Muzaev, Timur. *Ethnic Separatism in Russia*. 1999.
Warhola, James W. *Politicized Ethnicity in the Russian Federation: Dilemmas of State Formation*. 1996.

Basques

Euskal; Eskauldunak; Vascos

POPULATION: Approximately (2002e) 2,355,000 Basques in Europe, mostly in northern Spain, 1,615,000, and southwestern France, 740,000. Outside Europe, Basque communities numbering an estimated 500,000 live in the Americas, with smaller groups in Australia and New Zealand.

THE BASQUE HOMELAND: The Basque homeland lies in southwestern France, straddling the Franco-Spanish border on the Bay of Biscay, at the western end of the Pyrenees Mountains. The region is mostly mountainous, with the forested foothills of the Pyrenees in the east and part of the Cantabrian Mountains in the west. In the south is the valley of the upper Ebro River and its tributaries, a region famed for its orchards. The entire region, called Euskal Herria in the Basque language, forms two autonomous regions of the Spanish state— Pais Vasco (Euzkadi) and Navarra (Nafarroa)— and three districts of the French department of Pyrénées-Atlantiques (collectively called Iparralde in the Basque language)—Basse Navarre (Benaparroa), Labourd (Lapourdi), and Soule

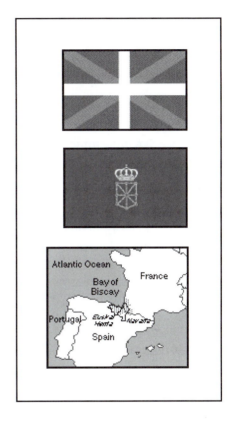

(Zuberos). The Basques call the French Basque Country Iparralde (from *impar*, meaning the north) and the Spanish part Hegoalde (from *hego*, the south). *Autonomous Basque Country (Pais Vasco/Euzkadi/Euskal Autonomia Erkidegoa)*: 2,803 sq. mi.—7,260 sq. km, (2002e) 2,099,000. *Autonomous Region of Navarra (Nafarroa)*: 4,024 sq. mi.—10,422 sq. km, (2002e) 551,000. Pays Basque (Iparralde): 1,270 sq. mi.—3,289 sq. km, (2002e) 371,000. *Euskal Herria* (the entire Basque Country in Spain and France): 8,055 sq. mi.—20,864 sq. km, (2002e) 3,021,000—Basques 73%, other Spanish and other French 27%. The spiritual capital is Guernica, called Guernika in Basque, (2002e) 19,000, the traditional site of the Basque assemblies. Other important cultural centers are Vitoria, Gasteiz in the

Basque language, (2002e) 218,000, the capital of the autonomous Basque Country in Spain; Bilbao (Bilbo), (2002e) 352,000 (metropolitan area 1,065,000), the region's largest city; San Sebastian (Donostia), (2002e) 181,000, the former summer residence of Spanish monarchs; Pamplona (Iruñea), (2002e) 189,000, the capital of Navarra; Bayonne (Baiona), (2002e) 40,000; and Biarritz (Miarritze), (2002e) 30,000 (Bayonne-Biarritz metropolitan area 152,000), the capital and major urban area of the French Basque Country.

FLAG: The Basque national flag, the official flag of the Pais Vasco in Spain and the unofficial flag of all the Basques, is a red field bearing a centered white cross backed by a green saltire. The flag is called the *Ikurriña* and forms an important part of the Basque identity. The flag of the Navarrese Basques, the flag of the Navarre region in Spain, is a red field bearing the traditional crest of chains surmounted by a crown.

PEOPLE AND CULTURE: The Basques, who call themselves Euskaldunak, are a unique national group, being almost certainly the oldest surviving ethnic group in Europe. Even the Basque blood-type differs from those of other Europeans. The origins of the Basques are still theoretical, with some experts claiming they are the descendants of early Iberian tribes, the pre-Celtic inhabitants of the region, while others connect them with wandering Caucasian nomads, and a third group claims they are a lost tribe of Israel. Many of the Basques are fair, blond with light eyes. Genetically and culturally, the Basque population has been relatively isolated and distinct, perhaps since Paleolithic times. The Basques have guarded their ancient customs and traditions in the isolation of their homeland, although they have been prominent in the histories of both Spain and France. Subgroups include the mainly Spanish-speaking Navarrese in the east and the French-speaking Gascons and Bearnese in the north. Traditional Basque culture has declined with urbanization and industrial development. In a 2001 poll, only 5% of Spanish Basques felt purely Spanish, 3% more Spanish than Basque, 41% equally Spanish and Basque, 17% more Basque than Spanish, and 23% purely Basque.

LANGUAGE AND RELIGION: The language of the Basques, Euzkarra, is the sole surviving example of the ancient languages that preceded the spread of the Indo-European languages. No relationship between Basque and any other language has been definitely established. The language is written in the Roman alphabet and is spoken in eight regional dialects— Guipuzcoan, High Navarese Septentrional, High Navarese Meridional, Biscayan, and Alavan in the Spanish Basque Country; Labourdin–Low Navarese and Souletin in French Euzkadi; and a number of subdialects. The eighth dialect, Batua, is a created variety used as the Basque literary language. The dialects are mutually intelligible, but there are significant differences between the dialects spoken in Spain and those spoken in France, particularly Souletin. The Basques are mostly bilingual, speaking either

Spanish or French in addition to their own language. A large minority, although in sentiment and culture considering themselves Basques, speak only Spanish or French, the result of decades of suppression and government policies.

The majority of the Basques are devoutly Roman Catholic, with a small Protestant minority, mostly among the Gascons and Bearnese in France. Evangelical Protestant sects, often represented by foreign missionaries, have won some converts in the region.

NATIONAL HISTORY: Prior to the Roman conquest of Gaul and Spain, the Basque tribes, loosely organized, extended north and south of their present homeland at the western end of the Pyrenees. Thought to predate the ancient Celts, the Basques are believed to have wandered into their homeland between 70,000 and 5,000 years ago. They are first mentioned as a people in Roman chronicles, as a nation difficult to subdue (though the region remained under Roman rule until the fifth century A.D.). The core tribes of the mountainous region resisted the Latinization of their culture and were only nominally under Roman authority.

Christianity, introduced between the third and fifth centuries, was slow to penetrate the Basque heartland, but once converted the Basques became fervent Christians. Although devout, the Basques retained a certain tradition of independence from both the Spanish and French church hierarchies.

During the barbarian invasions that followed the Roman collapse in the fifth century, Germanic Vandals and Visigoths passed through the Basque lands, destroying the last vestiges of Roman authority, but they failed to conquer the Basque strongholds in the Pyrenees Mountains. The Basques also withstood the Franks. In the sixth century, taking advantage of turmoil in the Frankish kingdom, the Basques expanded northward to take control of Vasconia, later called Gascony. Chronically at war with the Franks, Moors, and Visigoths, the Basques developed a warrior culture, defending their language and traditions against all intrusions.

The Germanic Franks finally overran Gascony and Navarre in the eighth century, but the Basques in the west successfully resisted the invaders. In 824 the western Basques returned to expel the Franks from the area south of the mountains, where they erected the kingdom of Navarre. Muslim Moors attacked the kingdom in the early tenth century and burned the capital, Pamplona, but by 937 the Basques had taken the offensive, later playing a prominent role in the Christian reconquest of northern Spain.

The most powerful of the Iberian kingdoms, Castile, conquered the western Basque country between 1200 and 1390; with the conquest of Navarre in 1512, the Basques lost their last independent territory. Granted special rights, the *fueros*, the Basques enjoyed broad autonomy in exchange for personal loyalty to the Spanish kings. Traditionally many Basques were fishermen and sailors; in 1492 a majority of the crews of Christopher Columbus came from the Basque region of Spain.

The northern Basques, incorporated in the French kingdom in 1601, were granted limited autonomy, a status they enjoyed until the French Revolution in 1789. The border between France and Spain, established in the Pyrenees and confirmed by a 1659 treaty, has remained unchanged to the present—although the frontier had little meaning for the Basques, who passed freely through the high passes in the Pyrenees Mountains.

The centralization of the French and Spanish kingdoms greatly reduced Basque autonomy. By the eighteenth century the prosperity of the region had also declined. Emigration became common, particularly to the Spanish colonies in the Americas. Other Basques, mostly sheepherders from France, migrated to the western territories of the United States or to the sheep-rearing regions of Australia and New Zealand.

Basque resistance to attempts by highly centralized governments to abrogate their ancient rights stimulated the growth of nationalism in the 1850s and 1860s. The national and cultural revival accelerated in the late nineteenth century, reversing centuries of assimilation and bringing the first demands for Basque self-determination and reunification of the traditional Basque territories. In 1873–74, during the Carlist Wars in Spain, the Basques resisted the Spanish Republican forces; in 1876 the *fueros* were abolished as a punishment. To regain their autonomy, the Basques habitually supported political movements opposing the central authorities in Madrid and Paris; by the 1890s a strong Basque nationalist movement had emerged on both sides of the international border.

Political turmoil in the Spanish state in the 1920s and 1930s strengthened the Basque national movement. In 1931, as virtual civil war paralyzed the Spanish government, the Basques of the three western provinces voted for secession. The Republic of Euzkadi, declared independent on 14 June 1931, was rapidly overrun and suppressed by troops sent by the government in Madrid.

Granted autonomy by a new leftist government in October 1936 at the outbreak of the Spanish Civil War, the Basques supported the Loyalist government against the fascist rebels, the Nationalists, and their German and Italian allies. The Spanish Civil War brought devastation to the region and divided the Basques, with some supporting the fascists. The town of Guernica, the site of a sacred oak tree, the symbol of Basque liberty, was deliberately destroyed by Nazi bombers in 1937. The destruction of the Basque's spiritual capital, commemorated by a famous painting by Pablo Picasso, marked the end of Basque autonomy and the imposition of harsh fascist rule under the Franco dictatorship. Thousands of Basques fled to France as the victorious fascists banned the Basque language, suppressed the culture, and instituted a policy of forced assimilation into Castilian Spanish culture.

The Spanish Basque region was industrialized by the Franco regime, eager to exploit its natural resources, and by the early 1950s the region had attained a standard of living comparable to the Benelux countries. Rapid economic development attracted thousands of migrants from Spain's backward southern provinces, their presence abetting the government's efforts to stamp out the Basque language and culture.

In 1952 a splinter group from the Basque Nationalist Party (PNV), calling itself Euzkadi ta Azkatazuna (Basque Homeland and Liberty)—but known by its initials, ETA—launched a resistance campaign. In France, a related group, Iparretarrak (IK, "Those of the North") became active. Spanish government pressure drove ETA underground, and in 1968, joined by its counterparts in French Euzkadi, ETA turned to violence and terrorism. In the early 1970s Basque nationalists often took sanctuary in the French Basque country, where the French government refused to extradite Basques wanted for political crimes in Franco's Spain. Under the slogan "Zazpiak bat" ("the seven are one," referring to the seven Basque regions), the nationalists won widespread support.

Franco's death in 1975 finally ended the dictatorship, and Spain rapidly democratized under a restored Bourbon monarchy. In 1978 the Basques were able to celebrate their national day for the first time since 1937. The Basque language, however, after four decades of suppression, was spoken by only 20% of Spain's Basques, as compared with 60% among Basques in France. The language experienced in the late 1970s and early 1980s a dramatic resurgence as part of the Basque's cultural renaissance.

The Basque provinces received a grant of autonomy in 1980, and a moderate nationalist regional government took control, with 70% support in local elections. The region of Navarre, Navarra in Spanish, was granted separate autonomous status and has strengthened ties to Euzkadi since 1988. The autonomous status of the Basques dramatically decreased support for the violent separatist organizations, with a corresponding rise in support for moderate nationalist political parties. The sacred oak of Guernica, grown from a branch of the original, again became the symbol of Basque sovereignty.

Nonetheless, militants in both Spain and France, vowing to settle for nothing less than full independence, continued their campaign of terror in the 1980s and 1990s. Since 1984 the Spanish and French governments have cooperated closely in a concerted antiterrorist crusade. A poll among the French Basques taken in 1990 showed that only 20% of the total Basque population in France considered themselves to be French.

In 1993, moderate nationalists in control of the regional government in the Spanish Basque Country put forward a plan for greater autonomy, which included closer official ties between Spanish and French Basques, and separate representation within the European Union. The French and

Spanish governments rejected the plan, but efforts to bring peace to the region began in earnest.

In 1998 the Spanish government and ETA, which sought to win greater political support in the region, agreed a cease-fire. ETA renounced the cease-fire in December 1999 and initiated a new round of bombings and other violent attacks in the Basque Country, Madrid, and other areas of Spain. Assassinations of political figures, both in the Basque Country and in other regions, particularly in Madrid and southern Spain, occurred on an almost monthly basis. The murder of members of Spain's ruling Popular Party (PP) and other politicians in the Basque Country and in southern Spain in 1999–2001 brought widespread condemnation, but public opinion seems not to faze the more militant Basque separatists. The Spanish government, controlled by the conservative PP, has refused to negotiate on the militants' major demand, full independence for the Basque Country.

Thousands of Basques marched through the cities of the French Basque region in September 1999. The demonstrators demanded a single Basque department to replace the three districts of Pyrenées-Atlantiques Department that now make up the French Basque Country. The proposed name for the new department is Iparralde, meaning North or Northern Basque Country.

In early 2000, increased autonomy for the Corsicans* stimulated new demands in the French Basque region for linguistic and political autonomy. The creation of a separate Basque province separate from surrounding non-Basque districts was put forward as a first step to an autonomous region.

Horrified by the indiscriminate violence, the vast majority of Basques have rejected armed confrontation and support moderate nationalist parties seeking greater independence within united Europe. The process of European unification has made the aspirations for the unification of the seven Basque provinces a more realistic possibility within the confines of a European federation. Although the militant groups have lost support, the political proxies of ETA won 18% of the Basque vote in 1998.

Although the Basque majority has rejected violence as a means to win greater independence, the small group of militants belonging to ETA continues to use terrorism to press their demands for separation of the Basque provinces from both Spain and France.

Support in the Basque region in Spain for the political allies of ETA fell from about 18% in 1998 to less than 10% in 2000. Continued violence has alienated many nationalists. In elections for a regional government in Spanish Euzkadi in May 2001, the Basques rejected both the Spanish government and the extremists of ETA, giving the moderate nationalists led by PNV 43% of the vote.

SELECTED BIBLIOGRAPHY:

Corversi, Daniele. *The Basques, the Catalans and Spain: Alternate Routes to Political Mobilisation.* 1997.
Heiberg, Marianne. *The Making of the Basque Nation.* 1989.
Jacob, James E. *Hills of Conflict: Basque Nationalism in France.* 1994.
Zirakzadeh, Cyrus E. *A Rebellious People: Basques, Protests, and Politics.* 1991.

Basters

Rehobothers; Rehoboth Basters

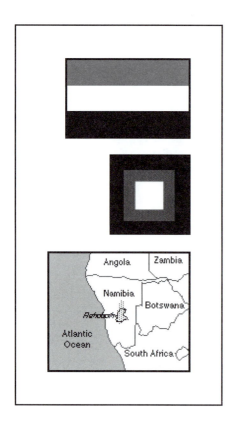

POPULATION: Approximately (2002e) 80,000 Basters in Namibia, concentrated in the Rehoboth region in central Namibia. Outside the homeland the largest community lives in Windhoek, the capital of Namibia, just north of the Rehoboth region.

THE BASTER HOMELAND: The Baster homeland lies just west of the Kalahari Desert in the central region of Namibia in southwestern Africa, an arid, sparsely populated region in Namibia's Central Highland. The homeland, an autonomous state prior to Namibian independence in 1990, is now divided between the regions of Khomas and Hardap. Baster nationalists have refused to recognize their incorporation into independent Namibia and continue to recognize their autonomous homeland. *Baster Gebiet (Rehoboth Gebiet/Rehoboth Baster Gemeente)*: 5,488 sq. mi.—14,216 sq. km, (2002e) 51,000—Basters 92%, other Namibians 8%. The Baster capital and major cultural center is Rehoboth, (2002e) 34,000, the traditional capital of the Baster homeland some 52 miles south of Windhoek, the Namibian capital.

FLAG: The Baster national flag, the flag of the nationalist movement, is a vertical tricolor of red, white, and black. The traditional flag of the Rehoboth homeland, adopted in 1872, is a square flag of overlaid squares of black, red, and white.

PEOPLE AND CULTURE: The Basters are the descendants of Afrikaners,* mostly of Dutch and French descent, and Khoi women they married in the Cape Colony. Later they intermarried with the local Namas but retained their European culture and traditions. They take pride in the name Basters, meaning Bastards, a name they were called by the white Afrikaner majority in South Africa. In Namibia the Basters are usually classified as "Colored," of mixed background, but they consider themselves distinct, though of similar origin to the Colored population. Modern Baster culture closely resembles the rural Afrikaner culture of the white South Africans, but many traditions and customs have been borrowed from the neighboring Namas.

LANGUAGE AND RELIGION: The Basters speak a dialect of Afrikaans, the language of the large Afrikaner population of South Africa. The language is a form of Dutch spoken in the Cape that gradually changed significantly from that spoken in Holland. The Cape dialect came to be called Afrikaans or Afrikaans, meaning the African language. The Basters share the language with the white Afrikaners but are separated from them by strong social and class distinctions.

The religion of the Basters is Christian, mostly Protestant sects brought to Africa by eighteenth and nineteenth century missionaries. The largest denominations are two Lutheran Churches, which together account for about half the Baster population. Smaller Roman Catholic, Dutch Reformed, and Anglican denominations exists mostly among the Basters living outside the Rehoboth region.

NATIONAL HISTORY: The Dutch began colonizing the southern tip of Africa in 1652, when a small company of employees of the Dutch East India Company was settled as a refreshment station for the sea route to the Far East. Dutch explorers after 1670 explored the region north of the Cape Colony, encouraging settlers to migrate to the new inland territories. During the eighteenth century, Dutch-speaking settlers, mostly young men looking for adventure or opportunity, took Khoi wives in the frontier districts. The first Baster communities emerged between the northwestern frontier of the British Cape Colony and the lower course of the Orange River in the 1790s. As an Afrikaans-speaking nation of mixed race, they were rejected by both the Afrikaners and the indigenous peoples of the region.

At the beginning of the nineteenth century, missionary organizations, such as the London Missionary Society and the Rheinische Missionsgesellschaft, established missions in Baster territory and supported local communities, called *gemeentes*, in developing written forms of regulations that had developed as customs over a long period. All community members were liable to pay taxes and levies, to attend church services, to send their children to schools, to register births and deaths, and to serve in militia units organized to protect the communities.

Like the Afrikaners, the Basters trekked north to escape discrimination and British rule. The Basters of Tuin in 1868 voted to emigrate beyond the borders of the British Cape Colony in order to find new places for settlement on the northern banks of the Orange River. The Tuin Council sent out an advance party under Hermanus van Wyk, who negotiated agreements with Nama and Herero tribal leaders for land for the settlement of the

Baster nation. The Tuin Basters trekked northwest in 1868, drafting a provisional constitution for their new national homeland during a stop at Warmbad on 15 December 1868. In the early 1870s, with their families and herds, other Basters trekked north out of British territory to join the new Baster nation. The difficult and dangerous trek became an important part of the Basters' national history.

The Baster communities in the Rehoboth region were Europeanized in military technology as well as in civil society and state organization, in keeping with the traditions of their Afrikaner forebears. In their new homeland, east of the Namib Desert, they established a national government with their own legislature and executive. A new constitution was promulgated on 31 January 1872 at Rehoboth proclaiming the region a republic. The constitution was amended and renewed in 1874, providing for an elected leader, the "kaptein," a council called the Kapteinsraad, and a parliament, the Volksraad. The Rehoboth Basters effectively constituted an independent nation, but as an isolated community they had few contacts with foreign powers.

The Germans established their authority in South-West Africa in 1885, but the Basters refused to recognize their authority in their homeland. The German colonial administration concluded a treaty of protection and friendship with the Baster nation. According to the treaty, the German emperor recognized the rights and freedoms acquired by the Basters of Rehoboth. The Basters insisted on a clause stating that any matters not covered in the agreement were to be resolved by agreement between the German and Baster governments. German troops won the help of the Basters in putting down resistance by native ethnic groups.

The colonial government, however, increasingly treated the Basters as yet another indigenous subject people, leading to Baster demands for German recognition of their independence. By the turn of the twentieth century, relations between the Basters and the German authorities had seriously deteriorated. In April 1915, during World War I, the Basters rebelled against the Germans, facilitating the occupation of German South-West Africa by South African troops.

The Basters' self-government remained unchanged during the period of South African occupation and in the first years after South Africa was granted a mandate over the former Germany colony by the new League of Nations. In 1923 several members of the Baster government signed an autonomy agreement with the South-West Africa administration, but a majority of the Basters rejected the agreement, claiming that it limited their right to self-determination and failed to restore lands confiscated by the former German regime. In 1924, because of disagreement among the Basters about an agreement concluded with South Africa concerning the administration of the district of Rehoboth, the South African government enacted a proclamation whereby all powers of the Captain, the courts and officials appointed by the Council, were transferred to the Magistrate and his Court, thereby suspending the agreement on self-government. Opposition led to open rebellion in 1924–25 and the formation of a new council determined to win independence. The Basters were defeated, and their self-governing community was only partly restored in 1928. Between 1925 and the early 1930s, the Basters sent a number of petitions to the League of Nations requesting the restoration of full self-government, but the petitions were blocked by the South African government.

After World War II, the League of Nations mandate in South-West Africa was transformed into a trusteeship agreement between South Africa and the United Nations. Administered as a "bantustan," or native homeland, under South Africa's increasingly restrictive apartheid laws, the Baster community suffered repression and discrimination from the late 1940s. In 1966 the United Nations attempted to terminate the trusteeship agreement, but the South African government continued to administer the region. In 1974, however, the South African administration allowed the Basters to resume full self-government.

In the late 1980s, the South African government finally agreed to allow the United Nations to prepare South-West Africa, renamed Namibia, for independence. The Basters, citing the 1885 treaty with Germany, demanded separate independence, but they were mostly ignored. They finally agreed to participate in the independence process, but without giving up their autonomy and self-determination. In the elections the Baster political party, the Federal Convention of Namibia (FCN), did poorly.

Namibian independence, under UN auspices, was scheduled for early 1991. Concerned about possible discrimination by the majority Ovambo and about securing their land from government confiscation, the Basters supported calls for independence rather than becoming part of multiethnic Namibia. Hans Diergaardt, the last kaptein, even bought up land in the hopes of linking Rehoboth to the ocean, in case his autonomy bid was successful.

Diergaardt, although not supported by the majority of the Basters, refused to give up the Baster government buildings in Rehoboth prior to the independence elections. On 19 March 1990 he declared Rehoboth autonomous under the constitution of 1872. In a referendum in the territory, 84.1% of the Baster voters were in favor of retaining control of their historical homeland. Diergaardt declared the independence of Rehoboth on the same day that Namibia was declared independent, 21 March 1991. The Baster rebellion was not taken seriously during the festivities of Namibian independence; however, a week after independence, the new Namibian president, Sam Najoma, warned the Basters that their attempts to break away from Namibia were illegal. Diergaardt and his supporters finally left the administrative buildings in Rehoboth in September 1991.

Under the excuse of eliminating the remnants of apartheid, the government of Namibia has, since independence, pursued a policy of treating all citizens of the state equally, dismantling the local governments that functioned under South African rule. The new Namibian constitution declared English to be the only official language, which meant the end of Afrikaans education and administration in Rehoboth. All assets of the previously recognized Baster Gebiet were confiscated, and all communal lands were transferred to the Namibian state, under the pretext that it had been public property under South African rule. The assets of the Rehoboth Development and Investment Corporation, worth about three million dollars, were sold to government allies and friends at greatly reduced prices. Immigration, mainly from the northern Ovambo region, the home of most government ministers, was promoted.

The Basters have refused to recognize their inclusion in independent Namibia, claiming that their autonomous homeland had never been annexed by the Germans or the South Africans and that their self-government had been recognized in treaties and agreements with the former governing powers. Fears that the Namibian government would confiscate their remaining lands for settlement by the excess Ovambo population in the north have disappeared, but distrust of the Ovambo-dominated government remains. These fears stimulated a nationalist movement in the late 1980s and early 1990s. The question of confiscated land remains a nationalist issue, with several claims still in the courts at the turn of the twenty-first century.

In October 1992, the Rehoboth Assembly declared the Baster nation as an indigenous people of the Republic of Namibia and demanded all rights to which autochthonous and indigenous peoples are entitled according to international practice and conventions. In 1993, the International Year of Indigenous Peoples, it appealed directly to the United Nations for recognition of the Basters' rights as a distinct nation predating the German, South African, and Namibian governments established in the region.

The Namibian High Court in 1995 denied an application by the Basters to force the government to return its traditional land in the Rehoboth region. The court ruled that the Basters' traditional lands had reverted to the central government upon independence. The Basters appealed to the Supreme Court, which agreed with the High Court. The Rehoboth Rate Payers Association, a new group formed in 1997, contested local elections in October 1997.

The Baster leader Hans Diergaardt died in February 1998. The community then decided to drop its long-standing legal battle over land. Elections for a new Baster leaders were controversial. Some Basters believe that a new leader is not needed because of the existence of the local council; others support the traditional leadership structure. In January 1999 the Basters elected a new leader, John McNab. With only 25% of the population participating in the election, McNab won with 41% of the turnout vote. He repeated the Baster demand for autonomy and self-determination.

In November 2000 several Baster activists complained to UN personnel of human rights abuses in the Baster region of central Namibia. The complaints were dismissed by the Namibian government, but protests and complaints of abuses continued in 2001–2.

SELECTED BIBLIOGRAPHY:

Bayer, Maximilian. *The Rehoboth Baster Nation of Namibia*. 1998.
Cliffe, Lionel. *The Transition to Independence in Namibia*. 1994.
Saul, John, and Colin Leys, eds. *Namibia's Liberation Struggle: The Two Edged Sword*. 1995.
Soggot, D. *Namibia: The Violent Heritage*. 1986.

Bavarians

Bayrisch; Bayerns

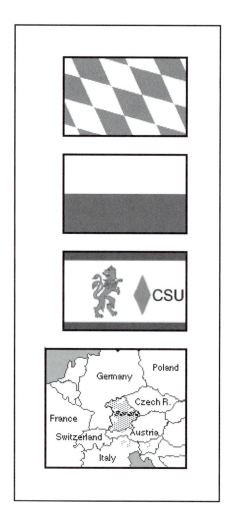

POPULATION: Approximately (2002e) 10,235,000 Bavarians in Europe, the majority in the state of Bavaria in Germany, but with small Bavarian populations in Austria and Italy. There are Bavarian communities in other parts of Germany, in France, and in the United States, Canada, Australia, and South America.

THE BAVARIAN HOMELAND: The Bavarian homeland occupies a mountainous region in Central Europe, traversed by the Danube River and its tributaries. The region is made up of fertile, softly rolling hills crossed by several important rivers, rising to the Bavarian Alps in the south. The Bavarian Alps contain Germany's highest mountain, the Zugspitze, at 9,729 feet (2,963 meters). Between the Alps and the Bohemian Forest lies the Franconian Jura, a plateau traversed by the Danube, Europe's longest river. Bavaria forms an autonomous state of the Federal Republic of Germany. *State of Bavaria (Länd Bayern)*: 27,239 sq. mi.—70,549 sq. km, (2002e) 12,221,000—Bavarians 80%, other Germans* 14%, Turks* 5%. The Bavarian capital and major cultural center is Munich, München in the German dialects, (2002e) 1,168,000 (metropolitan area, 2,349,000).

FLAG: The Bavarian national flag, the traditional flag of the Bavarians, is a lozenge pattern of pale blue and white. The official state flag is a vertical bicolor of white over blue, at times charged with the Bavarian coat of arms centered. The flag of the largest Bavarian political party, the Christian Social Union (CSU), is a white field with narrow green stripes at the top and bottom and charged with a gold lion rampant, a pale blue lozenge, and the initials of the party.

PEOPLE AND CULTURE: The Bavarians are a German people comprising three distinct groups that reflect the regional distribution of the early Germanic tribes—the people of old Bavarian stock in the south; the Bavarian Swabians* in the west; and the Franconians, the descendants of the Franks, in the north. Until the nineteenth century the Swabian and Franconian regions were separate, and they have distinct histories. Traditional differences among the three groups are still visible, but all see themselves as Bavarians first. After World War II there was an influx of refugees from the Sudetenland of Czechoslovakia and Eastern Europe, where many Germans had lived for centuries. A significant portion of the present Bavarian population, and often the most nationalistic, are descendants of these refugees.

LANGUAGE AND RELIGION: The Bavarian language, a dialect of High German, is more closely related to the German dialects spoken in neighboring Austria and Switzerland than to the standard German spoken throughout Germany. Only an estimated 40% of the Bavarian language is intelligible to speakers of standard German. The language is spoken in three dialects. North Bavarian is spoken in the region north of Regensburg and Nuremberg and east to the Czech border. Central Bavarian is spoken in the Alps; it is also spoken by some Austrians in Lower Austria and Salzburg provinces of the Austrian republic. South Bavarian is spoken in the Bavarian Alps, by the Tyroleans* in Austria, in Austrian Styria; it is called Heanzian in Austrian Burgenland and Carinthia. There are small pockets of Bavarian speakers in northern Italy and in the Gottschee in Slovenia. The Bavarians are the most nationalistic of the German peoples. Their national pride is based on over a thousand years of separate history and culture. Regionalism and nationalism remain a strong feature of the Bavarian nation. Although the Swabians and Franconians have separate histories, they remain staunchly Bavarian.

The majority of the Bavarians, about 70%, are Roman Catholic, with a Protestant minority, about 26% of the population. Religion in Bavaria has remained regional, with the Bavarians and Swabians in the south mostly Roman Catholic, and the Franconians in the north mostly Protestant, but with a large Catholic minority.

NATIONAL HISTORY: The earliest known inhabitants of the region were the Celts. They were later pressed between the Germanic tribes on the north and the Romans on the south. The Romans conquered the region and Latinized the Celts. Flourishing Roman colonies in the south were the forerunners of many present Bavarian cities. Germanic tribes crossed the Danube River, for five centuries the northern boundary of Roman rule, as Rome's power declined in the fourth and fifth centuries A.D. The tribes settled in distinctive regions and mixed with the remaining Roman and Celtic populations. The borders of Bavaria varied considerably during its long history, with the Swabian and Franconian territories often incorporated into neighboring states.

Named for the Bavarii tribe, the region formed a region tributary to the Franks in the sixth century; in 787–788 it came under the rule of Charlemagne's Frankish empire. Converted to Christianity in the eighth century, the Bavarians developed one of the five stem duchies of the Holy Roman Empire and one of the most powerful of the German states. In 911 a native dynasty again took power in the region. From the ninth to the eleventh centuries, the Bavarian dukes were often at the center of rebellions against the power of the emperors of the Holy Roman Empire, constantly extending their domains by conquest or purchase.

Due to its central location in Europe, foreign armies often invaded the Bavarian homeland. The Bavarian state, traditionally allied to neighboring Austria, became the most powerful of the southern German states; however, the Bavarian territories were often divided and subdivided among various rulers. By the fourteenth century the ruling family's various branches had divided Bavaria into three separate duchies. Neighboring states encroached on Bavarian territories, and the nobles ignored the authority of the dukes. Under Saxon rule in the twelfth century, the Bavarian Österreich (East Mark) separated in 1156 to become a distinct duchy, called Austria in English. In 1180 the Saxon lands were further divided by Frederick Barbarossa, who gave Bavaria to the house of Wittelsbach, which was to rule Bavaria until 1918.

The Reformation in the sixteenth century was opposed by the majority of the Bavarians, who fought in the Thirty Years' War on the Catholic side. In the south the Bavarians remained staunchly Roman Catholic, but the related Franconians to the north eventually accepted the Protestant Reformation.

Throughout the eighteenth century Bavaria was ravaged by wars. In the War of the Bavarian Succession, fought in 1779–79, Frederick II of Prussia prevented the Austrians from incorporating a large part of Bavaria to which it had a claim. Allied to France in the early nineteenth century, Bavaria was awarded by Napoleon additional territories in Swabia and Franconia; in 1806 Napoleon raised the Bavarian ruler, Maximilian I, to the status of king. The Bavarian king later deserted Napoleon and participated in the Congress of Vienna. The congress awarded Bavaria additional territory. The Bavarians participated in the Congress of Vienna, 1814–15, as a victor nation, retaining much of its territorial and political gains and becoming the third-largest German state, after Austria and Prussia.

The Bavarian kings, known for extravagant living and architectural fantasies, became increasingly out of touch with the Bavarian people. King Louis I, who ruled Bavaria from 1825 to 1848, had a famous affair with actress Lola Montez. King Louis II, 1864–86, was the patron of composer Richard Wagner. The brother of King Louis, Otto I, incurably insane after 1872, nevertheless succeeded Louis in 1886, when the king too was judged insane. Otto died under mysterious circumstances in 1913. King Louis III, who succeeded Otto, was dethroned following the German defeat in November 1918.

Politically and culturally closer to Vienna than to Berlin, Bavaria joined Austria to fight the hated Prussians in 1866, and with defeat paid a large indemnity and joined the Prussian-dominated German Empire in 1871, effectively ending Bavaria's independence. Pan-German nationalism, fostered throughout the empire, spread to Bavaria but without replacing Bavarian national sentiment. Bavarian nationalists remained adamantly opposed to the domination of the empire by Protestant Prussia. The Bavarians fought alongside the Prussians during the Franco-Prussian War of 1870–71 but refused to accept further integration into the Prussian-dominated German empire.

Bavarian armies fought for the empire as war engulfed Europe in 1914 and shared Germany's defeat in November 1918. As revolution swept Germany, revolutionaries deposed the Bavarian king and declared the kingdom a republic, thus ending one of the oldest of the European dynasties. By mid-November the major functions of government had come under the control of socialists led by Kurt Eisner, who declared Bavaria independent of Germany on 22 November 1918. Six days later the Bavarian government closed its legation in Berlin and severed all ties to the German government.

Kurt Eisner, a Jewish socialist and viewed as the one man produced by Germany's revolution who compared with his Russian counterparts, was assassinated by an embittered monarchist while on his way to open parliament on 21 February 1919. Without Eisner's leadership the socialist government faltered, its weakness a pretext for a communist coup. The coup ended Bavarian contacts with U.S. president Woodrow Wilson, established in an attempt to win international recognition of the Bavarian republic. The communists, inspired by Soviet Russia, declared the Soviet Republic of Bavaria on 7 April 1919. German troops called in by the deposed socialists invaded the state and defeated the communists in May. A new Bavarian government, firmly under the control of Pan-German nationalists, joined the recently inaugurated German federation, but the political scene remained unsettled, and in 1920 and 1921 there were unsuccessful attempts to take control of the Bavarian government. Traditional Bavarian nationalism, anti-Semitic and anti-Prussian, proved fertile ground for radical and reactionary political movements. In November 1923 monarchists attempted to seize the government, intent on secession and the restoration of the kingdom. A small, radical political group, the Nationalist Socialist Party (the members of which were called Nazis), pre-empted the planned monarchist coup and attempted its own takeover of the Bavarian government in the so-called Beerhall Putsch. For his part in the failed coup the group's leader, Adolf Hitler, received a five-year prison sentence. In the Bavarian prison he wrote *Mein Kampf*, his plan for world domination. In

German elections in 1932, the Nazis became the largest party in all German states except Bavaria, which was dominated by the Roman Catholic Bavarian People's Party. The Nazis, though enjoying strong support only in Bavaria's Protestant north, took control of the Bavarian government on 7 March 1933, dispatching paramilitary (SS and SA) troops to Bavaria on the pretext that the Bavarian government was unable to maintain order. The Bavarian premier was overthrown; to forestall separatism the Nazis took over all facets of government and closed all Bavarian legations in other countries. The first Nazi concentration camp was built in 1933 in Bavaria, at Dachau, near Munich. A Catholic separatist plot discovered in 1934 gave the Nazis a reason to eliminate ruthlessly all remaining Bavarian opposition.

Bavarians were enthusiastic in 1939 for war, which was presented as an anticommunist campaign, but their enthusiasm began to wane as Allied bombers reduced many cities to rubble. Bavaria was the scene of a famous anti-Nazi underground group, the White Rose. Several of the group's young members were beheaded in 1943. A resurgent nationalist movement attempted to win Allied support for separate independence at the end of the war, but the Bavarians ultimately settled for substantial autonomy within a reconstituted federal Germany.

Under American military occupation, a new constitution was adopted in 1946 based on the democratic principles of the Allies. The poorest of the states in 1949, when the new Federal Republic of Germany was proclaimed, Bavaria began an economic revival with industries relocated from communist East Germany. In the 1950s and 1960s the so-called German Miracle was interpreted in Bavaria as a Bavarian miracle. By 1972 Bavaria had become the richest of the German federation's states. The Christian Social Union, the successor of the prewar Bavarian People's Party, eventually became the leading party in Bavaria.

European integration and German reunification in 1990 rekindled Bavarian nationalism. Nationalists compared Bavaria's inclusion into united Europe (EU), as part of Germany, to the still-controversial incorporation of the state into Otto von Bismarck's Germany in 1871. For many Bavarian nationalists the German government has become an unwanted tier of government. Many Bavarians see the restoration of Berlin as the federal capital as the restoration of Prussia's leading rule in Germany.

In August 2000 Bavarian leaders, discussing the growing problem of an aging and declining population, urged Bavarians to have more children. Although immigration to Bavaria has been high, most leaders see immigration as a problem rather than a solution. However, although racism and xenophobia are growing problems, the Bavarians tend to be more tolerant than many of the other German peoples.

A meeting of European Union leaders in November 2000 was attended by delegates from the Bavarian government, who pressed for greater participation in the Union. The entrance of the Czech Republic and other former Soviet states in Central and Eastern Europe to the EU, planned for the first decade of the twenty-first century, would place the Bavarians in the center of the expanded European federation.

The separatist Bavaria Party is seeking sovereignty and eventual independence for the Bavaria, the largest of Germany's sixteen states. Many Bavarian politicians, not just the nationalists, believe that the trend in Europe is shifting governmental power to regional and local levels as national borders are erased while the economy of Europe becomes united. The nationalists continue to press for greater direct Bavarian participation in united Europe, while an increasingly vocal minority argues for the "European Option," Bavarian independence within the European federation.

SELECTED BIBLIOGRAPHY:

Dorondo, D. R. *Bavaria and German Federalism: Reich to Republic, 1918–33, 1945–49.* 1992.

James, Peter. *The Politics of Bavaria—An Exception to the Rule: The Special Position of the Free State of Bavaria in the New Germany.* 1995.

Kershaw, Ian. *Popular Opinion and Political Dissent in the Third Reich, Bavaria, 1933–1945.* 1985.

Nohbauer, Hans F. *Bavaria.* 1995.

Belongers

Turks and Caicos Islanders; Turcaicians

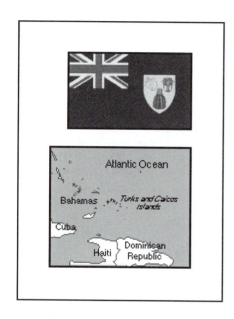

POPULATION: Approximately (2002e) 35,000 Belongers in the Caribbean, concentrated in the Turks and Caicos Islands. There are important Belonger communities in the Bahamas, about 17,000, and 10,000 in Florida, on the U.S. mainland.

THE BELONGER HOMELAND: The Belonger homeland is the Turks and Caicos Islands, an archipelago of 30 islands, of which eight are inhabited. The islands lie 575 miles southeast of Florida and 39 miles from the nearest of the islands of the Bahamas. The islands, including one of the longest coral reefs in the world, are relatively flat but, depending on the island, the terrain can vary from sand dunes to lush vegetation and mangrove swamps. The islands comprise two groups—the Turks Islands, with Grand Turk and Salt Cay; and the Caicos Islands, made up of South Caicos, East Caicos, Grand Caicos, North Caicos, Providenciales, West Caicos, and numerous small cays. The Turks and Caicos Islands are an overseas territory of the United Kingdom. *Turks and Caicos Islands*: 166 sq. mi.—430 sq. km, (2002e) 18,200—Belongers 91%, Bahamians 5%, others 4%. The Belonger capital and major cultural center is Cockburn Town on Grand Turk, (2002e) 5,000.

FLAG: The Belonger flag, the official flag of the Turks and Caicos Islands, is a blue field bearing the Union Jack as a canton on the upper hoist and a yellow shield charged with a conch shell, a lobster, and a cactus.

PEOPLE AND CULTURE: The islanders, calling themselves Belongers, are dispersed over the eight main islands. They are mostly the descendants of black slaves brought to the islands in the eighteenth and early nineteenth centuries, particularly to the cotton plantations of Providenciales. When slavery was abolished in 1834, most of the European planters left the islands, leaving their former slaves behind. A distinctive island culture developed, similar to that of the neighboring Bahamas, but with many local

302

traditions and customs. Tourism and annual subsidies from the British government has raised the standard of living to one of the most advanced in the Caribbean.

LANGUAGE AND RELIGION: The official language of the islands is English, which is spoken by nearly all the population; the language of daily life is a West Indian patois based on English but with considerable mixing with Spanish and African words and expressions. The Belongers are known as friendly, relaxed, and very hospitable.

The majority of the Belongers are Protestant, although religious beliefs and traditions brought to the islands by their ancestors continue hold the loyalty of many of the islanders. Religion is a major part of the Belonger culture, with participation in services, events, and ceremonies involving much of the islands' population. The major denominations are Baptist, Methodist, and Anglican.

NATIONAL HISTORY: The islands were inhabited by peaceful Arawaks, migrants from the South American mainland. The Arawaks settled the islands from the south, pushed north by the spread of the fierce Caribs.

According to local tradition, either Christopher Columbus or Ponce de Leon was the first European to visit the islands. The *Pinta*, one of Columbus's ships, is believed to have been lost in the islands in 1500. The islands were formally claimed by Ponce de Leon for Spain in 1512. By 1521 the islands were known as Spanish territory. The Turks Islands were named for the turk's head, a type of cactus that grows on the major islands.

Spanish rule, as in other areas of the Caribbean, decimated the indigenous population. Forced labor, slavery, violence, and disease virtually wiped out the Arawaks in the islands by the mid-sixteenth century. Having no economic interest, the islands were abandoned by the Spanish. The few inhabitants were pirates or the survivors of the many ships that were wrecked on the reefs between the sixteenth and eighteenth centuries.

The islands remained virtually uninhabited until they were settled by Bermudians* who arrived to work the salt ponds in 1678. A small English colony was settled; the local economy was based on the production of salt by evaporation of seawater in artificial basins. The islands were officially annexed to the British Empire in 1766. During the American Revolution, United Empire Loyalists fleeing the overthrow of British rule on the American mainland settled in the Caicos Islands and established cotton plantations. The planters imported black African slaves to work on the plantations, and the slaves were soon more numerous in the islands than the planters.

The Caicos Islands were administered from the Bahamas from 1799, while the Turks Islands were annexed to Bermuda in 1804. In 1848 the two island groups were united to form a presidency under the governor of Jamaica, becoming a dependency of Jamaica, some 400 miles (643 km) to the south, in 1873–74. Ships sailing between Britain and Jamaica used the ports, which were more convenient than Nassau in the Bahamas, thus facilitating communications and bringing modernization.

The abolition of slavery in the British Empire in 1834 ruined the plantation economy, forcing most of the planter families to leave the islands. The former slaves turned to subsistence farming, fishing, and salt production. Salt remained the main export until the twentieth century.

The islands remained poor, neglected, and underdeveloped. Their home islands damaged by severe hurricanes in 1925, 1928, and 1945, the Belongers struggled to survive, with only minimal aid from the British government. In the 1960s, the salt industry collapsed, leaving conch and shellfish as the chief exports.

In 1959 the islands formed a territory of the autonomous West Indies Federation, but they reverted to the status of a British crown colony when the larger members of the federation, Jamaica and Trinidad, opted for separate independence in 1962. Under a new constitution in 1969, the Belongers became self-governing as part of the Bahamas. The elected State Council unsuccessfully petitioned to join Canada in the early 1970s. In 1973 the Belongers opted to stay British when the Bahamas achieved independence. In the late 1970s, the British government promised independence whenever the Belongers wished.

Drug trafficking between the islands and the United States reached dangerous proportions in the 1970s, prompting a crackdown by the British and American governments. With relative peace, developers began to construct condominiums on Providenciales, as vacation homes. An international airport was constructed in 1983, allowing direct air links to Florida and other Caribbean islands. Tourism became the major industry, although many Belongers still go seasonally to the Bahamas to find work. The British government provides massive financial support, and the civil service provides most of the jobs outside the tourist industry.

Elections in 1976 were won by the People's Democratic Movement (PDM), which promised to negotiate independence if it won the next elections as well. In 1980 the British agreed to independence in 1982 if the pro-independence PDM won local elections. The leader of the party was killed in an accident, and the PDM lost the election to the pro-British Progressive National Party (PNP). In 1984 the elections were won by the pro-independence party, but popular opinion had turned against full sovereignty and the economic and political problems that it might bring.

In March 1985, the chief minister of the islands, Norman Saunders, was arrested in Miami on drug-related charges. His successor, Nathaniel Francis, was removed in 1986 by the British authorities for corruption. Ministerial government was then suspended; it was returned after elections in 1988.

The tourist industry is the mainstay of the Belonger economy, although offshore banking has become an important factor in the 1990s. There is a small traditional fishing industry, which continues mostly on the outer islands. Living conditions are generally poor, unemployment is high, and such basics as fresh water and electricity are limited. Health is good, with a hospital on Grand Turk and outpatient and dental clinics on the other islands. Education is free and compulsory at the primary level.

Both the government and opposition political parties spent most of 1996 trying to persuade the British authorities to remove the colonial governor, Martin Bourke, but their petition was rejected. The hostility to Bourke was based on his alleged abuse of power and his lack of respect for the Belongers. His term of office expired at the end of the year.

The Belongers have rejected independence for now, being content to remain under the financial and political security of the British. Although pro-independence groups continue to demand a referendum, popular opinion seems to favor the status quo.

In 2000, the British government floated the idea of extending British citizenship to the islanders, as long as they bring some of their more outdated laws into line with current British law. The idea, rejected by the pro-independence groups but welcomed by the pro-British, reawakened the dormant controversy over full independence for the Belongers.

SELECTED BIBLIOGRAPHY:

Boultbee, D. *Turks and Caicos Islands*. 1991.

Davies, Julia, and Phil Davies. *The Turks and Caicos Islands: Beautiful by Nature*. 2000.

Dowd, John. *Rare and Endangered*. 2000.

Stirling, Bill. *The Turks and Caicos: An Offshore Solution*. 1988.

Bermudians

Bermudans; Bermuda Islanders

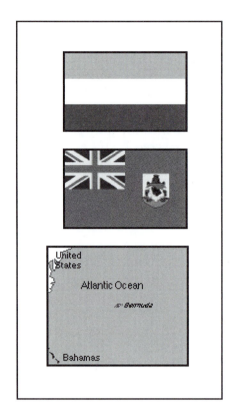

POPULATION: Approximately (2002e) 75,000 Bermudians, mostly living in the Bermuda Islands, but with sizable communities in Great Britain, the United States, and Canada.

THE BERMUDIAN HOMELAND: The Bermudian homeland is a group of small coral islands lying in the Atlantic Ocean about 580 miles (933 km) southeast of Cape Hatteras, North Carolina, and more than 800 miles (1,300 km) north of the West Indies. The island group is made up of about 360 small islands, although only 20 are inhabited. The archipelago is about 24 miles (40 km) long and averages less than one mile (1.6 km) in width. Geologically, the islands have a base of volcanic rock and are capped by coral formations. The main islands are clustered together in the shape of a fishhook and are all connected by bridges. Bermuda forms a self-governing state of the United Kingdom. *Bermuda*: 21 sq. mi.—53 sq. km, (2002e) 63,000—Bermudians 91% (black 49%, white 36%, other 6%), other British 9%. The Bermudian capital and major cultural center is Hamilton, (2002e) 1,500, urban area, 24,000.

FLAG: The Bermudian national flag, the flag of the national movement, is a vertical tricolor of pale blue, white, and green. The official flag of the state is a red field bearing the Union Jack as a canton and the state arms of Bermuda, which show the *Sea Venture* floundering on the rocks, on the fly.

PEOPLE AND CULTURE: The Bermudians are the descendants of early English settlers, later British civil servants, and slaves imported by the settlers from other British colonies and Africa. Some of the Bermudians are the descendants of British Loyalists who fled to the islands with their slaves from the rebellious mainland colonies between 1776 and 1781. The black Bermudian population is now the majority, but relations between blacks and whites are generally good, and a sense of Bermudian identity grew during the violence of 1977. The modern Bermudians are a sophisticated, well-educated people and are proud of the accomplishments of their small nation.

LANGUAGE AND RELIGION: The Bermudians speak English, often with an island lilt, although standard English is taught in the state schools and is the language of administration. Some of the black Bermudians speak an English patois similar to those spoken in the Caribbean. Education is widespread, compulsory, and well-organized, so the Bermudians are a literate people, with an estimated 99% literacy rate.

The majority of the Bermudians are Protestants, with the Anglicans accounting for 28% of the total; Methodists and Seventh-Day Adventists are the other large groups. Evangelical sects have gained converts in the islands since the 1970s. A Roman Catholic minority, about 15% of the population, is well integrated; religious tolerance is an island tradition.

NATIONAL HISTORY: According to early accounts, the islands were first sighted in 1503 by the Spanish explorer Juan Bermudez, for whom the islands were eventually named. The islands of the archipelago remained uninhabited until an English party bound for Virginia under Sir George Somers on the vessel *Sea Venture* became the unwilling founders of the colony when they were shipwrecked in 1609. The passengers and crew lived on fish and birds for a year while they built another ship, but the majority decided to stay. A British company was formed for the Plantation of the Somers Islands, as the islands were first called. The colonists created the House of Assembly, the first parliamentary body in the British possessions in 1620. In 1684 the English crown revoked the charter and took direct control of the archipelago, making Bermuda the first crown colony.

English planters imported African slaves to work the agricultural plantations that flourished on the islands. The Africans eventually became the most numerous group in the islands. The two groups remained separate, with little formal mixing, although a large number of mixed-race people appeared over the centuries.

Bermuda became the base of the Royal Navy's Atlantic fleet in 1767 and an important port on the trans-Atlantic trade routes. The prosperous colony, with its equitable climate, attracted settlers from the United Kingdom, and, unlike most of Britain's Caribbean colonies, it developed a sizable European population. During the Revolutionary War on the American mainland, many refugees, called United Empire Loyalists, left the rebelling colonies with their slaves and migrated to the islands.

The abolition of slavery in the British Empire in 1833 temporarily crippled the Bermudian economy, although events on the American mainland led to a rapid recovery several decades later. Madeirans* and Azoreans* were later imported as laborers, many staying to mix with the local population.

In 1861, during the American Civil War, Bermuda became an important trans-shipment port for Confederate blockade runners in the booming trade between the United Kingdom and the Confederacy. A number of Confederate blockade runners were based in the islands. Many Bermudians made fortunes in the trade until American warships tightened the blockade of the South and effectively curtailed the trade. At the end of the war some former Confederates, particularly Virginians, migrated to the islands.

The islands were used by the British government as a penal colony until 1862, with freed prisoners often settling in the islands. Bermuda became known for the number of wrecked ships lured onto the rocky shores by "wreckers," who then looted the valuable cargoes.

In the late 1800s Bermuda became a fashionable tourist resort for wealthy Americans. Passenger steamship lines operated between the islands and several large American ports. In 1908 automobiles were prohibited in the islands; Woodrow Wilson, a frequent visitor, was among the signers of a petition to the Bermuda government asking that the newfangled machine not be allowed to mar the tranquility of the islands.

The Volstead Act, which introduced prohibition to the nearby United States in 1920, led to a boom in the islands, which became one of the major sources of illegal shipments of alcohol into the States. The prosperity of the period resulted in a light rail system, which opened in 1931, and numerous bridges connecting the islands.

Under the terms of a lease signed in 1941, during World War II, the U.S. government was granted naval and air bases, which eventually covered 11% of the islands' territory. The Americans built an airfield and proper roads, which enabled tourism to expand rapidly after 1945. Thousands of young Bermudians served in the British military during the war, but a sense of identity also began to take hold as they increasingly saw themselves as distinct from the inhabitants of faraway Britain and the other territories of the empire.

Tourism increased dramatically in the postwar era, and in 1946 automobiles were allowed, although restricted as to size and power. The construction of many hotels and holiday homes ensured the prosperity of the islands in the 1950s. The short pants popular in the islands came to be called "Bermuda shorts" by the increasing number of tourists.

In the early 1960s there was a degree of sentiment for independence during the period of anticolonialism and the granting of sovereignty to British territories around the globe. The British government granted a new constitution in 1968 making the Bermudians self-governing, except for foreign affairs, defense, and internal security, and providing for the election of Bermuda's first prime minister. The Bermudian House of Assembly is

the oldest parliamentary body among the British and ex-British possessions.

The white minority who controlled the island government and economy
began to lose some of their privileges during the turbulent 1970s. The
black Bermudians, who normally held menial jobs in the tourist industry,
became increasingly discontent with the existing situation. Violence flared
on several occasions, most notably on 10 March 1973, when members of
a black pro-independence organization assassinated the British governor,
Sir Richard Sharples, and an aide. The execution of the assassins on 2
December 1977 resulted in a week of rioting. A state of emergency was
declared, and British troops were rushed to the islands to quell the rioting,
which left much of central Hamilton in ruins. The important tourist industry fell off for several years.

A royal commission meeting in London in 1978 recommended independence for Bermuda. The black majority, supporters of the Progressive
Labor Party (PLP), favored independence, but the powerful white minority
of the United Bermuda Party (UBP), who controlled the government, opposed the move as premature. In 1980 the UBP won elections and formed
a new government, again dominated by the white minority. The dissatisfied blacks called a four-week strike, which severely crippled the tourist
trade as thousands of visitors left the islands or canceled plans to visit.
Minority white control continued despite calls by the PLP for immediate
independence, inside or outside the British Commonwealth.

In 1989 the UBP, in power since 1968, received a much-reduced majority. The prosperous whites had been unwilling to share power with the
blacks and had imported professionals to manage the financial and tourist
industries. These temporary British residents were allowed to vote, which
helped to keep the minority white government in power.

The opposition PLP won elections in 1982 under Sir John Swan, the
first black Bermudian to hold the office of prime minister. His government
initially opposed immediate independence, although the PLP had long
advocated black majority rule and separation from the United Kingdom;
financial and administrative concerns curtailed support for separation in
the 1980s.

The islands have the highest per capita income of any island group in
the Caribbean or the western Atlantic. Lack of land and overpopulation
remain the major problems facing the Bermudians. In the 1980s the islands
became a major offshore banking center, and Bermuda remains the base
of the Atlantic and West Indies squadron of the Royal Navy. The wealthy
islands continued to prosper in the 1990s; local concerns involved not so
much money, as in other islands, but first-world problems such as crime,
drugs, housing, and prettiness. The islanders pay for any services that are
provided by the United Kingdom government.

On 15 August 1995, the Bermudians were asked to vote on the issue of independence. The opposition PLP, in the past pro-independence, called for a boycott, claiming that constitutional reform and a general election had to come first. Most Bermudians voted, but they voted 74% against independence, preferring to remain British. Sir John Swan, a convert to the pro-independence camp who had called the referendum, promptly resigned when the motion was resoundingly defeated. The PLP boycott dissuaded many from voting, and just 58% of registered voters took part in the referendum. The voters, mostly supporters of the ruling United Bermuda Party, divided along racial lines, with most whites rejecting independence and its uncertainties. Opinion polls showed that a majority of both whites and blacks were against premature independence, which could harm the lucrative tourist and financial industries.

In 1998 the PLP took 54% of the vote, with the UBP taking just 44%, but independence was left off the political agenda. The next elections, set for 2003, possibly will again address the question of Bermudian independence. The idea of full sovereignty remains potent for many Bermudians; yet, as they enjoy one of the highest per capita incomes in the world, they are reluctant to choose the unknown. The United Kingdom offers the islanders few advantages, and rich Bermuda pays for the services it provides, but tradition and uncertainty are against independence in the immediate future.

SELECTED BIBLIOGRAPHY:

Ahiakpor, James C. W. *Economic Consequences of Political Independence*. 1989.
Blagg, Daniel G. *Bermuda Atlas and Gazetteer*. 1992.
Boultbee, Paul G., and David F. Raine. *Bermuda*. 1998.
LaBrucherie, Roger A. *Bermuda: A World Apart*. 1996.

Bodos

Boros; Bodis; Baras; Mechis; Garos; Achiks

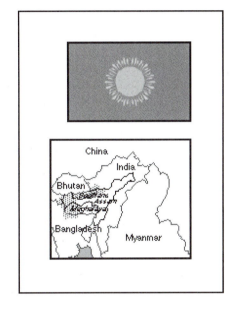

POPULATION: Approximately (2002e) 3,250,000 Bodos in northeastern India and northern Bangladesh, concentrated in the northwestern districts of Assam, north of the Brahmaputra River. The Garos and Rabna live south of the river in the mountainous region of western Meghalaya. Smaller communities live in adjacent areas of West Bengal and in Bangladesh. Bodo nationalists claim a national population of over six million in the region.

THE BODO HOMELAND: The Bodo homeland lies in northeastern India, concentrated in the northern areas of the Brahmaputra River valley, in the Kokrajhar, Nalbari, Bongaigaon, Darrang, Goalpara, Udalguri, and Sontipur districts of Assam, and in the Garo Hills district of Meghalaya. The region is mostly hilly, with teak forests and tea plantations north of the lowland plains of the Brahmaputra River valley. Part of the Bodo homeland was erected as an autonomous district, the Bodoland Autonomous Council (BAC), in 1993. *Bodoland Autonomous Council*: 3,220 sq. mi.—8,341 sq. km, (2002e) 2,400,000—Bodos 38%, Bengalis 35%, Assamese* 20%, Santhals* 7%. The Bodo capital and major cultural center is Dhubri, in western Bodoland, (2002e) 83,000. The other important cultural centers are Tezpur, (2002e) 69,000, and Barpeta, (2002e) 31,000. The major cultural center of the Garos is Tura, (2002e) 57,000.

FLAG: The Bodo national flag, the flag of the national movement, is a pale blue field bearing a centered yellow sun.

PEOPLE AND CULTURE: The Bodo-Garo tribes are a tribal people of early Mongolian extraction. They are fervently proud of their heritage and culture, and they feel that their language and culture are threatened by Assamese domination and Bengali migration. Most Bodos are settled farmers, although they formerly practiced slash-and-burn cultivation. The Bodo peoples are not culturally uniform and comprise a number of tribal groups, including the Cutiya, Plains Kachari, Garo, Rabnas,* Mech, Koch,

Dhimal, and Jaijona in the west; and the Dimasa or Hill Kachari, Galong, Hojai, Lalung, Tippera, and Moran in the east. The tribal groups are further divided into clans. Some tribes, such as the Garo and Rabna, are matrilineal, while others are patrilineal. Several tribes have been so influenced by Hindu social and religious concepts that at present they regard themselves as Hindu castes rather than as part of the Bodo nation. Their claim is not generally accepted, and many of the Hindu Bodos rank very low in the caste hierarchy.

LANGUAGE AND RELIGION: The Bodo language belongs the Baric (Bodo-Garo) branch of the Tibeto-Burman language group. The three major languages of the group of related dialects are Bodo, Garo, and Dimasa, spoken by about 75,000 in the highlands. The Bodo language was formerly written in the Assamese script, but nationalists increasingly demand the use of the Devanagair or Roman scripts, as part of their movement against assimilation. The language is spoken in two major dialects, Chote and Mech. The closely related Garo and Rabna, numbering about 900,000, speak the southern dialects in the Garo Hills of Meghalaya and the Mymensingh Plains. Garo has two major dialects, Achik in India and Abeng in Bangladesh.

The majority of the Bodos are Christian or Hindu, but a minority retain traditional beliefs, which include an extensive pantheon of village and household gods. Such institutions as community bachelor houses and many features of their religion link the Bodos to the Nagas* and other hill tribes of northeastern India, but Hindu and Christian influence has greatly modified existing beliefs, particularly among the Garos. Officially only 6% of the Bodos are Christians, but missionary activity since the mid-nineteenth century greatly influenced the religious beliefs and education in the region. The growing influence of Hindu ideas and customs results in a tendency toward assimilation into the rigid caste system of the Assam lowlands.

NATIONAL HISTORY: The Bodo-Garo tribes are thought to have settled the valley of the Brahmaputra River from the Tibetan Plateau over eight centuries ago. They settled the highlands north and south of the Aryan-dominated plains, dividing the region into tribally controlled regions. Much of the jungle-clad tribal area later came under the nominal rule of Hindu states in the lowlands, states that were influenced by the civilizations that flourished along the Ganges River.

Isolated from the mainstream of Indian civilization, the area lay outside most of the great states that arose on the subcontinent. In the early Christian era, the Hindus of the valley formed a state tributary to the Gupta Empire of northern India but were unable to bring the tribal regions under their rule.

In 1229 the region was overrun by invading Ahoms, a Thai people from present northern Burma-China border region. The Ahoms erected an independent kingdom and mixed with the conquered Aryans to form the

Assamese people, but like the former kingdoms they were unable to extend their rule effectively much beyond the Brahmaputra River valley. The Bodos withdrew to their jungle strongholds and maintained their control of much of present Assam.

The valley, after much fighting, finally fell to the Muslim Moguls in 1661–62, but their hold was tenuous, and they were quickly expelled by the Assamese. However, repeated invasions by the Burmans from the east had a more lasting impact on the Bodos. The Assamese requested aid from the British in Bengal against the Burmans in the early 1700s. In 1792 the Bodos rebelled against Assamese rule, and the Assamese again requested British help to put down the rebellion, setting a pattern for later confrontations.

The Burmans again invaded the region in 1822, one of the reasons for the first Anglo-Burmese War in 1824–26. The Burmans were forced to cede all of Assam, including the Bodo tribal areas, to British rule in 1826, when Assam became a British protectorate. The Bodo tribes were dominant in Assam until about 1825, when they too came under British domination. Other Bodo tribal areas were annexed in 1832–35. The Bodo territories, administered by British commissioners, formed part of British Bengal until 1874, when they were included in the new Assam province. Many Bodos were converted to Christianity by British and American missionaries in the nineteenth century.

Several Bodo leaders, educated by Christian missionaries, asked the British authorities for help in preserving their language and culture and for other small concessions in 1929. The date is considered to mark the birth of the modern Bodo national movement. In 1937 the Bodos first suggested the separation of their homeland from the province of Assam. During World War II, when Assam was the object of a Japanese thrust into India, the Bodos were at first courted as Japanese allies, but most joined the British forces fighting the Japanese. Since Indian independence in 1947, the Bodos have demanded greater autonomy.

The Nagas in northeastern Assam led a successful campaign to separate their homeland from Assam in 1961, followed by the Mizos* and Meghalayans, including the Garos, in 1972. The secession of the other hill tribes from Assam galvanized the nascent Bodo national movement in the 1970s. The major cause of the growth of nationalism among the Bodos is the fact that they are being outnumbered in their homeland by Bengali-speaking Hindu and Muslim immigrants and Santal tribal people, who settled in Assam from other parts of India. Encouraged by the Assamese self-assertion campaign of the 1980s, the Bodos launched a movement for greater autonomy and the expulsion of migrants from their homeland. Later other groups demanded separation and the creation of a separate Bodoland state.

The Bodos were once the sole inhabitants of upper Assam, the region north of the Brahmaputra, but immigration over the past century has reduced them to a minority in their homeland. Spokesmen for the Bodo national movement mobilized the Bodos to regain control of their affairs and territory, and they mustered enough weaponry to ensure that they could not be ignored. Bodo leaders assert that it is not possible for the Bodos to maintain their distinct ethnic identity and economic development if their homeland remains part of Assam. Militants demanded the expulsion of the Bengali Muslims and the Santhal tribal peoples who have settled in traditional Bodo territory.

In 1980 Bodo activists began to agitate for a separate Bodoland state within India. Less than a decade after a violent struggle for Assamese rights, the Bodos of northwestern Assam began to demand the same, threatening Assam's lucrative tea industry. The Bodo nationalists, led by the All-Bodo Students Union (ABSU), accused the Assamese government of insensitivity, like that of the federal government to Assamese demands, whereas the Assamese ultimately negotiated their way to state power. The campaign for autonomy turned violent in 1987, when Bodo guerrillas kidnapped tea plantation managers and held them for ransom.

In February 1989, the Bodos, to enforce their demands, called a five-day general strike that paralyzed the region. Many people were killed, and attacks on police, bombings, arson, and looting spread across the area. In August 1989 over 60,000 Bodos fled into neighboring Arunchal Pradesh to escape government reprisals. Since 1989 militants of the Bodoland Army and other factions have been fighting for the complete independence of Bodoland from India.

In 1993, the Assam state government agreed to give the Bodos an autonomous development council, the Bodoland Autonomous Council (BAC), which was to fulfill their aspirations for self-government. Although the deal did not cover all the areas claimed by activists, it seemed for a time that it might restore peace in the region. Rather than to accede directly to the demands of Bodo militants, the government created a 40-member Bodoland Executive Council (BEC).

The Bodo leaders who signed the accord later renounced it, claiming that the council was ineffective and excluded large tracts of Bodo territory. Violent clashes started between different Bodo groups, particularly between pro-state and pro-independence organizations. Meanwhile, the non-Bodos of the region, mostly Bengalis and Santhals, refused to accept Bodo authority in the autonomous region, with more violent clashes breaking out between the various ethnic groups. In 1994 the Bodos announced an ultimatum for the demarcation of the BAC boundaries. In 1994 militants of the Bodo Security Force (BSF) became allies of the Assamese separatist United Liberation Front of Assam (ULFA) to fight the government forces aligned against both groups.

In 1995 several Bodo groups agreed to talks on enlarging the BAC and modeling it on the more successful Darjeeling Gorkha Hill Council of the Gorkhas* in West Bengal. The Assamese government, preoccupied with the Assamese separatists led by the ULFA, refused concessions and rejected Bodo territorial claims. Most of the Bodo organizations ceased negotiations and revived their demands for a completely separate state within India or full independence. The Assamese government, controlled by former Assamese nationalists, is fiercely opposed to yet another division of the state; since Indian independence, parts of Assam have been hived off to create the separate states of Nagaland, Meghalaya, and Mizoram.

Militants in December 1996 formally requested that the Indian government present a plan to parliament for the creation of a separate Bodoland state. The government refused, and the Bodos launched a wave of bombings and kidnappings. In 1997, on the fiftieth anniversary of India's independence, the Bodo nationalists stepped up their campaign of violence, attacking trains, bridges, a telephone exchange, and other targets. Among the other demands of Bodo militants is that Bodo be declared as the official language of the Bodo areas and that it be recognized as one of India's national languages. The Bodos resorted to violence because they believed that violence was the only way for oppressed minorities to attract the attention of the distant central government of India.

Over 700 people have been killed in Bodo-related violence since 1986. In early 2000 over 200,000 Bodos and Santhals were living in relief camps, refugees from the escalating violence. Since 1996 the Bodo separatist campaign has become more violent as Bodo factions compete to demonstrate their strength. The divisions among the national movement are considered major impediments to a concerted campaign for a separate Bodoland.

In March 1999, the Assamese chief minister announced the finalization of the BAC boundaries to include 2,941 villages, fewer than the 3,031 villages demanded by the Bodos. The Bodos felt cheated by the autonomous area and its inefficient functioning and believed that the Assam state government was playing politics with their aspirations. The autonomy offer, rejected by a majority of the Bodo factions, was countered by growing demands for a 50–50 division of Assam.

The Indian prime minister, Atal Behari Vajpayee, during a visit to the northeastern states in January 2000, agreed to look into the issue of the division of Meghalaya into separate states for the Khasis* and Garos but refused to comment on Garo demands for separate statehood or amalgamation with the Bodos north of the Garo Hills.

The Bodo national movement remains factionalized, with one group, led by the Bodo Liberation Tigers Front (BLTF), fighting for a separate Bodo state within the Indian union to be created in about 50% of the territory of the state of Assam. The other group, the most important element being the National Democratic Front of Bodoland (NDFB), works for the creation of an independent Bodo state encompassing all the Bodo-related territories in India. In 2001 the Bodo leaders claimed that the Indian government has yet to implement the promises made by the agreement signed in 1993 that created a Bodoland Autonomous Council, which has driven many moderates to join in calling for a new state north of the Brahmaputra, including the Bodo language in the Indian constitution as an official language, creating district councils in Nilachal and Lalung on the south banks of the Brahmaputra, which have a sizable Bodo population, and giving the status of Scheduled Tribe to the Bodos living in the hills. The moderate Bodo nationalist faction has been encouraged by the Indian government's creation of new states such as Uttaranchal and Chattisgarh in 2000.

SELECTED BIBLIOGRAPHY:

Aluckal, Jacob, and Thomas Pulloppillil. *The Bodos: Children of Bhullumbutter.* 1997.

Bhattacharjee, Chandana. *Ethnicity and Autonomy Movement: Case of the Bodo-Kacharis of Assam.* 1996.

Datta, P. S. *Ethnic Movements in Poly-Cultural Assam.* 1990.

Mittal, A. C., and J. B. Sharma. *Tribal Movement, Politics, and Religion in India.* 1998.

Bougainvillians

North Solomon Islanders; Meekamuii

POPULATION: Approximately (2002e) 200,000 Bougainvillians in the Solomon Islands, most living in the North Solomons province of Papua New Guinea, but with over 30,000 in the neighboring Solomon Islands Republic.

THE BOUGAINVILLIAN HOMELAND: The Bougainvillian homeland lies in the southwestern Pacific Ocean, just north of Australia at the western tip of the Solomon Islands archipelago. Bougainville, 75 miles long and 40–60 miles wide, is the largest island of the archipelago. The province is just 4.5 miles (seven kilometers) from its nearest Solomon Islands neighbor but lies 310 miles (500 km) from the New Guinea, the center of Papua New Guinea. Bougainville forms the North Solomons province of the Republic of Papua New Guinea (PNG), which comprises the large islands of Bougainville and Buka and a number of small islands, including Kilinailau, Tauu, Nukumanu, Nuguria, and Nissan groups. *Province of Bougainville (North Solomons/Mekamui)*: 4,310 sq. mi.—11,165 sq. km, (2002e) 203,000—Bougainvillians (Melanesians) 93%, Polynesians 5%. The Bougainvillian capital and major cultural center is Arawa, (2002e) 19,000 (urban area, including the towns of Panguna, Kieta, and Toniva, 42,000).

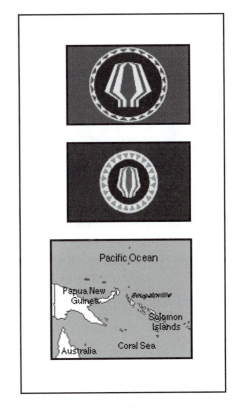

FLAG: The Bougainvillian national flag, the flag of the national movement, is a medium-blue field charged with a large centered black disc bearing a white and brown *upe*, the ceremonial headdress of the islands, within a green and white design representing *kapkap*, an abalone shell necklace. A variation of the flag, with the centered image compressed, is the official flag of the province of Bougainville in the Republic of Papua New Guinea.

PEOPLE AND CULTURE: The Bougainvillians are a Melanesian people, with some Polynesian admixture, geographically and culturally related to the Solomon Islanders just to the southwest but not ethnically nor culturally related to the Papuan peoples, the dominant group in Papua New Guinea. The Bougainvillian culture is a Melanesian culture with Polynesian borrowings, and it is known for colorful and elaborate ceremonies. The Bougainvillians have a village-based society, sustained mainly by food gardens and fishing. Much of the land is owned by women, and inheritance is through the female line. The islanders revere the land as a living spirit and see environmental damage as an attack on their beliefs.

LANGUAGE AND RELIGION: The Bougainvillians speak several Melanesian dialects. Along with a lingua franca used throughout the southwest Pacific, Pidgin—a patois of English, Melanesian, and Polynesian influences. The official language of Papua New Guinea is English, which is widely spoken in the region.

The majority of the islanders are Roman Catholic, with a large Protestant minority and smaller groups adhering to traditional religious beliefs, mostly in the less accessible areas. The Christian Bougainvillians have retained many of their pre-Christian traditions and beliefs, often mixed with the later Catholic and Protestant customs.

NATIONAL HISTORY: The islands, populated by Melanesians and some Polynesians in the coastal areas, were first sighted by Portuguese navigator Alvaro de Mendaña in 1567. The islands were later explored by Mendaña and others but the Europeans made no attempt to colonize the islands, and no Europeans visited for nearly two centuries. The next Europeans to visit the islands were those in a French expedition under Louis-Antoine de Bougainville in 1768. The leader of the expedition left his family name as the name of the largest island.

Fierce Melanesian resistance precluded colonization, and only a few traders and missionaries settled in the islands after 1845. Christian missionaries set up centers on Bougainville and Buka in the mid-nineteenth century. Church-sponsored education gave the islanders a head start in the region. At the turn of the twentieth century, the Bougainvillians were better educated and more prosperous than the other peoples included in what was by then a German colony.

Not fully explored until they came under the control of a German trading company in 1882, the islands became the object of a territorial dispute between Germany and Britain. In 1886 the European powers casually divided the Solomon Islands, with the northern islands of the Solomon group confirmed as a German possession. Bougainville's harbors and interior mines made it one of Germany's most valuable colonies. In 1898 Bougainville and Buka became part of the colony of German New Guinea.

The Germans attempted to fortify the islands when war began in Europe in 1914; their efforts were overtaken by an invasion of Australian and New Zealander troops. Australian civil administration of the islands was formalized at the end of the war under a 1920 League of Nations mandate. The Australians joined the North Solomons to the territory of New Guinea.

Occupied by the Japanese military forces from 1942 to 1944, the islands returned to Australian administration as part of a trust territory of the new United Nations at the end of World War II. The early missionary activity, and Australian development schemes in the 1960s and 1970s, made the North Solomons the most developed district of the New Guinea Trust Territory. An educated leadership formed a national movement in the 1960s. In 1968 the nationalists proposed a referendum on the choices available to the islands—independence, autonomy, or union with the neighboring British Solomon Islands.

In 1967 the Bougainville Copper Agreement was signed, giving an international consortium, headed by Australian mining giant Cozinc Rio Tinto, Ltd., and including Bank of America, over 50% ownership of the Panguna mine and most of the profits as well. The establishment of the mine in 1969 left 800 Bougainvillians landless and 1,400 without fishing rights. The land was seized by the mining company, and no law at the time compelled environmental-impact studies. Forests were poisoned, felled, and burned, then bulldozed directly into the major river, along with tons of rich organic topsoil. An Australian mining consortium began to exploit Bougainville's huge copper deposits in 1972. The company earned amazing profits from Panguna mine. The mining agreement was renegotiated in November 1974.

The Bougainvillians strenuously opposed the mining operations, which they claimed abused the spirit of the land. Following several clashes, the mining company hired an anthropologist to coordinate the mining operations with the islander's beliefs and traditions. The enormous profits from the mines, part going to the territorial government at Port Moresby, opened a dispute over the disposition of the funds. The Bougainvillians demanded a greater share of the profits for local development and for use in rehabilitating the lands desecrated by the mining operations.

The dispute over the Panguna mine was paralleled by rising ethnic tension between the Melanesians and Papuan workers brought in from New Guinea. Violence between the two groups increased as Papua New Guinea moved toward independence. On 1 September 1975, two weeks before Papua New Guinea's scheduled independence, Leo Hannet, the premier of the North Solomons, declared the islands independent as the Republic of the North Solomons. One of the first acts of the new government of Papua New Guinea, independent on 16 September, was to suspend the provincial government of the North Solomons and dispatch troops to occupy the islands.

Pro-independence violence again broke out in 1976, pushing the government to negotiate an autonomy agreement with island leaders, including the right to veto unwanted development. Secessionist sentiment declined with the restoration of provincial government. The island's copper mine developed as Papua New Guinea's major source of foreign currency and contributed over 40% of PNG's export earnings.

The rapid expansion of the mine, in the early 1980s, renewed ethnic tension between the islanders and the growing Papuan labor force. The Melanesians, holding all life sacred, were appalled by the almost daily Papuan murders. Ethnic tolerance turned to ethnic antagonism and racial slurs. The Bougainvillians call the Papuans *Skin i Red*, Redskins, while the Papuans refer to the islanders as *Bilong Suspen*, pidgin for "as black as the remains in the bottom of a saucepan."

Growing objections to the open-pit copper mine as an offense to the Bougainvillians' traditional reverence for the land, focused on the issue of damage to the island and the belief that when the copper is exhausted they will be left with just a huge hole, a ruined landscape, and extremely polluted rivers. In 1988 island leaders demanded $12 billion to repair the damage done by the mine, one of the world's largest man-made holes, some 2,000 yards (1.8 km) across. The copper mine, which was one of the PNG government's richest source of overseas revenue, functioned at the cost of destroyed villages, deforestation, and erosion. The mine employed few Bougainvillians, and little attempt was made to improve the island's infrastructure.

During the 20-plus years of the mine's operation, various forms of peaceful protest failed, including an attempt by local women to stop the bulldozers by lying in front of them. Ignored by the Papuan government, the Bougainvillians finally rebelled. The rebels, led by Francis Ona, raided the mine's armory and destroyed installations and finally forced the mine to close in 1989. A state of emergency was declared in December 1988. Threatened by government troops, the rebel leaders of the Bougainville Revolutionary Army (BRA) and its political wing, the Bougainville Interim Government (BIG), declared Bougainville independent of Papua New Guinea on 17 May 1990. The PNG government began an economic blockade of the islands but withdrew its soldiers after several bloody clashes. Government soldiers invaded and occupied Buka, the smaller island at Bougainville's northern tip. Much of Australia's $300 million in annual aid to Papua New Guinea was used to equip and train soldiers to fight in Bougainville to stop the secession of the islands and to reopen the lucrative Panguna mine.

In 1992 the government again sent soldiers to end the secession, but the invasion failed and degenerated into sporadic fighting. In March 1993 the island's nationalist leaders appealed to the United Nations for the dispatch of a peacekeeping force. Negotiations, the first in three years, began in August 1993 but soon collapsed over the issues of the mine and the Bougainvillians insistence on retaining their independence. Up to 70,000 Bougainvillians have been uprooted and resettled in "care centers" set up by the PNG government. During 1994 Australian human rights activists ran the blockade to bring in medicines and to bring out news of the conflict, about which little is known.

A new Australian government in 1996 recognized that the war on Bougainville could not be won, but the government of Papua New Guinea, under Julius Chan, declared an end to an eighteen-month cease-fire, and heavy fighting resumed. The new offensive, in central and southern Bougainville, was defeated by the rebels. The Chan government began hiring mercenaries through a British firm, Sandline International, bringing protests from human rights groups and the governments of Australia, New Zealand, and the United Kingdom.

The PNG government in April 1995 agreed to the creation of the Bougainville Interim Government, led by nationalist leaders Theodore Miriung and Martin Mirior, on government-held Buka. In October 1996, Miriung, a leading Bougainvillian voice for peace, was assassinated by identified PNG soldiers. In 1997 Miriori appealed to the international community to pressure the PNG government to abandon its use of foreign mercenaries to fight in Bougainville and for their replacement by international peacekeepers under a UN mandate. The conflict and the Australian-backed air and sea blockade had already cost the lives of over 20,000 people, many having died due to the lack of medical supplies and facilities. The war was already the longest and bloodiest in the Pacific since World War II.

The government of the neighboring Solomon Islands, although sympathetic to the aspirations of the Bougainvillians, has allowed few of the rebels and refugees sanctuary within its borders. Perhaps fearful of the larger and more powerful PNG, the Solomons have refused to provide overt support or to be drawn into the conflict.

An unofficial cease-fire has been in place since 1997, partly due to political unrest in New Guinea and partly due to efforts by the governments of Australia and New Zealand to broker a settlement. In January 1998, the rebel forces signed a declaration of peace, the Lincoln Agreement, and 250 unarmed monitors from Australia, New Zealand, Fiji, and Vanuatu were dispatched to ensure that the agreement was honored. The agreement provided for the election of a reconciliation government, which is to be autonomous until talks on the political future of the province begin, once peace is established. Peacekeeping troops from several Pacific states, including Australia and New Zealand, were sent to the islands to oversee the cease-fire.

Spokesmen for the Bougainville Copper, Ltd., discount the prospect of an early opening of the Panguna copper mine. Panguna was the trigger for the 1988 rebellion on the islands. Bougainvillian leaders oppose the opening of the mine until environmental issues and more equitable financial arrangements are addressed.

The Bougainvillians consider that they have now entered into a process of self-determination that will lead to eventual independence; however, delays and degrees of cooperation with PNG seriously divide the national movement. Elections, set for the end of 1998, have been repeatedly postponed. In May 1999, Joseph Kabui was elected president of the newly established Bougainville People's Congress, a peace forum organized by local leaders to aid the peace process. In January 2000, Bougainvillian leaders warned that further delay of the negotiations could jeopardize the region's fragile peace. Nationalists refused to discuss arms disposal until there was a government guarantee of a referendum on independence for the islands. The nationalists have agreed to greater autonomy in the interim, but they do not see autonomy within PNG as a lasting solution.

PNG agreed to a referendum on independence in March 2000. The agreement, the Loloate Understanding, would first establish a Bougainville Provincial Government, which would be allowed time to function and to be evaluated by the islanders. Later, an elected but autonomous provincial government with wider powers would be elected. The process is expected to take years, but it is viewed as a major step toward lasting peace.

In January 2001, the president of the Bougainville People's Congress, Joseph Kabui, and the governor of Bougainville, John Momis, announced a major breakthrough in the peace negotiations. At this occasion, the PNG government and Bougainville reached an agreement to give Bougainville a referendum on independence as part of peace negotiations seeking to end the civil war. The peace deal consists of a time schedule for a referendum that should be held between 10 and 15 years from the election of the first autonomous government of Bougainville. In April the Bougainvillian leaders participated in a new round of autonomy talks with the PNG government, leading to agreements that could be presented for approval to the PNG parliament. Several nationalist leaders threatened that if the referendum agreement was not approved, they would consider yet another unilateral declaration of independence or return to armed defense of their homeland.

SELECTED BIBLIOGRAPHY:

Brooks, Peter. *World Elsewhere.* 1999.
Larmour, Peter. *Legitimacy, Sovereignty, and Regime Change in the South Pacific: Comparisons between the Fiji Coups and the Bougainville Rebellion.* 1994.
Oliver, Douglas L. *Black Islanders: A Personal Perspective of Bougainville, 1937–1991.* 1991.
Rentz, John N. *Bougainville and the Northern Solomons.* 1988.

Bretons

Bretonants; Brezhoneg

POPULATION: Approximately (2002e) 2,825,000 Bretons in Europe, most in the historical Brittany region in western France. Breton communities also live in Paris and other regions of France. Outside Europe there are sizable Breton communities in Canada and the United States.

THE BRETON HOMELAND: The Breton homeland occupies a large peninsula in the Atlantic Ocean, between the English Channel on the north and the Bay of Biscay on the south. Brittany is traditionally divided into two distinct areas—Amor, the coastal regions, and Argoat, the hinterland. The coast of Brittany, particularly at the western tip, is irregular and rocky, with a number of natural harbors and numerous islands. The peninsula is the most southerly of three that traditionally have been held by Celts. To the north, across the narrow English Channel, are the peninsulas inhabited by the related Cornish* and Welsh* nations. Historical Brittany now comprises the French region of Brittany and the department of Loire-Atlantique, which forms part of the neighboring region of Pays de la Loire. One of the rallying points of Breton nationalism is the unification of their homeland in a single administrative unit. *Historical Region of Brittany (Breizh)*: 13,643 sq. mi.—35,344 sq. km, (2002e) 3,647,000—Bretons 72%, other French 28%. The Breton capital and major cultural center is Rennes, called Roazhon in Breton, (2002e) 210,000. The other major cultural center is Nantes, called Naoned by the Bretons, the capital of Loire-Atlantic Department, (2002e) 274,000, metropolitan area, 554,000.

FLAG: The Breton national flag has nine horizontal stripes of black and white charged with a white canton on the upper hoist bearing 11 black

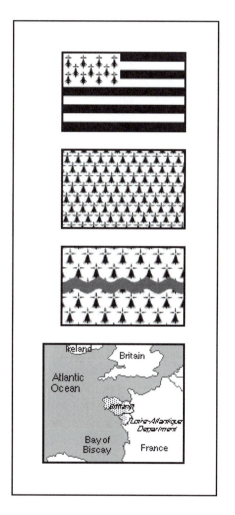

ermines. The historical flag of the Bretons, still used by some nationalist organizations, is a white field bearing over seventy black ermines. The flag of the disputed Loire-Atlantique department, also known as Eastern Brittany, is a white field with black ermines bearing a wavy pale-blue horizontal line across the center.

PEOPLE AND CULTURE: The Bretons are a Celtic people, the only Celtic-speaking nation in continental Europe. Closely related to the Celtic peoples of the British Isles, the Bretons are the descendants of fifth-century migrants from southwestern Britain. In their new homeland, the Bretons developed an extraordinary wealth of folklore and music. Throughout their history the Bretons have remained a conservative, religious nation, adamantly protecting their independent spirit and culture. The Breton nation is described as being as dreamy and passionate as the Irish, as whimsical as the Welsh, yet as tough and hard working as the Scots.* The last Celtic festival of the century was held in August 1999 in Lorient. With an attendance of over 400,000, the festival was one of Europe's largest.

LANGUAGE AND RELIGION: The Breton language belongs to the Brythonic branch of the Celtic group of Indo-European languages. Breton, spoken in western Brittany by about 700,000 on a daily basis, is also spoken in scattered regions in eastern Brittany. An estimated 1.5 million have some knowledge of Breton. The language, called Brezhoneg, is spoken in four distinct dialects—Leonais, Tregorrois, Vannetais, and Cornouaillais. Increasingly young Bretons are learning the language in schools, and speaking the language in daily life has become a matter of national pride. The French language is now the first language of the region, although Breton, predominant in the western departments, is rapidly being reestablished as Brittany's national language. The Breton language, like the other non-French national languages spoken in France, has no legal existence, and there is a strong movement demanding official recognition. In 1886, about two million people spoke Breton, but by 2000 only about 25% of the Breton population could read and write Breton. There is limited radio and television in the language.

The Bretons are overwhelmingly Roman Catholic, with a small but important Protestant minority, but they tend to be less religious than the French population in the region. In recent decades religious practice has declined as the Bretons have urbanized.

NATIONAL HISTORY: The Celtic peoples of northwestern Europe, divided by tribal and clan loyalties, developed a remarkable civilization. The Celts, armed with iron weapons, spread across most of Europe; Western European folklore is derived mainly from the Celts. On the Brittany Peninsula they mixed with the earlier inhabitants, the builders of the great stone monuments called *menhirs* and *dolmens*.

Subjugated by the Romans in 56 B.C., the western Celts were forced to adapt to the Latin culture and language, but they were never more than superficially Romanized and retained their Celtic culture and language. The region, under Roman rule, became part of the province of Armorica, a Latinized form of the Celtic word for seaside.

The gradual decline of Roman power, leading to the abandonment of nearby Britannia and the withdrawal of the Roman garrisons in A.D. 410, left the island open to invasion. Angles, Saxons, and Jutes, Germanic peoples from northern Europe, overran the island, driving the Celts into the western peninsulas, Cornwall and Wales, and eventually across the narrow channel to Armorica. Celtic refugees arrived in such numbers in the fifth and sixth centuries that the peninsula became known as Little Britannia, Britannia Minor, and later Brittany. Over the next three centuries the Celts were converted to Christianity by missionaries from the British Isles.

From the sixth to the ninth centuries, the Bretons successfully defended their peninsula against the Germanic Franks, who conquered all of present France except Brittany. The region was first united in the ninth century under the rule of Nomeno, now a national hero, who revolted against the Carolingians. Later they repulsed incursions by the Normans,* who went on to conquer England in 1066.

At the end of the twelfth century, Geoffrey, count of Rennes, took the title of the duke of Brittany and established his capital at Rennes, which vied with Nantes as capital of the Bretons until the French Revolution. In 1196 the title passed to Arthur I, who was apparently murdered by the English, who attempted to take control of the duchy. The French king recognized the title in 1213, but the extinction of the ruling house led to war. France and England contested control of Brittany and the two kingdoms backed rival claimants to the ducal title during the War of the Breton Succession, which devastated the peninsula from 1341 to 1365. The dukes of the Montfort family, who finally gained the title, attempted to maintain their neutrality between the English and French during the remainder of the Hundred Years' War.

Brittany became part of the French kingdom when Anne, heiress of Brittany, married two successive kings of France. In 1532 the French kingdom took control of Brittany, ending Brittany's golden age and over five centuries of independence. The French language was made obligatory in official and juridical institutions in 1539. The French kingdom annexed the duchy outright in 1589. Brittany became a French province, one of the last territories incorporated into the French kingdom. The province of Brittany retained considerable autonomy, with its own *parlement* at Rennes, from 1590 to the French Revolution in 1789. After 1794, the French language was the only language allowed in public life and administration.

Early adherents of revolutionary activity, the conservative Bretons soon turned against the revolutionary excesses, antireligious doctrines, and the centralization of all political power in Paris. In 1793 the Vendée uprising spread to most of Brittany, where it became a popular uprising, spurred by Breton nationalism, the outlawing of religion, and the imposition of universal conscription. The uprising, called the War of the Vendée, continued sporadically until the rebels were decisively routed in 1796. One of the rebel leaders, General Cadonal, executed in 1804 on Napoleon's orders, is considered the first martyr of Breton nationalism. The rebels were severely punished, with many sent to the guillotine. When that method proved too slow, others were shot in mass executions, but that method was still too slow; barges were loaded with prisoners and sunk in the Loire with their screaming, praying cargos.

Having lost all administrative and cultural autonomy during the French Revolution and the Napoleonic reorganization of the French state, the Bretons mobilized to protect their culture and language. The first Breton dictionary, published in 1821, led to a proliferation of poetry, novels, and history written in the Breton language. In 1829 the first pro-autonomy organization formed, the Association Breton. Fired by the cultural revival and the nationalism of their Celtic cousins, the Irish, the Bretons began to espouse nationalism in the 1870s, starting a reversal of the assimilation pursued by successive French governments. In the 1880s, the French government made education in the French language compulsory, and all publications in Breton were banned.

The first avowedly separatist group, called Strollad Broadel Breiz, formed in 1911, advocating the severance of all ties to the alien French government and the creation of a sovereign Breton state. In spite of German overtures, however, when World War I began three years later, the Bretons remained loyal to France. Another Breton national hero is France Laurent, a young soldier executed during the war for not obeying an order given in French, a language he did not understand. After the war, at the Paris Peace Conference in 1919, the Bretons presented U.S. president Woodrow Wilson, who advocated self-determination for Europe's minority peoples, a petition signed by over 800 prominent Bretons calling for a sovereign Brittany. The petition was, under intense French government pressure, later abandoned.

Breton nationalism grew dramatically during the turmoil and economic depression of the 1930s. In 1931, nationalists formed Given Ha Du (Black and White), modeled on the Irish Sinn Fein and named for the national colors. The organization carried out several violent attacks, including the bombing in 1932 of the statue in Rennes commemorating Breton union with France. In 1936 several nationalist groups formed the Front Breton, but as tension increased in Europe the French government outlawed the organization as subversive.

The Germans, during the World War II occupation of France, attempted to capitalize on Breton national sentiment by placing the region under separate administration and allowing broad cultural and linguistic rights. In spite of the German concessions, Nazi doctrine held little attraction for the majority of the conservative, devoutly Catholic Bretons. The German concessions to Breton-language education, publishing, and broadcasting were immediately withdrawn by the returning French authorities at the end of the war. Some 800 Bretons were shot for supposedly collaborating with the Germans. In 1947, the French minister of education, Marcel Nagelen, decreed that "the task of teachers in the Breton speaking regions is identical with that of teachers in Algeria: Assimilate the population at any price." Children speaking Breton at school were punished.

The postwar suppression of the Breton language and culture provoked a Breton cultural revival in the 1950s, with a parallel growth of nationalism over the next decade. The revival of the language and culture, including the standardization of Breton grammar, led to a renewed interest among the population. Numerous cultural, nationalist, and separatist groups emerged, the most militant employing violence and terrorism to press their cause of Breton independence.

The decline of the French share of North Atlantic fish stocks, and rural depopulation, led to a decline of the Breton population of 11% between 1910 and 1946, but after World War II the population began to increase. In the 1970s, however, the Breton region continued to decline, not sharing in the postwar French boom. Many young Bretons were forced to leave the region to find work. Among the general population, young, urban French-speaking Bretons began to embrace the Breton language as the first language of the family. The Bretonization of French-speaking Bretons became fashionable. In the late 1970s, emigration from the region began to reverse as many young Bretons refused to leave their homeland. The 1976 census showed more Bretons returning than leaving for the first time in the twentieth century.

The growth of industry and service industries accounted for much of population increase as young Bretons were no longer obliged to leave their homeland for greater opportunities in Paris or elsewhere in France. Formerly a region of rural subsistence farming, Brittany emerged as a major industrial and food-exporting region in the 1970s as trade increased with Britain and Ireland following their inclusion in the European Community in 1973. By 1975 only 21% of the Bretons were engaged in agriculture.

The activities of a number of Breton separatist organizations increased during the 1970s and 1980s, including the bombing of historic Versailles Palace near Paris. Several of the organizations, socialist and Marxist oriented, received military training from the Irish Republican Army (IRA). The largest of the groups, the Breton Republican Army (BRA) and the Breton Liberation Front (BLF), often included government functionaries and Catholic priests in their ranks.

In 1981 2.5 million people claimed Breton nationality in France. The partial decentralization of the French government, beginning the same year, returned some powers to regional authorities, including some the Bretons had not exercised since the twelfth century. However, the creation of regions loosely based on the historical provinces gave rise to yet another Breton nationalist grievance. The department of Loire-Atlantique, historically an integral part of Brittany and having one of the Bretons' most important urban areas, Nantes, became part of a neighboring region. Although by the mid-1980s most of the Breton nationalists had renounced violence, there was an increase in agitation, demonstrations, and public pressure, with demands for the recognition of their language and the reunification of their historical homeland.

In 1987 the effort to rescue the Breton language from extinction accelerated. After several generations of Bretons were punished for speaking their native language, younger Bretons took up the struggle to save Breton as the spoken language of the Breton nation. The French government finally allowed bilingual road signs and commercial advertising.

The nonviolent Breton nationalists have wide support for their campaign to win greater autonomy for a reunited Brittany. Resurgent Breton nationalism, supported by a network of flourishing cultural language schools, cultural centers, and the Breton media, remains a potent force in the region. The Bretons, having won the struggle to save their nation from extinction, now focus on finding a place for Brittany within united Europe.

In 1992 the Council of Europe passed the European charter of regional and minority languages, but the French government has, as of 2002, refused to sign. Late in 1992 a constitutional change reaffirmed French as the only legal language of the republic. In 1994 the regional council of Brittany, in defiance of Paris, announced its support for the Breton language and came out openly in favor of the reunification of historical Brittany.

In the 1990s, as France remained a determinedly centralized state, many Bretons left to live in other Celtic regions of Europe, particularly in the British Islands. Inspired by the government-sponsored language and cultural programs they encountered in Wales, Scotland, and Ireland, they demanded the same for their homeland. More than 56 propositions to recognize minority languages in France have failed. Minority languages in France still have no legal existence.

The French government rejected the European Union (EU) directive on local languages in July 1999, therefore withholding official support for Breton-language education and media. The first all-Breton-language television was inaugurated on 1 September 2000, transmitting from L'Orient. The television station, a private venture, is not government sponsored nor are other cultural advances. The Breton-language station gives the language a place in the cultural life of the region, particularly to the young

Bretons who grew up with television, but the language issue remains the focus of the Breton national movement.

SELECTED BIBLIOGRAPHY:

Barbour, Phillipe. *Brittany.* 1998.
Brustein, William. *The Social Origins of Political Regionalism: France 1849–1981.* 1982.
Ford, Caroline. *Creating the Nation in Provincial France: Religion and Political Identity in Brittany.* 1993.
Gallioui, Patrick, and Michael Jones. *The Bretons.* 1991.

Bubis

Bobes; Boobes; Adijas; Ediyas; Eris; Fernando Poans; Fernandians

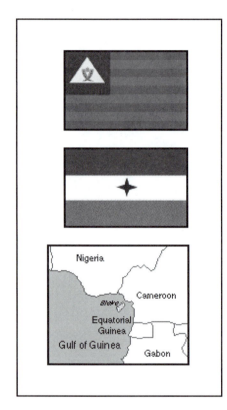

POPULATION: Approximately (2002e) 105,000 Bubis in West Africa, most living on the island of Bioko in the Gulf of Biafra, 40 miles (64 km) south of Nigeria on the African mainland and 100 miles (160 km) off continental Equatorial Guinea. Other Bubi populations, mostly exiles from political persecution, live in Nigeria and Benin on the mainland and in Spain. An estimated third of the total Bubi population live in exile.

THE BUBI HOMELAND: The Bubi homeland is the island of Bioko, lying off the coast of western Africa in the Gulf of Biafra region of the Atlantic Ocean. The island, just 45 miles (72 km) long and 22 miles (35 km) wide, is volcanic in origin and rises sharply to its highest point, Santa Isabel Peak, one of two volcanic mountains connected by a long fertile valley that accounts for most of the island's habitable area. Bioko, called Eri by the Bubis, forms two provinces, North and South Bioko, of the Republic of Equatorial Guinea. *Bioko (Eri)*: 779 sq. mi.—2,017 sq. km, (2002e) 124,000—Bubis 58%, Fangs 16%, Fernandinos 12%, Ibos* 7%. The Bubi capital and major cultural center is Malobo, (2002e) 53,000, the island's largest city and the official capital of the Republic of Equatorial Guinea.

FLAG: The Bubi national flag, the flag proposed for an independent Bubi state, has nine pale-green and red stripes bearing a blue canton on the upper hoist charged with a white triangle with the traditional tribal symbol in gold. The flag of the Bubi national movement is a vertical tricolor of pale blue, white, and green bearing a centered black four-pointed star.

PEOPLE AND CULTURE: The Bubi are a Bantu people thought to have developed as a separate people from small Bantu groups and refugees arriving on the island from the African mainland. The Bubi have retained their traditional culture, though they regained their numbers only in the twentieth century and were often under the control of stronger mainland tribes prior to colonial rule. A smaller group closely allied to the Bubis are the Fernandinos, descendants of freed slaves settled on the island in the nineteenth century. Most Bubis live by subsistence agriculture, but they often live in urban areas, particularly in the area around Malobo.

LANGUAGE AND RELIGION: The Bubi language is a Bube-Benga language of the Northwest Bantu languages of the Niger Congo language group. Laced with borrowings from Spanish, Portuguese, and Ibo, the language is spoken in three distinct dialects—North Bubi, Southwest Bubi, and Southeast Bubi. The related Fernandinos speak a dialect called Fernandino Krio, which has even more European admixtures, particularly English. Most educated Bubis also speak Spanish, the language of the former colonial power and now the official language of Equatorial Guinea. Pidgin English is also used in local commerce and is widely understood on Bioko.

The majority of the Bubis, after centuries of contact with Europeans, claim to be Roman Catholics, but most are only nominally Christians. Traditional beliefs, particularly belief in spirits, continues to permeate religious beliefs, particularly in times of crisis. In 1996 the government relaxed some restrictions on religious activities by foreign missionaries, and some Bubis have adopted evangelical Christianity. New restrictions on religious activities were instituted in 1997. Catholic priests of Bubi origin have suffered persecution in recent years. The government now requires Catholic priests to obtain government permission before celebrating mass.

NATIONAL HISTORY: Linguistic studies suggest the Bubi were among the first Bantu tribes to leave their Nigerian/Cameroon-area homeland, perhaps 5,000 years ago, and migrate southeast, settling on the coast of what is now southern Cameroon and northern Gabon. The faraway, green peaks of Bioko would have been visible to them on clear days, but any daring attempt to risk lives and travel across the fierce ocean would come only through great difficulty.

According to Bubi legend, some 3,000 years ago another tribe, more warring and more numerous, invaded the Bubi's coastal homeland, forcing them into hard labor and slavery. Those peaceful, mysterious peaks nearly 100 miles away began to hold the promise of peace and freedom. No African tribes were known as seafarers, but to escape the Bubis built large ocean-going canoes. According to legend, they sailed away under the cover of darkness over a period, each subtribe traveling together and settling a different part of the island.

The island, inhabited since prehistoric times, has received sporadic migrations of peoples from mainland Africa. The island's ancient inhabitants, representing several linguistic and cultural groups, gradually coalesced as a separate people, although inter-tribal and clan wars continued. Relatively isolated from the influences of the mainland, the Bubis developed many customs and cultural traits unique in Africa. To discourage incursions by mainland tribes, the Bubis developed a warrior tradition.

Encountered by Portuguese explorer Fernão do Pó in 1472, the island was originally *Formosa*, beautiful. The early explorers reported that the islanders were a hostile, savage people, which probably accounted for the relatively few Bubis captured and sent into slavery in the New World. The island served as a center of the growing Portuguese slave trade, a secure base physically removed from the coastal areas habitually raided for slaves.

In 1778 Portugal ceded the island to Spain as part of a series of agreements that settled colonial boundaries in South America. Almost totally ignored by the Spanish authorities, the island's only contacts with the outside world were occasional Spanish ships from the South American colonies.

In the eighteenth century, the island was frequented by slave traders and merchants from a variety of European states—Britain, Germany, France, and Holland. The Bubis are thought to have incorporated many small groups that migrated from the mainland in the eighteenth and nineteenth centuries, while incorporating ideas and cultural traits brought to the island by the slavers and the Europeans traders.

The colonial administration, seeing little commercial value in the island, allowed the British to take over the local administration in 1827. As a base for the ships involved in the suppression of the slave trade and as a center for colonization by freed slaves, the British established a mission at the site of Malobo in 1829. Between 1829 and 1843 the British landed the slaves taken from captured slave ships on the island, where they eventually came to be called Fernandinos. Returned to Spanish control in 1843, the island became a separate colony in 1858, and it united with the mainland colony of Río Muni in 1885.

Contacts with the Europeans decimated the Bubi people, and only a few thousand remained in the early twentieth century, though the Spanish authorities did not begin the systematic exploitation of the island until 1926. The island's rich volcanic soil favored plantation agriculture, but the native surviving Bubis resisted Spanish attempts to use them as plantation labor. Unused to plantation labor, the Bubis gained their living as small farmers and minor civil servants.

The resistance movement against the Spanish authorities was the forerunner of the later national movement. To overcome the resulting labor shortage, the authorities imported thousands of Ibo workers from nearby British Nigeria. Even though the Bubis resisted forced labor, they became the most pro-Spanish of the peoples of Spain's African territories, fearing that the end of Spanish rule would allow an invasion of the more numerous Fangs from the mainland.

The decolonization of Africa, begun with the independence of Ghana in 1957, exacerbated the ethnic tension between the more prosperous Bubis and the Fangs, the colony's largest ethnic group. In 1958 Bubi nationalists organized demonstrations demanding separation from the mainland area of Río Muni and autonomy for the island as part of the Spanish state. Pressured by the growing popularity of the nationalists, the Spanish authorities granted autonomy to the island in 1963. The majority Bubi population of Fernando Po was both administratively distinct from and economically more developed than the larger and more populous mainland Río Muni, with its Fang majority.

In the 1960s, Macias Nguema Biyogo Masie emerged as the spokesman for the colony's majority Fangs. The Republic of Equatorial Guinea became independent in 1968 under a federal system that guaranteed the island's autonomy and reserved a third of the seats in the federal parliament for representatives of the Bubi tribe. In 1969 severe rioting swept the new country over the perceived advantages enjoyed by the Bubi minority. Continuing political and economic turmoil allowed the state's first president, the mainlander Masie, to take control and to proclaim himself president-for-life in 1972. Over the next year he established a harsh one-party dictatorship that effectively ended all Bubi autonomy.

Masie's eleven-year reign was one of postcolonial Africa's most brutal. Most churches were closed in 1975, and in 1978 the Roman Catholic religion was officially banned. The country's 7,000 Europeans fled, and in 1976 the Nigerian government evacuated over 45,000 Nigerian citizens. The Bubi tribe of the richer island province, seen as a potential threat to the president's hold on power, lost an estimated third of its population to his reign of terror, which devastated the island's economy and decimated the Bubi leadership. In 1979 Theodoro Obiang Nguema, Masie's nephew, deposed his uncle and took control of the state. In 1985 Obiang, like his uncle before him, set up a one-party dictatorship. Pressed by aid donors and pro-democracy groups, presidential elections were held in 1988, which Obiang, as the only candidate in an openly fraudulent election, won with 99.98% of the vote.

Ethnic Fangs, members of the republic's dominant national group, have flocked to the island from Río Muni, continental Equatorial Guinea, and now hold most official and civil service positions on the island. Bubi nationalist organizations, mostly in exile in Spain, in 1989 stepped up demands for independence. Citing continuing human rights abuses and rising inter-ethnic violence, the nationalists claimed that the mainland Fang were colonizing and destroying the island. At independence in 1968 Fernando Póo was one of the richest areas of sub-Saharan Africa, but in the 1990s the island was one of Africa's poorest. The island receives 70% of its meager income from international aid, and corrupt government officials steal much of that before it reaches the island's coffers.

Pressured by the international community and the principal aid donors, the government began to introduce some of the trappings of democracy. In April 1991 President Obiang announced the formation of other political parties and in October 1992 legalized selected opposition groups. Bubi nationalist organizations calling for autonomy or independence remained illegal and persecuted, with most of their leaders remaining in exile. National elections held in 1993 were internationally condemned as fraudulent, and most Bubis refused to vote. In the 1996 presidential elections, Obiang Nguema, opposed by only one candidate, reportedly received over 99% of the vote.

Substantial oil deposits were discovered in waters around Bioko in 1995, and exploitation began in 1996. The economic factor has added to the nationalist fervor on the island, with the Bubis claiming that their natural wealth is being squandered by a corrupt government while they live in poverty and under repression.

In 1997, Spain's prime minister, José María Aznar, urged the Equatorial Guinean government to adopt democratic principles and to end the repression of political opponents, including the Bubi minority in the country. In spite of the Spanish appeal, government opponents continued to be harassed, detained, tortured, or otherwise ill-treated. The government later accused Spain's Radio Exterior of inciting armed rebellion in the country. Several Bubi leaders were arrested just for listening to Radio Exterior. Other Bubi leaders were forced to pay heavy fines or to join the ruling Democratic Party of Equatorial Guinea, the only recognized political organization in the country.

A group of Bubi nationalists on 21 January 1998 launched attacks on army and police installations on the island, killing several soldiers and civilians. In a series of reprisals attacks on Bubi villages, security forces broke into Bubi houses, raped Bubi women, and looted entire neighborhoods. In some instances soldiers threw household goods into the streets and encouraged passing Fangs to help themselves to the property. Bubi-owned stores and market stalls were also looted, and Bubi farmers were prevented from leaving Malobo to work their fields. The government did little to curtail gangs of Fangs who roamed the streets at night raping and looting. There were an unknown number of summary executions near the village of Belebu Belacha, but foreign journalists were prevented from visiting the region, and most were later expelled from the country. Over 500 Bubis were detained; many were reportedly tortured, and at least six died in detention. Most were detained solely on account of their Bubi origins.

In May 1998, over 110 people accused of involvement in the barracks attacks were tried in a grossly unfair mass trial. Most received sentences ranging from six to 26 years' imprisonment, but 15 of the accused, considered leaders of the rebellion, were sentenced to death. Their sentences were later commuted to life imprisonment. In 1999–2000 a number of peaceful opponents of the oppressive government were detained without charge or trial and were sentenced to long prison terms. Fang vigilante groups, unhindered by the government, established a virtual reign of terror on the island.

Equatorial Guinea, although nominally a multiparty republic, is in reality a dictatorship—a unitary, one-party state dominated by the Mongomo clan of the Fang tribe, the clan of Macias and Obiang. The government continues to refuse even to discuss the limited cultural and economic autonomy advocated by the most moderate of the Bubi nationalists, while a younger generation, less willing to compromise, takes over the leadership of the Bubi nationalist movement.

Discrimination against the Bubis has worsened since the 1998 rebellion on Bioko, with renewed suppression and curbs on the Bubis' basic rights, the most hated being restrictions on their movement. The Bubis are unable to move about freely on the island; roadblocks prevent them from traveling between towns and villages, even to visit family or country farms. New restrictions on religion also fuel the continuing unrest. The Catholic Church has repeatedly denounced human rights, violations, social injustice, and corruption in the country.

SELECTED BIBLIOGRAPHY:

Baule, E. *Equatorian Guinea: The Bubi Aspirations to Self-Government.* 1980.
Kelly, Robert C., ed. *Equatorial Guinea Country Review 1999/2000.* 1999.
Molino, Martain. *The Bubis: Rituals and Beliefs.* 1996.
Sundiata, Ibrahim K. *From Slavery to Neoslavery: The Bight of Biafra and Fernando Po in the Era of Abolition, 1827–1930.* 1996.

Burgundians

Bourgignons; Bourgognes

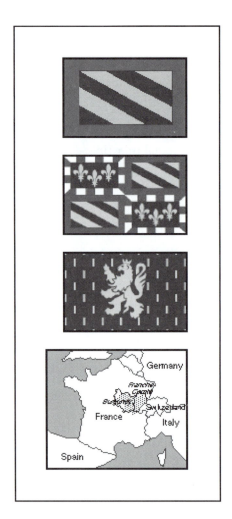

POPULATION: Approximately (2002e) 2,590,000 Burgundians in Europe, 2,375,000 in the historical region of Burgundy and with smaller communities in Paris and other parts of France and in Switzerland. Outside Europe there are small Burgundian communities in Canada and South America.

THE BURGUNDIAN HOMELAND: The Burgundian homeland lies at the confluence of influences from northern and Mediterranean Europe. The region is in east-central France, a mostly hilly area around the valleys of the Saône and the Rhône, which form the southern boundary of the historical region. In the east the land rises to the Jura Mountains, which form the international frontier between France and Switzerland, and in the north are the Vosges Mountains. A rich agricultural area, Burgundy is especially famous for wines of the Chablis region, the uplands of the Côte d'Or, and the valleys of the Saône and Rhône River valleys. The historical region of Burgundy comprises six French departments divided among three planning regions. The Department of Ain, which forms part of Rhône-Alpes region, Doubs, Haute-Saône, and Jura of the Franche-Comté region, and Côte d'Or and Saône-et-Loire departments of the Bourgogne region. *Historical Region of Burgundy (Bourgogne)*: 18,450 sq. mi.—47,784 sq. km, (2002e) 2,559,000—Burgundians 91%, Swiss Romands* 3%, other French 6%. The Burgundian capital and major cultural center is Dijon, (2002e) 147,000, the historical capital of Burgundy. The other important Burgundian center is Besançon, (2002e) 117,000, the historical capital of Franche-Comté, formerly the Free County of Burgundy.

FLAG: The Burgundian national flag, the historical flag of the region of Burgundy, has blue and yellow diagonal stripes within a border of red. The official flag of the French region of Burgundy has the historical flag on the upper fly and lower hoist; the other quadrants are blue with three gold fleur-des-lys surrounded by a red and white border. The flag of the region of Franche-Comté is a blue field dotted with gold lines and charged with a centered gold lion rampant.

PEOPLE AND CULTURE: The Burgundians are a French nation, the descendants of the early Germanic Burgundii that occupied the region in the fifth century A.D. The culture of the region, more oriented to Dijon and Geneva than to Paris, retains many traditions and customs unique to the Burgundians. Poverty and unequal land distribution forced many Burgundians to leave their homeland for Paris or other parts of France in the nineteenth and early twentieth centuries. Over the centuries the boundaries of the Burgundian homeland have changed greatly, but the Burgundians retain a sense of identity that transcends political borders. Much of the population remains rural, with about 40% living outside the urban areas. The Burgundian culture is based on the region's wine production, which dictates the seasonal occupations and regional festivals.

LANGUAGE AND RELIGION: The Germanic Burgundian language died out long ago, and the modern Burgundians speak standard French, along with two regional dialects, Bourgignon and Franc-Comtois, which differ considerably from the spoken French of Paris. The Burgundian dialects are further divided into a number of subdialects that mostly reflect the boundaries of the regional departments. The dialects have no official status and are mostly spoken in rural areas, but urbanized Burgundians have also maintained their linguistic traditions in spite of official French government opposition to regional languages.

The majority of the Burgundians are Roman Catholics, having successfully resisted the Protestant Reformation. A small, influential Protestant minority lives mostly in the east of the region.

NATIONAL HISTORY: Originally occupied by various Celtic tribes, the region was invaded by the Romans under Julius Caesar between 60 and 50 B.C. Harassed by Germanic invaders, the Celtic Sequanii appealed to Caesar for aid. The Romans established a permanent garrison at Vestontio, the present Besançon. Later the Sequanii, in an effort to expel the Romans, allied to the Gallic chief Vercingétorix. In 52 B.C. the Romans decisively defeated Vercingétorix at Alésia, and the region came under direct Roman control. Under Roman rule the region prospered, and the city of Autun evolved as a major Roman cultural center. Eventually Roman culture weakened and in the second century A.D. Christianity spread through the region. In the fourth century Roman power collapsed, and invading Germanic tribes overran the region.

In 480 the Germanic Burgundii, fleeing the advance of the Huns, conquered the region and expelled the other Germanic peoples. Mixing with the Romanized population, the Burgundii accepted Christianity, established a code of laws, the *Lex Burgundionum*, and established the first kingdom of Burgundy. At its height, the Burgundian kingdom included most of southeastern France and western Switzerland.

The Germanic Franks conquered the Burgundian kingdom in 534 and annexed the region to the growing Frankish kingdom. Throughout the Mergovingian period, Burgundy was subject to numerous partitions, although Burgundy survived as a political concept. At Charlemagne's death the Frankish empire was divided among his heirs, and two new Burgundian kingdoms were founded—Cisjurane Burgundy (or Provence) and Transjurane Burgundy in the north. In 933 the two kingdoms were united in the Second Kingdom of Burgundy, also called the Kingdom of Arles. A smaller area, roughly equivalent to present Burgundy, was created as a separate duchy of Burgundy by the Holy Roman emperor, Charles II, in 877.

In 1032 the Kingdom of Burgundy was incorporated into the Holy Roman Empire. As a transit area for much of Europe, Burgundy developed as a center of Roman Catholicism. Cluny became the headquarters of the Benedictine Order, which controlled over 1,200 monasteries and other religious sites across Europe during the twelfth century. The establishment of religious centers as centers of learning and culture aided the development of trade and agriculture in the region.

A local count, Raynald II, refused to honor the German king, Lothair, later the emperor of the Holy Roman Empire. Lothair supported a rival in Raynald's place, but after a decade of conflict, Raynald emerged victorious. Thereafter he was the "franc-comte," the free count, and his territory became known as Franche-Comté.

The golden age of Burgundy began in 1364, when John II of France gave Burgundy to his son, Philip the Bold, as a fief, beginning the Valois-Bourgogne dynasty. Philip and his successors, by conquest, treaty, or marriage, acquired vast territories, including most of the present Netherlands, Belgium, Luxembourg, and extensive regions in France and southwestern Germany. In the fifteenth century the Burgundians, through their partisans in France, dominated French politics. At that time Burgundy was the greatest European power and dominated the continent in trade, industry, and agriculture. The Burgundian court at Dijon was a center of European culture and art.

The wars of the ambitious Charles the Bold proved ruinous for the Burgundians. Opposed by the French and the Swiss, the Burgundians were defeated in several major battles in 1476–77, and Charles was killed. His daughter, Mary of Burgundy, married Emperor Maximilian I, bringing most of the Burgundian territories, excluding the original French duchy, under Hapsburg rule. Although divided between two empires, the Burgundians maintained their distinct identity and culture, while generally ignoring the political frontiers that traversed their homeland. In 1482 the Treaty of Arras ceded Franche-Comté to the *dauphin* of France on his betrothal to the daughter of the Austrian emperor. When the *dauphin* became king as Charles VIII, he renounced the betrothal and had to return Franche-Comté to Austrian Hapsburg rule. For the next 185 years, Franche-Comté remained a Hapsburg possession.

In 1556 the Burgundian territories of the Holy Roman Empire came under the control of the Spanish Habsburgs. Although some of the region's fortified towns were occupied by the French during the sixteenth-century wars of religion, the area was devastated by both Catholic and Protestant forces. In 1668 the French conquered the region, also called the Free County of Burgundy, and in 1674 finally obtained its cession from the Spanish Hapsburgs. The Burgundians of Franche-Comté had vehemently opposed the French invaders, and pro-Hapsburg feeling in the region lasted until the end of the eighteenth century. The two Burgundian regions, Burgundy and Franche-Comté, remained French provinces with regional *parlements* until the French Revolution.

Revolutionary violence in 1789 was especially targeted at the ecclesiastical centers in the region. The Abbey of Cluny was virtually destroyed, and other notable church structures suffered the same fate. In 1790 the regions were dissolved and replaced by departments in an effort to eliminate the strong regionalist feelings that permeated the French regions. All political and bureaucratic functions were centralized in Paris, ending centuries of autonomous rule in the Burgundian regions. Under Napoleon the government gave land tenure to the peasants and encouraged the growth of a middle class. Regionalist sentiment gave way to enthusiastic support for Napoleon's dream of a united Europe under French domination, but, with Napoleon's final defeat, regionalist sentiment again became a strong feature of local Burgundian society.

The construction of railroads ended the relative isolation of the Burgundians in the nineteenth century. Limited opportunities in their homeland drove the brightest and most talented to Paris, where all power in France was centralized. The need to leave their homeland to succeed in the arts, professions, or in academic life raised resentment and fed a growing regionalist movement demanding greater say over decisions involving the Burgundian homeland.

After World War I, an economic decline that began in 1918 accelerated, with young Burgundians forced to move to other, more prosperous parts of France. The rural depopulation that had begun in the late nineteenth century continued, as a lack of opportunity drove thousands to leave their homeland. The region's population declined by about 20% between 1870 and the end of World War II.

In the 1930s radical political groups gained followings in the region, which reflected the chaotic situation in France. Conservative groups intent on maintaining France's centralized government opposed populist regional leaders. In the late 1930s opposition to the growing power of Nazi Germany united the Burgundians behind the French government. In May–June 1940, the French government was ignominiously defeated by the invading forces of Nazi Germany. The Burgundians, under German occupation, were among the most active in the Resistance, using the rugged area of eastern Burgundy to maintain contacts with exile and anti-Nazi groups based in neutral Switzerland.

In 1968, regional Burgundian identity had nearly disappeared when student demonstrations against France's outdated educational system triggered widespread unrest among striking workers and farmers. In Dijon and other Burgundian cities the traditional Burgundian flag was displayed during demonstrations and marches and on barricades. Regionalist sentiment, spurred by anger at France's overly centralized and inefficient central government, grew throughout the 1970s.

A socialist government elected in 1981 and led by François Mitterand, who began his career in the region, devolved some limited powers to the reconstituted French regions, including Burgundy and Franche-Comté. Demands for the unification of the historical Burgundian territories, however, were ignored. The Burgundians have generally championed greater European integration, with its possibility of regaining their historical identity within a united Europe, but economic concerns have dictated voting patterns. Fearing for their important wine and agricultural industries, the Burgundians voted in 1992 against the Maastricht Treaty, which provided for closer economic integration of the member states of the European Economic Community (EEC).

In recent decades young Burgundians have left the region for greater opportunities in nearby Lyon or Paris, but the trend began to reverse in 1997, reflected in a slight overall population increase in the region. The Burgundians no longer wish to leave their homeland and have demanded more government attention to the region's economic problems. The lack of opportunities is one of the issues driving the growing regionalist movement.

In November 2001 several activists demanded the same statute of autonomy offered to the Corsicans,* including fiscal and cultural controls. The government ignored the demands, but with growing support the Burgundian regionalists continue to speak of a European dimension to their drive for autonomy.

SELECTED BIBLIOGRAPHY:

Coates, Clive. *Burgundy*. 1997.
Cobban, Alfred. *A History of Modern France*. 1967.
Hanson, Anthony. *Burgundy*. 1995.
Price, Roger. *A Concise History of France*. 1993.

Buryats

Buryat Mongols; Buriats; Byryats; Burguts; Northern Mongolians

POPULATION: Approximately (2002e) 464,000 Buryats in southern Siberian Russia, mostly concentrated in the Buryat Republic, the autonomous districts of Ust-Ordün and Agün, and other areas of Irkutsk and Chita oblasts. Outside Russia there is a Buryat population of about 50,000 in adjacent areas of Mongolia and some 70,000 in the Inner Mongolia region of China.

THE BURYAT HOMELAND: The Buryat homeland lies in southern Siberia, a complex of mountain ranges, including the Sayan Mountains, with plateaus, basins, and river valleys around huge Lake Baikal. The lake, sacred to the Buryats, represents 20% of the world's fresh-water reserves. Thick, poorly drained forests or taiga cover about 70% of the area, with fertile areas in the mountain valleys and the steppe lands. The largest portion of the homeland forms the Buryat Republic, a member state of the Russian Federation. Smaller Buryat units are the autonomous districts of Ust-Ordün Buryatia in Irkutsk Oblast and Agün Buryatia in Chita Oblast. *Buryat Republic (Burjaadaj Respublika)*: 135,637 sq. mi.—351,300 sq. km, (2002e) 1,024,000—Buryats 28%, Russians 70%. *Ust-Ordün Buryatia (Ust-Ordynskij Burjatskij Avtonomnyj Okrug)*: 8,494 sq. mi.—22,000 sq. km, (2002e) 142,000—Buryats 71%, Russians 23%.

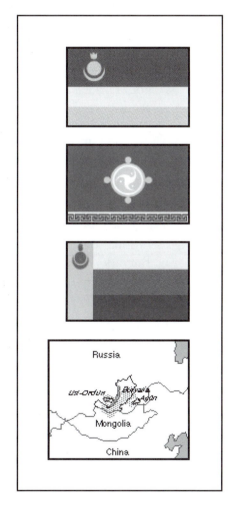

Agün Buryatia (Aginskij Burjatskij Avtonomnyj Okrug): 7,336 sq. mi.—19,000 sq. km, (2002e) 78,000—Buryats 55%, Russians 42%. The Buryat capital and major cultural center is Ulan Ude, (2002e) 371,000. The cultural center of the Ust-Ordün Buryats is the town of Ust Orda, (2002e) 15,000. The cultural center of the Agün Buryats is Aginskoye, (2002e) 12,000.

FLAG: The Buryat national flag, the official flag of the republic, is a vertical tricolor of blue, white, and yellow, proportions 2:1:1, charged with a yellow ideogram, the *soyonbo*, on the upper hoist, consisting of a yellow flame above a yellow sun and a crescent moon. The flag of Ust-Ordün Buryatia is green field bearing a centered Buddhist prayer wheel and a red-on-white design on the bottom. The flag of Agün Buryatia is a vertical tricolor of white, red, and blue with a vertical yellow stripe at the hoist bearing a blue *soyonbo* on the upper hoist.

PEOPLE AND CULTURE: The Buryats, the largest ethnic minority in Siberian Russia, belong to the Central Asian branch of the North Asian Mongol nations. Physically the Buryats are Mongols, but they also display many Turkic and Tungus physical and cultural traits. The origins of the Buryats have not been clearly established but are believed to include Mongol, Turkic, Tungus, Samoyed, and other strains. Historically the Buryats are a nomadic, pastoral people, herding cattle, horses, sheep, goats, and camels. Descent is traced through the paternal line, with patrilineal clans grouped into villages and clan confederations. The Buryats have been traditionally divided into five groups—Bugalat, Khora, Ekhirit, Khongodor, and Tabunut. Buryat subgroups include Buryatized Tuvans,* Evenks,* and the Karyms, of mixed Buryat and Russian background. The subdivisions among the Buryats, based on distinctive dialects, have eroded, with the only modern division of importance being that between those living west of Lake Baikal, the Irkutsk Buryats, and those to the east, the Transbaikal Buryats. Buryat culture has much in common with Mongol culture, including their favorite sports—wrestling, horse racing, and archery—and the enormously long *uligers*, or poems, that preserve the oral history of the Buryat nation. The ethnic and historical mixture that produced the Buryats has given the people a special quality. The old superstitions of the pre-Buddhist period and the later influences of Buddhism left the Buryats with a sense that avoiding conflict is far superior to engaging in it. The love of learning bequeathed by the lamas has served the Buryats well. They have achieved a high level of education that helps equip many for work in regional industries such as aircraft manufacture.

LANGUAGE AND RELIGION: The Buryat language is a northern subgroup of the Mongolian language group of the Altai language family. The language, also called Buriat or Northern Mongolian, is a dialect of Khori Mongol, spoken in two distinct regional dialects, Western and Eastern, that are further divided into nine subdialects. Eastern Buryat is less influenced by Russian and is more like the Khalkha Mongol, spoken in Mongolia. Until 1930 the Buryats used the traditional Uighur-Mongol written language, which was replaced in 1931 by a Latin-based alphabet by the Soviet authorities; in early 1939 the Cyrillic alphabet was made the only legal writing system. Only about 90% of the Buryats speak Buryat as their mother tongue, others having adopted Russian during the Soviet era, although Buryat is now taught in the region's schools. In Mongolia, where the Buryat language varies considerably, Khalkha Mongolian is used as the literary language. A Buryat cultural association in February 1994 issued a textbook that it hoped would allow Buryats quickly to learn or relearn their native language.

The Buryats west of Lake Baikal are mostly Russian Orthodox, while the Buryats of Transbaikalia, east of the lake, are mostly Buddhists, following the Tibetan Lamaism of the Tibetans.* Until the Soviet era Buddhist monasteries, called *datsans*, were famed ecclesiastical schools, workshops for the making of icons and sculptures, and printing shops. Many Buryat lamas were renowned scholars, with many physicians and astrologists. Traditionally the Buryats have adhered to an intricate combination of shamanistic and Buddhist traditions. Since 1991 there has been a rapid revival of shamanism. Since 1998, there has been a growing rift between the Buryat Buddhists who favor a break with the official, Russian-sanctioned Buddhist community and the more traditional Buddhists.

NATIONAL HISTORY: From ancient times different tribes and peoples inhabited the region around Lake Baikal. The Buryat origins can be traced back to small Karluk Turkic tribes in the region east of Lake Baikal, tribes loosely controlled by China until A.D. 754. Absorbed by successive waves of Mongol migrations from the south, the last of the Turkic tribes disappeared with the conquest of the region by the Mongols of Genghis Khan in 1205. Known as a separate Mongol people from 1207, the Buryats are first mentioned in 1240, in a Mongol manuscript. The various Buryat tribes formed part of the great Mongol empire until the fourteenth century. In the sixteenth century the last remains of Mongol power in the area ended, with the creation of an independent tribal confederation.

Cossacks, the forerunners of Russian expansion, reached the region around Lake Baikal, called Baigal by the Buryats, in 1643. The Russians gradually took control of the region, bringing the last of the Buryat tribes under their rule around 1700. Treaties signed by Russia and the Manchus* of China in 1689 and 1727 established definite boundaries and effectively cut off Buryat contact with the Mongol peoples to the south. The Buryat tribes attempted to throw off Russian rule in two revolts, in 1695 and 1696. In 1742 the imperial Russian government recognized Buddhism as an official religion, and the first *datsan* was constructed under Russian rule.

A violent schism within the Orthodox Church in European Russia at the end of the seventeenth century created a religious minority, Old Believers, called *Raskolniki* or *Semeiskye*, who suffered severe persecution in European Russia in the eighteenth and nineteenth centuries. Many of the Old Believers fled east to the new frontier districts around Lake Baikal to settle among the peaceful Buryats.

The Buryat tribes consolidated from various tribes and groups after the imposition of Russian control. In addition to the core Buryat tribes, the

Buryats assimilated other groups, including Oriots, Khalkas, and Tungus groups. The Russian authorities allotted tribal territories to each of the four major tribes—the Khori in the east, the Ekhirit and Bugalat west of Lake Baikal, and the Khongodor in the south. The remainder of the former Buryat lands were opened to colonization. Over the next century Russian colonists occupied the tribal lands, forcing the tribes west of Lake Baikal to abandon their lands and to migrate to the Selenga and Barguzin Valleys, east of the lake, in the eighteenth century. In the early nineteenth century the Khori lost their lands and moved south to the Aga Steppe region.

The Tibetan form of Buddhism, called Lamaism, spread through the Buryat tribes in the nineteenth century, the gentle doctrine quickly replacing their earlier shamanistic beliefs in all but the most remote areas. Although they shared religion, culture, and language, the Buryats remained a disunited and backward tribal people in the rural areas of Russia's Transbaikal region.

The Trans-Siberian Railroad reached Irkutsk, the major city of the Buryat region, in 1898. The railroad brought a massive influx of Russian peasants and finally united the Buryats in opposition to discriminatory Russian land laws. Serious Buryat revolts erupted in the region in 1903 and 1905, bringing Russian threats to demolish the Buryat culture. During the Russo-Japanese War, the Japanese government espoused a policy of "pan-Mongolism," making overtures to the Buryat leadership. A Buryat congress was held in Chita in 1905, issuing demands for linguistic freedom and self-government, but the movement was suppressed. Between 1907 and 1912 secret, then open, treaties between Japan and Russia recognized the Buryats as falling within Russia's sphere of influence.

Buryat life, revolving around the 48 *datsans* in the region, was virtually untouched by World War I until the Russian Revolution in February 1917. The Buryats then became effectively independent, as the tsarist civil government collapsed. Putting aside their remaining tribal differences, the Buryats united to drive all Russian officials from the region. A Buryat congress held at Irkutsk in April 1917 voted for independence and for closer ties to Mongolia. Ironically, the Buryat Buddhist monks were the first to divest the monasteries of their extensive holdings, distributing the lands to Buryat peasants in an attempt to return the religion to a more traditional form.

A Japanese intervention force, sent to keep eastern Siberia from falling to Bolshevik control, occupied Buryatia in early 1918. Encouraged by the Japanese, who envisaged a reconstituted Mongol federation under Japanese influence, the Buryats formed a national government and sent delegates to a pan-Mongol conference that endorsed a Buryat demand for the expulsion of all Slavs east of Lake Baikal. Threatened by the spreading Russian Civil War, the Buryat leaders declared Buryatia independent on 11 February

1919 and set about creating a state administered according to Buddhist teachings, but the region remained chaotic and the new state was unable to assert its authority.

The Buryats largely remained neutral during the Russian Civil War. The victorious Bolsheviks overran the state in 1920 and added Buryatia to the Far Eastern Republic, a communist-dominated buffer state. A Buryat-Mongolian Autonomous Region was set up within the Far East in 1921. The whole region was incorporated into the Soviet Union in 1922. The Buryat-Mongolian region was upgraded to the status of an autonomous republic within the Russian Federation in 1923. Between 1921 and 1928 Buryat Bolsheviks effectively ruled neighboring Mongolia, under orders from Moscow.

After the communist victory in Russia, the Buryats' open-pasture pastoralism was forcibly replaced by collective farms. The traditional pursuits of hunting and trapping were outlawed. In 1925, a campaign against religion in Buryatia was launched. The Soviet suppression of all religions led to the closure of all but a few temples and monasteries during the 1920s, the closures arousing strong Buryat resistance. In 1929 the Buryats rebelled against communist rule and the collectivization of their herds. The rebellion was quickly crushed by the Red Army; over 35,000 Buryats died, including thousands of monks, massacred on the orders of the Russian dictator, Joseph Stalin. Irreplaceable Buryat cultural treasures were arbitrarily destroyed. Accused of acting as Japanese agents, many of the remaining Buryats west of Lake Baikal were expelled. Buryat refugees in Mongolia joined the Khalkha Mongols in an anti-Soviet revolt in 1931–32, the so-called Shambhala War.

In 1937 Stalin, as part of a new purge that decimated the intelligentsia and the religious leadership of Buryatia, stripped Buryatia of about half its territory, arbitrarily separating two areas from the territory as new districts and reclassifying the local Buryats, called the Ust-Ordün and Agün Buryats, as separate nationalities. Stalin encouraged Slavic migration to the region in order to dilute the Buryat majority. During the Second World War, Buryat soldiers serving in the Red Army received more Hero of the Soviet Union medals than the soldiers of any other Soviet minority, but the devastation of western Russia accelerated the migration of Russians into Siberia and the heroes returned to a much-changed homeland; the Buryats were a minority in their homeland from the Second World War and onward. Attempts to revive Buryat Buddhism started during World War II, and the religion was officially reestablished in 1946, but under close Soviet control.

In 1948 the Soviet government launched a campaign to Russify and Sovietize Buryat culture. Fearing a rebirth of Buryat nationalism Stalin ordered over 10,000 Buryat leaders killed. Traditional art forms were banned, and Russian academics were put in charge of the education and assimilation of the Buryat population. Education in the Buryat language was forbidden. A Soviet policy of separating the Buryats from their Mongol roots included changing the name of the region from Buryat-Mongol Autonomous Soviet Socialist Republic to simply the Buryat ASSR, in 1958. Buryatia was declared a restricted area and access without special permission was denied, effectively cutting the Buryats off from outside contact. In 1976 there were only about 300 Buryat Buddhist lamas or monks, down from 16,000 before the Bolshevik Revolution, and only one officially sanctioned monastery.

The Buryat national movement, suppressed for over fifty years, resurfaced with the liberalization of Soviet life in the late 1980s. A group of Buryat intellectuals in 1991 denounced the administrative division of historical Buryatia during the Stalin era. The republic was unilaterally declared a member republic of the Russian Federation in 1992. Buryat officials in 1993 stated that they had no plans to secede from Russia, but the Buryat parliament declared the division of Buryatia in 1937 as unconstitutional. A new constitution was adopted in 1994, and a bilateral treaty with the Russian Federation was signed in 1995. In 1998 a Buryat, Sergei Aidaev, was elected as mayor of Ulan Ude, to become the highest-ranking Buryat in the Russian-dominated republican government.

The revival of the Buryat culture and the poor state of their sacred Lake Baikal are major nationalist issues in the late twentieth century. The severe pollution of the Buryat's Lake Baikal has become a rallying point for the small but growing national movement. At the present, any Buryat vote for greater autonomy is blocked by the fact that they form a minority in their own republic. Ethnic relations in the region have been relatively peaceful.

The resurgence of the Buryat's Buddhist religion, closely identified with Buryat culture, has led the peaceful Buryat national revival, with the reopened temples and monasteries serving as centers of Buryat culture and of national sentiment in favor of the reunification of the Buryat homeland and of the redrawing of ethnic borders in the region. The Dalai Lama indefinitely postponed a visit to Russia that was originally planned for September 1998, including stops in Buryatia. The trip was postponed because of the overall instability in Russia. In October 1999, a Buddhist school of higher learning opened in Ulan Ude.

In 2000, the official unemployment rate in the region was set at 2.7%, while unofficially a third of all Buryats between 16 and 19 were out of work. High unemployment is blamed for a dramatic growth in crime, particularly robbery, theft, and armed robbery. The declining standard of living continues to fuel unrest in the region. In February 2000, the executive director of Siberian Accord, a grouping that includes Buryatia and Aginsk-Buryat, announced that he area had not ruled out secession from Russia, in light of the region's low standard of living.

The Buryat territorial claims continue to animate the mostly peaceful national movement. In early 2001 activists again demanded the unification of the three Buryat ethnic divisions under one administrative unit of the Buryat Republic, as a first step toward the restoration of the former boundaries of the Buryat-Mongolian republic of 1937.

SELECTED BIBLIOGRAPHY:

Becker, Jasper. *The Lost Country: Mongolia Revealed.* 1992.
Matthiessen, Peter, ed. *Baikal: Sacred Sea of Siberia.* 1995.
Moses, Larry W. *The Political Role of Mongol Buddhism.* 1977.
Nicholas, Thomas, and Caroline Humphrey, eds. *Shamanism, History, and the State.* 1994.

Cabindans

Cabindese; Kabindans

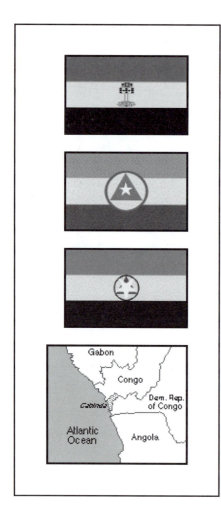

POPULATION: Approximately (2002e) 214,000 Cabindans in southwestern Africa, most in the enclave province of Cabinda of Angola, but with sizable refugee populations in other African states, in Europe, and in other parts of Angola. Nationalists claim a national population of between 400,000 and 600,000.

THE CABINDAN HOMELAND: The Cabindan homeland lies in southwestern Africa on the Atlantic Ocean, an oil-rich enclave separated from Angola by a strip of territory of the Democratic Republic of Congo. Cabinda has huge forests, especially in the wet regions in the vast Mayombe area, where gorillas still live under protection. These forests have the second richest variety of trees in the world after the Amazon region in South America, and the woods growing there, such as black wood, ebony, and African sandal wood, are of great value. The only Angolan province north of the Zaire River, the enclave of Cabinda has a 56-mile coastline and at its greatest width is about 70 miles (113 km). Cabinda forms a province of the People's Republic of Angola. *Province of Cabinda (Enclave do Cabinda/República de Cabinda)*: 2,794 sq. mi.—7,238 sq. km, (2002e) 202,000—Cabindans (Kakongo, Mayombe, Fiote) 88%, other Angolans 12%. The Cabindan capital and major cultural center is the enclave's capital, Cabinda City, called Tchiowa by the Cabindans, (2002e) 52,000, urban area, 90,000.

FLAG: The flag of the exile Republic of Cabinda is a vertical tricolor of pale blue, yellow, and black bearing a drawing of the Simulambuco monument, a *padrao*, a column of stone bearing the Portuguese *quinas* and topped by the Cross of Christ that the Portuguese sailors used to claim territories for Portugal. The flag of the major nationalist organization, Front for the Liberation of the Enclave of Cabinda (FLEC), is a vertical tricolor of pale blue, yellow, and red bearing a centered white five-pointed star backed by a green triangle encircled by a brown ring. The flag of Renovated FLEC, organized in 1996, is a vertical tricolor of red, yellow, and blue bearing a centered black ring enclosing a green triangle and an inverted white five-pointed star.

PEOPLE AND CULTURE: The Cabindans, who see themselves as a separate nation, are a Bantu people belonging to the tribes that make up the large Kongo* group in parts of Angola, Democratic Republic of Congo (Kinshasa), and Congo-Brazzaville. The two major divisions of the Cabindans are the coastal Kakongo and the minority Mayombe, who inhabit the region around Mount Mayombe in the interior. Although the Cabindans are a Kongo people, geographically and culturally they are separate and show little solidarity with the Kongo of northern Angola. The feeling of separateness from the rest of the peoples of Angola is deeply rooted among the Cabindans.

LANGUAGE AND RELIGION: The Ibinda dialect of Kikongo, the language of the Kongo peoples, is the first language of the enclave, although Portuguese and French, the official language in the adjacent areas of Zaire and Congo, are widely spoken. Both the coastal Kongo and the closely related interior Mayombes speak dialects of Kikongo that have substantial Portuguese and French admixtures. The Fiote, in the north, speak Fioti or West Kongo, which is understood with difficulty by the other Cabindans. Ibinda, formerly called Kiombe, is being promoted as a national language. Ibinda consists of several regional dialects, including Lindji, Oyo, Kotchi, Yombe, Sundi, and Lumbo.

The majority of the Cabindans, after long contact with the Portuguese, are now Roman Catholics. However, their religious beliefs have incorporated many pre-Christian traditions and customs that continue to have great importance to the population. A minority, mostly in the interior, adhere only to the traditional religious beliefs of the Kongos. In recent years evangelical Protestant sects, mostly spread by European and American missionaries, have had some success in the region.

NATIONAL HISTORY: The Kongo tribes, thought to have migrated from northeastern Africa, settled the vast basin of the Zaire River before A.D. 1100. A powerful kingdom of Kongo, united the tribes south of the Congo (Zaire) River in the thirteenth century and from there gradually expanded to control a number of tributary states north of the river. The culture and language of the Kongo became dominant across a wide region of southwestern Africa.

Portuguese explorers established contact with the Kongo kingdom in 1493, the beginning of the colonial expansion into the huge Congo River basin. The old Kongo kingdom was eventually divided between Portugal,

Belgium, and France, and its ordered life rapidly disappeared under the impact of colonial rule and the accompanying slave trade. Ports around the mouth of the Congo River became important centers for the export of slaves.

In 1883 Portuguese soldiers occupied the region north of the Congo River. The three European powers in 1884 demarcated and formalized the colonial boundaries. Portugal ceded part of its territory north of the Congo River to give the Belgian Congo an outlet to the Atlantic Ocean. The new colonial frontiers left the enclave of Portuguese Congo separated from Portuguese Angola by 25 miles (40 km) of Belgian territory.

The Portuguese authorities signed three treaties with the leaders of the local tribes—the treaty of Chinfuma in 1883; the treaty of Chicamba in 1884; and a treaty signed in February 1885 at Simulambuco establishing the region as a Portuguese protectorate, called Portuguese Congo. A monument was later built at the site, with three spears representing the three kingdoms of Kakongo, Loango, and Ngoyo that made up the colony. The monument is topped by a Portuguese cross and is modeled on the *padraos* constructed on lands claimed by the representatives of the Portuguese crown. The 1885 congress in Berlin recognized the division of the Congo territory into three parts—French Congo, Belgian Congo, and Portuguese Congo.

Portuguese Congo, administered as a separate colony from 1886, was the most neglected in Portuguese Africa, known principally for poverty and forced labor. A Kongo revolt in northern Angola in 1914 spread to the unhappy Kongo inhabitants of the enclave, where the revolt continued until 1917. The colonial revolt united the Cabinda clans and planted the seeds of the later Cabindan national movement. The 1933 Portuguese constitution recognized Cabinda as a separate colony, distinct from the Angolan territory to the south.

In 1954 oil explorations began in Portuguese Congo, which was for financial reasons administratively joined to Angola and renamed for its principal town in 1956. The enclave became the scene of serious nationalist agitation in the early 1960s. Fearing domination by the large Angolan tribes, the Cabindans agitated for a resumption of separate status, the agitation gradually evolving into a nationalist, anticolonial mass movement.

The Cabindans rebuffed overtures from Angola's rival nationalist organizations; by 1961 three separate nationalist organizations had formed in the territory. In 1963 the three groups united as the Front for the Liberation of the Enclave of Cabinda (FLEC) and demanded separate independence for the enclave. Incursions into Cabinda by other Angolan nationalist organizations were met with resistance by the Mayombes, whose territory they had to cross, and in central Cabinda by the newly formed forces of FLEC.

The Organization of African Unity (OAU) classified Cabinda separate from Angola as the 39th state of Africa on the list of territories to be decolonized. On 10 January 1967, the FLEC leaders created a government-in-exile in neighboring Congo-Kinshasa. Oil, discovered in 1966, greatly increased the economic importance of Cabinda and gave the nationalists a firm economic base. Despite a growing separatist war in the enclave, oil production began in 1968 and expanded dramatically over the next decade.

The Portuguese government, drained by long and costly colonial wars, was overthrown in a popular revolution in 1974. A new leftist regime in Lisbon, determined to rid Portugal of its colonial burden, moved to grant independence to the remaining possessions within two years. The Cabindans' petition for separate independence aroused fierce opposition from Angola's three rival nationalist organizations. The three Angolan groups agreed on very few points, but one of those points was that Cabinda, and its oil wealth, belonged to Angola.

The premature departure of the Portuguese administration left behind a three-way civil war in Angola but created an opportunity for the Cabindan nationalists. In February 1975, the new Angolan government declared it was ready to negotiate with the separatists in Cabinda. FLEC demands included the disassociation of Cabinda from Angola, recognition of FLEC as the only Cabindan liberation movement, and formal recognition of the Cabindans' right to self-determination. The government rejected the demands, and on 1 August 1975 Cabindan leaders declared the enclave independent, with Luis Ranque Franque, the leader of FLEC, as the country's first prime minister. The American firm pumping Cabinda's oil, its eye on future revenues, remained carefully neutral.

Angolan Marxists, aided by Soviet weapons and Cuban troops, gained control of most of Angola and dispatched troops to end Cabinda's secession and to secure its oil reserves. In spite of its continuing Marxist rhetoric the new Angolan government, hampered by a lack of expertise, did not nationalize Cabinda's oil production, thus creating a very curious anomaly—an oil installation in a communist country run by America's Gulf Oil Company and protected by Cuban troops against attacks by Cabindan separatists armed by Zaire (Congo-Kinshasa), an American ally.

The Cabindans remain among the poorest people in Angola, even though their province produces some 90% of Angola's export earnings. FLEC, reorganized in 1984, began operations against the Angolan government installations and foreign oil workers. In 1985, in a bid to undermine the nationalists' support, the Angolan government announced that 1% of Cabinda's oil revenues would be used for development projects in the enclave. Cabindan nationalists denounced the move as hypocritical, since the oil belongs to Cabinda and the Cabindans.

The oil reserves, which would give the citizens of an independent Cabinda incomes comparable to the oil-rich Middle East, back up the nationalists' claim that an independent Cabinda would be economically viable. Cabinda's oil wealth, pumped by a subsidiary of the United States–based Chevron Oil Company, which took over Gulf Oil's operation in the 1980s, mostly goes to the war effort against the rebels in Angola proper, to the south, and very little is returned for development in Cabinda.

The end of the Cold War, fought in party by proxy armies in Angola, greatly reduced outside political and military support for the combatants. Pressed by their former sponsors, the Angolans moved to end the civil war, but following negotiations and even elections, the war resumed. As part of the proposed democratic constitution for Angola, the Cabindans would have been granted autonomy in exchange for abandoning their goal of full independence.

In December 1991 five Cabindan factions met in Lisbon in an effort to end division and to foster closer coordination in the fight for independence. The following September a large majority of Cabinda's eligible voters honored a nationalist boycott of Angola's first free election. The election was later invalidated by the renewal of the civil war in Angola. The Cabindans' lack of unity has been a major obstacle to negotiations, with a number of separate factions representing regional and ideological differences. By 1993 nationalist rebels held most of the jungle interior, but the Angolan government controlled Cabinda City, with half of Cabinda's population, and the province's oil wealth.

Luis Ranque Franque, the president of FLEC, during talks in 1996 between the Cabindans and the Angolan government proposed a plan to end the conflict in Cabinda. He put forward a scheme for a special political and socioeconomic structure geared toward the development of the neglected province. The special status would allow the Cabindans their own political, administrative, economic, and cultural organizations. The proposal was rejected by the Angolan government and by other FLEC leaders, who subsequently formed rival nationalist organizations.

The Angolan government sent troops stationed in Cabinda into neighboring Zaire (Democratic Republic of Congo), where they assisted in the overthrow of the former President Mobutu. Later in 1997 Angolan soldiers helped to topple former President Lissouba of the Republic of Congo. The installation of new governments in the neighboring states ended much of the Cabindan separatists' outside support, while their bases in those countries were closed and the fighters dispersed. The Angolans, having cut off the Cabindans' support, launched an offensive in the province, resulting in heavy fighting in the northern districts. Angolan soldiers in Cabinda stepped up attacks on villages suspected of supporting the Cabindan nationalists, while troops in the Republic of Congo carried out raids on camps holding Cabindan refugees. Reports of torture, rape, and other abuses in early 1998 were ignored or denied by the Angolan government. Fighting spread to the Cabindan capital in March 1998. The Angolan authorities closed part of the border in Cabinda in response to crossborder movements and to a request by the Congolese government.

The Angolan government announced in March 1999 that it favored a resumption of negotiations with Cabindan nationalists. The talks, repeatedly postponed due to the resumption of fighting between government forces and the National Union for the Total Independence of Angla (UNITA) rebels in the north of the country and Angola's involvement in the spreading Congolese civil war, were called off following Cabindan demonstrations and protests over the conscription of young Cabindans to fight in the Angolan government forces.

Oil provides up to 90% of Angola's foreign earnings. Increasingly FLEC and other Cabindan nationalist groups have targeted government installation and oil personnel, including foreigners, in an effort to weaken Angolan control of the vital oil production

The Cabindans have paid a high price for their dream of an independent state. Over 70,000 people have been killed and more than 30,000 have fled overseas as refugees. Tens of thousands were detained and deported to Ba'a dos Tigres in southern Angola and many Cabindans were executed after summary trials and Angolan security forces extrajudicially executed thousands of unarmed civilians. In the perceived absence of commitment on the part of the Angolan government to seek a peaceful and humane solution to the military conflict, in 2000 separatists resorted to drastic action such as hostage taking to draw the former colonial power, Portugal, and the international community's attention to the injustice suffered by Cabinda. In July 2001 the last of the Portuguese hostages were released as a humanitarian gesture.

Many Portuguese are becoming more critical to the injustice of the 1975 Alvor Accords, which left the Cabindans to the mercy of the warring Angolan factions. Communiques issued in early 2001 by General Silvino Silverio Marques, former governor of the Portuguese administration in Cabinda, and by the pretender to the Portuguese throne, Duke Duarte Pio of Braganza, questioned the legality of Portugal's handling of the transfer of Cabinda to Angola.

Sporadic separatist violence continues in the province and nationalist leaders continue to press for a referendum on separate independence; however, most Cabindans have been careful not to provoke the level of violence evident in the rest of the country. As Angola tears itself apart, the Cabindans, who want no part of Angola's civil war, can only wait. Attempts to negotiate a cease-fire or to hold talks on the future of the enclave have so far failed, partly due to the Angolan fear of losing Cabinda's oil revenues and the Cabindans' refusal to renounce their goal of complete independence. The tragedy of Cabinda is that it once came very close to full independence, yet instead untold suffering was to be its destiny.

SELECTED BIBLIOGRAPHY:

Collelo, Thomas, ed. *Angola: A Country Study*. 1998.
Human Rights Watch. *Angola Unravels*. 1999.
Maier, Karl. *Angola: Promises and Lies*. 1995.
Martin, Phyllis. *Historical Dictionary of Angola*. 1980.

Cajuns

Cajans; Acadiens; Acadians*; Louisiana French

POPULATION: Approximately (2002e) 1,260,000 Cajuns in the United States, concentrated in the so-called French Triangle in southern Louisiana and eastern Texas. Outside the region there are sizable Cajun communities in New Orleans and other cities in southern Louisiana.

THE CAJUN HOMELAND: The Cajun homeland lies west of the Mississippi in the Mississippi River delta in southern Louisiana and southeastern Texas. Wooded marshes and swamps, the bayous, along the coast rise to plains and fertile prairies in the north. The Cajun area of Louisiana was officially designated in 1988 as Acadiana, embracing 22 parishes stretching from the Gulf of Mexico from south of New Orleans to the Texas border and north to Alexandria. The Acadian parishes include

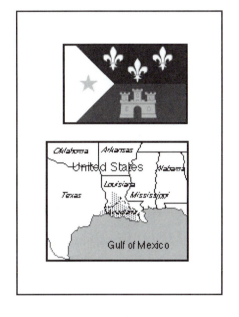

Calcasieu, Cameron, Jefferson Davis, Evangeline, Acadia, Vermilion, Ayoyelles, St. Landry, Lafayette, Pointe Coupée, St. Martin, Iberia, St. Mary, West Baton Rouge, Iberville, Assumption, Assension, St. James, Lafourche, Terrebonne, St. John the Baptist, and St. Charles. *Acadiana*: 17,759 sq. mi.—45,995 sq. km, (2002e) 1,754,000—Cajuns 52%, Islenos 10%, other Louisianans 38%. The Cajun capital and major cultural center is Lafayette, (2002e) 107,000, urban area, 178,000. Other important cultural centers are Alexandria, (2002e) 45,000, urban area, 126,000, and Lake Charles, 73,000, urban area, 182,000.

FLAG: The Cajun flag, the unofficial flag of Acadiana, is a vertical bicolor of blue over red with a white triangle extending from the hoist. On the blue stripe are three white fleur-de-lys; on the red stripe is a three-towered castle; and on the white there is a single yellow five-pointed star representing Our Lady of the Assumption, the patroness of the Cajuns.

PEOPLE AND CULTURE: The Cajuns are a Latin people, the descendants of eighteenth-century exiles from Canada. They remain clannish and exceedingly hostile to outsiders, known in the Cajun language as Teixannes, which stems from the discovery of oil and the influx of small-time Texan* robber-barons. "Teixanne" is a slang, almost scatological word for foreigner, which includes everyone but the Cajuns themselves. Their deep-rooted suspicion of the world beyond their bayous was not overcome until roads were build across the region in the 1930s and the Cajuns began letting strangers visit their homeland. In spite of rising prosperity and contact with non-Cajuns, their culture remains strong, with its distinct traditions, music, language, and cuisine.

LANGUAGE AND RELIGION: The Cajun language, called Cajun French or Français Acadien, is a bastardized version of French that incorporates archaic French forms with an anglicized syntax and idioms taken from English, German, and Spanish and with extensive borrowings from Indian and African languages. The language, spoken in three major dialects—Marsh French, Prairie French, and Big Woods French—is heard as far north as Avoyelles, Evangeline, Allen, and Calcasieu parishes in north-central Louisiana. Cajun speakers can to some degree understand standard French, but the dialect is almost incomprehensible to standard-French speakers. Many of the older Cajuns have only a limited knowledge of English, especially in rural areas, but younger Cajuns generally speak English as their first language, using Cajun with friends and family. Radio broadcasts in the language have helped to maintain the dialect; however, education in the region is in English and standard French.

The Cajuns are overwhelmingly Roman Catholic, but their beliefs are often mixed with old folk customs, pagan superstitions, and African spiritual practices brought to the region by African slaves and their descendants from the West Indies. Churches remain the cultural and social centers of rural Cajun life.

NATIONAL HISTORY: The region around the mouth of the Mississippi River was explored by the French in the seventeenth century. In 1731 the southern region, called Louisiana, became a French crown colony. Its population, about 8,000, included a French planter aristocracy and many black African slaves. The population of the colony grew rapidly with the arrival of the exiled Acadians from New France.

Descendants of Normans* and Bretons* had settled in New France or Acadia, in present Nova Scotia, and had come under British rule in 1713 during one of the frequent colonial wars. At that time the inhabitants were ordered to swear allegiance to the British crown or to withdraw to French-held Quebec. The Acadians did neither and continued to prosper in their small towns and rolling farmlands. They finally took the oath in 1730 but were exempted from bearing arms against the French and their Indian allies.

In 1755, for obscure reasons, the British forced between 6,000 and 8,000 Acadians at bayonet point to abandon their farms and villages and take passage on any ships leaving the region. The Acadian dispersal, called *Le Grande Dérangement*, was accompanied by great hardship. The Acadians scattered by sea to several points in British America, where they were persecuted as enemies and as Catholics. Most of the British colonies had laws prohibiting Catholics from settling within their borders, so many of the exiles sought refuge in the French Caribbean territories or moved west to live among the indigenous peoples. Others were deported to England, from where they eventually made their way back to France. Between 1756 and 1788 thousands of these Acadian exiles made their way to the French-speaking Louisiana from English-speaking regions throughout the British American possessions.

In French Louisiana the exiles established their own communities, rarely mixing with the French population of the territory. Confronted with a new land, new animals and plants, and new influences, the Acadians gradually changed their language and customs to fit their new circumstances. The indigenous peoples of the bayous, finding it difficult to pronounce "Acadian," began calling the new settlers Cajuns. The names Acadian and Cajun eventually were applied differently—Acadian describing all the descendants of the original Acadians, and Cajun referring only to Acadian exiles who came to Louisiana after 1755.

France ceded Louisiana to Spain in 1764, but the Spanish generally ignored the Cajuns, who had settled in the swampy delta region. In 1770 the Spanish authorities imported large numbers of Canary Islanders, later called Islenos. The Spanish retroceded Louisiana to French control in 1800. The French and Spanish built great fortunes in the river trade and on the inland plantations. Thousands of black slaves were imported to work the plantations and to serve in New Orleans and other Creole cities. The Acadian exiles from the beginning refused to engage in slave-supported plantation agriculture, continuing to farm small holdings in the European manner.

Fears that aggressive Napoleonic French would close the Mississippi River to American commerce led President Thomas Jefferson to offer to buy the Isle Orleans region at the mouth of the river. To his surprise the French government offered to sell all of the Louisiana Territory north to the Canadian border, including all of the French territories left in North America. In 1803 the Louisiana Purchase was finalized, and the United States took possession of the vast territory. The American authorities divided the territory; the Acadians were included in the new Territory of Orleans. The region remained dominated by the Creole aristocracy, joined by American planters moving west with their slaves.

The Cajuns were clannish and mostly rejected contact with other population groups. The Catholic Cajuns produced unusually large families. Between 1815 and 1880 the Cajun population rose from 35,000 to 270,000. The Cajuns remained *petits habitants* (small landowners), very religious, very self-sufficient, and isolated. In their rural parishes, the Cajuns developed a strong culture and dialect unlike those of cosmopolitan New Orleans. In 1847, *Evangeline*, a poetic commemoration of the hardships of the Acadian diaspora by Henry Wadsworth Longfellow, was published; it was widely read and quoted in the region.

In the first half of the nineteenth century, Louisiana experienced an economic boom generated by slave labor on flourishing plantations producing cotton and sugarcane. The political affairs of the state became seriously divided between the French and English speakers, between the planters and the small farmers, and between the slaveholders and the antislavery elements. A large sector of the Cajuns opposed Louisiana's secession from the Union in 1861. The secession was effectively ended with the occupation of New Orleans in 1862. The Cajuns, most supporting the Union, were dismayed at being treated as rebels along with the supporters of secession.

Louisiana's disrupted plantation system was replaced by sharecropping and small tenancy. In the latter half of the nineteenth century, while Louisiana slowly recovered from the effects of Civil War and the end of slavery, the Cajuns mostly lived in the bayou regions of the Mississippi Delta, working as fishermen or fur trappers. They continued to shun contact with outsiders.

In the first decades of the twentieth century the schools in the French Triangle, run mostly by Irish priests, forbade the speaking of French even in the playground. In 1921 the teaching of Cajun French was outlawed in all Louisiana schools. By the 1930s and 1940s Louisiana's large Creole population had been virtually assimilated, but the Cajuns remained separate and unassimilated.

In 1928 a local politician, Huey Long, became the virtual dictator of Louisiana, withstanding political foes and the federal government of President Franklin D. Roosevelt. Long, determined to end the isolation of the Cajuns, approved the building of roads into the bayous in the 1930s.

Oil and natural gas, discovered in the delta region at the beginning of the century, brought new prosperity to the Cajun region. Work in the new oil fields, particularly since the 1950s, became a staple of the Cajun economy. The new prosperity brought changes in attitudes, education, and also contact with the outside world. Much of Louisiana's oil and gas is in traditional Cajun areas.

A revival of the Cajun culture and language, begun in the 1970s, accelerated over the next decade. The Louisiana state legislature officially recognized the region of Acadiana for its unique Cajun and Acadian heritage. The first book written in Cajun, in 1986, was titled *Lâche pas la patate*, freely translated as *Hang in There*. Until the 1980s the Cajun language lacked literature, dictionaries, or grammar. Cajun children were unable to use the textbooks kindly sent by Québecois* as a gesture of solidarity; they had to use French textbooks from Ontario, designed for native English speakers. The University of Southwestern Louisiana, also called the

Université des Acadiens, began to offer Acadian studies as part of the ethnic revival. French was reintroduced to schools, but the Cajuns protested the move as standard French was being taught, not their cherished dialect. The French now taught in the region is the standard French of Paris, while the Cajun dialect, spoken across a wide area, is relegated to the status of a local patois.

The growth of nationalism in French-speaking Quebec raised fear that separatist sentiment might spread to the Cajuns. In 1988 a bill was passed by the Louisiana state legislature making the Cajuns a legal minority, therefore eligible for federal monetary assistance in spite of the general prosperity of the region.

In the 1980s and 1990s, the Cajuns have renewed their ties to the Acadians of New Brunswick, Nova Scotia, and Maine. Their new confidence has translated into political power, with the Cajun parishes regularly represented by Cajun politicians. Cajuns have dominated Louisiana politics for most of the period since the 1970s. Prosperity now depends on the number of oil jobs available and the ability of local politicians to lure new employers into Cajun areas.

Renewed contact with the Acadians and Québecois of eastern Canada in the 1980s and 1990s, particularly in the context of several Francophone organizations of French North American communities, stimulated interest in the Cajun language, heritage, and culture. Cultural contacts with other French-speaking communities, facilitated by technological advances in communications, have drawn many younger Cajuns back to their culture as interest increases in their unique history and traditions.

The Congrés Mondial Acadien-Louisiane, an international reunion of descendants of the Acadians was held in 1999 to chart the future of the Cajun nation. Negative stereotypes continue to endure, which many activists claim is the result of a lack of national status. Others demanded greater cultural, educational, and fiscal control and for real autonomy for the region known as Acadiana.

The Cajuns remain a nation within a nation, but, unlike so many of the world's other national groups, the Cajuns do not feel victimized. Cajun rights are protected, their language remains vital, and their culture, in spite of the allures of modern life, remains intact. The only Cajuns currently active in the nationalist cause focus on trying to get an apology from the British government for the harsh expulsion of their ancestors from Canada in 1755. Many Cajuns hope that Queen Elizabeth II will offer the long-awaited apology during a visit to Canada scheduled for the fall of 2002.

SELECTED BIBLIOGRAPHY:

Ancelet, Barry Jean, ed. *Cajun Country*. 1991.
Brasseaux, Carl A. *Acadian to Cajun: Transformation of a People 1803–1877*. 1996.
LeBois, Ruby. *Cajun*. 1999.
Post, Lauren C. *Cajun Sketches: From the Prairies of Southwest Louisiana*. 1990.

Californians

Californios

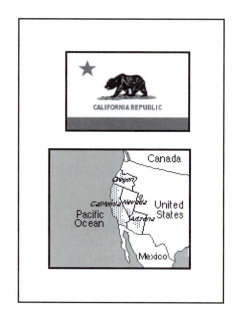

POPULATION: Approximately (2002e) 31,000,000 Californians in the United States, concentrated in the western state of California. Smaller communities live in neighboring states and as far away as Colorado and Idaho. Outside the United States there are Californian communities in Mexico.

THE CALIFORNIAN HOMELAND: The Californian homeland is known for its stunning contrasts, from the rainy northern coast to the arid Colorado Desert of the south. The mountains that divide California from the rest of the Union, the Sierra Nevada, exceed the Rocky Mountains in height. The highest and lowest points in the 48 coterminous states are in California—Mount Whitney at 14,494 feet (4,418 meters) above sea level and Death Valley at 282 feet (86 meters) below sea level. Despite its highly urbanized population, the Californians are the major agricultural producers in the United States. State of California: 158,706 sq. mi.—411,049 sq. km, (2002e) 34,341,000—white 54%, Hispanic 32%, Asian 10%, black 8%, native Californian 0.06%. The Californian capital is Sacramento, (2002e) 420,000, metropolitan area, 1,925,000. The major cultural centers are Los Angeles, (2002e), 3,761,000, metropolitan area, 16,438,000; San Francisco, (2002e), 781,000, metropolitan area, 7,035,000; San Diego, (2002e), 1,246,000, metropolitan area, 2,735,000; and San Jose, 978,000, metropolitan area, 1,732,000.

FLAG: The Californian flag, the Bear Flag, which is based on the original 1846 flag that was destroyed in the 1906 San Francisco earthquake and fire, is a white field bearing a centered California Grizzly bear with a broad red stripe and the former name of the state, California Republic, at the bottom and a single five-pointed red star on the upper hoist.

PEOPLE AND CULTURE: Californians are a people of mixed background, including in their ancestry peoples from all over the world and all over the United States. Assimilation of new arrivals, a long tradition in

California, continues, even though a quarter of Californians in 2000 had been born outside the United States. The influence of the Spanish settlers is evident in architecture and place names. The many Spanish surnames reflect the immigration from Latin America, particularly Mexico, during the twentieth century. Californian culture is marked by widespread public involvement in the arts and by enthusiasm for cultural trappings as symbols of achievement. Californians lavish expenditures on galleries, museums, and concert halls. Intermarriage among the various groups represented in the state is very high, reinforcing the regional Californian identity. There are about 200,000 native Californians, who represent the most neglected part of the population.

LANGUAGE AND RELIGION: The Californians mostly speak English, a primarily accentless American dialect incorporating extensive borrowings from Spanish. The language, as spoken in the state, also employs many words originating in Chinese, Japanese, and other languages spoken as second languages. The largest of the minority languages is Spanish, spoken by nearly a third of the population, although increasingly native Spanish speakers are bilingual, also speaking English fluently. In the 1990s, Californians voted down bilingual education in the state, over half the Hispanic population voting with the majority on the issue.

Only about a third of Californians list church affiliations, although generally Roman Catholicism is centered on the Bay Area of northern California, while Protestant sects predominant in those parts of southern California settled by migrants from the southern and midwestern states. The large Jewish population is concentrated in parts of Los Angeles and San Francisco. Los Angeles has long been famed for its exotic religious cults, television evangelists, and faith healers.

NATIONAL HISTORY: The early history of the native Californians is mostly unknown. As the descendants of migrants from northeastern Asia, little is known of their way of life before the Spanish arrived in the region in the sixteenth century. Population estimates of the indigenous population in the sixteenth century range from 130,000 to 275,000, making it the largest indigenous population of any part of the later United States. With small exceptions they were hunters and gatherers, living off the abundant bounty of the California landscape. Speaking at least 135 dialects, they never developed a warrior society like the more famous indigenous peoples of the Great Plains.

There is no definitive version of the origin of the name "California," but there is wide support for the contention that the name is derived from a 1510 Spanish novel that described an island paradise called California. A Spanish navigator, Juan Rodríguez Cabrillo, first sighted the coast in 1542. An adventurous merchant, Sebastián Vizcaíno, sailed along the southern California coast in 1602, sighting and naming San Diego, Santa Catalina Island, Santa Barbara, and Monterey Bay. The region was neglected by the Europeans for more than three centuries after its first sightings.

Gaspar de Portola led a disastrous 1769 expedition to California for the Spanish crown; about half his expedition died of malnutrition and scurvy. He wrote in his report that the Russians wanted California and that the Spanish government should let them have it. By 1820 only 3,750 Spaniards occupied California, which was a neglected and isolated part of the crumbling Spanish Empire. Mexico broke away from Spanish rule in 1821, and by 1825 the Californios had pledged loyalty to the new Mexican state. California went from a neglected Spanish territory to a neglected, isolated province of the Mexican Republic.

The Franciscan friar Junípero Serra established the first Spanish mission at San Diego in 1769. Forced labor, violence, and diseases introduced by the Europeans had decimated the indigenous population for decades after the Spaniards' arrival and by 1700 only an estimated 50,000 survived. Only in the mid-twentieth century did the native Californian population begin to increase. Spanish missionaries subjugated and converted the California Indians through a chain of missions stretching north to Sonoma. When the missions were secularized in 1833, some 30,000 native Californians were farming under the direction of priests and soldiers at 21 missions.

In 1831 the Mexican government sent Manuel Victoria to govern California. He attempted to rule by the heavy hand of Mexican law and opposed the secularization of church land. His oppressive rule was opposed by the Californios, who raised an army and fought the Mexican forces. Victoria was recalled, and a new governor, Nicholas Gutierrez, was installed. In 1833 the Californios and the mission Indians received the secularized church lands and assets, which were mostly parceled out to political favorites.

The Californios marched on the capitol of Monterey in 1836 and forced the governor to surrender. They declared California a free and sovereign state within the Mexican republic with broad powers of autonomy. The Mexican government conceded, and the Californio leader, Juan Alvarado, was named governor. For five years California functioned as a sovereign state, but in 1842 the Mexicans attempted to regain control. An army of *cholos*, former convicts employed as soldiers, led by Manuel Micheltorena marched on California, where he announced his new status as governor while moving on Monterey. His soldiers, raping, pillaging, and looting, took control of the territory, but in 1845 the Californians, having raised a new army, defeated Micheltorena, who fled back to Mexico.

The first organized group of American settlers arrived in California in 1841, having traveled overland from Missouri. Americans, called Anglos, had lived in California for decades, but in small numbers. Many had taken vows of loyalty to Mexico and to the Catholic Church and had married into the old California families. Generally relations between the Californios and the Anglos were good. In late 1845, John C. Frémont with a party of 60 men, having crossed the Sierra Nevada, arrived in California on an exploratory expedition. In spite of promises to leave the territory after wintering in the Central Valley, Frémont raised the U.S. flag and vowed to fight to defend it. The Californios raised a force of volunteers, and Frémont moved on to Oregon, leaving California in turmoil. Rumors spread that Governor Antonio Castro was organizing an army to expel all Anglos from California, and relations quickly soured.

Frémont returned from Oregon and encouraged a group of Anglos in the Central Valley to seize Californio soldiers. Another group, without Frémont's authority, seized the presidio of Sonoma and proclaimed the creation of the Bear Flag Republic. The Anglos defeated a Californio force sent against them. Frémont seized control of the new republic, not knowing that the United States and Mexico were already at war. U.S. forces invaded the territory and occupied Monterey on 7 July 1846. Modern California derives from the discovery of gold in 1848, discovered just nine days before the Mexican government signed the Treaty of Guadalupe, which ceded California to the United States. The Territory of California was admitted to the Union on 9 September 1850 as the 31st state.

The first settlers from the United States were mostly farmers of Anglo-Saxon descent from the Midwest. Following the discovery of gold at Sutter's Mill, near Sacramento, a more cosmopolitan population appeared. Ships full of immigrants sailed into San Francisco from the Atlantic ports of North America, from Europe, and from the Orient. In 1850 more than half the California population were in their twenties, mostly male and single. Large numbers of Irish, French, and Italians settled in San Francisco and the areas around San Francisco Bay.

Immigrants from Europe predominated in the first years of statehood. Only a few hundred Chinese lived in California in 1850, but two years later at least one out of every 10 was Chinese. Most Asians performed menial labor. Discrimination, particularly among the latest arrivals, was directed at the Asian population. An alien land law intended to discourage land ownership among Asians was not ruled unconstitutional until 1952. At one time the testimony of Chinese in courts was declared void. California law authorized separate schools for Asians until 1936, and not until 1943 was the Chinese Exclusion Act repealed.

As discrimination against the Chinese was rife, Japanese were encouraged to immigrate. In 1900 alone more than 12,000 Japanese entered California. Prospering as farmers, they came to control more than 10% of all California farmland by 1920, even though they constituted only 2% of the population. Los Angeles became the center of the Japanese-Californian community, while San Francisco's China Town became the Americas' largest Chinese settlement.

Discrimination against the Japanese erupted at the outbreak of World

War II, when some 93,000 Japanese-Californians, about 60%, called Nisei, had been born in the state. Most of the older Japanese were Issei, adults who had immigrated before the U.S. Congress halted the immigrant influx in 1924. During 1942 almost all of the Japanese-Californians, both Nisei and Issei, were rounded up and moved to isolated camps in inland areas where they were held under tight security until 1945. At the end of the war they found their properties had been sold for taxes or storage fees and their former neighborhoods were gone. After many years of litigation, about 26,000 claimants were finally reimbursed for their losses at about a third of the claimed values. In 1940 about 85% of the Japanese-Californians had been farmers, but with their lands stolen they became gardeners or laborers and eventually moved into businesses and the professions. In 1988 the U.S. Congress voted to grant $20,000 to each of those interned in 1942. Asian immigration to California again surged in the 1970s and 1980s, with Vietnamese, Filipinos, and Koreans the most numerous of the newcomers. By 1987 the Asian portion of the Californian population had grown to about 6% of the total.

Few blacks settled in California until World War II; however, between 1940 and 1980 the black population of the San Francisco Bay area grew from about 5,000 to over 86,000; the number of blacks in the Los Angeles area grew from 64,000 to around 900,000 in the same period. The number of black Californians increased rapidly, as blacks left the poorer southern states to settle mostly in California's growing urban areas. Problems between whites and blacks are less pronounced in California, a state that was largely formed after the abolition of slavery, than in the rest of America.

Thousands of Mexicans entered southern California illegally in the years up to 1987, when the U.S. Congress voted to grant an amnesty to those who could establish specific conditions of prior residence. By 1988 over 8,500,000 Hispanics in California had received temporary residence status under amnesty provisions. In April 2000 the Mexican government passed a law allowing the immigrants in the United States to hold dual citizenship, but very few Mexican-Californians applied.

The rapidly growing nonwhite population of California has confronted police and other officials, particularly in Los Angeles, protesting discrimination and high unemployment. Black riots leveled much of Los Angeles's mostly black Watts area in 1965 and race rioting in south-central Los Angeles in 1992 were the worst in the state's history.

Writers and artists in the late nineteenth century established a regional tradition in literature and the arts. Environmental writers extolled California's natural wonders, while socially aware writers detailed the many ills of Californian society in the early years of the twentieth century. An influx of literary figures worked as screenwriters in Hollywood in the 1930s and 1940s. The northern California towns of Carmel, Big Sur, and Sausalito are centers of diverse arts. Hollywood, responsible for the bulk of national television and film output, remains an international symbol of glamor.

California's spectacular population growth began to level off by 1970. Later migration was mostly from the crowded coastal cities to the smaller interior towns and rural areas. Californians also began to migrate to the cities of the northwestern states of Oregon and Washington and the mountain states, where Californian culture quickly took root. Demographers predict continued population growth in California, but these predictions have been scaled down from earlier years, although the state is likely to maintain its place as the United States' most populous state.

By the 1980s, Californians made up the most urban population in the United States, centered mainly along the coast, with some three-quarters of the Californian population concentrated in the Los Angeles, San Francisco, and San Diego urban areas. A profound disaffection with growth had set in throughout the state's urban areas, leading to a growing anti-immigrant movement and a new emphasis on the English language and assimilation.

A small national movement, demanding more self-government, evolved from this dissatisfaction. The nationalists claim that California, with a population larger than Canada's, would have the seventh-largest world economy, even though California now pays up to eight billion dollars more to the U.S. government than it receives in services. A minority within the national movement, seeking full independence, push for California to resume its status as an independent Bear Flag Republic.

The U.S. government, in what was seen as an insult to all Californians, reneged on a 1998 promise to provide two surplus coastal patrol craft in California and gave them to Ghana instead. Many Californians, not just the tiny nationalist movement, were outraged that the federal government felt that the West African state was more important to the United States than the state of California.

In 1998 the government of California announced that it would increase its unofficial embassies in foreign countries. The four new embassies will be in Singapore, South Korea, China, and Brazil. Californians have maintained foreign delegations since the 1960s, and by 1998 they had unofficial embassies in Mexico, South Africa, Germany, Indonesia, Hong Kong, Taiwan, and Japan. Although the delegations concentrate on Californian trade, they are gradually taking on other responsibilities.

California, at the turn of the twenty-first century, is the most populous state in the Union, and its per capita income is one of the highest in the world. The fluidity of the Californians' social, economic, and political lives gives California the aura of a laboratory for testing new modes of living. Early in the twenty-first century white Californians will become a minority in the state that was 90% white in 1900. In spite of serious racial tension, it is remarkable how little friction has occurred. Californians now represent one of the most polyethnic societies in the world, a new type of nation not based on ethnicity, language, or heritage but on shared experience as citizens of one of the world's most dynamic regions. In June 1998, Californians, including a majority of the Latinos, voted to end the state's bilingual education, under which non-English-speaking children had been taught in their own language for several years. Latinos, like many other Californians, see English as the language of advancement.

Anglo and Latino Californians have an intermarriage rate five times that of the United States as a whole. A striking number of native Californians continue to think that immigrants reinforce rather than undermine what is best in California. The Californians claim to have invented the new high-technology economy and are engaged in inventing a new society, one that has abolished class and race and that judges people purely on the basis of merit.

In the late 1990s and early 2000s, as immigrants pour into California, many Californians are migrating to neighboring states and into the mountain states farther east. The migration has fostered an economic boom in the regions, as the Californians bring their vitality and entrepreneurial spirit to what had formerly been considered California's hinterland. The regions where the Californians are settling are growth areas in their own rights and are becoming like the California of the 1980s.

The serious electricity crisis of early 2001 fueled resentment against the federal government and the neighboring states unwilling to aid during the crisis. Small nationalist groups began publishing a long list of California's production of fruits, vegetables, aerospace, and hi-tech that it exports to other parts of the United States, while neighboring states have refused to aid the state during its ongoing energy crisis. Plagued by power cuts, a sharp downturn in the technology industry has dented Californians' traditional optimism and raised questions of identity, with rival regional identities giving way to a new feeling of a common identity as Californians.

SELECTED BIBLIOGRAPHY:

Collier, Michael. *A Land in Motion.* 1999.
Hall, John, and Charles Lindholm. *Is America Breaking Apart?* 1999.
Maharidge, Dale. *The Coming of the White Minority: California's Eruptions and the Nation's Future.* 1997.
Sinclair, Nick. *California.* 2000.

Cambas

Cruceños; Kambas

POPULATION: Approximately (2002e) 2,500,000 Cambas in Bolivia, concentrated in the Oriente, the lowland provinces of Santa Cruz and El Beni east of the Antiplano, and the highlands plateau in the Andes Mountains. Outside the region there are Camba communities in the highlands, particularly in La Paz, and in adjacent areas of Brazil.

THE CAMBA HOMELAND: Santa Cruz occupies the Llanos, the subtropical and tropical lowlands east of the high Antiplano, the Bolivian plateau in the Andes Mountains. The region, called El Oriente, the East, the largest and most sparsely populated region of Bolivia, includes the upper reaches of the Amazon River basin in the northern districts. The Oriente forms the Bolivian departments of Santa Cruz and El Beni. *El Oriente (Santa Cruz)*: 222,554 sq. mi.—576,564 sq. km, (2002e) 2,410,000—Cambas 74%, Kollas (Highland Bolivians) 20%, Guarani 3%, Brazilians 2%. The Camba capital and major cultural center is Santa Cruz, (2002e) 1,092,000. The other important cultural center is Trinidad, (2002e) 82,000, the capital of El Beni.

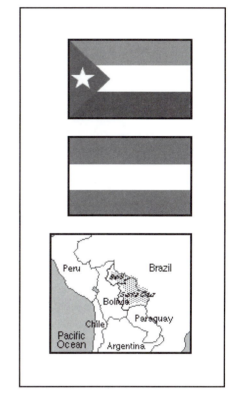

FLAG: The national flag, the flag of the former republic, is a vertical tricolor of green, white, and red bearing a pale blue triangle at the hoist charged with a five-pointed white star. The provincial flag of Santa Cruz has horizontal stripes of green, white, green. The El Beni provincial flag (not shown) is a field of solid green.

PEOPLE AND CULTURE: Cambas, also called Cruceños, are mostly of mixed European and Indian background, with a substantial unmixed population of European descent, and a Guarani minority in the southeast. The Cambas are further divided into the ruling class, mostly of white European descent, the mixed population, and the indigenous peoples. Physically, historically, and culturally separated from the highland Bolivian culture of the Andes Mountains, the Cambas are a lowland, tropical people. Mostly farmers in the fertile plains, a growing number of Cambas are involved in the drug trade, which is estimated to support over 750,000 directly and indirectly, almost the entire Oriente region. Indigenous peoples of mixed background are called Cholos, a term that connotes a person who is neither Indian nor "gente decente," the decent people, or the white Cambas. The Cambas are increasingly urbanized, leaving the poor rural zones to the Cholos and Indios. Racism and discrimination are widespread.

LANGUAGE AND RELIGION: The Cambas speak Spanish, in a dialect locally called Camba or Kamba, which combines influences from Portuguese and Guarani. Camba Spanish is less influenced by native languages than that of the Bolivian Antiplano, where Aymara and Quechua borrowings have developed a separate dialect. The majority of the Cambas speak standard Spanish but retain the antiquated dialect that has been spoken in the region for over two centuries. The Camba dialect is the language of the home and of intergroup communications, while standard Spanish is the language of education, media, and government.

The majority of the Cambas are Roman Catholic, with about 90% of the population stating that they are members of the Roman Catholic Church, although traditional adherence to religious practices is declining. Protestant sects, particularly evangelical groups, have been gaining adherents since the 1960s. A small Mennonite population has lived in the region since the nineteenth century.

NATIONAL HISTORY: Sparsely populated by Native American tribes, later called Indians, the region came under the influence of the highly advanced civilizations of the Andean highlands. In the early sixteenth century Spanish explorers crossed the region but, finding little gold or treasure, moved on. The Spanish, seeking riches not land, ignored the fertile region for decades. Spanish colonists moving north from Paraguay finally settled the area in the mid-sixteenth century, founding the town of San José de Chiquitos in 1561. The Spanish settlement was repeatedly attacked until 1595, when it was moved to a location along the Piray River and renamed Santa Cruz de la Sierra.

Physically isolated, the inhabitants of the Oriente developed their own cultural traditions and a character distinct from the centers of Spanish activity in the highlands. Dominated by Europeans and Cholos, the region became a producer of tropical produce, its main trade links being with the Rio Plate region to the south. In 1776 the Spanish authorities separated the region from the Andean provinces and added it to the Viceroyalty of La Plata, the colony governed from Buenos Aires. In 1782 it was organized as a separate intendency, or province, of La Plata.

The Cambas of Santa Cruz rebelled against Spanish rule in 1809, in one of the earliest colonial rebellions in Spanish America. Two years later, in 1811, the rebels drove the Spanish authorities from the province and declared Santa Cruz an independent republic. Spanish reinforcements ended the secession, but rebellions spread through the Spanish Empire as the Cambas joined with the Kollas, the highlanders of the Altiplano, to fight the Spanish. In 1825 the rebels triumphed, calling their new country Bolivia. Santa Cruz, organized as a Bolivian province in 1832, split ten years later, when El Beni was hived off as a separate province.

Isolated and restive under the domination of the highland Kollas, the region remained the domain of the European and mixed populations, unlike the largely Indian population of the Altiplano. The cultural differences created tension that erupted in Camba rebellions in 1892 and 1904. Each Camba uprising was ended by troops sent from the highlands, increasing the Camba resentment and support for separation from Bolivia.

Disputes between newly independent Bolivia and Paraguay over the Gran Chaco, the region just south of Oriente, increased in the late nineteenth century. The Bolivian government in the Altiplano, fearing that the Paraguayans would ferment revolution among the lowland Cambas, who had historical ties to Paraguay, increasingly garrisoned the region with Kolla troops, who were culturally and physically distinct from the local population.

A renewed revolt spread across the region in 1920, resulting in a virtual military occupation by Bolivian troops. On 25 May 1921 the Cambas resumed the rebellion, which quickly escalated into a civil war. The rebels held off Kolla troops, and Camba nationalist leaders declared the independence of Santa Cruz on 8 July 1921, but the breakaway republic fell to Bolivian forces less than a year later. Nationalists formed the Santa Cruz National Party to work secretly for the restoration of an independent republic. The Cambas, restive and unhappy under Kolla occupation, again rebelled on 1 July 1924. Fighting swept the region as rural Cambas joined the rebellion and the rebel forces tried to drive the Kollas from their homeland, but again they were defeated by the more numerous highlanders.

Tension between Bolivia and Paraguay over the territory called the Gran Chaco increased in the 1920s. In 1928 the two countries both laid claim to the region, believed to have substantial petroleum reserves. Four years later, in 1932, war broke between the two countries. In 1935, after three years of war, the Paraguayan government announced its support for an independent Camba republic in Santa Cruz. In May 1935 Camba prisoners of war requested separation from the other Bolivians. Over 150 officers and 6,000 men, released by the Paraguayans, swore allegiance to the proposed Camba state. On 22 May 1935 the leaders declared Santa Cruz independent of Bolivia. The end of the Chaco War and the negotiated partition of the Gran Chaco territory freed the Kollas to deal with the Camba secession.

Social divisions remained rigid and conservative until the 1940s. Since the initiation of major social reforms in 1952, a considerable portion of the Camba population has had access to schools, colleges, and universities. The descendants of Spanish settlers traditionally formed the region's ruling elite, mostly landowners, mine operators, and ranchers. In the post–World War II era, there has been increasing intermarriage between the Spanish and the population, and the division between the two groups has become blurred. Increasingly the Cambas see themselves as a separate people, and the former class structure is giving way to a revived regional identity.

Oriente remained isolated until the 1950s and the construction of a 422-mile (650 km) railroad linking the province to Brazil's Atlantic ports. Even though the region remained restive and a renewed rebellion broke out in 1961, settlers spread across the fertile plains. Lands traditionally held in the form of large estates, most dating from the days of the Spanish conquest, were largely broken up as part of a domestic colonization program aimed at alleviating overpopulation in the Altiplano. The opening of the Cochabamba–Santa Cruz highway in 1954 was crucial in ending Oriente's long isolation from the Andes. Development accelerated in the 1960s and 1970s, based on the fertility of the land, which yielded two crops a year without fertilizer. The exploitation of the region's natural wealth attracted thousands of poor highlanders, again raising tension between the Cambas and the Kollas.

A leftist uprising, led by Castroite Che Guevara, erupted in southern Oriente in 1967. Although Guevara failed to mobilize the Cambas, his appeal to the poorest of the region was a threat to both the Bolivian government and the Cambas. The rebellion ended when Guevara was killed by Bolivian troops.

In the 1970s Santa Cruz became a center of Bolivia's oil and natural gas production. A disproportionate amount of the profits from Oriente's natural resources, according to Camba sources, was used for development in the more heavily populated Altiplano. The discovery of oil brought a renewed influx of Kollas, attracted to the region's booming economic climate.

Attempts by the Bolivian government, supported by American antidrug funds and military equipment, to curtail the drug trade affected the entire region. The militarization of the region sparked a resurgence of nationalism as Camba leaders compared the situation to the military occupation of the 1920s and 1930s. Resistance to the antidrug effort has been fed by a steady trafficker-financed propaganda campaign depicting the U.S. antidrug agency and the Bolivian government as the oppressors of the Cambas. The provincial leaders denounced the government actions and declared that the drug trade would continue until a viable economic alternative became available to the Camba farmers.

The drug controversy and rising tension between the lowland Cambas and the Kollas of the Altiplano have fueled the region's nationalist resurgence. Rich in coca dollars, the Cambas have established close commercial relations with neighboring parts of Brazil, particularly the Corumba region, 390 miles east of Santa Cruz. Trade with Brazil has become much more important than the region's ties to La Paz and the Andes provinces. The settlement of over 15,000 Brazilian farmers in the region since 1985 has strengthened Oriente's ties to Brazil and further weakened the hold of the Bolivian government over the Camba lowlands.

In 1995, the Bolivian government proclaimed a state of siege in the Chapare region, where the government is waging an aggressive antidrug campaign. Unspecified threats to state companies operating in the Santa Cruz region led to a ban on all forms of protest. The Chapare coca growers are increasingly powerful in the region and are supported by trade unions, peasant organizations, and Camba regional groups. The antidrug crackdown led to a worsening of the economic situation in the region and raised resentment of the government's heavy-handed policies. The antidrug forces enjoyed wide powers and often abused locals, even those not involved in coca production. Thousands of people were reportedly imprisoned, and such abuses as rape, looting, and unprovoked attacks resulted in a backlash of antigovernment sentiment in the region. The state of siege was lifted in October 1995.

Economic policies that favored the Altiplano, the highland region of western Bolivia where 60% of the Bolivian population live, have led to protests and demonstrations. The protesters oppose a controversial land reform bill promoted by the National Institute for Agrarian Reform. The business community, indigenous peoples, and rural peasants united in a new organization, the Santa Cruz–El Beni Association, to work for the economic and political autonomy of the eastern lowlands of Bolivia.

General Hugo Banzer, who was Bolivia's dictator in the 1970s, was voted into power in June 1997 on promises to fight corruption, eradicate coca production, and modernize the Bolivian state. His return to power demonstrated how democratic aspirations are still shadowed by the lingering desire to for a firm administration by the Kollas of the Altiplano. Conflicts over land and regional differences increased rapidly in the late 1990s, with the government responding with an increased Kolla (highlander) military presence in the restive lowlands. Peasant unions blocked highways leading to the large cities in 1998, part of a widespread strike by workers demanding higher wages and modification of the land law. Camba landowners oppose the redistribution of land, leading to a growing conflict over land ownership.

Government economic reforms in the late 1990s have helped the economy but have done little to draw the two halves of the country closer together. Oil and gas from the Santa Cruz region promise even greater development, with a new $1.9 billion pipeline from Santa Cruz to Sao Paulo in Brazil, 1,950 miles (3,150 km) to the east. Agrobusiness is also growing rapidly, but Cambas complain that transportation links continue stifle the economy of their homeland.

In early 2000 Bolivia emerged from a virtual state of siege, but instability remains a serious problem not only in Bolivia but throughout the Andean region from Colombia and Venezuela to Ecuador and Peru. Recent events in Bolivia, South America's poorest country, have exposed fractures in the society between the power centers in the highlands and the increasingly separate and more prosperous tropical lowlands. The Andes region of western South America is rapidly becoming the "Balkans of Latin America."

With so many migrants arriving in the lowlands in such a short period of time, the previously isolated lowlanders are resentful and the fierce regionalism that has always existed has developed even further. Cambas have always felt resentment toward their western countrymen and the political and cultural dominance of the Andean regions. Their reaction is an extreme regionalism that in many cases converts into outright prejudice against Kollas, as with housing and creation of exclusively Camba neighborhoods. It is a response to the threat that so many migrants pose to the cultural autonomy and political independence that Cambas have always prized.

It is not simply a symbolic response. By promoting the bi-polarity of the Camba/Kolla identity, Cambas can use prejudice and a constructed ideology of race to keep political, social, and economic power in the hands of lowlanders. Cambas have little desire to share their wealth with the rest of the country simply for equality's sake since they do not think of their prosperity as tied to that of the rest of nation. The Cambas' independent pride is fierce.

The Kollas, mostly Quechua-Aymara* from highland Bolivia, have been relegated to the lowest rung of society in El Oriente. Menial jobs no longer done by the more prosperous Cambas continue to drag in the poor, undereducated excess population of the Altiplano. The growing antipathy between the Cambas and the Kollas is a serious threat to Bolivia's future.

The drug-fueled Camba economy, which increasingly separates the fertile lowlands from Bolivia's economic and political center in the Altiplano, has given the Cambas a new confidence. In spite of American-backed government efforts to eradicate cocoa production, the drug trade continues as the mainstay of the Camba economy and the reason for the continued growth of Santa Cruz. As Santa Cruz continues to grow, it will remain as a center of Camba sentiment, a forceful challenge to the traditional center of political, economic, and cultural power in the Andean highlands.

SELECTED BIBLIOGRAPHY:

Lagos, Maria L. *Autonomy and Power*. 1994.

Leons, Barbara, and Harry Sanabria, eds. *Coca, Cocaine and the Bolivian Reality*. 1997.

Lewis, Norman. *Eastern Bolivia: The White Promised Land*. 1978.

Stearman, Allyn M. *Camba and Kolla: Migration and Development in Santa Cruz, Bolivia*. 1985.

Canarians

Canarios; Canary Islanders

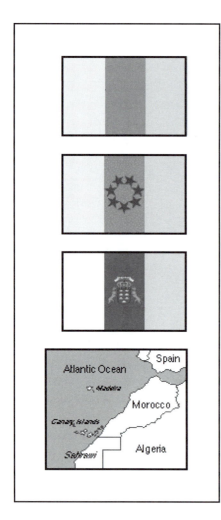

POPULATION: Approximately (2002e) 1,750,000 Canarians in Europe, the majority in the Canary Islands, but with substantial numbers living in mainland Spain, particularly in Andalusia* and the Madrid region. Outside Europe there are sizable Canarian communities in Venezuela and other Latin American countries and in the American state of Louisiana.

THE CANARIAN HOMELAND: The Canarian homeland, the Canary Islands, is an archipelago of 13 mountainous, volcanic islands, with the closest island lying 67 miles off the coast of southern Morocco and 823 miles (1,324 km) southwest of the Spanish mainland. The islands have constituted an autonomous region of Spain since 1982. The are divided into two provinces—Santa Cruz de Tenerife, which comprises Tenerife, La Palma, Gomera, and Hierro; and Las Palmas, with Grand Canary, Fuenteventura, Lanzarote, Alegranza, Graciosa, and Isla de Lobos. The last three islands are uninhabited. *Autonomous Region of the Canary Islands (Comunidad Autonoma de las Islas Canarias)*: 2,796 sq. mi.—7,242 sq. km, (2002e) 1,803,000—Canarian 90%, other Spanish and other Europeans 10%. The capital and a major cultural center is Santa Cruz de Tenerife, on Tenerife, (2002e) 218,000. The other major Canarian cultural center is the islands' major port, Las Palmas de Gran Canaria, on Grand Canary, (2002e) 367,000.

FLAG: The Canarian national flag is a horizontal tricolor of white, pale blue, and yellow. The same white, pale blue, and yellow flag, with the addition of seven green stars on the center stripe, is the flag of the largest nationalist organization, the Movement for the Autonomy and Independence of the Canary Archipelago (MAIAC). The official flag of the Canary

Islands is the same tricolor with the addition of the coat of arms, a centered blue shield flanked by dogs.

PEOPLE AND CULTURE: The Canarians, also called Islenos, are mostly descendants of colonists from mainland Spain in the fifteenth century. Although many diverse peoples have settled in the islands, the majority can trace their roots to the southern Spanish region of Andalusia. Among rural Canarians there is a high incidence of fair hair and eyes, considered holdovers from the archipelago's original Berber inhabitants. The Canarians often refer to people from the Spanish mainland as Goths, referring to the early medieval conquerors of Spain. Isolated from the Spanish mainland, the islanders developed a distinctive culture that incorporates traits and customs unique to the islands.

LANGUAGE AND RELIGION: The Spanish spoken in the islands is a separate dialect called Canario, which some experts consider a subdialect of the Andalusian dialect of Spanish; however, the dialect displays only a slight Andalusian accent and incorporates many words peculiar to the archipelago and even retains most archaic Portuguese influences. The dialect, which developed during the isolation of the islands until the early twentieth century, retains many antiquated words, expressions, and syntax that have disappeared elsewhere. The Canarians also speak standard Spanish, the language of education, government, and communications. In the New World, the Canarian dialect became known as Isleno.

The Canarians, considered the most conservative of the Spanish peoples, are overwhelmingly Roman Catholic. The religious traditions and rituals are often associated with archaic customs that have mostly disappeared from mainland Spain. Traditionally the village church was the center of Canarian life, both secular and religious. The migration to urban areas, beginning in the 1960s, has reduced the influence and power of the Church, but Catholic traditions, particularly the celebration and saints' days, remain part of the popular culture.

NATIONAL HISTORY: The islands, thought to mark the western limit of the world in ancient times, received their name from the Latin word for dog, *canis*, due to the fierce dogs encountered in the islands by ancient maritime peoples. Known as the Fortunate Islands, the archipelago was familiar to the ancient peoples of the Mediterranean, who often sailed west through the Pillars of Hercules. The Roman writers Pliny and Plutarch mention an expedition to the islands by Mauritanians from northwestern Africa around 40 B.C., when the islands were named.

Fair Berbers from North Africa, the Guanche, believed to have arrived in the islands with Phoenician colonists from ancient Carthage, were transported to the islands as workers or slaves. The Guanche regressed to a tribal existence when contact with the mainland ceased following the Roman destruction of Carthage in 146 B.C. The tribes were divided into small clan groups, and conflicts were frequent. Much of the earlier civilization of the islands was abandoned or destroyed. According to Arab chronicles, Arab traders landed on Grand Canaria in A.D. 999 and established a limited trade with the Guanche.

The islands were virtually forgotten as Europe entered the Dark Ages; the Portuguese rediscovered and claimed them in 1341, although they are shown on a map drawn by the Catalans* earlier in the century. Repulsed by the fierce Guanche warriors, the Portuguese abandoned efforts to colonize the islands. In 1344, a papal bull awarded the islands to the Spanish kingdom of Castile. In 1402 a Norman adventurer, Jean de Betencourt, supported by Castile, took control of Lanzarote. Two years later he proclaimed himself king of the islands. In 1406 he returned to Europe, leaving his nephew Maciot in charge.

The island of Gomera was the object of a Portuguese expedition in 1425, which began an intense Portuguese-Castilian rivalry in the islands. Colonists from impoverished Andalusia, newly reconquered from the Moors, settled some of the islands. By the Treaty of Alcacovas, endorsed by the pope and signed in 1480, the Portuguese government recognized the islands as Spanish territory. In 1496 the Berber Guanches were conquered, and Spanish authority was extended to all the islands. The Guanches, either assimilated or exterminated, soon disappeared completely from the islands.

Christopher Columbus replenished all four of his westbound fleets in the islands, which became important stations on the sea routes that the Spanish established to the New World in the early 1500s. Often attacked by pirates and privateers preying on Spanish shipping, the islands remained remote and isolated from mainland Spain. Sailing for England, Sir Francis Drake attacked the Canarian port towns in 1595; a Dutch attack followed in 1599.

During the seventeenth century, the islanders supplied wine in exchange for fish brought by New England sailors, a trade that sustained the islands following the establishment of more direct sea routes to Spain's American colonies. The Spanish government lost interest in the islands following the independence, in the early nineteenth century, of the majority of the Spanish colonies in the New World.

Ignored and neglected by the Spanish government, only locally produced wine provided the islanders with incomes—until grape blight ruined the vineyards in 1853. The Canarian vineyards were replaced by cochineal until aniline dyes came into use. Sugar cane then replaced aniline dyes as the island's economic mainstay. Unable to rely on the Spanish government, the Canarian culture and way of life developed a strong tradition of self-sufficiency, little-affected by the trends and influences of the Spanish mainland. To the Canarians, the Spanish monarchy was remote and exerted little influence.

In the early 1900s, a sense of their distinctive culture and lifestyle was born amid agitation for an end to their humiliating colonial status. The first stirring of modern Canarian nationalism emerged on the two major islands. A cultural society called Ateneo (Atheneum) raised the first auton-omist flag in 1907.

On 21 September 1927 the islands were formally incorporated into the Spanish state. The government, bowing to the rivalry between the two major islands, Tenerife and Gran Canaria, divided the islands into two sep-arate provinces ruled directly by Madrid. Provincial status, a disappointment to the Canarians, did little to alleviate the problems created by centuries of neglect and underdevelopment.

Francisco Franco, sent to the islands as captain-general in 1932, greatly resented his posting to the remote province, virtual exile for an ambitious officer. Franco's indignation influenced his later decision to lead the Span-ish Fascists in revolt and civil war. In 1936 Franco used the islands as the first base of the Nationalist revolt, which allowed him to consolidate his forces before embarking for nearby Spanish Morocco.

The islands, held by the Nationalists, were virtually unaffected by the civil war that swept mainland Spain from 1936 to 1939. Remote from mainland Spain and politically and economically isolated, the Canarians began to think of their islands as separate from mainland Spain. During the 1950s, the idea of a Canarian identity grew with increased education and the growth of nationalism in nearby Morocco. Tourism, beginning at the same time, brought much-needed income and development and gradually ended the is-land's insularity.

In the 1960s, as national liberation swept the rest of Africa, a national movement formed among the Canarians, claiming that the Spanish gov-ernment continued to treat the islands as a colony. In the late 1960s several small groups formed demanding autonomy for the islands, but the dic-tatorial Franco government soon outlawed them. Several of the small groups combined to form the first avowedly separatist organization, the Movement for the Autonomy and Independence of the Canary Archipel-ago (MAIAC). The Organization of African Unity (OAU) recognized the MAIAC as a legitimate African liberation movement in 1968. Considered by the OAU as an African territory still under foreign rule, many African states and organizations championed the decolonization and independence of the islands. In 1975 the MAIAC announced Libyan support after its secretary-general, Antonio Cubillo, paid a visit to Tripoli. The MAIAC increasingly turned to terrorism to win independence for the islands.

A separatist bombing at Las Palmas Airport on Grand Canary Island on 27 March 1977 forced a Pan American 747 en route from Los Angeles and New York to divert to the overcrowded Los Rodeos Airport on Ten-erife. A runway collision between the American jet and a Dutch 747 re-sulted in the deaths of 583 people, the worst disaster in aviation history. The disaster horrified the Canarians and caused a dramatic loss of support for the separatists.

Democracy returned to Spain at Franco's death in 1975, allowing the formation of regional, even openly nationalist, political parties. In 1979 the Canarians elected an openly separatist deputy to represent them in the new democratic legislature in Madrid. Granted autonomy in 1983, the islands experienced a rapid development of a territorial identity and a resurgence of national sentiment as the memories of the 1977 disaster faded. In 1982 the OAU again declared the islands an African territory still under foreign colonization.

An autonomous community was established on 10 August 1982, after years of Canarian agitation. Spain's entry into the European Economic Community in 1986 raised new issues; the islanders felt they suffered for decisions made far away in Brussels, while their concerns had to be channeled through an often unsympathetic national government in Madrid. Nationalists, with increasing support, advocated independence and bilateral ties to both Spain and the European federation. Supported by the income from over a million tourists a year, the Canarians became increasingly assured and less willing to accept decisions made far from their islands.

The populations of Tenerife and Gran Canaria have grown rapidly relative to the other islands of the archipelago during the twentieth century. The two major islands maintain a fierce rivalry that hinders the islands economically and politically. In late 1988, the proposed site of a new university rekindled the antagonism between the two islands, bringing over 700,000 demonstrators to the streets of Las Palmas and Santa Cruz.

The Canarians experienced a resurgence of culture and national pride during the 1980s and became increasingly more assertive in protecting their culture, dialect, and the fragile environment of their islands. In a further move to reclaim a separate Canarian culture, the regional parliament in April 1991 outlawed bullfights, the cruel and cherished symbol of mainland Spanish culture.

Moderate, pro-autonomy politicians have won support in the islands, and Canarian nationalist parties have become important partners in national coalition governments in Madrid. Canarian participation in the Spanish government in the 1990s eased the pressure for greater autonomy or independence; however, a new Spanish government, elected in early 2000, with a majority in the legislature no longer needed the support of the Canarian nationalist political parties. The decline of Canarian influence in Madrid led to a revival of demands for greater autonomy and financial aid to the poorer regions of the islands.

SELECTED BIBLIOGRAPHY:

Gravette, Andy. *Canary Islands*. 1996.
Lenning, Camille. *Notes from the Canary Islands*. 1996.
Mercer, John. *The Canary Islands: Their Prehistory, Conquest, and Survival*. 1994.
Yeoward, W. *Canary Islands*. 1981.

Cantabrians

Cantabru; Cantabrios; Cantabros; Cantabricos

POPULATION: Approximately (2002e) 620,000 Cantabrians in Spain, concentrated in the northern region of Cantabrian on the Atlantic Ocean. Outside the autonomous region, there are sizable Cantabrian communities in Madrid and other areas of central and Mediterranean Spain and in France, Germany, and Switzerland. There are small groups in Cuba and other parts of Latin America.

THE CANTABRIAN HOMELAND: The Cantabrian homeland lies on the Atlantic Ocean in northern Spain. The coastal plain in the north gives way to rolling hills that rise gradually into the Cantabrian Mountains that traverse the region. Almost half the land lies above 2,000 feet (600 meters), mostly in the southern part of the province. The valleys of Besaya and Pas lead through the mountains and connect Cantabria to Castile in the south. High tablelands mark the southern region of Cantabria and link the region to Spain's Meseta Central. Cantabria forms a province and autonomous region of the Kingdom of Spain. *Autonomous Community of Cantabria (Comunidad Autónoma de Cantabria)*: 2,042 sq. mi.— 5,289 sq. km, (2002e) 534,000—Cantabrians 88%, Basques* 6%, Asturians* 2%, other Spaniards 4%. The Cantabrian capital and major cultural center is Santander, (2002e) 184,000.

FLAG: The Cantabrian national flag is a vertical bicolor of white over red. The flag of the nationalist movement, the Labaru Cantabru, the flag of the largest nationalist organization of the same name, is a red field bearing a Celtic design, called the "Stela de Barros," in yellow. The official flag of the autonomous region is the white over red bicolor with the addition of the coat of arms, centered.

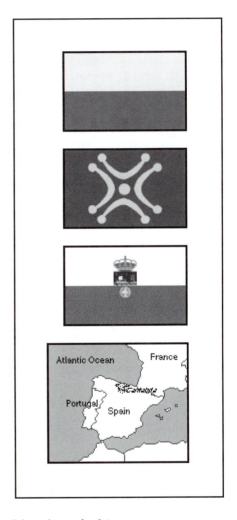

PEOPLE AND CULTURE: The Cantabrians are a Spanish nation of Celtic and Visigothic origins. Due to the isolation of their homeland they were little affected by the Muslim Moorish invasion and occupation of most of Spain. The Celtic heritage is evident in their culture, particularly in Cantabrian music, poetry, and popular culture; the Cantabrians see themselves as a Celtic nation. The Cantabrian population is concentrated along the coast, with more than a third living in the Santander metropolitan area. The rural population is widely scattered in isolated farms or small villages. Basque influence remains strong in the Cantabrian culture, including the typical beret, the *boina*, worn by men in both the Basque Country and Cantabria.

LANGUAGE AND RELIGION: The Cantabrians speak a dialect of Castilian Spanish, Cantabro-Astur, which retains many Celtic influences and is free of the strong Moorish influence of standard Castilian. Such words as *aban*, meaning river, still permeate the dialect. Dialectical variations are greater in the mountain valleys, although the dialect of Santander is considered the standard of the region. The dialect differs to such an extent that speakers of standard Spanish often encounter difficulties in understanding spoken Cantabrian. Castilian, the language now internationally known as Spanish, originated as the local dialect of Cantabria, which spread through Castile. After the merger of the kingdoms of Leon, Castile, and Aragon in the late fifteenth century, it became the standard language of all Spain. In the following centuries Castilian evolved separately, with the Cantabrian dialect considered archaic and less sophisticated. In the late 1970s new interest in the dialect led to the standardization of the Santander variety and to publication in the vernacular.

The Cantabrians are overwhelmingly Roman Catholic, priding themselves on the fact that they were among the first in Spain to embrace Christianity. Traditionally village life revolved around the church and the calendar of saints' days, but with increasing urbanization and modernization the influence of religion on daily life has declined.

NATIONAL HISTORY: Remains of Stone Age populations have been found in caves in the region. Some cave paintings have been dated at about 25,000 B.C. The Stone Age culture is often associated with the Basques, who may be the descendants of the prehistoric inhabitants of the area.

The early Iberian culture spread from the coastal plain into the foothills, protected by the barrier of the Cantabrian Mountains. Celts from the north settled the region between the sixth and eighth centuries B.C. The Celts absorbed the earlier inhabitants into their tribal groups. A powerful chiefdom of the Cantabri Celts emerged in the region, gradually extending its domination across the northern coastal plains. The name "Cantabria" is derived from the Cantabri, meaning "people of the mountains."

Roman power was fiercely resisted by the Celtic warriors in the second and first centuries B.C., but the Romans gradually won territory in the region. Epic battles were fought in the valleys leading through the Cantabrian Mountains, where the Celts held the Romans back for nearly two centuries. In 19 B.C. the Cantabri Celts were finally conquered by Emperor Augustus and added to Rome's Spanish provinces. The Roman colony of Portus Victoriae was founded on the site of present Santander. Roman culture and language was adopted by the lowland population, but the farmers in the foothills and the peoples of the mountain villages remained Celtic in language and culture.

Roman rule brought political unity, law, and economic prosperity to the region. Former tribal territories disappeared as the inhabitants adopted the Roman way of life. Christianity was introduced early, with most of the people adopting the new religion between the second and fourth centuries. Christian teachings were gradually carried into the isolated mountain regions, where the Celtic remnants adapted the religion to their earlier beliefs.

The decline of Roman political and military power in the fourth century left the region open to barbarian invasions. The first barbarian groups appeared in the coastal area in A.D. 409. The Romanized population of the coast mostly fled to strongholds in the mountains as chaos spread across the northern Iberian Peninsula. The mixture of the Roman and Celtic populations during the fifth and sixth centuries is considered to have given rise to the distinct Cantabrian nation.

The Visigoths drove the other invaders south and established a kingdom that included south Gaul and northern Spain, with its capital at Toulouse. Cantabria was created as a feudal fief of the kingdom. The Visigothic kingdom absorbed other areas of northern Spain following the loss of the French territories to the Franks in the early sixth century. The Visigoths, who adhered to Arianism (an early Christian heresy) until the late sixth century, and the Romanized population lived side by side under two separate sets of law. The fusion of the two cultures was very slow. In the seventh century a common law was adopted for all the subjects of the Visigoth kingdom.

According to the medieval Jesuit sect Fidel Fita, the Cantabrian nation came to the region from Asia and established itself in Spain. The people, originally from the Cantabras River region of India, were a Celtic people who founded the city of Canta-Iber. From there they spread through northern Spain.

The Muslim invasion of Spain and the collapse of the Visigothic kingdom in the early eighth century ended a period of relative peace. The Berber invaders, called Moors, swept north to conquer all of Spain except Asturias, Cantabria, and the Basque lands. Asturias and Cantabria, neither much affected by the Muslim conquest, became the centers of the Christian reconquest of Spain. Included in the kingdom of Navarre in the eleventh and twelfth centuries, Cantabria later formed the core of the kingdom of Castile that emerged at the breakup of Navarre. In 1212 the Castilians, including the Cantabrians, defeated the Moors at the battle of Navas de Tolosa and opened the way for the eventual reconquest of all of Muslim Spain by the Christian kingdoms of the north.

Cantabria formed part of the united kingdom of Castile and Aragon following the merger of the two states in 1479. Isolated behind their mountains, the Cantabrians had little to do with the Mediterranean empire or the final conquest of the Moors in Andalusia. Castilian grandees sent by the king to govern the region were resented as arrogant outsiders. Revolts against taxes or conscription were frequent, particularly in the mountains, in the fifteenth and sixteenth centuries. A neglected rural province, Cantabria declined as a backward farming and herding region. The only area of prosperity was the mining region in the foothills, which produced zinc and other minerals needed by the kingdom.

Increased prosperity followed the discovery of America. The port of Santander, formerly the port for the nearby mines, flourished as a result of the growing American trade. Many Cantabrians, poor and illiterate, took advantage of the closeness of the port to emigrate to the new lands in the Americas. Between 1600 and 1750, over 200,000 Cantabrians left the region to settle in Cuba and other colonies in the Americas.

In the eighteenth and nineteenth centuries the Cantabrians again slipped into a period of underdevelopment and poverty. The loss of Spain's American colonies in the early nineteenth century ended the era of prosperity for Santander. Many of the Cantabrian emigrants returned to the region from the Americas. Fanciful mansions built by wealthy returnees grew along the coast, often on lands bought from impoverished Cantabrian peasants.

A series of civil conflicts, the Carlist Wars, swept northern Spain between the 1830s and the 1870s. The period, marked by a series of uprisings, military coups d'etat, constitutions, and dictatorships, left Cantabria even poorer and less developed than a century before. The unhappy Cantabrians often supported any group that opposed the hated government in Madrid. The Syndicalist movement for the unionization of the Cantabrian mines in the late nineteenth century began a period of political mobilization. The workers' movement gave rise to a parallel movement for greater say in the local government and in the exploitation of their resources, particularly the important mines. By the end of the nineteenth century, the Socialist and Anarcho-Syndicalist parties began to gain wide followings, particularly in the mining districts.

Strikes and uprisings, often put down with great brutality, marked the first years of the twentieth century. Spain remained neutral during World War I, but wartime profits from the mines and the port at Santander led to a modest prosperity. The end of the war increased social and political unrest across Spain, leading to dictatorships and finally the establishment of a republic in 1931. There were serious Socialist and Syndicalist uprisings in Cantabria between 1931 and the outbreak of the Spanish Civil War in 1936.

The rebel forces of Gen. Francisco Franco took control of Cantabria in 1937, eliminating the local leadership and driving any remaining opposition into the high mountains. The imposition of the conservative Franco dictatorship, with the aid of Nazi Germany and Fascist Italy, ended a Cantabrian attempt to win autonomy within a democratic Spanish state. Opposition, particularly that associated with the leftists and syndicates, was vigorously suppressed. The historical center of Santander was destroyed by a fire, whipped into a firestorm by strong winds, in 1941. Anti-Franco forces in Cantabria blamed the fire on the government and its oppressive policy of eliminating regional cultures.

Agitation for autonomy began soon after Franco's death in 1975. Attempts by the authorities to add the Cantabrian region to neighboring regions in Asturias or Castile stimulated the growth of nationalism in the region in 1975–76. In 1977 nationalists formed the United Cantabria Association (ATROPU) in Santander. Other groups, some based on leftist ideologies, combined anti-Franco sentiments with demands for home rule.

The Cantabrian autonomous community was established by the statute of autonomy on 30 December 1981. The adoption of a national flag divided the Cantabrians, with the red and white flag of maritime Santander finally adopted over the opposition of the nationalists, who favored the adoption of the historical symbol of the Celtic Cantabri, which is featured on the flag of the nationalist movement.

Urbanization accelerated in the 1980s, with the city of Santander and its suburbs absorbing an influx from the rural regions of the province. Agriculture accounted for much of the economic activity up to the early 1980s, but manufacturing and mining became the most important activities after 1985. By 1995, farming accounted for only a small percentage of the Cantabrians' economic production.

The Cantabrians enjoyed the prosperity brought by the democratization and modernization of Spain, particularly Spain's entry in the European Economic Community (EEC), later renamed the European Union (EU), which provided development funds for poorer regions like Cantabria in the 1990s. Relative prosperity aided the reculturation that took hold in the late 1980s, mostly led by younger Cantabrians returning to the region from Madrid and other areas of Spain. No longer needing to leave the region to find work, they spearheaded a movement to revive the traditional Celto-Iberian Cantabrian culture.

In the late 1990s demands for greater autonomy fueled the national movement in the region. Seeing themselves as a distinct nation, like the Basques or Catalans,* the Cantabrians wanted the same self-government granted those nations. In 1998 nationalists demonstrated in Santander for local control of the mines, the major economic asset of their autonomous region. Some militants continue to demand complete independence for Cantabria, which they claim forms a distinct Celto-Iberian nation that could form a viable sovereign state within the framework of the EU.

SELECTED BIBLIOGRAPHY:

Caplan, R., ed. *Europe's New Nationalism: States and Minorities in Conflict.* 1996.
Facaros, Pauls. *Northern Spain.* 1999.
Kern, Robert W. *The Regions of Spain: A Reference Guide to History and Culture.* 1995.
Truscott, Sandra, and Maria Garcia. *A Dictionary of Contemporary Spain.* 1998.

Capers

Cape Bretoners; Cape Breton Islanders

POPULATION: Approximately (2002e) 170,000 Capers in eastern Canada, mostly living on the island of Cape Breton, in northern Nova Scotia, but with sizable communities in other parts of Nova Scotia, in the big Canadian cities of Toronto, Montreal, and Ottawa, and in the United States.

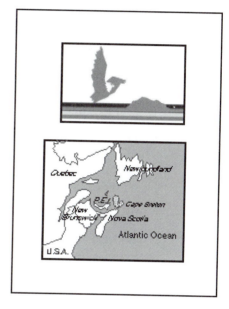

THE CAPER HOMELAND: The Caper homeland, Cape Breton Island, forms the northeastern portion of Nova Scotia. The irregularly shaped island is separated from the remainder of the province and the Canadian mainland by the Strait of Canso, two miles (three kilometers) wide. The center of the island is occupied by the Bras d'Or salt lakes. Cape Breton Island forms the counties of Cape Breton, Inverness, Richmond, and Victoria of the province of Nova Scotia. The island has a highly indented coastline and is most hilly and forested, rising to the Cape Breton Highlands. *Cape Breton Island*: 3,970 sq. mi.—10,282 sq. km, (2002e) 137,000—Capers 94%, Acadians* 2%, Micmacs* 2%, other Nova Scotians 2%. The Caper capital and major cultural center is the city of Sydney, (2002e) 24,000. The Sydney–Glace Bay urban area has a population of about (2002e) 100,000.

FLAG: The Caper national flag, the flag of the autonomy movement, is a white field bearing a stylized green bald eagle above five horizontal stripes of blue, green, yellow, gray, and white, with the green rising to a mountain on the fly.

PEOPLE AND CULTURE: The Capers, as the Cape Breton Islanders are called, are a people of mixed French, English, Scottish, and Micmac background, although most are descended from the Highland Scots who settled the island in the early nineteenth century. The islanders retain a very strong sense of regional identity, with Scottish and French influences much more obvious in the Caper culture than on mainland Nova Scotia. The island's unique music, crafts, and folklore display influences from all the peoples who settled the island, although the Highland Scots' traditions are predominant. Many Capers consider their small nation as a separate New World Celtic nation. A separate Cape Breton Island tartan of green, yellow, black, and white is widely used. The Capers' culture and way of life are closely tied to the maritime life of fishing, although farming is also important. The Gaelic College in St. Ann's, Cape Breton, fosters the traditional island folk arts, such as piping, singing, dancing, and handicrafts. Clan gatherings are held annually at the Gaelic College. The use of tartans, a tradition brought from Scotland, remains widespread.

LANGUAGE AND RELIGION: The language of the Capers is one of the Maritime dialects of English spoken in the Maritime Provinces of Canada. The language, spoken along with standard English, retains many borrowings from French, archaic English, Micmac, and Scots Gaelic. Most of the words unique to the dialect are related to fishing and mining, formerly the major occupations. French remains the first language of a minority, mostly in the more inaccessible coastal regions.

The majority of the Capers are Roman Catholic, the result of the original French and Highland Scots immigration. The island, relatively isolated until the twentieth century, was famed for its village churches, the centers of both social and religious life across the region. Religion remains a strong part of the regional Caper identity.

NATIONAL HISTORY: The island was originally settled by Micmacs who also inhabited the Nova Scotia Peninsula and the mainland regions now in the Maritime Provinces of Canada. Norse Vikings are thought to have visited the island about A.D. 1000, but the first sighting by later European explorers was by John Cabot in 1497. Cabot claimed the island for England, but a rival claim was established by the Frenchman Jacques Cartier in 1534. French settlers arrived in 1605 and adopted the Micmac name, Acadie, for the entire region. The French settlements were the first European settlements in North America lying north of Florida. The arrival of English and Scottish colonists between 1621 and 1629 opened a long conflict between England and France for control of the region. From 1623 to 1763 the island was part of New France.

By the terms of the Treaty of Utrecht in 1713, the Acadia region of New France was awarded to Britain, except for the island of Cape Breton, called Île Royale under French rule. In the southeast of the island the French built a large fortress, Louisbourg, which became one of the centers of French authority in North America. Hostilities between the British and French resumed in 1744. The Louisbourg fortress was captured by British colonial forces in 1745 but was later returned; the whole island was again captured in 1758. Along with Prince Edward Island, Cape Breton was formally ceded to the United Kingdom in 1763. The British name for the island was taken from its eastern cape, itself probably named for Cape Breton, near Bayonne, France, by Basque fishermen. Cape Breton was joined to Nova Scotia, but in 1784 it was made a separate British crown colony. It was rejoined to Nova Scotia in 1820.

British offers of free land attracted immigrants not only from the British Isles but also New Englanders* from the colonies to the south. Scots Highlanders, fleeing poverty and defeat, settled the island in large numbers. During the American Revolutionary War, the island served as a shelter for Loyalist refugees fleeing the overthrow of British rule farther south. Many of the immigrants purposely settled in remote areas, far from the centers of authority, beginning a tradition of independence and self-sufficiency that continues to the present.

The province of Nova Scotia received responsible government in 1848, including local government authorities on Cape Breton. In spite of opposition in the region, Cape Breton, along with Nova Scotia, joined the new union with Ontario, Quebec, and New Brunswick in 1867 to form the Dominion of Canada. The island remained isolated and mostly rural until the early years of the twentieth century.

In 1955 the island was linked to the Nova Scotia mainland by a causeway across the Strait of Canso, making it the eastern terminal of both the Trans-Canada Highway and the Canadian National Railway. The important coal-mining region around Sydney was the focus of growth and development throughout much of the nineteenth and early twentieth centuries. Coal mining became part of the region culture much as it had among the Welsh.* Coal mining and the related steel mills provided employment for generations of Capers until the industries began to decline in the 1970s.

Economic difficulties and continued friction between the Capers and the Nova Scotia government led to the creation of a regionalist movement in the early 1980s. An openly separatist organization, the Cape Breton Liberation Army (CBLA) was founded in 1982 with the aim of winning social and political justice and separation from Nova Scotia. A small splinter group advocated separate independence for the island and closer ties to the Celtic nations of Europe. In the late 1980s the nationalists called several large demonstrations, and thousands of Capers marched in support of autonomy.

In the 1990s the economic situation became even more serious as mines closed and steel mills laid off workers. Emigration from the island became the only alternative for many Capers. The decline of coal mining and steel production has left the Capers more heavily dependent upon such industries as fishing and fish processing.

Resentment of the need to leave their homeland to find work revived the Caper national movement in the early 1990s. Younger islanders refused to leave in search of jobs, straining local government resources. Many Capers blame the island's economic grievances on the government of Nova

Scotia, which they claim focuses on the mainland while neglecting the needs of the people of Cape Breton.

SELECTED BIBLIOGRAPHY:

Hornsby, Stephen J. *Nineteenth-Century Cape Breton*. 1992.
MacDonald, D. R. *Cape Breton Road*. 2000.
MacKinnon, Christy. *Silent Observer*. 1996.
MacKinnon, Neil. *This Unfriendly Soil: The Loyalist Experience in Nova Scotia, 1783–91*. 1989.

Carpatho-Rusyns

Carpatho-Russians; Carpatho-Ukrainians; Ruthenians; Ruthenes; Rusyns; Rusnaks; Rusins

POPULATION: Approximately (2002e) 1,950,000 Carpatho-Rusyns in Europe, the majority, 1,505,000, in Ukraine and another 330,000 in Slovakia and 100,000, called Lemkos or Lemkians, in Poland. There are smaller numbers in Romania, Yugoslavia, Hungary, and the Czech Republic. Outside Europe the largest communities live in the United States, Canada, Argentina, and Australia.

THE CARPATHO-RUSYN HOMELAND: The Carpatho-Rusyn homeland, historically called Ruthenia, Carpatho-Ukraine, or Subcarpathian Rus', lies in the heart of Europe, along the northern and southern slopes of the Carpathian Mountains where the borders of Ukraine, Slovakia, and Poland meet. The nation's heartland occupies part of the Carpathians, with long, fertile valleys leading into Slovakia. The Carpatho-Rusyn territory in Ukraine, except for the smaller region in northern Bukovina, forms an *oblast*, or province of Ukraine. *Zakarpats'ka Oblast (Transcarpathia)*: 4,942 sq. mi.—12,803 sq. km, (2002e) 1,280,000—Carpatho-Rusyns 69%, Hungarians 14%, Ukrainians 9%, Slovaks, Romanians, Russians, and Germans 8%. The Carpatho-Rusyn capital and major cultural center, Uzhgorod, called Uzhorod in Ukrainian, (2002e) 126,000, is the official capital of the oblast.

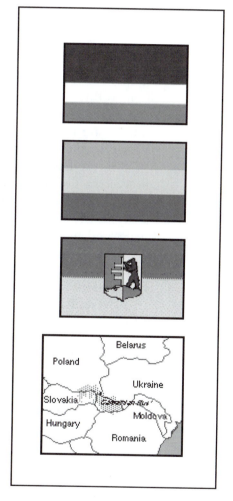

FLAG: The Carpatho-Rusyn national flag, the flag of the national movement, is a vertical tricolor of blue, white, and red, the blue twice the width of the other stripes. The flag of the Lemko Rusyns is a vertical tricolor of pale blue, yellow, and green. The flag of the provisional government, created in 1993, is a vertical bicolor of pale blue over yellow bearing the Carpatho-Rusyn coat of arms centered, divided vertically with a yellow cross on a blue background on the hoist and a red bear on a white background on the fly.

PEOPLE AND CULTURE: The Carpatho-Rusyns, calling themselves Po-Nashemy, or "our people," are a Slavic nation believed to descend from Slavic migrants and earlier Ruthene tribes of unknown origin. The name "Rusyn," an early designation for all Slavs, persisted in the isolated valleys of the Carpathians. The national name connects them to the east, as Rus' was the name given the inhabitants and territory of the medieval Slav state based on Kiev. The many names used by the Carpatho-Rusyns and the names they have been called by others—Carpatho-Russian, Carpatho-Ukrainian, Rusnak, Ruthese, Ruthenian, and Uhro-Rusyn—all relate to their traditional ties to the historical East Slav Rus'. In spite of the confusion over a national name, the nation itself prefers Carpatho-Rusyn, or simply Rusyn. In Poland the Carpatho-Rusyns call themselves Lemkos or Lemko Rusyns. In Slovakia, the Carpatho-Rusyns live in the Presov region of Eastern Slovakia province. Carpatho-Rusyns had traditionally lived in southeastern Poland, on the northern slopes of the Carpathians, an area known as the Lemko Region but now called Beskid Niski. After World War II, the Lemko Rusyns were deported from the Carpathians to Silesia in western Poland or the northern Polish provinces, for so-called security reasons. Several thousand have returned to their homeland, but the majority of the Lemkians remain scattered around Poland. Since 1991 many in Poland have begun to use the term Lemko Rusyn. In addition to dialectical and geographical divisions, the Carpatho-Rusyns are further divided between the *dolyshniany*, the lowlanders, and the *verkhovyntsi*, or highlanders.

LANGUAGE AND RELIGION: A long tradition of not mixing with neighboring peoples has safeguarded the unique Carpatho-Rusyn culture and dialect. The Carpatho-Rusyn dialects are classified as East Slavic and are closely related to Ukrainian, but they have been heavily influenced by Polish, Slovak, and Hungarian borrowings. Influences from both east and west, together with numerous inclusions from the Church Slavonic liturgical language and dialectal words unique to the Carpatho-Rusyns, are what distinguish the Carpatho-Rusyn language from the other East Slavic languages. The Carpatho-Rusyns speak four separate dialects, Lemko, Hutsul, Boiko, and Transcarpathian. The first three also designate the major divisions of the Carpatho-Rusyn nation.

The separate Carpatho-Rusyn Uniate Church, united with Rome by the Union of Uzhorod in 1646, is closely identified with Carpatho-Rusyn culture and national sentiment. Like their language and culture, the Carpatho-Rusyn churches share elements from both the eastern and western Christian traditions. Religion has traditionally been an important element in the lives of the Carpatho-Rusyns, and their churches have often been perceived as synonymous with the traditional Byzantine-rite churches. The separate

Carpatho-Rusyn Orthodox Church was legalized in 1990. In the last decade a growing number have joined the Jehovah Witnesses, the Baptists, and other evangelical sects.

NATIONAL HISTORY: Scholars believe that Slavic migrants, coming from the east, settled among the earlier Ruthene tribes in the high valleys of the Carpathian Mountains in the eighth century. Traditionally, Christianity was brought to the Carpatho-Rusyns by the so-called Apostles to the Slavs, Cyril and Methodius, two monks from Byzantium, around A.D. 860. Some scholars believe that the Carpatho-Rusyns, already Christian, settled the region after the conversion of Kievan Rus'. Their Carpathian homeland in the tenth and eleventh centuries formed part of Kievan Rus', the first great Slav state.

Although ruled by the Hungarians, the Carpatho-Rusyns remained within the Eastern Orthodox sphere, nominally under the authority of the patriarch of Constantinople after the Christian Church was divided in 1054. For centuries their Orthodox religion defined their people and distinguished the Carpatho-Rusyns from their Slovak, Hungarian, and Polish neighbors, who were mostly Roman Catholic or, later, often Protestant. They were also distinguished from their fellow Eastern-rite neighbors by certain practices and rituals borrowed from their Latin-rite neighbors, particularly the use of liturgical music.

The Carpatho-Rusyn homeland was officially annexed in 1382 by Hungary, where the non-Slav Magyar cultural influences in the region further distanced their culture from the other Slav cultures to the east. The Lemko region north of the Carpathians was divided until the mid-fourteenth century between the Galicia in the east and Poland. In the 1340s the entire Lemko region came under Polish rule.

The Protestant Reformation and the Catholic Counter-Reformation profoundly affected the Carpatho-Rusyns. The governments and local aristocracy of the region began in the late sixteenth century to try to bring the Orthodox Carpatho-Rusyns closer to the official Roman Catholic state religion of the two states that controlled their homeland, the Hungarian kingdom and Poland-Lithuania. The Byzantine-rite Uniate Church accepted the authority of Rome in 1586, and several bishops of the Carpatho-Rusyn population in northeastern Hungary organized the separate Carpatho-Rusyn Uniate Church in 1646. The first printed book, a Bible for the Carpatho-Rusyns, appeared in 1699.

The homeland remained divided, with Austria and Russia taking portions during the Polish partition of 1772. The Carpatho-Rusyns, without the territorial recognition accorded the other minority peoples of the Austrian Empire in the eighteenth century, remained divided among several counties in northeastern Hungary, the Presov region of Hungarian Slovakia, and the adjoining areas of Austrian Galicia. The majority, denied all cultural rights and under intense assimilation pressure, lived as illiterate peasants in near-feudal conditions on large estates. Without a clear ethnic identity, most identified with their church, around which Carpatho-Rusyn life revolved. Those under Russian rule were quickly reconverted to the Orthodox faith, and every effort was made to Russify the Carpatho-Rusyn population.

A small church-educated elite initiated a national and cultural revival that spread through the Carpatho-Rusyn lands in the mid-nineteenth century. The growing national self-awareness highlighted the misery of the Carpatho-Rusyns' daily life. To escape grinding poverty, cultural repression, and pressure on their exploited lands, the Carpatho-Rusyns turned to emigration. Thousands left, mostly for the Americas, with mass emigration beginning in the 1880s and continuing until the outbreak of World War I in 1914 blocked the emigrant routes.

Among Europe's poorest and most backward peoples, the Carpatho-Rusyns in the Austro-Hungarian Empire refused to support the Hungarian war effort during the First World War. Carpatho-Rusyn youths habitually fled conscription or deserted to the allies when the opportunity arose. Nationalist sentiment grew rapidly during the war, developing as an anti-Hungarian mass movement. In May 1917 Carpatho-Rusyn leaders demanded the creation of a separate Carpatho-Rusyn state within the empire, but they were generally ignored.

The nationalists mobilized as revolution overtook the defeated empire in November 1918. Rejecting claims to their homeland by the new states in the region, the Carpatho-Rusyn provisional government sent a delegation to the 1919 Paris Peace Conference to demand recognition under Point 10 of President Woodrow Wilson's Fourteen Points—self-determination for the peoples of the Austro-Hungarian Empire. Carpatho-Rusyn independence, emphatically opposed by the region's large Hungarian minority, was also opposed by the allies and the newly independent states of the region.

The nationalist leader, Gregory Zsatkovich, accepted an alternative proposed by the allies for the Carpatho-Rusyn heartland—the status of a trust territory, with broad autonomy, within the newly formed Czecho-Slovak state. Over nationalist protests, the Presov region and Subcarpathian Rus' south of the Carpathians became part of Czechoslovakia, except for about twenty towns and villages south of the Tisza River, which were incorporated into Romania. The Lemko region was added to newly independent Poland. A few Carpatho-Rusyn towns in the far south of former Hungarian territory became part of the new South Slav state later called Yugoslavia.

A number of autonomous governments were erected in the region. One of the least known, yet ironically perhaps the longest lasting, of these postwar "republics" was the Lemko Rusyn Republic (Ruska Lemkivska Respublyka), which existed for a full sixteen months from December 1918 to March 1920.

The Czechoslovak government created a new province, called Ruthenia, on 8 May 1919, with Gregory Zsatkovich as the first governor. The Paris Peace Conference in its Treaty of St. Germain recognized the union of the Transcarpathian region with Czechoslovakia, on the condition that Ruthenia be given broad autonomy. The Carpatho-Rusyns of the Presov region, under Slovak authority, and the Lemko Rusyns of Poland attempted to unite with the new Ruthenia but were blocked by the Czechoslovak and Polish governments. Zsatkovich resigned in 1920 to protest the abrogation of the autonomy agreement. Czechoslovakia's highly centralized government took control of most administrative functions and placed ethnic Czechs in most local government positions.

The Czech government, threatened by Hungary and Germany in 1938, sought to bind the Carpatho-Rusyns' loyalty by finally granting the long-promised autonomy. When Czechoslovakia was betrayed by its allies at the Munich Pact and transformed into a federal state made up of several autonomous units in October 1938, Ruthenia received full self-governing status. The Ruthenian government was first headed by Andrej Brodij and then by the pro-Ukrainian Avhustyn Volosyn (August Voloshin). Six months later, the dismemberment of Czechoslovakia by the fascist powers gave the Carpatho-Rusyns an opportunity: the nationalists mobilized to expel all Czech officials and to form a government under Voloshin. On 2 March 1939 the state, called Carpatho-Ukraine, declared its independence. The new government collapsed following a rapid invasion by Hungarian troops on 14 March, and two days later Hungary annexed the region and suppressed all signs of nationalism.

Soviet occupation of the region in October 1944 was aided by a pro-communist Transcarpathian National Council, which had been formed as the Hungarian civil government collapsed. At the end of 1945, under intense Soviet pressure, the Czechoslovak government ceded the region to the Soviet Union. The Carpatho-Rusyns lost their autonomous status, and the region was administered as an ordinary *oblast* of Soviet Ukraine. In the neighboring Presov region, in 1945, the Carpatho-Rusyns set up a national council and demanded self-rule but were blocked by the restored Czechoslovak government. In 1948 the communists took power in Czechoslovakia, and in 1949–50 the national council and the Greek-Catholic religion was disbanded and their leaders jailed. In 1952 the Carpatho-Rusyns were abolished as an official minority; the Czecho-Slovak government recognized them only as Ukrainians. About 12,000 were deported to the Transcarpathia region of Soviet Ukraine.

The new communist government in Poland, in an effort to end the problem of the Carpatho-Rusyn minority, deported in 1946–47 most of the estimated 178,000 Lemkos from their border homeland, sending about 80% to the Soviet Ukraine and the remainder to the former German lands taken by Poland after the war in the west ended. Following the deportations, the Polish government denied the existence of a distinct Carpatho-Rusyn national group on Polish soil.

One of the most immediate results of Soviet rule in Transcarpathia was the implementation of a government policy of Ukrainization. Similar programs were instituted in neighboring communist-dominated Poland and Czechoslovakia. The idea of a distinct Carpatho-Rusyn nationality was outlawed, and only the Ukrainian identity was recognized. The Carpatho-Rusyns suffered decades of religious, cultural, and political oppression under Soviet rule. A national revival, begun as an underground movement in the 1970s, began to emerge as a powerful force with the Soviet liberalization in the late 1980s.

The Lemkians of Poland, after decades of suppression, formed the first nationalist organization in 1989. The Lemko Association was permitted and officially recognized, though its position was that the Lemkians constituted an ethnic group distinct and separate from the Ukrainians. In 1990 the minority who consider the Lemkians part of the larger Ukrainian nation formed another organization, the Lemko Union. Lemkian organizations applied for the return of forests and fields that had been confiscated as a result of the deportations of 1947. Activists demanded a special charter of civil rights for the Lemkians of Poland, including the right to closer political and cultural ties to the Carpatho-Rusyns of Ukraine and Slovakia.

The Soviet Union collapsed in 1991, and Ukraine became an independent country, leading to demands by the Carpatho-Rusyns of Transcarpathia for a return to their historical status as an autonomous province. In a referendum on Ukrainian independence carried out on 1 December 1991, over 78% of Transcarpathia's inhabitants voted for regional autonomy within the newly independent Ukraine. When the Ukrainian government failed to fulfill the obligations of the December 1991 referendum, Carpatho-Rusyn leaders formed a provisional government of the Republic of Subcarpathian Rus' on 22 May 1993. Since the summer of 1994, the struggle for autonomy has taken place within the chambers of the 51-member Transcarpathian National Council, the local parliament. In 1992 nationalists advocating secession from Ukraine and the formation of an independent Carpatho-Rusyn state formed the first openly separatist political organization.

The collapse of communist governments in the neighboring states also raised demands among their Carpatho-Rusyn populations. Newly formed national organizations put forward demands for cultural autonomy in Slovakia, Poland, Hungary, Yugoslavia, and the Czech Republic. The major aim of these organizations is to have the Carpatho-Rusyns recognized as a distinct nationality and to codify a literary language for instruction in schools and for use in the press, radio, theater, and other cultural events. In March 1991 all these organizations, along with groups from Ukraine, the United States, and Canada, formed the World Congress of Rusyns, which meets periodically to formulate common goals for the preservation of the Carpatho-Rusyns. The result of these increased contacts among the politically divided Carpatho-Rusyns has, for the first time, allowed joint programs and close cooperation in cultural, scholarly, and economic endeavors, regardless of the country in which they live.

A language seminar held in Slovakia in 1992, known as the First Congress on the Rusyn Language, concluded that the Carpatho-Rusyns should develop four standards dialects based on the dialects spoken in Ukraine, Slovakia, Poland, and Yugoslavia, which would replace the dozens of regional dialects. The Carpatho-Rusyn language, as spoken in the Presov Region of Slovakia, was codified in 1995. The Lemkos of Poland have already published several grammar books as well as a dictionary of their dialect.

The largest Carpatho-Rusyn group, in Ukraine, is not recognized as a distinct national group, and consequently its language is officially recognized only as a dialect of Ukrainian. In January 2000, after seven years of failing to gain recognition and suffering official neglect, the self-proclaimed Carpatho-Rusyn government again called on the Ukrainian government to recognize the Carpatho-Rusyns as a distinct nation.

SELECTED BIBLIOGRAPHY:

Bonkalo, Alexander. *The Rusyns*. 1990.
Magocsi, Paul R. *Our People: Carpatho-Rusyns and Their Descendants in North America*. 1994.
Pekar, Athanasius B., et al. *The History of the Church in Carpathian Rus'*. 1992.
Shandor, Vincent. *Carpatho-Ukraine in the Twentieth Century: A Political and Legal History*. 1998.

Casamançais

Casamancois; Casamancians; Diola-Bainouks; Jolas; Jola-Balant

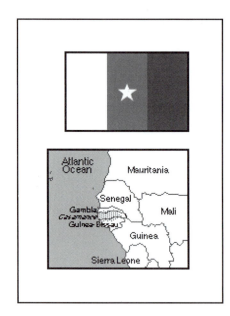

POPULATION: Approximately (2002e) 1,005,000 Casamançais (830,000 Diolas and 175,000 Bainouks) in Senegal. Other sizable populations live in the Senegalese capital, Dakar, and the neighboring states of Gambia and Guinea-Bissau.

THE CASAMANÇAIS HOMELAND: The Casamançais homeland lies in the basin of the Casamance River on the west coast of Africa. The most southerly region of Senegal, Casamance is heavily wooded and fertile; it is geographically separated from the rest of Senegal by the Gambia River and the state of Gambia. The only land connection is a corridor connecting eastern Casamance to Senegal proper. Casamance formed a province of Senegal until 1984 but now forms the regions of Ziguinchor (Lower Casamance) and Kolda (Upper Casamance). *Historic Region of Casamance*: 10,948 sq. mi.—28,355 sq. km, (2002e) 1,387,000—Diolas 60%, Mandingo (Mande) 23%, Bainouk 12%, Fulani 3%, Balante 2%. The Casamançais capital and major cultural center is Ziguinchor, (2002e) 205,000. The major cultural center of the people of Upper Casamance is Kolda, (2002e) 52,000.

FLAG: The Casamançais national flag, the flag used by the Movement of Democratic Forces of the Casamance (MFDC) and the other nationalist organizations, is a horizontal tricolor of white, green, and red bearing a centered five-pointed white star.

PEOPLE AND CULTURE: The Casamançais, or Casamancians, comprise two closely related peoples, the Diola in the coastal region and the Bainouk farther inland. The Diola and Bainouk have inhabited the Casamance region for over a thousand years, according to their legends and traditions. The two peoples speak closely related languages of the Niger-Congo language group and form a majority in the traditional region of Bas-Casamance (Lower Casamance) and a large minority in Haute-Casamance (Upper Casamance), where the Mande and Fulani populations are concentrated. Traditionally the Casamançais have remained aloof from other parts of Senegal, while their geographic isolation has allowed them to maintain their language and culture. Although the Diola and the closely related Bainouk are the predominant peoples among the Casamançais, they advocate a multiethnic cultural identity among the various Casamance peoples. Rice cultivation is closely tied to the culture and way of life in the Casamance region.

LANGUAGE AND RELIGION: The majority language of the Casamançais is Diola, a Northern Atlantic language of the Atlantic-Congo group. The language, often called Diola-Fogny, is spoken in five major dialects in Senegal and Guinea Bissau. In Senegal the language is recognized as one of the six national languages, although only Wolof and French are widely used in education, communications, and government. About 60,000 northern Diolas speak a related language, Diola-Kasa, spoken north of the Gambia River. A Portuguese patois is spoken by many of the residents of Ziguinchor and along the coast, where it is known as Cacheu-Ziguinchor Creole, or Crioulo.

The majority of the Casamançais are Christians or retain their traditional religious beliefs, although those in the eastern regions are mostly Muslims. The dominant people of the Casamançais, the Diola, are mainly animists, with a Muslim minority in the Fogni district. Christianity has made some inroads but is mostly restricted to the urban areas and along the coast. Religion is one of the causes of a separatist war in the region, as Senegal is over 80% Muslim. Both Christians and animists retain a local cosmology centered around initiation rites, a relationship with the earth, and with the invisible world of the nocturnal *kussay* spirits.

NATIONAL HISTORY: For centuries Diola kings ruled Casamance, often under the nominal rule of Serer or Wolof states to the north. Mostly rice farmers in the lush valley of the Casamance River, the Diola inhabited small towns and villages, each with a paramount chief. Isolated from the north, the Diola never developed the strong caste system prevalent among the other peoples of Senegal.

Portuguese navigators and slave traders, the first Europeans to visit the region in the fifteenth century, established trade relations with the king of Kasa and local Diola chiefs. They eventually constructed a permanent trading station at the mouth of the Casamance River. The Portuguese, from their colony of Guinea just to the south, remained the Diola's main European contact for several centuries. The region was later settled by migrants from the Mali empire. The name of the country, Cassamoukou, was changed by the Portuguese to Casamance.

British claims and the creation the colony of Gambia just to the north prompted the initial French interest in the Casamance region. Beginning in 1854 the French gradually increased their influence over the region, and in 1866 French troops expelled the Portuguese; the region was annexed to the French Empire. Although the other European powers recognized the French claim in 1870, the French generally ignored the isolated region.

The Portuguese authorities, under French pressure, officially sold the region to France on 12 May 1886. In 1888, to preclude incursions from neighboring European colonies, the French authorities in Senegal dispatched a force to occupy Ziguinchor, the Diola capital. Not until 1903 did the French begin to extend their authority beyond Ziguinchor. Resistance to French authority, particularly among the Diolas, continued until the 1920s.

Islam spread to the Diola and the Bainouk only after the European occupation, coming to the Casamance lowlands with traders and migrants from the Mande and Fulani peoples of Upper Casamance; the majority of the Casamançais retained their traditional religious beliefs. Partly motivated by religion, anti-French disturbances broke out in 1899 and continued sporadically for several years. Nationalists point to the early-twentieth-century disturbances as the beginning of the Casamance national movement.

Soldiers from Casamance were incorporated in the *tirailleurs Sénégalais* and participated in both world wars as French auxiliaries. Among them was a young Diola, Victor Dialla, who became the first African to receive a degree in literature in France in 1930. In 1947 he and three others founded the Movement of Democratic Forces of the Casamance (MFDC) to affirm the Casamance identity. He was murdered, possibly by French agents, on 20 November 1948.

Isolated from the rest of Senegal, and with the natural trade and transportation routes blocked by British Gambia, Casamance remained neglected and underdeveloped. During World War II, in response to French efforts to recruit laborers in the region, Casamançais resistance increased. In 1943 the French, to quell continuing disturbances, sent the Diola queen, Alinsitowe Diatte, into exile. Created as a district of French Senegal in 1920, the Casamançais continued to exist in relative isolation until the British finally allowed direct access across Gambia in 1947.

The diverse peoples of Casamance, impelled by common interests, began to unite in the early 1950s. The first openly separatist organization, the Casamance Autonomy Movement (MAC), led by Aleck Seck, formed to press for self-government and a separate administration within French West Africa. In 1959 the MAC formed the nucleus of a Casamance-based political party, the Parti de Regroupment Africain-Senegal, known as PRA-Senegal. The party openly opposed the centralizing policies of the Wolof-dominated Senegalese government and demanded a separate Casamance state within a federal Senegal. Following Senegalese independence in 1960 the party was banned as secessionist and forced underground.

The fertile region, receiving two or three times the rainfall of the rest of Senegal, became the main food-producing region, growing half of Senegal's rice, cotton, peanuts, and corn. Government policies that economically exploited the region but gave the Casamançais little in return led to confrontations and growing resentment in the 1970s. The sense of neglect in terms of infrastructure, education, and economic development was heightened by government insistence that all trade must pass through Dakar, not through Banjul in the Gambia, which is much closer to Casamance. Between 1968 and the early 1980s the marginalization of Casamance was accompanied by economic domination and exploitation.

The Casamançais nationalist movement resurfaced in the 1982, led by the MFDC, with the aim of separating Casamance from Senegal. Local resentment and a feeling of shared Casamançais identity superseded local Diola, Fulani, Mandingo, and Bainouk identities. The affirmation of Casamançais difference gave a stimulus to a spontaneous popular resistance against strangers to the region, accused of pillaging its natural resources and marginalizing its inhabitants, with the complicity of the government authorities.

The formation of the armed wing of the MFDC, the Atika, led to secessionist demonstrations. Severe rioting in December 1983 provoked the Senegalese government to abolish Casamance province and to divide the territory into two new regions—Ziguinchor, with a Diola and Bainouk majority; and Kolda, with a Mande majority. The division, denounced by nationalists as a government ploy to undermine the historical ties and the regional identity of the peoples of the Casamance, failed to end the growing separatist sentiment in the region. A number of regional leaders, including Augustin Diamacoune Senghor, a Catholic priest and the leader of the separatist movement, were jailed.

Senegal and Gambia in 1981 formed the Senegambia Confederation, which closely integrated their economies and political systems. The agreement was dissolved in 1989 over political differences and trade conflicts. The failure of the confederation adversely affected the Casamançais, as it was more lucrative and less troublesome to trade goods through Gambia's capital, Banjul, than to send them north to Dakar, the capital of Senegal. The dissolution of the confederation worsened the economic situation of the Casamançais, whose needs had been neglected by the Senegalese government.

The Casamance nationalists, spurred by the discovery of oil in the region, launched an armed separatist struggle in 1990. Mass demonstrations in favor of immediate independence rocked Ziguinchor and other Casamançais cities. Government troops, given wide powers to combat the threat, retaliated with a brutal suppression that pushed even the more moderate Casamance leaders into closer cooperation with the growing separatist movement. A cease-fire signed in May 1991 broke down after seven months, and the conflict resumed. By mid-1994 some 30,000 people had been displaced by the escalating violence, most having fled to refugee camps in Guinea-Bissau and Gambia.

The MFDC split into two factions in August 1992, the Front Sud and Front Nord. Front Sud continued to be the major Diola faction calling for independence, while Front Nord, with both Diolas and non-Diolas, favored further negotiations based on the 1991 agreement instead of full independence. The main reason for the split was fear by the non-Diola tribes of losing their cultural identity through domination by the Diolas, even though they shared the basic objective of greater political, cultural, and economic rights for the Casamançais.

In July 1993, a cease-fire was negotiated. Dissident nationalist organizations broke with the MFDC and launched a series of attacks on government soldiers. The increasing splits among the nationalist group reflects the division between those willing to discuss autonomy for Casamance and the more militant groups demanding full independence. The separatists have maintained bases across the border in neighboring Guinea-Bissau.

The Senegalese authorities have consistently denied the nationalists' assertion that documents from the colonial era indicate that France favored separate independence for Casamance. In December 1993 the French government, asked by Senegal for historical arbitration, issued a judgment that Casamance had not existed as an autonomous territory prior to the colonial period and that independence for the region had been neither demanded nor considered at the time of decolonization. The Senegalese government to justify the harsh methods employed by the military in the region has used the arbitration, dismissed by the nationalist leader Abbé Diamacoune Senghor as meaningless.

Government forces launched a full-scale invasion of the region in 1995. Senegalese soldiers drawn from the northern Wolofs and other peoples of central Senegal often mistreated the local population, making no distinction between Diola and Mandingo, Christian and Muslim, pro-separatist and pro-government.

The Casamance separatist conflict is closely tied to the civil war in the neighboring Republic of Guinea-Bissau. Conflict broke out there in June 1998, when Gen. Ansumane Mané was accused of smuggling arms to the separatist forces in Casamance. An alliance between the Casamançais nationalists and the rebels in Guinea-Bissau followed the Senegalese government's decision to send soldiers to intervene in the civil war in the neighboring republic. The rebels in Guinea-Bissau are sympathetic to the desire for independence of the Casamançais, as people on both sides of the border are of the same ethnic origins and lived in one territory until 1888. The war has further blurred the border as the two conflicts merged into one, with rebels in both countries fighting government troops without regard to the international boundary. The defeat of the Senegalese-backed government forces in Guinea-Bissau after eleven months of fighting brought a new government to power in Bissau, more disposed to aid the Casamançais, but the new government, under Joao Bernardo Viera, was overthrown in a coup in May 1999.

Government forces between April and June 1999 for the first time shelled the Casamançais capital, Ziguinchor. The shelling resulted in dozens of wounded and many dead among the civilian population of the city. Thousands fled the shelling, joining the 200,000 refugees from Senegal and Guinea-Bissau along the common border. The epicenter of the fighting shifted from Ziguinchor to the eastern Kolda region.

In December 1999, Casamançais leaders stated their demands for talks, land-mine clearance, free movement of people and goods, and the withdrawal of Senegalese soldiers sent to the region before 1979. In late 1999 talks were held in Banjul, Gambia, with an agreement to end the fighting immediately and to respect a cease-fire signed in 1993. The talks, which resumed in January 2000, reviewed the demands of the MFDC to be transformed into a political party, for the release of fighters, and for the lifting of all constraints on the free movement of people and goods in Casamance.

The talks' peace emphasized the transition of the Casamance Question from a violent confrontation to a political issue, but the Senegalese government's willingness to hold talks only with preconditions, including a refusal to discuss independence for Casamance, has delayed the start of negotiations. The negotiations are also complicated by the factionalism of the MFDC. Convincing the various factions to agree on a cease-fire or negotiations is extremely difficult.

Talks between the MFDC and the Senegalese government were opened with much fanfare in November 2000, but collapsed after only three hours. The leader of the MFDC, Abbé Diamacoune Senghor reiterated that he won't end the rebellion until the "country of the rivers," as he calls Casamance, is granted full independence, something no Senegalese government is going to offer. In March 2001 the rebel leadership signed yet another cease-fire with the Senegalese government, but by May heavy fighting had resumed, sending thousands of refugees fleeing into Guinea-Bissau. In November 2001 the resignation of the interim secretary-general of the MFDC led to a growing rift between independence factions, with criticisms of Abbé Diamacoune's seeming inability to bring a just peace or independence to Casamance.

SELECTED BIBLIOGRAPHY:

Baum, Robert M. *Shrines of the Slave Trade: Diola Religion and Society in Precolonial Senegambia*. 1992.

Clark, Andrew F, and Lucie Colvin Phillips. *Historical Dictionary of Senegal*. 1994.

Sharp, Robin. *Senegal: A State of Change*. 1994.

Villalon, Leonardo A. *Islamic Society and State Power in Senegal*. 1995.

Catalans

Catalonians; Valencians; Valencianos; Balearic Islanders; Mallorquins

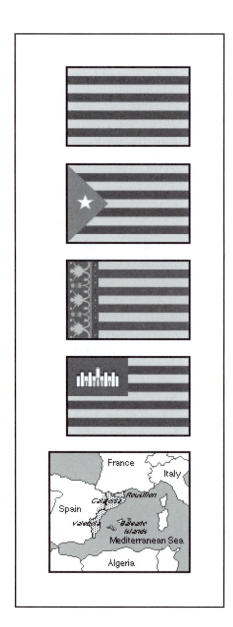

POPULATION: Approximately (2002e) 8,500,000 Catalans in Europe, concentrated in the Catalonia, Valencia, and Balearic Island regions of Spain and the Rousillon (Northern Catalonia) area of the region of Languedoc-Rousillon in France. Other sizable Catalan communities are in adjacent areas of Aragon (about 60,000), Murcia, and other parts of Spain, in Paris, and in Germany. Outside Europe there are Catalan communities in Latin America and the United States.

THE CATALAN HOMELAND: The Catalan homeland lies on the Mediterranean Sea in southwestern Europe, comprising a mainland region in Spain and France, and the Balearic Islands in the western Mediterranean Sea. The area, called Catalunya in Catalan, is traversed by the eastern spur of the Pyrenees Mountains, which form the international border between France and Spain. Greater Catalonia, called Països Catalans, consists of the autonomous regions of Catalonia, Valencia, the Balearic Islands, and Rousillon, in the French Department of Pyrénées Orientales. Spanish Catalonia was granted autonomy within the Spanish state in 1980. French Catalonia, joined to the region of Languedoc, was created as a planning region, with very limited autonomy, in 1981. *Autonomous Region of Catalonia (Comunidad Autónoma de Cataluña/Comunitat Autònom de Catalunya)*: 12,238 sq. mi.—31,930 sq. km, (2002e) 6,327,000. *Autonomous Region of Valencia (Comunidad Valenciana/Comunitat València)*: 8,998 sq. mi.—23,305 sq. km, (2002e) 4,177,000. *Autonomous Region of the Balearic Is-*

lands *(Baleares)*: 1,936 sq. mi.—5,014 sq. km, (2002e) 876,000. *Roussillon (Catalonie/Catalunya Nord)*: 1,589 sq. mi.—4,116 sq. km, (2002e) 409,000. *Països Catalans*: (2002e) 11,090,000—Catalan (Catalan, Valencian, Balearic Islanders) 76%, other Spanish and other French 24%. The Catalan capital and major cultural center, Barcelona, (2002e) 1,498,000 (metropolitan area, 4,450,000), is an important commercial center and port on the Mediterranean. The Valencian and Balearic capitals—Valencia, València in the Valencian dialect, (2002e) 741,000 (metropolitan area, 1,764,000), and Palma de Majorca, called Ciutat de Mallorca in Catalan, (2002e) 345,000—are other important cultural centers. The capital and cultural center of Roussillon, or Northern Catalonia (Catalunya Nord), is Perpignan, (2002e) 108,000, called Perpinyà in Catalan.

FLAG: The Catalan national flag, the official flag of the regions of Catalonia and French Catalonia, has nine yellow and red horizontal stripes. The yellow and red flag, with the addition of a blue triangle bearing a white star, at the hoist, is the flag of the Catalan nationalist movement. The Valencian flag has the nine yellow and red stripes with a broad pale-blue stripe at the hoist decorated with crowns and jewels. The Mallorquin flag is the same nine yellow and red stripes with a purple canton bearing a white building.

PEOPLE AND CULTURE: The Catalans are a Romance people, a mixture of early Pyreneean and Mediterranean strains. Known for their energy and intelligence, and for their clannish defense of their language and culture, they have created one of Europe's most dynamic regions. The Catalans form the largest non-Castilian nation of Spain and one of the largest of the non-state nations in Europe. Catalan culture, famous for art and architecture, has its roots in the Catalan Renaissance of the Middle Ages and is quite distinct from the Gothic and Moorish influences that prevail in most of Spain. The Catalan culture, suppressed during the decades of the Francisco Franco dictatorship, has recovered and strengthened since Spain's adoption of a democratic system in the late 1970s. In Northern Catalonia the culture has survived, but it also has suffered from the policies of the French government, which promotes centralization and homogenization of French society. Between 1900 and 1981 several million non-Catalans migrated to the region. They now form the vast majority of the unskilled and semiskilled workers, but most remain cultural outsiders.

LANGUAGE AND RELIGION: The Catalan language, officially Catalan-Valencian-Balear or Català, is a language of the Ibero-Romance group of Romance languages. Closer to Italian or the dialects of the Occitans* in southern France than to Spanish or French, Catalan is the first language of much of the population of northeastern Spain and French Catalonia. The language is spoken in three major dialects in Catalonia—Catalan-Roussillonese or Northern Catalan, Central Catalan, and Northwestern Catalan—with several subdialects. The other major dialects are

Valencian, spoken in Valencia, and Balearic, also called Mallorqui or Insular Catalan, with several subdialects in the Balearic Islands. The Valencian and Balearic dialects are 90 to 95% comprehensible to speakers of Catalan dialects. Catalan, with its major dialects, more closely reflects its Latin roots than most modern Romance languages. The high literacy in Catalan in Spanish Catalonia has developed only since 1975, although the literary language is a composite based on several dialects. Official documents were written in Latin or Catalan from 1212 to 1716, when the Catalan language was suppressed and Castilian imposed. Catalan re-emerged as the national language in 1975. A local movement in Valencia claims that Valencian is not Catalan but a distinct language; linguists do not agree.

The Catalans are mostly Roman Catholics, although they tend to be more skeptical and less devoted than neighboring peoples. Anticlerical sentiment, strong during the early decades of the twentieth century, continues to color religious observances. Since 1975 evangelical Protestant sects have been gaining converts in Spanish Catalonia.

NATIONAL HISTORY: Inhabited by small, independent Iberian tribes, the Mediterranean coast was colonized by the Greeks around six hundred B.C. In the third century B.C. the Carthaginians, under Hamilcar Barca and Hannibal, invaded the region. Absorbed by the Roman Empire in 218 B.C., after the fall of Carthage, the region became one of the first Roman possessions in Spain; the inhabitants mostly adopted Latin culture and speech. Under Roman rule the region became a wealthy province, with its capital at present Tarragona. The region flourished until the collapse of Roman power in the fifth century A.D. The weakness of the Romans left the region open to invasion by the Germanic Goths from the north. The Goths called the region Gothalonia, later changed to Catalonia.

Muslim Moors from North Africa, extending their empire to the north, conquered Catalonia in A.D. 711–714 but lost the northern districts to the Frankish king, later Holy Roman emperor, Charlemagne, in 795. The northern region was organized as the Spanish March of Charlemagne's empire in 801, with its capital at Barcelona, while the islands and Valencia, made a separate kingdom in the eleventh century, remained under Moorish rule.

Catalonia became an independent state, the County of Barcelona, in the ninth century. Ramon Berenguer IV, the count of Barcelona, married Petronila, the heiress of the neighboring kingdom of Aragon in 1137. The union of Catalonia and Aragon principally benefited the Catalans, who concentrated on their expanding Mediterranean empire while the Aragonese* protected the state against the expanding Castilians. The Catalans conquered Valencia and the Balearic Islands from the Moors in the thirteenth and fourteenth centuries and resettled the newly conquered regions with Catalan settlers. From 1230 to the fifteenth century a Catalan trading empire stretched as far east as the Balkan Peninsula, with extensive territories in the Mediterranean and north of the Pyrenees. Catalan wealth generated a golden age, accompanied by a great flowering of medieval Catalan arts and culture, that continued into the Renaissance. By the late Middle Ages, Catalonia, Aragon, and Valencia had joined together in a federation, forging one of the most advanced constitutional systems of the era in Europe.

In the early fifteenth century the male line of the counts of Barcelona became extinct, weakening Catalonia's position in the kingdom. Aragonese attempts to curtail Catalonia's autonomous rights incited a Catalan rebellion and led to civil war in the kingdom from 1460 to 1472. The war's devastation marked the beginning of a long decline that accelerated following the unification of the kingdoms of Aragon and Castile in 1479 and the centralizing of all government functions. The Catalans began a long struggle to preserve their culture and language.

The Catalans retained their autonomy and the Generalitat, the Catalan assembly, but by the seventeenth century their interests so diverged from those of the declining Spanish monarchy that separatism won widespread support. The Catalans rebelled, with French help, against the Spanish government of Philip IV during the Thirty Years' War. The rebellion lasted from 1640 to 1659. By the terms of the Treaty of the Pyrenees, France took control of northern Catalonia, Roussillon, and Cerdagne and established the northern boundary of Spanish territory in the middle Pyrenees. The Catalans sided with Archduke Charles of Austria against Philip V, the first Bourbon king of Spain, during the War of the Spanish Succession. In 1705 the Generalitat met for the first time to coordinate a Catalan rebellion intended to win Catalan independence from Spain, but in September 1714, after a long siege, the forces of Philip V conquered Barcelona. In reprisal for the rebellion, Philip deprived the Catalans of their constitution and all their traditional privileges. In 1716 the Spanish government banned the Catalan language and attempted to eradicate Catalan culture in the Spanish domains. Many Catalans emigrated to Spain's American colonies. In 1822 a western region of Catalonia, called the Franja de Ponente, or Eastern Strip, was transferred to Aragon, but the population remained Catalan in language and culture.

The suppressed Catalan culture and language began to revive with the spread of education and publishing in the 1830s, the revival leading to a resurgence of nationalism. A rebellion at Barcelona, in 1842, provoked renewed government efforts to stamp out the Catalan culture. The Catalan cultural revival resumed in the 1870s and over the next decades produced some of Europe's greatest artists, architects, and writers.

In the late nineteenth century, as part of the revival, nationalism again gained support in the region. In 1902 the first nationalist organizations demanded a separate administration and budget for Catalonia. Amid continuing turmoil in the Spanish state, the Catalans called a general strike, leading to yet another revolt in 1909. Nationalism gained support in the Balearic Islands and Valencia, with some groups seeking local privileges while others sought the reunification of the entire Catalan-speaking region in Spain and France, a region called the Catalan Countries, or Països Catalans. The Spanish Catalans by 1913 had won a slight degree of home rule.

The Spanish kingdom remained neutral during World War I, but between 1917 and 1919 separatist agitation swept the Catalan homeland. In 1919 the Catalan Union, the major nationalist organization, met in Barcelona and drafted a program for home rule. It sent a delegation to the Paris Peace Conference attempting to present a petition to President Woodrow Wilson of the United States, hoping for support under his proposal for self-determination for Europe's minorities. The Spanish government, by diplomatic means, was able to block the petition and to circumvent the issue of home rule for Catalonia.

A serious separatist uprising swept the region again in 1923, and in 1926 Catalan leaders were arrested in France while agitating for support in French Catalonia. The legislation conferring a degree of home rule was repealed in 1925 by the Spanish dictator Primo de Rivera, who attacked all manifestations of Catalan separatism. On 14 April 1931, while the Madrid government was in disarray, the republican leader, Louis Companys, declared from the balcony of Barcelona's city hall the independence of the Catalan Republic. On 9 June 1931, the Catalans convened the Generalitat for the first time in over two hundred years. A compromise was negotiated, and the Catalan government received the recognition of the new republican government in Madrid on 25 September 1931. In 1932 the statute of autonomy for Catalonia became law.

Continued interference by the Spanish government in the affairs of Catalonia caused increased tension between the Barcelona and Madrid. On 4 October 1934, the Catalan government declared the autonomous state independent of Spain, with Louis Companys as the first president. The government in Madrid responded by sending troops into Barcelona and other separatist centers. The Catalan leaders, including Louis Companys, were arrested, and all statutes of autonomy were rescinded.

A new leftist government in Madrid, elected in 1936, allowed the restoration of Catalan autonomy. Catalonia was granted broad self-determination with its own language, flag, anthem, president, and parliament, the Generalitat. To preserve their autonomy, the majority of the Catalans sided with the Loyalists against Franco's Fascist forces as civil war spread across Spain from 1936 to 1939. Aided by Germany and Italy, the Spanish Fascists conquered Catalonia in early 1939. The entire Catalan government, as well as officials of the Generalitat, were executed. Over 200,000 Catalans fled across the Pyrenees into exile, where many later died in Nazi concentration camps.

The triumphant Franco banned all demonstrations of Catalan culture, imposing severe penalties for publishing or teaching in the Catalan language.

Industrialization, particularly along the Mediterranean coast in the 1950s and 1960s, drew in a massive influx of peasant immigrants from Spain's backward southern regions. Dubbed "Franco's Legions" by the Catalans, the immigrants served the Spanish government in two ways—by providing a low-cost industrial workforce and by spreading the traditional Spanish culture approved by Franco's dictatorial government. Underground nationalist organizations became active, while Catalan writers, politicians, and educators were persecuted.

Franco's death in 1975, followed by the rapid democratization of Spain, allowed the Catalan culture to resurface. In 1978 the new democratic Spanish government granted limited autonomy to Catalonia. Promoted by a proliferation of autonomist, nationalist, and separatist organizations, the Catalan culture and language quickly revived and replaced the Castilian language and culture the Franco regime had attempted to impose on Catalonia.

The Catalans won full autonomy on 11 January 1980, but with less actual power than the autonomy statute of 1932. Valencia and the Balearic Islands became separate autonomous regions in 1982. The Catalans elected a government dominated by moderate nationalists determined to win the maximum possible independence within Spain. After over four decades of suppression, only about half the population could speak Catalan and only 16% were totally illiterate in the Catalan language. Following the restoration of the language, speaking and using Catalan and its regional varieties became a matter of pride.

Spain's entry into the European Economic Community (EEC) in 1986 changed the focus of Catalan nationalism. Since 1986, nationalism in the region has focused on independence within a united Europe and the reunification of the Catalan regions in Spain and France, as part of the new European integration. In 1988, the Catalan language, spoken by more Europeans than many official state languages, became an official language of the EEC. In April of 1988, the Catalans celebrated the millennium of the Catalan state and the proclamation of the second republic in 1931.

In 1991, previously violent nationalists, mostly in the Terra Lliure (Free Land) group, renounced violence and dedicated themselves to seeking independence through democratic means. The nationalist surge in Catalonia, unlike other parts of Spain and Europe, has remained relatively nonviolent.

Nationalist leaders claim that Catalonia, Spain's richest and most advanced region, is now more closely linked to the rest of Europe than to the rest of Spain. As the member states of the European Union (EU) draw closer economically and politically, the hold of the Spanish government over Catalonia is weakening. In February 1994 negotiations between Catalan leaders and members of the Spanish government centered on the

Catalan's desire to take up the status the region enjoyed before 1714—independence under the Spanish king, but not subject to the Spanish government.

In October 1998, the Catalan parliament passed a resolution confirming the right of the Catalan people to self-determination. The resolution, proposed by the Catalan Independence Party (PI), was supported by a broad spectrum of Catalan political parties. The Catalan regional government used the resolution to press for greater autonomy from the Spanish government.

To many Spanish Catalans, autonomy is only the first step to an independent Catalonia within the framework of a united Europe, while some already refer to the rest of the country as "Spain," as if they already formed a separate European state. Catalonia is Spain's most important industrial region, and its loss would be disastrous for the Spanish state; but with new European markets opening up, the Catalans could prosper and become a viable European nation-state. Opinion polls consistently show that Catalans in all regions reject violent nationalism but also that a majority continue to support the idea of attaining independence within a united Europe by peaceful, legal means.

SELECTED BIBLIOGRAPHY:

Balcells, Albert, et al. *Catalan Nationalism: Past and Present*. 1996.
Hargreaves, John. *Freedom for Catalonia?* 2000.
Sobrer, Josep Miquel. *Catalonia: A Self-Portrait*. 1992.
Wright, Sue, ed. *Language, Democracy and Devolution in Catalonia*. 1999.

Caymanians
Cayman Islanders

POPULATION: Approximately (2002e) 50,000 Caymanians concentrated in the Cayman Islands in the Caribbean Sea. Other sizable communities live in the United States, Canada, and the United Kingdom.

THE CAYMANIAN HOMELAND: The Caymanian homeland is a small group of islands in the Caribbean Sea. The islands consist of three low-lying limestone islands surrounded by coral reefs about 180 miles (289 km) northwest of Jamaica and 150 miles (241 km) southwest of Cuba. The group is made up of three islands, Grand Cayman, Little Cayman, and Cayman Brac. The islands, although covered with mangrove swamps, have no natural fresh water resources; all drinking water must be collected by rainwater catchment. *Cayman Islands*: 104 sq. mi.—289 sq. km, (2002e) 44,000—Caymanians 80%, expatriates 20%, mostly British and Americans. The Caymanian capital and major cultural center is George Town, (2002e) 27,000, on Grand Cayman.

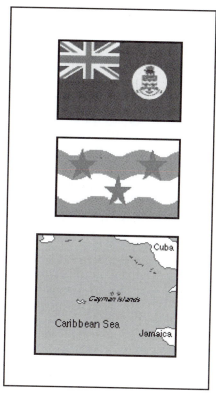

FLAG: The Caymanian national flag, the official flag of the dependent state, is a blue field bearing the Union Jack as a canton on the upper hoist and charged with the Caymanian coat of arms, which includes a pineapple and a turtle above a shield with three stars and the state motto, centered on a white disk on the fly. The flag proposed for an independent Cayman Islands is a field of wavy blue and white stripes charged with three green five-pointed stars.

PEOPLE AND CULTURE: The Caymanians are a Caribbean nation of mixed ancestry, with a large white population, the descendants of planters and farmers who remained after the abolition of slavery in the nineteenth century. The present population of the islands is estimated to comprise 40% of mixed background, 20% blacks, 20% whites, mostly of British background, and 20% non-Caymanians of various ethnic backgrounds. The remoteness of the islands and the integration following the emancipation of slavery in 1833 have resulted in a socially homogeneous society proud of its distinct island culture.

LANGUAGE AND RELIGION: The language of the Caymanians is English, spoken in a variety of dialects, including a Caribbean patois incorporating many African and Spanish words. The Caymanians have a very high literacy rate for the Caribbean, with about 98% able to read and write standard English. Spanish is often spoken as a second language.

Most Caymanians are Christians, with the largest portion belonging to the United Church (Presbyterian and Congregational). Other Christian sects include the Anglicans, Baptists, Roman Catholics, Church of God, and various Protestant denominations, including evangelical sects. The Presbyterians predominate on Grand Cayman and Little Cayman, while the Baptists are the largest congregation on Cayman Brac.

NATIONAL HISTORY: The uninhabited islands were discovered by Christopher Columbus on his fourth and last voyage to the New World on 10 May 1503. The Spanish named the islands Las Tortugas, for the numerous sea turtles found by the explorers, but by 1530 they were known as the Caimanas, or Caymanes, after the islands' large number of reptiles. The islands, although claimed as Spanish territory, were not colonized, partly due to the lack of water. For over a 150 years the islands were visited only by turtlers, loggers, and buccaneers of many nations. The Tortugas became a famous part of Caribbean pirate lore. No point stands higher than 60 feet (18.3 meters) above sea level, making the land almost invisible from the horizon—a perfect pirate hideout.

In 1670, by the Treaty of Madrid, the Spanish ceded the islands to England. The numerous colonial wars of the late seventeenth and early eighteenth centuries prevented English colonization of the Tortugas until 1734, when colonists from Jamaica settled in the islands and named their new settlement George Town, in honor of King George II. Most of the original settlers were British sailors and privateers, shipwrecked passengers, African slaves, and land-grant holders.

The colonists cleared plantations and farms, importing black African slaves as laborers. When the first settlers braved the Cayman Islands, their cattle suffocated as clouds of mosquitoes blocked their nasal passages. Beyond the white sand beaches much of the land was either dense bush or limestone plains, so jagged and shot through with holes that many abandoned the colony to return to Jamaica.

Slavery was outlawed in the British Empire in 1833; the large slave population was allowed to settle on small plots of land. The Cayman Islands were unusual in that many white planters and their families remained after the abolition of slavery. The ethnic mixture that resulted from the fusion of the two groups forms the basis of the majority of the present Caymanians.

At the end of the eighteenth century, uncontrolled fishing had eliminated the native turtle population, virtually the only resource available to the islanders. The Caymanians searched farther and farther away for new turtle grounds, but as international restrictions increased, turtle fishing was greatly reduced.

The three islands were governed as a dependency of the colony of Jamaica, with local authority exercised by justices of the peace. From 1900 to 1940 the islands remained a quiet backwater of the British Empire, remote and neglected. Economic development began only when the islands became accessible by air. The British-sponsored Federation of the West Indies, created in 1959, allowed the Cayman Islands to join as a unitary territory. The larger Caribbean islands opted for separate independence, and the federation was dissolved in 1962. The Caymanians, not wishing to become part of the new state of Jamaica, voted to remain British and were given a separate government as a British dependency.

The isolation of the Caymanians began to change in the mid-1960s, when the islands were discovered by tourists, especially divers on the coral reefs that ring the islands. Tourist development began with a few small hotels, but increasing numbers of tourists led to a building boom for hotels, condominiums, and vacation homes.

During the 1970s, as the island government collected no direct taxes, the islands became one of the major tax havens of the world. A new constitution, approved in 1972, provided for autonomy on most domestic issues. By 1980 over 300 banks and 12,000 foreign companies were registered in the islands. Tourism and financial services employed nearly all the Caymanian population and raised their standard of living to one of the highest in the Caribbean.

In February 1994 constitutional changes were introduced under which executive council members became government ministers. In spite of local support for the post of prime minister, the changes made no provision for a chief minister to be de facto head of the Caymanian government so that who should head the government remained unclear. In January 1995, the opposition People's Democratic Movement (PDM) defeated the Progressive National Party (PNP), winning eight out of 10 legislative council seats.

The island government's anti-money-laundering regime was approved by the Caribbean Financial Action Task Force in September 1996. The Caymans became the first territory in the Caribbean region to receive the organization's endorsement. The campaign against money laundering is part of the Caymanians' movement to become the premier financial center in the Caribbean, but without the financial scandals and accusations of money laundering that plague rival financial centers.

The Caymanians' new prosperity allowed them to relinquish all development aid from the British government. By the 1990s the Caymanians enjoyed virtually full employment in the financial and tourist industries, turtle and shark products, coconut farming, and lumbering. In 1997 the number of registered companies had grown to over 40,000, including about 600 banks and trust companies, making the islands one of the world's major financial centers. The Cayman Islands stock exchange opened the same year.

In the 1990s two of the major problems facing the Caymanians were illegal immigration and the arrival of Cuban refugees seeking to use the islands to reach the United States or Europe. The Caymanian government requested help from the British and American governments in dealing with the increasing numbers of Cubans arriving in the islands. Other immigrants, drawn to the booming economy, found work in construction or fishing, often illegally.

The Caymanians, at the turn of the new century, pay virtually no taxes, but import duties make the cost of living very high for islanders. About 95% of all food and goods must be imported. Despite the cost of living and although some 40% of the land is owned by foreigners, the Caymanians are content with their situation and control all aspects of their national life except military and foreign affairs, for which the government of the United Kingdom takes responsibility. The constitution, revised in 1994, provides for an assembly composed of the British governor, three official members, and 15 elected members. The Caymanians, in recent opinion polls, display no hurry to achieve full independence.

SELECTED BIBLIOGRAPHY:

Boultbee, Paul G. *Cayman Islands*. 1996.
Driver, Jenny. *Cayman Islands*. 2000.
Hannerz, Ulf. *Caymanian Politics: Structure and Style in a Changing Island Society*. 1974.
Williams, Neville. *A History of the Cayman Islands*. 1970.

Chagossians

Ilois; Iloise; Iloïs; Ilois des Chagos; Îloïs; Chagossiens; Chagossois; Chagosséens

POPULATION: Approximately (2002e) 6,000 Chagossians, most living in exile in Mauritius and Seychelles. Outside the region there are Chagossians living in the United Kingdom, Madagascar, and Switzerland.

THE CHAGOSSIAN HOMELAND: The Chagossian homeland is an archipelago of 65 tiny islands and many islets and atolls; it lies in the Indian Ocean, about halfway from Africa to Indonesia, southwest of Sri Lanka and 600 miles (966 km) south of the Maldive Islands. The islands, including Diego Garcia, the largest and southernmost of the islands, are flat and low-lying coral islands. The islands, an extension of the same geological formation as the Maldives and Laccadives, are remote and largely uninhabited. The entire archipelago is claimed by the Republic of Mauritius. The Chagos Archipelago forms a British dependency. *British Indian Ocean Territories (BIOT/ Chagos Archipelago)*: 24 sq. mi.—63 sq. km, (2002e) 2,500, mainly U.S. and British military personnel and civilian contract employees, mostly from the Philippines and Mauritius.

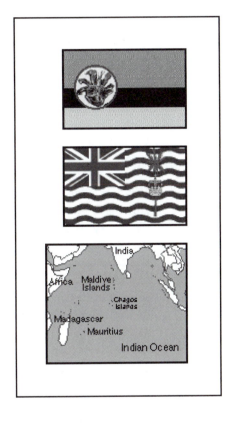

FLAG: The Chagossian national flag, the flag of the national movement, has three unequal horizontal strips of orange, black, and blue bearing a disk near the hoist depicting a drawing of Cocotier Crab, which is native to the islands. The official flag of the British Indian Ocean Territories has wavy white and blue stripes with the Union Jack as a canton on the upper hoist and a palm tree and golden crown on the fly.

PEOPLE AND CULTURE: The Chagossians are the indigenous people of the Chagos Archipelago in the Indian Ocean. Many are the descendants of slaves from Madagascar and Mauritius brought to the islands to work the copra plantations in the late eighteenth and early nineteenth centuries. Cultural influences from the Maldives, Sri Lanka, and India, brought to the islands by workers and fishermen, remain strong in the Chagossian traditions. The Chagossians are traditionally coconut farmers or fishermen, although about 40% are officially unemployed in Mauritius. The Chagossians are often called Ilois, from the French word for a remote islander. American sailor volunteers on Diego Garcia are now caring for the graves of the Chagossian ancestors in the islands, which is the focus of discontent.

LANGUAGE AND RELIGION: The Chagossians speak a French creole that is different from the patois spoken in the Seychelles or Mauritius. The dialect evolved from the fusion of the French of the former plantation owners and the languages originally spoken by the slaves and indentured workers brought to the islands. English is also widely spoken, although Chagossian remains the language of the group.

The majority of the Chagossians are Roman Catholic, although many non-Christian traditions are still observed. Customs originally brought from the African mainland and Madagascar have been mixed with later Christian traditions to form a distinct belief system. One of the aspects of Chagossian belief is veneration of their ancestors. Care of ancestral graves is an important duty for all Chagossian families.

NATIONAL HISTORY: Traditionally Turkish seamen sailing between Constantinople on the Asian spice trade routes discovered the uninhabited islands. Portuguese and Spanish explorers searched the islands, after the discovery of the sea route south around the Cape of Good Hope by Vasco da Gama in 1492. The Portuguese named the islands the Cinco Chagas, the five appearances of Christ. In 1532 explorer Diego Garcia discovered the most important island in the region, which now bears his name. In the seventeenth century English, French, and Dutch sailors changed the name of the island group to Chagos.

The islands, spread over a large area, were known to early mariners on the trade routes between the Cape of Good Hope and the northern entrance to the Moluccan Straits. The first inhabitants arrived in the islands in 1776, sent by the viscount de Souillac, the French resident at l'Ile de France, now Mauritius. By 1815, when Mauritius came under British rule, the islands had a population of about 2,000, mostly slaves of mixed Madagascar and African descent and indentured workers from India.

The islands were used as stopover points, and, after the introduction of steamships, as a coaling station on the Singapore route. With the opening of the Suez Canal in the 1850s, the islands, particularly Diego Garcia, were halfway between Suez and Australia. In the nineteenth century three large plantations were established on Diego Garcia, staffed by slaves from Mauritius. Later a leper colony was established in the islands; sufferers from Mauritius, Madagascar, and Seychelles were sent there until the facility was closed in 1835.

The end of slavery in the 1830s ended the plantation system, and commercial coconut plantations were established. The former slave and indentured workers remained when their masters left. They gradually formed a distinct culture, incorporating influences from Africa, Madagascar, and South Asia. The varied peoples gradually united around their island culture and distinct Creole dialect.

The British organized an island territory in 1965 by the amalgamation of Aldabra, Farquhar, and Desroches Islands, formerly part of the Seychelles, and the Chagos Archipelago. The island of Diego Garcia, the largest of the group, occupied a strategic location in the central Indian Ocean. The island is the site of a joint U.S.–U.K. military facility. The British government leased Diego Garcia to the United States in December 1966. The islands were separated from the Mauritius government and constituted the British Indian Ocean Territories (BIOT) in 1968. In June 1976, the former Seychelles Islands were retroceded to the independent Seychelles, and the Chagos Archipelago became a self-administering territory under the East African Desk of the British Foreign Office. The islands were officially recorded as uninhabited.

Between 1967 and 1973 the British government forced around 2,000 Chagossians into exile in Mauritius to make way for the U.S.–U.K. base on the island. Some were sent to the Seychelles, but the majority were dumped in Mauritius. The islanders were forced to abandon their homes, herded aboard overcrowded boats, and sent to Mauritius, over 1,245 miles (2,000 km) to the southwest. In Mauritius the Chagossians were left on their own, living in poverty and mostly rejected by the surrounding Mauritians, although the Mauritius government offered limited assistance. The Chagossians found it hard to obtain work, and some committed suicide. Only after seven years in exile did the British government offer any financial help for the resettlement of the exiles. In 1982 the British government offered further aid, provided that the Chagossians agreed to their "preclusion from returning to the Chagos."

Reefs off the islands are well developed and the most untouched in the Indian Ocean region, but they are being overfished and depleted. Although all but authorized people are barred from the region except by permit since 1971, pirate fishermen from Sri Lanka easily elude the Royal Navy's lone patrol boat and make off with huge catches of reef sharks and other large fish, virtually eliminating whole predator species, which could eventually cause the collapse of the reef ecosystem. Large-scale dredging and construction around the massive military base on Diego Garcia has already damaged the reefs around that island.

In the 1980s the younger Chagossians in Mauritius and the Seychelles began to mobilize in a campaign to return to their island homeland. The plight of the Chagossians, hidden by the British government and mostly forgotten by the world, began to win attention in the press and among international groups. In 1997 the Chagossians petitioned the British government for the right to return to the islands. In 1997–99 Chagossian representatives presented their case to the indigenous peoples seminars held by the United Nations in Geneva.

The High Court in London, in March 2000, gave a Chagossian leader, Louis Bancoult, the right to challenge the British government with claims that he and the other islanders were illegally forced into exile over 30 years ago. They will also be able to fight for the legal right to return to the Chagos Archipelago. The Chagossians, claiming their rights as British subjects, demand that the British government allow them to return to their home islands and to pay damages for the gross injustice of the Cold War politics. The High Court ruling gave the Chagossians hope that their long exile might one day end.

The Chagossians brought their case to court in London in July 2000. One of the major obstacles was the 1971 ordinance forbidding anyone to live in the archipelago permanently, which the Chagossians claim was enacted illegally and contravenes the European convention on human rights, which became part of British law in 2000. Another major problem is the U.S. government, loath to lose the important military base in the middle of the strategic Indian Ocean. The lease on the military base on Diego Garcia is in effect until 2017. The Chagossians have suggested that they be allowed to repopulate the other islands, leaving the issue of Diego Garcia for a later date. Others have demanded that the lease payments be turned over to the original inhabitants of Diego Garcia, or at least the island be shared with the returnees, who could replace the 1,500 contract workers employed at the military base.

There is not much left of the coconut plantations that once provided work and sustenance for the Chagossian population. They have long since been abandoned and are now overgrown and unproductive. Only Diego Garcia has piped water and electricity. There are doubts that the islands could support the 5,000 Chagossians the nationalists claim want to return to the islands. Although the exiles have produced official photographs detailing the life of the indigenous islanders in the 1950s, many in the British government continue to claim that there were never any native islanders, only Seychellois and Mauritians who returned to their home islands at the end of their coconut plantation contracts. Nationalists then ask why the British government gives the Chagossians temporary British dependent-territory passports but does not give passports to Seychellois and Mauritians.

In 2000 the issue was brought up in the European Parliament as concerning an overseas territory controlled by a member of the European Union (EU). Some members demanded that the Chagossians be given rights within the EU as the indigenous population of a territory dependent on an EU member state and be granted the right to return to the three largest of the Chagos Islands—Diego Garcia, Solomon, and Peros Banhos. Militants denounced the exile of the Chagossians as Britain's own "ethnic cleansing."

On 3 November 2000 the British High Court ruled that the Chagossians were illegally deported from their homeland but did not comment on their right to return. The Chagossians interpreted the ruling as sanctioning the return to their homeland.

The leader of the Chagos refugee group in Mauritius, Olivier Bancoult, in December 2000 announced that lawyers were preparing to sue the U.S. government for $6 billion in compensation. The U.S. government, following the Chagossians' winning of the right to return to their homes at the High Court in London in November 2000, has thrown up obstacles, finally conceding that it cannot prevent them returning to neighboring islands, but will not allow them on Diego Garcia, which has the only airstrip in the islands. Since the base opened, the U.S. government has brought in workers from the Philippines and Mauritius, but has never allowed any of the exiled Chagossians work. The British Foreign Office is also being sued for compensation.

A group of Chagossians, part of a displaced community in Mauritius, has staged a protest in front of the offices of the British High Commission in Port Louis demanding British citizenship in March 2001. British citizenship, long denied the exiles, would help them to press their case against the U.S. and U.K. governments.

SELECTED BIBLIOGRAPHY:

Chellapermal, A. *The Problem of Mauritius Sovereignty over the Chagos Archipelago and the Militarization of the Indian Ocean.* 1984.
Madeley, John. *Diego Garcia: A Contrast to the Falklands.* 1994.
Rao, P. Pattabhi Rama. *Diego Garcia: Towards a Zone of Peace.* 1988.
Walker, Iain. *Ethnic Identity and Social Change among the Ilois in Mauritius.* 1986.

Chamorros

Chamorus; Chamorris; Chaniolis; Tjamoros; Taotao Tano

POPULATION: Approximately (2002e) 120,000 Chamorros in the Pacific region, concentrated in the Marianas Islands but with a sizable population in the mainland United States, mostly in California, and in Hawaii.

THE CHAMORRO HOMELAND: The Chamorro homeland is an archipelago of volcanic and coral formation islands in the western Pacific Ocean 1,500 miles (2,400 km) east of the Philippines and 3,000 miles (5,000 km) west of the Hawaiian Islands. The islands extend 450 miles (725 km) north of the major island of Guam. Politically, the 23 Marianas Islands are divided into Guam, the largest of the islands and an organized unincorporated territory; and the 22 islands of the Northern Marianas, which constitute a commonwealth in political union with the United States. *Territory of Guam (Guahan)*: 208 sq. mi.—541 sq. km, (2002e) 164,000—Chamorros 48%, Filipinos 24%, mainland Americans 10%, Chinese, Japanese, and Koreans 18%. *Commonwealth of the Northern Marianans*: 184 sq. mi.—477 sq. km, (2002e) 75,000—Chamorros 35%, Filipinos 30%, Carolinians and other Micronesians, Caucasians, Japanese, Chinese, Koreans 35%. The capital and major cultural center is Agana, called Hagatna by the Chamorros, (2002e) 3,000, urban area, 55,000. The capital of the Northern Marianas is Chalan Kanoa, on Saipan, (2002e) 4,000, urban area, 40,000.

FLAG: The Chamorro national flag (not shown), the former flag of the Northern Marianas, is a pale blue field bearing a gray Latte stone surmounted by a five-pointed white star. The official flag of Guam is a blue field with a narrow red border bearing a centered shield with a tan beach, blue ocean, brown canoe, pale blue sky, and a green and brown palm tree. The official flag of the Northern Marianas is a pale blue field bearing a gray Latte stone behind a five-pointed white star surrounded by a flower wreath.

PEOPLE AND CULTURE: The Chamorros are Micronesians, descended from early Malay* settlers, with later admixture of Spanish, Mexican, Philippine, German, and Japanese strains. The Chamorros tend to be taller than most Micronesians and may be of early Polynesian origin. There are very few pure Chamorros in the islands, but all who identify with the culture and language are referred to as Chamorros. They call themselves Taotao Tano, meaning the People of the Land. The Chamorro culture, nearly wiped out under Spanish rule, has revived in the twentieth century, retaining a strong Spanish cultural influence. The Chamorro culture has been greatly influenced by American culture in the twentieth century. The majority of the Chamorros live in villages, with vegetable gardening as their main occupation, although there are sizable urban Chamorro populations on Guam and Saipan. The extended family is the main social unit. Strong family ties limit the desire of Chamorros to emigrate for employment opportunities, although over the last decades migration to the mainland United States has accelerated. In recent decades public and private groups have promoted traditional Chamorro music, dance, and other traditional cultural arts. The teaching of Chamorro cultural values, such as respect (for the elders, those in authority, and all others) and in-afa'maolek (caring for and getting along with others), are as important as teaching academic subjects. The Chamorros now form less than half the Guamanian population.

LANGUAGE AND RELIGION: The Chamorro language is a Western Malayo-Polynesian language of the Austronesian or Malayo-Polynesian language group. The language, more closely related to the languages of Indonesia and the Philippines than to the other languages of Micronesia, developed in the isolation of the islands and has been influenced by the languages of the peoples who controlled the islands. The distinct Chamorro language has its own vocabulary and grammar, mixed with many Spanish words and forms. The language is spoken in two major dialects, Chamorro and Rotanese Chamorro. English is widely spoken in the Marianas, being the language of government and instruction. In the Northern Marianas, 86% of the population speaks a language other than English at home. Chamorro became a modern literary language in the twentieth century, with works of history, science, and fiction.

The majority of the Chamorros are Roman Catholic, with many traditional beliefs and taboos mixed with the traditional Catholic teachings. An estimated 98% of the Chamorros adhere to Roman Catholicism; however, attendance at religious services, especially among younger Chamorros, has declined dramatically. Protestant sects, particularly evangelical groups, have made some inroads among the population since the 1950s.

NATIONAL HISTORY: The early history of the Marianas Islands is little known, but it is believed that the islands were first settled around 3000 B.C. by an ancient seafaring people from Asia, possibly from present

Indonesia. Later waves of migration arrived from Polynesia and Melanesia. By A.D. 800 the islanders had developed a complex society. The people eventually known as Chamorros developed a unique island culture, which included the construction of huge, mushroomlike capped pillars of stone called Latte or Taga stones. Their precise use remains a mystery.

A Portuguese navigator, Ferdinand Magellan, exploring for Spain, sighted the islands in March 1521. He made a landfall on Guam, claiming the islands for Spain. The theft of a small skiff by the islanders led to the islands' being named the Islas de Las Ladrones, the Islands of Thieves. The archipelago was later rechristened the Islands of the Lateen Sails, referring to the type of sails used by the Chamorros. The Spanish government formally claimed the island chain in 1565, although there was no European presence in the islands.

In 1668, when the islands were finally colonized, the name of the archipelago was changed to Las Marianas to honor Maria Anna of Austria, the widow of King Philip IV and at that time the regent of Spain. A Chamorro uprising against oppressive Spanish rule in 1670 set off 25 years of intermittent warfare called the Chamorro Wars, which ended only after considerable bloodshed. European diseases also played a part in the decimation of the Chamorro population. Jesuit priests who accompanied the colonists forcibly converted the surviving Chamorros to Catholicism. The Chamorros resisted conversion to Catholicism, which did not fit traditional beliefs.

The Spanish authorities, in order to control the indigenous population, moved the Chamorros into enclaves and segregated them into villages in the late seventeenth century. The entire indigenous populations of Saipan and Rota were forcibly relocated to Guam. Many islanders were killed in the process of relocation, but by 1698 the subjugation of the Chamorros was complete. The Chamorro population of the islands, estimated at 100,000 in the early sixteenth century, was almost wiped out by the brutal Spanish colonial administration. By 1700 only about 4,000 Chamorros survived. The Pacific island culture of the Chamorros was destroyed, but the language survived even though the population further declined to an estimated 1,500 in the mid-eighteenth century.

The Spanish developed Guam as a resupply station on the treasure routes in the Pacific. Spanish galleons traveling between the Philippines and Mexico regularly stopped at Guam for stores and food. Plantation agriculture, worked by slaves, produced tropical fruits and sugarcane. By the nineteenth century, the general pattern of life in the islands had evolved as a mixture of Chamorro and Spanish traditions.

Guam was ceded to the United States following the Spanish-American War in 1898. The defeated Spanish government, deciding to withdraw entirely from the Pacific, sold the northern Marianas to Germany in 1899. This period marked the permanent division of the Marianas between

Guam and the Northern Marianas. On 22 February 1900, the new American administration outlawed slavery on Guam. Modern medical facilities and education were introduced, and the Chamorro population began slowly to increase. From 1899 to 1950, naval officers appointed by the president of the United States served as governors of Guam.

The Japanese, an allied state in World War I, invaded the German-held Northern Marianas in 1914. Defeated Germany was stripped of all its overseas possessions in 1919. The Northern Marianas, turned over to the new League of Nations, were to be administered by the Japanese as a mandated territory. Japan withdrew from the League of Nations in 1935 after virtually annexing the northern Marianas Islands. To offset American military strength in the region, the Japanese built a large military base on the island of Tinian and began a program of civilian immigration to the islands. Thousands of Japanese, Okinawans,* and Koreans settled in the islands, creating an urbanized population that thrived on fishing and sugar production. The colonial population eventually outnumbered the Chamorros by a ratio of two to one. The Chamorro population was marginalized and mostly ignored.

The economy of the Japanese islands was diverse, and the islands became very prosperous, although the Chamorros were excluded from public life and were forced to learn Japanese. By 1935 the population of the Northern Marianas had reached 44,000, with over 30,000 in the flourishing capital city of Garapan, on Saipan.

Until World War II the Chamorro villages remained the basic social and economic units, preserving the surviving Chamorro customs plus many traditions and traits similar to those of nineteenth-century Spain. The village fiesta, held in honor of a patron saint, was the major social and religious event of each year, bringing together the extended Chamorro families. Divided by politics, the Chamorros maintained family ties between those living under Japanese rule and the inhabitants of American-controlled Guam.

Japanese troops landed on Guam just after the attack on Pearl Harbor, on 7 December 1941. They quickly overran the small American military force. American forces returned to invade the Japanese-held Marianas on 15 June 1944; some of the heaviest fighting of the war resulted, devastating the islands. Many Japanese civilians, believing propaganda that they would be executed and dishonored, joined Japanese soldiers in mass suicide, throwing their children and then themselves off high cliffs at the north end of Saipan.

In July 1944 the construction of military bases began. Guam was retaken in August 1944. The islands were prepared as forward bases for the invasion of Japan, but they were utilized instead for the bombing of the Japanese home islands. It was from an airfield on Tinian in the Northern

Marianas that the first nuclear weapon was dropped on the Japanese city of Hiroshima, by a B-29 aircraft called *Enola Gay*.

In 1947 the Northern Marianas were included in the UN Trust Territory of the Pacific Islands, which included the Micronesian islands to the east. The remaining Japanese nationals were re-patriated to Japan in 1946–47. The territory, now under American administration, was divided into several regions, including the Northern Marianas. The Organic Act of Guam, passed by the U.S. Congress in 1950, regulated the government of the island, under the U.S. Department of the Interior. The act made all Guamanian Chamorros American citizens but did not give them the right to vote in national elections.

The Office of Territorial Affairs, in the Department of the Interior, administered Guam, beginning in 1973. During the 1970s the island government gradually moved toward representative self-government. The first popularly elected governor ran for office in 1970, and in 1972 Guam gained the right to one nonvoting delegate to the U.S. House of Representatives. In 1973 the United Nations called on the United States to hold a free vote to allow the Guamanians to choose their own future. On 14 September 1976, the inhabitants of Guam voted 10,221 to 7,386 to continue as a U.S. territory. Of the five choices given the voters, full independence received the fewest votes. On 4 August 1979, however, the inhabitants of Guam voted five to one against a new constitution that made no provision for the return of traditional lands to the Chamorros.

In January 1978, the Northern Marianas became the first to leave the Trust Territory, becoming a self-governing commonwealth in political union with the United States. For the first time in over 400 years, the Chamorros of the Northern Marianas gained some measure of control over their own destiny.

In a September 1982 referendum in Guam offering six options, the option of commonwealth status won a plurality of 48% of the vote. The majority favored establishing a commonwealth relationship to the United States, similar to that of the Northern Marianas or Puerto Rico. The islanders approved a draft Commonwealth Act in 1987, and negotiations with Congress were initiated.

On 29 May 1986, the UN Trusteeship Council concluded that the United States had satisfactorily discharged its obligations to the Northern Marianas. Several months later, in November 1986, the inhabitants of the Northern Marianas were granted U.S. citizenship.

The Chamorros often felt neglected and misunderstood by the U.S. government and other world nations. Affected by the nationalism sweeping the Pacific in the 1970s and 1980s the Chamorros began a concerted effort to revive their flagging culture and began to demand greater self-government, including political and economic autonomy.

Typhoon Omar devastated the region in August 1992, damaging some

90% of the buildings in the islands. The reconstruction of the islands, particularly on Guam, revived the sensitive issue of land rights. Land taken from the Chamorros for defense purposes but no longer needed by the military became a nationalist issue. Land is intrinsically tied to the Chamorro culture, and the struggle for the return of traditional lands is seen as a spiritual quest to preserve the essence of the Chamorro identity. The U.S. and Guamanian governments own about two-thirds of the islands' land.

In the Northern Marianas nationalist sentiment focuses on the island of Tinian, the site of a major U.S. military base. In 1987 the inhabitants of the island demonstrated against plans to build three radar installations and against plans to build a major naval base at Tinian Harbor. The nationalists objected to the parts of the commonwealth agreement that gave the U.S. government rights to military installations in the islands. In 1996, in a dispute between Guam landowners and the government over former military land, the owners asked for Guam to be included on the UN list of non-self-governing territories. Inclusion on the list would bring official UN support for decolonization. In 1997 Chamorro nationalist leaders asked for Guam to be included on the UN non-self-governing territories. In December 1998, during a visit to the territory by U.S. President Bill Clinton, the Guamanians repeated their demands for commonwealth status, independence in association with the United States.

Demands for an end to the colonial status of Guam and for the reunification of the Chamorro nation have increased since the early 1990s. The nationalists point out the irony that democracy is taught in island schools and is held up as ideal, while representative democracy does not exist in Guam. Demands for commonwealth status, possibly in union with the Northern Marianas, are gaining support following the anniversary of a century of U.S. control in 1999.

Nationalists reiterated their demands for the return of traditional lands in early 2001. Lands seized by the U.S. military equal about one-third of the whole island of Guam. The Chamorros were compensated for the lands, but at values set by the military.

SELECTED BIBLIOGRAPHY:

Denfield, D. Colt. *Hold the Marianas: The Japanese Defense of the Marianas Islands.* 1996.

Kristen, Katherine, and Kathleen Thompson. *Pacific Islands.* 1996.

Rogers, Robert F. *Destiny's Landfall: A History of Guam.* 1995.

Wuerch, William L., and Dirk Anthony Ballendorf. *Historical Dictionary of Guam and Micronesia.* 1994.

Chams

Chamars; Chamshas; Tjams; Chiems; Chiem Thënh; Hroi

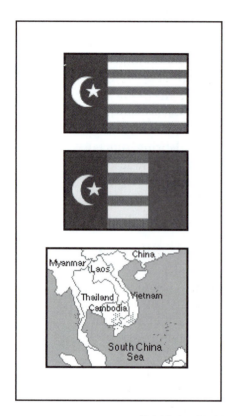

POPULATION: Approximately (2002e) 650,000 Chams in southeast Asia, concentrated in Cambodia, where some 250,000 live, and Vietnam, with a Cham population estimated at 240,000. Other sizable Cham communities include 20,000 in Laos, 10,000 in Malaysia, 5,000 in Thailand, and smaller groups in the United States, Canada, and Western Europe. Nationalists claim a Cham population of between one and 1.3 million in southeast Asia.

THE CHAM HOMELAND: The Cham homeland, Champa, lies in southeastern Asia, divided into two geographical regions—in Cambodia around Phnom Penh and along the Mekong River; and in Vietnam, the Mekong River delta, and the Central Highlands. The Western Cham regions in the Mekong Delta are mostly rice lands. Highland Champa, around the city of Dalat in southern Vietnam, is a high plateau rising from the coast. Champa has no official status in either country. The Cham capital and major cultural center in the Mekong Delta is Chau Doc in southwestern Vietnam, (2002e) 61,000. The capital and major cultural center of the Highland Chams is Dalat, (2002e) 124,000. The major cultural centers of the Cambodian Chams are Phnom Penh, the Cambodian capital, and the small town of Udong on the Mekong River.

FLAG: The Cham national flag, the flag of the former republic, has nine red and white horizontal stripes with a broad pale-blue vertical stripe at the hoist bearing a large white crescent moon and a five-pointed white star. The flag of the Champa Highland Liberation Front (FLHPC) is divided in thirds: the hoist is blue charged with a crescent moon and a five-pointed star; the middle consists of seven red and white stripes; the fly is green.

PEOPLE AND CULTURE: The Chams, the descendants of the people of ancient Champa, are a Malay* people; they are culturally, ethnically, and religiously distinct from their neighbors, although their precise origins are unknown. Historically and culturally the Chams are divided into two major groups—the Western Chams in Cambodia, Laos, and the delta provinces of southern Vietnam near the Cambodian border; and the Eastern Chams of the Central Highlands of southern Vietnam. Traditionally Cham society was matrilocal and matrilineal, but under Islamic influence they have become more patrilineal. Due to the number of Cham men killed in Cambodia between 1975 and 1979, the sex ratio is skewed, and women now perform many of the duties that once belonged to men. Even though they are descended from a warlike people, the present Chams are very timid, although group activism is increasing. They are known for their honesty; stealing and lying are virtually unknown among them. Even though they live among other nations, particularly the Khmers and Vietnamese, they rarely intermarry.

LANGUAGE AND RELIGION: The Cham language belongs to the Chamic group of the Malay branch of the Austronesian or Malayo-Polynesian languages. The language, called Cham-Chru, is considered a transition language between the Thai-Kadai languages of southern China and the Indonesian languages. The two major dialects, with some differences, correspond to the geographic separation of the Western and Eastern Chams. The language is written in an old Devanageri-based script, the alphabet used by many modern Indian languages. The earliest example of the Cham written language dates from A.D. 829, although some undated inscriptions are probably older. Exile communities in Europe and North America are considering adopting the Roman script.

Most Chams, particularly in Vietnam, practice a distinct version of Sunni Islam, mixed with the religious traditions of Shaioita Brahmanism, a religion derived from the Hindu religion of ancient Champa. The Chams are followers of Imam San who call themselves Kaum Juma'at, or the Friday group, because they pray only once every Friday. Most Muslims must pray several times daily. Although the Muslim Chams recognize Allah as the single, all-powerful God, they also recognize other, non-Islamic deities. In Brahman temples in Vietnam, *brahmanes*, with female mediums, perform rites in honor of deified heroes of the past and worship Shiva and Parvati. A special tradition is the burying of their dead twice. Immediately after death, the person is buried in a temporary grave, but after a year the bones are removed and reburied in a permanent grave. Since every action must be sanctioned by ancestral practices, progress of any kind tends to be very slow. Money from many Middle Eastern states has helped rebuild Cham mosques that were destroyed by the Khmer Rouge in Cambodia. Middle Eastern donors have tried to force their beneficiaries to adopt a more Middle Eastern style of Islam, but the Cham won't let the money sway their beliefs. A small number, mostly in Vietnam, are Christians, converted by missionaries working in the region before the Vietnam War.

NATIONAL HISTORY: Ancient Champa emerged as a separate kingdom in A.D. 192, during the breakup of the Han dynasty of China. The Han official in charge of the region established his own kingdom around the present city of Hue. The kingdom eventually expanded to control most of present south and central Vietnam. The Chams gradually came under Indian cultural influence and evolved a brilliant civilization. Administratively the kingdom was divided into four smaller states, named after regions of India—Amaravati (Quang Nam), Vijaya (Binh Dinh), Kauthara (Nha Trang), and Panduranga (Phan Rang). The Cham population was concentrated in coastal zones, where a powerful fleet carried out commerce and piracy.

Champa united under King Bhadravarman about 400 A.D., and the powerful Cham fleet raided the Chinese coast. In retaliation the Chinese invaded and again brought Champa under their rule in 446. A new dynasty, in the sixth century, threw off its allegiance to China. Champa entered a golden age of prosperity and artistic achievements. During this period the center of the kingdom began to shift to the south. In the late eighth century, the Chams were distracted by wars with the Javanese kingdoms, but in the ninth century they renewed their pressure on the Chinese-controlled provinces to the north.

The expansion of the coastal Cham kingdom brought it into conflict with the powerful Khmers in the south and the newly independent Vietnamese in the north. Beginning in the tenth century Champa fought a long series of indecisive wars with the Viet and Khmer states and with China. The Vietnamese kingdom of Dai Viet forced the Chams to relinquish Amarvati in 1000 and Vijaya in 1069. The Chams were able to withstand further Vietnamese and Khmer attacks, but in 1145 the Khmers invaded and conquered Champa. Two years later, a new Cham king, Jaya Harivarman I, established his authority and defied the Khmers. The Cham defeat of the Khmers by his successor and the sack of the Khmer capital, Angkor, in 1177, marked the Chams' apex as a military power.

Although the Chams were nearly always at war, their culture flourished. The sophisticated Cham civilization left behind magnificent and durable architecture, temples and public buildings as smooth as sandstone but constructed without mortar, as the bricks were baked after they were in place, in a construction process now lost.

Conquered by invading Mongols in 1262, Champa declined rapidly, its flourishing agriculture devastated and its magnificent cities in ruins. The Cham state slowly recovered, only to come into conflict again with Dai Viet. Decisively defeated by the Vietnamese in 1471–72, the kingdom lost all of its territory north of Danang. Cham refugees fled south to the remaining Cham lands around Dalat, Nhatrang, and Camranh.

One group of refugees, freemen and aristocrats, settled in the Khmer kingdom of Cambodia. Sometime between the fifteenth and seventeenth centuries they adopted the Islamic religion, brought north by Malay traders. The new religion gradually spread to Champa, where it mostly displaced Hinduism as the predominant religious sect. The decline of the kingdom changed the newly Muslim Chams from a prosperous seafaring power to an agrarian culture based on a system of advanced irrigation canals.

The Vietnamese, continuing to press Champa from the north, varied their method of conquest—sometimes marrying into the Cham aristocracy, other times launching offensives spearheaded by assault units of orphans raised by the state. In the seventeenth century a mighty Viet army pushed south into Champa and conquered all but the highland region around Dalat. The last Cham king fled into exile with the Viet conquest of Dalat in 1822. The Viet victory ended seventeen centuries of separate Cham existence. Massacres in the 1830s decimated the remaining Cham population, leaving only a few pockets of refugees in the highlands and along the Gulf of Thailand. The end of the Champa kingdom marked the demise of the only mainland Asian culture that had incorporated features of the Oceanic cultures. By 1810 the number of ethnic Chams in the region is thought to have fallen to around 45,000.

The French established a colonial administration in Vietnam and Cambodia in the mid-nineteenth century; the Cham survivors as protectors against the hated Vietnamese welcomed the powerful Europeans. The Chams, the most loyal allies of the French administration, provided many recruits for the colonial army and administration, and through contacts with other French colonies gradually established ties to other Muslim peoples. The Chams in the highlands traditionally mediated barter in salt and rare woods between the hill tribes, or Montagnards,* and the lowland Vietnamese; under French rule they became the representatives of the numerous highland tribes.

The Chams' renewed ties to the outside world began a process of national revival. Looking back on several periods of their history when conquered Champa had regained its sovereignty under Cham princes, national leaders began to press for an independent Cham state under French protection. In 1946 the French administration created an autonomous region in the highlands centered on the Cham metropolis, Dalat. The Cham populations in both Vietnam and Cambodia increased rapidly, and by 1970, according to Cham nationalists, their numbers totaled close to a million.

The French defeat by Vietnamese nationalists in 1954, followed by the French withdrawal and eventual partition of Vietnam, left the Chams without protection. Cham nationalists mobilized the population and formed the Champa Highland Liberation Front (FLHPC) to work for an independent Cham state. The Chams sent missions to the United Nations asking for assistance in reestablishing an independent, nonaligned Cham state. Their appeals to the United Nations were ignored, but the nationalist leaders on 19 February 1964 declared Champa independent of Vietnam. In 1965 South Vietnamese* government troops occupied the region, suppressed the Cham government, and ended the Cham bid for independence. In 1968 the head of the underground Cham government, Y-Bham-Huol, after nearly four years in hiding, was escorted to the Cambodian border and expelled. He and his followers joined the Cambodian Chams of the Cham National Liberation Movement (MNLC).

The communist Khmer Rouge tried, without much success, to recruit Cambodian Chams during the struggle with the Khmer Republic between 1970 and 1975. The vehemently anticommunist Chams suffered for their beliefs during the civil wars and foreign military incursions in both Vietnam and Cambodia that ended with communist victories in 1975. A Cham rebellion against the victorious Khmer Rouge in Cambodia ended with thousands massacred and the entire Cham population targeted for eradication. By the time the murderous Khmer Rouge had been driven from power in 1979, over a tenth of the Cham population of Cambodia had perished. Fearing a Khmer Rouge return to power in Cambodia, thousands emigrated illegally to the Cham heartland in southern Vietnam.

Cham nationalist groups, with the support of several wealthy Muslim countries, organized in the 1970s and 1980s to resist Vietnamese government plans to ease lowland population pressure by encouraging settlement in the minority-populated Central Highlands. Allied with the Montagnards and Khmer Krom,* and later joined by Vietnamese dissidents and religious minorities, the Chams encouraged a coalition of nationalist and anticommunist groups to form the United Front for the Struggle of Oppressed Races (FULRO), the only sizable resistance movement in Vietnam. Vietnamese government countermeasures, apart from military offensives, include the elimination of the official position of the *mufti*, the Cham religious leader, and the prohibition of participation in the Muslim pilgrimage to Mecca, measures that reinforced the Muslim Chams' determination to win cultural and political autonomy.

National pride, particularly among the Western Chams, has only begun to revive as the Cambodian and Laotian government liberalize their policies toward their national minorities. Promises of cultural and religious freedom have aided the ethnic revival. Renewed ties between the two parts of the Cham nation are encouraging a religious, cultural, and ethnic resurgence at the turn of the twenty-first century. Smaller groups, such as the Thai Chams, have only recently been recognized as ethnic Chams. They are thought to be descendants of Chams who fought in the Thai army some two centuries ago. The Chams base their case for unification and self-determination on their proud past and the vanished kingdom that lasted from the second to the seventeenth centuries.

SELECTED BIBLIOGRAPHY:

Dournes, Jacques. *Minorities of Central Vietnam*. 1980.
Gall, Timothy L. *Worldmark Encyclopedia of Culture and Daily Life*. 1998.
Maspero, Georges. *The Kingdom of Champa*. 1949.
Sheehan, Sean. *Cambodia*. 1996.

Chavash

Tavas; Chävash; Chuvash; Volga Bulgars; Bolgars

POPULATION: Approximately (2002e) 2,255,000 Chavash in Russia, mostly in the Volga River basin of eastern European Russia. Less than half live in the Chavash Republic of the Russian Federation, with large Chavash populations in neighboring republics and regions, as far east as western Siberia, and in the Central Asian republics of Kyrgyzstan and Uzbekistan.

THE CHAVASH HOMELAND: The Chavash homeland mostly lies on the right bank of the middle section of the Volga River. The region occupies the flat plains of the upland Chuvash Plateau, a wooded steppe in the western Volga River basin of eastern European Russia. The Chavash leadership declared the sovereignty of the republic on 26 October 1990, and in 1991 Chavashia became a member state of the newly independent Russian Federation. *Chavash Republic (Chävash Jen)*: 7,066 sq. mi.—18,301 sq. km, (2002e) 1,342,000—Chavash (Chuvash) 71%, Russians 24%, Tatars* 3%, Mordvins* 2%. The Chavash capital and major cultural center is Cheboksary, called Shupashkar by the Chavash, (2002e) 459,000.

FLAG: The Chavash flag, the official flag of the republic, is a yellow field with a narrow crimson stripe on the bottom and bearing a stylized "Tree of Life" and three stylized crimson suns in the center.

PEOPLE AND CULTURE: The Chavash, called Chuvash by the Russians, are the descendants of the medieval Bulgar people of the Volga River basin, with later admixtures of Turkic and Finnic strains. Considered a Turkic-Tatar people, the Chavash form an intermediate nation between the Orthodox Russians and the Finnic peoples on the one hand and Turkic Muslim Tatars and Bashkorts* on the other. The nation comprises two major divisions, the Anatri, or southern, group and the Viryal, or northern, group. The Chavash derive a strong identity from their Bulgar past, which makes their national identity somewhat resistant to assimilation by

430

other peoples. Though over half the Chavash live outside their national republic, they have proved less susceptible to assimilation than many larger groups and have preserved their unique culture intact. The strong link between their culture and national identity has sustained the suppressed Chavash nation for hundreds of years.

LANGUAGE AND RELIGION: The Chavash language, though of basic Turkic structure, is not considered to belong to any of the four Turkic language groups but to form a separate and distinct Bulgar branch of the West Altaic language group. Formerly, scholars considered Chavash to be a Turkicized Finno-Ugric language or an intermediary dialect between Turkic and Mongolian. The only modern descendant of the extinct Volga Bulgar language, it is a complicated mixture of Turkic, Finnic, Mongol, Russian, Farsi, and Arabic elements. The two major divisions of the Chavash correspond to the major dialects, Anatri (Lower Chavash) and Viryal (Upper Chavash). An estimated 82% use Chavash as their first language, and 80% are able to speak Russian as a second language. The old Chavash literary language used the Russian script, but a new writing system created in 1872 by I. Ya. Yakolev existed until 1933, when the Soviets replaced it with a modified Cyrillic alphabet. In 1938 the Russian Cyrillic was made the official alphabet. There is a movement to replace Cyrillic with the pre-Soviet Chavash alphabet, which is based on the Latin alphabet used in most of Europe.

The majority are Orthodox Christians; however, their religion and culture have been influenced by their pre-Christian beliefs and their proximity to Muslim peoples. The Chavash were originally Muslim but were forced to convert to Christianity by the Russians. A minority reconverted to Islam in the nineteenth and early twentieth centuries. Pre-Christian wedding and funeral rites survive, as does the veneration of their sacred tree of life, *kiremet*.

NATIONAL HISTORY: The ancestors of the Chavash were tribes of ancient Bulgars and Suvars living in the North Caucasus from the fifth to eighth centuries. In the seventh or eighth century, one part of the Bulgars left the region to emigrate to the Balkans. As early as the fifth century A.D., small groups began moving north to the middle Volga Basin, where they were joined by other clans over several centuries. The Volga Bulgars formed the ethnic foundation of the Chavash and Tatar nations. Other migrants moved northward, following the Khazar expansion in the seventh century and the Arab invasion of the Caucasus in the eighth century.

The Bulgars, called Black Bulgars, mixed with the earlier Finnic inhabitants and adopted many Finnic cultural traditions, establishing close ties to the neighboring peoples of the region. Descended from the mixture of the Finno-Ugric tribes of the middle Volga area and the Bulgar tribes of the Kama and Volga Rivers, the Chavash were identifiable as a separate people as early as the tenth century, when they converted to Islam brought north by traders and adventurers.

The Muslim Black Bulgars created an extensive early medieval state that eventually controlled many neighboring Finnic and Turkic peoples. The Mongols conquered the flourishing state in 1236; it never recovered, and the Black Bulgars later came under the rule of the Tatar Khanate of Kazan, a successor state established as Mongol power declined in the 1440s. Tatar raids on Chuvash communities forced the southern Chuvash to migrate northward out of their traditional homeland, abandoning their southern districts almost entirely from the fourteenth to the late sixteenth centuries.

Russian Orthodox monks, venturing into the unknown east in the fourteenth century, converted the majority of the Muslim Chavash to Christianity by 1500. Following their conversion, almost all traces of their earlier Islamic society disappeared. At the same time the Chavash mostly abandoned their former seminomadic life of cattle herding for more settled agricultural communities. The first mention of the Chuvash in Russian history is found in a chronicle dated 1521.

The Russian conquest in 1552 of Kazan, the center of the empire controlled by the Tatars, brought the Chavash under direct Russian rule. Russian attempts to assimilate the Chavash undermined the common bond of the Orthodox religion and provoked a strong anti-Russian movement among the Chavash population. In 1555 the Russians established a capital at Cheboksary and five years later created the position of the *namestnik*, the local Muscovite governor. Russian authority gave the Chavash protection against Tatar raids, and in 1600 they began to repopulate the abandoned southern territories.

Severe famine during a time of political chaos in Moscow sparked rebellions in the region in the seventeenth century. The Chavash, allied to the neighboring Maris* and Mordvins, attempted to throw off Russian rule in 1601–1603. Savage reprisals against the entire population accompanied their defeat by Russian troops, but the Chavash again rebelled, along with the other Volga nations, under the leadership of Stenka Razin in 1667–71. By 1750 the Chavash lands had been divided between the large Russian provinces of Kazan and Simbirsk. During this period, from the mid-eighteenth to the early nineteenth centuries, most of the remaining Muslim Chavash were forced to adopt the Russian Orthodox Christianity.

The consolidation of the Chavash nationality was advanced by the spread of literacy in the early nineteenth century. The first Chavash grammar was published in 1769. A more complete grammar and dictionary appeared in 1836. In 1868 the first Chavash secondary school was opened in Simbirsk. The development of the written language contributed to the strengthening of Chavash culture.

The Chavash, an impoverished rural minority dominated by Russian landlords, stubbornly clung to their language and culture throughout the nineteenth century. Serfdom, prevalent in most of Russia, failed in the region, as the Chavash traditionally located their villages in remote ravines to elude tsarist officials. Chavash resistance to Russian rule manifested itself in periodic disturbances, crop damage, illegal timber cutting, and the looting of Russian property. Russian attempts to force the Chavash into serfdom or to conscript Chavash men for military duty led to several confrontations between 1827 and 1860. Disturbances escalated following an influx of Russian peasants freed from serfdom in the western provinces 1861. Due to the domination of the region by Russian landlords, Chavashia remained economically backward, and illiteracy was widespread. Not until 1868, with the opening of the first Chavash school, did the culture begin to revive.

At least half of the Chavash rose during the 1905 Russian Revolution, attacking Slavic colonies, burning estates, and skirmishing with troops sent to restore order. Chavash guerrillas, operating from hidden villages, continued to harass the authorities for over two years, until finally routed in 1907. Up to World War I the Chavash remained primarily agricultural, with little development of their potentially important timber industry.

Living far from the front lines, the Chavash felt little of the immediate affects of World War I until conscription of minorities began in 1916. The Chavash resisted conscription, and skirmishes broke out with tsarist troops. When revolution overtook the conflict in February 1917, most Chavash soldiers deserted and returned home, bringing with them new ideas, including a new national sentiment that rapidly took root in the region.

Regional leaders convened a national congress to take over as civil government collapsed. The congress sent delegates to a conference of all the non-Russian peoples of the Volga-Ural region convened in late 1917 to discuss the Bolshevik coup and the future of the national groups. A majority of the Chavash supported the inclusion of their homeland in an independent Volga-Ural federation of states, the expulsion of Slavic settlers, and the return of all lands to the Chavash. Minorities favored a separate Chavash state or a federation only with the Orthodox Christian Maris and Mordvins. In February 1918, Bolshevik troops overran Chavashia before the Chavash had a chance to decide their own future. Devastated by heavy fighting between 1918 and 1920, the Chavash homeland witnessed some of the largest battles of the Russian Civil War. Thousands of Chavash died in the fighting and from hunger and disease.

The Bolsheviks, victorious in the Civil War, initially promised freedom of religion and cultural autonomy, but Chavash leaders advocating autonomy were quickly eliminated. The Chavash continued to make demands on the new government, including the incorporation of the town of Simbirsk, later called Ulyanovsk, into their region. On 24 June 1920, the Soviet government created the Chuvash Autonomous Region; however, ethnic Russians held all administrative posts in the newly created region. To diffuse growing Chavash anti-Soviet sentiment, the region was raised to the status of an autonomous republic within the Russian Federation on 21 April 1925. In 1926 the government changed the republic's boundaries to include a proletarian district that did not share the Chavash's bourgeois nationalist attitudes. The Chavash homeland was forcibly collectivized in the 1930s, during the Stalin era. The program, carried out with great brutality, was accompanied by purges of the Chavash cultural and political leadership for anti-Soviet "bourgeois" nationalism.

The Chavash, constituting over 80% of their national republic's population in 1965, experienced a modest cultural revival over the next decade, partly in response to increased Slavic immigration to the republic. The cultural revival, particularly important in publishing and in cultural studies, reinforced Chavash resistance to the government's assimilation pressure in the 1960s and 1970s. Chavash national sentiment was expressed in renewed interest in their unique history and in an emphasis on the purification and de-Russification of the Chavash language.

The Chavash national population grew rapidly in the 1970s and 1980s, increasing the number of Chavash living outside the Chavash republic. In 1979, only 52% of the Chavash population lived within the republican borders. The Chavash national revival, which spread to all Chavash populations, took the reunification of their nation in one administrative unit as an important national issue. In 1989 the Chuvash Public Cultural Center was founded to promote the Chavash culture. The revival took on nationalist overtones following the introduction of liberal reforms in the late 1980s, and it became openly nationalist with the disintegration of the Soviet Union.

Growing nationalist sentiment forced the local government to declare the republic's sovereignty and to change its name from the Russian to the Chavash version. In late 1991 the Chavash government unilaterally proclaimed the upgrading of the autonomous republic's status to that of a full republic, a member state of the newly democratic Russian Federation. On 21 January 1994, Nikolai Fedorov, a constitutional lawyer, was inaugurated as the first president of the Chavash Republic. Fedorov, a former Russian justice minister who had resigned in 1993 to protest the use of force in Chechnya, has had a stormy relationship with the Chavash legislature, which is dominated by leftist political parties. In January 1995, Fedorov signed a decree allowing citizens of the republic to refuse to participate in military activities in Chechnya.

In local elections in July 1998, the Communist Party, which had dominated the Chavash parliament since 1991, lost all but a few seats. The new legislature, with large numbers of reformers and Chavash nationalists, accepted economic and political reforms more easily and worked more closely with the Chavash president. Although the republican government concentrates on improving the economy, Chavash nationalism focuses on the consolidation of their traditional lands and the incorporation of all Chavash-populated territories in one state.

The storage of Soviet-era chemical weapons in Chavashia has become a major national issue. In 1998 the Chavash leadership demanded compensation, such as investment in local infrastructure, to compensate for their exposure to health risks due to the weapons' presence in their territory. The Russian government was to have begun destroying the weapons by December 1999 under international agreements, but a lack of funding delayed the start of the operation, adding to nationalist demands for the removal of all weapons of mass destruction from traditional Chavash territories.

The idea of joint sovereignty in the Volga River basin is gaining support, although the Christian Chavash are somewhat suspicious of too close ties to the Tatars and other Muslim peoples of the region. One proposal is for a union of the Chuvash, Mari, and Mordvin republics as part of a federation of Volga states.

Chavash claims to sovereignty are based on the long history of the Bulgar state. Nationalists estimate an ethnic population of over two million in Russia, making the Chavash one of the largest nations in the Russian Federation. Nationalists demand the abandonment of the Cyrillic alphabet in favor of the Latin script, the opening of Chavash-language schools, and the creation of a Chavash-language university.

SELECTED BIBLIOGRAPHY:

Bremmer, Ian, and Ray Taras. *Nations and Politics in the Soviet Successor States.* 1993.

Krueger, J. *Chuvash Manual.* 1997.

Olson, James S., ed. *An Ethnohistorical Dictionary of the Russian and Soviet Empires.* 1994.

Shnirelman, Victor A. *Who Gets the Past? Competition for Ancestors among Non-Russian Intellectuals in Russia.* 1995.

Chechens

Nokh; Nokhchi; Nakh; Nakchuo; Nokhchi; Chechenian; Shishan; Cecens

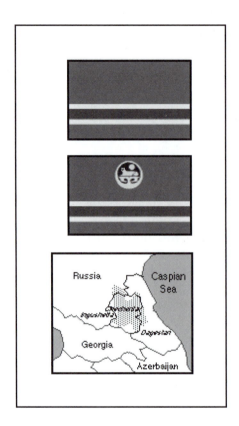

POPULATION: Approximately (2002e) 1,100,000 Chechens in Russia, the majority in the North Caucasus region of the Russian Federation, primarily in Chechnya or Chechenia, but also in neighboring Dagestan and Ingushetia and other Russian republics and regions, which includes a sizable population in Moscow. Smaller Chechen populations live in Azerbaijan, Ukraine, and an estimated 100,000 live in Central Asia, mostly in Kazakhstan.

THE CHECHEN HOMELAND: The Chechen homeland occupies the northern slopes of the middle Caucasus Mountains and extends into the flood plain of the Terek River in southern European Russia. The region is mostly rugged and mountainous, with steppe and sandy plains to the north. Chechnya is the site of the Grozni oil fields, one of Russia's major sources of petroleum. Chechnya's status remains undecided; officially it is a member state of the Russian Federation and in 2002 was mostly under Russian military occupation. Chechnya's independence was recognized internationally only by the Islamic Emirate of Afghanistan (the Taliban). *Chechen Republic/Chechen Republic of Ichkeria (Nokhchyïchuo/Noxçiyn Respublika Noxçiyçö)*: 6,210 sq. mi.—16,088 sq. km, (2002e) 542,000—Chechens 93%, Russians 2%, Ossetians,* Ingush,* Ukrainians, Terek Cossacks,* and Dagestanis* 5%. The Chechen capital and major cultural center is Grozni (Grozny), called Syelzha Ghaala (Sölz Ghala) in the Chechen language; it had a population of 411,000 in 1994, at the outbreak of fighting in the republic. The other major Chechen cultural center is Gudermes, called Gümse in Chechen, with a population of about 55,000 when the First Chechen War broke out in 1994.

FLAG: The Chechen national flag is a green field with three horizontal stripes of white, red, and white on the lower half. The same flag, with the addition of the traditional Chechen seal on the upper middle, is the official flag of the breakaway republic.

PEOPLE AND CULTURE: The Chechens, who call themselves Nakh or Nakchuo, as do the related Ingush to the west, are a Caucasian nation comprising 128 lowland and highland clans called *teips*, clanlike organizations that form the core of the Chechen nation. The mountain clans, traditionally the most powerful, are bound by strict traditions of hospitality and vendetta. Chechen society is strongly patriarchal, and the Council of Elders, drawn from the elders of each clan, remains very influential. The Chechens, and their neighbors the Ingush, constitute the Veinakh, or Vainakh, ethnic group. They have lived in the same region of the North Caucasus for over a thousand years, except for years spent in exile. The Chechen have retained an extremely high birthrate despite the urbanization of 40% of the Chechen population in recent years.

LANGUAGE AND RELIGION: The Chechen language, a dialect of the Vienakh or Vainakh, the northeastern branch of the Caucasian languages, developed as a literary language in the nineteenth century and is spoken by 98% of the Chechens as their mother tongue. The language, called Nokhchiin or Nokchiin Muott, is spoken in six major dialects and is the most widely spoken of the North Caucasian languages. The majority of the Chechens are bilingual in Russian. In 1992 a new Latin-based alphabet was adopted, and in 1997 the Chechen parliament enacted a law making Chechen the only official language in the republic.

The Chechens are overwhelmingly Sunni Muslim, adhering to the Shafi rite. Islamic sentiment has grown during the 1990s, fueled by Russian attempts to regain control of the region, in what is often depicted as an anti-Islamic campaign. Some of their early Christian heritage can be seen in their language. The word for Sunday translates as "God's Day," and the word for Friday translates as "Day of Mary."

NATIONAL HISTORY: The Chechens, thought to be descended from ancient Scythian tribes, have lived in the North Caucasus region since before 600 B.C. Some scholars believe that they have lived in the area for 6,000 to 8,000 years. Their homeland, straddling the main invasion route between Europe and Asia, knew many invaders.

Historical evidence shows that the region was relatively populous and prosperous in ancient times, drawing the attention of conquerors and invaders. From about 200 B.C. to A.D. 200, the region was under the domination of the Sarmathians, although Roman influence was felt in the territory from the Roman-held region just to the south. The region was controlled by the Huns from around 400 A.D. and was ruled by the Khazars from 650 to 750. Influenced by the Romans and later the Byzantines, most of the fierce mountain tribes had adopted Christianity by 1000 A.D.

The Mongols conquered the region in 1241, laying waste the Chechen lowlands. Withdrawing to mountain strongholds, the Chechens fought the invaders for over 50 years, finally throwing off Mongol rule in 1300. Over the next centuries the Chechens resisted Persian and Turkish attempts to dominate the region. Developing a warrior culture to hold their land against would-be conquerors, they were often at war with neighboring peoples.

Slavic Cossacks, the spearhead of Russian expansion, began to explore the region in the sixteenth century and in 1598 reached the Terek River, in Chechen territory. The Chechens, converted to Islam brought to the region from Dagestan about 1650, resisted incursions by the Christian Russians. In 1785, Sheikh Mansur, now a folk hero, led an assault upon Russian encroachment. For much of the nineteenth century, the Chechens resisted Russian efforts to extend their frontiers to the south. Grozni, founded in 1818 as a frontier fort, established a Russian foothold in the center of Chechen territory, where the Russians met the fiercest resistance to their conquest of the Caucasus.

The Chechens, under their political and religious leader Imam Shamil (Shamyl), fought an effective guerrilla war against the Russians from 1834 to 1859. Tens of thousands of Muslim warriors died in the final Russian conquest of the region. The surviving Chechens, driven from their fertile lowlands along the Terek River, lived in abject poverty in the high Caucasus Mountains. Hatred of the Slavs, particularly the Terek Cossacks* settled on their confiscated lands, provoked repeated revolts, especially severe in 1863, 1867, and 1877. In 1865, the Russians deported 39,000 Chechens to Ottoman Turkish territory.

The region was given added importance following the discovery of oil near Grozni in 1893. By 1900 the Grozni fields were the second greatest producers of oil in tsarist Russia, and they were the target of Chechen rioters during the 1905 Russian Revolution. The uprising was severely put down by Cossack troops; thousands of Chechens were deported to Russia's Siberian provinces.

Openly sympathetic to Muslim Turkey during World War I, the Chechens rejoiced as revolution spread across Russia in February 1917. Believing the revolution would redress old injustices and return their lost lands, the Chechen leaders sent petitions to the new democratic Russian government detailing their grievances. Ignored by Russia's beleaguered provisional government, the Chechens mobilized and launched an offensive against the Terek Cossack settlements on their traditional lands in the Terek River basin. In September 1917 a Chechen government took control of the local government and expelled all Slavic officials.

The Bolshevik coup in October 1917 ended Chechen attempts to win autonomy within a democratic Russia. On 27 October 1917, the first Congress of the Union of the North Caucasus was held at Vedens, Shamil's old capital. Alarmed by antireligious Bolshevik proclamations, the Chechens formed an alliance with their old enemies, the Terek Cossacks, but longstanding grievances soon ended the alliance. Proclaiming a holy war, a *gazava*, the Muslim warriors drove the Cossacks from Grozni, and a Chechen congress elected a national committee of sheiks, officers, and merchants to govern the region. The national committee declared Chechnya independent on 2 December 1917. It established a theocratic democracy headed by the Chechen emir Sheikh Ilzum Hadji, who at first formed an alliance with the anti-Bolshevik forces active in southern Russia.

Allied to the other Muslim peoples of the region, particularly the Dagestani peoples, the Chechens organized a republic called North Caucasia, which was proclaimed on 11 May 1918. In June 1918, the new state concluded a treaty with Turkey. The first capital of the new state, Vladikavkaz, called Dzaudzhikau, was captured in August 1918, by Cossack troops. The Muslims moved their capital to Nazra and later to Temir Khan Shura. Heavy fighting broke out across the region between the Muslim troops and the Whites, the anti-Bolshevik military forces who opposed the secession of any part of the former Russian Empire.

Seeking allies, the Muslims, led by the Chechens, who believed Bolshevik promises of independence, switched sides in the Russian Civil War. In November 1918, the Bolsheviks overran the Terek lowlands and began to redistribute confiscated lands to their Chechen allies. In January 1919, the White Volunteer Army of Gen. Anton Deniken invaded the region; despite a valiant resistance, the Chechens were finally defeated in the spring. The Chechens appealed directly to the allied nations, but while the Whites were exterminating Muslims in the region, the British, the only nation with forces in the region, refused to intervene.

The Bolshevik Red Army finally forced the Whites from the region in January 1920. The Chechens' communist allies attempted to take direct control and to incorporate the area into the new Soviet Russian state as a so-called Autonomous Mountain Republic. The Chechens rebelled and turned on their Red allies. The Chechens fought a vicious two-month war but were finally defeated in March 1920 and forced into the Mountain Republic. The Mountain Republic lasted only twenty months before ethnic tension caused its division. The Chechen autonomous region was established in November 1922.

The region, one of the last to be conquered by the Reds, remained a center of Muslim anticommunist activity. The Soviet government's antireligious stance provoked a widespread revolt in 1927. In 1934 Chechnya was joined with Ingushetia to form a larger region, which became an autonomous republic in 1936. In 1937, to avoid further disturbances in the region, the Soviets purged, killed, or deported the Chechens' entire religious, political, and cultural leadership. Under new leaders, however, a serious revolt again swept the region in 1939–40.

In World War II, a German drive on the Caucasus oil fields reached the border of the rebellious autonomous republic in 1942. The Nazi advance prompted a renewed Chechen revolt; many joined the Nazi's anti-communist campaign, while other Chechens formed anti-Nazi partisan groups or fought with the Red Army. In January 1943, the Red Army returned to drive the Nazis from Chechnya.

Stalin accused the entire Chechen nation, including the families of soldiers in the Red Army, of treason. Driven from their homes at gunpoint and loaded on cattle cars, the 408,000 Chechens suffered a brutal deportation to Central Asia. Those deemed "untransportable," mostly children, the elderly, and pregnant women, were massacred on the spot. Tens of thousands of Chechens died in the deportation or from hunger and disease when they were dumped in Central Asia and Siberia. Chechen soldiers in the Red Army, when they returned to their homes, were rounded up also and shipped east. Between 1940 and 1945 the Chechen population is estimated to have declined by at least 25%.

Officially rehabilitated and allowed to return to the Caucasus in 1957, the surviving Chechens arrived back in their homeland to find it occupied by Slavs and all traces of their culture eradicated. In 1958 severe Chechen rioting paralyzed the region, forcing the Soviet authorities to act on the Chechen grievances. Given limited cultural rights, the Chechen and the neighboring Ingush were united in a joint autonomous republic.

In the 1960s and 1970s the Chechen leadership suffered periodic purges, and their Muslim religion remained the target of suppression and persecution. An estimated half the Chechen men in the mid-1970s belonged to underground religious brotherhoods called *tariqat*. In 1978 two mosques were reopened, but the official policy of suppressing Islam in the region remained.

The Muslim Chechen population urbanized but without assimilating into the predominantly Russian urban culture. By 1979, 40% of the Chechen nation lived in urban areas. The liberalizing of Soviet life in the late 1980s allowed the urban Chechens to organize more openly. A popular front against communist rule was formed in 1988, and by 1990 there was an active pro-independence movement, motivated partly by a desire to secure control over Chechnya's lucrative oil industry.

The attempted coup against Soviet president Mikhail Gorbachev in August 1991 triggered a popular uprising in Chechnya. Maj. Gen. Djokar Dudayev exploited clan rivalries to take control of the government and to proclaim Chechnya an independent state. The Russian government imposed economic sanctions, which seriously affected Chechen living standards and helped make Dudayev unpopular in the republic.

Resistance increased against Dudayev's government, and in March 1992 a military coup, accompanied by widespread demonstrations, was attempted. In June the Ingush decided to separate themselves from Chechnya and reached an agreement with Moscow on a new status within the Russian Federation. All Russian troops stationed in Chechnya were withdrawn, leaving behind a large quantity of arms. In 1993 opposition to Dudayev's government increased, with many clans openly in revolt; however, expulsion of hundreds of Chechen traders and illegal residents from Moscow united the Chechens in fury against the Russians.

Opposition forces in the republic, with Russian government support, attempted to overthrow Dudayev in August 1994. In mid-August he ordered a general mobilization to combat the Chechen opposition and their Russian backers. Fighting between the Chechen government forces and the Russian-backed opposition broke out, and in December Russian troops moved into the republic. Sustained aerial bombing and artillery bombardments caused up to 80,000 deaths and created a severe refugee problem. Many Chechens became disillusioned with their unrecognized independence and were apprehensive about the future of their small nation; nonetheless, they refused to bow to Russian domination despite the ferocity of the so-called Chechen War. General Dudayev was killed in a plane crash and was replaced by Aslan Maskhadov. In August 1996, a cease-fire agreement ended the fighting and led to plans to withdraw Russian troops. The question of Chechen independence was to be postponed for a period of five years.

By early 1997 Chechnya was far more independent than many in Russia wished to admit, but far less independent than most Chechens desired. A treaty signed on 12 May 1997 effectively ended the Chechen War but again left the question of independence undecided. In July 1997, President Boris Yeltsin offered a power-sharing agreement similar to that between the Russian Federation and Tatarstan, but the offer was rejected.

A series of bomb attacks on Russian cities, including Moscow, in early 1999 was conveniently blamed on Chechen terrorists. Russian troops massed on the Chechen border intending to roll over the tiny republic, but Chechen resistance again proved stronger than anticipated. During the Second Chechen War in 1999–2000 Grozni and other cities were reduced to rubble, and over 200,000 Chechen civilians fled the fighting. By mid-2000 the Russian military controlled most Chechen territory, but determined rebel groups in the mountainous south continued to fight a bloody guerrilla war against the invaders. The Russian soldiers in the region faced a nightmare of ambushes and car bombings.

Yeltsin's successor, Vladimir Putin, appointed a Muslim cleric to head the Russian-controlled administration in the Chechen Republic in June 2000. The cleric, Akhmad Kadyrov, had initially favored Chechen independence, but after a dispute with Maskhadov he supported the Russian invasion of the republic. The Russian president followed a traditional formula—nomination of a "third way" leader loyal to Moscow but perhaps more acceptable to a large segment of the Chechen population.

In July 2000, the Russian army imposed an indefinite curfew across all of Chechnya following a series of suicide bombings. Fighting gradually ended, and a tense peace was maintained in the region. Elections for representatives from Chechnya to the Russian Duma were held in August 2000, with 15 Russian candidates put forward. In November 2000 the Russian government created a new department, headed by an ethnic Russian, to oversee affairs in Chechnya.

In mid-2001, despite criticism from the West, the Russian government maintained its stance in the region, continued war. The republic is now run by a fragile pro-Moscow administration whose authority extends only to areas held by the Red Army. Stalemated by the Chechen rebels, the Russians voiced their support for a coalition against international terrorism following the attacks in America on New York and Washington, DC on 11 September 2001. The Russians consider the Chechen groups fighting their troops in Chechnya to be terrorists closely tied to other Islamic groups. In October 2001 the Russian government announced that negotiations would begin with the Chechen leadership. Suspected ties to terrorist leader Osama bin Laden ended considerable sympathy in the West and muted criticism of Russian efforts to defeat the Chechens militarily; however, on 18 November 2001, the presidents of Russia and Chechnya had their first acknowledged meeting.

SELECTED BIBLIOGRAPHY:

de Waal, Thomas. *Chechnya: Calamity in the Caucasus*. 1998.
Hill, Fiona. *Russia's Tinderbox: Conflict in the North Caucasus and Its Implications for the Future of the Russian Federation*. 1995.
Lieven, Anatol. *Chechnya: Tombstone of Russian Power*. 1998.
Smith, Sebastian. *Allahs Mountains*. 1997.

Cherkess

Cherkes; Adyges; Circassians; Central Circassians; Cherkessians; Circasians

POPULATION: Approximately (2002e) 76,000 Cherkess in Russia, mostly in the northwestern Cherkess region of the Karachai-Cherkess Republic, a member state of the Russian Federation, and in neighboring areas of Stavropol Territory. There are large numbers of Circassians, including Cherkess, in Turkey, Syria, Jordan, Lebanon, and Israel.

THE CHERKESS HOMELAND: The Cherkess homeland lies in the foothills of the western spur of the Greater Caucasus Mountains in southern European Russia, mostly occupying the valley of the upper Kuban River. The rivers of Cherkessia drain to the Black Sea, not the Caspian, a simple geographical fact that early distinguished the Cherkess from other Caucasian peoples. The majority of the Cherkess inhabit the foothills of the Caucasus Mountains, with a continuing migration to Cherkess and the lowland. Officially Cherkessia remains part of the Republic of Karachai-Cherkessia; the Cherkess Republic, proclaimed in 1992, has not been recognized by the Russian government. *Cherkess Republic (Cherkess Respublike)*: 1,273 sq. mi.—3,297 sq. km, (2002e) 308,000—Russians 33%, Cossacks 25%, Cherkess (Circassian) 24%, Abaza* 10%, Ukrainians 7%. The Cherkess capital and major cultural center is Cherkessk, called Chérkéssk in the Cherkess language, (2002e) 122,000. Other important cultural centers are the towns of Besenei (Besenej) and Adyge-Khabi.

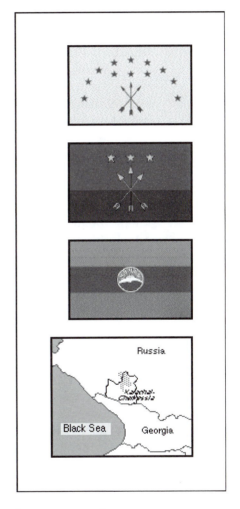

FLAG: The Cherkess national, the flag of their unrecognized republic, is a yellow field bearing three crossed red arrows surmounted by three red stars under an arc of nine red stars. The flag of the pan-Circassian national movement, Adyge Khase, is a vertical bicolor of red over green bearing three crossed yellow arrows surmounted by three yellow stars. The flag of the Karachai-Cherkess Republic is a vertical tricolor of pale blue, green, and red charged with a centered disk bearing a snowcapped mountain and a rising yellow sun.

PEOPLE AND CULTURE: The Cherkess are a Northern Caucasian people, one of the three divisions of the Circassian peoples, the others being the Adgye* and the Kabards.* The Cherkess have long been a subject of debate, but the modern Soviet and Russian classification includes only the Circassian group called Cherkess that inhabit the northern districts of the Karachai-Cherkess Republic. Tribal loyalties are strong among the Cherkess. The most prominent of the Cherkess subgroups are: Abadzekh, Besleney, Bzhedukh, Gatyukay, Yererukoy, Kemgoy, Kheak, Nadkhokuadzh, Shapsug, and Temirgoy. The Cherkess call themselves Adgye, as do the Adgye nation farther west, which indicates their relationship with the other Circassian peoples. In their traditional social organization, Cherkess princes and nobles controlled the herds and soil. Slavery was maintained until recent times, and women still occupy a low position in Circassian society. The majority of the Cherkess remain rural, an estimated 62% in 2000, although urbanization, particularly around the city of Cherkessk, is increasing.

LANGUAGE AND RELIGION: The Cherkess language, also called Adygebze or Central Circassian, is a Kiakh language of the Abzhazo-Adygheian group of Caucasian languages. The language is very close to Kabardian and similar to Adgye, although it is written in a different Cyrillic alphabet. The majority of the Cherkess speak Russian as their second language, and a smaller number speak Karachai.

The Muslim Cherkess mostly follow the Hanafi school of Sunni Islam. The religion, coming relatively late to the Cherkess, traditionally has been embraced in a less militant and more tolerant way than the Islam practiced by the Caucasian peoples farther to the east. Among the Cherkess the Adat, or custom law (the Adgye-Habze), has remained extremely powerful. Some pre-Islamic pagan rituals associated with thunder, fertility rites, and sacred groves have become part of the Cherkess religious observances.

NATIONAL HISTORY: The Cherkess are thought to be descended from a cluster of Caucasian tribes that originated in the Kuban Basin. Known to the ancient Greeks as Zyukhoy, the Cherkess probably settled the region of the North Caucasus before the sixth century B.C. Greek and Roman writers described tribes in the northwest Caucasus famed for their horse breeding and horsemanship. Possibly the earliest representative of the Caucasian peoples, the Circassians populated a wide area north of the Caucasus Mountains, a region that figured prominently in the legends of ancient Greece.

The handsome Cherkess, valued as slaves, developed a warrior society as protection against frequent invasions and raids by slavers. Cherkess women were considered especially beautiful and were valued in Turkish and Arabian harems. Cherkess warriors often hired out as mercenaries to powerful rulers.

Greek monks first introduced Christianity to the warlike Circassian tribes in the sixth century A.D. A common Christian religion help the Cherkess establish ties to the Byzantines to the south and to open trade routes to the early Slav state, Kievan Rus', in the north. By the late ninth century, regular trade and diplomatic ties existed with the Slavs. The Circassian tribes finally adopted Christianity as their national religion, while retaining much of their former pagan beliefs, during the eleventh and twelfth centuries. The newly Christianized tribes became known for their skill in commercial trading. The Cherkess carried on an extensive trade with Byzantium, receiving goods unavailable in their homeland in exchange for horses, furs, honey, and filigreed jewelry.

The Mongol Golden Horde invaded the region in 1241–42, ending contact with Byzantium and forcing some Circassians to move east toward the Terek River. The Circassians who stayed in the west became known as the Cherkess. The devastation caused by the Mongols greatly set back the consolidation of a single Circassian nation. Weakened by the Mongol conquest, the tribes came under the rule of Christian Georgia by the end of the thirteenth century. In the fifteenth century, the Cherkess resumed trade with the West, through Genoese merchants in the coastal towns.

In the sixteenth century, the Cherkess came into contact with the Muslim Ottoman Turks through the Crimean Tatars,* and by the eighteenth century they had adopted the Muslim religion. Circassian Kabard princes, from the fifteenth to the seventeenth centuries, dominated much of the North Caucasus as tributaries of the Ottoman Empire. The Muslim Cherkess, in the sixteenth and seventeenth centuries, were in a perpetual state of war with the Tatar Khanate of Crimea and with the Turkic peoples of the region—the Karachais,* Kumyks,* and Nogais.*

The mountains of the Cherkess homeland are relatively low and gentle, with no strongholds to which the Cherkess can retreat, like those of peoples farther east. For protection, the Cherkess, like other Circassians, alternately sought alliances with Ottoman Turkey and the expanding Russian empire. The Circassian peoples sent three diplomatic missions to Muscovy in the 1550s, producing what the Circassians called an "alliance" but the Russians termed a "voluntary union" with Russia.

The Russians, extending their frontiers to the south, came into conflict with the Ottomans in the Caucasus, setting off a series of wars that continued sporadically for centuries. Russian settlers, following the Cossacks into the region, began to settle in the region claimed as traditional Circassian lands. The Russo-Turkish Wars, mostly fought on Circassian territory, sealed the fate of the Cherkess. In 1790, Russian forces defeated the Ottoman troops of Batal Pasha on the upper Kuban River. In 1804 the Russians founded Balalpashinsk, later renamed Cherkessk, in the middle of Cherkess territory. From the fortified outpost the Russians carried out vicious reprisals against Cherkess who resisted Russian rule.

In 1864 the Russians, after years of fighting, triumphed over the Circassian warriors. Some 400,000 Circassians, including a majority of the Cherkess, rejecting Christian domination, fled or were expelled to Turkish territory between 1864 and 1878. Many Cherkess died during the Circassian exodus, which continued until the turn of the century. Of those who survived, some were assimilated, and some went farther south to settle in the Ottoman territories of Syria, Jordan, Palestine, and Lebanon. Russians, Ukrainians, and Armenians were settled in the depopulated Cherkess lands. By the beginning of the twentieth century only an estimated 20,000 Cherkess remained in the region. Although relegated to a marginal existence in rural areas, the Cherkess proved an enduring problem for the Russian military and civil authorities.

Openly supportive of the Muslim Turks when war broke out in 1914, the Cherkess enthusiastically welcomed the news that revolution had overthrown the hated tsarist government in February 1917. Cherkess appeals to the new government for religious freedom, political autonomy, and the reunification of the Circassian lands went unanswered. Responding to calls for Muslim solidarity, the Cherkess sent delegates to an all-Muslim conference in September 1917, seeking Muslim support for their demands.

The Russian Civil War expanded into the North Caucasus, with the Cherkess alternately attacked and courted by both Whites and Reds. White opposition to autonomy for the Caucasian nations prompted many Cherkess to join the Reds, believing the Soviet promise of sovereignty within a federation of Soviet states. In January 1920, the Red Army drove the last of the White forces from Cherkessia and joined the region to the newly created Mountain Republic, which lasted only twenty months.

The victorious Bolsheviks subjected the region to a seemingly endless round of administrative changes designed to keep the Cherkess separated from the other Circassian peoples and always outnumbered by ethnic Slavs. Soviet linguists devised three separate written languages for the Cherkess, Adyge, and Kabards in an effort to divide the three small Circassian nations further. In January 1922, Soviet authorities established the Cherkess Autonomous Oblast. The Soviets particularly repressed religion, closing all religious schools and most mosques in the region.

During the 1920s the Soviet authorities consolidated the Circassian peoples into two distinct groups, the Cherkess and the Kabards. Late in the 1930s the ethnic lines were again redrawn, with the Circassians being divided into three groups—the Adyge in the west, the Cherkess in the center, and the Kabards in the east. The regions were separated by Slav-colonized territories.

During World War II, the Nazi Germans, having taken the area during the Caucasus campaign of 1942, offered an alliance and promoted anti-communist solidarity. The Cherkess view that the Germans represented just another in a long series of invaders spared them the brutal deportations suffered by neighboring Karachai and other Muslim peoples of the Caucasus region following the return of the Soviet rule.

Regional and ethnic tension, suppressed for decades, emerged with the easing of Soviet restraint in the late 1980s. The three Circassian peoples, separated under tsarist and Soviet rule, demanded unification and the dissolution of the hybrid territories that the Cherkess and Kabards had been forced to share with the Turkic Karachai and Balkar peoples for most of the twentieth century. Demands for a separate Circassian republic within the Russian Federation accelerated with the disintegration of the Soviet state in 1991.

Growing tension between the Cherkess and Karachais mounted following the breakup of the Soviet Union. Demonstrators in Cherkessk demanded the withdrawal of the Cherkess from the parliament they shared with the Karachai. In March 1992 the local republican governments signed a new federal treaty regulating relations with Moscow, but Cherkess nationalists continued to demand a separate federal republic, reunification of the Circassian lands, and redress for past injustices. Militants proclaimed the creation of a Cherkess Republic, but the Russian government refused to recognize it. The republican government agreed, in a treaty with the Russian Federation in 1995, to a division of responsibilities.

One of the smaller of the Caucasian nations, the Cherkess look back on a long history; their sense of identity is equal to that of many larger nations. During the 1990s the appearance of a number of pan-Circassian groups seemed to point to the establishment of closer ties to the other Circassian peoples, ties that had been broken during the years of Soviet domination. The Karachai-Cherkess, Kabarda-Balkaria, and Adygeya republics set up an interparliamentary council in July 1997 to coordinate issues involving the three Circassian nations.

Several leaders of national and public movements representing the Cherkess and Abaza demanded that their territory be separated from Karachai and returned to Stavropol Kray, from which it had been separated in 1991. The leaders of the Cherkess and Abaza declared the autonomy of their regions in November 1998.

A contested election for the head of the republic in early 1999 led to a further deterioration of ethnic relations in the republic. Violent incidents became more common, and confrontations between Cherkess and Karachai became more serious. A congress of Cherkess and Abaza in August 1999 called for a restoration of Cherkess autonomy. In September 1999, organizations representing the Cherkess and other non-Karachai groups voted in favor of the restoration of the Cherkess Autonomous Oblast as part of the neighboring Stavropol Territory. The vote was taken after the inauguration of the new president of the Republic of Karachai-Cherkessia, Vladimir Semenov, whose defeat of the Cherkess candidate, Stanislav Derev, was seen as invalid by the Cherkess population of the republic. Derev had the important backing of Adyge Khase, arguably the most powerful nationalist organization in the North Caucasus.

The new Cherkess parliament named Derev to head the autonomous formation and charged him with forming its government. In November 1999, Cherkess nationalists staged demonstrations and pickets in Cherkessk to press their demands for separation from the joint republic. Although some Cherkess, supported by Russians, Abaza, and other non-Karachai groups, wanted to rejoin Stavropol Krai as an autonomous region, a growing number supported the division of the joint republic into two new republics—a Karachai republic in the highlands and a Cherkess republic in the foothills and the lowlands. In January 2000, eleven Cherkess and Abaza deputies walked out of the Karachai-Cherkess People's Assembly and refused to participate in debates in March and April, claiming that their participation would not be valid, as the Cherkess and Abaza would soon secede from the joint republic.

Militants of Adyge Khase have reiterated their demands for the formation of a united Circassian state in the northwestern Caucasus. The region, the traditional homeland of the Circassians, would include a large part of Caucasian Russia, including all or parts of Kuban, Stavropol, Karachay-Cherkess, Adygea, and Kabardino-Balkaria. As an interim measure, nationalists seek to separate the Cherkess homeland as a distinct republic in the lowlands, leaving the highlands to the Turkic Karachais.

SELECTED BIBLIOGRAPHY:

Abtorkhanov, Abdurahman, and Marie Bennigsen Broxup. *The North Caucasus Barrier: The Russian Advance towards the Muslim World.* 1992.

Cornell, Svante E. *Small Nations and Great Powers: A Study of Ethnopolitical Conflict in the Caucasus.* 1999.

Traho, R. *The Circassian History.* 1994.

Wright, John F. R., Suzanne Goldenberg, and Richard Schofield, eds. *Transcaucasian Boundaries.* 1996.

Cherokee

Tsalagi; Tsaragi; Tslagi; Yûñwiya; Aniyunwiya; Keetoowah; Entarironnen

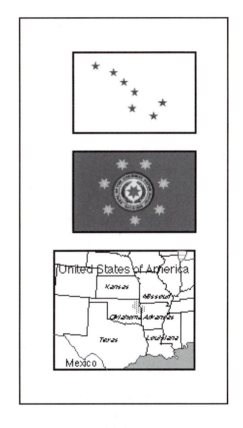

POPULATION: Approximately (2002e) 533,000 Cherokee, including part-Cherokee, in the United States. They are concentrated in the 14 northeastern counties of Oklahoma, with smaller communities in many areas of the United States, including North Carolina, Arkansas, Georgia, and Tennessee.

THE CHEROKEE HOMELAND: The Cherokee homeland in Oklahoma lies in the northeastern portion of the state, east of Tulsa, forming a 14-county jurisdictional area that replaced the former autonomous Cherokee state in 1906. The region, known locally as the Cherokee Nation, is called Ani-Yun'wiya in the Cherokee language. The Oklahoma Cherokee have no reserved lands and live in small towns or dispersed among the other population groups in the region. The only Cherokee reservation is in western North Carolina, where some 5,000 Cherokee, the descendants of those that escaped deportation, continue to live. Other groups of Cherokee live in Missouri, Alabama, Arkansas, Tenessee, and Georgia but do not currently enjoy federal recognition as members of the Cherokee Nation. The Cherokee Nation in Oklahoma has no territorial status recognized by the U.S. government. The Cherokee capital and major cultural center is Tahlequah, (2002e) 12,000. The other major cultural center is Muskogee, (2002e) 38,000. There is a large Cherokee community living in the Tulsa metropolitan area at the western edge of traditional Cherokee territory.

FLAG: The Cherokee peace flag—carried, according to tradition, by the deported Cherokee to Oklahoma—is a white field bearing the constellation the Big Dipper, or Big Bear, in red. The flag of the Cherokee Nation is a red field bearing the tribal seal surrounded by seven yellow seven-pointed stars and a single black star on the upper hoist.

PEOPLE AND CULTURE: The Cherokee are an Iroquoian people, the largest of the Five Civilized Tribes, which also include the Choctaw, Chickasaw, Creek, and Seminole. The Cherokee Nation, Tsalagihi Ayili, generally includes those of a quarter or more of Cherokee blood, but it also allows membership by anyone with Cherokee heritage. The Cherokee are the largest of the five nations that shared the misery of their deportation from the southeastern United States to Indian Territory, later called Oklahoma, in the 1830s and 1840s. The most assimilated of the Native American peoples, an estimated 45% of all Cherokee are not registered as Indians but retain family and cultural ties to the officially recognized tribal structures. Some scholars and tribal activists claim a Cherokee population of over a million. Traditionally the Cherokee are divided into seven clans, with descent through the female line. A minority of the Cherokee are black Americans, the descendants of slaves. Unlike the other Native American peoples in the United States, the Cherokee and the other nations of the Five Civilized Tribes have no reserved tribal lands. Despite all they have endured, the levels of education and living standards rank among the highest of all the indigenous American peoples.

LANGUAGE AND RELIGION: The Cherokee language belongs to the Iroquoian language group, although it differs significantly from the other languages of the group. Although the Cherokee are mostly English speaking, there is a movement to ensure the survival of their language and its alphabet of 86 characters. The preservation and perpetuation of the language is one of the most important aspects of the cultural survival of the Cherokee. The Cherokee language is still the language of the home for many in Oklahoma; it is used in church services and in private education. It remains one of the most widely spoken indigenous American languages. The language is spoken in four major dialects reflecting the regional distribution of the Cherokee.

The Cherokee are mostly Christians, with Methodist and Baptist denominations the most popular. Traditionally they were pantheists, holding in special reverence the sun, fire, and water. Their great yearly religious ceremony, which is still celebrated, is the Green Corn festival, a thanksgiving for new crops. Since the 1970s, younger Cherokee have taken a new interest in their traditional beliefs as part of their cultural revival.

NATIONAL HISTORY: The ancient inhabitants of southeastern North America, known as the Mississippian Culture, developed a sophisticated, centralized society ruled by an established elite of priests and chiefs. The tribal groups, living in fortified towns built around large temple mounds, spread across a vast area east of the Mississippi River. According to Cherokee tradition, their ancient ancestors migrated south after defeat by the Delaware and Iroquois* in the region of the Great Lakes. The Cherokee nation, part of the Mississippian Culture, eventually dominated in present

North and South Carolina, Georgia, Tennessee and in parts of Alabama, Virginia, and Kentucky.

The recorded history of the Cherokee begins with the Spanish expedition led by Hernan De Soto, which passed through the region of the Mississippian peoples in 1539–40. Armed with guns, the Spaniards looted temples and kidnapped women in the Choctaw and Chickasaw territories before moving into the Creek Confederacy. The more warlike Creeks resisted the Europeans and forced them to fight their way through to the Cherokee lands. Driven from the region by the Cherokee, the Spanish leader, De Soto, died after reaching the Mississippi River.

The Cherokee remained relatively isolated until after the settlement of Virginia by the English in 1609. By 1629 English traders and explorers had penetrated the Cherokee lands. Diseases introduced by the Europeans decimated the tribes, with an estimated 75% of the Cherokee dying in the epidemics that swept the region between 1650 and 1755.

The tribes, under pressure from settlers moving inland from the Europeans' coastal settlements, established relations and alliances with the British and French. In 1684 the Cherokee made their first treaty with the English of Carolina and eventually maintained a Cherokee ambassador at the Court of St. James. While broken treaties, war, and disease took their toll, the tribes increasingly adopted the lifestyle of the Europeans. Except for the Yamasee War in 1715–16, relations between the Cherokee and the Europeans were generally good. The Cherokee lived as well as, and usually better than, the European frontiersmen and settlers.

The first known Christian missionary, a French officer or agent possibly belonging to the Jesuit order, established himself among the Cherokee in 1736. He learned the language, organized the first tribal government beyond the village or town level, and taught the principles of Christian morality. Due to the intense rivalry between the British and French in North America, he was eventually arrested by the British authorities and conveyed to Charleston, South Carolina, where he died in prison. In 1801 the Moravians* established missions in Cherokee territory, soon followed by the Congregationalists, Presbyterians, and Baptists.

Encroachment on Cherokee lands by British settlers finally erupted in the Cherokee War of 1760–62. Settlers were massacred on the frontier, and a militia unit sent against the Cherokee was badly mauled. The French withdrawal from much of the region as part of the French and Indian War allowed the British to send more troops against the Cherokee. The British adopted a policy of killing all male prisoners but sparing women and children. The European troops destroyed the food the Cherokee needed for the coming winter in 1761, finally forcing Cherokee leaders to sue for peace. They were forced to cede most of their eastern lands in the Carolinas. White settlers poured across the mountains, once again encroaching on Cherokee territory.

Some Cherokee leaders, loyal to their British allies, fought against the colonists in the Revolutionary War, but the majority adopted a neutral stance in the conflict between the whites. Local militias and Continental regulars, who indiscriminately targeted both pro-British and neutral groups, revenged a series of attacks on colonial settlements. The Americans destroyed a number of Cherokee towns, killing every man, woman, and child they could find. By the end of 1776 Cherokee power had been broken, many villages had been destroyed, and the people had been dispersed. The Cherokee could win peace only by surrendering vast tracts of land in the Carolinas. New treaties in 1780–85 confirmed previous land cessions, and additional territories were yielded in Alabama, Kentucky, and Tennessee.

After 1800 the Cherokee were remarkable for their assimilation of white culture. An elected tribal government replaced the clan system, and in 1825 a new capital was established at New Echota. Education was widespread, and a majority lived much as their American neighbors did. The former ruling classes established themselves as slave-owning aristocrats, employing white tutors for their children. Many Cherokee were more prosperous and "civilized" than their increasingly envious white neighbors.

A Cherokee named George Guess, Sequoyah to his people, saw the writing of whites and set out to apply a similar system to the Cherokee language. He devised a phonetic table of 86 characters, the only such invention by a single man in history. The written language devised by Sequoyah in 1821 spread rapidly. Sequoyah's invention was used in education, publishing, and the republican constitution adopted by the tribe in 1827. The *Cherokee Phoenix*, the first newspaper published by an indigenous people, began publication using Sequoyah's syllabary in 1828.

Rapid acquisition of white culture did not protect the Cherokee against the insatiable land hunger of the settlers. When gold was discovered on Cherokee land in Georgia, agitation for the removal of the entire nation increased. President Andrew Jackson adopted in 1830 a policy of removing the Native American nations obstructing expansion. Establishing a dubious legality for removal by coercing chiefs or factions to sign removal orders, the American government branded those that resisted as rebels, revolutionaries, and traitors, subject to imprisonment or death. A long controversy with the state of Georgia, which claimed most of the Cherokee territory not already ceded, ended with the forced signing of the Treaty of New Echota by a small minority in 1835. The treaty bound all the Cherokee to leave their homeland, for a payment of five million dollars and seven million acres in Indian Territory in the west. The treaty obliged the Cherokee to leave their homeland within two years.

The overwhelming majority of the Cherokee repudiated the treaty and took their case to the U.S. Supreme Court. The court reached a decision favorable to the Cherokee, declaring that Georgia had no jurisdiction over the Cherokee and no claim to their lands. Georgia state officials ignored the court's decision, and when President Andrew Jackson refused to enforce the court's ruling, they prepared for the eviction of the Cherokee from their ancestral lands.

Sanctioned by the Georgia government, militiamen rode through the Cherokee lands burning, looting, and choosing mansions, plantations, and other valuable properties they would confiscate following the removal of the lawful owners. Driven from their homes, the Cherokee were herded into squalid camps, where disease, starvation, and filth decimated the weakest. In 1838 the Cherokee were forced westward on the so-called Trail of Tears. Some Christian missionaries accompanied the deportees, and a number of black slaves traveled west with the former plantation owners. Thousands died in the camps and on the forced migration to the area designated "Indian Territory." Those that survived endured torments and humiliations unequaled in modern history until the twentieth century.

When the survivors reached the zone set aside for them in what is now northeastern Oklahoma, they were met by new controversies, including a conflict with Cherokee expelled from Texas and earlier migrants from the Carolinas, who refused to accept the authority of the newcomers. Feuds and murders rent the tribe as reprisals were inflicted on the leaders who had signed the Treaty of New Echota, which had led to the latest deportation. The various groups finally united in the Cherokee Nation, which was recognized by the U.S. government in 1846.

During the American Civil War, the embittered Cherokee generally allied themselves to the Confederacy against the hated American government. In 1865 the Cherokee, having lost a quarter of their population, shared the South's final defeat. All treaties were set aside, and the Cherokee were restricted to the eastern part of the Indian Territory, the western districts being confiscated for the settlement of other dispossessed tribes. Stripped of power, the tribal government ceased to function except as an advisory council. In 1887 the U.S. administration forced the tribes to abandon communal lands for individual plots, producing a large quantity of surplus land that was confiscated by the federal government for distribution to white settlers.

Pressed by illegal land seizures, the tribal leaders of the Five Civilized Tribes met in Muskogee, the capital of the tribal confederation, on 21 August 1905 to debate their future. The council passed bills codifying tribal law and adopted a constitution for a proposed autonomous state, to be called the All-Indian State of Sequoyah, to include all the lands still designated Indian Territory. Representatives took the proposal to the U.S. Congress, which never acknowledged or acted upon the petition.

In 1906 Congress passed an enabling act that merged the Indian and Oklahoma territories and ended all tribal sovereignty. The Cherokee Nation was dissolved, and its members were given American citizenship in 1906. Some of their land was allotted to individual Cherokee; the rest was opened up to white homesteaders, held in trust by the U.S. government, or allotted to freed slaves. On 16 November 1907 Oklahoma was admitted to the Union as a state, and the former tribal lands were thrown open to thousands of settlers.

Neglected and ignored, the tribes began to mobilize in the 1940s, pressing their claims to former tribal lands. The present government of the Cherokee Nation was formed in 1948. A cultural revival, with renewed interest in the tribe's history, culture, and languages, led to a political revival and growing demands for self-government and for justice for the suffering of the past. Over the next decade the revival movement merged with the militant liberation movement of the 1960s, which translated into "Red Power" among the indigenous peoples.

University-educated activists in the 1960s and 1970s demanded that the government honor the treaties that recognized the Cherokee as a sovereign nation. The U.S. Claims Commission awarded the Cherokee Nation $15 million for lands confiscated in Oklahoma. In 1970 the tribal government was again authorized to elect its own leaders. Tribal activists joined the other indigenous American peoples in petitioning the United Nations to recognize the indigenous peoples of North America as sovereign nations, and in demands that the Red race, the only race not represented in the United Nations, be given a seat.

In the 1990 U.S. census, 369,305 persons identified themselves as Cherokee. Of these only about 15,000 were full-blood, and only some 95,000 lived in eastern Oklahoma. Another 10,000 lived on or near the North Carolina reservation. Cherokee tribal governments have fairly liberal membership standards, and some estimates in the late 1990s exceeded 500,000, which would make the Cherokee the largest indigenous group in the United States. Three Cherokee groups are currently federally recognized—the Cherokee Nation of Oklahoma, United Keetoowah Band of Cherokee in Oklahoma, and the Eastern Band of Cherokee of North Carolina. The Echota Cherokee are recognized only by the state of Alabama.

The renewed emphasis on self-determination, particularly strong following the disintegration of the Soviet Union and Yugoslavia in 1991, has given Cherokee activists new confidence in their fight to restore their nation's sovereignty. In October 1991, equating the deportations of the Five Civilized Tribes to the Stalinist deportations of Soviet minorities during World War II, Cherokee militants demanded the restoration of their homeland in eastern Oklahoma as a self-governing reservation.

In the late 1990s, the United Keetoowah Band, representing the Cherokee who settled in Oklahoma prior to 1828 (most having traded their lands in the southeast for territory in the west, initially in Arkansas), began negotiations for a federal government–approved move back to Arkansas. This move would make them the first indigenous group to relocate under government auspices in the twenty-first century. Many Cherokee, particularly younger members of the Cherokee Nation, are returning to their ancestral homes in Tennessee and North Carolina.

Cherokee Nation citizens living within the Cherokee Nation's 14-county jurisdictional area in Oklahoma were able to purchase tribal car tags beginning in October 2001. The Cherokee Nation Tribal Council voted to use revenue from the sale of car tags to fund road projects within the tribe's 14-county jurisdictional area. By committing 20% of tag revenues to road projects, the Cherokee Nation offsets the fears of some state officials that the state would lose significant amounts of money for roads. The tags, seen by activists as a symbol of sovereignty, are the first of several projects set to restore a measure of self-determination to the Cherokee.

SELECTED BIBLIOGRAPHY:

Ehle, John. *The Trail of Tears: The Rise and Fall of the Cherokee Nation*. 1988.
Long, Cathryn J. *The Cherokee*. 2000.
Lund, Bill. *The Cherokee Indians*. 1997.
Norgren, Jill. *The Cherokee Cases: The Confrontation of Law and Politics*. 1995.

Chukots

Chukchi; Chukchee; Chukcha; Luoravetlan; Luorawetlan; Lygoraveltlat

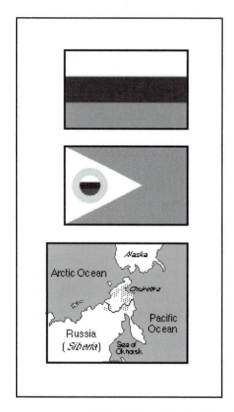

POPULATION: Approximately (2002e) 35,000 Chukots in northeastern Siberian Russia, concentrated in the Chukchi Autonomous Okrug, but with sizable populations in the neighboring Koryak Autonomous Okrug and the Lower Kolyma District of the neighboring Republic of Sakha.

THE CHUKOT HOMELAND: The Chukot homeland lies in extreme northeastern Siberian Russia, a huge region partly above the Arctic Circle. Mountainous and with a long coastline in the Chukchi, Siberian, and Bering Seas, the peninsula region in the northeast is less than 50 miles from Alaska, across the Bering Strait. Most of the region is tundra and taiga, which gives way to the northern forest in the inland districts. Officially Chukota forms an autonomous district of the Russian Federation, as the declaration unilaterally upgrading its status to that of a member state in the federation has not been recognized. *Chukot Autonomous Okrug*: 284,026 sq. mi.—737,700 sq. km, (2002e) 67,000—Russians 40%, Chukots 38%, Lamuts 8%, Sakhas* 3%. The Chukot capital and major cultural center is Anadyr, called Kagyrgyn by the Chukots, (2002e) 12,000. The town of Tavaivaam, recently annexed to Anadyr, is traditionally a major center of Chukot culture.

FLAG: The Chukot national flag, the flag of the self-proclaimed republic, is a vertical tricolor of white, cranberry red, and pale blue. The official flag of the region is a pale blue field bearing a white triangle at the hoist charged with a yellow disk around three horizontal stripes of white, blue, and red.

PEOPLE AND CULTURE: The Chukots are a Paleo-Asiatic people ethnically related to the Native American peoples. In the rural communities in the Arctic, the average lifespan is just 45 years, with tuberculosis, parasitic infections, alcoholism, and unemployment taking their tolls. Tribal groupings, important in the early history of the Chukots, remain as traditional divisions and cultural groupings. The most important groups are the Little Anyuy, Omolon, Chaun, Amguema, Onmylen, and Tuman. Traditionally the Chukot are divided into two groups based on occupations— the Reindeer Chukot or Chauchu, the more numerous reindeer herders of the plains and mountains of the interior; and the Maritime Chukot or Ankalyn, the fishing and hunting clans of the coasts. Collectively the Chukot call themselves Iygoravetlyan, meaning "true" or "genuine people." Traditionally, trade and population exchanges helped to maintain the Chukot culture and traditions shared by the two groups. Culturally the Chukot share affinities with the Koryak* and Inuit* peoples of the Arctic region.

LANGUAGE AND RELIGION: The Chukot language is part of the larger Chukotsko-Kamchatkan family of Paleosiberian languages. The language is related to that of the neighboring Koryaks and to the Inuit and Aleutian languages spoken by native Alaskans.* The language is spoken in two dialects, based on the Reindeer Chukot and the Maritime Chukot subgroups, and eight subdialects, although there is little dialectical difference. A curious feature of the Chukot language is a different pronunciation by men and women. The women's language lacks the "r" sound, which is regarded as unsuitable for women.

Traditionally the Chukots practiced a form of shamanism, with the role of shaman open to both males and females. Although many now profess Orthodox Christianity, shamanism and pre-Christian beliefs remain widespread among the Chukots. Shamans practice healing, divination, and sorcery. Chukot beliefs include invisible spirits that populate the universe, and sacrifices to these spirits are an important aspect of their shamanistic religion. Only about 2% of the Chukots are officially Orthodox Christians. Shamanism survived as most religious activity was in the home; with no stable religious hierarchy for the Soviet authorities to attack, it easily survived underground.

NATIONAL HISTORY: In prehistoric times the Chukot Peninsula formed the western extension of a land bridge that once connected Asia and North America. Beginning some 30,000 years ago, small bands of nomadic hunters began to migrate across the land bridge, following the mammoths and other large quarry. Clan groups eventually settled on the western end of the bridge, the ancestors of the Chukots, Lamuts, Inuits, and other native peoples. The Chukots were well adapted to the harsh climatic conditions; the seasons, the reindeer herds, and the availability of sea animals, fish, and other food regulated their traditional life. The Chukots did not engage in large-scale warfare, although they were formidable warriors. Small disputes, fighting, and raiding were common and captured enemies were enslaved, but most disputes were at the clan or village level.

Russian expansion, led by Cossack explorers and soldiers, reached the

Pacific Ocean in 1640. A Cossack explorer, Ivan Yerastov, first met the Chukots, on the Alazeya River, in 1642. Seven years later the Russians established Anadyr, called Novo-Mariinsk, as a fort and trading post on traditional Chukot land. Traders, hunters, government officials, settlers, explorers, and missionaries from several countries increased the contact between the newcomers and the native Chukots. Nominal Russian rule consisted of collecting an annual fur tax, leaving the native peoples to their traditional way of life. Between 1763 and 1800 the Russian Empire formally annexed the Chukot territories.

The introduction of firearms and the trade demands for valuable skins affected the Chukot way of life. The increased hunting of forest and sea animals by the Chukots and outsiders nearly caused extinction of these animals. New diseases took a toll on the small nation, and alcoholism became a problem, as Russians often paid with vodka. When conflicts arose, the Chukots most often lost, and many were killed in outbreaks of violence. In spite of enormous problems, the seminomadic Chukots effectively resisted Russian domination and continued to function as a semi-independent nation well into the nineteenth century.

After the sale of Russian Alaska to the United States in 1867, the Russian government hastened to tighten its hold on northeast Asia so that Russian businessmen could keep foreign, mostly American, merchants and traders at bay. In 1889 a special trading center was founded in Anadyr, but up to the end of World War I, British, American, and Norwegian ships and fishing boats were common in the area.

Orthodox missionaries introduced a system of education in the nineteenth century. Although usually limited to the sons of chiefs, the missionary education established a core of educated, modernizing leaders. Aided, and often studied, by educated political exiles sent to the remote region from European Russia, Chukot leaders began to demand the redress of past injustices. In the wake of the 1905 Russian Revolution, the nascent Chukot national movement focused on land and cultural rights. Until well into the twentieth century, the Chukots had only a very weak sense of common ethnicity but identified with regionally based tribal associations.

Virtually untouched by the war that engulfed European Russia from 1914 to 1918, the Chukots were dismayed by the news of the revolution that overthrew the empire. Slow to react, the Chukots began to mobilize only when the civil government collapsed. Pushed aside as rival Russian factions sought to win control of the strategic region at the eastern edge of Russian territory, most Chukots remained unsure what to do as the Russian Civil War spread to even the most remote corners of the disintegrating empire. In 1920 the victorious Reds expelled the last of the White forces and established Soviet rule in the Chukot homeland.

Outraged by clumsy Soviet attempts to collectivize their reindeer herds and to break the power of the shamans, small groups organized to resist, and in early 1921 violence broke out. Allied to other anti-Soviet peoples and groups, Chukot nationalists routed the small Soviet force at Anadyr and on 28 October 1921 declared Chukotka independent of Soviet Russia. The nationalists sought Japanese and American aid and recognition, but without success. A Soviet military force invaded the breakaway state, and on 21 October 1922 independent Chukotka ceased to exist. The Chukot nationalist leadership was imprisoned or killed. The rebellion and the brief period of independence established the basis of a united Chukot identity.

The Reindeer and Maritime Chukot were settled as collectives, and herds and fishing grounds were held in common. As part of the Soviet nationalities programs the authorities authorized a Chukot national area in 1930, but all power remained with the Soviet bureaucracy, which oversaw the vast chain of slave-labor camps established in the wilderness in the 1920s. After World War II, until the Cold War began, American traders and hunters from Alaska were active in the region.

During the Stalin era, between the late 1920s and 1953, thousands of political prisoners were sent to the area as slave labor. New roads and mineral extraction began to transform the region. Relationships between educated prisoners and Chukots in the labor camps reaffirmed ideas of identity and socialist self-determination, but for the majority of the Chukots the painful areas of politics and authority were carefully avoided.

In 1957 the Soviet authorities drove the Chukots off the tundra and into communal farms, where their reindeer-hide tents, *urangas*, were exchanged for prefabricated Soviet housing. The establishment of cultural bases, with schools, hospitals, day-care centers, and other amenities, served a dual purpose—to bring the Chukots into the Soviet culture and economy and to eliminate their traditional nomadism. In the 1960s there was a boom in mixed marriages, with many Chukots taking the ethnic identity of their spouses. By the early 1980s, most Chukots were living apathetic lives in a totally Russian-language environment.

The reforms introduced by Mikhail Gorbachev in the late 1980s stirred dormant Chukot nationalism. In early 1990 the first openly nationalist organization formed. Supported by the resurgent national movement and the regional parliament, the area's governor, Alexander Nazorov, unilaterally declared the upgrading of the region's political status in October 1990. Chukotka's self-declared status as a member republic of the Russian Federation has not received official recognition.

The disintegration of the Soviet Union in August 1991 fueled the rapid growth of nationalism in the region. In late 1991 the republican government sent a delegation to Moscow to seek recognition of Chukotka's status as a republic in the revamped Russian Federation. Rebuffed by the ministries and bureaucrats in Moscow, the delegation returned home, where the Chukots joined other native Siberian peoples in establishing the Association of Peoples of the North. In December 1992 the Chukot parliament proclaimed the republic independent of the provincial government of Magadan, the *oblast* it had been part of since 1953. In order to finance the republic's autonomy the Chukot government imposed a 10% tax on the production of gold. The Constitutional Court of the Russian Federation accepted the separation of Chukotka from Magadan Oblast in 1993.

The end of the Soviet command economy doomed many of the subsidized industries and mines, which once drew Russians from Europe with high wages and free housing. The uneconomical industries virtually collapsed, and thousands of the Russians returned to European Russia. The Chukots forced to work in the industries began to return to their traditional way of life, herding reindeer on the tundra.

Looking across the Bering Strait, the Chukot government established close political and economic ties to Alaska. Increasingly ignoring edicts and laws issued in faraway Moscow, the nationalist Chukot government entered into a number of joint commercial ventures with Alaskan companies and sought financial backing for oil exploration. Optimistic about the region's future, the government even participated in a feasibility study for a rail tunnel under the Bering Strait that would connect Chukotka, and its mineral wealth and natural resources, to the huge consumer markets of North America.

The Chukot homeland is rich beyond its needs. It sits on the second-largest reserves of gold in Russia and on significant reserves of coal, tin, and petroleum, and it has plentiful fish stocks off its long coast; yet the province must import everything from toilet paper to light bulbs from European Russia, paying with its earnings from the raw materials it exports. By 1998, as trading partners in other parts of Russia ceased buying, the value of the region's assets evaporated as part of an increasingly severe economic crisis. In 1999 only the "survival minimum" of food and fuel was delivered to the region. Power in most towns and villages was cut off for at least four hours every day during the long Arctic winter.

The region's population fell dramatically, from around 160,000 in 1990 to about 84,000 in 1998 and to 67,000 in 2002. Those who departed were the descendants of the original privileged Russian immigrants. The indigenous Chukots left behind made the best of what was left of their traditional way of life and work, as reindeer herders and fishermen. To the Chukots the preservation of traditional occupations and crafts was a matter of survival. Chukot activists demanded funds for promoting reindeer husbandry as a major source of traditional food in the region. Several organizations in Alaska took the lead in delivering aid to the Chukots, coordinated by the Alaskan Friends of Chukotkans. By 1997 Anadyr had become the most expensive city in Russia for food, fuel, and clothing.

The regional government in the late 1990s began to encourage the resettlement of the Slavs—called *prishliyw*, or immigrants, by the Chukots—

out of the area. The program attempted to induce the Russians to re-emigrate to other parts of the Russian Federation. The idea of establishing national parks, reservations, or some other form of protected territory for the exclusive use and occupancy by the Chukots has gained wide acceptance in the region and is supported by the Chukot national movement.

In 2000 both Russian government officials and clergy of the Moscow patriarchate spread the view that American Protestant missionaries in Chukotka were part of a U.S. government plot to transfer the region from Russian to American sovereignty. In June 2000, Bishop Anatoly Aksyonov of the Moscow patriarchate's diocese of Magadan and Chukotka published a letter he had received from a government official in the region detailing "a carefully planned system of measures by the U.S.A., now being executed over a long-term period, to wrest Chukotka away from the Russian Federation and make it part of the U.S.A." The letter stated that "no small part of this system is the religious invasion by a huge number of American Protestant preachers, who have recently been intensifying their activities in the Far East and particularly in Chukotka."

The election of Roman Abramovich, the former head of the state oil company in Siberia, Sibneft, as governor in January 2001 began to reverse Chukotka's long economic and demographic decline. Back wages are being paid and a program of transferring Russian pensioners to European Russia has liberated funds for development. Sibneft started tapping Chukot oil in mid-September 2001. The new Chukot government has promised increased funds for the development of the small Chukot nation.

SELECTED BIBLIOGRAPHY:

Mayer, Fred. *The Forgotten Peoples of Siberia.* 1994.
Slezkine, Yu. *Arctic Mirrors: Russia and the Small Peoples of the North.* 1994.
Yevtushenko, Yevgeny. *Divided Twins: Alaska and Siberia.* 1988.
Znamenski, Andrei A. *Native Encounters with Russian Orthodox Missions in Siberia and Alaska, 1820–1917.* 1999.

Cook Islanders

Rarotongans; Niueans

POPULATION: Approximately (2002e) 46,000 Cook Islanders in the South Pacific, concentrated in the Cook Islands, Niue, and New Zealand. Smaller communities live in Australia and the United States.

THE COOK ISLANDER HOMELAND: The Cook Islander homeland lies in the South Pacific, an archipelago of 15 islands scattered across 850,000 square miles northeast of New Zealand. The seven northern islands are low-lying and sparsely populated coral atolls, while the more heavily populated southern islands, including the central island, Rarotonga, are fertile and more mountainous. *Cook Islands*: 92 sq. mi.—238 sq. km, (2002e) 20,200—Cook Islanders 96% (Polynesians 81%, Polynesian-European mixtures 8%, Polynesian/non-European mixtures 7%), Europeans, mostly New Zealanders, 3%. Niue is also a self-governing territory, in association with New Zealand. *Niue*: 100 sq. mi.—259 sq. km, (2002e) 2,000, with about 13,000 living in New Zealand. The Cook Islander capital and major cultural center is Avarua, (2002e) 11,000, on the largest island of Rarotonga. The capital of Niue is Alofi, (2002e) 1,000.

FLAG: The Cook Islander national flag, the former official state flag, is a green field bearing a circle of 15 gold stars on the fly. The state flag since 1979 is a blue field bearing a circle of 15 white stars on the fly and the Union Jack as a canton on the upper hoist. The flag of Niue is a yellow field bearing the Union Jack on the upper hoist charged with five yellow stars.

PEOPLE AND CULTURE: The Cook Islanders are a Polynesian nation, related to the other Polynesian peoples of the South Pacific. With the exception of the inhabitants of isolated Pukapuka, who are predominantly of Samoan and Tongan descent, the majority of the Cook Islanders and Niueans are of mixed Polynesian ancestry. Intermarriage with European and Chinese traders and missionaries in the nineteenth century accounts for the large number of Cook Islanders of mixed ancestry. The rate of natural increase is high but is offset by continuing emigration to New Zealand, where more than twice as many persons of Cook Islands and Niuean ancestry live than in the islands.

LANGUAGE AND RELIGION: The Cook Islanders' Polynesian languages are closely related to the Maori* dialects spoken by the Polynesian population of New Zealand. Four main dialects are spoken in the islands—Penrhyn, or Tongareva, on Penrhyn Island, and Pukapuka on Pukapuka Island, by several hundred each; Rakahanga-Manihiki, spoken by about 6,000 people, half of them in New Zealand; and Rarotongan, also called Cook Islands Maori, spoken by about 17,000 in the islands and over 25,000 in New Zealand. Rarotongan is the literary language and is spoken in six major dialects. It is also the second language used throughout the archipelago. English is spoken by most Cook Islanders, and the literacy rate is over 90%.

The majority of the Cook Islanders belong to various Protestant sects brought to the islands by missionaries in the nineteenth century, with the majority belonging the Cook Islands Christian Church. Choral singing, introduced by the European missionaries, has become an integral part of the islands' culture. The Protestant churches have a very strong influence on everyday life in the islands.

NATIONAL HISTORY: Over 2,000 years ago the northern islands of the chain were populated by Polynesians arriving by canoe from Tonga and Samoa. The southern islands of the archipelago were populated by Polynesian explorers coming from the Marquesa Islands in the northern part of present-day French Polynesia. Signs of long habitation on Rarotonga included *marae*, or ancient temple platforms. The Polynesians colonized the islands and later expanded south to the large islands they called Aotearoa, New Zealand. About 1,000 high-ranking adventurers from Raiatea, in present-day French Polynesia, established their rule over the archipelago as a local aristocracy.

Europeans, mostly Spanish explorers, first visited the islands in the fifteenth and seventeenth centuries, but they remained virtually unknown until Capt. James Cook discovered them in 1773. Cook claimed the islands for the United Kingdom after visiting Rarotonga and the other southern islands. Capt. John Williams visited the other islands of the scattered group in the 1820s. The archipelago eventually adopted the name given by the Europeans, the Cook Islands, after the British discoverer.

English Protestant missionaries established themselves in the southern islands, where they converted many of the islanders to Christianity. The

London Missionary Society set up a virtual "missionary kingdom" in the islands, dictating the local administration, the clothing worn by the islanders, and many other aspects of island life. In 1888 the islands were made a British protectorate and were placed under direct British administration.

In 1901 the British government ceded the islands to newly independent New Zealand, which took over the administration and defense of the islands. Some of the more remote islands of the group were not discovered until New Zealander ships explored the scattered archipelago in the 1920s. The islanders, related to New Zealand's own Polynesian population, the Maoris, were granted New Zealand citizenship and allowed open immigration. Between the 1920s and World War II, thousands of Cook Islanders migrated to New Zealand in search of jobs or education.

During World War II, the islands were fortified by the New Zealanders in anticipation of a Japanese invasion that never occurred. In the postwar years the Cook Islanders were granted increased autonomy.

The anticolonial surge that swept the world in the 1960s fueled the growth of Cook Islander nationalism. In 1962 the New Zealand government offered four alternatives to the islanders—full independence; full integration with New Zealand; internal self-government with New Zealand responsible for foreign affairs and security; and membership in a (still non-existent) Polynesian Federation. By a nearly unanimous vote, the Cook Islands Assembly chose internal autonomy in association with New Zealand.

The New Zealand government in 1963 sent a commission to Rarotonga to work out the details of the association and the new Cook Islands constitution. The islands became a self-governing state, in free association with New Zealand, in 1965. The 1965 pact ended 65 years of missionary lawmakers followed by 77 years of paternalistic British, then New Zealander rule. Niue became a self-governing territory in 1974.

The autonomy agreement provided for a separate legislature, an advisory council of hereditary chiefs (the House of Ariki), and a premier, who is head of the Cook Islands government. The first elected premier, Sir Albert Henry, became increasingly nationalistic as neighboring island groups opted for independence. In 1974 Henry called for a referendum on independence but was blocked by the legislature. In 1978 parliamentary elections were held; Henry used public funds to fly in voters from New Zealand to support his reelection and his bid for independence. The Cook Islands government annulled the vote, and Sir Albert was convicted of conspiracy, stripped of his knighthood, and heavily fined. The local government in 1979 adopted a new flag more closely resembling that of New Zealand to replace the nationalist flag used by the Henry government. The former flag was adopted as the flag of the nationalist movement.

Tourism has become the major industry since a new jet airport opened on Rarotonga in 1974. Buoyed by the tourist income, the islands, while maintaining their ties to New Zealand, have taken on many of the trappings of independence, including membership in many international organizations. In the 1980s the government of the Cook Islands became active in Pacific politics, especially in opposing the French nuclear tests in French Polynesia. The emigration of Cook Islanders to New Zealand in large numbers in the 1970s and 1980s, with the resulting loss of skilled labor, was a problem.

The Cook Islanders, by following the procedure set out in the constitution, may terminate their relationship with New Zealand and attain full independence at any time. However, there is little likelihood that political independence would lessen the islands' economic dependence on New Zealand, which provides about 90% of the annual budget. The annual trade deficits are made up by remittances from Cook Islanders in New Zealand and by foreign aid, overwhelmingly from New Zealand. The second largest industry, after tourism, is international finance; the islands have become a major tax haven.

In a March 1994 general election, the Cook Islands Party, led by Sir Geoffrey Henry, Albert Henry's son, was returned to power in the Cook Islands, winning 20 of the 25 seats in the Legislative Assembly. Voters also endorsed the status quo with respect to the Cook Islands' name, national anthem, and flag. Henry won despite controversial financial dealings and allegations that the tax-haven facilities of the Cook Islands had been misused to disguise mismanagement and tax evasion by companies based in New Zealand. The Niue legislature passed, also in 1994, a bill to establish a tax haven, although on a more modest scale, hoping to make enough money from international financial services to replace some of the annual financial aid from New Zealand.

The Cook Islands government faced a grave financial crisis in 1996, with a huge deficit and the government near bankruptcy. The problems stemmed from the 1995 financial scandal and difficulties with the New Zealand government over allegations of tax avoidance by means of Cook Islands financial instutitions. The government declared bankruptcy, citing a $120 million debt. Efforts to expand tourism and the mining and fishing industries were not adequate to deal with the financial crisis. In an effort to stem a further deterioration of the economy, the government slashed public-sector salaries by 50%, shrank the number of ministries from 52 to 22, reduced the number of civil servants by more than half, and began selling government assets. The closing of all overseas diplomatic posts, except for the commission in New Zealand, became a nationalist issue in the late 1990s.

Prime Minister Henry resisted calls for his resignation over the financial scandals and the 1996 crisis. His party remains the governing party but has not pushed for full independence as Geoffrey Henry had once promised.

In July 2000, the Cook Islands and Niue were named as tax havens that harm trade and investment by the United States and later by other governments. Loose financial laws and a need for foreign currency have led to a growing financial sector, but little in the way of regulation.

SELECTED BIBLIOGRAPHY:

Banks, Sara Harrell. *A Net to Catch Time*. 1992.
Bevan, Stuart. *Cook Islands*. 1996.
Idiens, Dale. *Cook Islands Art*. 1990.
Keller, Nancy. *Rarotonga and the Cook Islands*. 1998.

Copts

Coptics; Coptic Christians

POPULATION: Approximately (2002e) 12,000,000 Copts in the Middle East, concentrated in Egypt, which has between six and 10 million. Other sizable Coptic populations live in Sudan, Libya, Syria, Israel, and Armenia. Outside the region an estimated 1.5 million immigrant Copts have established communities in many countries. The largest communities live in the United States, Brazil, Canada, Britain, and Ethiopia.

THE COPT HOMELAND: The Copt homeland lies in the Nile Valley in Egypt and northern Sudan, extending from near Khartoum to the Nile Delta. The Copts are most numerous in the middle Nile Valley regions of Asyut, al-Minya, and Qina in Egypt, where between 40% and 60% of the population is Christian. About a quarter of the total Coptic population lives in Cairo. The Copt capital and major culture center is Cairo (al-Qahira), (2002e) 7,746,000, metropolitan area, 16,210,000. The other major Copt cultural centers are Alexandria (al-Iskandariyah), (2002e) 3,743,000, metropolitan area, 4,310,000, and Asyut, in Upper Egypt, (2002e) 392,000.

FLAG: The Coptic flag is a white or black field bearing a centered Coptic cross. The flag of the Copt organizations that support secular government in Egypt and oppose calls for an Islamic government is a horizontal bicolor of white and yellow bearing a large yellow *ankh* on the white. The flag of the Coptic Pharaonic Movement has a central white inverted triangle bearing a red Coptic cross with blue and black stripes forming additional triangles on the hoist and fly.

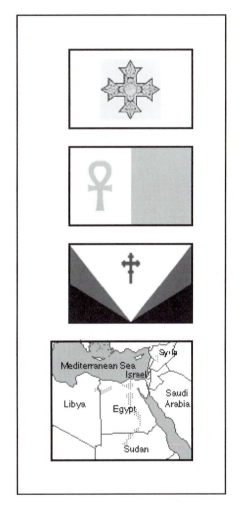

PEOPLE AND CULTURE: The Copts are an ethnoreligious Middle Eastern nation, Christians who have resisted conversion to Islam for over

14 centuries. They form the largest Christian presence in the Arab world and consider themselves the true descendants of the ancient Egyptians. The Copts are ethnically Egyptians, although, as a result of marrying almost exclusively within their community, many Copts preserve in their facial and bodily features the characteristics of the ancient population of Pharaonic Egypt. The Copts have traditionally been identified with certain handicrafts, trades, and professions, above all in finance, accounting, banking, commerce, and civil service. In Upper Egypt many Copts live in rural villages that are wholly Coptic or in mixed villages devoted to farming. The Coptic nation includes the majority Orthodox population, but also smaller Roman Catholic and Protestant elements. Although there is little physical difference between the Copts and the Muslim Egyptians, the former can be distinguished by their crosses worn around their necks or tattooed on their wrists, or by their Christian names. The Copts have a distinctive art and architecture, which developed as an early expression of their faith. Islam is the state religion of Egypt. It is illegal for Copts men to marry Muslim women. Muslims are not allowed to convert to another faith.

LANGUAGE AND RELIGION: The Copts speak the Egyptian dialect of Arabic, with the addition of many words and phrases preserved from their earlier language, which died out in the twelfth century. The language, called Coptic, is preserved as a ceremonial language, although Arabic is now used in the church services for most rituals. The Coptic language, the Boharic dialect of Alexandria, is still printed in Bibles and prayer books, with the Arabic text in parallel columns. Many Coptic churches, especially outside Egypt, have classes to teach the Coptic language, and many universities also teach the language. Activists would like to revive it as a national language.

The Coptic religion is an Orthodox Christian Church that officially adheres to Monophysitism. Less change has taken place in the Egyptian Church than in any other, either in ritual or doctrine. Some Muslim traditions—such as circumcision and dietary restrictions—are observed. The succession of Coptic patriarchs, bishops, and priests has been continuous since the time of St. Mark himself; His Holiness Pope Shenouda III is the 117th successor of St. Mark. The Copts pride themselves on the apostolicity of their church and on the fact that Egypt is the only land in the world honored and blessed by a long visit by the holy family. They are also very proud of their Egyptian saints, theologians, and scholars, who have always counted among the most distinguished figures of the Christian world. The Copts broke with the Eastern Church in the fifth century and since that time have maintained religious autonomy. The Coptic Catholic Church, a minority among the Copts, has been in communion with Rome since 1741 but maintains its Monophysite theology and Coptic rituals. The patriarchs of both the Coptic Orthodox and the Coptic Catholic Churches reside in Cairo. The Copts have their own primary and secondary schools in many areas of Egypt. There is a Coptic theological college attached to the Coptic Studies Institute. The Copts have more fasts than any other Christian community, fasting over 210 days each year, including all 40 days of Lent.

NATIONAL HISTORY: The pre-Arabic population of Egypt identified themselves and their language in Greek as *aigyptios*, in Arabic *qibt*, later called Copt. When the Egyptian Muslims ceased to call themselves Aigyptioi, the term was applied to the Christian minority. The Coptic Church was established by St. Mark in Alexandria in the year A.D. 62. St. Mark became the first Coptic martyr six years later; he was dragged by his feet all over Alexandria. Since that time the Copts have been persecuted by almost every ruler of Egypt.

Christianity spread throughout Egypt within half a century of St. Mark's arrival in Alexandria. In the fifth century the Coptic Orthodox Church broke its ties to the Eastern Church and has since maintained its autonomy, its belief, and its rituals. From its beginnings, Egyptian Christianity played a central role in Christian theology. The Bible was translated into the Coptic language in the second century.

The Coptic Church adhered to Monophysitism, acknowledging only one (divine) nature in Christ, and eventually called themselves the Egyptian Church. The Christian religion, espoused by the majority of the Egyptian population, was centered on Alexandria, the pre-Islamic metropolis of the country. In the fourth and fifth centuries a theological conflict arose between the Copts and the Greek-speaking Byzantines and their Eastern Orthodox Church, called the Melchites, or the Emperor's Men. The Council of Chalcedon declared monophysitism a heresy in A.D. 451. The Church of Alexandria was subsequently isolated.

After the Arab conquest of Egypt in 640–41, the Copts ceased to speak Coptic Greek, and the language barrier added to the controversy between their church and the Eastern Orthodox religion of the Byzantine Empire. Various attempts at compromise by the Byzantine emperors failed. Later, the Arab caliphates, although they openly favored the majority who adopted Islam, did not interfere overly in the internal affairs of the Christian church in Egypt. The Copts were alternately treated with tolerance or repression. As *dhimi*, or "people of the book," the Copts were officially tolerated under Islamic law, which can be interpreted in different ways to produce different levels of tolerance from autonomy to open persecution. For about three centuries after the Arab conquest of Egypt, the Muslims did not constitute a majority.

For more than 200 years, through the Umayyad and the 'Abbasid dynasties, Egypt was ruled by governors appointed by the caliphs. Religious unrest during the caliphate period was manifested in the form of political insurrections, especially when governors openly discriminated against the

Copts by forcing them to wear distinctive clothing, or even ordering their icons destroyed. Still, during the caliphate period, the official policy was tolerance, partly for fiscal reasons. In order to collect the higher taxes paid by the non-Muslims, the Arab governors discouraged conversion to Islam and even required those who did adopt Islam to continue paying the non-Muslim taxes. Even under the most tolerant of governments, the Copts were always second-class citizens.

In the ninth century, the caliph Mamun led an army from Baghdad to put down a rebellion raised by the Copts. The repression of the Christian Copts following their defeat in 829–30 is cited as an important factor in the increased conversion of Christians to the majority Islamic religion in Egypt. New restrictions were imposed on the Copts between 905 and 935. By the end of the twelfth century, Egypt changed from a predominantly Christian to a predominantly Muslim country.

The Coptic language remained the language of most of Egypt until the second half of the eleventh century. At that time the first Coptic-Arabic liturgical manuscripts were written. The first complete Arabic texts appeared in the thirteenth century, detailing the laws, cultural traits, and traditions of the Copts, more than 500 years after the Islamic conquest.

The Ottoman Turks, in control of Egypt in the Middle Ages, like the governments before them, employed Copts in the financial offices of the bureaucracy. Periodic persecutions of the Copts increased as the Ottoman Empire began to decline in the eighteenth century. Under Ottoman rule European missionaries were allowed to work in Egypt, but only among the Orthodox population. In 1741 a group of Copts established ties to Rome, while Protestant missionaries gained some converts, especially among the growing urban population.

Western influences in Egypt, in the nineteenth century, gave the Copts an opportunity to improve their status. Support by the Christian West also increased conflict with the Muslim majority. In the nineteenth and early twentieth centuries, the Egyptian Christians began to call themselves "Copts" and their church "Coptic Orthodox," to distinguish themselves from the other Christian sects in Egypt, mostly Greek Eastern Orthodox. In 1855 the *gezya*, the special tax paid by the Christians, was lifted, and the Copts accepted for the first time in the Egyptian army. Under Western influence, the Coptic Church developed a democratic system of government after the 1890s.

The conflict between the Copts and the Muslim Egyptians intensified when Egypt officially gained its independence from Great Britain in 1936. The Copts demanded equality in the new state, setting off a cycle of sectarian violence that continued until the coup that brought Abdul Nasser to power in 1952. Nasser's autocratic government suppressed the violence, but the Copts also suffered new restrictions and persecutions.

Persecution of the Coptic Christians in Sudan began in the 1980s, as part of the government's move to introduce Islamic rule. According to some sources, up to 700,000 Christians, including thousands of Copts, have been killed in Sudan and their churches, religious buildings, and homes burned or destroyed.

Sectarian tension in Egypt became serious when Mustafa Mashur, the leader of the fundamentalist Muslim Brotherhood, stated that Copts should not be allowed to serve in the Egyptian army and should be forced to pay a religious tax. The Copts felt that they were not trusted as Egyptians, a feeling that grew as attacks increased and anti-Copt violence spread throughout the country.

Attacks on Christians, particularly in the southern provinces of Upper Egypt, are mostly blamed on the fundamentalist militants of the el-Gamaa el-Islamiya, the Islamic Group, which became active in Egypt in 1992. Attacks have destroyed Coptic farms, businesses, and churches. Copts became a target of the fundamentalists who had organized to overthrow Egypt's secular government. Religious violence increased, often with the tacit approval of local officials sympathetic to the Islamic movement. In 1993, in a roundup of Islamic militants, government agents seized numerous books, cassettes, and videotapes calling for violence and increased discrimination against the Copts.

Thousands of Copts during the national elections in 1995 were illegally eliminated from the voting polls. In December 1995, however, Egypt's president, Hosni Mubarak, appointed 10 parliamentarians, using his constitutional privilege to enlarge the assembly with women and members of the Coptic community. In 1996, the leader of one of Egypt's largest fundamentalist organizations, the radical Jamaa Islamiya, denounced the attacks on Copts as contrary to Sharia law. The Islamic Brotherhood in 1997 announced itself in favor of segregating the Copts.

In August 1998, Pope Shenouda III, having previously criticized the Egyptian government for the lack of Coptic participation in Egypt's public life and abuses of voting rights, rejected U.S. interference on behalf of Egypt's Copts. The issue, arising from a bill on religious persecution supported by the American Coptic Union, stimulated demands for aid to the persecuted Copts, but the Coptic pope rejected all such aid and declared that there was no religious persecution in Egypt.

The Copts have an economic advantage in that they are disproportionately prosperous city dwellers engaged in commerce and the professions. In spite of their material advancement, however, they to suffer restrictions and persecution. Egyptian universities are reluctant to admit Copts, and the government has refused to allow a Coptic university to be created. They receive a disproportionately low amount of public funding, and there is clear discrimination in hiring, in both the public and private sectors. The Copts are excluded from the judiciary, even in matters of marriage, divorce, and inheritance. They are also subject to religious discrimination, both official and unofficial. The Egyptian government restricts Coptic broadcasting, public speech, holiday celebrations, and a number of Coptic institutions. Copts occupy 1% of judgeships and only 0.04% of ambassadorial positions. In recent decades many Coptic hospitals, schools, and church lands have been confiscated. The government strictly enforces an 1856 law making it illegal to build or repair a church without presidential approval, which is most often withheld.

Between 1990 and 2000, an estimated half-million Copts emigrated to escape the escalating violence and physical threats, against which the government takes no action. The situation of the Copts has worsened considerably since 1989. Most government action to combat the persecution of the Copts is in response to threats to the state and foreign tourists rather than out of any concern for the Copts. Government discrimination includes suspected underrepresentation of the size of the Christian community, discrimination in education, anti-Coptic themes in some Islamic television programs, and job discrimination in the police, armed forces, and other government agencies. As the recipient of the second-largest amount of foreign aid from the United States, however, the Egyptian government is susceptible to pressure exerted to improve the situation of the Coptic community.

In February 2000, fundamentalist violence against Copts in Upper Egypt was the worst in modern Egyptian history. The clashes again raised concern about discrimination against the Coptic minority, but Egyptian government spokesmen dismissed the possibility of discrimination. The Egyptian government was highly sensitive to suggestions of discrimination, particularly on the eve of Pope John Paul II's visit to Egypt in early 2000. During his visit, the Pope met with Orthodox Pope Shenouda III in Cairo.

In recent years activists gained support in a campaign promoting a Coptic identity separate from Arabs. They point to the fact that the Copts have every element of a nation—a separate culture, history, and language. They claim that the Copts share little with the Arab majority and should not be identified with them. A small group, the Coptic Pharaonic Movement, based in Europe, proposes a separate Coptic Pharaonic Republic in Egypt but has attracted little attention. Activists claim that a separate identity would decrease the persecution of the Copts, who are now identified only as Egyptians, making the violence and discrimination internal matters for the Egyptian government, about which governments or organizations outside the country can do little.

Following the terrorist attacks on the United States in September 2001, many Copts reported renewed discrimination, although the Egyptian government carefully supported the attack on the terrorists in Afghanistan. Several of the Islamic groups suspected of being behind the anti-Copt violence in Egypt since the late 1980s were named by the United States as terrorist organizations.

SELECTED BIBLIOGRAPHY:

Bengio, Ofra, and Gabriel Ben-Dor, eds. *Minorities and the State in the Arab World.*
　　1998.
Carter, B. L. *The Copts in Egyptian Politics.* 1986.
Kamil, Jill. *Coptic Egypt: History and Guide.* 1987.
Wakin, Edward. *A Lonely Minority: The Story of Egypt's Copts.* 1963.

Cordillerans

Igorots; Igorottes

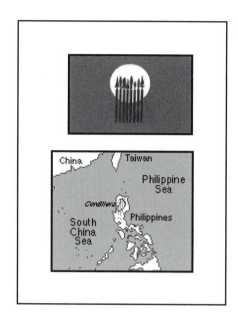

POPULATION: Approximately (2002e) 1,680,000 Cordillerans in the northern Philippines, concentrated in the Cordillera Central region of northern Luzon. Outside the region there are sizable communities in the south, particularly in Manila, and in Hawaii, where they migrated before and after World War II.

THE CORDILLERAN HOMELAND: The Cordilleran homeland lies in the northern Philippine island of Luzon in the Cordillera Central north of the Caraballo Mountains, between the South China Sea to the west and the Pacific Ocean on the east. Much of the region is rugged grassland and pine forests, with tropical forests in the foothills. The ancient rice terraces of the region have been declared monuments. Part of the Cordillera region, the provinces of Benguet, Ifugao, Bontoc (Mountain), Apayao, and Kalinga, has been included in a Cordillera administrative region. *Cordillera Administrative Region (CAR)*: 7,063 sq. mi.—18,293 sq. km, (2002e) 1,411,000—Cordillerans 74%, other Filipinos 26%. The Cordilleran capital and major cultural center is Baguio City, (2002e) 262,000.

FLAG: The Cordilleran national flag, the flag of the national movement, is a red field bearing a centered yellow disk behind eight black spears.

PEOPLE AND CULTURE: There are ten principal Cordilleran cultural groups, with numerous subgroups living in the Cordillera Central of Luzon. The Cordillerans, of Malay* descent, are collectively called Cordillera Peoples, or Igorots. The name Igorot, Tagalog for "mountaineer," was used for any group, often as a pejorative term, but the name is now used with pride as a sign of the Cordillerans' distinct national identity. The Igorots are broadly divided into two groups, the larger comprising the upland wet-rice cultivators—the Ifugaos, Bontocs, southern Kalingas, Kananays, Lepanto or northern Kananays, Ibalois, and Tinggians. The other group comprises the lower rain-forest groups, who grow dry rice in seasonally shifting plots—the Gaddang, northern Kalingas, and Isneg or Apayao. The Igorots are, like the other Filipinos, a blend of ethnic origins, although they did not as a rule have as much contact with the outside world as did the lowlands and although their cultures did not undergo Hispanization. They display great variety in social organization, cultural expression, and artistic skill; their levels of advancement ranged from that of the highly sophisticated Bontocs and Ifugaos, who engineered extraordinary rice terraces, to that of more primitive groups. There are no clans or tribes, and until recently political organization was generally limited to the village level. They also cover a wide spectrum in terms of their integration and assimilation into lowland Christian Filipino culture, but they share common cultural traits, religious beliefs, and languages. In the past, a number of the groups practiced forms of head-hunting, and intertribal wars were common, often resulting from disagreements over territory.

LANGUAGE AND RELIGION: Although the various groups that live in the region have similar cultures, they are divided into seven ethnolinguistic groups, in five provinces, speaking dialects with the common background of a language called Ilocano. The languages are mostly communal in nature; they have remained isolated from modernization and reflect a lifestyle based on survival. The Igorot languages belong to the Cordilleran subgroups of the Philippine language, which belong to the Austronesian (Malayo-Polynesian) language family.

Most of the Igorots are animists, believing in many gods and spirits who control life situations and circumstances. These deities are believed to have human emotions and to require appeasement by sacrifice and worship. They believe that these gods exist in both living and inanimate objects. Shamans, or mediums, utilize elaborate rituals to cure the sick by magic, to communicate with the gods, and to control events. Other groups, such as the Kalingas, believe that the spirits, called *anitos*, may be their deceased ancestors. In Kalinga-Apayao the forebears of the Kalinga and Apayao peoples practiced an unusual funeral ritual, stacking coffins made from tree trunks in the limestone karst cliffs and caves of the region. Christian missionaries have worked in the area for generations, and many Igorots are nominally Christian, but their beliefs coexist with their pre-Christian pagan beliefs.

NATIONAL HISTORY: Over the centuries the isolated highland tribes developed their own national identity. Elaborate rice terraces, sculpted from the steep hillsides, provided space for food production and protection from enemies. Their folk art was, in a sense, the last remnant of an indigenous tradition that flourished throughout the archipelago before Islamic and Spanish contact. Notorious for their wars and head-hunting, they were only partially subdued by the Spanish. In 1598 a Spanish garrison was established in Bangued to protect Ilocanos who had coverted to Christianity from raids by the highlanders. The ancient practice of mummification of the dead ended after the arrival of Christianity in the islands in the sixteenth century. The Cordillerans, isolated from the lowlands, kept the colonial saber and cross at bay for over 300 years of Spanish rule. Not until the mid-nineteenth century did the colonial government establish contact with some of the more remote groups.

The United States, victorious in the Spanish-American War, took control of the Philippines in December 1898. American troops moved into the Cordillera Central and eventually pacified the highland tribes. They stamped out head-hunting and put an end to the incessant warfare. American administrators promoted agricultural schemes and health care for the tribal groups, providing markets for their terraced rice crops and other products.

In the early 1900s, American colonizers introduced corporate mining and issued land titles to various village chiefs. This broke the traditional system of communal ownership of resources, and much of the tribal land was lost. American mining interests, backed by the government, opened mines, confiscated cultivated lands, and polluted rivers.

Over the decades, the Cordillera region remained backward, while a large landed class and multinational businesses took firm control of the region's natural resources at the expense of the often disunited and impoverished tribal communities. Lowlanders moving into the region insisted on individual landholdings and opposed the communal system still existing in some inland areas. In 1937 the foreign mining companies sparked a gold rush that brought thousands into the Cordillera area.

The Philippines were recognized as independent by the United States in 1946. Twenty years later, the Philippine congress passed a "separation bill," which divided the large Mountain Province into four new provinces to increase development in the area. In the 1970s, lowlands Filipinos, mostly Christian, grew in number and expanded into the interior of Luzon, isolating the upland tribal communities in tribal pockets.

Encroachments on their ancient lands by the lowland Filipinos in the latter half of the twentieth century forced the tribal peoples of the Cordillera to mobilize in defense of their communal interests. Chief Macliing Dulag inspired the Kalingas to rise up in the late 1970s to block a hydroelectric project on the Chico River, which would have drowned their villages. The government later abandoned the project, but the peaceful resistance reawakened the warrior spirit of the Igorots; many joined the communist guerrillas operating in the region.

Representatives of the indigenous peoples met in September 1983 to form the Consultative Assembly of Minority Peoples of the Philippines (CAMPP). The assembly served as a regular venue where leaders of indigenous populations met to share and discuss the problems and life struggles of their peoples. The period marked the first formation of local, provincial, and regional organizations of the indigenous upland peoples of the Cordillera. The Cordillera People's Alliance, a federation of indigenous people's organizations, was founded in 1984 as a protest against government development projects in the area.

The grievances of the tribal groups in northern Luzon are of recent origin, having been aroused by ill-considered development and dam-building schemes of the corrupt administration of Ferdinand Marcos. The dams entailed flooding valleys in the northern Cordillera, where the tribal groups lived. A revolutionary priest, Conrad Balueg, began a crusade for the rights of the Cordillera peoples in Abra. After negotiating a peace accord with Balueg's group in 1987, the Philippine government created the Cordillera Administrative Region (CAR) out of the Ilocano regions of Ilocos and Cagayan. This region encompassed the city of Baguio and the provinces of Abra, Benguet, Ifugao, Kalinga-Apayao, and Mountain.

A communist insurgency centered in the Cordillera area became a potent force in the late 1980s under the dictatorial rule of Ferdinand Marcos. By 1992 thousands of government soldiers were in the region fighting the communist insurgents, with devastating effects on the local Igorot peoples.

When Corazon Aquino came to power, she was confronted with a widespread rebellion by the Moros* of the southern Philippines and so mostly ignored the Cordillera. The Cordillera People's Liberation Army (CPLA), allied to the Communist New People's Army (NPA), was formed to lead the fight for indigenous rights after 1986. Aquino finally tackled the problem, supporting the creation of autonomous tribal regions in northern Luzon.

The Philippine congress passed a law creating a Cordillera Autonomous Region, but in a referendum held in the five core provinces—Abra, Benguet, Mountain, Kalinga-Apayao, and Ifugao—on 29 January 1990, the voters rejected it, except in Ifugao. The reasons were thought to be fear of the unknown and campaigning by mining companies that dreaded higher taxes. The act did not address the key tribal issues of ancestral landholdings nor issues of economic and political reforms. In 1991, the Philippine supreme court voided the autonomous region, ruling that the single province, Ifugao, could not constitute an autonomous region.

During most of the 1990s, the government remained generally indifferent to the region's problems, but it pressed development. President José Ramos signed a new mining code in 1995, giving mining companies 100% foreign ownership and giving them the right to displace and resettle people within their concessionary areas.

The government began to respond in early 1996 to growing pressure from tribal and human-rights groups. In October 1997, President Ramos signed the Indigenous Peoples' Rights Act, designed to protect indigenous peoples of the archipelago. The act also awarded ancestral lands on the basis of communal rather than individual ownership, impeding unilateral sale of lands by tribal leaders, and required a process of consultation and written consent to allow mining on tribal lands. The law assigned indigenous groups the responsibility of preserving forest lands, watersheds, and biodiversity areas in their domains. At the same time, new mining legislation and the opening up of tribal areas to international mining interests increased the threat to the indigenous communities.

Support for autonomy grew throughout the 1990s, including a consultation on autonomy that gained widespread support. President Ramos signed the Cordillera Autonomy Act in December 1997, to strengthen protection of the Cordilleran peoples of northern Luzon. However, patronage politics, still prevalent in the region, weaken enforcement of the tribal and forestry laws.

The Banaue rice terraces in Benguet Province, shaped by hand over centuries, are now considered one of the wonders of the world, but their survival depends on the survival of the people who created them. To survive, the terraces must be carefully maintained and their walls shored up against erosion. Uncontrolled mining and logging have caused landslides, burned patches of forest, and bared mountains like wounds on the once-lush countryside. Government officials blame earthquakes and typhoons for the ravages, but the Cordillerans assert that the mining industry and the cash-crop economy share much of the blame. In 1995 the Philippine government created the Ifugao Terraces Commission to try to ensure that development does not destroy the age-old rice terraces.

Many young Cordillerans are moving to the cities or going abroad to escape the chronic violence and the lack of opportunity for tribal peoples. Cordilleran leaders demand more autonomy and financial incentives to keep the young Igorots in the region. Although their region produces much of the Philippines' wealth, most of the region's roads are unpaved, electrical power is sporadic, and educational opportunities are limited. Thousands of Filipino soldiers remain in the area, mostly to protect development projects and control insurgent groups active in the region.

In January 1998, a group of lawyers representing mining interests announced that it would challenge the constitutionality of Republic Act 8438, which created the Cordillera Autonomous Region. A plebiscite was held on the issue in early March 1998; most Cordillerans voted for the autonomous region, but the non-Cordilleran groups outvoted them. A June 1998 survey of Cordilleran leaders revealed that they favored the current structure, the Cordillera Administrative Region.

In May 1999, the Igorots celebrated the recovery of the mummified remains of one of their ancestors—a mighty hunter, half human and half deity. They believe that the theft of the remains of the mummy, called Apo Annu, more than 80 years ago resulted in various kinds of natural calamities. The return of the mummy was celebrated with a three-day wake and ceremonies. Apo Annu was laid to rest in a mountain cave, where it is hoped that his return will end the cycle of earthquakes, disease, and bad harvests. Nationalists see his return as a sign that the time is ripe for the creation of an autonomous Cordilleran state.

In February 2001, President Gloria Arroyo spoke with officials from the Cordillera Administrative Region, and promised to start rebuilding the infrastructure and offered the Cordillera people financial assistance for development projects. The Cordillerans were surprised when they found out that Arroyo spoke fluently Ilocano. This apparently unknown fact may well prove to be an essential tool in improving mutual understanding and strengthening the dialogue between the Philippine government and the Cordillerans.

SELECTED BIBLIOGRAPHY:

Kessler, Richard J. *Rebellion and Repression in the Philippines.* 1989.
Perry, Richard J. *From Time Immemorial: Indigenous Peoples and State Systems.* 1996.
Razon, Felix, and Richard Hensman. *The Oppression of the Indigenous Peoples of the Philippines.* 1976.
Scott, William Henry. *The Discovery of the Igorots.* 1985

Cornish

Kerne; Cornishmen

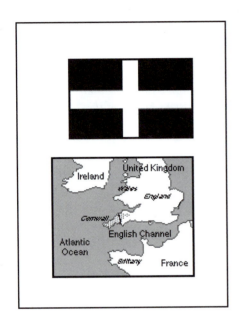

POPULATION: Approximately (2002e) 600,000 Cornish in the United Kingdom, most in the Cornwall region of southwestern England. Large Cornish populations, the product of Cornish emigration, live in the United States, Canada, Australia, South Africa, and New Zealand.

THE CORNISH HOMELAND: The Cornish homeland occupies a peninsula in southwestern England terminating in the rugged promontory of Land's End (Penn an Wlas). The traditional boundary of Cornwall is the Tamar River, 200 miles (321 km) west of London. The peninsula, marked by a rocky, indented coast, is England's most remote county and its only area of subtropical vegetation. Officially, Cornwall includes the Isles of Scilly, 140 small islands in the Atlantic Ocean west of Land's End. Cornwall forms a county of England and a separate hereditary duchy, the title held by the heir to the British throne. *County of Cornwall and Isles of Scilly (Mebyon Kernow):* 1,418 sq. mi.—3,673 sq. km, (2002e) 472,000—Cornish 86%, other English 10%, other British 4%. The Cornish capital and major cultural center is Truro, called Truru in the Cornish language, (2002e) 16,000. Other important cultural centers are the region's largest city, Camborne-Redruth (Kammbronn-Rysrudh), (2002e) 38,000, Penzance (Pennsans), (2002e) 21,000, near Land's End, and the former capital, Bodmin (Bosvenegh), (2002e) 13,000.

FLAG: The Cornish national flag, the flag of the national movement and the unofficial flag of the county, is a black field charged with a centered white cross, the cross of St. Pirin, Cornwall's patron saint.

PEOPLE AND CULTURE: The Cornish are a Celtic people, the descendants of the pre-Roman Celtic population of the British Isles and Western Europe. Although now mainly English-speaking, the Cornish retain their distinct character and remain separate from the English majority. The Cornish culture, which has survived in the isolation of their peninsula, is closely tied to the traditional Cornish occupation, tin mining. The working of the mines in the region goes back for over 35 centuries, but the mines were closed in the twentieth century, opening a debate on the Cornish nation and its future.

LANGUAGE AND RELIGION: The Cornish language, which died out in 1777, when the last native speaker died, has since the 1960s been revived as the national language. The language, Kernewek, belongs to the Brythonic branch of the Celtic languages and is closely related to the language of the Bretons* of Brittany, across the English Channel in northwestern France. The resurrection of Kernewek was so successful that in the late 1980s it became the fastest growing of all the Celtic languages. Church services are still held in Cornish, and there are evening classes, correspondence courses, children's play groups, and summer camps devoted to the language. It is now being taught in many schools, overseen by the Cornish Language Board. The English spoken in Cornwall is often considered a separate dialect, with a characteristic sing-song lilt and many Celtic borrowings. By 1990 Cornish was no longer in danger of extinction.

The majority of the Cornish belong to the Protestant Methodist faith, which has become closely identified with the Cornish culture. Although religious observances fell off during the mid-twentieth century, the revival of the Cornish culture has helped to revitalize the Methodist Church.

NATIONAL HISTORY: The Brythonic Celts migrated to the island of Britain from the European mainland in the first century B.C., later than the Celtic migrations to Ireland, Scotland, and the Isle of Man. The earlier Celtic migrants spoke Goidelic Celtic, while the later migrants, the ancestors of the Cornish, Welsh,* and Bretons spoke Brythonic Celtic, a linguistic division that has persisted to the present.

Romans conquered Britain in the first century A.D., and the Celts of Britannia assimilated into Roman life, becoming an urban, sophisticated population comfortable within the multi-ethnic Roman Empire. The decaying empire gradually abandoned Britannia in the fifth century. The withdrawal of the Roman garrison led to local squabbles, which further weakened the island's defenses. Germanic peoples from the mainland of northern Europe invaded, and many of the Romanized Celts fled west, leaving the eastern districts to the newcomers—the Angles, Saxons, and Jutes, the ancestors of the English population.

Celtic refugees settled the western peninsulas, present Cornwall and Wales, and even crossed the narrow channel to settle the peninsula later called Little Britannia, or Brittany. The southern peninsula in Britain, called Corn, the old Celtic word for "horn," referred to the horn shape of the peninsula; the name came to signify the Celts on the horn, or Cornwall.

In the eighth century Celtic Dumonia, later called Devon, fell to the Anglo-Saxons, leaving the peninsula isolated beyond the Tamar River.

Early medieval Cornwall became closely associated with the Arthurian legend, the mass of popular medieval lore that originated with the tales of a Celtic warrior who fought twelve victorious battles against the Saxon invaders.

The peninsula's many tin mines, known to the ancient Greeks and Phoenicians, sustained Cornish independence until their conquest by the Saxon king Athelstan in 936. Cornwall was the last part of England to submit to the Anglo-Saxons. Following the invasion of England by the Normans* in 1066, the Celts of Cornwall vigorously resisted Norman influence of their peninsula. In recognition of its separate character and history, Cornwall later became a separate duchy in 1337, an appanage of the royal heir in England.

The region's long isolation aided the survival of the distinct Celtic language and culture. For centuries the Cornish fiercely resisted assimilation, although English replaced Cornish as the language of daily life in the seventeenth century. Traditionally the Cornish were fervently Roman Catholic, and they were slow to accept the Protestant Reformation. In the sixteenth century, over 10,000 Cornish took up arms to protect their Roman Catholic religion against the advance of Protestantism, but two centuries later they finally abandoned Catholicism to embrace the teachings of the Wesleyan dissent. The Cornish converted en masse to the new Methodist sect and became extremely devout. Methodism became closely identified with the unique Cornish culture.

In the seventeenth and eighteenth centuries, the Cornish were scorned as backward peasants and punished for speaking their Celtic language. They struck back the only way they could—they turned to the ancient Cornish traditions of piracy and smuggling. Cornish "wreckers" lured English ships onto the rocky coast, then legally salvaged the cargoes. The practice became so widespread that the Cornish coast came to be called the "graveyard of ships."

Tin mining, closely tied to Cornish culture and the mainstay of the local economy, collapsed in 1866. Over 7,000 destitute Cornish families emigrated, mostly to the English-speaking countries—Canada, the United States, Australia, New Zealand, the Caribbean, and South Africa. Between 1860 and 1900 an estimated 13% of the Cornish population emigrated, mostly to countries in other parts of the world but also to other parts of England.

The unprofitable mines continued as the only important source of income until the worldwide depression of the 1930s ended all mining activity in Cornwall, which increased unemployment and hardship. A renewed demand for tin during World War II allowed the reopening of many of the mines, bringing a modest economic upturn that continued as Britain's access to colonial resources disappeared after the war. In the 1960s tourism replaced mining as Cornwall's economic mainstay. The visitors, drawn to

Cornwall's subtropical climate and unique culture, are called *emmets* by the locals, a Cornish word for the insects they resemble as they swarm across the Cornish Peninsula.

The Cornish, even before the reculturation that began after World War II, maintained that the land beyond the Tamar River was a separate country, Celtic Cornwall. Tourists at the border were given instructions telling them that they were entering a foreign country. Much of that Celtic attitude toward England remains; trips eastward across the Tamar are referred to as "going up to England."

Modern Cornish nationalism, spurred by increased inter-Celtic contract since the early 1960s, focused primarily on the Cornish language. A renewed interest in their language, beginning in the 1920s, prompted a parallel revitalization of the Cornish culture. The successful revival of Kernewek and the flourishing of the traditional Cornish culture fueled the growth of Cornish nationalism in the 1960s and 1970s. Nationalists demanded the same status within the United Kingdom accorded the other Celtic nations, Wales and Scotland.

The entry of the United Kingdom into the European Economic Community in 1973 opened a nationalist debate on Cornwall's future. Cornish nationalists claim that since 1979 too much power has been transferred from local centers to unelected *quangos*, quasi-autonomous organizations, or has been centralized in London. Decisions concerning Cornwall are increasingly made in London or Brussels, with little consultation with local Celtic leaders. Nationalists continue to demand the creation of a Cornish assembly to promote the best interests of Cornwall and to insist the teaching of Cornish in all country schools.

In early 1990, Cornish nationalists sold shares in tin mines to thousands of Cornish, which they claimed exempts them from paying English taxes, based on a charter granted the Cornish tin miners by Henry VII in 1508. The charter, ratified in 1511, exempted all tin miners and therefore shareholders in the mines from all English laws not ratified by the Stannary Court—an ancient tin miners' court that continues to function, now often as a forum for nationalist views. The original Latin copy of the charter was discovered in 1980.

The last active tin mine in Cornwall closed in March 1998, leaving the region increasingly restive. With the closing of the last five mines, unemployment in the region went up to 35% in some areas. With the end of tin mining, the Cornish feel that they are losing a basic part of their culture and identity. Economic hardships have reinforced local pride in being Cornish, but many are not overly proud of being British. Cornish miners are again looking for overseas mining jobs as their forebears had done in the past.

The Cornish consider the closing of the last mine not only an economic but also a cultural disaster. Economic and cultural grievances have added to the rising Cornish nationalism, the more militant asserting that the European Union (EU) begins at the Tamar River until the Cornish are recognized as a separate European people with their own state, under their black and white St. Pirin flag. Groups such as Cornish Solidarity work for the equality of the Cornish nation and the creation of a separate Cornish state within a federal United Kingdom.

In November 1998 the last tin mine to close was purchased by an investment company. In March 1999 the mine was reopened, with 250 workers. Nonetheless, mining, although an integral part of Cornish history, is now nearly extinct and has lost its importance to the Cornish culture.

Emigration remains the traditional answer to high unemployment and economic hardship, but the region's population has continued to grow due to the number of "foreigners" from other parts of the United Kingdom settling in the region. The population grew by about 10% between 1990 and 2000, even though the native Cornish population declined.

Cornwall is England's poorest county and has one of its highest rates of unemployment. Average weekly earnings in Cornwall are 23% below the national average. In 1999 Cornwall was officially awarded "Objective One" status, identifying it as one of the EU's poorest nations. The "Objective One" program will bring grants of EU funds, raising Cornish hopes that their economic plight might finally be alleviated.

The Cornish often cite Wales and Scotland, with greater autonomy and regional government, as examples of how Cornwall could prosper if given the same self-government. Although demands for a regional parliament, greater financial autonomy, and protection for the traditional Cornish culture and language have won support in the British government, Cornish calls for the same autonomy allowed neighboring Wales have mostly been ignored.

Cornwall's dual identity as a county and as a separate duchy became a focus for nationalists in 2001. The recovery of double tax charges on tin production in Cornwall imposed by the Duchy of Cornwall over centuries, amounting to £20 billion at 2002 values, was demanded with threats of law suits and a petition to the European Court of Justice.

The majority of the Cornish support demands for greater self-government. They claim that Cornwall belongs to the Cornish and has been so for the past three thousand years. Cornwall does not belong to the Southwest of England Regional Development Agency, the Government Office for the Southwest, English Heritage or English Nature. Activists want to restore Cornwall's own constitution based on the 1508 Royal Stannary Charter, which has never been abrogated. Expanding interest in the Cornish language mirrors growing support for devolution. There is a campaign to win support for Cornish to be included in the European charter of minority languages.

In May 2001 the government announced the opening, in 2003, of Cornwall's first university. At present, about 90% of young Cornish who leave for higher education do not return. In mid-November 2001 Cornish nationalist leaders stated a university is essential to the survival of the Cornish nation. They added that they viewed Cornwall as being in a similar position to Wales and Scotland and that they did not consider their homeland as part of England.

SELECTED BIBLIOGRAPHY:

Filbee, Majorie. *Celtic Cornwall.* 1996.
Guthrie, A. *Cornwall in the Age of Steam.* 1995.
Henwood, George. *Cornwall's Mines and Miners.* 1981.
Strong, Richard. *Cornwall.* 1998.

Corsicans

Corsu; Corce; Corse; Corsos; Corsi

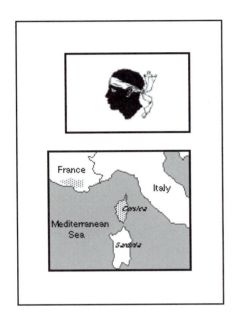

POPULATION: Approximately (2002e) 390,000 Corsicans in France, most living on the island of Corsica in the Mediterranean and the southern regions of mainland France. Smaller communities live in Paris and in Italy. Outside Europe, about 65,000 Corsicans live in the Americas.

THE CORSICAN HOMELAND: The Corsican homeland lies in the Mediterranean Sea 105 miles (170 km) southeast of mainland France, between the Italian mainland on the north and the Italian island of Sardinia on the south. It is the fourth-largest island in the Mediterranean and much of it is wild, mostly covered in thick undergrowth called *maquis* in French. The flowers of the *maquis* produce a fragrance that is carried far out to sea, giving the island the name "the scented isle." The island, called Corse in French, forms a region (*collectivité territoriale*) of France, divided into two departments. *Region of Corsica (Corsu)*: 3,352 sq. mi.—8,772 sq. km, (2002e) 261,000—Corsicans 55%, French 30%, North Africans 8%, Italians 5%. The Corsican capital and major cultural center is Corte, Corti in the Corsican language, (2002e) 15,000. The island's major cities are Ajaccio, Aiacciu in the Corsican language, (2002e) 48,000, and Bastia, (2002e) 41,000.

FLAG: The Corsican national flag, the flag of the national movement, is a white field bearing a centered black Moor's head in profile.

PEOPLE AND CULTURE: The Corsicans are an Italo-Romance people, their Latin heritage modified by the influences brought to the island by its many conquerors. Related to the mainland Italians and to the Sards* of Sardinia, the Corsicans have developed a unique Mediterranean culture. The islanders are known for vendettas, bitter prolonged feuds, that until recent decades were passed down from one generation to the next. The *maquis* provided a perfect hideout for bandits, members of an occupation that was traditional until suppressed by the French government. The clan system, formerly the basis of Corsican society, has also declined under French rule. Modern cultural life on the island has suffered from the emigration of the most gifted Corsicans to the French mainland, even though the Corsican diaspora retains the culture and preserves close ties to the island.

LANGUAGE AND RELIGION: The Corsicans speak a dialect of Italian, a Genoese dialect of the Tuscan group with a strong admixture of non-Italian borrowing, particularly French. The Corsican nationalists claim the language is a separate Romance language spoken in four dialects—Sartenais, Vico-Ajaccio, Northern Corsican, and Venaco. The literary language is based on the prestigious Vico-Ajaccio dialect. The language has been recognized as a separate language by the French government, but use of the dialect is still limited by France's traditional antipathy to non-French cultures and languages. The Corsicans are bilingual in French, but many are fluent only in Corsican. There is a movement for complete bilingual education on the island, but this is opposed by the French authorities. In spite of more teaching, television, and radio in the language, only about 60% of Corsicans can now speak the language correctly, against 80% in 1977.

Corsicans remain conservative and devoutly Roman Catholic, although the number of practicing Catholics has declined in recent decades. Their faith, which has sustained them through centuries of rule by outsiders, is an integral part of their unique Mediterranean culture.

NATIONAL HISTORY: The island was originally settled by Etruscans, the mysterious pre-Roman people of northern Italy, but it has a long history of domination by various Mediterranean empires. The ancient Phoenicians from present-day Lebanon held the island, followed by their successors the Carthaginians, from North Africa. In a series of campaigns from 259 to 163 B.C., the Romans conquered the island. Together with neighboring Sardinia, Corsica formed a province of the Roman Empire. Under Roman rule the economy flourished, and the Latinized population was prosperous and cultured.

The collapse of Roman power in the fifth century left the island virtually defenseless. Germanic Vandals, crossing from the mainland, destroyed the cities and drove the inhabitants inland, leaving the fertile coastal plains deserted. The island briefly returned to nominally Roman (actually Byzantine) rule in A.D. 534, but the eastern empire was unable to hold Corsica against successive invasions of Germanic tribes from the mainland. The island fell to the invading Goths, was taken by the Lombards* in 725 and eventually came under the control of the Germanic Franks.

Under constant threat by the Muslim Saracens from North Africa from the eighth to the twelfth centuries, Corsica was ceded by the Franks to the Holy See. Pope Gregory VII in 1047 gave the island to the maritime republic of Pisa. The Pisans began to develop the island and built hundreds of churches, but after a long and bloody struggle the island was taken by Pisa's rival in the Mediterranean, Genoa. The Ligurians* of Genoa expelled the last of the Pisan troops in 1347. A later struggle for control of the island pitted the Genoese against the Aragonese* kingdom. The bitter struggle between the Genoese and Corsica's feudal aristocracy further decimated the population of the island.

Genoese rule proved extremely harsh and unpopular. In the fifteenth century, the actual administration of the island was taken over by the Genoese Bank of San Gregorio. In the fifteenth and sixteenth centuries the French briefly controlled the island, bringing more a modern administration before returning the island to Genoese rule. Corsican nationalism originated during the four centuries of Genoese rule, particularly from the time of a nationalist rebellion led by Sampiero Corso that ended with renewed Genoese rule in 1567.

In 1729 the unhappy Corsicans launched a decades-long rebellion in response to a tax increase imposed by the Genoese authorities. Pasquale Paoli, whose military successes achieved virtual independence and the establishment of a Corsican republic, led the revolt after 1755. Paoli created a national government and opened a university to train the administrators needed by the new state. The military situation became a stalemate, with the Genoese confined to a few coastal towns, and the Corsicans holding the interior and many port towns. During the 14 years of his rule, Paoli led a Corsican revival, repressing the vendetta, establishing a Corsican printing press, and creating a Corsican navy. Unable to defeat the Corsican rebels, the Genoese finally sold their rights to France in 1768, just in time for Corsica's most famous son, Napoleon Buonaparte (later Bonaparte), to be born a French citizen at Ajaccio in 1769.

French troops invaded the island in overwhelming numbers and suppressed the Corsican resistance. The French colonial administration dissolved all Corsican institutions, and in 1770 forcibly closed the Corsican university, which is still today a nationalist issue. Sporadic revolts against French rule continued up to the French Revolution. The Corsicans again rebelled against the French authorities after the 1789 revolution and in 1793 drove the last French officials from the island. The rebel leaders requested British assistance and in 1794 organized a plebiscite that confirmed Corsican appeals for union with Great Britain. Reconquered by Napoleon's troops in 1796, the island fell to the British in 1814 during the Napoleonic Wars. Despite Corsican protests the 1815 Congress of Vienna returned the island to France.

Banditry, blood feuds, and attacks on French authorities continued to disrupt the island's administration, the *maquis* providing refuge for bandits and dissidents as it had for centuries. Clan rule, the major loyalty of the islanders, declined slowly under French administration, while a strong Bonapartist tradition and anti-Genoese sentiment helped to assure Corsican loyalty to France during most of the nineteenth century.

French rule brought the island education, in French, and relative order, but the economy was left mainly agricultural. The French language became predominant in the cities, but efforts to assimilate the Corsicans mostly failed. Neglected and underdeveloped, the island's inhabitants found it necessary to leave for the French mainland to find work. Resentment of this forced emigration coalesced national sentiment on the island in the 1920s. The first autonomist organization formed in 1927. Banditry was not fully eradicated until the 1930s.

Fascist Italian troops occupied the island after the fall of France in 1940 and initiated a program to Italianize the islanders. A Corsican uprising in 1943, aided by Free French forces, finally drove the Italians from the island. The triumphant Corsicans, preparing for independence, were gravely disappointed by the reimposition of French rule in 1945. The Corsican nationalists lost heart, and the nationalist movement became dormant. Despair spurred a massive postwar exodus to the mainland, finally forcing the French authorities to accelerate the island's development, mainly in tourism. Development of the island's tourist facilities continued intermittently under several French administrations.

The modern Corsican national movement stems from a failed insurrection in 1958, during the French colonial war in Algeria. The uprising was partly the result of the French policy of settling evacuated colonists and loyal Algerians on the island, some 17,000 between 1958 and 1963. The insurrection failed, but it sparked the rebirth of Corsican national sentiment that transcended class and regional differences. Numerous nationalist groups formed over the next two decades. Several nationalist groups turned to violence and terrorism, mostly directed at tourist installations owned by foreigners, including the French. In 1975, the Libyan government began monetary and training support for the largest of the nationalist organizations, the Corsican National Liberation Front (FLNC).

Socialists won the 1980 French general elections, and the Corsicans looked forward to the decentralization promised during the election campaign. Terrorism waned, and Corsican leaders entered into negotiations with the new socialist French government, demanding education in the Corsican language, the reopening of the Corsican university, closed since 1770, and the teaching of specifically Corsican history. In 1982 the French government passed a statute giving the island greater powers than the mainland regions but far fewer rights than demanded by the nationalists. Corsica became the first French region to elect its own government under the socialist decentralization scheme. Unsatisfied with the limited autonomy offered by the French government, the FLNC and other groups resumed their militant activities.

Terrorist incidents grew from 111 in 1974 to 238 in 1976, and a record

805 in 1982. The majority of the incidents involved the destruction of tourist homes or complexes owned by non-Corsicans. In January 1983 the government began a crackdown on nationalist activities and banned several organizations. The French government responded to continuing incidents and mass demonstrations by replacing Corsican police and officials with mainland French. In March 1986 the Corsican nationalists took their campaign to the mainland, perpetrating a series of bomb attacks across southern France.

Corsica remains virtually without industrial development, and unemployment would be much higher except for continuing emigration to the mainland. A lack of transportation and airports are among the main Corsican grievances. Since 1988 the majority of the Corsicans have supported more moderate nationalist political parties, with a concomitant loss of support for the violent separatist organizations. Several nationalist splinter groups have continued to attack holiday homes and businesses owned by non-Corsicans.

In 1991 French senators rejected key portions of a bill that would have recognized the Corsicans as a separate nation, voting instead to continue administering Corsica as part of metropolitan France. Despite opposition in the French General Assembly, a new statute was finally passed recognizing the Corsicans as a distinct people, only to be overturned by the Constitutional Court. Corsican frustration grew rapidly as the French government seemed unable or unwilling to meet even minimum demands. A 1991 poll of the islanders resulted in overwhelming support for some form of autonomy, with one third favoring immediate independence from France. In a move to appease separatists, the French government in 1994 began allowing students in schools and universities to study the Corsican language for three hours a week.

A poll taken in the spring of 1996 revealed that only 10% of the inhabitants of Corsica favored immediate independence. The majority favored various degrees of political, cultural, and economic autonomy. The poll did not allow for what the nationalists claim was the majority view, a gradual process leading to independence within the European federation.

A faction of the FLNC, the FLNC-Historical Wing, announced a planned cease-fire in advance of negotiations with the French government in 1996. In exchange, it demanded recognition of the Corsican nation, the use of Corsican as an official language, increased local-government control, and the establishment of a Corsican education system. The government rejected the offer.

A nationalist group claimed responsibility for a bomb that damaged the Bordeaux city hall in late 1996, raising fears that the Corsican conflict was moving to the French mainland. Other bomb attacks on mainland cities opened a new phase in the nationalist campaign. The FLNC showed its strength by bombing the tax office in Paris despite heightened security surrounding an official visit of the president of Iran in October 1999.

Feuds between the various nationalist factions, particularly between the FLNC and the Movement for Self-Determination (MPA) added a new and increasingly violent element to the conflict. A report released by the French government in September 1998 stated that the island was run by Mafia-like gangs who intimidated the authorities, carried out vendetta killings, and were involved in shady financial dealings. The report also denounced decades of French government attempts to buy off nationalists with public works and financial aid, most of which never reached its planned destination. The murder rate is three times that of the French mainland, and the number of violent crimes continues to climb. The French government has provided ample funds for public services and infrastructure but has failed to close the wide economic gap between the island and the mainland. In May 1999, several French police were arrested for setting off bombs and trying to blame nationalists.

The major Corsican nationalist groups signed a cease-fire with the French government in December 1999. The cease-fire held well into the new year, partly due to talks with the government. In April 2000, thirty Corsican leaders met in Paris with government officials for talks about a proposed new autonomy statute. The island's legislature had already passed the bill in March, with the majority of the island population favoring autonomy. The large Corsican population living in mainland France mostly preserved their national identity and returned to vote in regional elections, giving the nationalists, both moderates and militants, greater support than the demographics of the island would suggest.

The Corsican national movement suffers from factionalism and rivalries. The small number of innocent casualties limited damage to native Corsicans has allowed it to thrive without a significant counter-movement. Relatively few Corsicans protest to stop the separatist violence, and there is little impetus for the groups involved to change their tactics or to negotiate. On the government side, the island is seen as a haven of criminal gangs, which reinforces the policy of negotiations without comprise.

The French government took the first step in May 2001 toward granting partial autonomy to Corsica when the national assembly began debating a revolutionary package of laws aimed at ending more than 25 years of separatist violence on the island. Any changes to Corsica's status would be the first since 1769. The bill would temporarily transfer the administration of areas such as culture, regional development, education, agriculture, and infrastructure to the Corsican assembly, which after presidential and parliamentary elections in 2002 would have the power to modify certain laws passed in Paris. Nationalists continue to demand that their language be included in the bill and be offered on the curriculum in primary and middle schools. Some groups are threatening to abandon the peace plan unless all "political prisoners" are released.

The peace plan for Corsica, adopted in 2000, though welcomed by most Corsican nationalist groups, has not brought peace. Murders, extortion, and other crimes continue to take place in the murky world shared by both separatists and gangsters. The Corsicans want peace, but also the right to live as Corsicans.

SELECTED BIBLIOGRAPHY:

Carrington, Dorothy. *The Dream-Hunters of Corsica*. 1996.
Taylor, Theo. *Corsica*. 1994.
Thrasher, Peter A. *Pasquale Paoli: An Enlightened Hero*, 1725–1807. 1970
Wilson, Stephen. *Feuding, Conflict and Banditry in 19th Century Corsica*. 1988.

Cree

Eythinyuwuk; Eeyou; Eenou; Iynu

POPULATION: Approximately (2002e) 148,000 Cree in North America, concentrated in eastern and central Canada. Outside Canada the largest community, numbering about 9,000, is in the United States.

THE CREE HOMELAND: The Cree Homeland, called Eeyou Istchee or Eenou Astchee, meaning "our land" or "people's land," comprises a number of separate regions from Quebec in eastern Canada to Alberta in the west. Much of the area lies in the subarctic region, in the forest belt and north of the tree line. A royal proclamation of 1763 confirmed common title to the Cree lands, but that right has been challenged many times. The capital and major cultural center of the Woodland Cree is the town of Baie-du-Poste, Quebec, called Mistissini in the Cree language, (2002e) 2,000. The other important cultural center is Moosonee, Ontario, (2002e) 1,000. Other important centers are the cities of Saskatoon, Saskatchewan and Winnipeg, Manitoba.

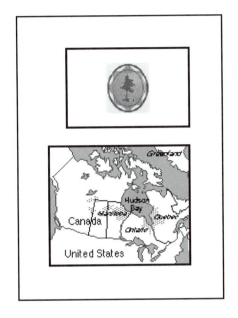

FLAG: The Cree national flag is a white field bearing a centered oval with a tan center representing a skin charged with a single green tree.

PEOPLE AND CULTURE: The Cree are a Native American people living in east-central Canada. Cree is a contraction of Cristino, or Kenisteno, the name given them by the neighboring Ojibwas. The Cree are the largest and most important native group in Canada and one of the largest north of Mexico. The Cree assumed the living patterns of those with whom they came in contact; there developed two major groups—the Woodland Cree, also called the Swampy Cree or Maskegon, and the Plains Cree. The Woodland Cree culture was essentially an eastern woodlands type, although the cool environment precluded corn cultivation and forced reliance on hunting and trapping. The Plains Cree, moving onto the Great Plains, became bison hunters. The Woodland Cree and Plains Cree are each subdivided by bands that are differentiated by slight peculiarities in dialect and tradition. Traditionally, social organization was based on bands of related families, though large groups pulled together to face threats. Old beliefs, hunting customs, and kinship relations persisted throughout the fur-trading years but began to fade in the second half of the twentieth century.

LANGUAGE AND RELIGION: The Cree language belongs to the Algonquian language group spoken in eastern Canada and the United States. The language is spoken in three major dialects that correspond to the geographical distribution of the Cree nation—Central Cree, also called York Cree, with two major dialects, Moose Cree, spoken in the southern tip of James Bay, and Swampy Cree, in northern Ontario across to northern Manitoba; Coastal or Eastern Coastal Cree, spoken in Quebec on the eastern coast of James Bay, and Inland Eastern Cree, a dialect of Eastern Coastal Cree, spoken from southern James Bay to Lake Mistassini in Quebec; and Western Cree, spoken in northern Manitoba across Saskatchewan into Alberta, divided into three major dialects—Woods Cree, Plains Cree, and Western Swampy Cree. In October 2001 a two-volume dictionary of the Cree language was published, a labor of 15 years.

French Jesuit priests converted many of the eastern bands to Catholicism, and the majority are now devout Roman Catholics. A minority were converted by Protestant missionaries who arrived in the area in 1820. Their principal myths centered on a supernatural hero called Wisukatcak. They also believed in conjuration and witchcraft, and they had an influential priestly order. Their greatest religious ceremony was the annual sun dance ceremony.

NATIONAL HISTORY: The Cree are believed to have inhabited the subarctic region south of Hudson Bay since the glaciers receded about 5,000 years ago. French Jesuit missionaries first encountered the Cree about 1650 east of James Bay. The Cree maintained friendly ties to both the English and the French. Traders, attracted to the potential wealth represented by fur-bearing animals in the region, began to expand into the Cree regions. Obtaining firearms from European trading posts established in their territory in the 1670s, they began to push out into the open plains to the west, driving other tribes before them. They eventually reached the Mackenzie River and the Rocky Mountains, but an epidemic of smallpox brought by the Europeans greatly reduced their numbers in 1781. Wars with the Sioux* and Blackfoot and severe smallpox epidemics in 1784 and 1838 further decimated the scattered Cree nation.

The Plains Cree, after acquiring horses and firearms, became more warlike than the Woodland Cree. Raiding and warring against many other tribes, the Plains Cree developed a warrior society. Divided into twelve bands, each with its own chief, the Plains Cree had an integrated military society that united the bands.

The first permanent mission among the Plains Cree was established at

St. Boniface, opposite present-day Winnipeg, in 1818. One of the later missionaries, Father Albert Lacombe, produced a monumental Cree grammar and dictionary, and translated religious tracts into the Cree language. A Protestant missionary, Reverend James Evan, invented a Cree syllabary in the mid-nineteenth century.

Until the Cree were confined to reservations, their various bands held most of the extensive territory about Lakes Winnipeg and Manitoba, the lower Red and Saskatchewan Rivers, and eastward to the Maskegon country around Hudson Bay. The Cree lands were included in the vast territories claimed by the Hudson Bay Company. In 1870 the Canadian government purchased the Hudson Bay Company's rights. Canadian government presence was slow to be felt, but as grievances went unanswered the Canadian authorities were increasingly resented. The Plains Cree, led by Chief Poundmaker, took part in the Riel Rebellion in 1885, an uprising of Indians and Métis* against the Canadian government.

In the late nineteenth century, most Cree lands were brought under provincial governments. In 1898 and 1912, the boundaries of Quebec were extended northward to include the formerly separate Ungava region, which included part of the historical Cree homeland. The Canadian and provincial governments neglected to obtain the consent of the aboriginal peoples to these transfers. In the 1920s, provincial governments began to intervene in the Cree regions, particularly in response to a crisis created by overtrapping by nonindigenous trappers.

During the 1960s, although some schooling had been provided earlier, a significant portion of Cree children began to attend school. The trauma of schooling away from the Cree reserves, in programs not significantly adapted to Cree culture, created a sense of dislocation. The longer Cree children remained in school, the harder it was for parents and children to understand each other.

In 1975 the Cree signed the James Bay and Northern Quebec agreement. The agreement was Canada's first modern treaty with indigenous nations. The agreement provided for construction of water systems and sanitary facilities, but they have not been provided. The Quebec government, despite repeated appeals, refused to provide the agreed-upon facilities, even though ample funds were available from the sale of electricity from dams on rivers in Cree territory. Only after the Cree presented their case to the United Nations in 1981 did the Canadian government begin to provide clean water supplies.

Representatives of the Grand Council of the Cree presented their case for rights to the territory and natural resources of their traditional homeland to the Commission on Human Rights in Geneva in 1985. Their traditional way of life—hunting, fishing, and trapping—was greatly disrupted in Quebec by the construction in the late 1970s near James Bay of a major hydroelectric project that had the potential to flood a large part of their land. Work on the huge project was begun without consultation or discussion with, or approval by, the Cree. When the Cree raised objections, they were told by both the Quebec and Canadian governments that they were considered "squatters" and had no title to the land—which had never been ceded, surrendered, or conquered. Overcoming great difficulties, the Cree brought the matter before the judicial system and, as construction on the project continued, argued that they had never surrendered their land. They won in one court, only to be overruled by a higher court.

Because of legal appeals, the Canadian and Québecois* governments agreed to negotiate Cree land claims in the region with the Grand Council. However, during the negotiations construction on the hydroelectric project proceeded, transforming the area and forcing many Cree to find new livelihoods. The Cree realized that even the most favorable legal decisions would never bring back the land and animals destroyed by the project; therefore, they attempted to minimize the damage to their nation and way of life. The federal and provincial governments were unwilling to share even a small part of the great wealth from the sale of electricity produced by the system of dams. Eventually the Cree won limited rights to continue traditional hunting and trapping activities, but some of the rivers they had fished were now dry, while newly created lakes were contaminated with mercury and had become sterile.

The Meech Lake Accord, a package of amendments to the Canadian constitution aimed at settling the controversy over Quebec's status, included an agreement that aboriginal peoples would be included in all future constitutional negotiations. Ratification of the accord was blocked in Manitoba by a filibuster by a Cree legislator, because it failed to recognize Canada's native peoples as a distinct society; the legislator took advantage of a provincial rule that require public hearings before the ratification of a constitutional amendment. The accord collapsed in 1990.

Faced with the inevitability of change in their homeland, the Cree attempted in the negotiations to establish the basis for a Cree nation that would offer a viable alternative that incorporates their traditional way of life and participation in the new wage-earning economy that was being imposed from outside. They continued to fight for environmental protection and guaranteed hunting and fishing rights. They also demanded Cree-controlled education facilities and modern Cree-administered health services.

Chief Ted Moses, of the James Bay Cree, told a UN commission in 1991 that if Quebec seceded from Canada, the Cree would in turn declare their homeland in Quebec an independent nation. The objections of the Cree went largely unmentioned in the furor that surrounded the secession vote in Quebec in 1995. They voted by more than 95% to stick with Canada, partly because Quebec separation would divide the Cree nation between two sovereign states. The Quebec government declared that it would not respect the outcome of any native-run referendum that gave indigenous communities a mandate to secede from an independent Quebec. A plan by the Quebec government to increase the Québecois population in the James Bay region was denounced by Cree leaders as "ethnic occupation." The James Bay region, the major focus of Cree activism, is now officially called the Radisonnerie region by the Quebec government.

In Alberta, in western Canada, questions of jurisdiction and native land claims focused on the Lubicon Cree, south of Lesser Slave Lake. The Lubicon Cree resisted a proposal to import toxic waste from across North America. The small Lubicon band had been fighting for land rights for well over half a century. Contested jurisdiction over natural resources, including natural gas, oil, and minerals, has pitted the Cree against provincial and federal agencies and multinational mining and petroleum companies.

In 1998, the Quebec government invited the Cree and other indigenous groups to define a structure of self-government, to include sending representatives to the provincial legislature. The new strategy aimed to ease the mistrust between the native peoples and the Québecois. The framework of negotiations included taxation powers as well as the possibility of sharing revenues from new projects, such as hydroelectricity, mining, and forestry, in traditional territories. Cree leaders welcomed the move but warned that the process of negotiation would be long. They also objected to the many references in official documents to the territorial integrity of Quebec. A group of Cree filed suit in the Canadian Supreme Court in February 1998 asking for the right to remain part of Canada in the event of secession by Quebec.

The Cree claim that Canada, with its well-respected democratic institutions, does not protect indigenous rights or recognize formal land claims settlements negotiated in the 1970s and 1980s. The Cree were the first Canadian indigenous group to sign a land claims settlement and are now the only indigenous group to have self-government legislation, but the agreements have never been fully implemented. Throughout the long years of negotiations, the Cree have never relinquished their claim to jurisdiction over their traditional territories.

Each summer the Cree hold a general assembly, which all Cree are eligible to attend. These meetings are based on the tradition that different Cree bands have traditionally gathered at an appointed place to share food, information on hunting, and generally celebrate the abundance of the season. The modern meetings, held in a different community each year, are now devoted to reports on the events of the past year, the progress of land claims, and the movement for Cree autonomy.

After years of tense relations, the Quebec government and the Crees of northern Quebec signed an agreement in October 2001 that will ensure native communities jobs, development funds, and control over natural resources for a period of 50 years. The agreement is approved by most Cree organizations being the first seen by the Cree as negotiated nation to nation.

SELECTED BIBLIOGRAPHY:

Grand Council of the Crees. *Never without Consent: James Bay Crees' Stand against Forcible Inclusion into an Independent Quebec.* 1997.
Richardson, Boyce. *People of Terra Nullius.* 1993.
———. *Strangers Devour the Land.* 1991.
Salishbury, Richard F. *A Homeland for the Cree.* 1986.

Crimean Tatars

Krym-Tatars; Krym-Turks; Crim Tatar; Krymskije; Attars; Kirim; Tatarlarnin Evi

POPULATION: Approximately (2002e) 550,000 Crimean Tatars in the countries of the former Soviet Union. The largest population lives in Crimea, in the southern Ukraine, with large populations still living in exile in Central Asia, particularly Kazakhstan and Uzbekistan. There are smaller Crimean Tatar populations in Russia, Romania, Bulgaria, Poland, Finland, and the United States. Nationalists claim that over five million people of Crimean Tatar descent live in Turkey.

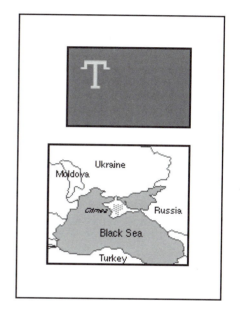

THE CRIMEAN TATAR HOMELAND: The Crimean Tatar homeland lies in southern Ukraine, a large peninsula in the Black Sea connected to the mainland by the Isthmus of Perekop, five miles (8 km) wide. The fertile peninsula, with its pleasant climate, was a favorite resort of tsarist aristocracy and afterward Soviet hierarchy. Officially the Crimean Peninsula forms an autonomous republic in Ukraine, but the region's future is disputed by the Ukrainian government, the peninsula's Russian majority, and the indigenous population, the Crimean Tatars. *Republic of Crimea (Kïrïm)*: 10,425 sq. mi.—27,001 sq. km, (2002e) 2,084,000—Russians 55%, Ukrainians 30%, Crimean Tatars 13%. The Crimean Tatar capital and major cultural center is Bakhchisaray, called Bahçesaray in the Crimean Tatar language, (2002e) 33,000. The peninsula's largest cities are Sevastopol, called Akyar by the Tatars, (2002e) 344,000, and Simferopol (Akmescid), (2002e) 330,000.

FLAG: The Crimean Tatar national flag, the flag of the national movement, is a light blue field bearing the *tarak tamga*, the national emblem, a yellow device resembling a scale, on the upper hoist.

PEOPLE AND CULTURE: The Crimean Tatars, the indigenous nation of the Crimea Peninsula and the mainland area formerly known as Tauria, are a Turkic people belonging to the southern branch of the Turkic peoples, the Orguz. In Soviet censuses the Crimean Tatars were included with the larger group of Tatars* of the Volga region, but the culture and language of the Crimean Tatars are quite different. The Crimean Tatars are divided into three subgroups based on historical geography—the Steppe-Tatars, the Hill-Tatars, and the South Coast Tatars. The Krymchaks, numbering about 60,000, are the descendants of the inhabitants of the adjacent mainland region of Tauria. The Crimean Tatars have a deep love of song and music, which has helped to united the scattered exile communities. About 91% of the Crimean Tatars marry within the group, a very high percentage for the former Soviet nations.

LANGUAGE AND RELIGION: The Crimean Tatar language, called Krym or Crimean Turkish, is a Turkic language belonging to the Kipchak or Western Turkic group of languages. The language is spoken in three major dialects that correspond to the major ethnic divisions—Northern or Steppe Crimean, Central Crimean, and Southern or Coastal Crimean. The differences between dialects are quite distinct, as they have been influenced by the languages of the Nogais* in the north and the Turks in the south. The Crimean Tatars have been denied schools of their own; about 75% of the children cannot read their native language. The oldest Crimean Tatar texts date from the thirteenth century. Until 1927 the literary language was based on the southern, Turkicized dialect, but it was then switched to the central dialect. The language was written in the Arabic script until the 1920s, the Latin alphabet until 1938, and finally the Russian Cyrillic alphabet.

The Crimean Tatars are mostly Sunni Muslims, but a large number, while retaining Muslim culture and practices, do not practice their religion. Religious friction among the Crimean Tatars returning from exile and the Slav majority of the Crimea has given rise to fundamentalist sentiment and to calls for stricter religious adherence.

NATIONAL HISTORY: The many peoples who conquered and settled the peninsula left behind an ethnically and religiously diverse population. Turkic tribes and Mongol Tatars of the Golden Horde entered the region from the ninth century A.D. The Crimean Tatars first emerged as a distinct national group in the thirteenth and fourteenth centuries. The Byzantines were ruling the multi-ethnic Crimea when the Turkic and Mongol hordes overran the region in 1239. The Turkic tribes took control of the coastal cities and extended their authority across the peninsula. In 1443, following the disintegration of the Horde, the local Turkic peoples, called Tatars, erected a separate Tatar khanate under Haci Giray Khan. The Giray dynasty ruled the region continuously for over three centuries.

Although the Crimean khanate eventually became nominally tributary to the Ottoman Empire, it expanded to control much of southern Russia, Ukraine, and eastern Poland. The khanate formed a buffer between the Ottoman Empire and the expanding Muscovite and Polish-Lithuanian states. The Tatars established trading links to most of the Mediterranean and beyond, through the contacts and ties of the large Genoese and Greek populations of their southern port cities. The Crimean Tatar state developed an advanced administrative bureaucracy, a codified legal system, and hierarchical political institutions. The Crimean Tatar slave trade, sustained by raids on the Slavic peoples to the north, delivered captives to the Ottoman provinces on the southern shore of the Black Sea.

The decline of the Ottoman Empire allowed the Russians to push south. A Russian military leader, Prince Vasily Golitsyn, made two failed attempts to invade the region in 1687 and 1689; finally, in 1696, Peter the Great captured Azov, on the mainland, giving the Russians access to the Black Sea. The khanate, rich on trade, developed a brilliant and sophisticated civilization even as its outer provinces fell to the expanding Russian empire. In 1736 invading Russians conquered all except the Tatar heartland, the Crimean Peninsula and mainland Tauria. The Russian empress Catherine the Great forced the declining Ottoman Empire to recognize the independence of the khanate, which she then annexed in 1783. The annexation opened the way for the Russian conquest of the remaining territories in 1792–93, without risking war with the still-powerful Turks. Due to centuries of slave raids and incursions by the Tatars, who constituted 98% of the peninsula's population, there was deep Slavic hostility toward the newly conquered nation.

Deportations and expropriation of land, especially in the 1850s and 1860s, forced an estimated million Tatars to seek refuge in Turkish territory, leaving large parts of the newly annexed region virtually depopulated. Government-sponsored settlement brought an influx of Slavs to settle the mainland Tauria. Over the next century, the local authorities pressed an official policy of assimilation. Tatar architecture was destroyed, and ancient cultural monuments disappeared. By 1897 the devastated Tatar nation accounted for only 34% of the population of Taurida province, which comprised the Crimean Peninsula and mainland Tauria.

After 1860 the Russian government enrolled Tatar children in Russian schools. Eventually a Tatar intelligentsia emerged, separate from the traditional Muslim hierarchy. Education, which led to modernization, spurred the growth of national consciousness and fueled demands for greater rights within the Russian Empire. The Crimean Tatar national movement was nurtured by the parallel rise of pan-Islamic and pan-Turkic movements.

The opening of a Tatar press in 1883 stimulated a Tatar cultural revival and the growth of nationalism. The Crimean Tatar revival was suppressed in 1891, forcing many nationalists to flee to Turkey. In 1909 Crimean Tatar students in Constantinople formed Vatan, a nationalist organization dedicated to the creation of an independent Crimean Tatar state. Openly favoring the Turks during World War I, the nationalists mobilized. By the time revolution swept Russia in February 1917, Vatan had underground cells in most Crimean Tatar towns and villages.

A Crimean Tatar congress convened in September 1917 rejected the

Bolshevik coup in October, seeing it as just another form of Slavic oppression. Threatened by local Bolsheviks, nationalists under the leadership of Numan Celebi Cihan declared Taurida independent on 10 December 1917. Fighting soon broke out between Tatar nationalists and the pro-Bolshevik soldiers and sailors who took control of Sevastopol; in January 1918 the poorly equipped Tatars suffered defeat.

German troops took control of the region in March 1918, and Tatar leaders emerged from hiding to organize an independent state on the Crimean Peninsula. On 16 May 1918 they declared the Crimean Democratic Republic, independent of both the Russian factions, as civil war swept across the disintegrating Russian Empire. Defeated by the Red Army in 1919, the peninsula was quickly occupied; the independent republic collapsed.

The new Soviet government, unable fully to suppress Crimean Tatar nationalism, decided in 1921 to allow the Crimean Tatars, like the other large Soviet nationalities, to have their own national republic. The Crimean Tatar culture flourished under the leadership of Veli Ibrahimov, but after 1927 the Crimean Tatars suffered the same oppression as the other Soviet peoples. During the collectivization of 1928–29, thousands of Crimean Tatar peasants were deported or slaughtered. Food was confiscated for shipment to central Russia, while more than 100,000 Crimean Tatars starved to death; tens of thousands fled to Turkey or Romania. Ibrahimov and other leaders were charged with "bourgeois nationalism" and executed. Thousands were arrested, including most independent farmers, who were deported. The government campaign led to another famine in 1931–33. No other Soviet nationality suffered the sharp population decline of the Crimean Tatars. Between 1917 and 1933 an estimated half the total Crimean Tatar population were killed or deported, and the intellectual class was completely exterminated. Study of the Crimean Tatar language and history was forbidden, and all Crimean Tatar publications and press were banned.

Although many welcomed the Germans as liberators during the Nazi invasion of the Soviet Union in 1941, the Crimean Tatars mostly remained loyal. The Germans recruited and outfitted about 1,500 Crimean prisoners of war into 14 companies, but 20,000 served in the Red Army. The Soviet dictator, Joseph Stalin, later alleged, however, that the entire Crimean Tatar nation had been guilty of treason. Six days after the last German troops evacuated Crimea, on the night of 17–18 May 1944, the entire Crimean Tatar population, numbering about 400,000, living on the peninsula was rounded up and deported in sealed cattle cars. An estimated 46% of the deportees, mostly children, elderly, and women, died during transport and in the first two years of resettlement in "special zones" on the Central Asian steppes and in concentration camps in the Sverdlovsk region in the Ural Mountains. Crimean Tatar soldiers released from the

Red Army were arrested on their return to the peninsula at the end of the war; they followed their families into exile.

The Soviet authorities obliterated all historical, linguistic, and cultural traces of the Crimean Tatar nation. Place-names were changed, and the history of the Crimean Tatars was rewritten, portraying them as no more than nomadic brigands. The Soviet government made a gift of the peninsula to the Ukrainian Soviet Socialist Republic in 1954, on the 300th anniversary of Ukraine's union with Russia.

Stalin's death in 1953 began a period of improvement in the condition of the Crimean Tatars. Restrictions on the movement of the Tatars were lifted, and Tatar organizations began to assemble. Not rehabilitated with the other nations deported by Stalin in 1956–57, the Crimean Tatars launched a campaign to win the right to return to their homeland. From the 1960s to the late 1980s, the Crimean Tatar national movement was the only mass ethnic movement in the Soviet Union. Thousands dared to sign petitions and took part in demonstrations. Many activists were arrested and sent to labor camps or prison.

On 8 September 1967 the Crimean Tatars were officially rehabilitated, but permission to return to their homeland was not granted, and they were not recognized as a separate people. Nominally autonomous districts were created in Uzbekistan with the aim of making the Crimean Tatar resettlement permanent, but the Tatars rejected the plan. For the purposes of official censuses, all Tatars in the Soviet Union were considered one people. The persistence of the Crimean Tatars finally resulted in their being counted as a separate national group in the last Soviet census, in 1989.

From the 1960s to the 1980s the revival of the culture accelerated, with the participation of Crimean Tatar newspapers, publishing houses, and organizations. A Soviet government commission appointed in 1987 finally addressed the issue. In 1990, after 46 years in exile, the Crimean Tatars' right to return to their homeland was finally granted, but with no dates given nor financial assistance offered. On 30 June 1991 the Mejlis, the elected national congress, declared the sovereignty of the Crimean Tatars and adopted a national anthem and flag.

The disintegration of the Soviet Union, resulting in the establishment of an independent Ukrainian state, opened a bitter conflict over the fate of the region and dealt a blow to the Crimean Tatars' right to a national homeland. Russian claims to the Crimea, particularly to the large former Soviet naval base at Sevastopol and the ships stationed there, quickly strained relations between Russia and Ukraine. Both governments attempted to use the Crimean Tatars in the dispute, while carefully avoiding the issue of the Tatars' ancient claim to the peninsula.

The returning Crimean Tatars, numbering over 270,000 by 1993, found themselves relegated to marginal lands or the shantytowns around their former capital and other cities. The harsh condition of the lives of the returnees gave new impetus to the national movement. In July 1993 a number of nationalist organizations joined to demand the resurrection of the independent Crimean Tatar state and to reiterate the Tatar claim to the entire peninsula—a claim that, Crimean Tatar nationalist leaders point out, predates both the Russian and the Ukrainian claims to the region.

In January 1994, in an effort to enlist Crimean Tatar support in its dispute with the Russians, the Ukrainian government increased tenfold its allocation for construction of housing for the returning Crimean Tatars; however, the government also continued to demolish Tatar refugee settlements. In February 1995, the leaders of the Tatars demanded a quota for the Crimean Tatars in the Ukrainian parliament, to overcome the electoral disadvantage of their dispersed demographics.

The three claims to the peninsula, Russian, Ukrainian, and Crimean Tatar, could lead to violence in the region; however, the Tatar leader, Mustafa Cemioglu, is a firm believer in nonviolence and was a close friend of former Soviet dissident Andrei Sahkarov. The Tatars remain loosely allied with the Ukrainian authorities in opposition to the Russian majority in the region, although the Ukrainian authorities have made obtaining Ukrainian citizenship difficult for many returnees. Tatar claims for special status as the indigenous population of the Crimean Peninsula are yet to be addressed.

In February 1999, Crimean Tatars, waving their national flag, demonstrated in several cities to demand an end to repression and discrimination. They also demanded representation in the Crimean parliament and in state offices. Crimean Tatar leaders blamed the deteriorating condition of their people on the continuing domination of the peninsula by former communists and a lack of concern for the indigenous Tatars on the part of the Ukrainian president and parliament. In May demonstrators descended on Simferopol, the republic's capital, to carry their protests to the Crimean republican government. Nationalist leaders continue to caution restraint, arguing that the Crimean Tatars would lose everything if violence broke out.

Most of the estimated 250,000 Crimean Tatars still living in exile plan to resettle in Crimea over the next few years, but financial and social problems have prevented many from returning. The Russians and Ukrainians do not dispute the Crimean Tatars' right to return, but the resettlement of over a quarter of a million people, with the likelihood of an equal number arriving over the next few years, is a daunting task for any administration, particularly in a country undergoing wrenching economic and social reorientation.

In late 2000, Crimean Tatar leaders reiterated their demand for recognition by the Ukrainian and Crimean constitutions of their status as the indigenous nation of the Crimean Peninsula. Recognition would give the Crimean Tatars effective representation in all organs of state power on the peninsula. The precarious position of the population is aggravated by the fact that thousands have not been granted Ukrainian citizenship, many are considered stateless, and only about 3,000 returnees have been naturalized.

SELECTED BIBLIOGRAPHY:

Allworth, Edward A., ed. *Tatars of the Crimea: Their Struggle for Survival.* 1988.
———. *The Tatars of the Crimea: Return to the Homeland.* 1998.
Fisher, Alan W. *The Crimean Tatars.* 1978.
Kirimli, Hakan. *National Movements and National Identity among the Crimean Tatars (1905–1916).* 1996.

Crucians
Virgin Islanders

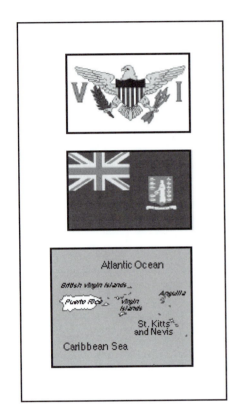

POPULATION: Approximately (2002e) 85,000 Crucians in the Caribbean, concentrated in the Virgin Islands. There are sizable Crucian populations in the United States, Puerto Rico, and the United Kingdom.

THE CRUCIAN HOMELAND: The Crucian homeland is a mountainous island chain with an inviting subtropical climate at the northeastern end of the Greater Antilles, about 40 miles (64 km) east of Puerto Rico. The islands, collectively called the Virgin Islands, are administered in two groups, the Virgin Islands of the United States and the British Virgin Islands. The U.S. Virgin Islands consist of the islands of St. Thomas, St. Croix, St. John, and about 50 islets and cays. The islands are an organized, unincorporated territory of the United States. *Virgin Islands of the United States*: 133 sq. mi.—345 sq. km, (2002e) 151,000—Crucians (West Indian blacks and mulattos) 74%, whites 13%, Puerto Ricans* 5%. The British Virgin Islands (BVI), lying north and east of the U.S. Virgin Islands, comprise four larger islands—Tortola, Anegada, Virgin Gorda, and Jost Van Dyke—and 32 smaller islands. The BVI are a dependent territory of the United Kingdom. *British Virgin Islands*: 59 sq. mi.—153 sq. km, (2002e) 21,000—Crucians (West Indian blacks and mulattos) 90%, whites 8%, Asians 2%. The Crucian capital and major cultural center is Charlotte Amalie, on St. Thomas, (2002e) 16,000, urban area, 45,000, the largest city in the Virgin Islands. The capital of the British islands is Road Town on Tortola, (2002e) 9,500. The other important cultural center is Christiansted, on St. Croix, (2002e) 5,000.

FLAG: The flag of the U.S. Virgin Islands is a white field with a modified U.S. coat of arms centered between two large blue initials V and I. The flag of the British Virgin Islands is a blue field with the Union Jack as a canton on the upper hoist and the BVI coat of arms, depicting a woman flanked on each side by a vertical column of six oil lamps, on the fly.

PEOPLE AND CULTURE: The great majority of the Crucians are blacks and mulattos, descendants of African slaves and their white owners. The Crucian name originally was applied only to the inhabitants of St. Croix but has since been used for all the inhabitants of the Virgin Islands. There are strong historical and cultural ties between the inhabitants of the two administrative zones. Whites constitute a small minority, some, such as the French Huguenots on St. Thomas, having lived on the islands for many generations. The white population has grown rapidly since 1960, as has the overall population. The U.S. Virgin Islands had a population of just 32,000 in 1960 but over 100,000 in 1980. The general health of the islanders is good, and literacy is almost 100%. Unemployment is very low, and the majority work in the growing tourist industry.

LANGUAGE AND RELIGION: The language of the islands is English, the official language of both administrations and the chief tongue of the Crucians. The language, as spoken in the Virgin Islands, is a Caribbean dialect called Calypso, which incorporates many borrowings from African, Spanish, Portuguese, and other languages and varies somewhat from island to island. Spanish, spoken by the Puerto Rican minority on St. Croix, is widely spoken as a second language throughout the archipelago.

The religious affiliation of the Crucians is mostly Protestant, with a large Roman Catholic minority, about 34%, in the U.S. Virgin Islands. In the BVI Protestants make up 86% of the population; the largest single denomination is Methodist, while the Baptists dominate in the U.S. Virgin Islands. Religious freedom in the islands has existed since the 1600s.

NATIONAL HISTORY: Peaceful Arawaks who originally inhabited the islands had been displaced by the warlike Caribs by the time Christopher Columbus visited the islands in 1493. He named the group for St. Ursula and the Eleven Thousand Virgins. In 1555 a Spanish force was dispatched to claim the islands, and by 1596 most of the Caribs had fled or had been exterminated, although the Spanish did not stay to colonize the group.

The islands became an early center for Caribbean pirates and buccaneers. Dutch pirates occupied Tortola in 1648 and held it until English planters took control of the island in 1666. In 1672, Tortola was annexed by the British Leeward Islands. The Dutch, English, French, and Spanish occupied or colonized the islands. In 1773 the planters were granted civil government with an elected assembly.

The Danes took control of St. Thomas in 1666 and formed the Danish West India Company in 1672 to supply the mother country with sugar, cotton, indigo, and other island products. Slaves from Africa were first introduced in 1673, and the islands quickly became important sugar producers, with a prosperous planter aristocracy. From St. Thomas the Danes occupied St. John in 1684 and purchased St. Croix from the French in

1733, the same year that a massive slave revolt broke out on St. John. The revolt lasted for eight months, and many plantation families were killed before the Danes were able to restore order.

The Danish king acquired St. Thomas from the West India Company in 1754–55, and the capital, Charlotte Amalie, was declared a free port, open to international shipping. The neutrality of the islands during the Napoleonic Wars made them the center of Caribbean trade and the largest slave market in the Western Hemisphere. The British took control of the islands in 1801 and again in 1807–15 but later returned them to Danish rule.

Falling sugar prices after 1820 led to a decrease in profits and trade. The slave-based sugar plantations further declined after slavery was abolished in the British islands in 1833 and in Danish territory in 1848. In 1872 the British islands became part of the colony of the Leeward Islands.

American interest in the islands began during the Civil War period, but the U.S. Senate refused in 1870 to approve the purchase from Denmark of St. Thomas and St. John. A firm offer to purchase the islands came during World War I, when they were seen as strategically important to the control of the main passage through the Caribbean to the Panama Canal. The Danes, fearing seizure of the islands by the allies or conquest by the Germans, were willing to sell. In 1917 the United States purchased the three Danish islands for $25 million.

An act passed in 1927 granted U.S. citizenship to most of the Crucians, and another in 1932 provided citizenship rights to Crucians and their descendants living elsewhere in the Caribbean or on the U.S. mainland. A revised act adopted in 1954 provided for substantial self-government. In 1970 a bill was introduced that allowed for direct popular elections for governor and lieutenant governor, for four-year terms.

The British Virgin Islands remained part of the colony of the Leeward Islands until it was divided and defederated in 1956; the British Virgin Islands became a separate colony. In 1958 the West Indies Federation was established, but the Crucians of the BVI rejected membership in order to retain their close economic and cultural ties to the American islands. Because of traditionally close ties to the U.S. Virgin Islands, the British islands have used the dollar as its official currency since 1959.

The U.K. government announced in March 1994 the enlargement of the British Virgin Islands Legislative Council, adding four new seats to the existing nine. The move, made to broaden the representative government in the islands, was a response to local demands for a greater say in the government of the islands.

The economy of the islands, one of the most prosperous in the Caribbean, is highly dependent on tourism, which generates an estimated of 45% of the national income in the BVI. In the 1980s, the government began offering offshore registration to companies, and incorporation fees now generate substantial revenues. An estimated 250,000 offshore companies were registered in the BVI by 1997.

The U.S. Virgin Islands are administered by the Office of Insular Affairs of the U.S. Department of the Interior, through a governor elected by universal suffrage to a four-year term. The British Virgins have an elected government under a constitution adopted in 1967 and amended 10 years later to allow for greater autonomy in internal affairs.

The Crucians have the highest per capita income in the Caribbean region and a sizable middle class, which has effectively precluded support for independence or a change in the islands' status. In 1970 and 1981 the inhabitants of the U.S. Virgin Islands resoundingly rejected home rule. There has been little demand for autonomy in either zone, mostly because of fears of disrupting the lucrative tourist industry and the increase in taxes that autonomy would entail. There are small independence movements, but the majority prefer the status quo; statehood for the U.S. Virgin Islands is not a popular option.

A 1982 referendum was held in the U.S. zone to consider a new constitution and a new flag, but voters overwhelmingly favored no change. In 1986, a black Democrat won the governor's race, but about a third of the voters opted for the Independent Citizens Movement, which questioned present ties to the U.S. government and tapped into black discontent at not sharing in the prosperity of the white and mulatto populations.

In recent years there has been increasing tension between the Crucians and people from other parts of the Caribbean. The newcomers are called "Down Islanders," or Garotes, after the tropical bird that migrates from island to island in the Caribbean. They immigrated, mostly from the former British islands farther south, to the islands seeking jobs and better living conditions. Particularly in the U.S. Virgin Islands—where an estimated 30% of the population are West Indian, born elsewhere in the Caribbean, and 45% are represented by the native Crucian population—tension has been increasingly intense since the 1990s. There is a parallel movement by the Crucian majority of African descent for a greater role in the economic and social decisions and in the administrations of the islands.

SELECTED BIBLIOGRAPHY:

Lunatta, Karl. *Virgin Islands Handbook*. 1997.
Martel, Arlene R. *The United States Virgin Islands*. 1998.
Mauer, Bill. *Recharting the Caribbean: Land, Law, and Citizenship in the British Virgin Islands*. 2000.
Wallace, Walter. *British Virgin Islands: Report of the Constitutional Commissioners 1993*. 1994.